The Rise and Fall of Modern Empires, Volume II

The Rise and Fall of Modern Empires
Series Editor: Philippa Levine

Titles in the Series:

The Rise and Fall of Modern Empires, Volume II
Colonial Knowledges

Edited by

Saul Dubow

Queen Mary, University of London

Routledge
Taylor & Francis Group

LONDON AND NEW YORK

First published 2013 by Ashgate Publishing

Published 2016 by Routledge
2 Park Square, Milton Park, Abingdon, Oxon OX14 4RN
605 Third Avenue, New York, NY 10017

First issued in paperback 2022

Routledge is an imprint of the Taylor & Francis Group, an informa business

Notice:
Product or corporate names may be trademarks or registered trademarks, and are used only for identification and explanation without intent to infringe.

Publisher's Note
The publisher has gone to great lengths to ensure the quality of this reprint but points out that some imperfections in the original copies may be apparent.

British Library Cataloguing in Publication Data
The rise and fall of modern empires.
  Volume II, Colonial knowledges.
  1. Imperialism–History. 2. Intellectual life–History.
  I. Dubow, Saul.
  325.3'2–dc23

The Library of Congress has cataloged the printed edition as follows: 2012953507

ISBN 13: 978-1-4094-3666-9 (hbk)
ISBN 13: 978-1-03-240266-6 (pbk)

DOI: 10.4324/9781315237336

Contents

**PART V   INDIGENOUS KNOWLEDGE: ENVIRONMENT, MEDICINE,
              LANDSCAPE**

PART VI THE CIRCULATION OF KNOWLEDGE

Acknowledgements

Ashgate would like to thank our researchers and the contributing authors who provided copies, along with the following for their permission to reprint copyright material.

Boydell & Brewer Ltd for the essay: Patrick Harries (2007), 'Natural Sciences', in *Butterflies and Barbarians: Swiss Missionaries and Systems of Knowledge in South-East Africa*, Oxford: James Currey and Athens: Ohio University Press, pp. 123–54.

Cambridge University Press for the essays: T.O. Beidelman (1974), 'Social Theory and the Study of Christian Missions in Africa', *Africa*, **44**, pp. 235–49. Copyright © 1974 Cambridge University Press; C.A. Bayly (1993), 'Knowing the Country: Empire and Information in India', *Modern Asian Studies*, **27**, pp. 3–43. Copyright © 1993 Cambridge University Press; Archie Mafeje (1971), 'The Ideology of "Tribalism"', *Journal of Modern African Studies*, **9**, pp. 253–61. Copyright © 1971 Cambridge University Press; Keletso E. Atkins (1988), '"Kafir Time": Preindustrial Temporal Concepts and Labour Discipline in Nineteenth-Century Colonial Natal', *Journal of African History*, **29**, pp. 229–44. Copyright © 1988 Cambridge University Press.

Copyright Clearance Center for the essays: Tony Ballantyne (2001), 'Race and the Webs of Empire: Aryanism from India to the Pacific', *Journal of Colonialism and Colonial History*, **2**, pp. 1–35. Copyright © 2001 Johns Hopkins University Press Journals; Benjamin Schmidt (1997), 'Mapping an Empire: Cartographic and Colonial Rivalry in Seventeenth-Century Dutch and English North America', *William and Mary Quarterly*, **54**, pp. 549–78. Copyright © 1997 Institute of Early American History of Culture.

Manchester University Press for the essays: David Arnold (1988), 'Introduction: Disease, Medicine and Empire', in David Arnold (ed.), *Imperial Medicine and Indigenous Societies*, Manchester: Manchester University Press, pp. 1–26; Richard H. Grove (1990), 'Colonial Conservation, Ecological Hegemony and Popular Resistance: Towards a Global Synthesis', in John M. Mackenzie (ed.), *Imperialism and the Natural World*, Manchester: Manchester University Press, pp. 15–50; Saul Dubow (2001), 'A Commonwealth of Science: The British Association in South Africa, 1905 and 1929', in Saul Dubow (ed.), *Science and Society in Southern Africa*, Manchester: Manchester University Press, pp. 66–99.

Museo de América, Madrid for the image: Juan Revenet, 'View of Mexico City from Guadalupe' (1971).

Oxford University Press for the essay: Robert A. Stafford (1999), 'Scientific Exploration and Empire', in Andrew Porter (ed.), *The Oxford History of the British Empire*, Vol. 3: *The Nineteenth Century*, Oxford: Oxford University Press, pp. 294–319.

Oxford University Press India for the essays: Bernard S. Cohn (1985), 'The Command of Language and the Language of Command', in Ranajit Guha (ed.), *Subaltern Studies IV*,

Publisher's Note

The material in this volume has been reproduced using the facsimile method. This means we can retain the original pagination to facilitate easy and correct citation of the original essays. It also explains the variety of typefaces, page layouts and numbering.

Series Preface

In the modern world, empires have been a constant and characteristic element of the political landscape. While the fact of colonial conquest is by no means unique to the modern period, the empires of the past three hundred years or so share some fundamental characteristics. These were empires much of whose dominance was based on technological prowess; they were principally the province of Western nations; and they frequently claimed a humanitarian impulse connected to the technology that also helped them succeed in conquering other lands. They were also, for the most part, white empires ruling principally over peoples considered inferior, not least because of their racial difference from their European overlords.

We can trace some critical changes in the nature of empire over time, a shift from colonies of settlement intended to absorb population from Europe to colonies of extraction never intended as sites where large numbers of Europeans would settle permanently. There is no simple linear chronology to this: the two always co-existed but at the same time, there is no doubt that in the nineteenth century there was a growing emphasis on the model of extraction, especially where raw materials for industrial production were available, even while settlement continued.

The colonized adopted a variety of tactics in the face of conquest. Many chose to collaborate, a tactic that could certainly enrich and empower a lucky or canny few. Collaboration came in many forms ranging from enforcement of colonial laws to securing a Western education or converting to Christianity. Just as many, however, adopted the opposite route of resistance, and this, too, had many guises from outright rebellion to slow work routines. We need to remember, too, that many people remained unaware or barely cognisant of a colonial presence, especially in places where colonial officials were sparse on the ground. There was a world of difference between colonies such as French Algeria or British India, where a substantial European population influenced everything from available foodstuffs to architecture, from labour opportunities to town planning, and much of sub-Saharan Africa where a mere handful of colonial officials housed in modest dwellings, and often itinerant, was often the only visible manifestation of colonial rule.

These four volumes are closely concerned with all aspects of modern colonial rule. We have divided the volumes into four broad but inevitably overlapping areas. The four over-arching themes that we thought best captured the breadth and depth of this critical historical phenomenon are Social Organization, Colonial Knowledges, Economics and Politics, and Reactions to Colonialism. All four volumes offer analyses of the experience of both the colonized and the colonizer, and pay as much attention to ideas as to events, to the materiality of politics and economics as to the cultures that developed around colonial practice. All take seriously the need to explore the impact of empires locally and globally – that is, in the places which were colonized, in the places responsible for that colonization and in the complex and multiple global ramifications of empire-building. For at every level, the fact of empire shaped political and diplomatic relations, the pursuit of both knowledge and profit, the contours of resistance as well as the quotidian rhythms of life in many parts of the world.

We should recognize, moreover, that while the age of formal imperialism may be over, its consequences have been tenacious. The legacies of colonialism haunt a considerable number of our contemporary political conflicts and have shaped the economics of many locations around the world. Policy debates in the early twenty-first century have been profoundly shaped by a neo-imperialist lobby that argues for a continued relevance for a humanitarian imperialism. These four volumes offer a comprehensive assessment of the impact, effects and legacies of modern imperialism.

PHILIPPA LEVINE
University of Texas at Austin, USA

Introduction[*]

The claim that we are all part of a 'Knowledge Society' is a contemporary truism. Politicians are fond of reminding voters that our continued prosperity depends on acquiring skills relevant to knowledge-based economies. Fashionable it may be today, but the idea of knowledge as empowerment has a long ancestry. When the English Renaissance statesman and philosopher Francis Bacon referred to knowledge as the 'worthiest power', he was making a case for the virtues and practical possibilities of empirically based science. A key figure in the 'scientific revolution', Bacon saw knowledge as an active means to improve society through the mastery of nature; he may also have seen it as a means to enlarge the power of the Elizabethan English state and to realize the ideal of the 'New Atlantis'.

Whether Bacon conceived of scientific knowledge as serving the interests of an expanding imperial state or as an international enterprise potentially serving the interests of all humanity is debatable.[1] A contemporary restatement of this question might ask whether knowledge confers universal benefits rather than serving sectional interests. If knowledge knows no boundaries and circulates frictionlessly through the digitized ether, is it global, local or both? There are many ways of addressing these problems. Here we do so through the prism of empire and colony.

This volume is entitled '*Colonial Knowledges*'. Why? One clue lies in the adjective 'colonial', which alerts us to the fact that knowledge is shaped by historically specific power relationships. Another hint lies in the plural form, 'knowledge*s*', indicating an emphasis on the interplay between different, often competing, cognitive systems. The reference to Bacon is a reminder that the association between knowledge and power, including colonial power, is centuries old. Yet the term 'colonial knowledge' is itself of fairly recent coinage, emerging as an academic descriptor or subfield sometime in the 1990s.

One constant of intellectual history is that ideas are seldom new. They always have progenitors and require critical mass and currency before they take hold. Very often swirling currents of thought are distilled by the title of an article or book. In our case, two books published in 1996 by leading scholars of India – one American, the other British – foregrounded the concept of colonial knowledge and did much to shape subsequent debate: Bernard Cohn's *Colonialism and its Forms of Knowledge: The British in India* and Christopher Bayly's *Empire and Information: Intelligence Gathering and Social Communication in India, 1780–1870*.[2] In

[*]   I am grateful to Keith Breckenridge, Trevor Burnard and Margot Finn for helpful suggestions for inclusions in this volume. I only wish I could have included more of them. Vinita Damodaran, Ian Duncan, Ramachandra Guha, Patrick Harries, Sujit Sivasundaram, Andrew Thompson, Kim Wagner and Richard Wilson made sharp comments on this introductory chapter. My special thanks to Philippa Levine for her constant vigilance and consummate professionalism.

[1]   See, for instance, the entry on Bacon by Markku Peltonen in *Oxford Dictionary of National Biography*.

[2]   Bayly used the term 'colonial knowledge' in chapter 4 of *Empire and Information* (1996).

a review of Bayly's book, David Arnold, himself a leading historian of knowledge interaction in the context of Indian colonial medicine, stated the problem succinctly:

> The question of what constitutes 'colonial knowledge' has been at the heart of recent debates about empire. To what extent did the colonial powers 'know' the subjects and societies over which they ruled? Did they invent or impose their own understanding of alien peoples and places? Or was colonial knowledge the product of a mutual exchange of ideas and impressions rather than the one-sided product of imperial imagining? (1997, para 1)

These questions were already the subject of considerable discussion, mostly on the part of non-historians. From a theoretical perspective, the complex relationship of knowledge to power had been thoroughly explored by the hugely influential French post-structuralist thinker Michel Foucault. In the field of post-colonial studies, Edward Said's *Orientalism* (1978) used Foucauldian and Gramscian analysis to examine how the interests of imperialism were served by intellectual experts who imposed their categories or 'constructs' on the Islamic and Arab worlds. Although their objectives and methods differed, Foucault and Said both opened up key questions about the relationship of cultural and social ideas to structures of power. Terms like representation, hegemony and governmentality offered an alluring conceptual language which helped to fix ideas already in circulation. Proponents of the 'linguistic turn' in the social sciences – the assumption that reality is substantively constituted by language rather than being independent of it[3] – were also highly receptive to such ideas.

Traditional historians of empire were often hostile to, or dismissive of, the new theoretical language. Even those who were more receptive to the new wave tended to eschew the abstract and overarching claims made by post-colonialists, not least because of the homogenizing manner in which the 'West' and the 'Other' were sometimes presented. But the power of these arguments could not be ignored and a gradual process of acceptance ensued. Neither Foucault nor even Said were concerned to analyse how colonialism actually worked 'on the ground', and so they largely failed to cast light on the last of the questions raised by Arnold, namely, the extent to which colonial knowledge could be said to have been the product of multiple agency and interaction, and thus not only a source of subordination but also a matter of disputation and resistance.[4] This approach was germane to the interests of historians in India and in Africa, and also to those 'new' imperial historians who, from the 1980s, were keen to consider the cultural, social and ideological aspects of empire from new perspectives.

While the lines of descent are neither direct nor always clearly acknowledged, the leading progenitors of colonial knowledge were also absorbing long-standing ideas in the sociology of knowledge. French postmodern thinkers drew freely on the insights of forebears like Emile Durkheim who ascribed a central role to the understanding of classificatory schemes and symbolic language as a means of understanding society. These insights were subsequently developed by such scholars as Lucien Lévy-Bruhl, Roland Barthes and Claude Lévi-Strauss, whose structuralist anthropology began to transform the field of linguistics and communication theory from the 1950s. An important claim in Lévi-Strauss's work is the idea

---

[3]   This idea was developed by analytic philosophers long before it spread to the social sciences.

[4]   For useful critical discussions of Said's concept of 'orientalism', see, for example, Mackenzie (1995) and Irwin **(2006).**

that all societies, bound as they are by symbolic language, are knowledge-based, and that all humans are fundamentally alike in their capacity to think and process information. Lévi-Strauss did, however, distinguish between the different degrees of abstraction involved in concrete or embedded and scientific modes of thought, apparently without seeing one as more valid than the other.[5]

The term 'sociology of knowledge' is connected above all with Karl Mannheim, the Austro-Hungarian philosopher, and with Max Scheler, both of whom explored this conception from the 1920s. Mannheim drew on Marxist understandings of ideology, which hold that knowledge is geared to the reproduction and legitimation of the class system, in order to argue that all thought was socially produced and tied to particular historical conditions. Unlike the anthropological approach of Durkheim and Lévi-Strauss, Mannheim was particularly concerned with the role of intellectuals, who he believed constituted a distinct social stratum in the class system.

Connections between knowledge, power and society were also powerfully explored in the United States where modern sociology and psychology were distinctively shaped by variants of Dewey's philosophy of pragmatism. At Columbia University, where the sociologist C. Wright Mills spent much of his career, pragmatism was strongly evident in the social sciences. Mills also drew on Weber and Marx, as well as the American sociologist Thorstein Veblen, to analyse the influence of power elites on public policy. According to Mills (1956), control of social knowledge and communication, principally through the media, was one of the key ways in which the American Power Elite – institutional leaders in the corporate, political, and military domains – exercised decisive influence.[6] The early, optimistic Mills believed that knowledge could be a force for democratic good, but his disillusionment grew as he became preoccupied with the role of intellectuals in supporting elites – and providing succour to America's aggressive foreign policy (for example in Mills, 1960).

Mills's critical sociology made a great impression on Anglo-American new left thought in the late 1960s, just as the approaches of Foucault and Bourdieu to the understanding of knowledge and power did for European radicals.[7] The confluence of these ideas fed into the anti-war movement in the United States and, slightly later, the rise of 'third world' global anti-colonialism. This provided a fertile context for heterodox interpretations of knowledge, focusing either on its role as a tool of governance or its function in manufacturing consent.

---

[5]   Arun Agrawal (1995) takes the view that Lévi-Strauss anticipated, but failed to resolve, the dichotomy between indigenous and Western scientific knowledge.

[6]   For a succinct discussion, see Summers (2006).

[7]   Whereas Mills was chiefly interested in the ways in which elites actively exercised their power in order to dominate, the theoretical approach of Foucault and Bourdieu (and Gramsci) was far more concerned with the manner in which 'hidden' ideology serves to ensure that the hegemony of the powerful cannot readily be understood, let alone challenged. For an imaginative reading, see Burawoy (2008).

The Colonial Situation

Anthropologists in the United States and Britain were highly attentive to these 'new left' currents of thought. In 1968, Kathleen Gough announced that anthropology was the 'child of western imperialism' (1968, p. 403). This approach was strongly articulated in *Anthropology and the Colonial Encounter* by Talal Asad, who argued that anthropology was 'rooted in an unequal power encounter between the West and the Third World ... [an] encounter that gives the West access to cultural and historical information about the societies it has progressively dominated' (1973, p. 16). In the same collection, Richard Brown began his essay on the work of anthropologists at the Rhodes-Livingstone Institute in Zambia with a quotation from C. Wright Mills: 'The problem of knowledge and power is, and always has been, the problem of the relations of men of knowledge with men of power' (Brown, 1973, p. 173). Yet Brown's analysis was also concerned to stress ambiguities that complicate the relationship between anthropology and colonial rule. He remarked on the complexity of the 'colonial situation', a phrase that referenced the French anthropologist George Balandier's classic discussion of this problem in 1951.

Writing before the battle of Dien Bien Phu and the start of the Algerian War, a moment at which colonialism was already arousing political passions, Balandier (Chapter 1) set out his conceptual innovation, which was, as Frederick Cooper (2002) puts it, to see colonialism as a 'totality': a set of relationships, the analysis of which requires integrating social, economic, political and cultural aspects in a single field or 'complex'. Balandier's approach was highly original in its desire to integrate history, economics and sociology, though it has clear forebears in Southern African anthropology, for example Max Gluckman's path-breaking 1940 study of a 'social situation' in Zululand. Alice Conklin has shown how Balandier's work emerged out of a specifically French matrix of specialist research and governmental institutions, as well as his own personal experience as a state-employed ethnologist in West Africa. In her view, Balandier's conceptualization of the 'colonial situation' foreshadowed the issue of anthropological 'complicity' in colonialism and continues to demonstrate that 'we still have much to learn about colonial forms of knowledge, as they emerged on the margins of a scientizing empire and a professionalizing science' (Conklin, 2002, p. 31).

Balandier's insight that the colonial situation involved understanding colonizers as well as colonized is applied in Thomas Beidelman's 1974 essay, 'Social Theory and the Study of Christian Missions in Africa' (Chapter 2). Beidelman begins by observing that anthropology is no longer concerned with the study of 'alien, exotic societies' (p. 31) but is instead concerned with processes such as nation-building and modernization. However, he observed that this shift in method did not yet extend to the study of colonial groups like administrators, missionaries and traders. In Beidelman's view, it was vital to understand not just the convert but also those responsible for conversion and for instilling colonial ideas – in other words, to know the knower.

Of particular relevance here, in Beidelman's view, is the ethnicity, class, economic and cultural background of missionaries, as well as their denominational theology and conversion strategies. Beidelman's broadly Weberian analysis, informed also by Durkheim, draws attention to the web of tensions and contradictions involved in missionary activity. His keen observation that missionaries could be 'prisoners of their concepts and unable to grasp the full implications of their policies and actions' (p. 42) illuminates the problem of colonial intentionality and provides a means to understand why it was that these key intermediaries helped to pave the way for colonialism while also instilling values that equipped Africans to challenge colonial rule. This approach to the missionary encounter points to an underlying ambiguity in colonial knowledge (be this knowledge of the bible or mission education): that it is a resource which can be put to quite different uses.[8]

The link between history and anthropology, so important to our appreciation of colonial knowledge, is exemplified in the work of Chicago University anthropologist Bernard Cohn. His concern with the connections between colonial authority, knowledge, and power, led him to offer a striking interpretation of the development of the Indian caste system as an institution which, though predating British rule, was significantly modified through its codification by the colonial state. Cohn's method involved understanding caste and the institutions of colonial law in ways that allowed him to conceptualize the significance of 'Orientalism' in advance of (and perhaps with greater precision than) Said's totalizing analysis of colonial 'Othering'. As Ranajit Guha put it in his introduction to Cohn's collection, *An Anthropologist among the Historians and Other Essays* (1987), the fact that colonists and colonized lived in a relation of mutuality means that 'the interpenetration of power and knowledge constitutes the very fabric of colonialism' (1987, p. xx).

Language and Control

In Chapter 3, 'The Command of Language and the Language of Command', Cohn makes the striking claim that the 'conquest of India was a conquest of knowledge' (p. 49). Using the records of the East India Company he shows how the British gradually began to use their knowledge of Indian languages to construct a system of rule. Grammars, dictionaries, guidebooks and treatises were all part of this 'apparatus'. Together, they invaded the 'epistemological space' occupied by Indian scholars, priests, clerks and merchants, transforming these groups into sub-agents of colonial rule. In the process, North India's 'vast social world' was 'classified, categorized and bounded' to facilitate state command and control (p. 57). While Cohn allows that this process was not always conscious and often had unintended effects, the British were nonetheless purposeful and deliberate in their project of ordering and managing Indian languages and indigenous knowledge (cf. Leylveld, 1993).

A complementary but strikingly different approach to the question of knowledge and power in India is taken by Christopher Bayly in 'Knowing the Country: Empire and Information in India' (Chapter 4). Bayly focuses not so much on the formal construction of knowledge as on extant networks of intelligence and information, upon which the British Raj depended.[9] He reveals the social complexity of eighteenth- and nineteenth-century India's 'densely-knit', 'information-rich' society (pp. 109, 107): traders, clerks, boatmen, prostitutes, Sufi mystics

---

[8]   For a more extended and theoretical treatment of the missionary encounter, see Comaroff and Comaroff (1991).

[9]   Peter Burke (2000, p. 11), adapting a distinction made by Lévi-Strauss, suggests that information of practical or specific use is 'raw' whereas knowledge is 'cooked' or processed.

and Hindu pilgrims, as well as spies, collectively possessed a range of valuable, if fragmented, knowledge which the colonial state sought to assemble into usable form.

This analytical perspective complicates Cohn's hierarchies by revealing the British Raj to be merely one competing force among others. Categories like caste, class and tribe appear far more indeterminate when viewed through covert and local sources of knowledge, or via the disorder of the bazaar. Centres of power, be they the Mughals or the East India Company, were not always equipped to test and validate the information they accumulated. Only in the nineteenth century did the trained experts of the centralizing Raj succeed in controlling and ordering its flow. But even so, their 'expert' grasp of intelligence remained incomplete – there were no reliable warnings of the 1857 uprising – and 'knowledge panics' or misunderstanding could arouse anxiety and result in disproportionate responses. Bayly's long historical perspective deepens our understanding of knowledge production and utilization by analysing these processes in the context of India's dense, sometimes impermeable and always contested, social structures. In doing so, his contribution serves as a pointed (if oblique) reminder against over-generalization. Crucially, it draws attention to the difference between colonial knowledge in practice and colonial discourse in theory.[10]

Ranajit Guha, one of the founders of the 'subaltern' group of Indian social and cultural historians, is similarly interested in the inchoate nature of colonial knowledge, namely, in its silences as well as its overt expression. A decade before Bayly, Guha's essay on 'The Prose of Counter-Insurgency' (Chapter 5) pursued one of the central objectives of the subaltern school – that is, the attempt to destabilize established nationalist narratives of resistance. The term 'subaltern' was borrowed from Gramsci for whom it denoted marginalized people and groups whose lack of power was best understood in terms of the hegemony (ideological dominance) of ruling elites on both sides of the colonial/nationalist divide.

Guha extends Gramsci's concept of hegemony (with explicit reference to the work of Barthes and Foucault) in order to demonstrate that colonial knowledge of the 1855–56 Santhal revolt systematically misread the meaning and motives of the rebels, notably by treating insurgency as irrational fanaticism. In Guha's view, this 'blind spot' is not only a function of the ideological assumptions embedded in primary and archival texts. Historians, he maintains, are apt to misread resistance when it does not fall neatly into the categories (such as Marxist units of analysis) that they are conditioned to recognize or validate.[11]

To correct this deficiency, Guha makes extensive use of linguistic theory to demonstrate that language, texts and discourse are never neutral. There was a vigorous reaction on the part of Marxist and social historians to this critique, suggesting that Guha had fallen into a hermeneutic circle whereby language becomes a closed system, rendering the author 'incapable of proceeding beyond the discourse of the participants themselves' ('Subaltern Studies II', 1984, p. 5; see also O'Hanlon, 1988). Whatever the merits of such criticisms, Guha's essay remains a provocative intervention in discussions around elite representations

---

[10]   In his review of their 1996 books in *History and Theory*, William R. Pinch (1999) argues that the different approaches to colonial knowledge taken by Cohn and Bayly are ultimately incompatible.

[11]   Oddly, Guha does not refer to the work of the British Marxist historians E.P. Thompson and Eric Hobsbawm, though Hobsbawm's analysis of 'primitive' rebels shaped Guha's own work at this time, most notably his *Elementary Aspects of Peasant Insurgency in Colonial India* (1983).

of resistance as well as a thoughtful contribution to strategies of reading colonial texts with a view to restoring consciousness and agency to neglected historical agents.

In this quest, the subalternists were in close sympathy with Africanists, for whom the recovery of historical agency among colonized subjects had been a central motivating factor since the 1960s. Yet, despite the subaltern school's determination to examine resistance in all its many different facets, their growing preoccupation with discourse analysis generated a view of state power that made it seem ever more extensive and insidious, prompting Ramachandra Guha's wry remark that subaltern studies had morphed into the study of elites – what he teasingly dubbed 'Bhadralok Studies' (in reference to the Bengali intelligentsia) (1995, p. 2057). The growing influence of Foucault on historians, together with the ever-thickening documentary source base available to Indianists, encouraged this tendency to focus on literate elites.

Categorical Knowledge

A great deal of writing about colonial knowledge is concerned with the manner in which ideas serve the interests of power. Some view the relationship in close, instrumental terms, whereas others deduce it through a process of inference and analogy. Reference has already been made to allegations of anthropology's complicity (intentional or otherwise) with colonial governance. One line of argument, focusing on the role of interwar British anthropology, was that anthropologists had no real power, or that they worked within the colonial system to protect the interests of the people they lived among and studied. Others turned the accusation on its head, arguing that the emphasis should be less on how anthropologists served the interests of colonialism and more on how the discipline of social anthropology was reliant on colonial institutions, including universities, who half-bought into the promise that the science of applied anthropology would yield practical benefits.[12]

Talal Asad is a strong proponent of the view that anthropological knowledge is historically enmeshed in colonialism. Chapter 6, 'Two European Images of Non-European Rule', is his ambitious, if schematic, effort to characterize perceptions of traditional rule in Africa as well as Islamic societies in the Middle East. Conceived within a broadly Marxist tradition, where ideology is assumed to be an expression of underlying class interests, Asad's idea predates Said's culturally oriented work, while sharing certain assumptions with this approach – in particular, the view that the colonial encounter generates images (or representations) of other people in order to devalue or subordinate them. Asad is alert to the difference in approach between 'functional' social anthropologists in Africa, who tend to characterize the 'tribal system' in terms of reciprocity and consensus-building, while emphasizing the underlying rationality of African cultures, with an older 'Orientalist' view of Islamic societies that stresses the capricious use of absolute power to assert the 'basic irrationality of Islamic history' (p. 201). Despite these differences, both readings rely on ahistorical 'essentialisms': an emphasis on societal continuity in the former and historical stasis in the latter. Although the disciplines of social anthropology and Orientalism developed at different moments in European history,

---

[12] For a good overview and discussion, see Kuper (1973, ch. 3).

it is Asad's contention that both helped to justify colonial domination as part of the unequal 'power encounter between the West and the Third World' (p. 204).

Archie Mafeje's 'Ideology of "Tribalism" in South Africa' (Chapter 7) offers another powerful critique of anthropology's complicity with colonialism. The author, who was denied a lectureship at the University of Cape Town in 1967 on account of his colour,[13] entered the debate on 'tribe' at a moment when its status as a legitimate category was already being questioned by anthropologists such as A.W. Southall. Born and educated in the Transkei, Mafeje was expelled from the University of Fort Hare, which was then in the process of being turned into a 'tribal' university by the South African government, for political reasons. Both as scholar and activist, Mafeje saw 'tribe' as a conceptually weak, ideologically loaded idea that obscured more than it revealed. He did not deny the existence of tribalism but instead read it as 'a mark of false consciousness' (p. 211) created by anthropologists and colonial administrators and adopted by members of the African middle class to further their own material and political interests.

Comparisons with the critique of caste in the Indian context are highly apposite, yet the connections between British rule in these two continents were seldom, if ever, made at this time.[14] In the African context the critique of 'tribe' in the 1970s was more often than not written from a historical materialist or an empirically informed historical point of view, whereas postmodern and deconstructionist arguments were increasingly fashionable in South Asian scholarship at this time. It took time for these literatures to intersect.

This point bears on one of the key themes of this volume, the global circulation of knowledge. Ironically, the circulation of key ideas may have been quicker in the era before the emergence of extensive networks of universities – for the highly specialized nature of academic work means that congruent literatures are often generated in a relatively closed self-referential system, defined by discipline or region and consumed by audiences whose starting points and assumptions may be very different. It is misleading, therefore, to assume that the ever greater volume of knowledge, and its ever quicker circulation, equates to its being uniformly absorbed or understood.

Even more than 'tribe', 'race' was pre-eminently the category used to define and legitimate social hierarchies. Modern conceptions of race, while not produced solely to justify colonialism, are inseparable from the history of European global domination and therefore fit squarely within our conception of colonial knowledge. Tony Ballantyne's discussion of 'Aryanism' (Chapter 8) fits particularly well in this collection because he demonstrates the adaptability of this idea as it travelled from India to New Zealand, having been theorized in the metropolitan centres of Germany and Britain by Max Müller and William Jones.

As applied to Maoris, the so-called 'white savages' of colonial New Zealand, Aryanism provided a convenient way to explain that country's distinctive view of itself as a bi-cultural settler nation. Ballantyne usefully situates his discussion in the context of debates around

---

[13]   The university's decision to rescind this appointment prompted student protests in 1968 against the university administration on grounds of its alleged complicity with the government. Mafeje went into exile and continued his academic career in Tanzania and Egypt.

[14]   Compare Dirks's important 'The Invention of Caste: Civil Society in Colonial India' (1988) with the equally important Africanist collection by Vail, *The Creation of Tribalism in South Africa* (1989).

Orientalism and the power–knowledge relation. Moreover, he offers his own interpretation of the circulation of transnational knowledge by deploying the spatial metaphor of 'the web' as a means to challenge older unilinear notions of metropolitan–colonial transmission. The utility of the Aryan idea, its flexibility and its pervasiveness (rather like the application of the Hamitic myth in Africa[15]), offers an excellent case study in the plasticity – and hence utility – of racial ideology. It shows, too, that the idea of race has its foundations in religious and cultural as well as biological habits of thought, and that the appeal of the concept has as much to do with its capacity to generate spurious taxonomical gradations as to define others in the binary terminology of black/white.

Measurement and Mapping

Colonial cognitive control often took less direct forms. The capacity to map, measure, time and enumerate are some of the more important technical devices that have been used to support purposes of governance. Cartography was key not only to the effective control of imperial space, but to its very definition, and its impact was as much symbolic as practical. Chapter 11, Benjamin Schmidt's study of Dutch–English colonial rivalry in seventeenth-century colonial North America, shows how competing colonial claims were asserted by map-makers eager to imprint names as well as boundaries on public consciousness. Dutch pre-eminence in map-making showed up the technical deficiencies of competing English efforts at a time when both nations were seeking to confirm their footholds in North America. Schmidt asks whether this 'patriotic cartography' mattered, concluding that ultimately it did not – for maps neither constituted the primary cause of conflicts nor served as the main determinant of their outcomes. Nonetheless, conflicts over 'geographic protocol' and the capacity to name were important as ideological expressions of sovereignty; key to ordering and exerting order, the right to name was taken seriously by those who exercised power – as the diplomatic struggle for authority waged between British ambassador Downing and Dutch Governor Stuyvesant in the 1660s shows so vividly.

The early nineteenth century saw an explosion of scientific map-making dealing with the oceans and the heavens as well as the earth. Imperial aspirations figured strongly in the production of naval hydrographic charts, astronomical surveys of the skies of the southern hemisphere (Herschel) and the Great Trigonometrical Survey of India (Lambton and Everest), which determined the height of the Himalayan mountains and the precise extent of India's landmass.[16] Below ground level, geological and stratigraphical surveys disclosed information vital for mineral extraction. These ventures also established 'deep time' sequences that

---

[15]   See, for example, Macgaffey (1966). The Hamitic theory, which was fully elaborated by linguists and scientists of race in the nineteenth century, rests on the biblical story of Ham, who is said to have been punished for dishonouring his father, Noah. Hamites are seen as black Africans (typically pastoralists) who, though cursed, are nonetheless 'superior' to Bantu-speaking 'negroids' by virtue of being of having 'caucasoid' ancestry. This highly flexible racial mythology was widely applied in Africa, and has been cited as one of the deep-rooted causes of division in the 1994 Rwanda genocide.

[16]   For a stimulating discussion of the triangulation survey of the Indian subcontinent, see Keay (2000).

proved the earth's antiquity, and were in turn used to validate theories of evolution and inform racially inflected notions about the peopling of the world. The mapping impulse was in part prompted by scientific curiosity; it also served powerful economic and political interests. All these aspects are distilled in Robert Stafford's study of 'Scientific Exploration and Empire' (Chapter 12), which pays close attention to the Royal Geographical Society (established in 1830) and its role in sponsoring many highly publicized feats of heroic exploration in Africa. These ventures aroused popular support for imperialism and helped to legitimize territorial expansion and control of newly 'discovered' lands.

Mapping established multidimensional matrices of potential power, but it was only with the creation of colonial bureaucracies that 'cadastral politics' took full shape. This term, as used by Arjun Appadurai in 'Number in the Colonial Imagination' (Chapter 9), shows how routine acts of administrative enumeration were ideologically rooted in a quest to order, categorize and control. Drawing on Cohn's influential analysis of the population census in India, Appadurai considers the colonial state's fascination with numbers. Counting, classifying and taxonomizing native bodies, as well as the land and its resources, was vital to the administration's ability to comprehend, objectify and manage the exotic and unfamiliar. The statistical enterprise was also important as a means of '*translating* the colonial experience into terms graspable in the metropolis, terms that could encompass the ethnological peculiarities that various orientalist discourses provided' (p. 255; emphasis in original). It was one thing for colonial authorities to count and order the unfamiliar so as to render sovereignty meaningful and manageable from the point of view of officialdom, quite another to ensure that such units of measurement were recognized and internalized by (often unwilling) subjects. The regimentation of time posed a particular problem.

In 1967, the British social historian E.P. Thompson published a leading article dealing with the ways in which the English working class was habituated to the discipline and work rhythms of industrial capitalism. In Chapter 10, Keletso Atkins applies these ideas to Nguni-speaking Zulu agriculturalists responding to the labour requirements of sugar planters in nineteenth-century colonial Natal. Time, she argues, 'was at the nexus of the "kafir labour problem"' (p. 270). European labour contracts did not accord with African modes of temporal reckoning which, Atkins maintains, were oriented to the moon and the stars and seasonal cycles. There was no direct equivalent in isiZulu to the European idea of a calendar year, nor any agreement on the length of the working day since the period between sunrise and sunset varied from summer to winter. The inability of employers to impose industrial work rhythms on the sugar estates was one reason that Indian indentured workers were employed in Natal from 1860. In urban areas, employers proved more successful in instilling the concept of work-time or 'clock consciousness', but this was not a simple victory: conflicts about the length of the day and permissible leisure time on weekends prompted protests and strikes.[17]

---

[17]   Note the parallels with James C. Scott's *Weapons of the Weak* (1987) published just before Atkins's essay. For a major new study, see Nanni (2012).

Indigenous Knowledge

As well as being about the interplay of knowledge and power, Atkins's treatment raises the broader issue of the interaction between colonial and indigenous knowledge, a term that usually refers to local, culturally based knowledge systems pertaining to food cultivation, human and animal medicine, and understandings of the environment. The concept came to prominence in the 1970s as development theorists and anthropologists challenged the widespread modernizing assumption that traditional knowledge was an obstacle to progress and contended instead that locally based 'participatory' knowledge was key to achieving sustainable development and poverty alleviation.

As descriptors of particular kinds of knowledge, the adjectives 'colonial' and 'indigenous' are of recent coinage. Curiously, there is as yet no entry for 'indigenous knowledge' in the *Oxford English Dictionary*, although it is a widely used term in international development agencies where it is commonly abbreviated as IK or IKS (the last letter referring to systems).[18] The attractiveness of the concept has to be understood in part as a reaction against so-called 'Eurocentric' assumptions that 'Western' science or knowledge is neutral or objective.[19] Indeed, one of the chief ways in which conquest was justified during the colonial era was the claim (or faith) that colonialism involved imparting knowledge, secular as well as religious, to save those who lacked it.

We now have a much more sophisticated understanding of the ways in which the conversion of oral forms of knowledge into print helped enable colonial modernity. This goes along with greater appreciation of the importance of orality, and the resilience and potential of diverse indigenous forms of knowledge.[20] Historians of colonized regions of the world are thus much more disposed today to view knowledge as mutually 'co-produced' or syncretic.

Whether opposed to each other as antonyms or conjoined in notions of hybridity and interpenetration, we should resist reifying 'indigenous' and 'colonial' forms of knowledge. These terms may be helpful for heuristic purposes, yet they are too diverse and complex to be treated as unitary bodies of thought. Indigenous knowledge is neither innate nor unchanging, nor can it be assumed to be the exclusive or collective property of particular groups. It is no less constructed than any other form of knowledge. We should not ignore the fact that 'indigenous' (sometimes 'ethno-') is often a synonym for 'native' and therefore tends to be used to refer to areas of the globe that fell under the shadow of colonialism. A certain kind of privileging seems to be operative here.

It is therefore worth considering why 'indigenous', 'local' knowledge has found acceptance in extra-European contexts, in preference to words like 'folk' 'everyday', 'popular', 'tacit' or 'artisanal' knowledge – formulations that commonly occur in studies of early modern Europe where the spectre of 'primitiveness' intrudes rather less.[21] Anthropologists and

---

[18] But the term 'ethno-' as in 'ethno-botany' does occur in the *Oxford English Dictionary*.

[19] The *OED*'s etymological entry for 'eurocentric' includes a 2005 quotation from the *Big Issue* in South Africa: 'The trouble with science is that it's Eurocentric – and this is Africa.' For useful discussions of indigenous knowledge, see Ellen et al. (2000) and Agrawal (1995).

[20] For a recent discussion, see Ballantyne (2011). In the African context, see Hofmeyr (2003) and Barber (2006).

[21] Helen Tilly (2010) makes a case for the use of 'vernacular science'.

sociologists have long provided sophisticated refutations of the categorical or distinction between indigenous and Western knowledge systems. Historians also have an important role in relativizing these concepts through situating them in time depth. As Peter Burke has shown in his social history of knowledge, there exists a plurality of knowledges in every culture, and distinctions between different kinds or levels of knowledge are always relative. Europe, too, had its 'margins', as well as its marginalized groups, whose expertise was drawn upon in development work – for instance the women labourers whose indigenous knowledge was utilized in helping to construct the Canal du Midi in seventeenth century France (Burke, 2000, ch. 1; Mukerji, 2007; Schmidt and Smith, 2007, p. 8). It follows that we should endeavour always to treat indigenous knowledge in Africa, India or Latin America as part of a universal or global process of historical enquiry rather than as the unchanging property of particular ethnic or cultural groups.

The fact that the encounter between colonial and indigenous knowledge systems frequently took place in situations structured by conflict and unequal power is of central importance, notwithstanding the emphasis that many writers place on mutuality and exchange. Relations of power and matters of status are therefore significant. In the imperial encounter attitudes to nature and land were always deeply contested. In some cases (such as Australia and parts of North America) the doctrine of terra nullius ('land belonging to no one') was invoked to deny that indigenous peoples had any sovereign rights to land. Where the presence of natives could not be denied, colonists arrogated to themselves the right both to exploit nature and to interpret and protect it, often presuming that indigenous peoples were thoughtlessly destructive of their environments. It followed that scientific experts were best placed to inform colonial decision-making in fields as diverse as agricultural practices, soil erosion, forestry management and game preservation. Over the last two decades a powerful counter-view has been articulated, which insists that indigenous people were often the best custodians of the land and that their knowledge, acquired over multiple generations, was frequently more appropriate and effective than the prescriptions of colonial science (see, for example, Fairhead and Leach, 1996).

Chapter 15, Richard Grove's bold attempt to achieve a 'global synthesis' of the literature on colonial conservation, argues that contestation over resources and resource management is essential to our understanding of resistance to imperialism. He discerns a pattern of 'ecological power relations' as early as the mid-seventeenth century, which became subject to acute contestation at the height of imperial expansion in the mid-nineteenth century. Colonial scientists were key agents in imperial expansion and, indeed, the concept of scientists as state employees developed on the colonial periphery rather than originating in the metropoles.

Many of these experts were stationed in different colonial locations over the course of their careers, thereby accumulating comparative knowledge and speeding up the circulation of conservationist theories. Ecological crises, human-made or natural, were often proximate causes of popular resistance, especially if they resulted in famine or loss of land. In response, colonial conservation strictures were used to contain political challenges arising out of population pressures and hunger. In the twentieth century, nascent nationalist movements responded to popular protests rooted in ecological crisis, though sometimes incorporating these movements in ways that ultimately betrayed their causes. For Grove, the imposition of colonial knowledge in the form of conservationism is therefore crucial to our understanding of conquest and resistance.

The field of environmental history, at both a local and a global level, has burgeoned and matured in the last two decades, as William Beinart's distillation of his own and others' work on Africa amply shows (Chapter 16). Like Grove, Beinart draws inspiration from the formative work of Alfred W. Crosby, who explored the global impacts of European expansion on human history in his 1986 book, *Ecological Imperialism*. Beinart, too, is concerned with themes of human agency and resistance, key ideas in African historiography. He shares in the growing consensus that Africans' alleged culpability in environmental degradation has been much exaggerated; there are many instances in which the local knowledge acquired by African women and men has proved a better guide to environmental management than the advice offered by technical experts. Nevertheless, Beinart cautions against a simple inversion whereby all local knowledge and custodianship is applauded and all interventionist wisdom is condemned. He eschews simple attributions of blame for environmental crises and allows for the possibility that state-led strategies may be essential for recuperation. Similarly, he points out that African ideas and practices have undergone significant change often in dialogue with colonial scientists who displayed sensitivity to African viewpoints. The logic of Beinart's carefully considered argument points strongly to seeing systems of knowledge as 'porous and plural over a long period' (p. 447).

Comparable arguments about the interconnections between indigenous and colonial medicine have been advanced by David Arnold, a founding member of the subaltern school, with broad interests in science and the colonial body. Chapter 13, Arnold's introduction to the key 1998 collection, *Imperial Medicine and Indigenous Societies* (one of an important series of books inspired by the pioneering cultural historian of empire John Mackenzie), demonstrates that medicine was as much about ideology as it was a scientific means of curing disease.

In Arnold's conception, the historical study of disease and medicine is a means of illuminating broad themes in imperial and colonial history. Crucially, it concerns power and authority. Attitudes to disease were strongly conditioned by preconceptions about the racial or cultural backwardness of indigenous people, and in many cases worked to reinforce such racial prejudices. Reciprocally, epidemics and ill-health might be interpreted by indigenous people as evidence of colonial malevolence. For Europeans, too, fears about 'tropical' diseases reflected broader anxieties about threats posed by the environments and peoples they were colonizing. Rather like scientific expertise in agronomy and conservation, Western medicine was assumed by Europeans to be self-evidently a gift of colonialism. Some Africans and Asians were persuaded by its benefits and trained as doctors, nurses and auxiliaries. Yet, in disrupting or denigrating indigenous conceptions of health, Western medicine and pharmacology challenged strongly held ideas and cosmologies. This in turn provoked suspicion and resistance.

Evidence of mutual suspicion in the colonial encounter is not hard to come by, as incompatible cosmological views of the world were forced into some form of mutual engagement. Luise White offers a vivid example of such dissonance from colonial East Africa in her suggestive essay 'Cars out of Place' (Chapter 17). Here she addresses the persistent belief of many Africans in the existence of vampires, which were often associated with colonial institutions and symbols of modernity: typically, hospitals, red cars and fire engines. For White, such fears illuminate much about the colonial encounter that otherwise lies submerged. Vehicles, which conspicuously alter spatiotemporal boundaries, may become vectors for older folkloric anxieties as well as symbols of power relationships. It was not only ordinary people who found technology fearsome; skilled workers might also be mystified by aspects of the machines they used, or else use the secret knowledge they acquired for personal advantage. White abjures any simple explanation of vampiric phenomena; the meanings of mechanical devices were layered, contradictory and complex. Vampires, she suggests, were 'new symbols for new times' (p. 469).

In other cases, the gulf between knowledge systems was not so much a source of incomprehension and conflict as a spur to understanding borne of mutual curiosity. Patrick Harries's study of the activities of Swiss missionaries in south-east Africa (Chapter 14) shows how European intellectuals sought to accommodate Africa and Africans into their own mental landscapes. H.A. Junod, an enlightened missionary anthropologist from the Swiss Romande, arrived in Lourenço Marques in 1889. Already grappling with the powerful concept of evolution, and the desire to reconcile science with religion, he sought to do something similar with respect to African and European conceptions of knowledge. Science offered Junod a powerful methodology to study African society; it also offered knowledge brokers, like his informant/collaborator Elias 'Spoon' Libombo, opportunities to secure their own position as part of an emerging local elite.

Harries's work demonstrates how the intellectually receptive Junod developed an international reputation as an entomologist and anthropologist. He depended on the botanical expertise of Africans and respected their skills, while believing that Africans would have to adopt European scientific rationality in order to progress. Junod disavowed social Darwinism, in part because his religious beliefs disposed him to reject simple materialism, but also because he considered that all humans were susceptible to improvement. Thus, he likened the superstitions of Africans to those of uneducated rural Swiss. A striking feature of the chapter included here from *Butterflies and Barbarians* is the way in which Harries demonstrates the hybridity of new knowledge in formation: 'one root of modern science', Harries concludes, 'has to be located in the messy, everyday encounters' (p. 393) between missionaries, their converts, and indigenous custodians of knowledge such as diviners and rainmakers.

The Circulation of Knowledge

The scientific life of H.A. Junod, who enjoyed a wide correspondence and exchanged artefacts with museums around the world, is just one example of how 'universal' knowledge was co-produced on the frontiers of empire. Indeed, it serves as a useful reminder that a great deal of European science was practised outside of Europe, and that European science would have been much the poorer without such field laboratories, which often allowed scientists unparalleled scope to investigate and experiment. Seen in this way, Harries's essay is one of many rejoinders to George Basalla's modernizing model of the diffusion of Western science (1966) from a few, select, hubs to the extra-European world.[22]

---

[22]   Basalla allowed for, but showed no interest in, the existence of 'ancient, indigenous scientific thought' (p. 611) in India, Japan and China. He did not even consider that there might be any systems of scientific thought extant among 'the primitives encountered elsewhere' (p. 622).

Basalla's sequential, mechanical, outline (sometimes imagined as a radiant lighthouse, as radial spokes on a wheel or in terms of imperial core and colonial periphery) was decisively challenged in 1982 by Roy Macleod, in a widely cited article 'On Visiting the "Moving Metropolis"'. Macleod approached the generation of global knowledge in polycentric terms and questioned the assumption that 'colonial' science was derivative, inferior or valuable only for its fact-gathering function.[23]

By colonial science, Macleod was primarily thinking of settler societies like Australia. But his decentred approach is applicable far more widely and has in turn prompted many alternative ways of understanding the spread of knowledge. The historical geographer David Livingstone argues that knowledge is always produced in particular locales and has to be understood contextually. In his view, science does not disperse evenly across the world: 'As it moves it is modified; as it travels it is transformed' (Livingstone, 2003, p. 4). In this sense, science is always 'local knowledge' (Livingstone, 2003, p. 81). Spatial relationships and trajectories are also stressed by Alan Lester and David Lambert (2006) who follow the imperial careers of particular individuals to demonstrate how ideas were transplanted, connected and sustained.

Imperial institutions like Kew Gardens, with its affiliate botanical gardens spread throughout the globe, formed part of this system of knowledge exchange, as did a thick array of print culture (newspapers, periodicals, journals) and institutions (circulating libraries, museums). Centres like London, Edinburgh, Paris and Berlin played key roles as originary centres and brokerages but there is a wealth of evidence to show intercolonial exchange too. The assumption of unidirectional flows of knowledge controlled by a limited number of metropolitan-based 'centres of calculation' has thus yielded to a much more networked, delegated and hence reciprocal understanding of knowledge accumulation, dispersal and exchange. Analogies and metaphors like mapping, networking and the web have begun to supplant rigid conceptions of diffusion from key points of origin. Words like 'hybridity', 'fluidity' and 'interpenetration' proliferate.

Nevertheless, this growing consensus has not gone unchallenged. Lewis Pyenson, for example, continues to insist that scientific knowledge differs little from one place to another while denying that science is in any significant sense 'national'. According to Pyenson (2002, 2011), the influence of postmodernism has allowed relativism to run rampant, meaning that small differences in scientific 'style' are wildly exaggerated.

Several essays in this collection implicitly question the assumption that Western science should constitute the paradigm against which other knowledge systems ought to be assessed. In Chapter 18, 'Global Knowledge on the Move', Neil Safier makes this explicit, by raising the problem of whether indigenous and Western knowledge systems are mutually comprehensible or epistemologically commensurable. Drawing on the history of exploration of eighteenth-century Amazonia, Safier suggests that indigenous conceptions of time and place may simply not translate into, or be comparable with, linear imperial models of scientific production. He argues that an integrated history of the encounter between knowledge systems ought not be constrained by reference to scientific and political institutions, or 'intercivilizational' contact – which Basalla took for granted in his conception of the spread of Western science. In Safier's view, imperial models of knowledge acquisition and dissemination ought to give

---

[23]   Macleod borrowed the phrase 'moving metropolis' from W.K. Hancock, the great Australian historian of empire/commonwealth.

way to alternative conceptual schemes that allow far more expansive definitions of global scientific enterprise.

The questions raised by Safier do not turn on the normative value or worth of different knowledge schemes as much as on the problems we wish to consider. If our primary interest is in the nature of the phenomenological encounter between Western and indigenous knowledge systems, the methodology we employ is bound to be different from one that seeks to understand the spread of knowledge, its explanatory force and its relation to centres of economic and political power. It is one thing to ask what is specifically Western about Western science, a question nicely posed by Marwa Elshakry (2010), quite another to ask, ontologically, what scientific knowledge is, as Safier seems to be doing.

Daniela Bleichmar's discussion of visual culture in the Hispanic enlightenment (Chapter 20) overlaps temporally with Safier. It, too, concerns knowledge generated through exploration, in this case expeditions led by the Spanish physician and botanist José Celestino Mutis (1732–1808). As a botanist, Mutis drew on local expertise, but he was mostly dismissive of popular knowledge. He engaged large teams of artists to record flowers and plants in great detail. The huge visual archive he oversaw on an industrial scale was intended to collapse the distance between Spain and its colonies, to represent what was unique about South America, but without taking much account of local cultural or environmental contexts. It was driven by a desire to exploit the economic potential of South America's resources, and the desire to affirm the cognitive reach, power and universality of the Linnean system.

Bleichmar's analysis would place Mutis firmly in the tradition of Enlightenment imperial science, yet she observes that he is celebrated today as a founding figure of Colombian national science and therefore as a source of patriotic pride. This points to a difference, evident particularly in work on settler societies, between imperial and *colonial* science, one that is frequently occluded in post-colonial writings.

The distinction is clearly evident in work on the British dominions where settlers deliberately sought to re-create the societies they had left behind.[24] As they expanded over the world, settlers initially saw themselves as agents of imperialism. But, over time, many deliberately acquired a form of indigeneity (partly in order to deny the rights of native peoples) and came to express local forms of patriotism that challenged aspects of the dominance of the imperial metropole. This phenomenon is conspicuous in the loosely linked network of neo-British settler colonies (Australia, New Zealand, Canada and South Africa) that achieved self-governing Dominion status in the first decade of the twentieth century.

I address this issue in Chapter 19, 'A Commonwealth of Science', which compares the visits of the British Association for the Advancement of Science to South Africa in 1905 and 1929. Whereas the purpose of the first excursion was to reiterate the power and universality of British-based science, in order to draw a recalcitrant rebel nation back into the imperial fold, a quarter century later accommodations had to be made to rising Afrikaner nationalism in South Africa. This was also a key moment in the transmutation from empire to the (white) commonwealth of nations. The 'South Africanization' of science, offered by senior politicians as a reason for whites to exhibit common national patriotism and pride, was thus closely linked to a dual political effort to transcend ethnic tensions between English- and Afrikaans-

---

24   It is a clear subtheme in Macleod's 'On Visiting the "Moving Metropolis"' (1980). See also Macleod (2009). My own ideas are elaborated in *A Commonwealth of Knowledge* (Dubow, 2006).

speakers in the interwar period, and thereby reinforce the political subjugation of African peoples. The development of colonial racial science was very much part of this process.

Conclusions

Any collection must be selective and this one is no exception. The aim of this volume has been to include a mixture of foundational and newer texts which were either intended to speak to each other or can be shown to do so. Selection applies to themes as well.

One omission has been the literature on gendered knowledge, beginning with the question as to whether knowledge is implicitly masculine. In the case of scientific knowledge, the assumption would be that knowledge is neutral in respect of gender, just as it is supposedly value-free. But even if this implausible claim has some merit, it can hardly be sustained in respect of medicine, midwifery, sorcery and so on. In Australia, secret or special women's knowledge became a major point of legal and political contestation in regard to land claims affecting the Ngarrendjeri people during the 1990s when the controversial Mabo and Wik judgments dealing with indigenous 'native title' to land reached the High Court (Howden, 2001).

This question about the gendering of colonial knowledge suggests another omission, namely colonial jurisprudence, especially as this affected marriage, property and family. The law has not been included in this volume, since it is a large and specialized subfield that necessitates taking account of a diverse and technical set of concepts ranging from terra nullius and customary law to individual versus collective rights.

Turning back to the questions that this volume does set out to address, what observations or tentative conclusions can be made?

The approach here turns on the notion of the 'colonial situation', a formulation suggesting that European global expansion occasioned multiple fields of social and intellectual interaction and that these require analysis in an integrated, synchronic manner. Many historians attempt to do precisely this, but we are still only beginning to look at the connections between different colonial situations. In an age of heightened awareness about globalization, there is a tendency to assume that information circulates seamlessly and to restate a much older assumption that knowledge knows no boundaries. Yet knowledge and information are not identical, precisely because knowledge is processed to a higher degree than raw empirical data. This may result in the formulation of widely applicable abstract principles but it is just as likely to be specific to particular contexts.

The specificity of knowledge can be reinforced rather than diminished by academic disciplines, schools and specialisms which, as they become more developed and self-referential, may serve to concentrate scholarship at the cost of the broad dissemination of ideas. The example of the near simultaneous, but largely discrete, discussions about the invention of caste in India and of tribe in Africa has already been noted. The apparent failure to make connections between the study of indigenous or local knowledge in colonial formations on the one hand, and pre-modern European societies on the other is also worth considering. The convergence of critical and 'new left' thinking about knowledge as a form of power in France, Germany and the United States in the 1960s and 1970s stands as a partial counter-example, but in fact it took quite some time for insights generated by sociologists, anthropologists and historians to coalesce, for example in the post-structuralist and post-colonial approaches of Foucault and Said.

Even where debates and discussions appear to mirror each other so closely as to be connected, it is not always clear that we are talking about the same thing. However universal in reach and application, Darwin's theory of evolution did not resonate in quite the same ways in Britain as it did in Germany or the United States, let alone in Egypt or in Japan (see, for example, Elshakry, 2008; Livingstone, 2006; Numbers and Stenhouse, 1999). Likewise, the message of the Christian Bible was not promoted in the same way, nor understood identically, in Africa, Asia or Latin America, or indeed within those continents.

The colonial knowledge encounter in India, which was often characterized by interactions between literate elites from different cultures, differs substantially from encounters with non-literate societies in Africa, Latin America or Australasia, where local peoples' initiatives and agency can only be surmised through the records compiled by those responsible for their conquest. As we have seen, this challenge has been taken up by Ranajit Guha's 'Prose of Counterinsurgency' (Chapter 5), a remarkable effort to illuminate ideological 'blind spots' in the Indian colonial archives. The challenge is made even more difficult in situations like Amazonia where, as Neil Safier points out in Chapter 18, indigenous knowledge systems may be entirely incommensurable with those of European colonizers.

Clearly, different techniques and approaches have to be developed to speak meaningfully about such colonial situations. One historian who takes up the challenge is Greg Dening, whose brilliant treatment of colonial encounters on the beaches and islands of the Pacific makes cognitive dissonance and epistemological uncertainty the very substance of his investigations. Dening's form of 'reflective history' is powerfully evocative but fundamentally indeterminate as he 're-presents' the past in literary forms that border on the speculative and fictive. He advocates going beyond the 'texted past' so as to understand colonial knowledge in terms of symbolic exchanges, signs and inscriptions (see, for example, Dening, 1980, 1988; for an appreciation, see Griffiths, 2009).

Though not so radical or experimental as Dening, several essays in this collection tend to a 'soft' relativism at least insofar as they demonstrate that knowledge is neither unitary nor culture-free. Running in parallel with this view is the assumption that knowledge and power are intimately connected and, indeed, that the acquisition and utilization of colonial knowledge was designed to underwrite colonial dominance, whether directly or indirectly. The essays by Asad, Atkins, Guha and Appadurai lean strongly towards this view. Other contributions, for instance those by Arnold, Bayly, Beinart and White, are more attuned to the constraints on colonial power and its failure in given colonial situations to displace other competing knowledge systems. Sujit Sivasundaram (2012) expresses this as the 'thesis of limits' in his chapter in the *Ashgate Research Companion to Modern Imperial Histories*. In different ways, Beidelman, Bleichmar, Dubow and Harries suggest that colonial knowledge had as much to do with self-understanding and colonial identity formation as with exerting power and control over others.

Perhaps all we can conclude is that colonial knowledge was never just one thing, that it served different interests at different times, and that its calculating intentions were significantly offset by incalculable consequences.

References

Agrawal, Arun (1995), 'Dismantling the Divide between Indigenous and Scientific Knowledge', *Development and Change*, **26**, 3, pp. 413–39.

Arnold, David (1997), 'All Ears to the Ground', *Times Higher Educational Supplement*, 21 April.

Asad, Talal (ed.) (1973), *Anthropology and the Colonial Encounter*, London: Ithaca Press.

Ballantyne, Tony (2011), 'Paper, Pen, and Print: The Transformation of the Kai Tahu Knowledge Order', *Comparative Studies in Society and History*, **53**, 2, pp. 232–60.

Barber, Karin (ed.) (2006), *Africa's Hidden Histories: Everyday Literacy and the Making of the Self*, Bloomington: Indiana University Press.

Basalla, G. (1967), 'The Spread of Western Science', *Science*, **156**, 3775, pp. 611–22.

Bayly, C.A. (1996), *Empire and Information: Intelligence Gathering and Social Communication in India, 1780–1870*, Cambridge: Cambridge University Press.

Brown, R. (1973), 'Anthropology and Colonial Rule: The Case of Godfrey Wilson and the Rhodes-Livingstone Institute, Northern Rhodesia', in Talal Asad (ed.), *Anthropology and the Colonial Encounter*, London: Ithaca Press, pp. 173–99.

Burawoy, M. (2008), 'Intellectuals and their Publics: Bourdieu meets Mills', at: http://burawoy.berkeley.edu/Bourdieu/8.Mills.pdf.

Burke, Peter (2000), *A Social History of Knowledge*, Cambridge: Polity Press.

Cohn, Bernard S. (ed.) (1987), *An Anthropologist among the Historians and Other Essays*, Delhi: Oxford University Press.

Cohn, Bernard S. (1996), *Colonialism and its Forms of Knowledge: The British in India*, Princeton: Princeton University Press.

Comaroff, Jean and Comaroff, John L. (1991), *Of Revelation and Revolution*, Vol. 1: *Christianity, Colonialism, and Consciousness in South Africa*, Chicago: University of Chicago Press.

Conklin, Alice L. (2002), 'The New "Ethnology" and "La Situation Coloniale" in Interwar France', *French Politics, Culture & Society*, **20**, 2, pp. 29–46.

Cooper, F. (2002), 'Decolonizing Situations: The Rise, Fall and Rise of Colonial Studies, 1951–2001', *French Politics, Culture & Society*, **20**, 2, pp. 47–76.

Crosby, Alfred W. (1986), *Ecological Imperialism: The Biological Expansion of Europe, 900–1900*, Cambridge: Cambridge University Press.

Dening, Greg (1980), *Islands and Beaches: Discourse on a Silent Land, Marquesas 1774–1880*, Honolulu: University of Hawai'i Press.

Dening, Greg (1988), *History's Anthropology: The Death of William Gooch*, Lanham, MD: University Press of America.

Dirks, Nicholas B. (1988), 'The Invention of Caste: Civil Society in Colonial India', CSST Working Paper #11, University of Michigan, Ann Arbor, October.

Dubow, Saul (2006), *A Commonwealth of Knowledge: Science, Sensibility and White South Africa, 1820–2000*, Oxford: Oxford University Press.

Ellen, Roy, Parkes, Peter and Bicker, Alan (eds) (2000), *Indigenous Environmental Knowledge and its Transformations*, Amsterdam: Harwood Academic.

Elshakry, Marwa (2008), 'Knowledge in Motion: The Cultural Politics of Modern Science Translations in Arabic', *Isis*, **99**, 4, pp. 701–30.

Elshakry, Marwa (2010), 'When Science Became Western: Historiographical Reflections', *Isis*, **101**, 1, pp. 98–109.

Fairhead, James and Leach, Melissa (1996), *Misreading the African Landscape: Society and Ecology in a Forest-Savanna Mosaic*, Cambridge: Cambridge University Press.

Gluckman, M. (1940), 'Analysis of a Social Situation in Modern Zululand', *Bantu Studies*, **14**, pp. 1–30, 147–74.

Gough, K. (1968), 'New Proposals for Anthropologists', *Current Anthropology*, **9**, 5, pp. 403–407.

Griffiths, T. (2009), 'Greg Dening (1931–2008)', *History Workshop Journal*, **67**, 1, pp. 292–96.

Guha, Ramachandra (1995), 'Subaltern and Bhadralok Studies', *Economic and Political Weekly*, 19 August, pp. 2056–58.

Guha, Ranajit (1983), *Elementary Aspects of Peasant Insurgency in Colonial India*, Delhi: Oxford University Press.

Guha, Ranajit (1987), 'Introduction', to B.S. Cohn (ed.), *An Anthropologist among the Historians and Other Essays*, Delhi: Oxford University Press, pp. vii–xxvi.

Hofmeyr, Isabel (2003), *The Portable Bunyan: A Transnational History of the Pilgrim's Progress*, Princeton: Princeton University Press.

Howden, K. (2001), 'Indigenous Traditional Knowledge and Native Title', *University of New South Wales Law Journal*, **24**, 1, pp. 60–84.

Irwin, Robert (2006), *For Lust of Knowing: The Orientalists and their Enemies*, London: Allen Lane.

Keay, J. (2000), *The Great Arc: The Dramatic Tale of How India was Mapped and Everest was Named*, London: HarperCollins.

Kuper, Adam (1973), *Anthropology and Anthropologists: The Modern British School*, London: Routledge & Kegan Paul.

Lambert, David and Lester, Alan (eds) (2006), *Colonial Lives Across the British Empire: Imperial Careering in the Long Nineteenth Century*, Cambridge: Cambridge University Press.

Leyleveld, D. (1993), 'The Fate of Hindustani: Colonial Knowledge and the Project of a National Language', in Carol A. Breckenridge and Peter van der Veer (eds), *Orientalism and the Postcolonial Predicament: Perspectives on South Asia*, Philadelphia: University of Pennsylvania Press, pp. 189–214.

Livingstone, David N. (2003), *Putting Science in its Place: Geographies of Scientific Knowledge*, Chicago: University of Chicago Press.

Livingstone, David N. (2006), 'The Geography of Darwinism', *Interdisciplinary Science Reviews*, **31**, pp. 32–41.

Macgaffey, Wyatt (1966), 'Concepts of Race in the Historiography of Northeast Africa', *Journal of African History*, **7**, 1, pp. 1–17.

Mackenzie, John M. (1995), *Orientalism: History, Theory and the Arts*, Manchester: Manchester University Press.

Macleod, R. (1980), 'On Visiting the "Moving Metropolis": Reflections on the Architecture of Imperial Science', *Historical Records of Australian Science*, **5**, 3, pp. 1–16.

Macleod, R. (2009), *Archibald Liversidge, FRS: Imperial Science under the Southern Cross*, Sydney: University of Sydney Press and the Royal Society of New South Wales.

Mills, C. Wright (1956), *The Power Elite*, New York: Oxford University Press.

Mills, C. Wright (1960), *Listen, Yankee: The Revolution in Cuba*, New York: Ballantine Books.

Mukerji, Chandra (2007), 'Women Engineers and the Culture of the Pyrenees: Indigenous Knowledge and Engineering in Seventeenth-Century France', in B. Schmidt and P. Smith (eds), *Making Knowledge in Early Modern Europe: Practices, Objects and Texts, 1400–1800*, Chicago: University of Chicago Press, pp. 19–44.

Nanni, Giordano (2012), *The Colonisation of Time*, Manchester: Manchester University Press.

Numbers, Ronald L. and Stenhouse, John (eds) (1999), *Disseminating Darwin: The Role of Place, Race, Religion and Gender*, Cambridge: Cambridge University Press.

O'Hanlon, Rosalind (1988), 'Recovering the Subject: Subaltern Studies and Histories of Resistance in Colonial South Asia', *Modern Asian Studies*, **22**, 1, pp. 189–224.

Pinch, William R. (1999), 'Same Difference in India and Europe', *History and Theory*, **38**, 3, pp. 389–407.

Pyenson, L. (2002), 'An End to National Science: The Meaning and the Extension of Local Knowledge', *History of Science*, **40**, pp. 251–90.

Pyenson, L. (2011), 'The Enlightened Image of Nature in the Dutch East Indies: Consequences of Postmodernist Doctrine for Broad Structures and Intimate Life', *Historical Studies in the Natural Sciences*, **41**, 1, pp. 1–40.

Said, Edward (1978), *Orientalism*, London: Routledge & Kegan Paul.

Schmidt, B. and Smith, P. (eds) (2007), *Making Knowledge in Early Modern Europe: Practices, Objects and Texts, 1400–1800*, Chicago: University of Chicago Press.

Scott, James C. (1987), *Weapons of the Weak: Everyday Forms of Peasant Resistance*, New Haven, CT: Yale University Press.

Sivasundaram, Sujit (2012), 'Science, Medicine and Technology', in P. Levine and J. Marriot (eds), *The Ashgate Research Companion to Modern Imperial Histories*, Farnham: Ashgate, pp. 549–66.

'Subaltern Studies II: A Review Article' (1984), *Social Scientist*, **12**, 137, pp. 3–41.

Summers, John H. (2006), 'The Deciders', *New York Times*, 14 May.

Thompson, E.P. (1967), 'Time, Work-Discipline, and Industrial Capitalism', *Past & Present*, **38**, pp. 56–97.

Tilly, Helen (2010), 'Global Histories, Vernacular Science, and African Genealogies; or is the History of Science Ready for the World?', *Isis*, **101**, 1, pp. 110–19.

Vail, L. (ed.) (1989), *The Creation of Tribalism in South Africa*, London: James Currey.

Part I
The Colonial Situation

[1]

THE COLONIAL SITUATION:
A THEORETICAL APPROACH (1951)

G. Balandier

One of the most striking events in the recent history of mankind is the expansion throughout the entire world of most European peoples. It has brought about the subjugation and, in some instances, the disappearance of virtually every people regarded as backward, archaic, or primitive. The colonial movement of the nineteenth century was the most important in magnitude, the most fraught with consequences, resulting from this European expansion. It overturned in a brutal manner the history of the peoples it subjugated. Colonialism, in establishing itself, imposed on subject peoples a very special type of situation. We cannot ignore this fact. It not only conditioned the reactions of "dependent" peoples, but is still responsible for certain reactions of peoples recently emancipated. The *colonial situation* poses problems for a conquered people—who respond to these problems to the degree that a certain latitude is granted to them—problems for the administration representing the so-called protective power (which also defends that power's local interests), problems for the newly created state on which still rests the burden of colonial liabilities. Whether currently present or in process of liquidation, this *situation* involves specific problems which must arrest the attention of a sociologist. The postwar period has clearly indicated the urgency and importance of the colonial problem in its totality. It has been characterized by difficult attempts at reconquest, by the granting of independence to some, and by more or less conditional concessions to others. It has announced a technical phase in colonialism in the wake of a political-administrative phase.

It was only a few years ago that a rough but significant estimate

SOURCE. G. Balandier, "La Situation Coloniale: Approche Théorique," reprinted from *Cahiers internationaux de sociologie*, XI, 1951, pp. 44–79, by permission of the Presses Universitaires de France.

noted the fact that colonial territories covered at that time one-third of the world's surface and that seven hundred million individuals out of a total population of some two billion were subject peoples.[1] Until very recently the greater part of the world's population, not belonging to the white race (if we exclude China and Japan), knew only a status of dependency on one or another of the European colonial powers. These subject peoples, distributed throughout Asia, Africa, and Oceania, all belonged to cultures designated "backward" or "pre-industrial." They constituted the field of research within which anthropologists or ethnologists carried on—and still carry on—their investigations. And the scientific knowledge that we have of colonial peoples is due in large part to the efforts of these scholarly investigators. Such studies, in principle, could not (or should not) ignore such an important fact as colonialism, a phenomenon which has imposed, for a century or more, a certain type of evolution on subjugated populations. It seemed impossible not to take into account certain concrete situations in which the recent history of these peoples evolved. And yet it is only now and then that anthropologists have taken into consideration this specific context inherent in the *colonial situation*. (We have substantiating evidence to present in a study presently in preparation.) On the one hand, we find researchers obsessed with the pursuit of the ethnologically pure, with the unaltered fact miraculously preserved in its primitive state, or else investigators entirely absorbed with theoretical speculations regarding the destiny of civilizations or the origins of society. And on the other hand, we find researchers engaged in numerous practical investigations of very limited scope, satisfied with a comfortable empiricism scarcely surpassing the level of using a technique. Between the two extremes the distance is great—it leads from the confines of a so-called "cultural" anthropology to the confines of one described as "applied" anthropology. In one case, the colonial situation is rejected as being a disturbing factor or is seen as only one of the causes of cultural change. In the other case, the colonial situation is viewed only in certain aspects—those immediately and obviously relating to the problem under investigation—and never appears as a force acting in terms of its own totality. Yet any *present-day* study of colonial societies striving for an understanding of current realities and not a reconstitution of a purely historical nature, a study aiming at a comprehension of conditions as they are, not sacrificing facts for the convenience of some dogmatic schematization, can only be accomplished by taking into account this complex we have called the *colonial situation*. It is precisely this situation that we wish to describe. But first it is necessary to sketch the essential outlines of this system of reference that we have invoked.

Among recent studies undertaken in France, only those of O. Mannoni assign an important role to the notion of *colonial situation*.[2] But as

Mannoni was intent on treating the subject from a purely psychological or psychoanalytical point of view, he offers only an imprecise definition of the phenomenon we refer to. He presents it as "a situation of incomprehension," as "a misunderstanding," and, accordingly, he analyzes the psychological attitudes that characterize the "colonizer" and the "colonized," attitudes that permit an understanding of the relationship maintained on both sides.[3] This is not enough, and O. Mannoni seems to recognize the fact when he cautions against "under-estimating the (capital) importance of economic relationships." Moreover, he concedes having selected a rather ill-defined aspect of the colonial situation. We, for our part, assume an opposite position from his. We are biased in favor of dealing with the question as a whole, believing there is something deceitful in examining only one of the many facts implied in this situation.

Such a situation as that created by the colonial expansion of European states during the last century can be examined from different points of view. Each one constitutes an individual approach to the subject, a separate analysis with a different orientation depending on whether the point of view is that of a colonial historian, an economist, a politician and administrator, a sociologist preoccupied with the relationships of foreign cultures, a psychologist concerned with a study of race relations, etc. And if one is to hazard an over-all view of the problem, it seems indispensable to discover what can be gleaned from each of these individual specialties.

The historian examines the various periods of colonization with respect to the colonial power. He enables us to grasp the changes that occur in the existing relationships between that power and its territorial dependencies. He shows us how the isolation of colonial peoples was shattered by a caprice of history over which these peoples had had no control. He evokes the ideologies which, at different times, have been used to justify colonialism and have created the "role" adopted by the colonial power, and he reveals the discrepancies separating facts from theories. He analyzes the administrative and economic systems which have guaranteed "colonial peace" and permitted an economic profit (for the metropole) from the colonial enterprise. In short, the historian makes us understand how, in the course of time, the colonial power implanted itself in the heart of its colonial societies. Acting in this manner he furnishes the sociologist with his first and indispensable frame of reference. He reminds the sociologist that the history of a colonial people has developed as a result of a foreign presence while at the same time he elucidates the different aspects of the latter's role and influence.

Most historians have insisted on the fact that the pacification, the organization, and the development of colonial territories were carried out "with respect to the interests of the western powers and not with local interests in mind . . . by assigning (the needs) of native producers to a position of secondary importance." [4] They have shown how, in less than a century, the European absorption of Asia, Africa, and Oceania "transformed the shape of human society through force and the imposition of reforms, often bold reforms." They have shown how such upheavals were made necessary by "colonial imperialism (which) is merely one manifestation of economic imperialism." [5] They have reminded us that economic exploitation is based on the seizure of political power—the two characteristic features of colonialism.[6] Thus historians enable us to see to what extent a colonial society is an instrumentality of the colonial power. We can observe this instrumental function in the politics practiced by the European power, which consists in compromising the native aristocracy by tempting it with inducements calculated to appeal to its self-interest: "Enlist the ruling class in our cause," said Lyautey; [7] reduce the native chiefs to the role of "mere creatures," said R. Kennedy; and the evidence is even more obvious in the policies pursued in transplanting populations and in the recruitment of workers, all based exclusively on the economic interests of the colonial power.[8] By reminding us of certain "bold" measures—population transfers and the policy of "reserves," the transformation of traditional laws, and questioning the ownership of resources, policies requiring a certain level of productivity, etc.—the historian draws our attention to the fact that "colonialism was literally at times an act of social surgery." [9] And this observation, more or less valid, according to the peoples and areas under consideration, is of great interest to a sociologist studying colonial societies. It indicates to him that these societies are, in varying degrees, in a state of latent crisis, that they are involved to some extent in a kind of social pathology. It is valuable evidence of the special features of the sociology of colonial peoples and suggests the practical and theoretical results one may expect from such a discipline. We shall have occasion to note its importance elsewhere in our analysis.

But after having noted this external pressure applied to colonial societies, the historian points out the various kinds of reactions that have resulted. The reactions of Far Eastern peoples, the Arab world, and Black Africa have often been the subject of comparative studies. In general terms we learn of the opposition of "closed societies" in the Far East despite outward appearances of westernization; the tense relations with Islamic society which refuses to abandon a notion of superiority and maintains "a competitive spirit that can be veiled and silent but nevertheless remains at the heart of the problem"; the "openness" of the black world which is explained by "the African readiness to imitate," by a lack of "confidence in the depths and resources of its own past." [10] And in a rather special case, the history of Africa, the colonial continent *par excellence*, reveals important differences in ways of resisting the ascendancy of European nations within the very heart of Black Africa. After having exposed the importance of "the external factor" with respect to transformations affecting colonial societies, the history of colonialism confronts us with an "internal factor" inherent in social structures and subjugated societies. At this point the history of colonialism touches on territory familiar to the anthropologist. But in offering a picture of the varied responses to the colonial situation, history shows us how much that situation can reveal to us. Colonialism appears as a trial, a kind of test imposed on certain societies or, if we may call it such, as a crude sociological experiment. An analysis of colonial societies cannot overlook these specific conditions. As certain anthropologists have perceived,[11] they reveal not only the processes of adaptation or rejection, the new guideposts set up for a society whose traditional models have been destroyed (the "patterns" of Anglo-American authors), but they also disclose "the points of resistance" among colonial peoples, the fundamental structure and behavior of such a people. They touch society's bedrock. Such information offers unmistakable theoretical interest (if we consider the colonial situation as a fact calling for scientific observation, independent of any moral judgments it may provoke), and it has a truly practical importance: it shows the fundamental premises in terms of which each problem must be conceived.

The historian reveals the way in which the colonial system was established and transformed. He describes, according to differing circumstances, the various political, juridical, and administrative aspects of the system. He also enables us to take due note of the ideologies used to justify colonialism.[12] Numerous studies emphasize the gap that has existed between announced principles and actual practices, between "the civilizing mission" (*la mission civilisatrice*—a phrase used with particular emphasis under Napoleon III)—and the desired "utility" that Eugène Etienne, the "colonialist of Oran" defined in 1894 as "the sum total of profits and advantages accruing to the metropole" from any colonial enterprise.[13] H. Brunschwig calls attention, in his history of French colonization, to the long series of misunderstandings (nay, outright lies) that stand out so conspicuously. L. Joubert reminds us of "the gulf that separated facts from theories following the formal declarations of responsibility for civilizing the subject peoples; the rupture between these alleged objectives and their application, if not the blatant hypocrisy which, in the name of humanitarian principles, condoned exploitation pure and simple. . . ."[14] The colonial situation thus appears to have assumed an essentially spurious character. It sought continually to justify itself by means of pseudo-reasons. In his study entitled "The Colonial Crisis and the Future," R. Kennedy shows how each characteristic of "colonialism"—the *color line*, political dependency, economic dependency, virtually non-existent "social" benefits, the lack of contact between natives and "the dominant caste"—is predicated on "a series of rationalizations"; for example: the superiority of the white race; the inability of the native population to govern itself correctly; the despotism of traditional chiefs; the temptation for present leaders to form "a dictatorial clique"; native inability to develop their own natural resources; the feeble financial resources of colonial peoples; the need to maintain national prestige, etc.[15] In the light of such evidence, the sociologist understands the extent to which a European colonial power, motivated by a dubious doctrine whose historical development can be traced, condemned to resort to deceit and hypocrisy, and wedded to a fixed image of the native population, acted upon colonial societies in terms of these concepts. We have called attention elsewhere to the importance of this fact.[16] No valid sociological study of colonial peoples is possible which ignores this attention given to ideologies and to the more or less stereotyped behavior they produced.

The historian reminds us that contemporary colonial societies are the product of a dual history. Thus in the case of Africa, the one history is entirely African: "these societies, so stable, so seemingly immobile, all resulted, or almost all, from the variable combinations of diverse peoples who were thrown together, clashed with one another, or were superimposed on each other by historical events" [17]—a history that "brought together (in a relationship of domination or assimilation) homogeneous social forms"; [18] while on the other hand, the other history, largely conditioned by European domination, "brought into contact social forms that were radically heterogeneous" and presented a picture of "disintegration." "Three forces," says Ch.-A. Julien, "have disintegrated Africa: governmental administration, missionaries, and the new economy." [19] Any current study of these societies can be made only by viewing them in terms of this dual history.

It is customary to recall that colonialism, broadly speaking, has involved the interplay of three closely inter-related forces—an historical association, as R. Montagne has pointed out by observing that "the effort to spread the Christian gospel has been tied historically to European expansion in the commercial, political, or military spheres." [20] The economic, governmental, and missionary objectives have been experienced by subject peoples as closely associated activities,[21] and it is in terms of these factors that anthropologists have usually analyzed "social changes." But in an effort to describe modern European colonialism and to explain its appearance, certain historians have been inclined to place the greatest emphasis on one of these aspects—the economic factor. "Colonial imperialism is but one form of economic imperialism," Ch.-A. Julien has written in an article on this subject.[22] At this point history impinges on another point of view that is indispensable for understanding the colonial situation.

The propaganda for political expansion based its arguments, in part, on economic arguments. In 1874 P. Leroy Beaulieu argued France's need to become a colonial power. J. Ferry wrote in 1890: "Colonial policy is the child of industrial policy . . . colonialism is an international manifestation of the eternal laws of competition. . . ."[23] It was economic reasons that colonial powers invoked to justify their presence—the resources that were developed and the equipment built were regarded as property as of right—and economic advantages were the last to be surrendered even after more or less genuine agreements for political independence had been arrived at. Even before the studies of Marxist writers appeared, certain analyses devoted to "imperialism" revealed its economic characteristics.[24] Lenin was the first Marxist to offer a systematic theory in his famous work: *Imperialism: the Highest Stage of Capitalism.* Ch.-A. Julien stressed its central thesis by recalling that "colonial policies are the offspring of monopoly, of the exportation of capital and the quest for spheres of economic influence."[25] Whether it involve colonization or an economic protectorate, a Marxist discovers one and the same reality, one that is linked to capitalism and must disappear with it. The close ties that exist between capitalism and colonial expansion have prompted certain non-Marxist authors to compare the "colonial question" with the "social question" and to observe, like J. Guitton, "that they are not fundamentally different because the *metropole-colony* relationship is in no sense different from the *capital-labor* relationship, or the relationship Hegel has termed *master-servant*.[26] Note the possible identification of "colonial peoples" with the "proletariat." "In both cases," P. Reuter writes, "we are dealing with a population that produces all the wealth but does not share in its political or economic advantages and constitutes an oppressed 'class.' "[27]

For a Marxist there is no doubt whatsoever about this common identity. Politically, it justifies the combined action of the proletariat and the colonial peoples. Stalin devoted a number of studies to the colonial question and, after having showed that "Leninism . . . destroyed the wall separating Whites from Blacks, Europeans from Asiatics, the 'civilized' from the 'non-civilized' slaves of imperialism," he recalled that "the October Revolution *inaugurated* a new era, the era of *colonial revolutions in the oppressed countries* of the world, in *alliance* with the proletariat and *under the direction* of the proletariat."[28] The colonial peoples themselves stress the economic aspect of their condition more than its political aspect. An African journalist from the Gold Coast writes on this subject: "Nations whose economic power is preponderant are precisely those whose political influence predominates. . . . As of now the authorities have made no effort at all to encourage native populations in their colonies to reach an economic level commensurate with their political advancement."[29]

Without envisaging the colonial situation exclusively in terms of its economic manifestations, a sociologist who tries to understand and inter-

The Colonial Situation: A Theoretical Approach (*1951*)   **41**

pret colonial societies must recognize the importance of such demonstrable facts. They will remind him that the structures of these societies are not explained simply in terms of contacts between a technically advanced civilization and a primitive, nontechnical society. They will indicate that between the colonial power and the colonized population certain relationships exist which connote tension and conflict. (We have already referred to the instrumental nature of relationships in the colonial society.) This observation would have proved useful to the theoretical views of Malinowski. When the famed anthropologist established the doctrine of "a practical anthropology," he declared that a "wise" control of the forces for change "can guarantee a normal and stable development," [30] and this misunderstanding of the extremely antagonistic nature of the situation led him, according to one commentator, to pose the problems "in the most naïve terms." [31]

The economic aspect of the colonial situation has been expressed in general terms by certain anthropologists or geographers who have specialized in tropical countries. R. Kennedy (in a previously mentioned study) has indicated its principal characteristics: [32] the quest for raw materials by colonial powers for utilization in the metropolitan industrial complex—a fact that explains the inferior (if not in fact nonexistent) [33] industrial equipment in colonial territories; large-scale exploitation and import-export trade are entirely within the hands of "societies" which reap all the profits for themselves; [34] the "distance" separating the Europeans from the colonial peoples (the latter essentially reduced to the role of peasants, laborers, and domestics), explaining the native's difficulty "in raising himself economically"; and finally, the economic stagnation of the indigenous masses.

Among French-language studies, those dealing with Indo-China are particularly valuable (indeed, they are the only ones which have real depth). That they are the work of geographers like Charles Robequain and P. Gourou [35] is quite indicative of the current disregard for the present that has characterized French ethnology. "Peasants" represent 90 to 95% of the Indo-Chinese population, and these studies are essentially concerned with the peasantry. Aside from the importance attached first of all to available technical means (which were not improved, or only slightly improved, by the colonial power) emphasis is placed on the loss of property holdings,[36] on "property dispossession" producing an uprooted and proletarian population. And we find, as a concomitant trend, the establishment of a bourgeoisie (essentially agrarian in origin) born "like the proletariat, from contact with western civilization and from a weakening of traditional values." The growth of this class results almost always "from exploitation of the rice fields and the system of money-lending associated therewith." [37] The observations dealing with business (native businesses are broken up into many small and unimportant enterprises while big businesses and export trade are in the hands of Europeans or foreigners—Chinese and Indians) and the observations concerning industry (a stagnation of local industry, a lack of any industrial processing, and a negligible growth of the work force—since 1890 the average annual increase in the work force was only 2,500 according to Charles Robequain—and the low level of skilled workmen) all substantiate the general picture presented by R. Kennedy. It is on the basis of such facts that P. Naville could give a precise and strictly Marxist interpretation of the economic and political conditions of the Vietnamese revolution.[38]

Studies relating to Africa, especially Central and South Africa, disclose the same kinds of facts. These studies are primarily by Anglo-American anthropologists rightly concerned with "practical anthropology." The situation created in South Africa by a European minority is well known: territorial segregation imposed by the *Native Land Act* of 1913 (*native areas* comprise only 12% of the entire territory of the Union of South Africa); social segregation legalized by the *Colour Bar Act* of 1926 which restricts black workers to jobs requiring manual labor only; the disproportionately small share of national income enjoyed by the Negroes (representing 69% of the population, they receive only 20% of the national income, whereas the Whites, who make up 21% of the population, receive 74% of the income); the racial bases and racist premises of economic and political structures; the profound contradictions in a policy that establishes segregation (the Whites fearing to be overrun by the Blacks) while at the same time it must "sound the call for native workers,"[39] thus provoking a rural exodus resulting in "proletarization" and "de-tribalization" of the indigenous population. The special situation in South Africa, in some ways almost a caricature of these conditions, shows the extent to which economic, political, and racial questions are closely interrelated.[40] And it shows, too, how these questions cannot be ignored by anyone undertaking a study of present-day conditions in the Union of South Africa. It is in the light of these facts that we reaffirm the compelling need to consider the *colonial situation* as a single complex, as a totality.

Anglo-American anthropologists have assigned an important role to economic facts considered as one of the principal "forces" responsible for "culture-change." In her celebrated work, *Reaction to Conquest*, Monica Hunter examines the transformations that occurred in Pondo society (in South Africa) in terms first of the economic factor and then of the political factor ("which, historically speaking, has an economic origin, whatever non-Marxists may say about it"). But these studies, already quite numerous on the question of Africa alone,[41] are conducted solely along economic lines, analyzing the "primitive" social organization and economy with regard to the dislocations brought about by a "modern" economy and the problems created by the latter. They fail to relate these to the colonial economy, the colonial situation. They fail to convey the notion of reciprocity of outlooks existing between the colonial population, on the one hand, and the colonial power, on the other. The studies inspired by Malinowski are conspicuous for these shortcomings since they reveal only the results of "contact" between "institutions" of the same nature, and scarcely go beyond a simple description of certain transformations and the enumeration of certain problems. This explains why they are concerned primarily with rural questions, with changes affecting the village and "the family," with rural depopulation. In this field, they have outlined significant patterns of "culture-change": destruction of the extended family, predominance of economic values, the emancipation of the younger generation, the establishment of a monetary economy which upsets personal relationships, the threat to traditional hierarchies (wealth and rank no longer always being closely associated), etc. Certain special research fields—such as that relating to living standards [42]—have been developed, but important facts—such as the new social groupings resulting from the dislocation of traditional groupings, the appearance of social classes, the nature and role of the proletariat, etc.—are touched on only in very general terms, and the conflicts they imply are rarely analyzed.[43]

Yet it is precisely these aspects of the problem that are given highest priority in studies inspired by the condition of crisis that exists in colonial societies and by the political and administrative implications deriving from this crisis. In this area of study, the declarations made by a Marxist observer find common ground with those of the highly placed colonial administrator. Each, for different reasons, draws attention to the degradation of the peasantry, to the constant increase of a colonial proletariat, and to the antagonisms arising therefrom. With respect to French North Africa and French Black Africa, we call the reader's attention to two general studies that complement or reinforce each other, one by geographer J. Dresch and the other by High Commissioner R. Delavignette.[44] The movement of dispossession on the one hand ("730,000 rural families are totally deprived of land and must be regarded as indigent," J. Dresch writes), of "uprooting" the peasantry, and the correlative increase in the proletarian population, measured by the accelerated growth of urban centers, are analyzed within the framework of local conditions. Elsewhere the accent is on those characteristics peculiar to the colonial proletariat. "The natives of North Africa are becoming proletarians, but unskilled proletarians, colonial proletarians, judged equally good and equally unfit for any kind of employment, servants of an elementary and speculative economy, threatened by crises alternately produced by droughts and the uncertainty of sources of raw materials" (J. Dresch). The proletariat "is the vehicle for racism, imbuing the class struggle with a fierce degree of violence by linking it with a racial struggle," and, in the face of this threat there is a mounting temptation on the part of "certain Europeans" to keep the peasantry as long as possible in a primitive state (which they think) is one of tranquility" (R. Delavignette). Such observations indicate to what extent the colonial population, in its urban as well as its rural aspects, together with the colonial power, form a system, a whole. There is a need for any study dealing with one of these elements to take cognizance of the whole. Such observations also draw attention to the antagonisms existing in the very heart of this situation as a result of a stratification by classes that is achieved at the expense of traditional social structures, and to the conflicts that can be explained only within the framework of the colonial situation. In other portions of these studies we find that the concept of "crisis" is at the very root of these preoccupations ("a crisis that strikes a dislocated society and, little by little, destroys it," to quote J. Dresch). These observations enable us to discover—by singling out and even perhaps exaggerating the situation— this pathological aspect of colonial societies to which we have called attention.

Elsewhere in these same studies considerable attention is given to the role of the judicial and administrative apparatus charged with maintaining this domination. One critic, after having denounced its "arbitrariness," talks of the actions of an organization "that has separated peoples of the same ethnic origin and the same social structure and has thrown together dissimilar ethnic groups of different social structures. . . ." The arbitrary nature of the colonial boundaries and administrative divisions, between and within colonies, results in—or aims at—fragmenting important ethnic groups, breaking up political units of any significance, and artificially juxtaposing incompatible or antagonistic ethnic groups.[45] Certain recent actions on the part of colonial peoples can be explained as a reaction to such conditions as, for instance, the manifestation of a desire to restore former social groupings. In the case of Black West Africa alone, we can point out: the demands for unification among the Ewe (divided between French and British Togoland); the attempts to establish tribal federalism in the South Cameroons; the more or less explicit desire for regrouping evidenced by the African churches—known by the name of Kimbangism—occurring in the Ba-Kongo country (in the Belgian Congo and in the French Congo).

The maintenance or creation of this type of "balkanization" with its attendant rivalries or hostilities among ethnic groups, treated as pawns of administrative policies, have imposed on these groups, within the framework of the colonial situation, a particular history which no sociological analysis can afford to ignore. And a recent study dealing with the Malagasies indicates how this desire to weaken an ethnic group (for fear of encountering a national consciousness) is often accompanied by the desire to destroy the group's historical record (for fear of providing a basis for "pride in being a malagasy and thus justifying a sense of nationalism," as the author puts it.[46] We again come upon the already mentioned question of ideologies. The effort to pervert a people's history affects their collective memory, provoking an inevitable backlash, and thus we see the possible importance of such facts in any effort to understand colonial peoples. . . .

In the light of these basic facts, it is easier to establish and evaluate the contributions of sociology and social psychology as applied to colonial society. In a recent work devoted to "colonies," E. A. Walcker calls our attention to the fact that the former are made up of "plural societies." [47] He demonstrates that the "colony" (as a global society) "is composed in general of a number of groups more or less conscious of their existence, often opposed to one another on the basis of color, and who seek to lead different kinds of lives within the limits of a single political framework." And Walcker adds: these "groups, who speak different languages, eat different kinds of food, are often engaged in quite different occupations in keeping with their laws or customs, wear different types of clothing . . . , live in different kinds of dwellings, cherish different traditions, adore different gods, and maintain different ideas about good and evil. Such societies are not communities." To these observations he adds a useful element for our analysis when he writes, with regard to the *color bar*, that it "reflects the world-wide problem of minorities in tropical terms, with this difference that, almost everywhere in the colonies, the lower class constitutes a majority."

These observations offer a point of departure. The interesting fact is not the existence of pluralism (a characteristic of any global society), but the indication of its specific features: the racial basis of "groups," their extreme dissimilarity, the antagonistic relationships this entails, and the necessity imposed on them to co-exist "within the limits of a single political framework." Also important is the attention given to the colonial power as the dominant minority (minority in the numerical sense). In a study that is primarily of political interest, H. Laurentie, for his part, has defined the "colony" as a country in which a European minority has imposed itself on an indigenous majority whose civilization and behavior are different from the European; this European minority exercises its influence over the native population with a force disproportionate to its numbers. This force, if you will, is extremely contagious and, by its nature, causes social distortions." [48] This active "minority," with its distorting influence, predicates its domination on the basis of an incontestable material superiority (it imposes itself on nonindustrial societies), on a legal status established in its own favor, and on a rationale with a more or less racial foundation (for certain authors, like R. Maunier, the colonial phenomenon is primarily a "contact" between races). The European minority reacts all the more aggressively as it becomes more firmly intrenched, and all the more hostile to racial intermingling as it feels itself threatened by demographic pressures from colored peoples. Thus in South Africa the white population "is beginning to view its situation as a minority problem whereas the Blacks view theirs as a colonial problem and one of trusteeship." [49] The same holds true in North Africa. This fact of "beginning to view its situation as a minority problem" is interesting. It reminds us clearly that this numerical minority is not a sociological minority, and risks becoming such only by an upheaval in the colonial situation.

Certain sociologists have already made this observation. L. Wirth, in defining a minority and establishing a typology of minorities, has insisted on this point: "the concept is not a matter of statistics," and he cites the example of Negroes living in the southern states of the United States who, in several states, are a numerical majority but nevertheless constitute a minority "by being socially, politically, and economically suppressed." He notes the situation created by the colonial expansion of European nations, establishing the Whites as "dominant groups" and colored peoples as "minorities." [50] The quantity of a group is not enough to make it a minority even though "it may have some effect on the laws and on its relations with the dominant group." The characteristic feature of a minority is a certain way of life in the larger society. Fundamentally, it implies the relationship of the dominated to the dominant. We have constantly encountered this kind of relationship in our previous analysis in depicting the colonial society as an "instrument" in the hands of the colonial power (the historical perspective), the relations between the exploiter and the exploited, the close parallel between "the metropole-colony and the capital-labor relationship" (the economic perspective), the "relations of domination and subjection" (political perspective). This description of a minority (in the sociological sense of the word), as applied to colonial populations, indicates rather clearly to what extent the latter must be considered in terms of the other groups comprising the colony—a necessity we have underscored on several occasions by pointing out the importance of examining the colonized population and the colonial power from reciprocal perspectives. But that does not indicate wherein a colonial population is distinguishable from other minorities (the American Negroes, for instance) who are placed in a different situation. The first step to be undertaken is to clarify the precise position of the "colony" in the larger society.

If we set forth in a very schematic fashion the various social groupings brought together by the colonial situation, classifying them, starting with the colonial power (the dominant group) and ending with the colonial population (the subject group), we find: (*a*) the colonial power, not including foreigners of the white race; (*b*) white "foreigners"; (*c*) the "coloured"—to use the English expression which is defined broadly;

(*d*) the colonized population, namely, all those whom the British call "the natives." We find a distinction and a hierarchy based, first of all, on criteria of race and nationality, implying as a sort of postulate the excellence of the white race, and more especially, of that fraction which is the colonial power (its supremacy is given as a fact of history, established by nature).

Of course this is only a rough outline which needs to be filled in. R. Delavignette has devoted a chapter of his book to a study of colonial society [51] (that is, its European component). He recalls certain general characteristics that define it: a society "of European origins, oriented to the homeland," constituting a numerical minority, middle class in character, given to the "notion of heroic superiority" (a doctrine partially explained by the greater percentage of males—and, for the most part, young men especially numerous during the early stages of colonization). Above all we are dealing with a society whose function it is to achieve political, economic, and spiritual domination. In the words of R. Delavignette, this society tends to instill in its members "the feudal spirit." The important fact is that this dominant group constitutes a numerical minority to a very large degree. There is a great imbalance between the mass of the "colonizers" and the mass of those "colonized." And there is a more or less persistent fear of seeing the hierarchy re-established on the sole basis of the size of the masses. This fear is revived in times of crisis and explains seemingly inexplicable reactions such as the "events" in Madagascar. And L. Wirth offers an oversimplified judgment when he declares, with respect to colonial situations, that "the dominant group can maintain its superior situation simply by utilizing its military and administrative machinery." So great is the disproportion between civilizations! [52] He underestimates thus a number of important aspects—the means by which the European population renders itself untouchable: (*a*) keeping contacts at a bare minimum (segregation); (*b*) offering the European as the model for emulation, while effectively blocking any means to that end (assimilation is held out as the basis for equality—because it is known full well that assimilation is either impossible of attainment or is restricted to a very limited few); (*c*) maintaining ideologies justifying the position of the dominant group; (*d*) employing political tactics designed to preserve the imbalance in favor of the colonial power (and its European homeland); (*d*) more or less deliberately transferring to certain groups the attitudes and feelings provoked by political and economic domination: thus, for example, to the Lebanese-Syrians in French West Africa (where they represent about one-fourth of the population designated administratively as "European and assimilated") or regularly to the Indians and "Coloured" in the Union of South Africa (at the time of the troubles in 1947, 1948, and 1949, the Africans attacked only Asians). To the extent that the distance between cultures is less, the relative size of the groups plays a greater role. Force alone no longer suffices to maintain control, and more indirect methods are resorted to—the element of "misunderstanding" comes into play (a fact that struck H. Brunschwig in his historical analysis and O. Mannoni in his psychoanalytical one). These indirect methods use most frequently, depending on individual circumstances, racial or religious differences of an antagonistic nature (as in India during the heyday of British colonialism). It must be remembered that the European colonial society is not perfectly homogeneous. It has its "factions," its "clans" (the "administrators," the "private sector," the "military," and the "missionaries," according to the terminology used in French territories). These groups are more or less self-contained, more or less competitive (antagonism between the administration and the missions, or between the administration and the commercial sector occurs frequently). Each group practices its own native policies (indeed, to such an extent, that certain English anthropologists have regarded each one of them as "an agent" provoking "cultural change"). They cause widely varied reactions. In other respects the European colonial society is essentially a closed one, more or less remote from the colonized population. But a policy of domination and prestige demands that it be closed and aloof, a situation that does not facilitate mutual understanding and appreciation, a situation that allows (or encourages) the easy recourse to "stereotypes." Isolated in the "colony," this society has also partially severed its connections with the homeland. R. Delavignette has made due note of this fact in writing about "the colonials": "Europeans in the colony, they become colonials at home . . . ," "they seek to channel their energies into a jealous sort of particularism. . . ." [53]

This particularism is seen first in relations with "foreigners" of the white race. The latter constitute a minority in the full sense of the word, numerically and sociologically. They may hold an important economic post, but they are nonetheless subject to administrative controls. They are suspect by virtue of their nationality. A distrust of foreign religious missions, for example, is common in colonial states. They are often cut off from the real colonial society. In French West Africa, for instance, the Lebanese-Syrians are not accepted in "good society" except for a very few who happen to be quite wealthy. To the extent that they are rejected, they regroup into ethnic minorities and enjoy closer relationships with the indigenous population. This greater degree of "familiarity" and their minority status explain the ambivalent reactions towards them on the part of the indigenous population (a certain intimacy tinged with scorn) —reactions to be noted with regard to the Lebanese-Syrians, the Greeks, and the Portuguese in French West Africa.[54] The resentments of colonial peoples can be directed against them with a certain impunity. They offer outlets for hostilities at minimal cost or risk. At the time of the troubles in certain French West African cities after 1945, it was only the Lebanese-Syrian minority that was affected. They are one of the most constantly threatened groups in this fragile edifice that is the colonial social structure.

Among the groups discriminated against by those in control, colored people (mixed breeds and colored foreigners) are held in the lowest esteem. For what amounts to an essentially racial reason, the colored man is rejected both by the colonial power and by the colonial peoples themselves. He has few contacts with either. His isolation becomes even greater (by means of discriminatory measures) reducing him to the role of an "exotic" community, as he achieves greater economic importance. The Indian problem in South Africa is thus explained by the fact that certain Indians "have become too rich and are surreptitiously acquiring positions held by the Whites." [55] Here we see clearly an overlapping of facts of a racial nature and facts of an economic nature. In the case of half-breeds (*métis*), the isolation is even more absolute because of their racial impurity—"a racial compromise." Only in rare instances do they succeed in regrouping and forming a viable society. The case of the "Bastards of Rehoboth" in former German Southwest Africa is especially famous. And a very strict isolation was imposed on this group. As A. Siegfried has noted with regard to the "Cape coloured," these half-breeds are forced "into the hands of a black race with which they do not want to be identified." They aim at becoming assimilated by the colonial society which remains closed to them (more or less, according to local circumstances), or which grants them a special status [56] conferring a legal recognition of their particular position. If they are "a racial compromise," they are in no sense "a social compromise." One can scarcely regard them as being a liaison between the colonial power and the colonized population. Their political alliance with the élite of a colonial society was never durable. Thus, for example, the *Conference of Non-Europeans,* created in 1927 in South Africa, which tried to unite in a common endeavor Coloureds, Indians, and Bantus, produced no effective results and was short-lived. The "Coloureds" are more in conflict than in agreement with the colonized population, because of their improved economic and social condition and because of the racial factor. They cannot pretend thus to leadership of the colonial peoples.

The colonial population presents two salient characteristics: its overwhelming numerical superiority [57] and the rigid control to which it is subjected. While a numerical majority, it is nevertheless a sociological minority. In the words of R. Maunier, "colonialism is a fact of power": it involves the loss of autonomy and "a legal or *de facto* trusteeship." [58] Each sector of the controlling society has as its function to maintain the domination of the colonial power in some specific domain (political, economic, and, almost always, spiritual). This domination by the European power is an absolute one owing to the absence of any advanced technology or material power other than sheer numbers. It finds its *de facto* expression in practices which, while not codified into laws, incur sharp and immediate disapproval if they are not respected, whereas other practices are given legal sanction. As we have already mentioned several times, colonial domination is based on an idealogy, on a system of pseudo-justifications and rationalizations. It has a racist foundation, more or less acknowledged, more or less obvious. A colonial people is subjected to the pressures of every group comprising the colony. All exert their pre-eminence in some area with the result that a colonial people is made to feel all the more keenly its subordinate status. The agencies of the colonial power regard the colony itself as essentially a productive source of wealth (whereas the colonial people keep only a very small part of that wealth despite their greater numbers). This fact conditions in part the relations it maintains with the other groups (who derive from the colony their economic advantages). These relations, however, are not simple. They are not merely the relationship of the exploiter to the exploited, of the dominant to the dominated. They are not that simple because of the lack of unity among colonial peoples themselves and, above all, because of the extremely heterogeneous character of the culture (or rather, the cultures) which are to be found in the society.

The colonial population is divided ethnically. The divisions are rooted in the society's own history but are utilized by the colonial power (we recall the utility of that old principle: "Divide and rule"), and these divisions are complicated by the arbitrary colonial "divisions" and by administrative "splitting up" of tribes within the colony. These ethnic divisions not only orient the relations of each ethnic group with the colonial power [for example, the peoples who acted as "intermediaries" during the period of African slave trade and the establishment of trading settlements (*comptoirs*) tried to transfer their role from the economic to the political plane and became "militant" minorities], but these divisions likewise orient their attitude with respect to the culture introduced by the colonial power (some ethnic groups are more "assimilationist" or more "traditionalist" than certain neighboring groups, a reaction, in part at least, to the attitudes adopted by the latter). The colonial population is spiritually divided. Spiritual divisions may have preceded European colonization and be associated notably with the waves of Islamic conquest. But we are familiar with the tactics adopted by European colonial powers. The strategy of English domination in India is well known. In many places colonialism brought about religious confusion by opposing Christianity to traditional religions, while Christian churches presented differences among themselves. We mention in this connection an African of Brazzaville who recalled "this state of affairs whose only effect is to create a lamentable confusion in the individual's moral and psychological development" and who added: "The Black African, whoever he is, has the rudiments of a religion. To deprive him of them by introducing atheism or a confusion of religious doctrines can only result in completely unhinging him." [59] The author almost went so far as to ask the "colonizer" to impose unity! This serves to illustrate the extent to which these new divisions, added to the old ones, have had the most painful effects on certain groups. But colonization has brought other divisions we may designate as social in nature, products of administrative and economic action and of educational policies: the separation of city dwellers from rural groups,[60] the separation of proletariat from bourgeoisie, of the "élites" (or "*évolués*"—groups who have *evolved*, according to the usual expression) from the masses of the population,[61] and that between generations. We have touched on all these factors and indicated their importance in various parts of our analysis. Each of these fragmented groups participates differently in the world society. The contact between races and civilizations, which colonization has brought about, has neither the same meaning nor the same consequences for any one of them. The contact must be studied in the light of this diversity (for which it is partly responsible in the first place, but which is now in turn partly influenced by the very conditions it helped bring about).

Conditions among the colonial population differ greatly from those prevailing in the European colonial society. In race and culture, the differences are unmistakable. They are reflected in a language that opposes "the primitive man" to the civilized man, the pagan to the Christian, a technically-advanced society to a backward society. More than the colonial situation, it is this fact that stands out clearly.—it is the contact between heterogeneous civilizations that has attracted the attention of anthropologists in recent decades, and, above all, the shock that it has produced, "the clash of cultures" noted by English authors. We have shown elsewhere how, starting with this observation, new studies have developed called *acculturation* in the United States and *culture contact* in England, with the aim of determining the most dynamic aspects of cultures placed in confrontation and of discovering, if possible, the essential features of the whole of cultural reality. The stages of the "contact" have been set forth in a more or less simplistic and arbitrary manner: the phases of conflict, adjustment, syncretism, assimilation (or a counter-acculturation reaction) to be found in the writings of North American anthropologists; phases of opposition, of imitation (from "top to bottom" and from "bottom to top") and of aggregation as analyzed by R. Maunier in his *Sociologie Coloniale;* the appearance of a new culture ("the *tertium quid* of contact"), different from those placed in confrontation, according to B. Malinowski and others. We will not dwell at this point on all the criticisms such writings and doctrines call for. We call attention to these works only to illustrate, on the one hand, that the relations between colonial peoples and colonial powers cannot be envisaged solely in the economic and political terms emphasized by these authors who are *engagés*. And we do so, on the other hand, to remind the reader that the contact between civilizations takes place at the moment of a very special situation, the colonial situation, which becomes transformed historically—that the contact is made by means of social groups (and not among cultures existing in the form of independent realities) whose reactions are conditioned internally (according to the type of group affected) and also externally. In this respect, a precise typology of the groupings comprising this global society, the colony, is at the basis of any accurate and fairly comprehensive investigation. We have frequently insisted on the necessity for such by pointing out how the sociologist was obliged to view the colonial population and the European population in reciprocal fashions. Similarly, we have suggested in an earlier study the special kind of evolution that the colonial situation imposes on sociocultural facts. And we have shown notably how the "crises" created by colonialism have in part oriented this evolution.

Most studies dealing with present-day colonial societies stress the state of crisis affecting them and "the arduous and complex problems" they pose. To a greater or lesser degree, they are regarded as sick societies,[62] which is true to the extent that the colonial power opposes any genuine solutions. For it is an apparent fact that, among colonial peoples, the quest for norms coincides with the quest for autonomy. And this fact imposes on the sociologist an analytical method that is in some measure clinical. We have indicated, in the previously mentioned study, how an approach to the question of colonial societies, concentrating on their specific crises, constitutes "an unexcelled standpoint for analysis," "the only point at which one can grasp *the evolution of indigenous social structures placed in the colonial situation.*"[63] Such crises force reexamination of the society as a whole, its institutions as well as its component groups and symbols; the social dislocations provide opportunities for the analyst to penetrate and explore from within, and not merely arrive at some abstract notions of the phenomena arising from the contact between a colonial power and a colonial people. The analyst will be better able to understand the latter in its traditional forms by discovering certain systems and weaknesses (as we shall indicate in the case of the Fang of Gabon, a people among whom the colonial situation encouraged certain ruptures already inherent in its previous social structure), or certain unshakeable structures and collective representations (thus, for example, a study of the religious crisis and of "Negro churches" characteristic of Bantu Africa would reveal what remains of traditional religions despite all the other pressures brought to bear—the irreducible element). Each crisis, affecting the global society as a whole, constitutes a point of insight into that society and the relationships it implies.[64] Looking at such crises permits of that concrete and comprehensive approach already recommended by Marcel Mauss. And to complete the illustration just given, we recall a recent thesis devoted to "the Negro churches" and the activities of Bantu prophets (in South Africa) in which the author, B. G. M. Sundkler shows that the problems posed are not only of a religious nature, but raise the question of Bantu reactions as a whole to White domination, and that the study of these "churches" leads to a study of all the social problems characterizing the Union of South Africa.[65]

At first glance these crises are noteworthy for the radical changes in, or the outright disappearance of, certain institutions and certain groups. But a sociological analysis cannot limit itself to these aspects of the social picture—its institutional or structural forms—and merely note the changes and disappearances, locating new social structures and describing them. It is indispensable to go beyond these considerations and to reach for "the forms of sociability," to borrow the expression of Georges Gurvitch.[66] For it seems quite apparent that certain "ways of forming links," certain social ties persist, even when the structures within which they operate are radically altered or destroyed, while at the same time new ties appear as a result of the colonial situation and the social conjunctures it creates. These social ties can co-exist and impart to the innovations conceived by the colonial society those characteristics that are both traditionalist and modernist, that peculiar state of ambiguity noted by several observers.

We have frequently alluded to the importance of race relations, the racial basis for social groupings, to the racial coloration of political and economic facts (current literature confuses or associates racism and colonialism) in the framework of the colonial situation. And various authors insist on the interracial nature of "human relationships in overseas territories," on the fact that, beneath "the political or economic causes still dividing the white race and the colored peoples, there is almost always a racial motive." These authors insist that the society remains "interracial" even when national independence is acquired.[67] We have several times indicated that colonial anthropologists have paid little attention to these racial facts and problems and given little room to them in their research projects. This is explained by the greater attention given to cultures rather than to societies and can be attributed to the more or less conscious desire on the part of these anthropologists to avoid questioning the very foundations (and ideology) of the society to which they belong, the society of the colonial power.[68]

We find just the reverse situation among anthropological studies carried out in the U.S.A. and in Brazil. These are largely devoted to the subject of race relations and racial prejudices, especially to the relations between Whites and Negroes. These facts cannot be brushed aside because the vast differences in civilization, language, religion, and customs (so conspicuous in the colonial situation) do not exist to any comparable degree in America (or Brazil) and cannot therefore serve to mask or complicate the true facts of the matter. The Negro's inferior status and a justification for racial prejudice cannot be made to appear rooted in nature, precisely because cultural differences are virtually imperceptible and a common identity of rights has been affirmed (which explains, among other reasons, why American society appears "confused, contradictory, and paradoxical," to quote Gunnar Myrdal [69] . . .), because these facts represent what remains to be liquidated from a colonial past. And it was precisely at the moment of liquidation that they gave rise to violent conflicts (in the United States, it was during the period called the Reconstruction). At times such studies emphasize the economic implications and, at other times, the sexual implications of various forms of racial behavior. They show the connection between racial reactions and cultural reactions, as R. Bastide [70] has clearly indicated. We refer in particular to his analysis of Negro messianism in the United States, which shows how closely messianism is linked to racial conflicts and to a "psychology of resentment." These find their expression in a variety of behavior patterns corresponding to the circumstances producing them.

We have risked offering this hasty reminder since it reveals ties and relationships that cannot be disregarded, and it illustrates the utter impossibility of separating the study of cultural contacts from that of racial contacts, and the impossibility of contemplating such studies, in the case of colonial peoples, without referring to the colonial situations themselves. . . .

We have just considered certain facts which Anglo-American writers place under the headings of "the clash of civilizations" or "the clash of races," but we have shown that, in the case of colonial peoples, these "clashes" (or "contacts") occur under very special circumstances. To these collective circumstances we have given the name *colonial situation.* The latter may be defined by singling out and retaining the most general and most obvious of these conditions: (1) the domination imposed by a foreign minority, racially (or ethnically) and culturally different, acting in the name of a racial (or ethnic) and cultural superiority dogmatically affirmed, and imposing itself on an indigenous population constituting a numerical majority but inferior to the dominant group from a material point of view; (2) this domination linking radically different civilizations into some form of relationship; (3) a mechanized, industrialized society with a powerful economy, a fast tempo of life, and a Christian background, imposing itself on a nonindustrialized, "backward" society in which the pace of living is much slower and religious institutions are most definitely "non-Christian"; (4) the fundamentally antagonistic character of the relationship between these two societies resulting from the subservient role to which the colonial people are subjected as "instruments" of the colonial power; (5) the need, in maintaining this domination, not only to resort to "force," but also to a system of pseudo-justifications and stereotyped behaviors, etc. But this enumeration by itself is inadequate. With the help of the particular "views" offered by each discipline, we have preferred to grasp the colonial situation as a whole, and as a system. We have set forth the elements in terms of which any specific situation can be described and understood and have shown how these elements are interrelated, with the result that any analysis of a part is necessarily distorted. This oneness raises doubts about the reality of the "groups" comprising "the global society" (the colony) as collective representations peculiar to each of these groups. This sense of totality is felt at all levels of social reality. But owing to the heterogeneous character of the groups, of the cultural "models," of the various representations confronting each other, and owing to the changes that occur in the system responsible for maintaining artificially the conditions of domination and subordination, the colonial situation becomes greatly modified, and at a rapid pace. This fact requires that the situation be studied in an historical manner, that the dates be specified.

The colonial population, as it interests the anthropologist (who calls it "primitive" or "backward," etc.), participates in the colonial situation to a greater or lesser degree, depending on its size, its economic potential, its cultural conservatism, etc. It is one of the groupings that make up "the colony." And he is misguided who thinks that a present-day study of this society can be made without taking into account this dual reality, "the colony," a global society within which the study must situate itself, and the colonial situation created by "the colony." This is especially true of any study whose avowed purpose is to set forth the facts resulting from "the contact" and the phenomena or processes of evolution. Whenever a study proceeds in a unilateral fashion and reveals these facts only in terms of a traditional premise (or a "primitive" concept), it can do little more than enumerate and classify them. And the same is true of investigations that limit themselves to examining "the contact" between "institutions" of the same nature (as B. Malinowski has recommended). The fact is that "modernist" aspects (once they are located) become intelligible only with respect to the colonial situation. Certain English anthropologists (Fortes, Gluckman) are moving in the direction of recognizing this fact by taking the view that, in the case of colonial black Africa, both the white and black societies participate integrally in a single whole and by thereby moving toward the concept of "situation." [71] Similarly, R. Bastide has noted the importance of "the situation in which the process occurs" in his studies concerned with the inter-penetration of cultures. We have tried to go beyond the framework of these simple indications by showing how a colonial situation can be "approached" and what the situation implies. We have tried to make clear that any current sociological problem regarding colonial peoples can only be studied in the light of this totality. The notion of "situation" is not the exclusive property of existentialist philosophers. It has forced itself on various specialists in the social sciences, whether they use it under the name of "social situation," as H. Wallon does, or in the expression "particular social conjuncture," as G. Gurvitch has done. The idea of "a total social phenomenon," as elaborated by Mauss, laid the basis for thinking in such terms.[72]

It is rather significant that many anthropologists, operating within the structure of a colonial society and preoccupied with its current aspects and problems, have avoided (unconsciously, in most cases) describing the concrete situation applicable to such a society. Out of a more or less conscious fear of having to take into consideration a specific kind of "system" and society: the society of the colonial power to which they themselves belong. They have dealt with less compromising systems—"western civilization" and "primitive cultures," or else have confined themselves to limited problems for which they have proposed solutions of a limited nature. And it is because of a refusal to accept this attitude, which they regard as inevitable and profitable only to the colonial power, that certain anthropologists decline to treat their discipline as "an applied" science.[73] We are confronted here with a fact that belongs in the framework of critical judgment in the domain of human sciences and one which suggests the extensive critical preparation incumbent upon anyone who contemplates offering an analysis of colonial societies.

We have frequently noted the somewhat pathological character of colonial societies, the *crises* marking the stages of the so-called process of "evolution"—crises that do not correspond to necessary phases of this process, yet which have nevertheless specific characteristics in relation to the type of colonial society under consideration and the nature of the colonial society (the Islamized Africans do not react like "animist" Africans or pseudo-Christians; African societies of the same type do not react in the same manner to "the French presence" and "the British presence," etc.) By focusing clearly on those facts that characterize a society subjected to colonial domination, and on those facts that characterize the colonial situation in its particular aspects, these "crises" enable a sociologist to achieve a comprehensive analysis since they constitute the only points of reference from which one can grasp, in a global sense, the transformations occurring among a colonial people under the influence and actions of the colonial power. They are conducive to reaching over-all views, an awareness of essential ties and relationships. They allow one to avoid fragmentary analyses (changes in the economic life, in the political life, etc.) which are both incomplete and artificial and can only lead to an academic sort of description and classification. We have already indicated that these "crises" constitute so many vantage points from which to view not only the phenomena of contact, but also the colonized society in all its traditional aspects. We must add that they also permit in this manner an analysis which takes into account, simultaneously, "the external milieu" and "the internal milieu"—and takes them into account in terms of existing conditions and relationships, in terms of actual life experiences.

We may be criticized for having resorted, in a more or less explicit manner, to the dangerous notion of the pathological and be asked to define the criteria characteristic of colonial crises. Our answer is to refer the critic to all the passages in this study which set forth the antagonistic aspects of relations between a colonial people and a colonial power, between a native culture and an imported culture—aspects tied to the relationships between domination and subjection, to the heterogeneous nature of societies and cultures in contact with each other—and in which the critic will find a suggestion as to the way in which these conflicts are felt by the individuals involved. The history of colonial societies reveals periods during which conflicts are merely latent, when a temporary equilibrium or adjustment has been achieved, and periods during which conflicts rise to the surface and are apparent on one level or the other, according to circumstances (religious, political, and economic). But conflicts expose at the same time the totality of relationships between colonial peoples and colonial powers and between the cultures of each of them (as we have reminded the reader in the case of Negro churches in Bantu Africa), moments when the antagonism and the gulf between a colonial people and a colonial power are at their maximum and are experienced by the colonial rulers as a challenge to established order, but by the colonial peoples as an effort to regain their autonomy. At each of these moments, which can be clearly delineated throughout the history of a colonial people, the latter present an unmistakable state of crisis, and it is precisely at such moments we can study the colonial society in terms of the concrete colonial situation. Paris.

(Translated from the French by Robert A. Wagoner, State University of New York Maritime College.)

NOTES

1. R. Kennedy, "The Colonial Crisis and the Future," in R. Linton, ed., *The Science of Man in the World Crisis*, 1945, p. 307.

2. O. Mannoni, *Psychologie de la Colonisation*, Editions du Seuil, 1950. This author did not however originate the expression which is found with different connotations in previous works, notably, in studies by the American sociologist, L. Wirth, devoted to the "typology of minorities." (This book is translated in English as *Prospero and Caliban*—Ed. note.)

3. We refer the reader to our summary of O. Mannoni's work published in the *Cahiers Internationaux de Sociologie,* vol. IX, 1950, p. 183 to 186.

4. L. Joubert, "Le Fait colonial et ses prolongements," *Le Monde non-chrétien,* 15, 1950.

5. Ch.-A. Julien, "Impéralisme économique et impéralisme colonial," in *Fin de l'ère coloniale,* Paris, 1948.

6. Cf. R. Kennedy, *op. cit.,* pp. 308–309, and R. Grousset, "Colonisations," in *Fin de l'ère coloniale.*

7. Quotation appears in the excellent book by H. Brunschwig, *La Colonisation française,* Calman-Lévy, 1949.

8. For example, the displacements carried out on behalf of the *Office du Niger* which gave rise to the most heated controversy; see P. Herrart's pamphlet, *Le Chancre du Niger,* with a preface by André Gide, Gallimard, 1939.

9. E. Chancelé, "La Question coloniale," *Critique,* no. 35, 1949.

10. Cf. L. Joubert, *op. cit.,* part II.

11. Cf. L. P. Mair, "The Study of Culture Contact as a Practical Problem," *Africa,* VII, 4, 1934.

12. Cf. J. Harmand, *Domination et Colonisation,* Flammarion, 1910, as a "classic" example of a juridical type of justification.

13. Quoted from H. Brunschwig, *op. cit.,* p. 64.

14. *Ibid.,* p. 265.

15. R. Kennedy, *op. cit.,* pp. 312–318.

16. G. Balandier, "Aspects de l'évolution sociale chez les Fang du Gabon," *Cahiers Internationaux de Sociologie,* vol. IX, 1950, p. 82.

17. R. Montagne, "Le Bilan de l'oeuvre européenne au-delà des mers," in *Peuples d'Outre-Mer et Civilisation Occidentale,* Semaines Sociales de France, 1948.

18. G. Balandier, *op. cit.,* p. 78.

19. Ch.-A. Julien, *Histoire de l'Afrique,* Collection *Que sais-je?,* Presses Universitaires de France, 1944, p. 123.

20. R. Montagne, *op. cit.,* p. 49.

21. Cf. especially Pham Nhuam, "Appel," in *Que pensent les étudiants coloniaux,* Le Semeur, Dec. 1947, Jan. 1948.

22. Ch.-A. Julien, "Impérialisme économique et impérialisme colonial," *op. cit.,* p. 25.

23. P. Leroy-Beaulieu, *De la colonisation chez les peuples modernes,* 1874, 1st edition; J. Ferry, preface to *Le Tonkin et la Mère-Patrie,* 1890.

24. Cf. A. Conant, *The Economic Basis of Imperialism,* 1898, and J. A. Hobson, *Imperialism, A Study,* 1902 (whose worth was recognized by Lenin), both works quoted by Ch.-A. Julien, *op. cit.*

25. Ch.-A. Julien, *op. cit.,* p. 29. Cf. on the subject of Africa, S. H. Frankel, *Capital Investments in Africa,* 1936.

26. J. Guitton, "Crises et valeurs permanentes de la Civilisation occidentales," in *Peuples d'Outre-Mer et Civilisation Occidentale,* p. 61.

27. P. Reuter, "Deux formes actuelles de l'Impérialisme colonial: protectorat économique et pénétration communiste," in *Peuples d'Outre-Mer . . . ,* p. 142.

28. J. Stalin, *Le Marxisme et la question nationale et coloniale*, éd. française, Editions Sociales, 1949, p. 179 and 247.

29. *The African Morning Post*, June 2, 1945, quoted in *Univers*, "L'Avenir de la colonisation," October 1945.

30. B. Malinowski, *The Dynamics of Culture Change*, Yale University Press, 1945.

31. Cf. the excellent analysis of M. Gluckman, "Malinowski's 'Functional' Analysis of Social Change," *Africa*, XVII, April 2, 1947.

32. R. Kennedy, *op. cit.*, pp. 309–311.

33. Cf. L. Durand-Reville, "Le Problème de l'industrialisation des territoires d'Outre-Mer," *Le Monde non-chrétien*, 13, Jan.–Mar. 1959, where this aspect is suggested and in which the author, a member of the French parliament from Gabon, sets forth the changes made necessary by the last war as well as present-day needs.

34. For facts concerning French Africa we refer the reader to the excellent studies of the geographer, Jean Dresch.

35. Cf. especially Ch. Robequain, *L'Evolution économique de l'Indo-chine française*, Paris, 1940, and P. Gourou, *L'Utilisation du sol en Indochine française* and *Les Pays Tropicaux*, Paris, 1948.

36. For a comprehensive study of this phenomenon see *Land Tenure in the Colonies*, V. Liversage, 1945; quoted by P. Naville, *La Guerre du Viet-Nam*, Paris, 1949.

37. Cf. Ch. Robequain, *op. cit.*

38. P. Naville, *op. cit.*, Paris, 1949; cf. especially, "La Politique française en Cochinchine," "La Bourgeoisie cochinchinoise," "Les Paysans annamites et la Révolution," "Le Développement de la classe ouvrière et de l'industrie."

39. J. Borde, "Le Problème ethnique dans l'Union Sud-Africaine," *Cahiers d'Outre-Mer*, no. 12, 1950; an excellent over-all view and bibliography.

40. Cf. W. G. Ballinger, *Race and Economics in South Africa*, 1934.

41. For South Africa we mention I. Schapera, M. Hunter; for East Africa, L. P. Mair, Audrey Richards, M. Read, M. Gluckman; for West Africa, M. Fortes, D. Forde, K. L. Little. We regard their works as the most important.

42. Cf. M. Read, *Native Standards of Living and African Culture-Change*, London, 1938.

43. K. L. Little, "Social Change and Social Class in the Sierra-Leone Protectorate," *American Journal of Sociology*, 54, July 1948. An important study.

44. J. Dresch, "La Prolétarisation des masses indigènes en Afrique du Nord," in *Fin de l'ère coloniale, op. cit.*, p. 57–69, and R. Delavignette, "Les Problèmes du travail: Paysannerie et Prolétariat," in *Peuples d'Outre-Mer et Civilisation Occidentale*, p. 273–291.

45. G. D'Arboussier, "Les Problèmes de la culture," *Afrique Noire*, special edition of *Europe*, May–June 1949.

46. O. Hatzfeld, "Les Peuples heureux ont une histoire. Etude malgache," *Cahiers du monde non-chrétien*, 16, 1950.

47. *Les Colonies, passé et avenir*, chapter entitled: "Colonies tropicales et sociétés plurales."

48. H. Laurentie, "Notes sur une philosophie de la politique coloniale française," in a special issue of *Renaissances,* Oct. 1944.

49. J. Borde, "Le Problème ethnique dans l'Union Sud-Africaine," *op. cit.,* p. 320.

50. L. Wirth, "The Problem of Minority Groups," in *The Science of Man in the World Crisis,* pp. 347–372. By the same author on this subject: *The Present Position of Minorities in the United States.*

51. *Les Vrais chefs de l'Empire,* a new edition under the title *Service Africain,* 1946; chapt. II, "La Société coloniale." [Translated as *Freedom and Authority in French West Africa,* 1950]

52. *Op. cit.,* p. 353.

53. *Op. cit.,* p. 41.

54. There is a significant proverb: "God created the White Man, then the Black Man, and finally the Portuguese." And also: "There are three kinds of men: Whites, Blacks, and Portuguese" (a proverb in the Belgian Congo).

55. Cf. A. Siegfried, *Afrique du Sud,* Armand Colin, 1949, p. 75. Also, *Handbook on Race Relations in South Africa,* E. Hellmann, 1949, and J. Borde, *op. cit.,* p. 339–340.

56. As was attempted before 1939 in territories under French control: in French West Africa (1930), in Madagascar (1934), in French Equatorial Africa (1936), and in Indo-China (1938).

57. For Black Africa alone, R. Delavignette gave, in 1939, the following proportions in respect to the population designated as European: the Union of South Africa (25.0%, former German Southwest Africa, 10.0%), Rhodesia (4.5%), Angola (1.0%), Kenya (0.5%), Belgian Congo (0.2%), French West Africa and French Equatorial Africa (0.1%); *op. cit.,* p. 36. Concerning the latter territories, since 1945 the increase in European population has been important.

58. Cf. R. Maunier, *Sociologie Coloniale,* p. 19, 30, 33.

59. J.-R. Ayouné, "Occidentalisme et Africanisme," in *Renaissances,* special edition, October 1944, p. 204.

60. We call attention to Brazzaville where the African population rose from 3,800 inhabitants in 1912 to 75,000 in 1950; that is more than one-tenth of the population of the Central Congo.

61. Cf. Dr. L. Aujoulat, "Elites et masses en pays d'Outre-Mer" in *Peuples d'Outre-Mer et Civilisation Occidentale, op. cit.,* p. 233–272.

62. Cf. L. Achille, "Rapports humains en Pays d'Outre-Mer" in *Peuples d'Outre-Mer et Civilisation Occidentale, op. cit.*

63. G. Balandier, "Aspects de l'Evolution sociale chez les Fang du Gabon; I. Les implications de la situation coloniale," *op. cit.*

64. Monica Hunter had come close to making this observation. She wrote: "The study of culture contact makes very clear that society is a unity, and when one aspect is modified, the whole is affected."; *Reaction to Conquest,* p. 552. She was content simply to make this observation and did not seek to explore its implications or discover its consequences in a methodical manner.

65. B. G. M. Sundkler, *Bantu Prophets in South Africa,* London, 1948.

66. Cf. *La Vocation Actuelle de la Sociologie,* in particular, pp. 98–108.

The Colonial Situation: A Theoretical Approach (*1951*)   **61**

The definition of sociology and its essential distinctions are set forth. Chapters III and IV are devoted to microsociology, whose true founder is Georges Gurvitch.

67. Cf. L. Achille, *op. cit.,* pp. 211–215.

68. A carefully reasoned and concise critical analysis was given by M. Leiris in a lecture entitled "l'Ethnographe devant le colonialisme" in 1950, later published in *Les Temps Modernes.*

69. Gunnar Myrdal, *An American Dilemma,* New York, 1944.

70. Cf. especially R. Bastide, *Sociologie et Psychanalyse,* Chapt. XI: "Le Heurt des Races, des Civilisations et la Psychanalyse," Paris, P.U.F., 1950.

71. Cf. M. Gluckman, "Analysis of a Social Situation in Modern Zululand," in *Bantu Studies,* vol. XIV, 1940; and Malinowski's controversy on this subject in *The Dynamics of Culture Change,* p. 14 ff.

72. G. Gurvitch, moreover, associates the three terms in his "Prefatory Remarks" written for the section entitled "Psychologie Collective" for *L'Année Sociologique,* 3rd series, 1948–1949. Likewise, a psychiatrist like Karen Horney emphasizes the fact that all neuroses, individual or collective, can be explained by a process involving *all* personal and socio-cultural factors; cf. Dr. Karen Horney, *The Neurotic Personality of Our Time,* New York, 1937.

73. Cf. F. M. Keesing, "Applied Anthropology in Colonial Administration," in R. Linton, ed., *op. cit.*

[2]

SOCIAL THEORY AND THE STUDY OF CHRISTIAN MISSIONS IN AFRICA[1]

T. O. BEIDELMAN

IN the past anthropology was concerned with alien, exotic societies such as Indians, Africans, and Pacific Islanders. Today it is in vogue to do the anthropology of modern societies. Abroad this is termed the study of nation-building and development; at home it becomes the study of various sub-cultures with attention towards ethnic minorities and deviant groups rather than upon the more powerful and prominent segments of our society. Anthropologists tend to neglect those groups nearest themselves, and in the scurry to conduct relevant research, a broad area of great theoretical interest has been passed by. Almost no attention was ever paid by anthropologists to the study of colonial groups such as administrators, missionaries, or traders. Today we can read anthropological studies of the impact of such groups upon native populations, but the focus of such work dims with the colour line. Thus, an anthropologist has studied the machinations of the members of a Nigerian emirate but not the tactics of the British Resident and his staff. Another applied potted Weberian bureaucratic theory to Soga local government but neglected to discuss the British district officers in the same chiefdom. Another asked how Christian Tswana behaved, but not about those missionaries who had converted them. Anthropologists may have spoken about studying total societies, but they did not seem to consider their compatriots as subjects for wonder and analysis.[2] In the studies of Christianity in Africa, consideration was mainly in terms of the relations of the convert to his traditional society, to the process of social change, or sometimes to the development of native separatist churches. It never included the missionaries who had made the conversions or described everyday affairs at the mission station, clinic, or school.

Study of such agents of change would be useful in four different but complementary areas of social theory and research. First, this helps complete the historical picture of Africa's recent past. Native societies responded to policies and values deriving outside themselves. Behaviour making little sense from the African

[1] Over the past sixteen years, as part of a wider anthropological study of Kaguru society, I have been engaged in a study of the Church Missionary Society in Ukaguru, Tanzania. I presented a brief set of comments on this topic in my recent book, *The Kaguru*, Holt-Rinehart-Winston, New York, 1971. With the support of a Wenner-Gren Foundation Research Grant in 1973 I consulted the C.M.S. Archives in London. I hope to publish a historical monograph on this topic within the next few years. Since this will be, to the best of my knowledge, the first such missionary study by a social anthropologist, I have delayed publication until I have better appreciated some of the complex historical and religious issues involved. The present essay formed the basis of various lectures given at Harvard University, Cornell University, State University of New York (Stonybrook), and the School of Oriental and African Studies, University of London. I should like to thank Professor Marion Kilson, Professor Martin Kilson, and Professor John Middleton for reading drafts of this manuscript.

[2] I have drawn my examples from Africa and therefore consider the neglect of British, French, and Belgians as subjects of study. However, Americans have shown themselves no better in their neglect of the Bureau of Indian Affairs, traders, and missionaries when studying contemporary American Indian life.

236   SOCIAL THEORY AND THE STUDY OF CHRISTIAN MISSIONS

perspective may become clear once it is related to the values and motives of missionaries or administrators. Second, colonial administrators and missionaries can now be studied with relative safety, freedom, and some dispassion although, of course, the former can no longer be studied *in situ*. It is questionable whether comparable leeway would be allowed researchers inquiring into contemporary governmental groups which have now taken over in the new, developing states. The parallels between these two types of agencies seem striking and it is reasonable to hope that we can gain insights into less accessible contemporary agencies through historical analysis of their predecessors. Third, the problem of planned social change, of communication, and exercise of power between culturally different groups, remains one of the most important and pressing sociological issues. No better documented cases are available for such study than those found in the colonial record, particularly since these have considerable historical depth. Finally, colonial structures may be viewed as variants of a far broader type, that of the complex bureaucratic organization. Many would agree with Weber that this is the prevailing mode of organization in modern life and as such its study in its many different manifestations provides extremely valuable comparative data. Colonial study would provide provocative new perspectives into some of the problems of the relation between 'rational' social organizations and 'non-rational' cultural values, an issue only recently appreciated by some sociologists and political scientists.

Current historical interest in the study of missionaries in Africa is generally credited to the influence of Roland Oliver, although a stronger case might be made for Bengt Sundkler.[3] Many British-trained historians and sociologists cite Oliver's work as inspiring their own, while Sundkler's pioneer studies have inspired the writings of many Scandinavian and German scholars as well as British.[4] Unfortunately, none of these works conveys much about the ordinary activities and organization of these missionaries at the grassroots, still less about their social backgrounds, beliefs, and day-to-day problems, economic attitudes, or patriotism. Instead we have broad historical narratives of missionary exploits on a national or regional basis or we have a discussion of various theories about the proper method of missionizing. Nowhere do we gain any idea of how any particular station was run or what a typical day at a mission station was like. There is no description of the career of any rank-and-file missionary. In general, the historical studies of missionaries represent a

[3] Roland Oliver, *The Missionary Factor in East Africa*, Longmans, London, 1952; Bengt Sundkler, *Bantu Prophets in South Africa*, Lutterworth, London, 1948; *The Christian Ministry in Africa*, Swedish Institute of Missionary Research, Uppsala, 1960. Edwin Smith may have been in the minds of some, but he is rarely cited these days.

[4] The best of the British-trained or influenced are: J. F. A. Ajayi, *Christian Missions in Nigeria 1841–1891*, Longmans, London, 1965; E. A. Ayandele, *The Missionary Impact on Modern Nigeria 1842–1914*, Humanities, New York, 1967; F. K. Ekechi, *Missionary Enterprise and Rivalry in Igboland 1857–1914*, Cass, London, 1971; M. W. Murphree, *Christianity and the Shona*, Athlone, London, 1969; R. L. Rotberg, *Christian Missionaries and the Creation of Northern Rhodesia*, Princeton University, Princeton, 1965; A. J. Temu, *British Protestant Missions*, Longmans, London, 1972; R. L. Wishlade, *Sectarianism in Southern Nyasaland*, Oxford University Press, London, 1965; Marcia Wright, *German Missions in Tanganyika 1891–1941*, Clarendon Press, Oxford, 1971.

Examples of Sundkler's influence may be found in the various publications of Studia Missionalia Upsaliensia, including P. Beverhause and C. F. Hallencreutz (eds.), *The Church Crossing Frontiers*, 1969; C-J. Hellbert, *Missions on a Colonial Frontier West of Lake Victoria*, 1965; S. von Sicard, *The Lutheran Church on the Coast of Tanzania 1887–1914*, 1970; and in B. A. Pauw, *Religion in a Tswana Chiefdom*, Oxford University Press, for the International African Institute, London, 1960.

SOCIAL THEORY AND THE STUDY OF CHRISTIAN MISSIONS   237

rather dull form of scissors-and-paste history devoid of the kind of social theory that can make events meaningful, convincing, and relevant to current problems. There have, of course, been some highly sophisticated studies of missions by missionaries themselves. Unfortunately, none of these writers appears to have had any interest in relating his findings to theories or problems outside the mission community.[5] To the best of my knowledge there have been no proper sociological or anthropological studies of European missionaries anywhere.[6]

The remainder of this paper aims at presenting some of the basic theoretical issues involved in the study of Christian missions in Africa. In doing so I hope to raise questions which are relevant to the analysis of other types of social organization in Africa and elsewhere. For the most part I do not present this material with reference to the writings of other scholars. Those writing in detail on missions, whether historians or missionaries, have shown so little concern for social theory that this seems justified. Those concerned with any theory that might be relevant, such as Max Weber and Robert Michels among the classic sociologists, or Michel Crozier, Alvin Gouldner, and Chie Nakane among those writing today, have shown no direct interest in colonial societies. Furnivall seems one of the very few concerned with colonialism who also exhibits theoretical sophistication.

My discussion is organized along six broad, analytical themes, each allowing for the organization of data in a manner pertinent not only for missionary study but for relation to some basic sociological theories. I indicate the kind of data required and then suggest the broader issues to which these data might relate. At times I draw illustrations from my research on the Church Missionary Society (henceforth, C.M.S.) in Ukaguru; however, this is in no way intended as an analysis of that system. That will follow in a later, full-scale historical monograph.

I. Some Secular Attributes of Missionaries

It is essential to consider any missionary group in terms of its ethnicity, class, and economic background. This involves two aspects: the cultural background of

---

[5] Sundkler and those influenced by him apply sociological theory when describing African separatists, but they become highly subjective and far less critical when examining their fellow European missionaries and the basic features of the Christian church. The literature by missionary groups is immense. A few examples of useful studies on the church in Africa are: E. Andersson, *Churches at the Grassroots*, Friendship Press, New York, 1968; H. W. Mobley, *The Ghanaian's Image of the Missionary*, Brill, Leiden, 1970; F. Rubingh, *Sons of Tiv, a Study of the Rise of the Church among the Tiv of Central Nigeria*, Baker Book House, Grand Rapids, 1969; N. Smith, *The Presbyterian Church of Ghana 1835-1960*, Ghana University, Accra, 1966; J. V. Taylor and D. A. Lehman, *Christians of the Copperbelt*, SCM, London, 1961; J. V. Taylor, *The Growth of the Church in Buganda*, SCM, London, 1958; F. B. Welbourn, *East African Rebels*, SCM, London, 1961.

[6] The symposium volume, C. G. Baëta (ed.), *Christianity in Tropical Africa*, Oxford University Press, for the International African Institute, Lon-

don, 1968, is most disappointing, both in the lack of new insights and in the superficiality of most of the papers. No studies specifically of missionaries seem to be in progress to judge from recent issues of *African Religious Research*, African Studies Center, University of California, Los Angeles. *The International Review of Missions* (since 1970, *International Review of Mission*) contains few essays of sociological use, but the bibliographical survey published in each issue is essential for anyone in mission studies. The number and range of material cited in each issue indicate the staggering volume of material continually published on this topic. It is remarkable that despite this, little reflects any grasp of sociological principles. Other relevant journals are *The Bulletin of the Society for African Church History*, the *Journal of Religion in Africa*, and *Practical Anthropology* (now *Missiology*) which have encouraged publication on missionary problems but nothing has appeared which could be called a sociological study of missionaries or a mission station.

238   SOCIAL THEORY AND THE STUDY OF CHRISTIAN MISSIONS

missionaries as this influences their behaviour in ways not logically determined by their Christian beliefs and work and also as this relates to the larger colonial milieu in which missionaries function. The C.M.S. in Ukaguru provides a useful illustration. Most of their members appear to be recruited from the working and lower middle class. Their views on the roles of men and women, on thrift, and on conspicuous consumption and even on the aims and qualities of education all appear highly coloured by their broader socio-economic experience at home; certainly they contrasted even in the 1960s with American Roman Catholic teaching missionaries such as Jesuits and Maryknolls and even with English Protestants such as the U.M.C.A.[7] The ethnicity of the C.M.S. had varying significance through their stay in Ukaguru, and it is surprising that this variable is underplayed in most missionary studies. Thus, during the earliest period of mission contact, the British exerted political influence at Zanzibar and Mombasa. Without such connections the C.M.S. would not have been tolerated in their repeated meddling in Arab-African affairs at that time. During the period of German colonial rule, British ethnicity was a considerable disadvantage. Not only were the missionaries unwilling to learn German until compelled to do so, but early reports abound in criticism and misunderstanding between the German administration and the British missionaries. The C.M.S. were never so critical of colonial rule or so defensive of Kaguru interests as during this period when such rule was by a foreign power rivalling their homeland. After the British mandate, the missionaries in Ukaguru became strong supporters of the colonial doctrine and tended to equate African nationalism with materialism and ungodliness. If from time to time they had differences in their relations with the British colonial authorities, these related to class differences and life-style. As a further illustration of ethnic variables, one might contrast the former Belgian Congo with Tanzania. In the Congo the Belgian Roman Catholic orders were closely integrated into the colonial power structure and until shortly before independence, relatively uncritical of the colonial regime, whereas Protestant groups, mainly from outside Belgium, sometimes reflected views far less sympathetic to the *status quo*. In contrast, in Tanzania Roman Catholics, rarely of British background, were unsympathetic to colonial rule and shortly before African independence they even appear to have been involved in nationalist political activities, whereas the Protestant groups, mainly of British background, were singularly conservative and uncritical.

Even the finances of a mission group have implications far beyond the mere needs for support and expansion of missionary activities. Missions with large international backing, such as some Roman Catholic orders, or with rich funding such as some American, Swiss, and German groups, were able to provide capital investment, salaries, and life-styles both in the metropolitan training establishments and in the field which encouraged a set of attitudes and a manner of behaviour far different from poorer missions. This sometimes determined the kind of models of modernization provided by missionaries for converts as well as reinforcing attitudes about materialism and well-being. A pervading sense of subdued life-style and pinching thrift

---

[7] The issue of class experience can even affect attitudes about methods of discipline and education. For example, the harsh measures taken by missionaries at Livingstonia, in what is now Malawi, must be seen in part as a reflection not of racist cruelty against Blacks but of the pervading philosophy of harshness in discipline reflected in the prisons and schools of Victorian Britain.

SOCIAL THEORY AND THE STUDY OF CHRISTIAN MISSIONS   239

permeates the past accounts of the C.M.S. in Ukaguru and continues into the recent period. Its effect on missionary morale and on the image missionaries presented to Africans (as contrasted to the images of American and Dutch Roman Catholic missionaries and British civil servants) should be obvious.

Christianity is framed in universal terms which ideally override ethnicity, nationality, class, and income. Ideally then missionary activities should reflect basic similarities regardless of these social variables. Such an assertion is about as realistic as contending that a shoe factory in Bombay should resemble ones in Manchester, Kansas City, and Leningrad. Organizations clearly vary, not simply in terms of their scale and tasks, but in terms of the cultures in which they are set. Similarly, French Protestants and English Protestants may both organize missionary groups to save souls, but English and French exhibit very different styles of social behaviour. The structure of a mission (even within the same religious order) must still be acted out in terms not entirely defined by rational, formal belief, and organization. Notions of security, self-interest, esteem, honour, privacy, sexuality, age, and status vary with national culture and also with class, educational background, and family income. How strange then that nearly all studies of colonial administration and of missionary activities ignore these features and tend to consider missionaries (or administrators and traders) as essentially all the same.[8]

II. Religious Beliefs

Most studies of Christian missions in Africa consider all missionaries as members of a general class. A few select a particular missionary group for study but then this tends to become mere anecdotal narrative. Rarely, a writer discusses the competition between certain missions, such as Protestants and Roman Catholics. None undertakes a review of the relation between religious beliefs and the organization and character of missionary activities, even though this would be a primary line of inquiry if the writer were describing an African tribal group. The greatest contrast in missionary beliefs involves the difference between Protestant and Catholic conceptions of a religious leader as a priest or pastor. In general, priests are required to undergo a far greater educational and social commitment than pastors. Invariably Roman Catholic priests have the educational equivalent of a college degree whereas Protestant pastors may vary greatly, depending upon their group, from college to primary school education. For example, in Ukaguru White pastors had college education but Kaguru pastors had only primary school education and could not read or speak English. In contrast African priests in neighbouring areas had college educations with knowledge of English, French, Latin, and Greek. While this contrast is somewhat extreme, it indicates that whereas Protestant sects embrace a wide range of standards, sometimes with a double standard for European and native clergy, the sacerdotal power of the Roman Catholic priesthood has required a higher and more consistent set of standards. The issues involved are more than theological. Religious leaders serve as role models for Africans, as well as agents to represent African interests to secular agencies. African pastors and priests gain much of their prestige

---

[8] I am aware of the works of Robert Heussler, but these exhibit almost no appreciation of sociological aspects of class, authority, or power: see *Yesterday's Rulers*, Syracuse University Press, Syracuse, 1963; *The British in Northern Nigeria*, Oxford University Press, London, 1968.

240 SOCIAL THEORY AND THE STUDY OF CHRISTIAN MISSIONS

and leadership powers from secular skills and qualities such as familiarity with European languages, facility in communication with Europeans and Europeanized Africans, and skill and familiarity with modern technology. These are often symbolized by the assumption of European life-style in dress, mannerisms, transport, and home accommodations. Not only is education required to carry this off, but the economic support necessary to sustain such a life-style is less easily justified when clergy are poorly educated and therefore arguably less entitled to pay equal to more educated Europeans. For such reasons, Kaguru pastors were forced to cultivate to make ends meet and lacked modern furnishings, shoes, and stylish clothing. This may have contributed a note of Christian simplicity, but for Kaguru, conversion was associated with gaining access to modern skills rather than with cultivation of homely virtues as defined by a kind of romantic Christian atavism on the part of European missionaries. Furthermore, the investment in time, psychological commitment, and effort required of the priesthood is by and large greater than for a Protestant pastor and this in turn leads to stronger incorporation into the religious organization. Finally, the celibacy of priests has had profound implications for White–Black relations on mission stations. George Orwell once remarked on how *mem-sahibs* soured the romantic paternalism of colonial life. Certainly the inclusion of European wives and children at mission stations produced a new and more entrenched form of domestic colonialism, a concern over sexual accessibility, and the demands for frequent home-leave and familial disruption on the grounds of health and education. No such complex domestic–colonial infrastructure developed in Catholic missions. We see that the theological issues of the priesthood, prolonged sacerdotal training, and celibacy led to unforeseen and far-reaching developments in secular affairs.

Theology also influenced the speed and ease of conversion of ordinary church members, as well as the training of clergy. Protestants emphasized enthusiasm, spirit, and self-dedication rather than more formal and complex sets of ritual and belief. This often, though not always, lent itself to more rapid, facile conversions than in the case of Roman Catholicism. This is especially clear in the case of revivalism, common in Protestantism but unacceptable as a recruiting device among Catholics. Revival provides a cheap, speedy mode of dramatic conversion with considerable potential for propagandistic public display. It has been especially prominent during periods when there was poor economic support of more routine conversion measures. The length and degree of proselytization are closely related to the degree that the convert is incorporated into the new system and also to the rate of relapse into pagan practices. A contrast between deeds and ritual, on the one hand, and zeal and spirit, on the other, is an over-simplification of the differences between Roman Catholics and Protestants. Yet the shades of emphasis along these lines clearly affected the ways in which potential recruits were absorbed and members defined as being in good standing or as falling outside the group. Missionaries entertained inconsistent notions about the signs of right conscience or the nature of Christian conduct. They described their goals as essentially spiritual and religious, yet in Ukaguru we find missionaries legislating against wearing Muslim or pagan dress, against beer, tobacco, and dancing, against wearing traditional jewellery, against use of traditional names, against traditional cosmetics and hair-styles, and endorsing consumption of European

SOCIAL THEORY AND THE STUDY OF CHRISTIAN MISSIONS 241

cotton goods and Western hygiene. Clearly missionaries viewed Christian life as a totality, involving every facet of cultural life, from domestic organization and inheritance to forms of punishment, amusement, and grooming. Much of this is, of course, in no way prescribed by the formal literature of Christian teaching, any more than the underlying notions of reasonability, propriety, and goodwill are delineated in legal literature, even though these affect many aspects of legal interpretation. We must examine the culture of the missionaries themselves to determine how they extended their Christian beliefs into a broader framework of social life. The character of such a picture clearly varied not only with the theology but with the class, economic, and national attitudes of the missionaries. Here are two simple illustrations. (1) In the nineteenth century Protestant missionaries in Ukaguru came from lower and lower middle class homes in Britain and Ireland where drinking was a serious and constant menace, if only as it was observed in others as a sign of their failure to come to terms with modern industrial life. The C.M.S.'s violent condemnation of drink was in sharp contrast to the views of the neighbouring French fathers, and, for that matter, with other, 'High Church' Anglicans. (2) Throughout its stay in Ukaguru, the C.M.S. resisted training Africans in practical skills such as carpentry, printing, tailoring, and metalwork. Other missionaries, Protestant and Catholic alike, fostered such training and brought out artisan missionaries, much to their advantage in securing converts and in developing their stations. It is not entirely clear why the C.M.S. at the London headquarters held to this impractical and self-defeating line, but it may be that these policy-makers were influenced by C.M.S. difficulties with craftsmen–trader missionaries and converts during the West African expansion of the C.M.S. some decades earlier. It may be that a tinge of unworldliness and militant anti-materialism survived as a product of the earlier 'conversion' of leading members of this group into evangelical activities. Clearly the reasons for these policies relate to values and beliefs not essentially part of basic Christian theology.[9] It is obvious that cultural factors must be considered in determining the full implications and variations in the beliefs and policies of any missionary group.

III. Theories of Conversion

Conversion has been the subject of considerable theorizing. Missionaries write trying to determine the means which best conform to their own aims. Religious historians consider the reasons leading to conversion, the historical confrontation between cultures, while social anthropologists or psychologists consider this as an example of social or personality change.[10] Of course, all these approaches overlap and

[9] Ekechi remarks on similar conduct by the C.M.S. in southern Nigeria (1971: 183–6). He argues that this relates to their general hostility towards higher education and secular skills in that this involved teaching in English rather than the vernacular; Ekechi rightly observes that the C.M.S. emphasized vernacular education as a means to reading Scripture translated into the vernacular. In this sense, there was a doctrinal basis for C.M.S. policies related to their antagonism towards higher education, in contrast to Roman Catholics who had no such commitments and who quickly accommodated themselves to the colonial government's needs for more secular

education.

[10] Perhaps the most sociologically perceptive study by a missionary is Louis George Mylene, *Missions to Hindus*, Longmans, Green, London, 1908; the sociologist D. R. Heise makes much of this in 'Prefatory Findings in the Sociology of Missions', *Journal for the Scientific Study of Religions*, 6 (1967), 49–63. A somewhat similar position, contrasting the static-self-contained mission station with the expanding, open mission community was made by the missionary D. A. McGavran, *The Bridges of God, a Study in the Strategy of Missions*, World Dominion, London, 1955. Few anthropologists have seriously

242   SOCIAL THEORY AND THE STUDY OF CHRISTIAN MISSIONS

complement one another. It is remarkable that no one other than missionaries has provided any analysis of the various theories of conversion, much as one would provide a sociological exposition of any other theory of knowledge and conduct. Just as we study a cosmology in order to understand the ways members of a society act, so we must comprehend a missionary's theories about conversion before we can determine why he proceeds along a certain course in his attempts to convert others. Such an analysis may be conveniently divided into two parts: the stereotypes which a missionary holds about the objects of his efforts, and his theories about what tactics would best achieve his ends. The first detailed anthropological accounts of the Kaguru were provided by C.M.S. missionaries in their attempts to secure information to facilitate conversion. They were part of a plan to uncover the character of Kaguru society. It is to these ends that we owe the missionaries' pioneer study of the Kaguru language. Their views about Kaguru mentality, custom, and the structure of Kaguru society led them along certain lines of missionizing. Indeed, the need to missionize makes sense only if one has a basically negative, evolutionary view of the culture one is trying to change.

Missionary views about the process of conversion itself ultimately amount to a whole theory of social change. It is therefore remarkable that despite the profusion of theory and descriptive writings on social change, on the whole missionary activities have remained outside the scrutiny of social scientists. In one of the few perceptive studies of missionary tactics, Mylene, himself a missionary, dichotomizes between missionaries that aim at changing individuals and who then segregate these converts into a special community in order to provide a new social environment for a different way of behaviour, and those missionaries who seek to subvert the entire existing community in order to prevent old ideas from being perpetuated. Clearly any theory of conversion involves aspects of both procedures, and in this the Christian missionary resembles the political revolutionary. Missionary theories of society are, in large part, reflections of the particular cultures and segments of society from which the missionaries themselves have sprung, perhaps far more than being any reflections of the actual states of the societies on which these have been applied.

IV. Careers and Routinization

Missionary careers parallel those of early colonial adminstrators in their problems of routinization. It is only appropriate that the most recent official history of the C.M.S. is entitled *The Problems of Success*.[11] In all such ventures, the very success of the movement, the increase in numbers of personnel and range of activities, poses serious problems.

The term *routinization* was originally coined by Weber to describe the process by which charismatic authority was converted into rational–legal authority. All this can be fitted into certain stereotypes. The initial colonial contact was by romantic adven-

considered missionaries or conversion. I. Schapera studied Tswana conversion but paid little attention to the missionaries, 'Christianity and the Tswana', *J.R.A.I.* 88 (1958), 1–10. More recently Robin Horton has attempted to reconsider conversion anthropologically, 'African Conversion', *Africa*, 41 (1971), 85–108, and has been criticized by H. J.

Fisher, 'Conversion Reconsidered', *Africa*, 43 (1973), 27–40. None of these writers has displayed much sensitivity to the conduct of missionaries themselves, much less to their notions about conversion.

[11] Gordon Hewit, *The Problems of Success*, SCM, London, 1971.

SOCIAL THEORY AND THE STUDY OF CHRISTIAN MISSIONS   243

turers exploring an area. The exploits of early missionaries such as David Livingstone, or, on a lesser dimension, J. T. Last in Ukaguru, were of interest to geographers, linguists, and ethnographers as well as to evangelists. During the early phase the missionary usually lacked a station and lived among the natives, learned the local tongue, and spent long hours in arduous travel over the countryside. The same was true of the very first colonial administrators. This stereotype certainly appealed to many early missionaries who sometimes seem as much repressed adventurers as spiritual leaders. In many cases, both Roman Catholics and Protestants built early stations as centres for runaway slaves or even secured converts by purchasing, educating, and freeing the slaves. This posed peculiar social and ethical problems. With success, direct contact with natives decreased. In the case of British colonial administration, an African Native Authority was established. Henceforth, the major task of a colonial administration was to oversee Black administrators, not to administer directly themselves. Similarly among missionaries, as converts increased and as success allowed the establishment of schools, clinics, and shops, and as native clergy and teachers were trained, Europeans took on the tasks of administering this African cadre. As this happened, the qualities most desirable in missionaries were no longer those of charismatic charm and leadership or spellbinding preaching but ones of administrative skill and record-keeping. Missionaries had less and less occasion to deal directly with the ordinary native. This led to some serious problems in missionary thinking, especially pronounced because these issues could not be clearly recognized and formally stated without jeopardizing the missionary mystique.

For example, long after C.M.S. missionaries became almost totally absorbed with administrative and technical duties, missionary training and literature (both that which indoctrinated missionaries and that designed to encourage donations and support from home) continued to picture missionaries as directly encountering natives, speaking the language of savages, and saving souls, even when missionaries rarely encountered untutored and illiterate Africans outside the fixed routine of a work or service situation in which most prolonged proselytization was between Africans. Yet Christians abroad were mainly drawn into missionary work with such a romantic spiritual vision in mind. Certainly without considerable affect and dramatization of the conversion situation, few Europeans[12] would be willing to sacrifice the economic and social comforts which they do (in contrast to life either at home or in comparable secular activities on the colonial scene). They need the intangible recompense of an affectual order, highly coloured with those aspects of altruism, paternal guidance, and sentiment congenial to close and prolonged personal contact with another, less advanced ethnic group. Missionary reports and missionaries themselves still dwell upon their evangelical experiences, their trials in an exotic and challenging environment, and the generally unsecular motivations behind their work. Yet for the most part, today their careers consist in writing reports and records, supervising a large cadre of African staff, and in preoccupation with a great many technical activities far removed from preaching the Gospel, although, of course, clinics, classrooms, bookstores, and pharmacies are clearly related to the key activities by which missionaries were and still are able to secure contact with unbelievers and

[12] I follow African usage and label all Whites as Europeans regardless of whether they come from Europe, America, or the Antipodes.

244   SOCIAL THEORY AND THE STUDY OF CHRISTIAN MISSIONS

thereby preach their faith. The history of various mission stations records such transformations as part of their success. Missionaries' own contradictory assertions (at times poignant and touching, at other times obfuscating and seemingly hypocritical) stem from the fact that missionaries themselves have had considerable difficulty in coming to terms with this transformation, both in their activities and in the resultant image they hold of themselves. These ambiguities are particularly sharply illustrated by the next set of social issues, those involving the problems of separating secular and sacred activities.

V. Compartmentalization and Total Social Phenomena

The actual practice of missionizing is itself grounded in profound and insoluble contradictions. At a broad level this is experienced in all social life, but is particularly pronounced in spheres such as missions and newly formed religious (or political) communities where there is an especially keen awareness of the gap between ideal (sacred) and actual or necessary (secular) behaviour. In his classic study of Christianity, Ernst Troeltsch points this out in terms of the incompatibility between the two poles of an ideal egalitarian commune of spiritual brotherhood and the everyday practical demands for a hierarchical, authoritarian church. In *Professional Ethics and Civic Morals* Durkheim expresses these two antithetical trends in his contrast between justice and charity. The issue touches most serious social analysis. In the study of Christian missions and similar idealizing movements this takes on two closely interconnected aspects.

The first relates to the idea of what the missionary is trying to do, his view of society in general and his appraisal of native cultures in contrast to his own. Essentially it involves the unrealistic dichotomization of secular and sacred affairs. Perhaps the best way to appreciate the issues is to consider the recent history of the mission. Thus, the C.M.S. reached Ukaguru in 1876 as part of a broader process of Victorian unrest and expansion. Modern science, the industrial revolution, and even the new Biblical criticism had deeply undermined Christian life, so that traditional values, especially those associated with religion and morality, were profoundly shaken. This was a time when Christianity was greatly discredited and of diminishing account in social life. Perhaps for these reasons missionaries may have felt impelled to go abroad to implement their vision of what society should be since this seemed unattainable at home. Whatever their motives, their activities could not elude the same secular forces that had disturbed Europe and America and indeed the missionaries themselves made use of such forces even while condemning them. They presented Christianity as an essential element of Western culture. The force of weapons, skill in manufacturing medicine and textiles, and widespread literacy were all implied somehow to be part and parcel of the same cultural package, even though in many respects these secular forces had worked to undermine religious faith. Missionaries were keen to present most aspects of European life as integrally related, as though the kind of minds that theologized about sin and salvation were necessarily those which could develop vaccines, lead conquering troops, or organize a productive textile mill. Protestants and Catholics alike were quick to use education and medical facilities as vehicles for proselytization. In early C.M.S. reports from Ukaguru, Africans were described as being evangelized even as they were medically treated, and on occasion were told

SOCIAL THEORY AND THE STUDY OF CHRISTIAN MISSIONS 245

that illness and sin were related.[13] Even in recent times those assembled for treatment at a local C.M.S. clinic first witness a brief religious service before medical treatment is begun for the day. Similarly those attending mission schools are required to take religious instruction.[14] Throughout their history in Africa missionaries have recognized that education provides the most powerful means to convert Africans. In their first decade, the C.M.S. made very little headway in Ukaguru; however, once the Germans had set up colonial rule and required educated natives to serve as petty officials, clerks, soldiers, and craftsmen, Kaguru flocked to mission schools and were converted. Since the C.M.S. monopolized education in Ukaguru during German times, Kaguru had no choice but conversion if they were to gain the education required for access to posts of power in collaboration with the new colonialists. A European colonial officer once remarked to me in Ukaguru that one of the few issues on which Protestant and Roman Catholic missionaries agreed was in their steady opposition to government secular schools. The C.M.S. pioneered in the study of the Kaguru language, compiling a grammar and Kaguru hymnbook, as well as publishing numerous Swahili readers, but their professed purpose in teaching literacy was to enable Kaguru to read the Bible, not to teach them about modern life.

A second aspect is that the missionaries had acted in a contradictory and unrealistic manner, as indeed they had over much of Africa. They had utilized secular features of European culture as means to interest Africans in religious matters. Yet later a C.M.S. missionary was to complain about the Kaguru, '. . . the subtle forces of materialism and bitter nationalism impose a new kind of bondage on the heart and minds of the African. As another missionary put it: "Our battle to-day is not with the bad old things but with the bad new things".'[15]

The missionaries instilled attitudes and values which they later condemned, mainly because they themselves had a poor comprehension of their own assumptions and activities. In part too this was the result of a double-standard in missionary perceptions about themselves and Kaguru. Earlier Professor Winter and I wrote:

The European missionaries on their part see the spirit of materialism in many Africans but particularly among their own employees, who constantly desire higher salaries and who, as we have seen in the case of the teachers, are unwilling to contribute even 10 per cent of their salaries to the church. We can understand the distaste and discouragement felt by Europeans in the face of such attitudes and actions on the part of the Africans only when we appreciate the notions of service and sacrifice which play such an important role in the lives of the missionaries. The strength of these ideals can be seen, for example, in the case of a mission physician who earns a mere fraction of the amount he would earn at home, or, for that matter, in Tanganyika itself if he were in the government medical service. As a result of the low salaries which they receive, financial questions are a continual source of anxiety to most European missionaries, particularly to those who are married and who are faced with problems such as clothing and educating their children. By contrast, they see the upper echelons of the African employees of the mission occupying positions of great prestige in their own society and enjoying incomes which are fantastically high in comparison

---

[13] *Proceedings of the C.M.S.* (1892–3), 53.
[14] Of course, in recent times in Tanganyika (Tanzania), Government insisted that in state-subsidized mission schools, students could not be forced to receive such religious instruction, but in practice such niceties were not usually observed.
[15] *Proceedings of the C.M.S.* (1947–8), 11.

246   SOCIAL THEORY AND THE STUDY OF CHRISTIAN MISSIONS

with the mass of the local population. From the European point of view, the Europeans engaged in missionary work are leading a life of poverty and sacrifice while the Africans who work for the church—far from sacrificing anything—are gaining wealth and enjoying previously unknown amenities.

While the Europeans view these matters in a comparative context, the Africans view them against an absolute scale. To the African clergyman or school teacher, the most obvious fact is that the standard of living and salary of the European missionary are higher than his own. The European missionaries . . . live in superior houses which are better furnished . . . and they have the use of an automobile. While many people in America or in Australia, for that matter, would be extremely loath to exchange their lot with an Australian missionary in Tanganyika, it must be remembered that for many Kaguru the standard of living now enjoyed by the missionaries remains the ultimate goal to be achieved either in their lifetime or that of their children.[16]

Missionaries were inconsistent in their use of the concept of a total society. Where it served their purposes, Western society was presented by missionaries as a functional whole and material attainments were considered signs of Christian civilization. At other times missionaries picked and chose between 'good' and 'bad' elements of modern life, though differently for themselves and for Kaguru.

The missionaries tried, on occasions, to separate themselves from the secular aspects of European colonialism. During the colonial period, the C.M.S. tried to present themselves as 'different' from Roman Catholic missionaries, and also unlike the drinking and partying colonial administrators and estate managers. As independence neared, they tried to present themselves as 'different' from the colonial rulers who would soon be leaving. Of course, this was at odds with their previous stance, especially as it was recalled by Africans how missionaries utilized colonial funds and authority for implementing their policies.

Over thirty years ago Evans-Pritchard wrote a masterpiece which revealed how the Azande could entertain inconsistent interpretations about behaviour and events. An intensive analysis of missionary beliefs (or those of any colonial group, for that matter) would provide rich data illustrating similar aspects of compartmentalization, rationalization, and circular thinking along lines long ago suggested by Pareto. Missionaries too can be prisoners of their concepts and unable to grasp the full implications of their policies and actions.

VI. Colonial and Bureaucratic Structure

This is the most important theoretical aspect of missionary studies. The study of bureaucratic structures as pioneered by Weber provides the seminal core for most advanced analysis of organizations within modern complex societies. The size and scope of modern organizations pose difficulties for analysis, but the task is further complicated because these structures are based upon profound contradictions and ambiguities. Such organizations are framed in rational terms, yet being staffed by human beings they necessarily become arenas for the exercise of power, prestige, and self interest, all elements essentially outside the terms of rationality *per se* and deter-

---

[16] E. H. Winter and T. O. Beidelman, 'Tanganyika', in *Contemporary Change in Traditional Societies* (ed. J. Steward), University of Illinois, Urbana, 1967, pp. 185–6.

SOCIAL THEORY AND THE STUDY OF CHRISTIAN MISSIONS   247

mined by cultural values and sentiments. Equally important, though strangely neglected in social analysis, is the relation between colonial structures and bureaucratic ones. Colonial systems exhibit bureaucratic features—a civil service, school systems, banks, large estates, missionary enterprises. What is generally described as 'colonial' is exhibited in all modern societies.

Colonial societies may be conveniently described by the model of a pyramid in which a minority at the apex controls and exploits large numbers at the base, with the aid of a medial cadre group which manifests characteristics of both ruler and ruled. For example, British administrators governed Ukaguru through a Native Authority whose cadre were local Africans. A sisal estate was controlled by Europeans or Asians and worked by Africans, while the foremen, supervisors and clerks who transmitted orders and reported the activities of workers were Africans trained to mediate between the aims of their alien masters and the acts of fellow African subordinates. Similarly, European missionaries proselytized and taught a large mass of Kaguru by means of an educated, converted African cadre of teachers, evangelists, pastors, nurses, and others. In each case the size of the group controlled was thought to require a rationalized, centralized hierarchical structure. This size and the scope of the technical tasks involved fostered considerable cultural differences between those at the top and base of the pyramid. Thus, the cultures of a doctor and his patients are usually very different, at least within the sub-world of a hospital, and a comparable gulf exists between the directors of a factory and those in an assembly line. In each situation we have a cadre which stands ambiguously between both extremes of the structure; nurses, headmen, foremen, catechists, prison guards, all share medial attributes. A cadre's roles are ambiguous in terms of their cultural identity and pivotal in terms of their transmission of information, orders, and needs. The emphasis upon procedure, uniforms, and rank all suggests this precariousness. Without uniforms, Kaguru Native Authority agents look and behave like any other Kaguru, and prison guards often resemble their prisoners culturally. Some of these structural features were long appreciated by anthropologists in their concern with the roles of chiefs and headmen in colonial authorities. The same features are displayed within missions. In Ukaguru before Tanzanian independence, the C.M.S. was directed by an Australian bishop resident far outside the chiefdom, just as the European District Commissioner, Provincial Commissioner, and Governor fashioned administrative policy but resided far from Ukaguru. Various European missionaries supervised educational, medical, and evangelical activities which were actually carried out by an African staff of teachers, medical aids, catechists, and clerks, just as African government staff were supervised by European technical officers. Just as Ukaguru had a paramount chief, subchiefs, and headmen staffing its Native Authority, so the C.M.S. mission had an African assistant bishop, archdeacon, pastors, and catechists, and just as the African government staff was far less trained than their European supervisors, so it was with these African churchmen.

The difficulties faced in these colonial groups resemble those in other bureaucratic organizations. Those at the top had little direct contact with the grassroots, usually not even knowing the local languages and certainly not residing near those they governed. These leaders depended upon their staff for the information on which to formulate and carry out policies. African pastors and catechists reported the moral

248   SOCIAL THEORY AND THE STUDY OF CHRISTIAN MISSIONS

states of their neighbours and indicated the community's needs. The local community rarely if ever approached the topmost European mission leaders directly but moved through the appropriate channels of African leadership. All this fostered the power of the cadre whose main advantage derived not so much from its formal authority as from its mastery of the flow of information between the base and apex of the system. The organization took on functions far different from those for which it was said to exist. Native Authorities did not exist simply to govern nor missions only to save souls. Both might be viewed as fields in which persons could gain security and advantages. These became systems existing in their own rights, their functions being to perpetuate themselves and therefore fill the needs of their staff. This helps to account for the extreme conservatism of bureaucratic structures which tend to perpetuate the very situations they were said to be working to efface. Tribal Authorities were said to be working to train Africans so that they could gradually rule themselves in detribalized states and missions were said to be converting pagans to become true Christians. Eventually the Native Authority should be transformed into independent national government and a mission into an autonomous church. If this were to happen, the structures would so alter that those in power in the original organization would lose their posts, for they occupied their particular positions, especially in the case of the African cadre, because of, not in spite of, their limited acculturation. In the mission literature there is rich evidence of the unwillingness of European missionaries to yield posts to Africans and an encouragement of double standards in filling posts and organizing activities. When the successful missionary had accomplished his task, he was theoretically supposed to pass on to other fields of endeavour. In actual practice, the successful missionary desired to head the new church he had created, confusing the roles of missionary and church leader.

Conclusion

   The study of colonial societies has generally been the sphere of historians and those political scientists and economists concerned with the social changes of recent decades. With the elimination of most formal colonial systems, academic interest has greatly waned. Apart from the work of Furnivall, little theoretical writing has emerged from this topic, even though at one time colonialism involved about half the world's population. It is remarkable too that analysts have seen little to connect colonial structures with modern social organization in general.[17] Colonial societies exhibit qualities little different from those of most large-scale modern organizations. There is a cultural gulf separating the top administrator from the masses administered in a large city administration, a hospital, or an army. All such groups utilize a cadre culturally medial between the administrative leaders and the administered masses. The problems of resentment, exploitation, and lack of communication which characterize classic colonial societies clearly pervade modern life for very similar reasons. The colonial record provides a largely unconsidered wealth of data from which we can gain insight into the present dilemmas of our own social world. Missionary studies are among the most neglected of a wide area of potential colonial research. Even more than the study of economic and political colonialism, the history of

---

[17] In a somewhat muddled way this seems the point of an essay by R. H. Davis, 'Interpreting the Colonial Period in African History', *Afr. Affairs*, lxxii (1973), 383–400.

SOCIAL THEORY AND THE STUDY OF CHRISTIAN MISSIONS 249

missionary enterprise would sharply illustrate the fundamental dilemma of modern social life, the failure of professed values and world-view to provide a meaningful reference for social action.

Part II
Language and Control

[3]

The Command of Language and the Language of Command

BERNARD S. COHN

The records generated by the East India Company—in their published form found in series such as *The Letters Received from its Servants in the East,* or *The Fort William India House Correspondence,* and the manuscript records stored in the India Office Library and Records, and the National Archives of India—are the primary sources utilized by all historians to reconstruct the facts of the British conquest of India and the construction of the institutions of colonial rule. These archival publications are a tribute to the extraordinary labours of thousands of employees of the Company who produced this seemingly endless store of information. These records are 'tribute' in another sense of the word. To quote *Webster's Collegiate Dictionary* (1948), tribute is 'a payment paid by one ruler or nation to another, either as an acknowledgment of submission, or of the price of protection'.

In this essay I will argue that the tribute represented in print and manuscript is that of complicated and complex forms of knowledge created by Indians, but codified and transmitted by Europeans. The conquest of India was a conquest of knowledge. In these 'official' sources we can trace the changes in forms of knowledge which the conquerors defined as useful for their own ends. The records of the seventeenth and eighteenth centuries reflect the Company's central concerns with trade and commerce; one finds long lists of products, prices, information about trade routes, descriptions of coastal and inland marts, and 'political' information about the Mughal empire, and especially local officials and their actions in relation to the Company. Scattered through these records are mentions of names and functions of Indians employed by the Company or with whom they were associated, on whom they were dependent for the information and knowledge to carry out their commercial ventures.

The Command of Language and the Language of Command 277

The titles of some of these functionaries in the anglicized forms include *Akhund, Banyan, Dalal, Dubashi, Gomastah, Munshi, Pandit, Shroff,* and *Vakil.* The titles varied with the location of the Company's factories, but the Indians bearing these titles all had specialized forms of knowledge, some about prices and values of currencies, the sources of specialized products, locations of markets, and the networks along which trade goods flowed; others knew about local and imperial governments, diplomatic and political rules, and the personalities of the rulers on whom the British were dependent for protection. All of these specialists were multilingual and had command of specialized languages necessary for the various levels of communication between foreigners and Indians. The Dubashi of the Coromandel coast had his function embodied in his title, which means 'two languages'. In Bengal the Akhund, sometimes referred to as a 'Muhmadan School teacher', was employed 'in composeing, writing and interpreting all letters and writings in the Persian language.'[1] The Akhund was frequently trusted with diplomatic missions as well as with delivering letters and various documents to Mughal officials. Vakils were confidential agents who, like Akhunds, were frequently involved in negotiations with Indian officials and were not only Persian-using, but had to be familiar with court formalities and personalities. They frequently advised the Company officials on courses of action in relation to the Company's continuing need to negotiate various legal and commercial matters with the Mughal state.

During the decade of the 1670s in Surat, the Company carried on repeated diplomatic negotiations with the Maratha ruler, Sivaji, seeking reparations for property lost in his attack on the Company's factory at Rajapur, and to establish trading rights in Sivaji's territories. The Company was well served during this period by a number of Indians, especially two brothers, Rama Shenvi, Portuguese writer, and Narayan Shenvi, the Company's linguist.[2]

Almost from the inception of their trading efforts in India, the British had sought legitimacy and protection from Indian rulers, primarily the Mughal emperor. To this end in 1615 Sir Thomas Roe

---

[1] Sir Richard Temple, ed., *The Diaries of Streynsham Master, 1675–1680* (London, 1911), vol. I, pp. 446–7.

[2] D.V. Kale, ed., *English Records on Shivaji* (Poona, 1931), pp. 195–6, 205, 266; Sir Charles Fawcett, ed., *The English Factories in India* (New Series, Oxford, 1936), vol. I, pp. 29, 69, 106.

was jointly dispatched to the Mughal's court by the Company and James I to obtain a treaty or pact which would guarantee 'constant love and peace' between the two monarchs.[3] Roe read the political world in which he found himself in terms of his own system of meanings; it was one which he thought compelled himself to undergo a 'thousand indignities unfit for a quality that represents a Kings Person', and in which he could not accomplish his ends 'without base creeping and bribing'.[4] Roe was plagued by a lack of knowledge of Persian, the court language, and did not have anyone whom he thought he could trust to properly translate the letters he had brought from his king, which were to be presented to Jahangir. Roe complained to his employers:

> Another terrible inconvenience that I suffer: want of an interpreter. For the Broker's here will not speak but what shall please; yea they would alter the Kings letter because his name was before the Mughals, which I would not allow.[5]

Roe employed as interpreters at various times during his stay at the court of Jahangir, a Greek, an Armenian, an eccentric Englishman, and on at least one occasion an Italian who knew Turkish but no Persian. Roe spoke to this interpreter in Spanish, a language he had learned in the Caribbean; the Italian then would translate this into Turkish for an officer of Jahangir's court who knew both Turkish and Persian.[6]

The British realized that in seventeenth-century India Persian was the crucial language for them to learn. They approached Persian as a kind of functional language, a pragmatic vehicle of communication with Indian officials and rulers through which, in a denotative fashion, they could express their requests, queries and thoughts, and through which they could get things done. Persian was a language which required highly specialized forms of knowledge, particularly to draft the many forms of documents which were the basis of official communication throughout much of India. Persian as a language was part of a much larger system of meanings which was in turn based on cultural premises which led to Indians constructing

---

[3] Sir William Foster, ed., *The Embassy of Sir Thomas Roe to India, 1615–19* (Oxford, 1926), p. 129.

[4] Ibid., p. 100.

[5] Ibid.

[6] Ibid., p. 130.

The Command of Language and the Language of Command **279**

action in ways far different from those on which the British based
their own.

Europeans of the seventeenth century lived in a world of signs
and correspondences, while Indians lived in a world of substances.
Roe interpreted the court ritual of the Mughal in which he was required to participate as a sign of debasement rather than an act of incorporation in a substantive fashion which made him a companion
of the ruler. Relations between persons, groups, 'nations' (*quam*),
and ruler and ruled were constituted differently in Europe and India. The British in seventeenth century India operated on the idea
that everything and everyone had a 'price'. The presents through
which relationships were constituted were seen as a form of exchange to which a quantitative value could be attached, and which
could be translated into a 'price'. Hence, the cloth which was the
staple of their trade was seen as a utilitarian object whose value was
set in a market. They never seemed to realize that certain kinds of
cloth and clothes, jewels, arms and animals had values that were not
established in terms of a market-determined price, but were objects
in a culturally constructed system by which authority and social relations were literally constituted and transmitted.

Hindus and Muslims operated with an unbounded substantive
theory of objects and persons. The body of the ruler was literally his
authority, the substance of which could be transmitted in what
Europeans thought of as objects. Clothes, weapons, jewels and paper were the means by which a ruler could transmit the substance of
his authority to a chosen companion. To be in the gaze or the sight
of one who is powerful, to receive food from or hear sounds emitted
by a superior, was to be affected by that person.

Meaning for the English was something attributed to a word, a
phrase or an object, which could be determined and translated,
hopefully with a synonym which had a direct referent to something
in what the English thought of as a 'natural' world. Everything had
a more or less specific referent for the English. With the Indians,
meaning was not necessarily construed in the same fashion. The
effect and affect of hearing a Brahmin chanting in Sanskrit at a sacrifice did not entail meaning in the European sense; it was to have
one's substance literally affected by the sound. When a Mughal
ruler issued a *farman* or a *parwana*, it was more than an order or an
entitlement. These were more than messages or, as the British
construed them, a contract or right. Rather, they were a sharing,

through the act of creating the document, in the authority and substance of the sender. Hence, in the drawing up of a document, a letter, a treaty, everything about it was charged with a significance which transcended what might be thought of as its practical purpose. The paper, the forms of address, the preliminary invocative phrases, the type of script, the elaboration of the terminology, the grammar, the seals used, the particular status of the composer and writer of the document, its mode of transmission, and the form of delivery, were all meaningful.[7]

In addition to cultural blocks to the British acquisition of knowledge of Indian languages, their mode of living in India furthered difficulties. From the middle of the seventeenth to the middle of the eighteenth century there were comparatively few covenanted servants of the Company. In 1665 there were 100 officials of the Company in India,[8] in 1740 approximately 170,[9] in 1756, on the eve of the Battle of Plassey, there were 224.[10] The majority of the Company's servants lived in the cosmopolitan port cities, generally within the confines of their factories. Most of their social contacts were with other Europeans. The Indians who worked for them as domestic and commercial servants appear to have known some English or Portuguese, the coastal trade language of India. Most British found they could manage their affairs with these languages and with some knowledge of a pidginized version of 'Moors', the lingua franca of India. Most of the Company servants lived for a limited time in India, some succumbing to disease or serving, as was the practice in the Company, for five years and then returning to Great Britain. The Europeans most likely to have known Indian languages well were the Portuguese, and 'country born' Europeans, many of whom were engaged in small-scale trading activities or found employment with the East India Company in subordinate positions.

[7] Mohiuddin Momin, *The Chancellery and Persian Epistolography under the Mughals, from Babar to Shah Jahan* (Calcutta, 1971); Riazul Islam, *A Calendar of Documents on Indo-Persian Relations, 1500–1750* (Karachi, 1979), vol. I, pp. 1–53.

[8] W. Foster, ed., *English Factories in India* (Oxford, 1925), vol. XII, p. 14; Temple, ed., *Diaries*, vol. II, pp. 16–20.

[9] G.W. Forrest, ed., *Selections from the Bombay Records* (1887), vol. I, pp. 169–71; Madras Presidency, *Records of Fort St. George, Diary and Consultation Book, 1740* (Madras, 1931), pp. 224–6; Peter Marshall, *East Indian Fortunes* (Oxford 1976), p. 11.

[10] Forrest, (1887), vol. II, pp. 202–9; Madras Presidency, *Records*, vol. 85, pp. 209–303; S.C. Hill, ed., *Bengal in 1756–57* (London, 1905), vol. III, pp. 411–13.

The Command of Language and the Language of Command 281

The Directors looked with suspicion on this latter category as they felt they were untrustworthy and likely to put their own interests ahead of those of the Company.

In 1713 when the Company wished to obtain a *farman* [royal order] from the Mughal empire to reduce taxes on their internal trade in India and to make permanent a whole series of grants they had received at various times from the Mughal, they had no one in their Bengal establishment who knew sufficient Persian to carry out the negotiations and had to depend upon an Armenian merchant for this vital function. John Surman, head of the embassy, eventually learned Persian, but not before their interpreter had lead them into a number of difficulties. The embassy was successful, but Surman died soon after his return to Calcutta, and the knowledge of Persian went with him.

It was not until the 1740s and '50s that any significant number of officials of the Company knew any of the Indian languages, a result of more and more of them serving up-country in Company stations and having longer and longer careers in India. James Fraser, who was on the Surat establishment for nineteen years, learned Persian well enough to write a contemporary history of the court of Nadir Shah, based on a Persian account and 'constant correspondence' with Persians and Mughals. He had learned his Persian from a Parsi, and had studied with a scholar who was famous for his knowledge of Muslim law in Cambay.[11]

In mid century there were increasing numbers of British officials with knowledge of Persian and what the British termed 'Indostan' or 'Moors', as well as other 'vulgar' languages of India. Hastings had learned Persian and Moors while serving in Kassimbazar in commercial and diplomatic positions.[12] J.Z. Howell knew enough Bengali or Indostan to serve as judge of the zamindar's court in Calcutta, and, at the time of the capture of Calcutta by Siraj-ud-daula, was translating into English an Indostanee version 'of a shastra'. Those British immediately involved in the negotiations with members of the Nawab of Bengal's court that led to his

[11] James Fraser, *The History of Nadir Shah* (London, 1742), pp. iii-vi; William Irvine, 'Notes on James Fraser', *Journal of the Royal Asiatic Society*, 1899, pp. 214–20; L. Lockhart, *Nadir Shah* (London, 1938), pp. 304–6.

[12] For Hastings's language skills see Peter Marshall, 'Hastings as Scholar and Patron', in Anne Whiteman *et al.*, eds, *Statesmen, Scholars and Merchants* (Oxford, 1973), p. 243.

overthrow—William Watts, Henry Vansittart and Luke Scrafton—were linguistically well-enough equipped to outwit even such a canny political operator as Omichand. The architect of the Bengal revolution, Robert Clive, however, appears not to have known any Indian language with the exception of the Portuguese trade language, and he was dependent on his Banyan, Nubkissen, for translating and interpreting in his dealings with Indian rulers.[13] It was to be the British success at Plassey and the subsequent appropriation of the revenues of Bengal that would provide the impetus for more and more British civilians and military officers to learn one or more of the Indian languages.

Indian Languages and the Creation of a Discursive Formation

The years 1770–85 may be looked upon as the formative period during which the British successfully began the program of appropriating Indian languages to serve as a crucial component in their construction of the system of rule. More and more British officials were learning the 'classical languages of India' (Sanskrit, Persian and Arabic), as well as many of the 'vulgar' languages. More importantly, this was the period in which the British were beginning to produce an apparatus: grammars, dictionaries, treatises, class books and translations about and from the languages of India. Some of the leading texts of this period include: Alexander Dow, *The History of Hindostan*, 1770; Sir William Jones, *A Grammar of the Persian Language*, 1771; George Hadley, *The Practical and Vulgar Dialect of the Indostan Language Commonly Called Moors*, 1772; N.B. Halhed, *A Code of Gentoo Laws, or, Ordinations of the Pundits*, 1776, and *A Grammar of the Bengal Language*, 1778; John Richardson, *A Dictionary of English, Persian and Arabic*, 1780; William Davy, *Institutes Political and Military of Timour*, Oxford 1783; Francis Balfour, *The Forms of the Herkern*, 1781; Charles Wilkins, *The Bhagvet Geeta*, 1785; William Kirkpatrick, *A Vocabulary, Persian, Arabic and English; Containing Such words as have been Adopted from the Two Former Languages and Incorporated into the Hindvi*, 1785; Francis Gladwin, *Ayeen i Akberry or the Institutes of the Emperor Akbar*, 1783–6; John A. Gilchrist, *A Dictionary English and Hindustani, Part I*, 1787.

The argument of this essay is that the production of these texts

---

[13] Mark Bence Jones, *Clive of India* (London, 1974), p. 225.

The Command of Language and the Language of Command 283

and others which follow them began the establishment of discursive formation, defined an epistemological space, created a discourse (Orientalism), and had the effect of converting Indian forms of knowledge into European objects. The subjects of these texts were first and foremost the Indian languages themselves, re-presented in European terms as grammars, dictionaries and teaching aids in a project to make the acquisition of a working knowledge of the languages available to those British who were to be part of the ruling groups in India.

Some of these texts, such as Balfour's *Herkern* and Gladwin's *Ain*, were to be guidebooks; the one to the epistolary practice of professional scribes, the other to the administrative practices of the Mughal empire. The translations by Dow and Davy of Persian chronicles were intended to be expositions of the political practices and the failures of the imperial predecessors of the British conquerors. Halhed's *Gentoo Law* and Wilkins' *Geeta* were translations thought to be 'keys' with which to unlock, and hence make available, knowledge of Indian law and religion held tightly by the 'mysterious' Brahmins.

Seen as a corpus, these texts signal the invasion of an epistemological space occupied by a great number of a diverse variety of Indian scholars, intellectuals, teachers, scribes, priests, lawyers, officials, merchants and bankers, whose knowledge, as well as they themselves, were to be converted into instruments of colonial rule. They were now to become part of the army of babus, clerks, interpreters, sub-inspectors, *munshis*, pundits, *kazis*, *vakils*, schoolmasters, *amins*, *sharistidars*, *tahsildars*, *desmukhs*, *darogahs*, and *mamlatdars* who, under the scrutiny and supervision of the white sahibs, ran the everyday affairs of the Raj.

The knowledge which this small group of British officials sought to control was to be the instrumentality through which they were to issue commands and collect ever-increasing amounts of information. This information was needed to create or locate cheap and effective means to assess and collect taxes, maintain law and order, and it served as a way to identify and classify groups within Indian society. Élites had to be found within Indian society who could be made to see that they had an interest in the maintenance of British rule. Political strategies and tactics had to be created and codified into diplomacy through which the country powers could be converted into allied dependencies. The vast social world that was India had to be classified, categorized and bounded before it could be hierarchized.

As with many discursive formations and their discourses, many of its major effects were unintended, as those who were to be the objects produced by the formation often turned it to their own ends. None the less the languages which the Indians were to speak and read were to be transformed. The discursive formation was to participate in the creation and reification of social groups with their varied interests. It was to establish and regularize a discourse of differentiations which came to mark the social and political map of nineteenth-century India.

I have chosen to utilize a mode of exposition which is obviously influenced by the work of Michel Foucault. My effort will be to try to locate the kinds of questions his work directs us towards by rehearsing a history, much of which is familiar to students of Indian history. It is a recounting of some of the details of how the English, during the period from roughly 1770 to 1820, went about learning Indian languages and of how they developed a pedagogical and scholarly apparatus for this purpose. It does not aim to be complete, nor will it even deal with what might be thought of as its most important texts, its most famous or leading figures, or its most important institutions—such as the College at Fort William and the College at Fort St George. This account proceeds by presentation of a series of examples selected purposely to illustrate the arguments I have begun to outline above.

Persian: The Language of Indian Politics

A knowledge of Persian was needed immediately after the Battle of Plassey to recruit and train an Indian army, to develop a system of alliances and treaties with native independent princes and powers to protect 'the rich and fertile territories' in Coromandel, Upper India and Bengal, which the Company had conquered.[14] William Davy, who as a military officer in the Bengal army had found the development of knowledge of Persian highly lucrative, thought that the important job of translation could not be entrusted to Indian interpreters. In describing the talent needed for this important task, he wrote:

[14] Great Britain: Parliament, *Third Report from the Committee appointed to Enquire into the Nature, State and Condition of the East India Company* (London, 1803), vol. III, p. 379, originally published in 1773.

The Command of Language and the Language of Command 285

> A Persian interpreter should not only be able to speak fluently in the
> language, but to read all such letters as he may receive, . . . to answer
> them with his own hand, if the importance of the subject, of which they
> treat should render it necessary. Otherwise the secret negotiations and
> correspondence of government are liable to be made public through the
> medium of the native Munchees, or writers, whom he will be obliged to
> employ and trust.[15]

Davy appears to have learned his Persian from a munshi, and without the aid of a Persian–English dictionary or a grammar. The only
dictionary of Persian then known was one in Latin by Franciscus
Meninski, which was so scarce in India that Davy paid 100 guineas
for a copy he found in Calcutta in 1773. This was not much use to
him as Meninski, Davy thought, did not know Persian, but he did
have an extensive knowledge of Turkish on which he based his Arabic, Turkish and Persian lexicon. The result, Davy felt, was that

> words in one language, bearing a variety of significations, are given
> through the medium of words in another, having also various meanings,
> and many directly contradictory, were translated by words in a third,
> which in many significations, differs totally from both.[16]

There had been a Chair in Arabic established at Oxford in the late
seventeenth century and there were on the continent a few scholars
of Persian, who, according to Sir William Jones, 'had confined their
studies to minute researches of verbal criticism'. Jones further complained that the learned 'have no taste, and the men of taste, have no
learning'.[17] There was no patronage for literary and scholarly research on oriental languages. Jones wrote that Meninski's work may
have 'immortalized' him as a savant but it 'ruined him financially'.[18]
Jones thought the Persian language 'rich, melodious and elegant',
with important works in poetry and history, which was due for a
great interest now that India had become 'the source of incredible
wealth to the merchants of Europe'.[19] Jones wrote:

> The servants of the company received letters they could not read and
> were ambitious of gaining titles of which they could not comprehend the

[15] William Davy, *Institutes Political and Military of Timour* (Oxford, 1783), pp.
li–liii.

[16] Letter from William Davy to John Richardson, dated 8 March 1780, in John
Richardson, *A Dictionary, English, Persian and Arabic* (Oxford, 1780), vol. ii, p.
xv.

[17] Sir William Jones, *A Grammar of the Persian Language* (London, 1771), p. i.

[18] Ibid., p. viii.

[19] Ibid., p. ix.

meaning; it was found highly dangerous to employ the natives as inter-preters, upon whose fidelity they could not depend; and it was at last discovered that they must apply themselves to the study of the Persian language . . . The languages of Asia will now perhaps be studied with uncommon ardour; they are known to be useful, and will soon be found to be instructive and entertaining.[20]

Sir William Jones' *Grammar of the Persian Language*, published in London in 1771, was very successful and went through six edi-tions by 1804. Although it was recommended by the Court of Directors to their employees, they did not, as with many subse-quent publications on Indian languages, subsidize it.

Jones in constructing his *Grammar* was centrally interested in Persian poetry, and the descriptive statements on which the gram-matical rules were based were 'poetry composed in the shiraz liter-ary "dialect" between the tenth and fifteenth centuries A.D.'[21] The *Grammar* provided for its time a useful description of the phonolo-gy, morphology and syntax of the language he was describing.[22]

Jones supplied his readers with advice on how to learn Persian, which was premised on the availability of a native speaker of Per-sian. The student should learn to read the characters with fluency and 'learn the true pronunciation of every letter from the mouth of a native'. He then should memorize 'the regular inflexions of nouns and verbs'. He recommended using Meninski's dictionary, but warned the learner 'that he must not neglect to converse with his living instructor and to learn from him the phrases of common discourse'.[23]

After six months, Jones recommended, the student should move on to reading 'some elegant History or poem with an intelligent native'.[24] He should get his munshi to transcribe a section of the Gulistan or a fable of Cashefi, 'in the common broken hand used in India'.[25] In a year's time, the reader was assured, if he worked according to Jones's plan, he would be abe to 'translate and to

---

[20] Ibid., p. x.

[21] K.D. Bhargava, ed., *Fort William–India House Correspondence* (Delhi, 1969), vol. VI, pp. 110–11.

[22] Garland Cannon, *Oriental Jones* (Bombay, 1964), p. 24; see also Garland Cannon, 'Sir William Jones' Persian Linguistics', *American Oriental Society Journal* (1958), vol. 78, pp. 262–73.

[23] Jones, *Grammar*, pp. xiv–xv.

[24] Ibid., p. xvi.

[25] Ibid., p. xiv.

The Command of Language and the Language of Command 287

answer any letter from an Indian Prince, and to converse with the natives of India not only with fluency but with elegance.' However, if he aspires to be 'an eminent translator' he will have to learn Arabic as well, 'which is blended with the Persian in so singular a manner'.[26] Another benefit for the would-be official of the East India Company would be a knowledge of 'the jargon of Indostan, very improperly called the language of the Moors', which, Jones reports, 'contains so great a number of Persian words that I was able, with little difficulty, to read the fables of Pilpai, which are translated into that idom.'[27]

The prestige of Persian as the best language for an ambitious cadet or junior writer continued into the early nineteenth-century. Hastings, who had lobbied unsuccessfully in 1765 for the establishment of a Chair in Persian at Oxford,[28] vigorously argued that Persian and Arabic should be the keystone of the curriculum at the newly-established Company's College at Fort William:

> To the Persian language as being the medium of all Political intercourse the first place ought to be assigned in the studies of the Pupils; and as much of the Arabic as is necessary to shew the principles of its construction and the variations which the sense of the radical word derives from its inflections, to complete their knowledge of the Persian, which in its modern dialect consists in a great measure of the Arabic . . . the Persian language ought to be studied to perfection, and is requisite to all the civil servants of the Company, as it may also prove of equal use to the Military Officers of all the Presidencies.[29]

Through the first fifteen years of the College the Persian Department was the most prestigous and best supported. These young officials who did well in Persian were frequently slated for the best beginning jobs, which frequently led to lucrative and influential positions in the central secretariat in Calcutta. In addition it would appear that, as Persian and Arabic were the 'classical languages' of India, they were worthy to be studied by gentlemen whose English education stressed the learning of the European classical languages, Latin and Greek, as the emblem of an educated man fitted thereby for rulership.

---

[26] Ibid., p. xvii.

[27] Ibid., p. xviii–xix.

[28] Marshall, 'Hastings as Scholar', p. 245.

[29] W.H. Hutton, ed., 'A Letter of Warren Hastings on the Civil Service of the East India Company', *English Historical Review* (1929), vol. XLIV, p. 635.

Sanskrit: The Language of Indian Law and Lore

In India there was also another classical language, Sanskrit, which was seen by the seventeenth and eighteenth-century British to be a secret language 'invented by the Brahmins to be a mysterious repository for their religion and philosophy'.[30] There was considerable curiosity about the religion of the Gentoos among the Europeans, and there had been scattered and discontinuous efforts to learn Sanskrit, particularly by Catholic missionaries in the seventeenth century, of which the British in the eighteenth century seemed unaware. James Fraser, J.Z. Howell, and Alexander Dow had all made unsuccessful efforts to learn Sanskrit. What knowledge the British had of the learning and religious thought of the Hindus came from discussions with Brahmins and other high-caste Indians, or from Persian or 'Hindustani' translations of Sanskrit texts.

John Z. Howell, who in his thirty years' experience in India had learned Persian, Bengali and 'Indostan', wrote an extended account of the 'religious Tenets of the Gentoos', published in 1767.[31] This account was based on an unidentified 'Gentoo *Shastah*' (*shastra*), which he was translating at the time of Siraj-ud-daula's capture of Calcutta in 1756. Howell at this time lost 'curious manuscripts' as well as a translation of 'an Hindustani version of a shastra'. In addition to the translation of a shastra, Howell alluded to conferences with 'many of the most learned and ingenious amongst the laity of the Koyt.'[32]

Howell criticized all his predecessors' views that the 'Hindoos' are 'a race of stupid and gross idolaters'. Most of the more recent accounts of 'Hindoos', he argued, were by those of the 'Romish communion', who had a vested interest in denigrating Hindus, as they wanted to convert them to Catholicism. Howell stigmatized Roman Catholic religious tenets as 'more idolatrous' than those of the Hindus. He not only castigated 'Popish authors', but also most others who had written only on 'exterior manners and religion' of

---

[30] Alexander Dow, 'A Dissertation Concerning the Customs, Manners, Language, Religion and Philosophy of the Hindoos', in *The History of Hindostan*, 3rd edition (London, 1792), vol. I, p. xxvii; also reprinted with a commentary in Peter Marshall, ed., *The British Discovery of Hinduism in the Eighteenth Century* (Cambridge, 1970), pp. 107–39.

[31] Published in John Z. Howell, *Interesting Historical Events Relative to the Province of Bengal and the Empire of Indostan* (London, 1767).

[32] Marshall (1970), p. 46, notes a and b.

The Command of Language and the Language of Command 289

the Hindus. The casual observer or traveller, Howell suggested, had to get beyond 'his own ignorance, superstition and partiality' and the provincialism involved in thinking that anything 'beyond the limits of their native land' was greatly inferior in comparison with their own.' Howell castigated travel writers as superficial:

> His telling us such and such a people, in the East or West-Indies, worship this stick, or that stone, or monstrous idol; only serves to reduce in our esteem, our fellow creatures, to the most abject and despicable point of light. Whereas, was he skilled in the language of the people he describes, sufficiently to trace the etymology of their words and phrases, and capable of diving into the mysteries of their theology; he would probably be able to evince us, that such seemingly preposterous worship, had the most sublime rational source and foundation.
> The traveller, who without these essential requisites, (as well as industry and a clear understanding) pretends to describe and fix the religious tenets of any nation whatever, dishonestly imposes his own reveries on the world; and does the greatest injury and violence to letters, and the cause of humanity.[33]

The motivation for the British in India to learn Sanskrit had a dual basis: at one and the same time there was a scholarly curiosity to unlock the mysterious and perhaps curious knowledge of the Ancients, and an immediate practical necessity as well, fuelled by Warren Hastings' plan of 1772 for the better governance of Bengal. In writing to the Court of Directors explaining this plan he stated that his plan would establish the Company's system of governance on a 'most equitable, solid and permanent footing'. The plan was based on

> principles of experience and common observation, without the advantages which an intimate knowledge of the theory of law might have afforded us: We have endeavoured to adapt our Regulations to the Manners and Understandings of the People, and the Exigencies of the Country, adhering as closely as we are able to their ancient uses and Institutions.[34]

In Hastings' plan the theory was clear: India should be governed by Indian principles, particularly in relation to law. The practical question arose as to how the British were to gain knowledge of the

---

[33] Howell, reprinted in Marshall (1970), pp. 48–50.

[34] Letter from Governor-General and Council to Court of Directors, Fort William, 3 November 1772, printed in Great Britain: Parliament, *Reports from Committees of the House of Commons*, vol. IV (East Indies, 1772–3; reprinted London, 1804), pp. 345–6.

ancient 'usages and institutions'. The answer was easy enough to state. The Hindus, Hastings averred, 'had been in possession of laws which continued unchanged, from remotest antiquity'. These laws, he wrote, were in the hands of the Brahmins, or 'professors of law', found all over India, who were supported by 'public endowments and benefactions from every and all people'. These professors received a 'degree of personal respect amounting almost to idolatry'.[35] In each of the criminal courts established, the kazi, *mufti*, and two *moulvi*s 'were to expound the law, and to determine how far the delinquents shall be guilty of a breach thereof.' In the civil courts,

> suits regarding inheritance, Marriage, caste and other religious usages and institutions, the Laws of the Koran with respect to Mahometans, and those of the Shaster with respect to the Gentoos shall be invariably adhered to.[36]

For officers of a commercial company it was clearly the laws which the civil courts were to administer which were most crucial, as they would hear disputes 'concerning property, whether real or personal, all cases of inheritance, marriage and caste; all claims of debt, disputed accounts, contracts, partnerships and demands of rent.'[37] The Company's government through this plan was to become the guarantor of what Hastings and the other eighteenth-century British saw as the basic rights of Indians, oddly enough in a polity which was supposed to be despotic and hence without such rights.

In his discussion of his plans Hastings was translating for a British audience theories and practices from one culture to another. India had an ancient constitution which was expressed into what came to be thought of as two codes, one Hindu and the other Muslim. Pundits were 'professors', and some even came to be conceived of as 'lawyers'. For the demonstration of law there were also experts, 'kazis', 'judges' who knew the appropriate codes to apply to particular cases. Following current practice in Bengal, which was a Muslim-ruled state, the British accepted Muslim criminal law as the law of the land, but civil law was to be Hindu for Hindus and Muslim for Muslims. Hastings and the Council at Fort Williams'

---

[35] George R. Gleig (comp.), *Memoirs of the Life of the Right Honorable Warren Hastings* (London, 1841), vol. I, p. 400.
[36] House of Commons, (1772–3), vol. IV, pp. 348–50.
[37] House of Commons, (1772), vol. IV, p. 348.

The Command of Language and the Language of Command 291

decision was to have profound effects on the future course of the judicial system in India.[38]

If the British were to administer Hindu law with the guidance and assistance of 'Hindu Law officers' (pundits), they had to establish some fixed body of this law, one which they hoped could become authoritative and which could be translated into English, so that the judges would have some idea of the nature and content of this law.

In order to establish what was the Hindu law, Warren Hastings persuaded eleven of the 'most respectable pandits in Bengal' to make a compilation of the relevent shastric literature. Hastings appointed H.B. Halhed to supervise this compilation and to translate the resulting text into English.[39] Halhed described the manner in which the text, *A Code of Gentoo Laws or Ordinations of the Pundits* (published in London in 1776), was compiled and translated:

> The professors of the ordinances here collected still speak the original language in which they were composed, and which is entirely unknown to the bulk of the people, who have settled upon those professors several great endowments and benefactions in all parts of Hindostan, and pay them besides a degree of personal respect little short of idolatry, in return for the advantages supposed to be derived from their studies. A set of the most experienced of these lawyers was selected from every part of Bengal for the purpose of compiling the present work, which they picked out sentence by sentence from various originals in the Shanscrit language, neither adding to, nor diminishing any part of the ancient text. The articles thus collected were next translated literally into Persian, under the inspection of one of their own body; and from that translation were rendered into English with an equal attention to the closeness and fidelity of the version.[40]

---

[38] J.D.M. Derrett, 'Sanskrit Legal Treatises Compiled at the Instance of the British', *Zeitschrift für Vergleichende Rechtswissenschaft*, 63 (1961), pp. 72–117; 'The Administration of Hindu Law by the British', *Comparative Studies in Society and History*, vol. IV (1961), pp. 10–52; *Religion, Law and the State in India* (London, 1968); Marc Galanter, 'The Displacement of Traditional Law in Modern India', *Journal of Social Issues*, 24 (1968), pp. 65–91; Lloyd and Susanne Rudolph, 'Barristers and Brahmans in India: Legal Cultures and Social Change', *Comparative Studies in Society and History*, vol. 8 (1965), pp. 24–49; Ludo Rocher, 'Indian Reactions to Anglo-Indian Law', *Journal of the American Oriental Society*, vol. 92 (1972), pp. 419–24.

[39] Rosane Rocher, *Orientalism, Poetry, and the Millennium: The Checkered Life of Nathanial Brassey Halhed, 1751–1830* (Delhi, 1983), pp. 48–73.

[40] Halhed, *Gentoo Law*, p. x.

The compilation was known in Sanskrit as the *Vivadarnavasetu* (bridge across the sea of litigation). The manner in which the translation was made, and the authoritative nature of the compilation, came into question within the next fifteen years. Halhed had only a very limited knowledge of Sanskrit and depended on an explication of passages in the text done in Bengali or Hindustani by the pundits, which discussions were then abstracted into Persian by a munshi, and from this Halhed did the final translation into English.[41]

Sir William Jones, who had been appointed a judge in the Supreme Court of Judicature in 1783, thought the *Gentoo Code* was like a Roman law digest, consisting of 'authentic texts with short notes taken from commentaries of high authority.'[42] He praised the work as far as it went, but it was too diffuse, 'rather curious than useful', the section on the law of contracts too 'succinct and superficial'. But if the Sanskrit text itself was faulted, the translation he felt was useless:

> But, whatever be the merit of the original, the translation of it has no authority, and is of no other use than to suggest inquiries on the many dark passages, which we find in it: properly speaking, indeed, we cannot call it a translation; for, though Mr. Halhed performed his part with fidelity, yet the Persian interpreter had supplied him only with a loose injudicious epitome of the original Sanscrit, in which abstract many essential passages are omitted . . . All this I say with confidence, having already perused no small part of the original with a learned Pandit, comparing it, as I proceeded, with the English version.[43]

On his arrival in Calcutta Jones had no plans to undertake the study of Sanskrit; he complained to Wilkins, 'life is too short and my necessary business too long for me to think of acquiring a new language.'[44] Jones's curiosity about Indian thought and his role as a judge of the Crown Court in Calcutta, however, led him to undertake the learning of Sanskrit. After being in India less than a year, Jones journeyed to Benares where he met 'Maulvies, Pandits and Rajas', among whom were Ali Ibraham Khan, long regarded by the British as a distinguished scholar and judge. Jones had hoped to obtain from Khan a Persian translation of the 'Dherm Shastr Menu Smrety', which was considered to be the authoritative source of

---

[41] Rocher, p. 51.

[42] Jones to Cornwallis, 19 March 1788, in Garland Cannon, ed., *The Letters of Sir William Jones* (Oxford, 1970), vol. ii, p. 797. Hereafter, *Letters*.

[43] Ibid.

[44] Jones to Wikins, 24 April 1784: ibid., p. 646.

The Command of Language and the Language of Command 293

Hindu law. Although Khan obtained a Sanskrit text, Manu's *Dharmashastra*, the pundits refused to assist Khan in translating it into Persian.[45]

Jones became increasingly frustrated in having to depend on defective Persian translations of Hindu law books. He reported to William Pitt the Younger in February 1785 that he was almost 'tempted to learn Sanskrit, that I may check on the pundits in the Court.'[46] A month later he was complaining to Wilkins 'that it was of the utmost importance that the stream of Hindu law should be pure: for we are entirely at the devotion of the native lawyers, through our ignorance of Sanskrit.'[47] In September 1785 Jones had gone to Nadiya, a centre of Sanskrit learning sixty miles north of Calcutta on the Hugli river, where he hoped 'to learn the rudiments of that venerable and interesting language'.[48] In October he was back in Calcutta, with 'the father of the University of Nadya', who, Jones explained, was not a Brahmin, but who had instructed young Brahmin students in grammar and ethics. He would serve Jones's purpose as a teacher, as he lacked the 'priestly pride' which marked his students.[49] A year later Jones could report that he was 'tolerably strong in Sanskrit', and getting ready to translate a law tract ascribed to 'Menu, the Minos of India'.[50]

By October 1786 Jones had enough confidence in his own knowledge of Sanskrit, for he was correcting his own court pundits' interpretations of legal texts by translating to his own satisfaction 'the original tracts' on which they based their decisions.[51] Jones was now to go on to plan a much bigger project which he believed would free the British judges in India from dependence on what he thought was the venality and corruption of the Indian interpreters of Hindu and Muslim law. This was the legal counterpart to the effort a few decades earlier of the British, through knowledge of Persian, to free themselves from the akhunds, munshis and *kayasthas* who translated and interpreted political documents. Jones now

[45] Sir William Jones, ' "Preface", Institutes of Hindu Law . . .', in *The Works of Sir William Jones* (London, 1807), vol. VII, p. 37.

[46] Jones to Pitt, 5 February 1785: *Letters*, p. 664.

[47] Jones to Wilkins, March 1785: ibid., p. 666.

[48] Jones to Russell, 8 September 1785: ibid., p. 680

[49] Jones to Macpherson, October 1785: ibid., p. 687.

[50] Jones to Hastings, 23 October 1786: ibid., p. 718.

[51] Murray B. Emmenau, 'India and Linguistics', *Journal of the American Oriental Society* (1955), vol. 75, p. 148.

proposed to compile from the best available sources a digest of Hindu and Muslim law, which could then be translated into English and which would provide the European judges a 'check upon the native interpreters'. Jones wanted a means by which 'the laws of natives' could be preserved inviolate, and the decrees of courts made to conform to 'Hindu or Mahomedan law'.[52]

If the system which Jones hoped to see implemented was to succeed, it would require that several forms of knowledge become codified and public. The English judges and other officials would require access to what Jones and others believed at the time was '*the* Hindu and *the* Mahomedan law', which was locked up in the texts and the heads of pundits and maulvis. There had to be found a fixed body of knowledge which could be objectified into Hindu and Muslim law. This body of knowledge could be specified, set into hierarchies of knowledge, linearly ordered from the most 'sacred' or compelling to the less powerful.

Jones and others had the idea that there was historically in India a fixed body of laws, codes, which had been set down or established by 'law givers', which over time had become corrupted by accretions, interpretations, and commentaries, and it was this jungle of accretions and corruptions of the earlier pure codes which was controlled in the present by those Indians whom the British thought of as the Indian lawyers. An *ur* text had to be found or reconstituted, which at one and the same time would establish *the* Hindu and Muslim law as well as free the English from dependency for interpretations and knowledge on fallible and seemingly overly susceptible pundits and maulvis. The task also had to be accomplished somehow by using the knowledge which their Indian guides, the mistrusted pundits and maulvis, seemed to monopolize. Jones, even before arriving in India, seemed to distrust Indian scholars' interpretations of their own legal traditions: a distrust which grew with experience in India. He wrote to Cornwallis, the Governor-General, in 1788, that he could not with 'an easy conscience, concur in a decision, merely on the written opinion of native lawyers in any case, in which they could have the remotest interest in misleading the court.'[53] Jones wanted to provide the English courts in India, Crown and Company, with a sure basis on which they could render

[52] *Letters*, pp. 643–4; and Garland Cannon, 'Sir William Jones and Edmund Burke', *Modern Philology* (1956/7), vol. 54, pp. 165–86.

[53] Jones to Cornwallis, 19 March 1788: *Letters*, p. 795.

The Command of Language and the Language of Command 295

decisions consonant with a 'true' or 'pure' version of Hindu law. Then the pundits, Brahmins and Indian 'lawyers', Jones believed, henceforth could not 'deal out Hindoo law as they please, and make it at reasonable rates, when they cannot find it ready made.'[54]

In advocating his ambitious plan for a digest of Hindu and Muslim law Jones deployed a discourse which made a direct connection between the British future in India and the late Classical Roman past. In discussing his plans he explained that his mode of proceeding would be that of Tribonian, the compiler of the Justinian code, with only 'original texts arranged in a scientific method'.[55] The analogy to Justinian was spelled out for Cornwallis by Jones, who, he hoped, was to become 'the Justinian of India', and Jones, by implication, would become the Tribonian. The British government would give to the natives of India 'security for the due administration of justice among them, similar to that which Justinian gave to his Greek and Roman subjects', he wrote to Cornwallis.[56] The main subject of the digests would be the laws of contract and inheritance, and, as Jones was time and time again to reiterate, these subjects were at the heart of the establishment of rights in property, 'real and personal'.[57]

Jones did not live to see the completion of his ambition to become the Tribonian of India, but to this day he stands in stone in St Paul's Cathedral, a statue commissioned by the Court of Directors, dressed in a toga, with pen in hand and leaning on two volumes which are 'understood to mean the Institutes of Menu'.[58] Visual reminders of the British as Romans can still be found in the gardens of the Victoria Memorial, where we find Warren Hastings in the toga of a Roman senator, standing above a Brahmin pundit with a palm leaf manuscript, and a Muslim maulvi poring over a Persian manuscript.

Classical Models and the Definition of the 'Vulgar' Languages of India

N.B. Halhed, the translator of the *Gentoo Code* and author of the first English grammar of Bengali, drew heavily on analogies be-

---

[54] Jones to Chapman, 28 September 1785: ibid., p. 684.

[55] Jones to Rouse, 24 October 1786: ibid., p. 721.

[56] Jones to Cornwallis, 19 March 1788, ibid., p. 798.

[57] Ibid., p. 799.

[58] George Lewis Smyth, *Monuments and Genni of St. Paul's Cathedral and Westminister Abby* (London, 1826), vol. II, p. 631.

tween the eighteenth-century English in India and the Romans. His grammar was part of a larger project which would stabilize and perpetuate British rule in Bengal. The 'English masters of Bengal', wrote Halhed in 1778, needed to add its language to their acquisitions, like the Romans, 'people of little learning and less taste', who applied themselves to the study of Greek once they had conquered them. So the British in Bengal needed to cultivate a language which would be the 'medium of intercourse between the Government and its subjects, between the natives of Europe who are to rule, and the inhabitants of India who are to obey.' In addition, the English needed to know the language to explain 'the benevolent principles' of the legislation which they were 'to enforce'.[59]

The British in late eighteenth-century Bengal found what was for them a complex language situation. Few of the British knew Bengali; rather, they used 'Moors' and Persian in many of their transactions. This of course reflected the political situation in Bengal and the language-use of many of their Indian associates and subordinates.

H.P. Foster, who produced an English/Bengali and a Bengali/English dictionary between 1799 and 1802, provided a hypothetical example of the results of the dependence on Persian in the courts of Bengal at the time. A Dom, who, he informed his British readers, is from 'the lowest and most illiterate classes', goes to a darogah, a minor police official, to make a complaint. According to Foster the darogah's knowledge of Persian was restricted to reading *Tales of the Parrot*, a popular class book of the time. The Dom delivers his complaint in the 'vulgar' dialect of Bengali, and it gets written down by the police official in 'bad Bongalee in Persian characters with here and there a mangled Persian phrase'. This document may then get translated into Persian, and finally, if the case makes its way up to the Nizamat Adalat, the documents that have accumulated are translated into English.[60] If the British learned Bengali, says Foster, it was because it was the language spoken around the major cities, such as Murshidabad, Dacca, and Calcutta, which were the 'seats of foreign governments and the rendezvous of all nations', where the language spoken was much influenced by 'Hindostanee or Moors', and this was the language which the British adapted as their

[59] Nathaniel Halhed, *A Grammar of the Bengali Language* (Hoogly, 1778; facsimile reprint, 1969), pp. i–ii.

[60] H.P. Foster, *A Vocabulary in Two Parts, English Bongalee and Vice a Versa, Part I* (originally published Calcutta, 1799; reprinted Calcutta, 1830), p. iv.

The Command of Language and the Language of Command 297

'medium of communication' with the people of Bengal.[61]

William Carey observed that the Indian servant, personal and official, in speaking Bengali with Europeans 'generally intermixes his language with words derived from the Arabic or Persian and with some few corrupted English and Portuguese words.'[62] Carey warned his countrymen that dependence on poor interpreters and the continued use of the 'jargon of Moors' limited their ability to deal directly with 'men of great respectability' as well as the common folk of Bengal, who could 'provide information on local affairs'.[63]

The *Grammar* which Halhed produced of the Bengal language was organized in terms of European grammatical categories, the parts of speech, elements and substantives, pronouns, verbs, words denoting attributes and relations, numerals, syntax, orthography and versification being the title of his chapters. Halhed took pride in being the first European who related Bengali to Sanskrit: 'The following work presents the Bengal language merely as derived from its parent Shanscrit', with all the words from the Persian and Hindostanic dialects expunged.[64] He warned, though, that those who wanted to be accurate translators would have to study the Persian and 'Hindostanic' dialects, 'since in the occurrences of modern business, as managed by the present illiterate generation, he will find all his letters, representations and accounts interspersed with a variety of borrowed phrases or unauthorized expressions.'[65] Halhed based his knowledge of Bengali grammar on 'a pandit who imparted a small portion of his language to me' and readily 'displayed the principles of his grammar'.[66]

The speakers of pure 'Hindustanic' are found in Upper India and in Western India, where they still use this language for purposes of commerce. Halhed drew an analogy between 'Hindustanic' and Bengali:

> What the pure Hindostanic is to upper India, the language which I have here endeavoured to explain is to Bengal, intimately related to the Shans-

[61] Ibid., p. i.

[62] William Carey, *Dialogues Intended to Facilitate the Acquireing of the Bengali Language* (Serampur, 1801), p. v.

[63] William Carey, *Grammar of the Bengali Language* (Serampur, 1805), p. iv.

[64] Halhed, *Grammar*, p. xxi.

[65] Ibid., p. xxii.

[66] Ibid., pp x–xi; see Muhammad Abdul Qayyam, *A Critical Study of the Early Bengali Grammars: Halhed to Houghton* (Dhaka, 1982), for a highly sophisticated analysis of the linguistic and historical context of Halhed's *Grammar*.

crit both in expressions, construction and character. It is the sole channel of personal and epistolary communication among the Hindoos of every occupation and tribe. All their business is transacted, and all their accounts are kept in it; and as their system of education is in general very confined, there are few among them who can write or read any other idiom: the uneducated, or eight parts in ten of the whole nation are necessarily confined to the usage of their mother tongue.[67]

Halhed prefigured Jones's statement on the relation of Sanskrit to Latin and Greek. Halhed was astonished

> to find the similitude of Shanscrit words with those of Persian and Arabic, and even of Latin and Greek . . . in the main ground work of the language, in monosyllables, in the names of numbers, and the appellations of such things as would be discriminated at the immediate dawn of civilization.[68]

In Halhed's introduction to his *Grammar* of Bengali, he developed a social historical argument to account for the current language situation as he found it in Bengal. In addition to Sanskrit and Bengali, he identified two other important languages in Bengal, Persian, and 'Hindustanic', which had two varieties, one which was spoken over most of Hindustan proper and 'indubitably derived from Sanskrit', with which it has exactly the same connection as the modern dialects of France and Italy with pure Latin.[69]

The other variety of 'Hindustanic' was developed by the Muslim invaders of India, who could not learn the language spoken by the Hindus, who, in order to maintain the purity of their own tongue, introduced more and more abstruse terms from Sanskrit. The Muslim invaders introduced many 'exotic' words from their own languages which they superimposed on the 'grammatical principles of the original Hindustanic'. Halhed refers to this form of 'Hindustanic' as a compound idiom which was spoken by Hindus connected with Muslim courts. There were those Brahmins and other well-educated Hindus 'whose ambition has not overpowered their principles', who continued to speak and write the pure form of 'Hindustanic' and who wrote it with Nagri characters rather than with the Arabic script.[70]

Halhed's introduction to the *Grammar* stands as a prime text

[67] Halhed, *Grammar*, p. xii.
[68] Ibid., p. iii.
[69] Ibid., p. ix.
[70] Ibid., pp. xi–xii.

which both summarizes and constitutes knowledge which the British were beginning to develop regarding Indian languages. It prefigures much that was to happen in the next thirty years. As a classically educated man he was concerned to find general principles about Indian languages, and these were to be found in Sanskrit, the treasury of knowledge about India. Languages for the English were to be learned for practical reasons, but this was best done through some knowledge of the 'classical' languages which underlay the contemporary dialects, jargons, vernaculars, and idioms.

Halhed's view that the languages currently spoken in Bengal and Upper India were 'fallen', 'broken', or corrupt versions of some 'pure', 'authentic', coherent, logically formed prior language, was one of course shared by his Hindu and Muslim instructors, who frequently had contempt for the spoken languages and favoured the sacred and literary languages of Sanskrit, Arabic and Persian.

The Establishment of Hindustani as the British Language of Command

Until the late part of the eighteenth century the British in India had done little to systematically study the wide variety of languages spoken in India. Portuguese, German, and Danish missionaries, as well as the Company's Dutch and French trade rivals, had produced grammars and dictionaries of one or another of the Indian languages. The British appear to have been ignorant of these efforts. The classifications used by the British of the Indian languages were vague and shifting, reflecting both geography and function. 'Malabar' referred to the language spoken by fishermen and boatmen on both the Malabar and Coromandel coasts and was by extension used as a label for the language spoken in what is today Tamilnad. 'Gentu' or 'Telinga' was found in what is Andhra, but was also widely diffused in South India, reflecting the presence as mercenaries of large numbers of Telingas in the South Indian armies. 'Banyan' was at times used to refer to Gujarati, reflecting the fact that many of the merchants within the west coast were Gujaratis. Calcutta, Bombay, and Madras were heterogeneous and polyglot cities. Reflecting the political history of the seventeenth and eighteenth centuries, Marathi, Persian and 'Moors' were looked upon by the British as important languages in the south of India.[71]

[71] For early British ideas about Indian languages see: John Fryer, *A New Account of East India and Persia* (London, 1909), vol. I, p. 95; vol. II, pp. 41–2, 103; J. Ovington, *A Voyage to Surat in the year 1689* (London, 1929), p. 147; Tho-

From their first exposure to the Mughal court the British were aware of the central importance of a language spoken there and elsewhere in India. Reverend Terry, who had accompanied Sir Thomas Roe, described this language in the following terms:

> The language of this Empire, I mean the vulgar, bears the name of it, and is called Indostan; it hath much affinitie with the Persian and Arabian tongue . . . a language which is very significant, and speaks much in few words. It is expressed by letters which are different than those alphebets by which the Persian and Arabic tongues are formed.[72]

For the next two hundred years this language, or variants thereof, carried a bewildering variety of labels: 'Moors', 'Indostan', 'Hindoostanic', 'Hindowee', 'Nagreeo', and 'Koota'. Most generally the British labelled it 'Moors' and pejoratively referred to it as a jargon.[73]

In the immediate post-Plassey period, even before there were published grammars for this language, notes and manuscripts were circulating as aids for the Company's officers, particularly military ones, to acquire a working knowledge of this language. The first grammar of Moors published in England was that of Edward Hadley, an officer in the Bengal army who had found it 'impossible to discharge my duties . . . without a knowledge of the corrupt dialect' spoken by those troops he was to command.[74] Hadley rejected the prevalent idea of the 'Eastern Literate' that Moors was so irregular that it did not have a grammar. He demonstrated that the verbs in Moors were not declined as they were in Persian, and that its grammar was derived from some other language, which, he speculated, was derived from India's northern invaders, the Tartars.[75] Hadley's grammar, revised by a number of authors, was to go through seven editions by 1809, at which time it was superseded by a series of

---

mas Bowrey, *A Geographical Account of the Countries Around the Bay of Bengal* (Cambridge, 1903), vol. xviii, p. 6; H.D. Love, *Vestiges of Old Madras* (London, 1913), vol. ii, p. 147; vol. iii, p. 128; Temple, *Diaries*, vol. ii, p. 192.

[72] Edward Terry, *A Voyage to East India* (London, 1655), p. 232.

[73] G.A. Grierson, 'On the Early Study of Indian Vernaculars in Europe', *Journal of the Asiatic Society of Bengal* (1893), vol. 62, pp. 41–50; see also G.A. Grierson, 'Bibliography of Western Hindi, Including Hindostani', *The Indian Antiquary* (January 1903), pp. 16–25; (February 1903), pp. 59–76; (April 1903), pp. 160–79.

[74] George Hadley, *Grammatical Remarks on the Practical and Vulgar Dialect of the Indostan Language Commonly Called Moors* . . . (London, 1772), p. vi.

[75] Ibid., pp. xii–xiii.

The Command of Language and the Language of Command 301

works of John Borthwick Gilchrist, who is generally regarded as the creator of what was to become the British language of command in India—Hindustani.

In 1782, at the age of twenty-three, after studying medicine in Edinburgh, John Gilchrist arrived in Bombay, where he obtained an appointment as an assistant surgeon and was attached to a regiment in the Bengal army.[76] Gilchrist wrote that on his arrival at Bombay in 1782:

> I instantly foresaw that my residence, in any capacity, would prove as unpleasant to myself, as unprofitable to my employers, until I acquired an adequate knowledge of the current language of the country, in which I was now to sojourn. I therefore sat resolutely down to acquire what was then termed as the *Moors* . . . During the march with the Bengal troops under the command of Col. Charles Morgan from Surat to Futigurh [*sic*], I had innumerable instances in every town and village we visited of the universal currency of the language I had been learning.[77]

Within two years Gilchrist had left the army and was settled in Faizabad, where he grew a beard and 'assumed for a period the dress of the natives'. Here he began, with the assistance of several 'learned Hindoostanees' (a term he was careful to point out referred to Hindus and Muslims alike in Upper India), an effort to prepare a dictionary and grammar of their language.[78] His associates could not supply him with a dictionary of this language, so he began to extract from them 'viva voce' every known word in their voluminous tongue. He did this by instructing his munshis to 'furnish [him] with every signification they possibly attach to such words as *a*, *ab*, *abab*, *abach* . . . and so on.' The syllables he wrote led the way to a 'numerous tribe of words'.[79] He found this system of establishing a corpus for his dictionary too cumbersome and resorted to using

[76] For Gilchrist's biography and selections from his works see M. Atique Siddiqi, *Origins of Modern Hindustani Literature: Source Materials: Gilchrist Letters* (Aligarh, 1963), and Sadiq-Ur-Rahman Kidwai, *Gilchrist and the "Language of Hindoostan"* (New Delhi, 1972). For the history of the East India Company's College at Fort William see Sisir Kumar Das, *Sahibs and Munshis: An Account of the College of Fort William* (Calcutta, 1978), and David Kopf, *British Orientalism and the Bengal Renaissance* (Berkeley, 1969).

[77] Siddiqi, p. 21.

[78] John B. Gilchrist, 'Preface', *A Dictionary English and Hindoostanee* (Calcutta: part I, 1786; part II, 1790). The preface was reprinted as 'Appendix' to the *Grammar and Dictionary* (Calcutta, 1798). References in this paper are to the 1790 edition.

[79] Ibid., p. vii.

Johnson's English dictionary. Gilchrist would explain the English term as best he could to the Hindustanis, who then 'would furnish the synonymous vocables in their own speech.'[80]

Gilchrist quickly discovered that his 'learned associates', rather than providing him with 'the most easy, familiar and common words', would let their 'mind's eye' roam for far-fetched expressions 'from the deserts of Arabia, or they would be beating and scampering over the mountains of Persia.' Others would search 'in the dark intricate mines and caverns of Sanskrit lexicography'.[81] Not only did Gilchrist have difficulties with glossing, he kept insisting that there must be a written grammar of the language they were studying. His collaborators replied to his question with one of their own, asking 'if it was ever yet known in any country that men had to consult vocabularies and rudiments for their own vernacular speech.'[82] Only after many enquiries did his 'coadjutors' produce a 'Tom Thumb' performance, a *Khalig Baree*, which the Indians called a 'vocabulary' but which Gilchrist slightingly referred to as 'old meagre school vocabulary'.[83]

What Gilchrist took to be the failure of his associates to take seriously their own vernacular speech, he attributed to the favourite British explanation of a conspiracy on the part of educated Indians to prevent the British from having access to the great mass of the Indian population. He theorized:

> that it is not at all improbable, that the cormorant crew of Dewans, Mootsuddies, Sirkars, Nazirs, Pundits, Munshis and a tremendous roll call of harpies who encompass power here see with jealous solicitude every attempt in their masters to acquire the means of immediate communication with the great mass of the people who those locusts of the land conceive their lawful prey.[84]

Why was Hindostanee so badly studied and ignored by Gilchrist's European predecessors? Throughout the 'Preface' he builds a complicated argument to answer this question. At base the problem was that of the British having labelled the language 'a jargon', and the conflation of what Gilchrist began to call Hindustani and that language which the majority of Europeans in India referred to as

[80] Ibid., p. xiv.
[81] Ibid.
[82] Ibid.
[83] Ibid.
[84] Ibid., p. xxvi.

The Command of Language and the Language of Command 303

'Moors'. 'Moors' today would be termed a pidgin. Gilchrist
thought of Moors as a

> barbarian gabble [which] exists nowhere but among the dregs of our ser-
> vants, in their snip snap dialogues with us only. Even they would not
> degrade themselves by chattering the gibberish of the savage while
> conversing with or addressing each other in the capacity of human
> beings.[85]

Gilchrist and the Definition of Hindustani

The Hindustani language has three levels or 'styles' which Gilchrist
identified as the 'High Court or Persian Style', 'the Middle or
Genuine Hindostanee Style', and the 'vulgar or the Hinduwee'.

The Court or Persian style is found in the elevated poems of
Sauda, Wulee, Meer Durd, and other poets. This is the 'pompous
and pedantic language of literature and politics', wrote Gilchrist,
and it draws heavily on Arabic and Persian. The second level of
Hindustani is what Gilchrist wants to establish as the standard lan-
guage, and it can be found in the elegy of 'Miskeen, the satires of
Sauda', in Kirkpatrick's, and the translation of the articles of war.
The third level, or the vulgar, is, Gilchrist writes,

> evidenced in Mr. Forster's translation of the Regulations of Government
> . . . in the greatest part of Hindostanee compositions written in the
> Nagaree character, in the dialect of the lower order of servants and Hin-
> doos, as well as among the peasantry of Hindoostan.[86]

Gilchrist was very much aware that he was dealing with shadings,
fluctuations, and a language which was 'evanescent'. What made his
task all the harder, he felt, was that those Indians, Hindu and Muslim, who professionally used languages and had a knowledge of
languages were dominated by what he felt was 'pedantry': 'In a
country where pedantry is esteemed [as] the touchstone of learning,
the learned Moosulman glories in his Arabic and Persian . . . The
Hindoo is no less attached to Sunskrit and Hinduwee.'[87]

Gilchrist explained the emergence and fixing of these language
styles by constructing a history. He believed that before the 'irrup-
tions, and subsequent settlement of the Mossulmans there was a language spoken all over north India, referred to by Hindus as Brij

---

[85] Ibid., p. v.
[86] Ibid., p. xli.
[87] Ibid.

Bhasa, a pure speech . . . the language of the Indian Arcadia.'[88] This language was referred to by the Muslims as 'Hinduwee', the language of the Hindus. In his construction of a history of the Indian languages, Gilchrist compared Hinduwee to the language of the Saxons before their conquest by the French. Hinduwee, like Saxon, was then deluged by Arabic and Persian. After repeated invasions of Muslims, this resulted in the creation of the language which Gilchrist termed Hindustani. Muslims referred to this language as 'Oorduwer', in its military form, 'Rekhtu' in its poetical form, and 'Hindee' as the everyday language of the Hindoos.[89]

As a cover term for this language Gilchrist chose the term 'Hindustani', which had a geographic referent, Hindustan, which could denote in the eighteenth century the whole of the South Asian peninsula, or, in its more restricted sense, India north of the Vindhyas. Gilchrist intended through the use of the term Hindustani to denote a language spoken by the people, Hindu and Muslim, who inhabited Hindustan. For Gilchrist this was a term like 'British or European . . . a conciliating appellation for people in other matters very dissimilar, consequently the most applicable also to the grand popular connecting language of vast regions of the East.' He very consciously chose the term 'Hindustani' to refer to the modern or the contemporary spoken language of India, and preferred this to labelling the language 'Hindee', 'lest it be confused with Hindwee, or Hindoee, which belongs here exclusively to the Hindoos.'[90]

In Gilchrist's theory Sanskrit, 'the dead, sacred, mysterious tongue of the Hindoos', plays little part. He thought that Sanskrit was derived from 'Hindouwee', which was spoken over much of India before the Muslim invasions.[91] The other languages which he distinguished in North India were Bengalee, Rajpootee and Poorbee (Bhoj Puri). He thought these languages were very different in both spoken and literary forms than that language he was classifying as Hindustani. Other languages found in India included: Dukhunee, the language spoken by Muslims in South India, Ooreea (Oriya), Mulwaree (Marwari), Goojaratee (Gujarati), Tilungee (Talinga, Telugu), and Kismeere (Kashmiri). These languages Gilchrist thought had been derived from Hinduwee, Brij Bhasha or Bhakha.

[88] Ibid., p. xx.
[89] Ibid., pp xix-xx.
[90] Ibid., p. xx.
[91] Ibid., p. iv.

The Command of Language and the Language of Command 305

Gilchrist noted that the subdivisions of Indian languages were almost endless, with many local names. Some of the variations he thought of as varieties. Dukhunee and Punjabee, were varieties of Hindustani, while others like Bungal Bhasa were specific dialects and, he implies, derived directly from the parent Hinduwee.[92]

Gilchrist theorized that there were 'three grand indigenous languages which were to be found in India.' Two were 'orally current', Hinduwee and Hindostanee; the third was Sanskrit,

> which really is the dead letter of civil and religious policy, is the consecrated palladium of science and the priestcraft among the Hindoos. The Hinduwee and Hindostani have produced in the several kingdoms and states through which they range territorial varieties or dialects.[93]

The historical ordering of these three languages, Gilchrist speculated, was first Hinduwee, then Sanskrit, and most recently Hindustanee. Sanskrit was not a natural language but a 'usurpation' on Hinduwee, a 'cunning fabrication' of Hinduwee by 'the insidious Bruhmans'.[94] The logic by which Gilchrist came to believe that Sanskrit was historically posterior to the Hinduwee was based on a general theory of language development. If Sanskrit was the original parent language of the other two, why is it so 'inextricably perplexing' by implication to the Europeans, and why does its name imply that it is 'polished or artificial'?[95] He further wondered how such a language could be developed in 'the earliest stages of civilization'. The answer was that the cunning grammarians created Sanskrit out of a pre-existing language that was the language of the folk themselves. From this folk language they constructed 'a mystical, but splendid factum factotum for the reception of the priest craft.' The language of the priests was part of a conspiracy or plot, which resulted in the creation of a double yoke of 'a mild despotism', and an 'insatiable catholick religious persuasion'. The language and its creators, the Brahmins, used their knowledge to enslave the Hindu population of India. The Brahmins he characterized as 'a villainous priesthood' whose teachings are nothing but the 'sonorous inarticulate bellowings of Brahmanical wolves'.[96]

Gilchrist, with the publication of his *Dictionary* (which appeared

[92] Ibid., p. xxiii.
[93] Ibid., p. xxii.
[94] Ibid.
[95] Ibid., p. xxiii.
[96] Ibid., p. xxiv.

in parts and with great difficulty), began to become more and more vociferous in his attacks on both Indian and British scholars of Indian languages, especially those who insisted that one or another of the Indian 'classical' languages was the prerequisite for learning Hindustani. In 1799 Gilchrist wanted to establish an Oriental seminary in Calcutta to teach the newly-appointed Company servants Hindustani. This was to replace the then current practice of granting Company appointees a Rs 30 allowance to enable them to hire a munshi to teach them the country languages. This system he deemed ineffective since few of the munshis spoke English and there were no adequate teaching materials. Simultaneously with the establishment of Gilchrist's seminary, the Governor-General, Lord Wellesley, had published a notification that starting 1 January 1800 no civil servant

> should be nominated to . . . offices of trust and responsibility until it shall be ascertained that he was sufficiently acquainted with the laws and regulations . . . and the several languages, the knowledge of which is required for the due discharge of the respective function of such offices.[97]

The seminary was quickly replaced by Lord Wellesley's ambitious plan for the College at Fort William, established in 1800, at which Gilchrist was appointed Professor of Hindustani. Here he supervised a staff of Indian scholars who were engaged in an extraordinary burst of scholarly, literary and pedagogical activities directed towards making available to students at the College a corpus of works from which they could learn to read and write and speak Hindustani.[98] At the College there was a distinct split in the European faculty, with some stressing the study of classical languages and others emphasizing the spoken languages. Gilchrist and William Carey led the spoken language group. Each published 'Dialogues' or phrase books to convey to the neophyte something of the flavour of the languages, as well as introducing the young officials

---

[97] IOLR, Board's Collection 1981, vol. 97.

[98] There is no agreement on the exact number of books published in Hindustani, Braj and Urdu under the auspices of the College. Kidwai (1972) lists 60 Urdu books published between 1800–4, p. 25; Das (1978) lists 44 books in Hindustani produced at the College between 1802–20. A. Locket, Secretary of the College, listed 28 works in Braj, Urdu and Hindustani, published at the expense of the Government between 1800–12. IOLR, Board's Collection 10708, vol. 446.

The Command of Language and the Language of Command 307

to the 'manners and customs' of the Indians among whom they were going to work.[99]

Carey's *Dialogues* begins with a *khansaman* or *sirkar* talking with a European. The dialect is one in which there are mixed Persian, English and Persian phrases. The topics covered in this dialogue include phrases necessary to set up and run a household. The sahib learns how to berate his servants for slovenly attire and behaviour. He learns brief commands to obtain food, requisites while travelling, and to have a garden laid out for his home.[100] The rest of the work presents dialogues between various types of Indians: a Brahmin talks in an elevated dialect about rituals and the family, and the sahib learns something about kinship terminology and the religious practices of Indians. There are also examples of the common talk of lower orders, fishermen and lower-caste women, whose dialect is characterized by Carey as the 'greatest instance of literal irregularity'.[101] Carey compiled his work 'by employing sensible natives' who composed dialogues 'dealing with subjects of domestic nature'. Sisir Kumar Das identifies the Bengali associates of Carey in this work as probably being Ramram Basu and Mrityunjay Vidyalamkar.[102]

Gilchrist published his first set of Hindustani conversations in 1798 in the *Oriental Linguist*. These were reprinted and revised in 1809 and 1820. In the 1809 version of the *Dialogues*, Gilchrist provides the young Englishman in India specific rules on how to talk with Indians, all of whom in his work seem to be servants.[103] The European must begin by learning how to get the native's attention, and this is accomplished by the command, 'sunno'. This, Gilchrist tells his reader, serves the function of putting the servant 'on his guard'. The commands issued should be as simple as possible, he advised; do not say 'give me a plate', just utter the command, 'plate'.

---

[99] William Carey, *Dialogues*. For discussion of the significance and a partial linguistic analysis of these dialogues, see Sisir Kumar Das, *Early Bengali Prose: Carey to Vidyasagar* (Calcutta, 1966), pp. 68–75, and Das, *Sahibs*, pp. 74–5.

[100] William Carey, *Dialogues*, pp. v, 1–31.

[101] Ibid., pp. vi, 53–61.

[102] Das, *Sahibs*, p. 74.

[103] John Borthwick Gilchrist, *Dialogues, English and Hindustanee calculated to promote the Colloquial intercourse of Europeans on the most useful and familiar subjects, with Natives of India Upon their arrival in That Country* (London, 1809, second edition).

The European should always use the imperative plural, 'we want such and such'. The asking of casual questions should be avoided since 'the Hindustani is too apt to conceive the most innocent of queries only so many traps set to catch him in some villainy or other.'

The *Dialogues* covers the following topics: eating and the preparation of food (31 pages); personal service, such as dressing and preparing for bed (18 pages); travelling, both locally and long distance (43 pages); sports and leisure activities (27 pages); the 'memsahib' and her dealings with servants (only 7 pages); studying (14 pages); commercial transactions (13 pages); expostulating and abusing servants and eliciting information (13 pages); time and weather (5 pages); polite enquiries (2 pages); necessary military activities (5 pages); dialogues about health and medicine and consulting of local doctors (40 pages, perhaps reflecting Gilchrist's original profession as a surgeon). The tone of the dialogue is mainly declamatory: 'bring me this or that', 'take everything away', 'get the breakfast ready'. The sahib, following Gilchrist's instruction, would quickly learn a considerable range of admonitions: 'let me see them every morning on my table without fail, or I shall turn you off, as a good-for-nothing fellow'; 'take care! or the House of Corrections will be your lot'. Food sellers have to be constantly 'warned' about the quality of the provisions. We get phrases like 'the bread has sand in it'. In almost all the dialogues the mishap, mistake, or stupidity of the Indian servant is the theme: soup is served without a spoon, food is either too hot, cold, thick or thin. 'In the future', the servant is told, 'do not dress these Hindustanee dishes with so much spice, this tastes of nothing but pepper.' The wine is never properly cooled.

The real disasters seem to strike when the sahib ventures forth. Walking only needs 21 phrases, but riding or going about in a carriage or palanquin requires 134 phrases. The sahib seems to get lost a lot, servants are sent to make enquiries. While travelling everything seems to get misplaced, the wine especially. There are innumerable delays, people sleep when they should be working. But there are pleasures as well. The servant is sent off to find out from a local villager if there is game in the neighbourhood; there is, but it turns out that it is dangerous to hunt there because of the large number of tigers. Orders have to be given to the local zamindar 'to have his people beat up the game for us.'

The Command of Language and the Language of Command 309

Language as command was not only a domestic or personal matter, but a matter of state. Lord Minto, in addressing the annual prize ceremony at Fort William College in 1808, explained to sixteen young officers that the nature of their relationship to Indians would be mediated by language:

> You are about to be employed in the administration of a great and extensive country in which . . . the English language is not known. You will have to deal with multitudes; who can communicate with you, can receive your commands, or render an account of their performance of them; whose testimonies can be delivered, whose engagements can be contracted; whose affairs, only in some one or another of the languages taught at the College of Fort William.[104]

The Englishmen's honour and self-respect were also involved, as Minto echoed the statements of the Court of Directors and the Governor-General and language teachers for the past sixty years on the evils of interpreters. Without proper knowledge of the language of the people they were ruling, there would arise an 'unlimited dependence on native and subordinate officers, which inevitably leads to oppressive vexation, extortion, and cruelty towards our native subjects.' Without the knowledge of languages, the European is delivered into a 'helpless and dependent thraldom' of a native assistant. The officers' 'fair fame' would be threatened, there would be public loss and calamity and the officer would suffer individual shame and ruin.[105]

The Englishman needed not only to speak with grammatical precision, but had to learn to 'manage his own language' in a manner most conducive for the execution of orders and the gratification of his own wishes on every occasion.[106] Those who would follow Gilchrist's methods of teaching were assured that they would have the means to start their careers in India by not only making rapid progress in learning the vernacular, but in doing so would acquire 'local knowledge' and daily increase their 'stock of general information'. This Gilchrist contrasted with those who began with the study of the 'classical' languages, who might find themselves diminishing 'those intellectual powers, and that common sense which are fre-

---

[104] Quoted in Gilchrist's *Dialogues*, p. lxxx.

[105] Ibid., p. lxxi.

[106] J.B. Gilchrist, *The General East India Guide and Vade Mecum . . . Being a Digest of the work of the Late Cap' Williamson with Many Improvements and Additions* (London, 1825), p. 536.

quently sunk under a heavy load of sheer pedantry and classical lore, very different indeed from real science and practical wisdom.'[107] What emerges from reading Gilchrist is the idea of the Englishman in India as he who commands, the one who knows how to give orders, how to keep the natives in their proper place in the order of things, through the application of 'real science and practical wisdom' rather than pedantry and classical knowledge.

The emphasis on the use of language as the key to understanding Indians, hence being able to control them, was stressed frequently in Lt. Col. John Briggs's *Letters Addressed to a Young Person in India*, a book written in the form of letters by an old hand in India to two brothers, one in the military, who is older, and a younger brother who is a civil servant.[108] Briggs sets out to instruct the civil servant in proper behaviour. The older brother who has already been in India for a few years has made all the mistakes, which the younger brother is to avoid. He fails to learn languages, gets into debt, selects the wrong type of servant, beats and abuses his servants, and generally make a mess of things. In the letters to the young civilian not only are the failures of his brother the constant reminder as to what may happen to shame the individual, but, more importantly, to shake the foundations of British rule in India. Briggs instructs his younger readers in these principles, as laid down by Major General Sir John Malcolm

> Almost all who, from knowledge and experience, have been capable of forming any judgment upon the question, are agreed that our power in India rests on the general opinion of the natives of our comparative superiority in good faith, wisdom, and strength, to their own rulers. This important impression will be improved by the consideration we show to their habits, institutions, and religion—by the moderation, temper, and kindness, with which we conduct ourselves towards them; and injured by every act that offends their belief or superstition, that shows disregard or neglect of individuals or communities, or that evinces our having, with the arrogance of conquerors, forgotten those maxims by which this great empire has been established, and by which alone it can be preserved.[109]

The only way to gain the knowledge and sympathy which Mal-

---

[107] Ibid., p. 537.

[108] John Briggs, *Letters Addressed to a Young Person in India* (London, 1828).

[109] 'Instructions by Major General Sir John Malcolm, To Officers Acting under His Orders in Central India, in 1821', in Sir John Malcolm, *The Political History of India, from 1784–1823* (London, 1826), vol. II, appendix VII, pp. cclxiii-iv.

The Command of Language and the Language of Command 311

colm's instructions required was through the languages of the people. 'The veil which exists between us and the natives can only be removed by mutual and kind intercourse.'[110] There might be kindly intercourse with the natives, but language was also the 'channel of communicating of your wants, and of obtaining information', Briggs advised.[111] Knowledge of Indian languages was the means of gaining a more complex knowledge, that of the strange customs, codes and rules of the Indians, who were in most instances docile, co-operative, and quite willing to obey the orders and commands of the sahibs, except when ignorance led them to offend the prejudices of the natives. The newcomer seemingly had to be instructed in the simplest and most obvious of distinctions, that between Hindus and Muslims. Gilchrist informed his readers that Muslims were larger, bearded and more fierce and robust in appearance than Hindus. One had to learn how to distinguish the differences in dress by the way they tied their garments, by their facial marks, by the varied use of beads, rings, and ornaments, by the form of hair-style and turban, and above all by their names and their food habits.

Unlike Briggs and Malcolm, whose careers were amongst the peoples of Central and Western India—and hence who were instructing their juniors in proper behaviour towards not only their Indian servants, domestic and civil, but to learned men, chiefs, opulent bankers and merchants and peasants—Gilchrist's image of Indian society seems to have been largely restricted to domestic servants and lowly assistants. No matter how one tried, apparently in Bengal there were occasions when even the most knowledgeable and even-tempered European would be driven 'by the stupidity, perverseness, and chicanery' of natives to 'want to beat his servants'. But Gilchrist advises: 'let the storm blow over' with a volley of abusive words directed at the miscreant.[112] The normal good manners of the European can be tested, according to Gilchrist, in all sorts of situations, for example when invited to a wealthy Indian's house for an entertainment. On such an occasion one should not condemn the music, dancing and singing, or if a dramatic pantomine particularly offends the European's sense of modesty he should retire in silence rather than offer vociferous exclamations such as 'beastly stuff'. Quiet withdrawal in such situations, writes Gilchrist, 'will do more

[110] Briggs, *Letters*, p. 9.
[111] Ibid., p. 50.
[112] Gilchrist, *East India Guide*, pp. 536–9; *Dialogues*, pp. 174–81.

to establish our superiority in breeding and morality.'[113]

The European has to learn to insist on proper performance of the Indian's social and verbal codes in dealing with superiors. One should not let an Indian subordinate get away with behaviour or speech acts which would be offensive not only to the European but to an Indian of superior quality. Gilchrist, as did most Europeans in India, reduced what was and is an extremely sensitive, well-ordered and complex system of deference and demeanour codes which Indians follow to what for the Europeans were highly charged symbolic acts revolving around the wearing of various foot coverings.[114] Gilchrist explained that Europeans uncover their heads as a mark of respect, while Indians take off their slippers while performing worship in a mosque or a temple or on entering a home or office. Yet he observes that natives

> intrude on the British inhabitants of Calcutta and environs, without the slightest attention to this act of politeness, most scrupulously observed amongst themselves, as if they were determined to trample us under the pride of Caste, by evincing, that to a Hindoo or Moosulman alone, it was necessary to pay the common marks of civility or respect.[115]

The wearing of shoes by Indians in the houses of Europeans was seen as part of a larger effort on the part of Indians to establish equality or even superiority with, or over, the European. This intent was directed to gaining advantage not only over the European, but also of particular Indians over other Indians by appearing to be on a footing of equality with Europeans.

Indian languages, with their graded grammatical systems of polite forms and forms of various degrees of familiarity and respect, also could be a source of disrespect to the Europeans. For the unwitting European in India, some servants and menials would use the singular pronoun in addressing the sahib. 'It is rather surprising that servants and sipahees, etc., should be allowed to take such advantage of their master's ignorance of the language and customs of the country, as to *too* and *tera* them on every occasion: a liberty they dare not take with one another.'[116] The insult of the use of familiar forms by

[113] Gilchrist, *East India Guide*, p. 546.

[114] V.C.P. Chaudhary, 'Imperial Honeymoon with Indian Aristocracy'; Patna, *Kashi Prasad Jayaswal Research Institute, Historical Research Series*, no. 18 (1980), appendix 13, pp. 425–36.

[115] Gilchrist, *East India Guide*, p. 551.

[116] Ibid., pp. 564–5.

The Command of Language and the Language of Command 313

the servant to the sahib was not just a personal insult but had a much greater consequence for the loss of dignity for his country and nation. Gilchrist stressed that the necessary knowledge of indigenous language and custom was not one of just the sahib getting proper respect; it also entailed the sahib avoiding unwittingly acting in a disrespectful manner towards the Indian when he did not intend it.

Two issues require some commentary on the discussion of the use of what Gilchrist tried to establish as the British language of command. The first is—how well did the British learn this or any other Indian language? And the second, how fixed did the standard which Gilchrist hoped to establish remain? Until the middle of the century there were recurrent complaints about the lack of sophisticated knowledge which the British had of Hindustani, or Urdu as it became more generally known. F.J. Shore, who had considerable empathy with Indians and who was continually critical of both the policies of the Company's government and the behaviour of his fellow countrymen towards Indians, ridiculed the level of knowledge of Hindustani which most 'judges, magistrates and military officers' had attained even after a number of years' service in India. He likened them to the broken English of Frenchmen or Italians, who are made objects of fun or contempt on the stage. This lack of capacity to speak properly, he felt, encouraged Indians to be equally slovenly or mannerless in their dealings with the sahibs. He cited a hypothetical case:

> Two or three English are out hunting or shooting; one of them who speaks broken Hindustanee, asks a peasant some questions relative to the sport: the native answers him in a careless way, perhaps without stopping his work; and sometimes without even looking up from it, after the first glance; omitting, at the same time, the respectful terms of speech. Should another of the party, who can speak in a gentlemanlike manner, address the peasant, in an instant the latter will rise up, or stop his work, make a salaam, and reply in the most respectful language. Were the native asked by any one to whom he could speak freely, why he made such a difference in addressing the two gentlemen, his answer would be something to the following effect: 'Two gentlemen! Do you call the first a gentleman; if so, why did he not speak like one? The second evidently was so, by his language, and I answered him as such.'[117]

The Englishman with a limited grasp of Hindustani indeed received

[117] Frederick John Shore, *Notes on Indian Affairs* (1837), vol. I, p. 27.

answers to his questions. The issue which Shore raises is not about communication, but about behaviour and status, and I think this issue continued through much of the history of the British in India. There were obviously those British who spoke and understood the standard or even the literary registers of the varied languages of India, and hence could manage their official persona as F.J. Shore would have wished they did. I would speculate, however, that the majority knew only very restricted and specific codes, which were adequate to specified contexts, e.g. running their households, dealing with their subordinates, in the courts and offices, and in giving orders in the military.

The battle between the Classicists and Vernacularists in relation to Hindustani was to continue throughout the nineteenth century. Each new dictionary or grammar that would appear caused argumentation. The missionaries soon joined the officials of the Company and questions of the scripts and the source of borrowings for lexical items and for grammatical refinements became politically charged issues. In the 1860s Indians, some of whom had added a sophisticated knowledge of English to their own 'classical' educations, began to argue, organize and eventually to demand in the name of history and religion that the Government favour one or another script and associated literatures.[118]

British Power and Indian Knowledge

On the eve of the fiftieth anniversary of the founding of the Asiatic Society of Bengal, W.C. Taylor, in an address to the Royal Asiatic Society in London, declared it was the British who in the last decades of the eighteenth century were responsible for the 'literary treasures of Hindustan being opened to the wonder and admiration of the world.'[119] He went on, like a twentieth-century counterpart

[118] Christopher King, 'The Nagari Prachaini Sabha . . .', Ph.D. dissertation, University of Wisconsin (1974); Rajendralal Mitra, 'On the Origin of the Hindvi Language and its Relation to the Urdu Dialect', *Journal of the Asiatic Society* (1864), vol. 33, pp. 489–515; John Beames, 'Outline for the Plea for the Arabic Element in Official Hindustani', *Journal of the Asiatic Society* (1866), vol. 35, pp. 1–13; M.A. Growse, 'Some Objections to the Modern Style of Official Hindustani', *Journal of the Asiatic Society* (1866), vol. 35, pp. 172–81.

[119] W.C. Taylor, 'On the Present State and Future Prospect of Oriental Literature Viewed in Connection with the Royal Asiatic Society', *Journal of the Royal Asiatic Society of Great Britain and Ireland*, vol. II (1835), p. 4.

The Command of Language and the Language of Command 315

in the UK or the US, to appeal for funds to support continuing research and publication by linking the knowledge gained through the study of Oriental literature to success in 'the pursuit of Oriental commerce'. He clinched his argument by citing the aphorism 'KNOWLEDGE IS POWER'.[120]

Warren Hastings in 1784 explicated for Nathaniel Smith, Chairman of the Court of Directors, the relation of knowledge to power in the establishment of British rule in India:

> Every accumulation of knowledge and especially such as is obtained by social communication with people over whom we exercise dominion founded on the right of conquest, is useful to the state . . . it attracts and conciliates distant affections; it lessens the weight of the chain by which the natives are held in subjection; and it imprints on the hearts of our countrymen the sense of obligation and benevolence . . . Every instance which brings their real character (i.e. that of the Indians) home to observation will impress us with a more generous sense of feeling for their natural rights, and teach us to estimate them by the measure of our own. But such instances can only be obtained in their writings: and these will survive when the British dominion in India shall have long ceased to exist, and when the sources which once yielded of wealth and power are lost to rememberance.[121]

Hastings drew a contrast between the 'benevolent and sympathetic interest' which the British had shown towards the Brahmins, the keepers 'of the mysteries of their own learning', and the previous rulers, the Muslims, who had systematically derided the religion of the Hindus and who sought from their studies 'arguments to support their own intolerant principles'. Hastings believed that as a result of the conciliatory nature of British rule, the pundits were now 'no less eager to impart their knowledge, than we are to receive it.'[122]

Twenty years later Sir James Mackintosh, a Benthamite and legal reformer who was Recorder of Bombay, struck a somewhat harsher note in addressing the first meeting of the Bombay Literary Society. He urged his colleagues to 'mine the knowledge of which we have become the masters'.[123] He went on to remind his listeners 'that all

---

[120] Ibid., p. 9. Capitals in original.

[121] The letter is printed as part of the introduction to Charles Wilkins (ed.), *The Bhavat-Geeta or Dialogues of Kreeshna and Arjoon* (London, 1785), p. 13.

[122] Ibid., p. 15.

[123] Sir James Mackintosh, 'A Discourse at the Opening of the Literary Society of Bombay, 26 November 1804', *Transactions of the Literary Society of Bombay*, vol. I (1819), reprinted 1877, p. xiv.

Europeans who visit remote countries . . . are detachments from the main body of civilized men sent out to levy contributors of knowledge, as well as gain victories over barbarism.'[124]

H.T. Colebrook, in a letter to his father, described the ambivalence which characterized much of the British reaction to Indian culture:

> The further our literary enquiries are extended here, the more vast and stupendous the scene which opens to us; at the same time that the true and the false, the sublime and the puerile, wisdom and absurdity, are so intermixed, that at every step, we have to smile at folly, while we admire and acknowledge the philosophical truth, though couched in obscure allegory and puerile fable.[125]

British studies of Indian languages, literature, science, and thought produced three major projects. The first involved the objectification and use of Indian languages as instruments of rule to better understand the 'peculiar' manners, customs, and prejudices of Indians, and to carry out enquiries to gather information necessary to conciliate and control the peoples of India. The second project entailed what the Europeans defined as 'discoveries' of the wisdom of the ancients, the analogy being to the restoration of Greek and Roman thought and knowledge in the fifteenth and sixteenth centuries. This was a European project, the end being to construct a history of the relationship between India and the West, to classify and order and locate their civilizations on an evaluative scale of progress and decay. The third project involved the patronage of institutions and religious and literary specialists who maintained and transmitted—through texts, writing, recitations, performances, painting and sculptures, rituals and performances—that which the British conquerors defined as the traditions of the conquered. To appear legitimate in the eyes of the Indians the British thought they had to demonstrate respect and interest in those Indians and institutions that were the carriers of the traditions.

There were to be consistent differences in the valuation of the three projects between the two centres of decision making, one in London in the Court of Directors, representing the 'owners' of the East India Company, and the Board of Control which had been established by Parliament to exercise political control over the

[124] Ibid., p. xi.
[125] H.T. Colebrooke, *Miscellaneous Essays*, edited by Sir T.E. Colebrooke, vol. i (London, 1873), p. 61, letter dated April 18, 1794.

The Command of Language and the Language of Command 317

affairs of the Company. In India there was a theoretically subordinate group of officials, headed by the Governor-General in Council, and the Governors of Bombay and Madras, which supervised the functioning of the instrumentalities of colonial rule. Given the distance and time which separated India and London, and the growing weight and power of senior civil servants, Calcutta, Madras and Bombay frequently acted independently of the owners of the Company and the Home Government.

London tended to put the question of language learning at the top of its priorities. The construction of 'European' knowledge was increasingly left to semi-official bodies such as the Asiatic Society of Bengal, and to professional scholars in the colleges and universities. The issues entailed in the construction of the legitimacy of the Company's rule through the preservation and patronage of Indian knowledge caused a political and epistemological battle between London and Calcutta over the allocation of resources, and a financial and moral battle about the forms of knowledge and the shape of institutions which could most effectively preserve and transmit to Indians their own and European thought.

Education and the Preservation of the Past

In September 1780 a delegation of Muslims of 'credit and learning' called upon Warren Hastings to urge him to establish a madrassa for the instruction of young students 'in Mahamadan law and other sciences'.[126] The visit had been occasioned by the arrival in Calcutta of a famous teacher and scholar, Muiz ud din, whom the petitioners hoped the Government would employ to direct the madrassa.[127] Hastings, in justifying the expenditure of the Company's funds to support a madrassa in Calcutta, painted a bleak picture of decaying remains 'of these schools which could be seen in every capital, town and city of Hindustan.' The Calcutta Madrassa, Hastings hoped, would preserve and further knowledge, provide training for future law officers of the Company, contribute to the 'credit' of the Company's name, and 'help soften the prejudices excited by the growth of British dominions.'[128]

[126] 'Minute by Governor General Warren Hastings, 17 April 1781', in H. Sharp (ed.), *Selections from the Educational Records*, part I, 1781–1939 (Calcutta, 1920), p. 8.

[127] Ruth Gabriel, 'Learned Communities and British Educational Experiments in North India: 1780–1830', Ph.D. dissertation, University of Virginia (1979), p. 109.

[128] Glieg, *Memoirs of Warren Hastings*, vol. III, p. 159.

The Madrassa, under the direction of Muiz ud din, appeared to have got off to a good start, with ninety students pursuing a wide range of studies. However, within a few years the maulvi was accused of mishandling Company funds, favouritism in appointments, and losing control over the students. A committee of British officials was appointed to supervise the administration of the college, the maulvi was dismissed, and the college was reorganized along European lines, although the subject matter studied remained Islamic.[129]

A similar history repeated itself at the Sanskrit College in Banaras which owed its inception to the initiative of Jonathan Duncan, Resident in Banaras. He recommended that surplus revenue, expected to accrue to the Company from the Permanent Settlement of the Banaras Zamindari, be applied to the establishment of 'a Hindoo College . . . for the preservation and cultivation of Laws, Literature and Religion of that nation, at this centre of their faith.' Such an institution, Duncan felt, 'would endear our Government to the Native Hindoos'. There were, he observed, 'many private seminaries' for the study of various forms of Hindu learning, but as the Company's college would be the only 'public' institution dedicated to this purpose the reputation of the Company would be enhanced. In addition to its teaching functions, Duncan noted that as an institution it could without too much expense build a 'precious library of complete and correct treatises . . . dealing with Hindoo religion, laws, arts and sciences'.[130]

Perhaps influenced by the history of the Madrassa, Duncan drew up a set of rules which made the Resident, acting on behalf of the Governor-General, responsible for the payment of stipends for those students being educated at Government expense, hiring and firing of faculty, and the dismissal of students. Duncan was to attend the quarterly examinations, at least in those subjects which were not considered to be sacred—for these he would appoint a committee of Brahmins who would examine students in the 'more secret branches of learning'. Within ten years of its founding, accusations similar to those of financial mismanagement and favouritism that had plagued the Madrassa led to a more intensive British supervision of the Sanskrit College.[131]

[129] Gabriel, pp. 112–120.
[130] Letter from Jonathan Duncan to Lord Cornwallis, 1 January 1792, in Sharp (ed.), *Selections*, pp. 9–11.
[131] Sharp, *Selections*, pp. 33–6.

The Command of Language and the Language of Command 319

The history of the British experiments with the Calcutta Madrassa and the Sanskrit College in Banaras are symbolic of wider issues entailed in the establishing of educational institutions under the colonial state. The British conceived of education as taking place in 'institutions', meaning a building with physically divided spaces marking off one 'class' of students from another, as well as teachers from students. There were to be fixed positions of professors, teachers and assistants, who taught regular classes in subjects. The students' progress had to be regularly examined to measure their acquisition of fixed bodies of knowledge. The end of the process was marked by prizes and certification which attested to the students' command of a specifiable body of knowledge. Even with the undoubted good will and best intentions on the part of Duncan, Hastings and others, a British metalogic of regularity, uniformity, and above all fiscal responsibility, could not help but participate in the erosion and transformation of what the British wanted to preserve; i.e. Hindu and Muslim learning.

The political project of enhancing the credit of the Company and the British nation as the protector and preserver of indigenous knowledge was to lead them to become keepers of a vast museum which would, in turn, lead to providing definitions of what should be preserved, as well as to developing a programme for locating and classifying the specimens to be maintained. The substance of Lord Minto's remarks on the decay of Indian science and literature was to echo throughout the nineteenth century:

> It is a common remark that science and literature are in a progressive state of decay among the natives of India. From every inquiry which I have been enabled to make on this interesting subject that remark appears to me but too well founded. The number of the learned is not only diminished but the circle of learning even among those who still devote themselves to it appears to be considerably contracted. The abstract sciences are abandoned, polite literature neglected and no branch of learning cultivated but what is connected with the peculiar religious doctrines of the people. The immediate consequence of this state of things is the disuse and even actual loss of many valuable books; and it is to be apprehended that unless Government interpose with a fostering hand the revival of letters may shortly become hopeless from a want of books or of persons capable of explaining them.[132]

Lord Wellesley, who had a magisterial and imperial vision of the Company's rule in India, conceived in 1800 a plan for the education

---

[132] 'Minute by Lord Minto, 6 March 1811', in Sharp, p. 19.

and training of the young men appointed to the Company's civil
service. No longer should these appointees be thought of 'as agents
of a commercial concern', he declared. They should be trained as
'ministers and officers of a powerful sovereign'. Wellesley, without
the permission of the Court of Directors, established the College at
Fort William to provide the education which he thought was required. He wrote to the Court of Directors that the education
should impart a knowledge of 'those branches of literature and science' such as was included in the education of persons 'destined for
high offices in Europe'. In addition, the young men required special
instruction in the codes and regulations of the Company, as well as
in the 'true and sound principles of the British constitution'. As
they were to be rulers of an alien race they had to obtain 'an intimate acquaintance with the history, languages, customs, laws and
religions of India'. As if this wasn't enough for a group of sixteen-
and seventeen-year olds, the College had to shape their moral character so they would be armed with the virtues of 'industry, pru-
dence, integrity, and religious sensibility' which would help them
guard against the 'temptations and corruptions' they would be exposed to because of the Indian climate and the 'peculiar depravity'
of the people of India. Their education, Wellesley claimed, had to
form a natural barrier 'against habitual indolence, dissipation, licen-
tiousness and indulgence' which had marked the behaviour of most
of the employees of the Company.[133]

To accomplish this awesome educational project Wellesley planned a residential college where the young men's lives could be properly supervised. It was to be staffed by a European faculty of eight
to ten which could teach Indian languages as well as the European
curriculum. To set the proper moral tone the Vice-Provost was to
be a clergyman of the Anglican faith. To teach the Oriental subjects
fifty munshis were employed and divided into four departments:
Sanskrit-Bengali, Arabic, Persian and Hindustani. Each department
had a European professor, a chief munshi, a second munshi, as well
as subordinate munshis. The pay of the European faculty ranged
from Rs 1600 to Rs 500; for the Indian staff the range was Rs 200 for
the four chief munshis, Rs 100 for the second munshis, and Rs 60

[133] Lord Wellesley, 'Notes with Respect to the Foundation of a College at Fort
William', in Montgomery Martin (ed.), *Despatches and Minutes . . . of the Marquis
of Wellesley . . . In India* (London, 1836), vol. II, pp. 329–30.

The Command of Language and the Language of Command 321

for the subordinate munshis.[134] The duties of the munshis involved providing individual tutorials, preparing (in collaboration with the European professors) teaching materials, preparing and publishing grammars and dictionaries, as well as undertaking extensive projects in publishing 'classic' works of Indian literature.

The Court of Directors, when they learned of the very ambitious plans, quickly cut back on the European part of the curriculum and barred the building of a residential college. Their central concern was with the college as a language-teaching institution. They did, however, establish in England the East India Company's Training College at Haileybury for the education of their appointees to the civil service in India. Here they received an education in European subjects and some Indian language work.[135]

The College Council, which was the governing body of the College at Fort William, was estimated by the Court of Directors to have spent upwards of £40,000 to subsidize the editing, writing, and publishing of eighty-eight 'Oriental works' in the period 1801–12.[136] The vast bulk of the funds was spent on works in or about Persian (Rs 110,000), Arabic (Rs 52,000), and Sanskrit (Rs 44,000). The Company informed their servants in Calcutta that any work subsidized showed 'value and merit' in the teaching of languages. The Court complained of 'The very heavy expense to which you have subjected us by the encouragement, which seems to have been indiscriminately afforded to publications, several of which are very ill executed, or of no use as class books, nor are they in any other way objects which call for the patronage of your government.'[137]

The Indian staff recruited for the College included a number of distinguished scholars such as Mrityunjay Vidyalamkar from Midnapur and Maulvi Allah Daud from Lucknow. In addition several, such as Ram Ram Basu, Mir Amin and Lalljilal from Gujarat, made major contributions to the prose literatures of Bengali, Urdu and Hindi. Some made a major scholarly and intellectual impact on their European counterparts. Mathew Lumsden, whose Persian *Gram-*

---

[134] Sisir Kumar Das, *Sahibs and Munshis* pp. 7–21.

[135] Bernard S. Cohn, 'Recruitment and Training of British Civil Servants in India 1600–1800', in Ralph Braibanti (ed.), *Asian Bureaucratic Systems Emergent from the British Imperial System* (Durham, 1966), pp. 116–40.

[136] For list see IOLR, *Board's Collection*, vol. 465, # 110708; for the entire period of the College see Das, appendix E, pp. 155–66.

[137] IOLR, *Board's Collection*, vol. 465, # 11252.

mar was published in 1810, described Maulvi Allah Daud 'as the master under whom I have studied', and acknowledged his great debt to 'his knowledge and industry'.[138] Lumsden assured his European readers that though he was the author of the *Grammar*, 'the more arduous task of supplying the information devolved . . . onto Daud.'[139]

Lumsden's remark I think typifies the relations between Indian and British scholars who were engaged not only at the College, but in other settings as well, transforming Indian knowledge into European information. The Indians were sources or 'native informants' who supplied information, *viva voce*, in English or Indian languages, who collected, translated and discussed texts and documents, and who wrote exegeses of various kinds which were classified, processed and analysed into knowledge *of* or *about* India.

As Das points out, in the College there were two separate categories, *Sahibs* and *Munshis*. There was indeed mutual learning going on, there was respect and some amicability in the relations between the two categories of persons, but it was the British who set the agenda and who had the authoritative voice in determining what was useful knowledge to be processed for European projects: 'The Indian scholar knew he was superior to his European Master in respect of Indian languages, [but] he was primarily an informant, a mere tool in the exercise of language teaching to be handled by others.'[140]

The differences between the Indian scholars and their British counterparts were based on more than the social and political relations which had made the British dominant; there was a major epistemological gulf between the two cultures as well. Those British who sought to produce grammars, dictionaries, or translations of literary or 'practical' works, such as law codes, frequently complained about the way in which Indian scholars worked and thought. C.P. Brown, who spent forty years working on Telugu, writes of working with Brahmins who nearly 'shipwrecked' him with their 'pedantry'. He complained that the Brahmins valued only the abstract and abstruse and despised 'all that is natural and in daily

---

[138] Mathew Lumsden, *A Grammar of the Persian Language* (Calcutta, 1810), p. xxviii.

[139] Ibid.

[140] Das, p. 107.

The Command of Language and the Language of Command 323

use'.[141] He rebelled against their instructions to 'learn by rote long vocabularies, framed in metre' while he was trying to construct his dictionary of Telugu. The Reverend Robert Caldwell claimed that the learning of 'versified enigmas and harmonious platitudes' resulted in Indians developing a great capacity for patient labour, 'and an accurate knowledge of details', but this also prevented the development of a 'zeal for historical truth' and the 'power of generalization and discrimination'.[142]

The development of the capacity for memorizing was part of the education which the British received as well. Brown complained of his pundits' demands to memorize, but also took pride in the fact that they thought he 'knew the Bible, Shakespeare, and Milton by heart'. What baffled the British the most about the prodigious feats of memorization of the Indians was that it appeared to them that the Indians did not know the meaning of what they had internalized so effectively.

A.D. Campbell found in Bellary district in 1823 that great attention was being paid in the schools to proper pronunciation of syllables of a 'poetical' language but not to 'the meaning or construction of words' in this language. He found that the teachers themselves could not 'understand the purport of the numerous books which they thus learn[ed] from memory'. The result was that the students had a 'parrot-like capacity to repeat, but not to understand what they had learned, they gained little from their education, as they did not have the means' to expand their general stock of useful knowledge.[143]

William Adam, in his reports on vernacular education in Bengal and Bihar, believed that the education in the local schools was 'superficial and deficitive [sic]'. Even at the Sanskrit colleges at which grammar, law, rhetoric, literature and logic were taught, following William Ward's assessment, few attained very high levels of knowledge and only five out of one thousand students in the colleges

---

[141] 'Some Account of the Literary Life of Charles Philip Brown, Written by Himself', in C.P. Brown, *English-Telugu Dictionary* (1866, second edition, Madras, 1895), p. xiv.

[142] Robert Caldwell, *A Comparative Grammar of South Indian Family of Languages* (1856; third edition, reprinted New Delhi, 1974), pp. xii–xiii.

[143] 'Report of A.D. Campbell', 17 August 1823, in House of Commons, *Committee on the Affairs of the East India Company*, 1832–33, appendix, Public 1.2, vol. 12, p. 353.

knew anything of the philosophical systems of the Veda, even though they could chant from memory long passages in Sanskrit.[144]

One of the few Europeans of the early nineteenth century who was not dismissive of the Indian form of education based on memorization was Francis W. Ellis of the Madras civil service. Ellis, who had a career as judge and collector in South India, was one of the most accomplished and sensitive of the early Orientalists.[145] Ellis was one of the founders of the Company's College at Fort St. George in 1812, which differed significantly in its purpose from the College at Fort William, since, in addition to training the British in South Indian languages, it also included the training of Indians in Hindu and Muslim law as part of its responsibilities. As in North India, the Company's courts administered Hindu and Muslim personal law, but in Madras they found that few of the South Indian Brahmins appeared to know the Dharmashastric literature. Ellis had drawn up a list of what he thought were the most useful and important compilations of Sanskrit works for the purpose of forming a 'practical guide' for the administration of Hindu law in the Madras Presidency. He recommended that these works be translated into 'Tamil verse' for the use of the Hindu students in the College. He explained that only if they were translated into Tamil prose would they have any authority for the Indians.[146] Ellis argued that 'the mode of study prevalent among the natives of India [was] the best means of conveying the law.' He went on to state that all knowledge and science in India 'from the lowest to the highest form of logic and theology' were 'acquired by committing to memory technical verses'. These memorized verses were like a 'tap root', which the scholar or pundit could draw upon to 'explain, illustrate or enforce dicta'.[147]

What Ellis was pointing to was that the Indian mode of knowing and thinking was radically different from what the British assumed

---

[144] William Adam, *Reports on Vernacular Education in Bengal and Behar*, ed. J. Long (Calcutta, 1868), p. 20.

[145] F.W. Ellis, 'Note to the Introduction', in A.D. Campbell, *A Grammar of the Telagu Language* (Madras, 1820), pp. 1–2; for a discussion of Ellis's work and significance see Walter Eliot, *Indian Antiquary*, vol. IV (July 1875), pp. 219–21 and (November 1878), pp. 274–5; R.E. Asher, 'Notes on F.W. Ellis and an unpublished Fragment of his Commentary on the Tirukkural', *Proceedings of the First International Conference Seminar of Tamil Studies* (April, 1966), pp. 513–22.

[146] IOLR, *Board's Collection*, vol. 12, # 549, letter dated 12 May 1814, p. 19.

[147] Ibid., p. 47.

The Command of Language and the Language of Command 325

was the natural or normal form, and which they used as a standard by which they could adjudge Indian forms of knowing as marred or inadequate, rather than different. Indian reasoning was based, Ellis wrote, on 'the habit of their education' which rested on the memorization 'of concentrated not diffuse knowledge', which was easier to comprehend in verse form.[148] The use of Tamil in its verse form also 'would diminish the influence of the Brahmans', who were regarded with 'jealousy' by the Sudras in South India, who could study law in their own 'language'. It would also enable the pleaders in their courts to 'read' the law, and would secure a more 'impartial administration of justice'. In addition, as the English judges were required to learn Tamil in Madras, they could discuss issues directly in a language common to themselves and their law officers.[149]

Conclusion: The Reordering of the Nature of Indian Knowledge

The British conquest of India brought them into a new world which they tried to comprehend using their own forms of knowing and thinking. To the educated Englishman of the late eighteenth and early nineteenth centuries the world was knowable through the senses, which could record the experience of a 'natural' world. This world was generally believed to be divinely created, knowable in an empirical fashion, and constitutive of the 'sciences' through which would be revealed the 'laws of Nature' that governed the world and all that was in it. Unknowingly and unwittingly they had not only invaded and conquered a territory, but, through their scholarship, had invaded an epistemological space as well. The British believed they could explore and conquer this space through translation: establishing correspondences could make the unknown and the strange knowable.

At one level they found this could be done relatively easily and quickly through labels which served to locate the strange in a frame of reference with which they were familiar. Brahmins became 'priests', and the *Kosha* of Amarasinha was a 'Dictionary of the Sanskrit Language'. Since all languages had a grammar, the commentaries on Indian languages could be turned into tools to enable the sahibs to communicate their commands and gather information. They quickly found and utilized extraordinarily able guides, aides, and assistants who knew highly specialized forms of Indian know-

[148] Ibid.
[149] Ibid., pp. 49–51.

ledge and could be interpreters, sources and transmitters of this knowledge to the new rulers. The Victorian successors to the first generation of scholars were more likely to describe their goals as 'scientific and historical'; the wonders which had excited Jones, Wilkins, Halhed and Ellis now had to be normalized and located in a discourse which would make India into a 'case' of an archaic civilization, or a museum of ancient practices, from which earlier stages of universal world history could be recovered. A theory and method had been created by Europeans through which India could be hierarchized into a case.

Sir William Jones, in his declaration of the relationship of Latin, Greek and Sanskrit in 1785, provided the impetus for the development, largely by German scholars, of comparative philology, which in turn supplied the 'scientific' model for the comparative study of law, religion and society. The comparative method, as it became formalized in the middle of the nineteenth century, drew together many strands of eighteenth-century thought and scholarly practice. It promised answers to the persistent European quest for the 'origins' of things. In its linguistic and literary forms it utilized techniques for the collation of texts in order to construct the original and pure versions which could then be used to establish a linear chronology. Europeans had utilized these critical methods of textual reconstruction to establish the documents, records, and texts by which they constituted their own 'true' history. They now were prepared to give to the Indians the greatest gift they could give anyone — the Indians would receive a *history*.

The theory of language implicit in the comparative method is that there are 'genetic' or 'genealogical' relations among languages which have been determined to belong to a 'family'. What is posited is that there was once a single, original language from which all the languages in the family descend. The establishment of the membership in the language family was based on the comparison of *formal* features, displayed lexically, syntactically, morphologically, and phonetically, in the language. The goal of the method was to establish a *history*; those features which appear from formal comparison as the most common in the family of languages were thought to be the most 'authentic'. The end of the exercise was the reconstruction of 'the unrecorded languages of the past'.[150]

---

[150] Thomas R. Trautman, 'The Study of Dravidian Kinship', in Madhav M. Desh-

The Command of Language and the Language of Command 327

The Reverend Robert Caldwell, a Church of England missionary in Tinnevelly, applied the methods which had been so successful in reconstructing the history of the Indo-European family of languages to the South Indian languages, which he labelled the Dravidian language family. Caldwell had two goals, the first being to add to European knowledge of the languages of the world and, in particular, to establish the significance of Dravidian in relation to other Indian language families. The other was to stimulate the 'native literate' of South India 'to an intelligent interest in the comparative study of their own languages'. He noted, as had many British before, that Indians had long studied grammar, but in a regressive and unscientific way. They were more interested in mystifying the knowledge of languages than contributing to the 'progressive refinement' of it, making it the means of clear communication. By studying the Dravidian languages comparatively the native literate would come to realize that 'language has a history of its own which, throwing light upon all other history', would thereby be capable of 'rendering ethnology and archaeology possible'.[151]

The power of the comparative method was that it enabled the practitioner to classify, bound and control variety and difference. At a phenomenological level the British discovered hundreds of languages and dialects, and these could be arranged into neat diagrams and tables which showed the relationship of languages to each other. As with genealogies, which could represent all the members of a 'family' or descent group visually as a tree with a root, a trunk, branches and even twigs, so could dialects and languages be similarly represented and grouped. Significantly, the trees always seemed to be Northern European ones, like oaks and maples, and the British never seemed to think of using the most typical South Asian tree, the banyan, which grew up, out and down at the same time.

The comparative method implied linear directionality: things, ideas, institutions could be seen as progressing through stages to some end or goal. It could also be used to establish regression, decay, and decadence, the movement through time away from some pristine, authentic, original starting point, a 'Golden Age' in the past. The decline rather than the progress model came increasingly to be applied by the Europeans and some Indians to the textual

---

pande and Peter Edwin Hook (eds.), *Aryan and Non Aryan in India*, Michigan Papers on South and Southeast Asian Studies, no. 14 (Ann Arbor, 1979), pp. 153–4.
[151] Caldwell, pp. xi–xii.

traditions of India. In this view the present, because of the conquest, was seen as a period of dissolution and retrogression. This could be reversed by the re-establishment of 'authentic' and pure versions of the great sacred works of the ancient Hindus.

C.P. Brown, in constructing a Telugu dictionary, after several false starts decided to establish his corpus of lexical items by standardizing several texts, one of which was Manu Charitra. He assembled a group of learned assistants and collected upwards of a dozen manuscript versions of the texts. These manuscripts, he wrote, 'swarmed with errors', which his assistants 'adjusted by guess as they went along'. Brown had copies made of each manuscript, leaving alternate pages blank with the verses numbered. He had a number of clerks with several copies of the manuscript in front of them, as well as 'three professors', masters of 'grammar and prosody, both Sanskrit and Telagu'. The verses were then read out, discussed by the pundits, with Brown deciding which version was correct, 'just as a judge frames a decree out of conflicting evidence.'[152]

Brown, through this procedure, was creating what he thought of as an 'authentic' text. With the advent of printing in India, which was simultaneously developing along with the European ideas about how texts were constituted and transmitted, this was to have a powerful effect in standardizing the Telugu language and its literature. Implicit in this process were several European assumptions about literature. In European theory texts have authors who create or record what had previously been transmitted orally or through writing. Before the advent of printing it was assumed that texts 'swarmed with errors' because of the unreliability of the scribes, leading to the corruption of the original and pure version created by the author.

Europeans in the nineteenth century saw literature as being conditioned by history, with an author building on and knowing great works of thought which he or she, through an act of genius and originality, could affect. Kamal Zvelbil has recently argued that Indians do not order their literature in a temporal linear fashion, but rather by structures and type. 'Literature' in India 'has a simultaneous existence and composes a simultaneous order.'[153] He has also pointed out that persons are constituted differently in India

[152] Brown, p. xv.
[153] Kamil Zvelbil, 'Tamil Literature', in Jan Gonda (ed.), *A History of Indian Literature*, vol. x, fasc. 1 (Wiesbaden, 1974), p. 3.

The Command of Language and the Language of Command 329

than in the West. In India they are less unique individuals and more incumbents of positions in a social order which has pre-existed them and which will continue to exist after their deaths. A poet or writer before the nineteenth century, Zvelbil states, did not invent or create a poem or a literary work, rather they could only express 'an unchanging truth in a traditional form' and by following 'traditional rules'.[154]

The delineation of the cumulative effect of the results of the first half-century of the objectification and reordering through the application of European scholarly methods on Indian thought and culture is beyond the scope of this essay. The Indians who increasingly became drawn into the process of transformation of their own traditions and modes of thought were, however, far from passive. In the long run the authoritative control which the British tried to exercise over new social and material technologies was taken over by Indians and put to purposes which led to the ultimate erosion of British authority. The consciousness of Indians at all levels in society was transformed as they refused to become specimens in a European-controlled museum of an archaic stage in world history.[155]

[154] Ibid., pp. 3–4.

[155] This paper has been long in gestation, much of the research having been done as part of a larger project concerned with British representations of India. This research has been supported by the National Science Foundation, the National Endowment for the Humanities, Research School of Pacific Studies of the Australian National University, and the Lichstern Research Fund of the Department of Anthropology at the University of Chicago. Parts of the paper were presented in a number of institutions since 1978, including Sydney University, the Australian National University, the University of Chicago, Brown University, and the University of California at Santa Cruz. The paper could not have been done without the collections of the Regenstein Library of the University of Chicago and I owe a special debt to Robert Rosenthal, Curator of Special Collections, and Maureen L.P. Patterson, South Asian Bibliographer.

Many colleagues and friends have read and commented on parts of earlier versions of the paper, or have discussed with me the issues which I have tried to explore in this work. These include Michael Silverstein, Ronald Inden, S.N. Mukherjee, A.K. Ramanujan, Aditi Nath Sarkar, C.M. Naim, James Clifford, David Pingree, David Lelyveld and Roger Keesing. My greatest debt is to Ranajit Guha and his colleagues who invited me to present the penultimate version in Canberra in November 1982. Special thanks are due to Ms Julie McCarthy, who has miraculously made sense out of my ill-typed, ungrammatical and mis-spelt final draft.

[4]

Knowing the Country: Empire and Information in India

C. A. BAYLY

University of Cambridge

Kingsley Martin's critique of imperialism was born out of socialist rationalism and long overseas lecture tours. But in Leonard Woolf, his friend and periodic replacement at the offices of the *New Statesman*, we have a confidant who had, for several years before 1914, abandoned the rarefied circles of Bloomsbury, to become a civil administrator in Ceylon. Woolf's experience of colonial government had soured him from the beginning. He came to feel that the British were eternally shut out from knowledge of the lives of the Ceylonese subjects by an almost palpable curtain of ignorance and racial prejudice.[1] Those temples of accumulated colonial knowledge, the district offices where he worked, were 'great monuments of official incompetence, bottle-necks of delay'. When he tried to galvanize into action these places of sacred lore, the squeals of rage, from Briton and Ceylonese alike, were louder than if he had trespassed into the holiest Buddhist shrine. Yet, for all that, Woolf remained a devout believer in the individualist myth that sustained colonial rule: the ideal of the lone colonial officer and sage, standing at the centre of a web of untainted knowledge, the man who 'knows the country'. British rule might be saved from damnation if liberal judgement were based on pure information. The problem was that, at some level, information had to come from a

This paper was originally given in May 1990 as the annual Kingsley Memorial Lecture under the auspices of the Centre of South Asian Studies, University of Cambridge. I am greatly honoured that the Committee of Management asked me to give the lecture. I am indebted to my Cambridge colleagues for help, and especially, to Dr Susan Bayly, Dr Seema Alavi, Dr Katherine Prior and Dr Radhika Singha. I have also benefited from the comments of members of seminars at the Queen's University, Belfast, and the School of Oriental and African Studies, University of London. Professor Michael Fisher has done pioneering work on the Persian newsletter system. It is hoped that our papers strengthen one another.

[1] L. Woolf, *Autobiography*, vol. i, *1880–1911*, pp. 162–5.

4   C. A. BAYLY

'native informant', an agent, a spy, an 'approver' who turned King's
Evidence, and, by their very nature, such agencies could not be
trusted.

It is because of this dilemma, one feels, that the world of the news-
collector, the spy and the exotic informant exercised such a strong
fascination for the British mind in the East. It is a thread running
through the few classics of Anglo-Indian literature. Meadows
Taylor's, *Memoirs of a Thug*, published in 1839, concerns the secret lore
of the stranglers. *Kim* was trained as a spy for the Great Game of
espionage against the Russians in central Asia. John Masters, an
underrated author, returned constantly to the theme of Englishmen or
Eurasians who penetrated oriental knowledge in novels such as *The
Night Runners of Bengal*, which concerns the Mutiny, and the *Venus of
Konpara* which deals with the subtle machinations of 'tribal' people
within a native state.

These literary themes had an early and classic statement in a
revealing passage at the beginning of Sir John Kaye's great history of
the Indian mutiny and rebellion of 1857–59. 'We know little of Native
Indian society', he wrote,[2] 'beyond its merest externals, the colour of
the people's skins, the form of their garments, the outer aspects of
their houses. That History while it states broad results, can often only
surmise causes . . .'. Indeed, 'our' ignorance was matched by 'their'
subtle lines of information and secret knowledges. 'It is a fact that
there is a certain description of news, which travels in India, from one
station to another with a rapidity almost electric'; it conveyed 'an
uneasy feeling—an impression that something had happened,
"though they [the British] could not discern the shape thereof" '. It
was as likely as not to have been conveyed by a venerable, bearded
'native of respectable aspect . . . who salaamed an English gentleman'
from his ambling pony as he passed, though all the while he was the
veritable 'messenger of evil'. The passage suggests that, for Kaye, the
'respectable native' is a Muslim *maulavi* or a learned servant of a
native court. Kaye goes on later to implicate in clandestine communication that other great agent of malign intelligence for the British, 'the
Dharma Sabha of Bengal', 'the Great Brahminical Institution'.[3]

The theme of this paper is the creation and atrophy of channels of
information between subject and ruler in colonial south Asia, which
made Empire possible, but also defined the roles of some important
groups in its society. Yet this issue touches not only the British

[2] *Kaye's and Malleson's History of the Indian Mutiny of 1857–8*, i, Sir John Kaye (1897–
98; reprint, London, 1971), 361.   [3] *Ibid.*, p. 363.

Empire. Indigenous Indian polities, it will be argued, were constituted to an unusual degree through their networks of espionage and information collection, and peculiarly vulnerable to the distortion or contamination of these networks.

Here we can do little more than survey a large area of evidence and scholarship. But the paper suggests that to view south Asian society and its states from the perspective of the accumulation and transmission of information might bring significant benefits. This approach might help, for instance, to focus more usefully the debate between those who see south Asian regimes, including the British Raj, as loose, superficial structures and those who see in them powerful agents of centralization. Any 'centralization' of military or fiscal resources implies some prior collation of information about their distribution and the knowledge to determine their optimal use. So networks of information gathering, spies, informers and collaters of gossip, were more than useful adjuncts to power and legitimacy. They were integral to them.

Again, an approach to the problems of south Asian government and society along these lines may help to demonstrate how 'oriental knowledge' was actually generated in detail, and to illuminate in particular the role of 'native informants' in its creation.[4] How, and by whom, one might ask, were the 'decentred discourses' of Indian society 'centred' and formed into those knowledges which, it is asserted, sustained colonial power?

Intelligence Agencies in Indian Political Theory and Practice

Several historians have noted that traditional Indian sources consider the issue of intelligence and political communication in considerable detail. From the time of the *Artha Shastra*, Hindu texts elaborated on the importance of intelligence-gathering by ambassadors in enemy kingdoms, and of spies and informers within the home kingdom.[5] The

---

[4] See, e.g., Shahid Amin (ed.), W. Crooke, *A Glossary of North Indian Peasant Life* (reprint, Delhi, 1989), editor's introduction, pp. xxx–xxxiii; B. Cohn has been concerned with British knowledge of Indian society throughout his career: see, *An Anthropologist among the Historians and Other Essays* (Delhi, 1987); more recently, 'The command of language and the language of command' in R. Guha (ed.), *Subaltern Studies*, iv (Delhi, 1985). Dr Sandria Freitag has recently been writing on the approver (criminal informer) system in unpublished papers. For the anthropological interest in the 'native informant', M. Fisher, *Writing Culture* (London, 1988).

[5] Wendy Doniger with Brian K. Smith (ed., trans.), *The Laws of Manu* (London, 1991), pp. 151, 225–6.

6   C. A. BAYLY

king's cunning knowledge (*rajniti*) was generated by his success in
training his spies, his 'eyes and ears'. His enlightened knowledge
(*buddhi*) was then to work on the pool of information created by able
sleuths. For instance, a Hindu treatise of the fifteenth century A.D.,
derived ultimately from the *Artha Shastra*, remarked on the duties of
ambassadors:

> An ambassador should secretly communicate with the spies of his own lord
> stationed in places of pilgrimage, hermitages and temples, in the guise of
> hermits pretending to study the sastras [holy books].[6]

> As, in a sacrifice priests are guided by the Vedic Sutras [chants or hymns],
> so the king can undertake any action guided by the spies. Spies should be
> carefully fashioned for their assignments like vessels for a ritual.[7]

> Wandering spies may be of reckless type, mendicant or recluse type,
> sacrificer or black magician type and poisoner type, or in the guise of persons
> of noble character.[8]

Spies, then, are more than the 'low informers' of Tudor England,
more even than the 'secret servants' of the Hanoverians; in the world
of Indian statecraft they were a vital adjunct of kingship. Mobile
spies, like a secret army, should concert with other intelligence agents
and penetrate enemy coalitions at key points of social and political
fracture. They should approach, particularly, 'disaffected officers,
frontier guards and foresters'.[9]

This tradition, and the texts associated with it, highlight important
aspects of Indian conceptions of surveillance, spying and information-
collection. First, despite the popular conception that the
Arthashastric tradition was 'machiavellian'—that is that it begins
with an assumption that all men are 'evil'—there is no suggestion that
covert political arts stand outside dharmic morality, let alone raj-
dharma. Secondly, the tradition, by mentioning the Sutras, the
Shastras and the Hindu holy places, indirectly associates one level of
intelligence and information-gathering with brahminical or high caste
status. By later convention, the best and 'most intelligent' spies were
brahmins, whose activities could be masked by their residual priestly
role. This was a tradition noted by Europeans, including the British,
who in the later eighteenth century began to recruit Indian intelligence experts to their service.[10]

---

[6] Rajendra Lal Mitra (ed.), *The Nitisara [Elements of polity] by Kamandaki* revised
with an English translation by Sisir Kumar Mitra (Calcutta, 1982), p. 262.
[7] *Ibid.*, p. 269.   [8] *Ibid.*   [9] *Ibid.*, p. 266.
[10] Note by Agnew to Sloper, ? 1787, regarding Col. Fullarton's reorganization of
the Hircarrah System, Home Miscellaneous vol. 84, Oriental and India Office

On the other hand, the texts associate the king through tracking and spying during military campaigns with the forests, and by implication with 'tribal' people. Tribals (*atavika bala*) are mentioned as a branch of the royal army.[11] Yet the terms 'tribal' and 'forester' are inadequate translations. What is indicated in the texts is the inhabitants of the domain beyond the arable, the domain of magic, hunting, asceticism and the arts of tracking and spying on animals and man. Kings, and even gods, might take on the characteristics of huntsmen to track their enemies through the jungle. There are several occasions in the Mahabharata and Ramayana when gods and kings in double disguise penetrate the enemy's camp by pretending to be a 'forester'. Indeed, rather than being marginal, the domain of the forest lay quite close to the heart of kingship. Kings formed their armies, in part, from the men of the forests who traditionally added auspiciousness to his reign by placing the *tilak* mark on his brow and employing magic (a covert ritual art) and spying (a covert political art) on his behalf. In recent times a close relationship continued to exist between king and 'tribal'. For instance, there was a ritual and military bond between the Maratha kings and the Bhils,[12] and between the kings of north Malabar and the Kurichiyar and Kurumba hillmen. These people sustained the famous freedom-fighter Kerala Varma, the Palassi Raja, for many years in his guerrilla war against the British between 1798 and 1806, warning him of the enemy's approach and showing him the pathways.[13]

The great importance of surveillance and information-collection for Indian kingship was a reflection of social complexity. Despite its great size India was an information-rich society. From an early period large proportions of the population travelled long distances in connection with marriage, pilgrimage, and networks of trade and marketing.

Records, London (OIOR) (hereafter, Home Misc.), pp. 911–23; S. C. Hill's notes in the Home Misc. series catalogue records under this item that de Souza had also reported the employment of Brahmins as intelligence agents at the time of the first Portuguese contact with India.

[11] Mitra (ed.), *Nitisara*, pp. 389, 397 (but 'foresters' by their very nature are not to be trusted).

[12] A. M. Deshpande, *John Briggs in Maharashtra: A Study of District Administration under Early British Rule* (Delhi, 1987), pp. 70–110, briefly mentions arrangements between Maratha rulers and the Bhils; Briggs's report on Maratha–Bhil relations is in Pol. and Secret Cons. vol. 60, 22 June 1825, OIOR, cited in Stewart N. Gordon, 'Bhils and the Idea of a Criminal Tribe in Nineteenth-century India', in Anand A. Yang (ed.), *Crime and Criminality in British India* (Tucson, 1985), pp. 128–39.

[13] William Logan, *Malabar* (reprint Madras, 1951), i, 542, 546, iii, 364–7, for Kurichiyars, Kurumbas and the Palassi Raja; see also, A. D. Luiz, *The Tribes of Kerala* (Delhi, 1962), p. 110; for a general narrative of the revolt, Home Misc. vol. 607.

8   C. A. BAYLY

Amongst the higher castes rules of endogamy and exogamy imposed patterns of long-distance marriage which required continued communication with distant towns and villages. The repute of the great all-India pilgrimage centres was spread by word of mouth and texts in their honour. From the sixteenth century at least bodies of pilgrims as large as 100,000 traversed huge distances from central and south India to attend the great centres of the Ganges.[14] Money was generally used in these networks from the thirteenth century or before. The variety of local coinages did not imply a lack of economic integration. Flows of written communication between merchants dispersed and collected information on the prices of metals and produce, and on local events which might impinge on trade.

Even the physical means of transport were more developed than it might appear, at least during the dry season. The people of the north Indian plains had devised a variety of forms of fast wheeled transport using camels, ponies and small horses.[15] River transport was also well developed. During the height of the Mughal empire there were more than 200,000 river boatmen on the route between Delhi and Bengal alone.[16] On the eve of the introduction of railways a British postal official demonstrated that traffic on the major north Indian roads was considerably higher than that on European roads before the coming of the railways; as much as ten per cent of the population per annum was estimated to have undertaken a journey that required staying away at least one night.[17] Social communication was proportionately dense. All the great Indian states and empires attempted to foster and organize these extensive networks through systems of runners and intelligence-gatherers (*harkaras* lit. 'do-alls', factotums, and *kasids*, Arabic for runner).[18] Along with the provision of mints, or of resthouses and serais for merchants, the smooth functioning and protection of the runner system was itself an important manifestation of successful kingship.

However, flows of information and news were unevenly distributed in space, in time, and between different social groups. For one thing,

[14] See, e.g., S. M. Bhardwaj, *Hindu Places of Pilgrimage in India. A Study in Cultural Geography* (Berkeley, 1973); K. H. Prior, 'The British Administration of Hinduism in North India, 1780–1900', unpubl. Ph.D. diss., University of Cambridge, 1990.

[15] J. Deloche, 'Wheeled Transport in North India', paper given at the Leiden–Amsterdam conference on technology transfer, June 1991.

[16] H. K. Naqvi, *Urban Centres and Industries in Upper India* (London, 1968).

[17] [A. Postmaster], *Project for a Railway in India* (London, 1846), pp. 10–20.

[18] H. Yule and A. Burnell, *Hobson-Jobson* (London, 1903), pp. 430, 262–3; H. H. Wilson, *A Glossary of Judicial and Revenue Terms* (London, 1855), p. 199.

the monsoons had a profound impact. During a full four months of the year—from late May to September in north India—roads were often impassable, warfare changed tempo, trade and pilgrimage were severely curtailed. By tradition the king retreated into his monsoon palace, adopting a reclusive, almost priestly character and storing up spiritual energy. The cycle of social and ritual life slowed almost to a dead stop. Information from outside was often reduced to a trickle. Small kingdoms went through an annual metamorphosis. A British report of 1799 contends that it was necessary to more than double the numbers of runners on a given communications route during the monsoons;[19] even during the dry season runners should be no more than six miles apart in difficult terrain.[20]

The great aspirants to continental empire, the Mughals in the sixteenth and seventeenth century, the Marathas and the British in the eighteenth century, could not afford the luxury of this altered state. Their armies and siege trains had to be ready to move to a specified place immediately the rains ended to snuff out the enemy coalitions that took to plunder as the floods went down. Otherwise the campaigning season was too short. Worse, they would lose control of the first or autumn harvest upon which all wealth and power depended. These Indian emperors crossed the Rubicon not once, but every year as the flood plains dwindled. In order to know where to dispatch their massive forces, and against whom, in this annual military gamble, the great kings desperately needed regular and prior news reports despatched by secret pathways which bypassed the floods.

Secondly, the cultural, linguistic and religious heterogeneity of the country put a premium on accurate intelligence. India was a densely-knit society, never a 'subsistence economy' for at least two millennia. But information tended to pass along specialist networks in inaccessible forms. Merchants, for instance, had their professional knowledge. While account books had attained a pattern common to most parts of India by the seventeenth century, individual merchant groups and families within them, employed different types of merchant shorthand and argot (*mahajani*) which cloaked their secrets. Travelling Islamic sufi mystics or Hindu ascetics on pilgrimage, carried large quantities

[19] W. Palmer, Resident at Poona to Lord Mornington, 6 July 1799, Home Misc. vol. 574.
[20] Resdt Mysore to Sec. Govt, Fort St George, 20 Nov. 1799, 'Refusal of the Peshwa to admit the establishment of a post through their territory', 1659, Board's Collections, OIOR (hereafter BC).

of information, but their networks did not merge, even if they crossed. Periodic migrants carried information about particular communities in local languages. Public knowledge, if we can call it that, was dense, but it was specialized and the lines of communication which brought it were fragmented. Empires and states therefore positioned news-writers and spies carefully, to tie together bundles of information from different cultural networks, and to pass them to the centre, the imperial cities or camps.

Surveillance and Moral Suasion: The Heart of Indian Government

Under the Emperor Akbar, the flow of information was at times very rich. Even Aurangzeb, who tried in his first twenty years to recon-solidate the Empire on personal loyalties and Islamic piety, received huge quantities of written reports. Consequently, resources could be collected and used effectively. By contrast, the failure of Empire after 1680 was reflected in, possibly even implicated with, a failure of knowledge, of the flow of information, and of the central ruling elite's canny understanding of local circumstances. The same can be said about the more effective of the 'successor states' of the Mughal dominion through to the kingdom of Ranjit Singh in the early nineteenth century.

The formal structure has often been described.[21] Imperial news-writers (the *waqyanavis*) collected and processed the information col-lected by the newswriters placed in every subdistrict throughout the Empire. These men wrote regular reports on the doings of officials and local magnates, on plunderers and malefactors, occasionally on the affairs of merchants. They gathered material from other officials: local judges and the officers commanding in the cities. The emperors and provincial governors also maintained sets of secret agents and writers (the *khufia navis*) who could act as a check on the other writers and postal officials.[22] The newsreports (*akhbarat*) were copied to the imperial centre and to other officials. Officials routinely divulged their contents to other literate men, so that the contents of the weekly or even daily newsreport, fleshed out in private newsreports and mer-

---

[21] M. A. Nayeem, *Evolution of Postal Communications and Administration in the Deccan (from 1294 A.D. to the Formation of the Hyderabad State in 1724 A.D.)* (Hyderabad, 1969), provides one of the best overviews; *Ain-i-Akbari*, trans. Francis Gladwin as *Ayeen Akbery or the Institutes of the Emperor Akber* (London, 1800), i, 213.

[22] Nayeem, *Postal Communications*, p. 5.

chant letters, were the main item of discussion in the morning bazaar. As in the Hindu texts on kingship, so in the great administrative manuals of the empire, including the *Ain-i-Akbari*, the function and duties of the newswriters are detailed with care. Fragmented and increasingly farmed out to private hands, this system was still capable of mobilizing a huge amount of information as late as the 1850s, when the newsreports were still being read by the oriental linguists of the English East India Company. The mass of official documents and orders along with private letters was transported across the country by a dense network of runners and camel *harkaras* maintained by village cesses or by the funds of private individuals. Akbar reorganized the runner or *harkara* system and strengthened the powers of the networks of *dak darogas* or 'postmasters general' who forwarded official letters and reports alongside private ones.[23]

The effectiveness of the system depended not only on the loyalty, conscientiousness and sophistication of the personnel who manned it, but also on the social context in which it was set. At the height of the Mughal Empire in north India, literacy in both reading and writing was probably not notably high by east Asian or European standards. Judging by the situation in the late eighteenth century, admittedly after a century of political flux, and only in north India, perhaps 8% to 10% of the adult male population could read and write.[24] Yet the interleaving of Hindu commercial intelligence and book-keeping with the tradition of Indo-Muslim aristocratic literacy made the pool of talent a powerful one. Nor in this culture was the collection of information divorced from more abstract and structured thought. Important Mughal historians, for instance, were sons or relatives of newswriters.[25] Practical skills such as accountancy (*siyaq*) attracted increasing numbers of manuals.[26] Local descriptions and histories, once rather formal lists of holy men, rulers, climes and products in the Islamic classical style, appear to have become more complex, and more cognisant of local economic and social conditions in the seventeenth and eighteenth centuries.[27]

[23] M. F. Lokhandawala (ed., trans.), *Mirat-i-Ahmadi* (Baroda, 1965), pp. 357–8.

[24] Little work has been done on this issue but see J. Hagen, 'Indigenous Society . . . and Education in Patna District, 1811–1951', unpubl. diss. University of Virginia, 1981.

[25] A. Schimmel, *Islamic Literatures of India; History of Indian Literature*, viii, i (Wiesbaden, 1973), 47.

[26] *Siyaq* or accountancy was a science which linked the world of the Hindu merchant and the Muslim *mutsaddi* or manager.

[27] C. Curwen (ed.), *The Balwantnamah or Tuhfa-i-Toza* (Allahabad, 1875) and

12   C. A. BAYLY

The world of the Indo-Islamic literati was not only subject to a system of reportage, it also initiated a dialogue on rights and duties with its rulers. The local memorial attested often by 'the Sheikhs, Sayyids, *karoris* [local office-holders] and *mahajans* [respectable merchants] of a locality incorporated and enhanced the sense of the neighbourhood, of the *qasbah* and its dependencies.'[28] Such memorials (*mahzars* and *surathals*)[29] were not simply by-products of 'government'; they were the essence of righteous rule, a dialogue on rights and duties between subject and ruler. The ideology of *sharia* afforced by Hindu and local custom was the informing spirit of the state. Terms such as 'recalcitrant' and 'stiff-necked' seen in these documents were not simply terms of abuse, they were statements that the zamindars and magnates referred to lay outside the discourse of Timurid rule and Mughal respectability. The good subject was to submit himself voluntarily to the will of the ruler, as a son to a father, or a believer to God.

Systems which historians have tended to classify as 'administration' and 'police' are better seen as agencies of surveillance and persuasion, and both exhortation and information-collection were equally important. The hierarchy of rural 'police' running down from the circle chief (*daroga*) to the inspector (*thanadar*), the armed constable (*barkandazi*), and police *harkara* was one such agency. In major cities the *kotwal* headed a similar chain of command which connected with the watchmen of the different city quarters.[30]

Indo-Persian political culture had also thrown up more specialized surveillance systems. Two important examples of these were irrigation canal guards and moral regulators (*muhtasibs*). Canal guards for the great Ali Mardan Khan system near Delhi were drawn from the Rajput communities of the eastern Gangetic plain (the *Purbiyas*). This was probably an attempt to avoid collusion on the part of the guards with local zamindars who were constantly seeking to make illegal

Khairuddin Muhammad Illahabadi, 'Tarikh-i-Jaunpur' (trans.), Cambridge University Library, MSS; cf. for a statistical and topographical work similar to that of European contemporaries, Bahadur Singh, 'Yadgar-i-Bahaduri', MS Add. 30786, British Library.

[28] G. N. Saletore (ed.), *A Calendar of Oriental Records: U.P. State Records Series*, iii, pp. 1–13 for examples of *mahzars* from 1658–1813.

[29] See Wilson, *Glossary* p. 494; *surathals* were still in use, attested by the law officers and *raises* in the early days of British rule; see, e.g., attested *surathal* from Pargana Daroga Cowreea Telhanee, 12 Oct. 1803, 'Disturbances in the Conquered and Ceeded Provinces', 2954, Board's Collections, F/4/169, IOL (hereafter, BC).

[30] Statements by the Indian judges of Mirzapur and Benares on the 'police' of the cities, 1786–90, published in G. N. Saletore (ed.), *Banaras Affairs*, i (Allahabad, nd.), pp. 63–138.

cuttings in the canals and drain off the water.[31] The *muhtasib*'s function or duty of moral surveillance was reinforced by Aurangzeb in the late seventeenth century.[32] His target was drinkers, prostitutes, eunuch-makers, hoarders, forestallers, forgers, and others who violated God's law. However, as the famous eighteenth-century Bengali statesman Hakim Reza Khan acknowledged, the rigorous application of *sharia* by the *muhtasib* agency was impossible given the constant complaints of the 'tribe of Hindus'.[33]

There is little early evidence on the detailed working of these systems, but written correspondence between darogas and their subordinates during the early stages of the Gurkha War, 1814–16, in Gorakhpur, Tirhut and adjoining parts of Awadh, reveals the surveillance authorities at work before British rule had significantly altered their operations.[34] Surprisingly, even the lower levels of these officials communicated with their seniors by letter, and filed complex reports. The constable or *daroga*'s *harkaras* in turn gleaned their information from community watchmen (*pasobans*)[35] and also from 'foresters' (*bantirias*).[36] These were persons, often from hunting and pastoralist backgrounds themselves, who held land revenue grants in the Terai in

[31] G. Blane, Superintendent of the Canal, to Ochterlony, Resident at Delhi, N. K. Sinha (ed.), *Selections from Ochterlony Papers (1818–25) in the National Archives of India* (Calcutta, 1964), pp. 122–35. Blane mentions 'Buxarie' and 'Porubee' mutsaddis and bildars associated with the Mughal Daroga of the canal in the early eighteenth century; J. F. Richards (ed.), *Document Forms for Official Orders of Appointment in the Mughal Empire* (Cambridge, 1986), doct 224b.

[32] M. Z. Siddiqi, 'The Muhtasib under Aurangzeb', *Medieval India Quarterly* 5 (1963), 113–19.

[33] Murshidabad Procs, 2 July 1771, Range 69, OIOR, cited in A. M. Khan, *The Transition in Bengal. A Study of Saiyid Mahomed Reza Khan* (Cambridge, 1976), p. 279.

[34] See, e.g., report from the Daroga of Bansee 20 Jan., 1815, Home Misc. 651, OIOR, ff. 625, and extensive correspondence between inferior 'police' officials in British territory in Awadh in Home Misc. 649.

[35] *Pasobans* were often Pasis, a ritually low caste in Hindustan; another village spy and the runner, associated with the *patwari*, who often appears in the correspondence was the *goret*. Runners (*daurias* here) of the *dak* in pre-colonial Benares were supposed to be Chamars, a low caste, but in the cities Chamars had apparently compounded their service and had people employed on the sums they raised (see, Saletore (ed.), *Banaras Affairs*, i, p. 88, reply by Ibrahim Ali Khan. In Maharashtra village watchmen were Mahars who removed dead cattle, ran errands for village officers, kept watch on the village property and 'were generally principal witnesses in disputes about boundaries of fields, etc.' (I. Karve and V. Dandekar, *Anthropometric Measurements of Maharashtra* (Poona, 1951), p. 35); this association of the lowest level of information collection with low caste, or outcaste tribal status, paralleling the role of the Brahmin at the apex, also applied to runners, see below fn. 69.

[36] Translation of a Report from Daroga of Pallee, Gorakhpur, 28 Dec. 1814, Home Misc. 649; for *bantiria*, see Wilson, *Glossary*, p. 157.

return for their services as intelligence agents. The *daroga* and his men also made use of the informal networks of information run by the local landholders, the pupils of Vaishnavite 'monasteries' and people going on pilgrimage. In fact, the whole operation bore a remarkable similarity to the one described in the arthashastric texts.

Some preliminary points about the role of intelligence-gathering in pre-colonial polities do seem to emerge. Intelligence was designed to alert the ruler to infractions of moral law and true obedience rather than simply to punish 'crime'. For the latter was really the preserve of the community. The agents of intelligence were also the agents of persuasion and compromise, the men who sought to reassure the populace of the omniscience of the emperor's gaze. To this end the armed constable carried the badge of the emperor (the *mohur* or royal image). John Richards recently described the Mughal system as a 'powerful' and 'centralising' one.[37] Others, from contemporary observers to recent historians, have seen it as weak and ineffective. The impression of weakness has arisen partly because people have assumed that the absorption of a vast amount of revenue in 'collection charges' and service grants was similar to what the British in the nineteenth century saw as 'defalcations from the revenue': dead losses to the state. However, if we see Indo-Persian 'administration' as an exercise in surveillance and persuasion, then its workings indeed seem powerful, flexible, and intricate. It resembled a delicate filature of information and guidance threading in and out of complex local patterns of communication and loyalty. On the other hand, the weakness of the system was its over-dependence on a few key individuals and their loyalty, and on a general inclination to submit to royal authority. The boundary between flexibility and breakdown could be easily crossed.

There is one final point about the language of communication in detail within the lower echelons of the state: description by caste played an important if not yet dominant part in it. In the ordinary language of *mahzars* and *surathals*, caste names are used routinely, especially for the poor and for Hindus.[38] In the *darogas*' cor-

---

[37] Richards, *Document Forms*, p. 10; for the alternative view, e.g. as early as 1678, Charnock wrote that the 'King's *husbul-hukm* [exalted order] is of as small value as an ordinary governor's', cited in Ian Bruce Watson, *Foundation for Empire. English Private Trade in India, 1659–1760* (Delhi, 1980), p. 284.

[38] See, e.g., Arzee of Thanadar of Lowtun (?) nr. Nichlour, 13 Jan. 1815, Home Misc. 651, pp. 460–1. Here the Thanadar's and Daroga's reports list the castes of villagers who have lost their property to the Nepalis; cf. Saletore, *Oriental Records*, iii, 34 (sale deed, 1677), 50 (agreement, 1801); in documents such as these, caste attribu-

respondence caste names are one part of a grid which also includes landholding status and Mughal conceptions of honour and respectability. The use of all these social markers made it possible for an official or a resident body to convey to the ruler very precise social information—the feel of a village or a local conflict—with great ease and dispatch. Before jumping to conclusions about the colonial 'creation' of caste categories, historians and sociologists might well note that caste description had already become an aspect of administrative language in pre-colonial states, and one which was abstracted from hierarchical relations in the locality.

From the locally resident bodies of scholars and officials the information networks available to the state threaded out into the wider society: bazaar writers, beggars, holy men, midwives, informers, professional forgers, prostitutes and temple-dancers plied information-rich trades between communities and regions. Within communities, in turn, barbers, midwives, bards and the messengers of caste panchayats trafficked in the information which kept the community itself informed and self-conscious. From time to time, these agencies were coopted into the service of indigenous and colonial authority. Indeed, the source of the power and influence of several problematic groups or categories in Indian society becomes clearer if we consider them in relation to transactions in information. Here three groups, already alluded to, seem noteworthy: religious specialists and astrologers, women and so-called Indian tribal people.

The Sufi orders, those mystical adepts of Islamic knowledge, played an important part in indigenous medicine. They gave counsel to the barren, disturbed and mentally-ill, but had their finger on the pulse of the whole social body.[39] Astute kings and nobles took trouble to consult their assessments of local feeling as well as their religious knowledge. Manucci, the Venetian, mentions the throngs of 'worldly mendicants' (*fakhirs*) who made assignations and passed information, especially among the women's quarters of the great households.[40] Again, astrologers and sooth-sayers, a critical social group unduly ignored by scholars, provided a vast private intelligence service on day-to-day matters, as well as the motions of the stars: 'even the bazaars swarm with these folk, and by this means they find out all

tions are used unsystematically, but by the 1830s they are invariably used in criminal cases.

[39] Sudhir Kakar, *Shamans, Mystics and Doctors. A Psychological Enquiry into India and its Teaching Traditions* (Delhi, 1982).

[40] Niccolao Manucci, *Storio do Mogor, or Mogul India, 1653–1703. Translated by W. Irvine* (London, 1907), ii, 11–12.

that passes in the houses.'[41] Some groups acahieved quite an extra-ordinary geographical range. The *unani hakims* or itinerant doctors of Peshawar ventured annually as far afield as Bokhara and the Deccan, dispensing medicine, spiritual advice and magical spells. One of the most knowledgeable groups in Indo-Muslim society, they were suc-cessfully pumped for information by members of Elphinstone's mis-sion to Kabul, 1808–11. [42]

In a society characterized by extended marriage networks and upper-class polygamy, women in general were a critical source of intelligence, not simply carriers of wealth or political alliance. Women retained connections and sources of information in their far-distant home territories. Newsreports were read in princely harems;[43] royal ladies were judged by their ability to act as intermediaries in diplo-matic manoeuvring; the emperors married often, and with care, to maximize intelligence as much as to secure support. Within com-munities midwives could convey and collect information, usually hid-den from the eyes of the male ruler. In fact, women's influence in pre-colonial society was greatly enhanced by their access to, and collation of, political and community information.

As we have suggested, one of the richest sources of all were the so-called 'tribal people' of the Indian subcontinent. This 'difficult cate-gory' of nomads, hunter-gatherers, archers and people who just don't fit into anybody else's models, are often defined in both histories and anthropologies as outsiders. They were supposedly cut off from Hindu and Muslim society by language, religion or kinship structure. At best they are conceded military prowess and the capacity to make dangerous magic. Yet, paradoxically, until recent times 'tribals' were found right at the heart of state power. It becomes easier to under-stand them if we consider the cunning skills they had, and could deploy in the wider society. Tribal people knew the paths, the route-ways, the products of the forest, the care of animals, the backways, the location of water and forage, the quickest way to move men and information from one place to another: not surprising, then, that the classical texts refer to tribal people as another critical limb of army and state.

---

[41] *Ibid.*, i, 213.

[42] Reports on Elphinstone's mission to Kabul, Home Misc. 658, f. 383.

[43] Nayeem, *Postal Communications*, p. 6, notes that the intelligence reports were generally read by the Mughal Emperor at night in his private quarters; rulers had traditionally used marriage to wives from different regions to increase knowledge and surveillance, see e.g., H. K. Sherwani, *The Bahmanis of the Deccan* (Hyderabad, 1953), pp. 144–5.

One particular group, the Bedas[44] of the central Indian plateau are an instructive case. They played an important part in the emergence of the kingdom of Mysore to subcontinental power in the eighteenth century, but also founded their own ruling houses. On the face of it, it is difficult to understand them at all. They appear at different points as hunters, archers, sappers and miners, and as magicians; their women are sometimes temple dancers and courtesans. What was most important was not their lineage structure, relative purity, or magical prowess—the staples of historical anthropology—but the fact that all their activities formed an interlocking package of skills in information, spying, and the use of long-distance connections. As 'foresters' their knowledge of wood made them adepts at archery and the making of props for siege tunnels. Their movement with armies made it possible for them to place their women as temple dancers or as great men's concubines. Since the ability to read songs and ballads was a prerequisite for a successful singer and dancer, these women were among the few members of their sex who were both literate and had regular access to men.[45] They became an important information network. 'Tribal' people were also disproportionately represented among the official runners and spies. The spy-masters appear to have been Brahmins or Muslims operating from large cities, mosques and temples. But the runners themselves were drawn from tribal people such as the Ramnad Kallars in south India,[46] Bhils and Kolis in the west, and Kurumbas in the southwest.[47]

Caste, class, 'tribe', state, 'colonial discourse'—all those incubuses of Indian history and anthropology, and presumably of the sociology of other societies too—appear in a significantly different light from the vantage point of transactions in information and special knowledge.

Information and Political Decline

What of limitations and decay of Indian states? The argument is not simply that the decay of information was an important and revealing

---

[44] *History of Ayder Ali Khan Nabob-Behadur*, by N.N.D.L.T. [de la Tour] (London, 1784), i, 40 on the 'Bayaderes'; cf. Hamilton Buchanan, *A Journey from Madras through the Countries of Mysore, etc.* (London, 1811), i, 178–9.

[45] See Balfour's *Encyclopedia of Southern Asia* . . . (Madras, 1873), i, 925, 'Deva Dasa'.

[46] Fullarton's Hircarrahs, Home Misc. 84.

[47] Tribal people from the Western Ghats were employed as runners and escorts of the pepper crop along the hill routeways; later they were recruited as guides and pioneers in the war against the Palassi Raja. W. Logan, *Malabar Gazetteer*, iii, 364–7; Home Misc. 607; cf. *Mirat-i-Ahmadi*, p. 780.

aspect of what is called the decline of the Mughals. But more: that Indian polities (and here I would include the East India Company) were *peculiarly* vulnerable to the decline of their agents of information; that the Mughals' access to knowledge, for instance, may in some cases have decayed more rapidly than their military or financial resources.

The first point is the simple one: that the links between the rich pools of local information and the imperial centre were highly vulnerable. The colonies of literate men planted in a huge hinterland—the men who provided the newsreports and memorials—were sometimes easily isolated and silenced. After 1670, the Mughal Empire foundered into crisis in central India. It was fighting the powerful mobile army of the Hindu Marathas. The Marathas, a fighting peasant alliance, rich in local knowledge, were able to intercept the imperial messengers, suborn the merchant firms and their postal systems, and displace the newswriters and imperial agents from the networks of small towns. Despite the large amount of information mobilized by surveillance agencies at their height, the emperor might find himself without 'eyes or ears'.[48]

More ominously, the sectional interests of the information-gatherers might pollute and frustrate the imperial system itself. John Fryer, who visited the Emperor in the 1680s, remarked that the great nobles and administration 'live[d] lazily and in pay',[49] during the protracted campaigning. They had an interest in keeping the war spluttering on. So did the newswriters and literati whose wealth and influence were sustained by war. 'Notwithstanding all the formidable numbers' of the Mughal army, 'while the generals and *Vocanovices* [newswriters] consult to deceive the Emperor, on whom he depends for a true state of things',[50] the Emperor could never deliver a decisive blow. When, in 1683, the Moghuls stumbled into war with the English East India Company, the Emperor claimed, probably quite genuinely, that he simply had not been informed that serious conflicts had arisen between the English factors and his local governors.[51] Both parties were attempting to conceal their illicit profits.

---

[48] J. N. Sarkar, *The House of Shivaji* (Delhi, 1940), p. 150, Shivaji was able to use merchant networks to convey his jewellery and private notes between Agra and Aurangabad. The Emperor sent messengers to search all fakhirs and tried to close the *ghats* (presumably through his Bhil feudatories).

[49] J. Fryer, *A New Account of the East Indies and Persia* (reprint London, 1909), ii, 49, 52, cited in Ian Bruce Watson, *Foundation for Empire. English Private Trade in India, 1659–1760* (New Delhi, 1980), p. 282.

[50] Fryer, *New Account*, ii, 52.   [51] Watson, *Foundation*, p. 283.

Thirdly, overstrained imperial agents of control seem to have been diverted into the pursuit of information of a largely symbolic or ideological sort. One need not assume, of course, that the newswriter or memorialist system was ever simply a matter of practical reason or an empirical data-search. It was always, in part, a symbolic affirmation of the omnipresence of the imperial gaze. The Emperors wanted prior warning of faction and disorder not so much to administer but to anticipate infractions of religious law and insults to royal honour. After 1671 the Emperor Aurangzeb devoted an important part of his intelligence system, including the revived *muhtasib* agency, to extirpating moral crime, particularly drinking and the propagation of false Islamic beliefs. What might be called an 'information panic' set in. The functioning of the intelligence agencies of the Empire were set lumbering off at a tangent in the search for 'drinkers' and 'heretics', as the bases of legitimacy of the empire were reorientated.[52]

Such weaknesses and distortions might be fatally intertwined as they were in the Punjab where, after 1704, the Mughals were grappling with the formidable Sikhs. Rumours were heard that Hindu newswriters had connived with the Sikhs, and were allegedly denying the imperial armies vital information about the whereabouts of the enemy's cavalry forces. The centre therefore ordered that all Hindus, many of whom were Khattris with contacts to the local business communities and the Sikh Panth itself, should be dismissed from the office of newswriter, and that all newswriters should be forced to have their beards cut in the Muslim style.[53] Hereafter, the imperial forces were steadily worn down and defeated in the Punjab. Muzaffar Alam's work suggests that, in important respects, this was because they no longer knew what was happening, estranged as they were from a set of people who had unique access to both political and commercial intelligence.

Clearly problems of the raising and deployment of resources remained central to the failure of the Timurid empire. In Rajasthan during the imperial crisis following Aurangzeb's death imperial ambassadors and informants progressively failed to perform their surveillance duties because the centre was unable to mobilize the will and resources to pay them.[54] Nevertheless, the speed of the Mughal

---

[52] Richards, *Document Forms*, no. 230b ('abolisher of forbidden beliefs').
[53] Muzaffar Alam, *The Crisis of Empire in Mughal North India* (Delhi, 1986), pp. 197–9.
[54] G. D. Sharma (ed.), *Vakil Reports Maharajgan (1693–1712 A.D.)* (New Delhi, 1987), see, e.g., nos 68, 78, 79, 81, 86.

debacle is still in need of explanation, particularly since some historians have painted a rosy picture of its health as late as 1700. It may well be that a system whose effectiveness depended so heavily on the twin tactics of surveillance and persuasion was liable to degenerate particularly fast when a few key men, albeit deeply rooted in the community, were removed. To return again to the Gurkha war episode, when this system was still working in the fringes of the province of Awadh, it is notable that the Gurkhas themselves went to considerable trouble to seize the *darogas* and *thanadars* in person.[55] If these eyes, ears and representatives of the enemy state could be eliminated, the whole delicate politics of moral suasion of communities would unravel.

Surveillance and Control: The Eighteenth Century

With the decline of the Mughal empire, the centrally controlled system of newswriters began to disintegrate. In its place a multilateral system, linking together the major post-Mughal polities, began to emerge. The great rulers—the Nawab Vazir, the Nizam, the Marathas and the East India Company—all continued to maintain *vakils* or ambassadors, and alongside them newswriters, at each others' courts. Official newswriters appointed by the respective rulers disseminated information on the courts' daily round, its devotions and major political events. In parallel with this, newswriters assigned by the foreign powers also transmitted private political information to their employers. Confidential agents working on behalf of states, and individual political leaders, submitted further political intelligence and undertook secret missions for their principals. The complex factional politics of the eighteenth century depended on an intricate underpinning of agencies of information—and disinformation—staffed at the senior levels by Muslim literati and Hindu pensmen, mainly Kayasthas and Khattris.

The emergence of regional states within the penumbra of Mughul legitimacy did not necessarily bring about the breakdown of those patterns of inter-regional communication which were accessible at least to the more privileged subjects. Postal systems spanned regional and local states, though, with the decline of Mughal authority, conflicts over their control could be intense. Right at the end of the

---

[55] See, e.g., translation of a report from Motilal, Thanadar of Natchloul, 25 Jan. 1815, encl. in R. Martin to John Adam, 29 Jan. 1815, Home Misc. 649.

century, for instance, Muhammad Waris was daroga of the dak at Cuttack. His establishment of runners regularly sent the letters of the Cuttack agents of local Indian bankers to their Agarwal principals in upper India.[56] He also despatched the letters of the Maratha rulers of Orissa throughout eastern India. In due course, he had been appointed postmaster by the British to link together their agencies in Madras and Bengal. In this way tacit agreements by ruling powers to patronize the same postmasters could keep an integrated mail and intelligence system working. But there were strains. Muhammad Waris, a wealthy shipowner and trader,[57] flourished until he was inveigled by the British into intercepting and passing on to them the Maratha mails. When the Maratha governor of Cuttack accidentally got to know of this, he seized Muhammad Waris's property and threatened to blow him from a gun. Nevertheless, interstate postal systems such as this continued to cross huge distances and zones of war. Despite a generation of troubles throughout the northwest, in 1808 the runner from Kabul still brought newsletters and information to Benares in forty days. He was able to report on events even further to the west in Persia.[58]

Some disruption to long-distance communication inevitably occurred. Agents working within the ambit of the Mughal political culture, for instance, appear to have found it difficult to obtain reliable information on events occurring in the Punjab or the Jat territories for long periods of the eighteenth century.[59] Merchants were sometimes unable to maintain commercial relations over relatively short distances when war had interdicted the movement of commercial letters. In 1801–03, for instance, it was difficult to procure in Benares a credit note on Muttra and Agra only a few hundred miles away.[60]

---

[56] 'Donation to Mohamed Wauris in consequences of the losses he sustained in the performance of his duty as Dawk Moonshee of Cuttack', Aug. 1808, 5444, BC F/4/236.   [57] Examination of Mahomed Wauris, *ibid.*

[58] Edmonstone to Elphinstone, 5 Dec. 1808 encloses, T. Brooke, Benares, to Edmonstone, 20 June 1808, Home Misc. 657; Edmondstone's minute, 'Memorandum respecting the credibility of the supposed intrigue between Raja Runjeet Singh and Amrut Row', 28 Aug. 1808. Home Misc. 592. There were doubts whether the runner could actually have travelled these vast distances (Lahore Benares in 35 days; Kabul Agra in 38 days) in the time stated, but not that communications were still open.

[59] S. Gole (ed.), *Maps of Mughal India drawn by Col. Jean-Baptiste-Joseph Gentil* . . . (London, 1988). Gentil's maps, drawn from indigenous local sources, have almost no information relating to the Jat territories.

[60] Agent to the Governor-General, Benares to Military Secretary to Commander in Chief, 25 Nov. 1804, Benares, Agency Proceedings, U.P. Central Record Office, Allahabad.

Within their respective territories, the regional states attempted to
maintain or enhance the existing methods of surveillance and suasion.
Awadh and Bengal deepened the newswriter and *muhtasib* systems
alongside effective postal services until they were eroded or closed
down after British annexation. The British, for instance, considered
Shuja-ud Daulah, Nawab of Awadh, 'the best informed man in
Hindostan'. In the state of Jaipur, a dense volume of reporting on
revenue and political matters reached the court until about 1755.[61]
Rulers also continued to manipulate informal networks of communication with great skill. In Mysore, Haidar Ali and Tipu Sultan appear
to have made good use of the extensive contacts of sufi brotherhoods[62]
to gather information and even recruits for their military activities. At
the same time they tapped into the special knowledge of the 'tribal'
people of the Deccan upland.

How did the widespread resort of the regional states to the practice
of 'farming-out' revenue to great magnates affect the flow of information? This policy was designed to maximize revenue and minimize the
risks of collection in times of adversity. But one of its many disadvantages was that it might erode the knowledge-base of ruler. It may be
significant, for instance, that the decline in regular reporting by local
officials to the Jaipur durbar after 1750 coincided with the entrench-
ing in the state of the revenue-farming system.[63] Again, in Awadh
after 1775, the regime appears to have colluded in staunching the
flows of revenue and political information from the outlying revenue-
farming magnates precisely in order to deny the British knowledge of
where the state's resources were hidden.[64] What happened to the local
newswriter system in areas ruled by revenue-farmers remains unclear.
However, it is interesting to note that one of the baits offered to the
British by a would-be usurper of the throne of Awadh in 1807 was
that, along with customs receipts, the Company would have newswriters 'stationed with every aumil [revenue-farmer]'.[65] This was an

[61] M. Bajekal, 'The State and the Rural Grain Market in Eighteenth-century
Eastern India', in S. Subrahmanyam (ed.), *Merchants, Markets and the State in Early
Modern India* (Oxford, 1990), pp. 90–121, gives a good indication of the range of
detailed revenue and agricultural information coming into Jaipur.
[62] W. Kirkpatrick, *Select Letters of Tipoo Sultan to Various Public Functionaries* . . .
(London, 1811), pp. 304–5, circular letter 16 May 1786 to Pirzadas at shrines outside
Mysore; cf. p. 385.
[63] Bajekal, 'State and Rural Grain Market' (see note 61).
[64] R. Barnett, *North India Between Empires, Awadh, the Mughals and the British, 1720–
1801* (Berkeley; 1980), pp. 213–22.
[65] Enclosure (3) in Resdt. Lucknow to Govt. 24 Oct. 1807, 'Intrigues by members
of the Vizier's family against him', BC 5584 (1807), F/4/248.

indication, perhaps, that the system had been deliberately allowed to atrophy in some parts of the territory.

One final point should be noted. The greater fluidity of politics and the precarious state of some channels of communication in conditions of fiscal 'decentralization' may have enhanced the importance of any agent who could combine an effective supra-local intelligence with access to money or military power. By the mid-eighteenth century, 'private' (or rather patrimonial) intelligence services operated by Indians, Armenians, and French, English and Eurasian entre-preneurs were beginning to make the running. Individuals such as Jean-Baptiste Gentil[66] the French representative in Awadh, William Bolts[67] and his Armenian agents, or Beni Ram Pandit,[68] the Maratha agent in Benares, have usually been studied as 'private traders'. But one of the most important functions they served was the provision of political and commercial intelligence, sometimes on a purely competi-tive basis. It was to take the East India Company many decades to reverse this 'privatisation' of intelligence and information services.

It would be illuminating to examine the nature of the eighteenth-century Maratha states in terms of their mobilization and use of political and military information. Most interpretations of their suc-cess rely, not altogether convincingly, on assertions about their 'guerrilla warfare', wiry Deccan horses, or cultural homogeneity in the face of an effete Mughal Empire. But even a cursory inspection reveals the great density of written materials and of political and social infor-mation upon which their leaders could draw. The Peshwa's Daftar (Chancellery) at Poona was one of the richest archives in south Asia. Massive details on revenue, political and social issues, down to infrac-tions of caste rules at village level are recorded here. Maratha leaders, notably Nana Farnavis, had some of the most effective personal systems of information available to Indian politicians. In addition, the rapid transfer of information was guaranteed by a well-rooted system of public informants, runners and spies (*jasus=harkaras*) maintained by a cess on villages (the *jasudpatti*).[69] The *naiks* or headmen of the guild of runners and spies ('the Jasud Runners') represented a fusion

[66] For Gentil, see Gole, *Maps of Mughal India*, intro.

[67] *Ibid.*, p. 4, for Bolts' role in supplying the British, Awadh and the French with information; for Bolts' career see P. J. Marshall, *East Indian Fortunes* (Oxford, 1976), pp. 115, 122, 123, 191–2.

[68] For Beni Ram Pandit see T. S. Shejwalkar (ed.), *Nagpur Affairs [a selection of Marathi letters from the Menavli Daftar]* (Poona, 1954), intro. p. xxiv.

[69] Wilson, *Dictionary of Judicial and Revenue Terms*, p. 234: The confusion of 'spy' and 'runner' perhaps explains the odd remark by Alexander Walker that in Gujarat

of the newswriter and spy systems. In the 1780s, they carried on 'a regular post between Poona and Nagpur and report[ed] on the daily activity of the Nagpur Court.'[70]

Why this density of information flow? What does it tell us about the society of western India in the eighteenth century? Popular literacy does seem to have been somewhat higher here than in richer north India. Brahmin writers, literate intermediaries and village accountants were thickly clustered in the Maratha countryside. This was a relatively open society, both geographically and socially mobile. If not formally literate the Kunbi villager was well acquainted with the instruments of literacy, especially the songs and ballads associated with the saints of devotional Hinduism who had once flourished here. A dense pattern of pilgrimage tied the region together.[71]

In Marathi-speaking territories the Marathas were able to build their state from the bottom up, as it were. There was a constant exchange of information on everyday happenings, rights and duties, between the village leadership, the local Brahmin, the village accountant and the superior controllers of the state, now increasingly Brahmin literati. Many of these lineages and corporate bodies had their own archives, which in turn increased the level of knowledge available to the courts.[72] For the Marathas information was agglutinative, stuck together by cultural contact, and by intense competition over the title to shares in produce. For all their sophistication, outside the northern plains the Mughals never did create more than islands of special correspondents and informants in a vast rural sea. But even the Marathas were vulnerable when, in 1761, they ventured apparently without route plans and clear information into northern India. Here, traversing an alien cultural zone, their armies were starved of intelligence, harried and ultimately crushed on the field of Panipat.[73]

'spies' were also public executioners (thus attesting to their low or outcaste status), and rewarded by taking a handful of meal from sacks in the bazaar, Walker of Bowland Papers, Ms 13819, National Library of Scotland. I am indebted to Dr Dilip Menon for this reference.

[70] Shejwalkar, *Nagpur Affairs*, p. li.

[71] See, e.g., G. A. Deleury, *The Cult of Vithoba* (Poona, 1960); M. J. Murray, 'Pandharpur', *Indian Antiquary* 11 (1882), 149–56.

[72] Laurence W. Preston, *The Devs of Cincvad. A Lineage and the State in Maharashtra* (Cambridge, 1989).

[73] T. S. Shejwalkar, *Panipat 1761; Deccan College Monograph Series* (Poona, 1946), pp. 47, 69–70, the Peshwa received no letters from the Maratha camp during the crucial days before Panipat; they were all intercepted by Abdali patrols, or those of their local allies.

The East India Company and Indigenous Information Systems

With this contrast in mind, we can now pass on to the British Empire and the proud boast of the colonial official to 'know the country'. In the earliest days of the Company's factories, the English had already begun to use the *harkara* and *kasid* system of communication with each other, other Europeans and the Indian rulers. Dutch and English 'cussids' are frequently mentioned in the Fort William House Correspondence and other early sources. In one of the most dramatic examples of the 'sorry we haven't written' letter, the Surat Factors explained in 1665 that their silence could be explained by the fact that their runner had been consumed by 'a tyger'.[74] Alongside established runners, informal networks of Indian merchants passing into the interior and of the native women whom Company servants were wont to keep, supplied important local information. Finally, of course, the *dubash*, literally, master of 'two tongues', first emerged in his guise of interpreter.

However, as incidents such as the war with Aurangzeb and the Surman embassy to the Mughal Emperor revealed, the British knew little and understood less about the great states of the interior. This lack was progressively remedied between 1757 and 1820 as the Company drew into its orbit the main Indian intelligence systems and the critical clusters of native informants. The charge that the British never really understood what was happening in India, vigorously advanced by today's anti-orientalists, has some truth perhaps as far as deep sociological knowledge is concerned. By contrast, it was the very effectiveness of the British in penetrating Indian information systems at a pragmatic political and economic level which explains the speed and effectiveness of conquest. As Holkar, the Maratha chief wrote (somewhat disingenuously) in 1816: 'It is a favourite object of the British government to receive intelligence of all occurrences and transactions in every quarter'.[75] How was this penetration effected?

In the first place, the superiority of British resources told quite early. *Waqyanavis* and writer families throughout India, suffering from the decline of Mughal patronage, turned to British service to maintain the honour of their lineages. The family of the once-powerful Mughal Faujdar of Hughly, for instance, staffed many of the most important

[74] Sir W. Foster, CIE, *The English Factories in India, 1665–67* (London, 1923), p. 83 (?) Karwar Factors to Surat, 29 Aug. 1665.
[75] 'Objections to Kurreem Oollah', 5447, BC F/4/236.

confidential embassies between 1780 and 1820.[76] The British built up an efficient system of newswriters and intelligence agents around every one of their major residencies at Indian courts, as Michael Fisher shows.[77] The staff of agents to the Governor General residing at communications centres such as Benares and Delhi, collected and read the products of the newswriters stationed at different courts by the Indian powers. British skills in reading and interpreting the meaning of indigenous diplomatic papers also increased rapidly. From 1759 the large 'Persian correspondence' of the Bengal government was gradually systematized. A Persian Secretary and staff were appointed, separate from the Foreign and Political Department in the 1790s, and the Governor General's own private office developed its own matching expertise in 'country correspondence', or communication with the Indian powers.

To an extent it was the greater financial resources of the British which allowed them to buy their way into the news and postal services. Money talked; skilled newswriters were paid as much as Rs 300 per month,[78] while the most important native diplomatists and informants were given large landholdings in *jagir* at the termination of their services. These British gentlemen were, moreover, quite skilled at unravelling the chains of cultural connection that ran through the Asian aristocracy: the connections of Gosains, and hill Brahmins, of Mughals and Afghan horse-fanciers. The Delhi Residency, for instance, secured the services of the nephew of the Chief Minister of Afghanistan as a spy between 1803 and 1806.[79] It is also no doubt important that the British did, formally at least, inherit the legitimacy of the Mughal empire through their control of the Diwani of Bengal, and this gave a degree of legitimacy to their manipulation of the imperial systems of surveillance and information gathering.

Much the same was true of the downward-thrusting systems of surveillance represented by the sub-provincial newswriters, the *muhtasibs*, *darogas*, and other imperial officers. In due course, many of

[76] For the interconnections in British confidential service of descendants of the Faujdar and Kazi of Hooghly see, Secretary's Report on the examination of Mahomed Saudik and Mirza Bauker, Bengal Pol. Cons. 4 Jan. 1808, 5584, BC F/4/248.

[77] E.g., list of personnel of the intelligence department of the Delhi residency, 1814, see, Sinha (ed.), *Selections from the Ochterlony Papers*, p. 89; for an example of a newsletter, Michael H. Fisher, *A Clash of Cultures, Awadh, the British and the Mughals* (New Delhi, 1987), appendix iii, pp. 261–2.

[78] Rs 300 per month appears to have been standard for high grade writers and agents.

[79] 5565, BC F/4/247.

these offices were edged aside and replaced by agencies supposedly more directly dependent on British judges and magistrates. But before 1780 regular interrogation of indigenous officials on matters of revenue (*kanungos*), moral surveillance, (*kotwals* and *darogas*) and political infractions (*waqyanigars*) filled the British district archives with evidence which was put to effective use later, as the collectors slowly gained some degree of control over their charges.

We have already mentioned the emergence in the eighteenth century of 'private' information services associated with magnates and political servants who maintained interests over a wide area. These men and their descendants also played a critical role as the generation of 'native informants' who tied together the British conquest of India with their intrigues and contacts. Many came from traditional Islamic literati backgrounds. They included Mahomed Reza Khan,[80] a whole group of informants, diplomatists and *munshis* (secretaries) associated with the families of the former Kazi and Faujdar of Hughly,[81] or Maulvi Abdul Kader Khan, confidential agent for the Marathas at Benares, who used his contacts in Nepal and upper India to the British advantage.[82] This lineage of native experts passed on into the nineteenth century, culminating with the 'one-eyed Maulvi' from Ambala who helped William Hodson penetrate the defences of rebel Delhi,[83] and Maulvi Amir Ali who established a great network of collaborating magnates throughout Bihar and eastern India during the worst times of 1857.[84] But the British were also able to win over men from the writer-Brahmin connections in both north and south India whose acquaintance with Hindu patterns of pilgrimage, in particular, made them excellent intelligence officers.[85]

By the turn of the century the first generation of old 'India hands'

[80] Khan, *The Transition in Bengal.*

[81] See n. 76 above; another similar figure was Izatullah Khan, munshi of the Delhi residency who accompanied Moorcroft.

[82] For the history of Kader Khan see 'Conduct of Molavee Abdool Kader in accepting from the late Nabob Vizier a jaghier whilst confidentially employed by the Resident at His Excellency's court', 5585, BC F/4/248; Wood to Fagan, 21 Jan. 1815, encloses minute by Abdul Kader Khan on the Terai, Home Misc. 649; his report on trade in Nepal, Benares Agency Records, 22 Jan. 1796, U.P. Records Office, Allahabad.

[83] G. H. Hodson, *Twelve Years of a Soldier's Life in India; being Extracts from the Letters of Major S. W. R. Hodson, B.A.* (London, 1859), p. 197.

[84] Amir Ali was an official of the Patna court; his family was rewarded with a substantial zamindari.

[85] E.g., the attempts by Thomas Rutherfurd, Superintendent of the Postal and Intelligence Department, to use the hill Brahmin connections in intelligence activity against Nepal, 1814–16, Home Misc. 644–53.

28   C. A. BAYLY

among the British themselves was beginning to emerge. These were linguists and cultural experts—progenitors of the later official anthropologists—with a wide range of indigenous contacts who were often drawn from outside the main lines of civil and military officialdom. Several such as Hamilton Buchanan,[86] Thomas Rutherfurd,[87] and much later, E. G. Balfour[88] (all surgeons) and William Moorcroft (superintendent of the Pusa Stud in Bihar)[89] had scientific backgrounds. Often associated with the generation of high 'orientalist knowledge', these men were as important by virtue of the detailed pragmatic knowledge in geography, disease, and Indian material life which they could provide to the expanding Empire. Hamilton Buchanan's statistical and topographical works have been mined by scholars seeking the lineage of British administrative treatises and ideological preconceptions. Less well known is the detailed information on routes, bridges, rivers and the location of villages which he gave to the invading Company armies during the Nepal War of 1814–16.[90]

The significance of Indian merchants to the British in moving their financial resources around the subcontinent has been stressed in recent works.[91] But merchants were also able to provide European officials and traders with an excellent general picture of economy and politics because their own information system was one of the fastest and most flexible in the country. Merchant-bankers, moreover, were one of the most reliable sources of information. In general, their material interests appeared to run parallel with those of the Company. But they were also totally dependent on it for the security of their families, homes and property and could afford no 'treachery'.[92] For this reason one of the main functions of Jonathan Duncan and later Agents to the Governor-General in the commercial centre of

[86] Marika Vicziany, 'Imperialism, Botany and Statistics in Early Nineteenth Century India. The Surveys of Francis Buchanan (1762–1829)', *Modern Asian Studies* 20, 4 (1986), 625–61.

[87] See, e.g., T. Rutherfurd to J. Adam, Sect. to Govt., 8 July 1814 and following correspondence, Home Misc. 644; R. H. Phillimore, *Historical Records of the Survey of India, ii, 1800–1815* (Dehra Dun, 1950), 40, 82, 90.

[88] Editor of *Encyclopedia of India and Southern Asia* (repr. Madras, 1873).

[89] W. Moorcroft to Adam, 17 Oct. 1814, and later corr. Home Misc. 646; G. Alder, *Beyond Bokhara. The Life of William Moorcroft, Asian Explorer and Pioneer Veterinary Surgeon, 1767–1825* (London, 1985).

[90] J. Adam to F. Buchanan, 28 July 1814; Buchanan to Adam, 19 Aug. 1814, Home Misc., 644, ff. 281–333.

[91] See, e.g., Lakshmi Subramanian, 'Banias and the British', *Modern Asian Studies* 21, 3 (1987), 473–511; C. A. Bayly, *Rulers, Townsmen and Bazaars* (Cambridge, 1983).

[92] Adam to P. Bradshaw, 30 Sept. 1814, Home Misc. 644.

Benares was regularly to interview members of the great local firms such as that of Bhaiaram Gopal Das and Kashmiri Mull. With their continent-wide correspondents, they could explain how exchange rates were expected to affect British military and naval operations throughout India, the location of enemy armies and much other information and gossip that came their way.

This success in tapping into Indian information systems was not simply a feature of British relations with the Indian elites. The military, in particular, learned, admittedly somewhat slowly, to manipulate the *harkara* system on a massive scale to defend their vulnerable columns against the light cavalry attacks which were the hallmark of Mysore and Maratha warfare, and posed such a threat to the revenue-bearing villages held by the British. Col. Fullarton's recruitment of a huge Guide Establishment of 'hircarrahs' and Brahmin controllers from the Kallar 'tribal' state of Ramnad began to turn the tide of the 1780–84 Mysore war in favour of the British.[93] Runners and spies, often recruited from groups beyond the margins of the arable also played an important part in the Maratha campaigns of Wellesley, of Alexander Walker against the Palassi Raja, and of Ochterlony against the Gurkhas. From this point of view, the British recruitment of irregular cavalry regiments during the final wars of conquest, 1790–1818, should be seen as an attempt to enhance their intelligence gathering capacity as well as an augmentation of their simple military force.

British Control and Manipulation of Information

It would be wrong to think that the British simply 'hacked into' the Mughals' information systems and left them as they were. Significant changes, amounting in some sectors to a conceptual revolution, took place in the use of the products of surveillance.

The Mughals and later Indian powers had controlled the collection and use of information in two basic ways. First, they had appointed new and more reliable agencies to keep a check on ones that seemed to be failing. Moral suasion and punishment had been used to keep officers on the straight and narrow. In exceptional circumstances new 'intendants' might be established, like the ones set up by Aurangzeb

---

[93] Fullarton's Hircarrah system, Home Misc. 84, ff. 911–23. Fullarton obtained from the Tondaiman Raja of Ramnad, 'a body of colleries [kallars] who were perfectly acquainted with all the bye-ways of the country'.

to prevent the dissemination of Ismaili views, or of drinking. Secondly, the tone of the discourse of royal rights and popular obligations had a kind of corrective tendency. To be castigated as a 'troublemaker', a *fitna*-monger, or stiff-necked in imperial pronouncements undoubtedly had some impact in an aristocratic society thirsting for royal honour.

In the days of Clive and Warren Hastings notions of personal loyalty and the discourse of royal rights were deployed by the British to check the doings of their officers of surveillance and others in much the same way. The Company was used to its Indian officers resorting to intrigue and faction against it. But personal reprimand and disgrace do not seem to have been afforced strongly with the western European concept of 'treason'.[94] Amongst its own officers the Company allowed a good deal of latitude for personal correspondence even with potential enemies (though anything concerning the French was more severely controlled). Again, if the content of transactions and communications often concerned somewhat sordid matters of personal perquisites, the contemporary ideologies of 'improvement' and 'enlightenment' did set limits to what could be known and disseminated among Company officials. James Hicky's *Calcutta Gazette* was given a lot of latitude, but its lurid details of the financial and sexual peccadillos of the British in Bengal finally broke the patience of government.[95]

With Cornwallis and Wellesley we find the Company, now under pressure from both European and Indian enemies, deploying a more strident rhetoric of imperial loyalty and racial superiority to control the boundaries of political language and information.[96] At the same time the government began to resort to a much more direct control of information agencies both Indian and European. If strict control of what people can know is one of the hallmarks of the modern state, then it was between 1790 and 1820 that such a state emerged in India. Military officers were refused permission to correspond with newspapers on 'public matters',[97] and there began the long duel

---

[94] See, e.g., the case of Nand Kumar, letter out 24 Feb. 1761, *Imperial Record Department. Calendar of Persian Correspondence* (Calcutta, 1911–), ii, p. 67. He had engaged in 'treasonable behaviour' by dealing with the Company's enemies, but his actions 'did not come under the tenor' of the Company's law, so he was merely 'disgraced' for what turned out to be a short time.

[95] *Bengal Gazette*, 21 April 1781; M. K. Chanda, *History of the English Press in Bengal* (Calcutta, 1987), pp. 1–4.

[96] C. A. Bayly, *Imperial Meridian. The British Empire and the World, 1780–1830* (London, 1989).

[97] Circular by P. A. Agnew, 4 Dec. 1799, Home Misc. 457, p. 176.

between the Anglo-Indian press and officialdom which rumbled on into the later nineteenth century.[98] Under Wellesley a stricter control over secret information was one of the main impetuses towards the creation of the Governor-General's private secretariat.[99]

The Company meanwhile adopted a number of important innovations in its political relations with Indian states. The Intelligence and Postal Departments of the major residencies and of the Company's army were generally expanded in size and importance. Efforts were made to strengthen and develop postal communications directly under control of the Presidency governments.[100] In conquered and ceded territories there was discussion of the suppression of 'native dauks' in order to bring all postal communications within the Company's orbit.[101] In general this was not effected, though in time Indian-run postal systems did tend to give way to official ones, which directly benefited the government's finances through the sale of stamps. There is a good deal of research waiting to be done on the implication of postal charges for the passage of information within the Indian population. But the high cost of postage stamps throughout the early nineteenth century suggests that the benefits of improved basic communications may well not have trickled down to the middle and poorer strata of the population.[102]

The fiercest battles over information took place with the Indian states. After 1793, for instance, the British used the excuse of Awadh's dire financial situation to persuade it to give up appointing its own newswriters to the Maratha court and those of other Indian states.[103] This followed a general policy by which the Company sought to try to restrict bilateral and multilateral communications between native

[98] See, e.g., J. Natarajan, *History of Indian Journalism* (New Delhi, 1955); S. P. Sen (ed.), *The Indian Press* (Calcutta, 1967); N. G. Barrier, *Banned. Controversial Literature and Political Control in British India, 1907–47* (New Delhi, 1976), intro. For the liberalization of the press see J. W. Kaye (ed.), *Selections from the Papers of Lord Metcalfe* (London, 1855), p. 197. Minute of 16 May 1835; for connection of government servants with the press, Minute of 29 Dec. 1829, *ibid.*, p. 311.

[99] 'New arrangements of the Governor-General's Private Office and of the Secretary's Office of the Political Department', 2375, BC F/4/128.

[100] See, e.g., A. G. Sen, *The Post Office of India, or a Historical Review of its Rise, Progress, Regulation and General Administration* (Calcutta, 1875).

[101] Actg Magt, Mirzapur to Postmaster General, Calcutta, 11 October 1810, Mirzapur Judicial Records issued vol. 74, U.P. Central Records Office, Allahabad. The report said that an ancient and effective dak existed in Awadh; six people in Mirzapur alone ran postal services for merchants and others and retained 'cossidars'.

[102] *Benares Recorder*, 8 Jan. 1846, comments on heavy postage on indigenous newspapers.

[103] Cherry to Shore, 11 Aug. 1795, Home Misc. 577.

powers and insert itself as the only channel of information between them. For their part, Indian powers did attempt to prohibit the spread of Company intelligence-gathering and postal arrangements on their own territories. Between 1799 and 1801, for instance, the Peshwa held at bay attempts to establish postal communications from Bombay to Poona and Mysore to Poona.[104] Not only were postal *harkaras* a possible source of enemy intelligence during war, but one imagines that since protection of *dak* was a prerogative of kings, this arrangement would have cast doubt on the Peshwa's sovereignty. Ultimately, *force majeure* settled the issue and by the end of the Maratha wars in 1818 western India was fully incorporated into the Company's information systems. The issue, however, was not a simple one of cause and effect. It was the very penetration of British intelligence-gathering systems and the effectiveness of the *harkara* establishment which helped the British to gain the military upper hand in the first place.

It was also during this period that communication and contact with enemies during times of war, previously perfectly compatible with the Indian notion of political intrigue or *fitna*, was outlawed. Henceforth all contact by ambassador, post or confidential agent with an enemy power was deemed sedition by the Company. The *cause célèbre* was the discovery of 'treasonable' correspondence between the Nawab of Arcot and Tipu Sultan after the fall of Seringapatam in 1799. This discovery led on directly to the fall of the Arcot regime, now tainted with disloyalty in British eyes.[105] It was to no effect that the advisers of the Peshwa's house claimed that it was commonly accepted in the 'practice of native powers' that enemies might carry on communication during times of war.[106] Now the state had established impermeable boundaries during wartime and their transgression was criminalized.

What is equally important is the use to which the Company officials put the vast accumulation of data from this continental intelligence and diplomatic system. Men such as N. B. Edmonstone or H. T. Prinsep who ran the Persian Department of the Government of India and the Persian branch of the Secret and Political Department in the early nineteenth century were some of the best linguists of the age.

---

[104] Palmer to Mornington, 10, 31 Dec. 1798, Home Misc. 574.

[105] Clive to Wellesley, 11 Aug. 1801, Home Misc. 464; for *fitna* cf. 'treason' see, A. Wink, *Land and Sovereignty in India* (Cambridge, 1986).

[106] Remarks of Nana Farnavis reported in Palmer to Mornington, 2 July 1799, Home Misc. 574.

They were also managers of information, who worked in a style derived from the inquisitorial methods of British departmental committees and Treasury Boards.[107]

It would be unwise to underestimate the 'archival depth' of the eighteenth-century Indian powers or the capacity of the Indo-Muslim literati to convey information rapidly across political boundaries. It does seem, however, that the Company was able to manage the information it had collected in more complex and sophisticated ways. The Company instituted a system of cross-referencing and purposive distribution of written Indian intelligence which marked a considerable advance on earlier regimes. Information from newsletters, or residents' and ambassadors' reports was sorted into subject files and extensive political biographies were built up. It may be that well-informed individual officials of Indian states had been able to give interpretative depth to the disaggregated information available from the complex reports they received. But the Company's routine processing of these records into widely disseminated printed packages marked a decisive break. After 1790 periodical literature such as the *Asiatick Researches, Asiatic Annual Register,* filling out the government gazettes, fed the products of Indian reports and newsletters to the wider European public.[108] This created an information-rich administrative and military service, but also identified private interests with those of the Company state, with which they had often been at odds in earlier periods. With the Napoleonic, Mysore and Maratha 'threats' all merging into one, empire loyalism and deference to officialdom provided an idiom in which this new rapprochement could be expressed.

However, the conceptual reach of the information accumulated and disseminated also changed. The few available studies of the form of indigenous records suggest that these could be statistically rich. Yet they were single-purpose, devoted to the taxation of houses in a bazaar or the computation of land-revenues, or separate political intelligence. The Company, however, began to build up banks of multi-purpose social data in conformity with the new European science of statistics. Indian data had apparently been 'flat' historically

---

[107] I am indebted to Joanna Innes for information on this issue and also to her unpublished paper 'The Collection and Use of Information by Government [in England] *circa* 1690–1800.'

[108] See, e.g., Home Misc. 556, 557, 577, 'Notes on Europeans and Asiatics', and other similar personal intelligence files used both in London and Calcutta; cf. *The Asiatick Annual Register, or a View of the History of Hindostan for 1799* (London, 1800).

in general, looking back to rights and duties previously established. Company data was adjusted to fit ideas of economic and moral improvement which could potentially rank all societies, within and outside India, in a global hierarchy and pattern of development. The information so collected might or might not be used actually to prosecute such improvement, but it certainly had the effect of reinforcing Europeans' notions of their own historical superiority. Of course, earlier Arabic and Persian travelogues detailing the practice of savage people in unfriendly climes may well have exhibited a kind of sociological map of mankind to give meaning to the 'flatness' of their written records,[109] but the scale of the European effort was vastly greater.

Not only did the British accumulate information and interrogate society more systematically than their predecessors, but their knowledge also acquired a new territorial, truly three-dimensional form. James Rennell's surveys of the Company's territories of the 1760s and 1770s had not quite been modern maps.[110] They had been visual depictions of routes, which pinpointed rivers, villages, wells and other geographical features which a military party might encounter on a march through a territory. They were similar to the route maps which Mughal commanders used.[111] However, after 1818, the Survey of India generally introduced trigonometrical methods. The boundaries of villages, subdivisions and districts were fixed. This was partly an aspect of the assertion of sovereignty. An eighteenth-century Indian ruler had rejected a British Survey on the grounds that it would 'cause a diminution of his dignity and honour in the eyes of neighbouring powers and foreigners'.[112] In the early nineteenth century, the trigonometrical pole replaced the Mughal's oxtail standard as the symbol of authority. The survey was also clearly an aid to the practical aim of the collection of territorial revenue. To be a subject came to mean inhabiting a certain piece of land.

The ideal of informed British rule was beautifully illustrated in 1816 by the artist, Thomas Hickey's portrait of Colin Mackenzie, a

---

[109] Persian works such as the *Ain-i-Akbari*, or *Dabistan* which devotes much of their text to Hindu practices, or even topologies such as the 'Yadgar-i-Bahaduri' deploy 'sociological' information as part of a discourse of rule.

[110] For Rennell's methods see his *Memoir of a Map of Hindoostan, or the Moguls Empire* (2nd edn, London, 1785), pp. i–viii.

[111] Gole, *Maps of Mughal India*.

[112] R. H. Phillimore, *Historical Records of the Survey of India*, iv vols (Dehra Dun, 1945–58), i, 23; for the implications of the use of trigonometrical surveys, see, D. Ludden, *Peasant History in South India* (Princeton, 1985), pp. 12–13, 177–8.

noted orientalist and first Surveyor-General of India, which hangs in the India Office Library.[113] The redcoated Scotsman is shown surrounded by his Indian 'native informants'. They offer him a telescope with which to view the surveying poles, and bundles of Indian manuscripts. On a hill in the background stands the colossal tenth-century Jain statue of Bahubali at Shravanabelagola near Mysore, which Mackenzie has just surveyed and drawn. Thus the arcane knowledge of India, purely mysterious to an earlier age, is now reduced to scientific information. The Indian informants and learned men who are painted here helped Mackenzie draw up his reports. They include a Maratha Brahmin, a Jain and a Telugu Brahmin from the south. The pictures intend to show how the British had placed themselves at the centre of the richest skeins of oriental information and intelligence.

Epilogue: Colonial Data Panics and Imperfections

It would be tempting to leave the story there with European intelligence firmly in control of the subcontinent, the myriad channels of information from newswriters and native informants, approvers, spies and 'canny people' merging into great rivers of knowledge which flowed past Fort William in Calcutta. But that whiggish picture of the growth of information and the mobilization of state, and ultimately nation, by the steady accretion of communications—the model elaborated in the theories of the sociologist Karl Deutsch[114]—seems inappropriate to the history of India. Company, Crown and even, in a sense, the Indian National Congress, continued to be vulnerable to the atrophy of their information systems or their infiltration by middlemen with contrary interests. False information might give rise to damaging official convulsions, while true intelligence of danger was routinely misinterpreted or ignored. Despite fifty years of filling up red ledgers and blue books, or penning maps, the British were caught unawares by the mutinies and rebellions of 1857, and took months to rebuild an adequate intelligence service, despite the fact that they now possessed the electric telegraph.

The colonial power did, of course, throw a stronger and more regular beam into many areas of Indian life, but their knowledge of others was exiguous. Despite heroic exceptions, the British excluded themselves from the women's quarters and their associated networks

[113] Thomas Hickey, 'Colonel Colin Mackenzie and his assistant', OIOR.
[114] K. Deutsch, *Nationalism and Social Communication* (Cambridge, Mass., 1966).

of domestic information after 1800. Indo-Portuguese Christians and Eurasian officers such as James Skinner, who retained kinship links with Indians, remained useful, but were gradually excluded from a more racially conscious expatriate society.[115] Again, well-informed officials sometimes made attempts to enlist the aid of information-rich servants of local communities, such as barbers, midwives and itinerant doctors. But usually the material such contacts could produce was subtly reworked by the time it reached the judge or collector, having been passed through the hands of many Indian agents.[116] The British found it particularly difficult to make use of the knowledge of religious institutions, let alone the wandering religious mendicant. Indeed, these last were often treated as enemies and suspected of being agents of Thugs, Pindari raiders or disaffected Indian powers. Even the role of the canny knowledge of the tribal diminished in importance as warfare changed form and commercial logging speeded up. In turn, the distancing of these networks of information from the centres of political power depressed the significance of the groups whose importance they had once sustained. For instance, as royal women and the associated circles of literate ladies lost access to the arenas of power growing up around the British residencies, women in general lost part of their significance as independent political actors.[117]

Tapping into the dense webs of commercial and social knowledge which revolved around pilgrimage and the great fairs, the seed-bed of local politics, was to remain quite difficult for the British. Kipling's intelligence officers dressed as wandering holy men were, in general, a delicious invention. Instead, the colonial officials adopted two dubious procedures. First, they paid huge sums of money to spies or informers and empowered subordinate officials to collect information for them on matters of domestic life and family property. Innumerable petitions and depositions after riots denounce the Company's reliance on 'people of low character' who poke their noses into the business of

---

[115] This point has been made by Seema Alavi; the 'invalid thana' which she discusses below was evidently also useful as an intelligence gathering institution.

[116] One Guzra Bye, royal midwife, in Baroda supplied A. Walker with an account of female infanticide there, *c.* 1804, Walker of Bowland Mss 13651, National Library of Scotland (I am indebted to Dr Dilip Menon for this reference), but generally speaking, the British appear to have relied on reports from inferior police in their attack on infanticide.

[117] There were, however, a few cases where British residents retained intimate contacts with Indian women formed in the course of official surveillance, see, e.g., the case of J. Kirkpatrick, Home Misc. 464.

the wealthy and respectable. The slow demise of the elite newswriter and the attested reports of the local notables was matched by the rise of the professional spy and official snooper and the hanger-on of the police *daroga*, a figure much nearer now to those despised 'spies' and informers of Stuart England. Orthodox outrage at the banning of *sati* was redoubled because it was the police *daroga* or his even lowlier agents who were to investigate reports of the practice.[118] Officials of the Excise Department and poorly paid local police, the lowest of the low to many Indians, became key sources of social and political intelligence.

New and arbitrary centres of power were created by the amalgamation of surveillance systems which had previously been separate and designed to keep a check on each other. Despite the enormous volume of paper generated, attempts to gain control of village registrars and local revenue officials were frustrated by landlords' command of the networks of information. Networks of power and surveillance which under Indian powers had been kept separate, and endowed with moral and religious legitimacy, were unified under the influence of local magnates or the chief clerks of district offices. These agents regularly colluded in denying information to the distant British official struggling to maintain the coherence of correspondence in Persian, English and often a third regional language. The link between surveillance and moral suasion was now attenuated as the ruling power forfeited many of the props of cultural and religious legitimacy which had sustained pre-colonial rulers.

Secondly, since the British often found it difficult to secure reliable and regular sources of information from the great towns and bazaar villages, their own establishments were periodically convulsed by panics about the passage of arcane and esoteric knowledge between Indians. Before the 1857 Mutiny and Rebellion the famous *chapatis* passed from hand to hand and village to village were supposed to have signalled uprising. Fifty years later, in 1907, on the anniversary of the Mutiny, the European community across India was terrified by the prospect of wandering holy men smearing cow dung on trees. Was this another signal for a general massacre of Europeans?[119]

[118] *Parliamentary Papers on Hindoo Widows and Voluntary Immolations*, xviii, 1821, pp. 335ff; for the rising power of darogas and their informers, see J. R. McLane, 'Bengali Bandits, Police and Landlords after the Permanent Settlement', in Yang (ed.), *Crime and Criminality*, pp. 42–3.

[119] Home Pol., July 1907, 24D, National Archives of India; the fear of Mutiny, cow protection, the old enemy the Holkar dynasty of Indore and Brahmins all gells into a nightmare here.

38   C. A. BAYLY

Throughout the nineteenth century the British worried about the arcane worshippers of the Goddess Kali, or later, radical Indian nationalists who passed easily along the lines of communication supposedly inaccessible to the European.[120]

Far from being rational responses to the needs of the modern state, 'knowledge panics' sent official agencies through curious parabolas of growth. New agencies were formed. They built up huge data-bases and armies of informants. They developed their own lore, often in isolation from other departments of government. They then atrophied and became obsolescent. The Thuggee and Dacoitee Department, founded to suppress the ritualized strangling of travellers, went through many surprising metamorphoses. When the British were totally wrong-footed by the Mutiny—fighting again 'without eyes and ears'—Col. Hodson's Intelligence Department boomed,[121] but later atrophied. In the 1900s, the Indian CID with its finger-printing and magic ink, enjoyed a brief period of fashion.[122] Where the sensibilities of domestic and Anglo-Indian opinion converged in time, particular issues provoked the accumulation of masses of data: strangling and widow-burning before 1840, the 'demon drink' and excise violations in the 1800s and again in the 1880s[123]—here there are clear echoes of the concerns of the Mughal Emperor Aurangzeb—'plague' in the 1890s.

It was not only special departments of this sort which fell into information-sclerosis. In some respects the whole vast apparatus of British rural control and reporting through the land-revenue systems was of a similar order. The blue books, survey and settlement reports which flooded into Calcutta could become curiously ritualized documents. The administration and its 'native informants' were habituated to discussion of certain well-worn topics. Striking social changes were often not reported to the administration because it did not ask. It remains uncertain how far the enormous volume of reporting on rent-

---

[120] Valentine Chirol, *Indian Unrest* (London, 1910), pp. 18, 27, 102, 103, 345–6.

[121] See Hodson, *Twelve Years of a Soldier's Life*; Kaye and Malleson, *History*, ii, 136; iv, 55, 205, 207, 208.

[122] R. Popplewell, 'The surveillance of Indian Revolutionaries in Great Britain and on the Continent', *Intelligence and National Security* 3, Jan. 1988, 56–77.

[123] Official debates about drink always appeared to have shown a dual aspect. Under the Mughals drinking was an infraction of moral law and an assault on the emperor's authority; Wellesley's campaign about illicit stills was connected with fears for revenue, but expressed in the language of evangelicalism; by the 1870s, the language was of moral purity, but an underlying concern was discipline among plantation workers. In each case surveillance systems displayed both moral and practical applications and could slip easily between these concerns.

rates, revenues and tenures was ever used for anything. It was not so much that the statistics and reports were flawed, though they probably were; or that the Government of India was a 'mighty machine for doing nothing'. It was more often that it was very good at doing things it had done for many years, because they had been important many years before. In some departments, of course, the state did receive regular and untainted flows of information. But even here the social isolation and political biases of officials often meant that the intelligence was not read aright.

Then there was bureaucratic politics. Kipling's short-story 'Pig' in *Plain Tales from the Hills* charts the course of a definitive survey of the Pig population of the Punjab. What drove the enormous machine of intelligence was Nafferton's desire to be revenged on his colleague Pinecoffin, who had sold him a mad horse. Nafferton pestered him for more and more details on the distribution, food and welfare of the horrid, black *sus indicus* until Pinecoffin 'sat up nights, reducing Pig to five places of decimals for the honour of his Service'. Kipling observes 'Our Government is peculiar, it gushes on the agricultural and general information side. . . . The bigger man you are the more information and the greater trouble you can raise.'[124] Reality was even stranger. Several North-Western Provinces Censuses contained a multi-page report on the sub-district distribution of caste and tribe of eunuchs.

The fragmented, uneven and esoteric nature of these empires of information led Lord Curzon at the end of the century to abolish the vast mass of paper coming into the imperial administration. He saw clearly that the capacity of government to act was being eroded by its own information system. Atrophy of intelligence at the local level was paralleled by an overload of exotic information at the centre which was routinely misinterpreted because of the growing isolation of the official and European community from the mass of the population. As Lord Salisbury put it, with his usual mordant precision, the British were being overwhelmed by 'Paper and "damned nigger" ', that is by the accumulation of useless information and growing racial prejudice.[125]

A more serious problem for the future of the empire was the increasing capacity of its opponents within Indian society to mobilize their own sources of knowledge and information, to 'discover India' themselves. The rapid spread of lithographic and printing techniques at

[124] R. Kipling, 'Pig', *Plain Tales from the Hills* (London, 1911).
[125] Cited in D. Dilks, *Curzon in India*, i, *Achievement* (London, 1969), pp. 221–48.

first benefited European critics of the Government of India. Heavy
fines on erring editors and publishers were maintained even when
freedom of the press was formally conceded.[126] In general the
burgeoning Indian press was viewed benignly. In the 1830s, when
Lord William Bentinck was considering control of the infant vernacular press, the head of the Persian Office felt that there was little danger
from the fourth estate. Indian newspapers had a circulation limited to
the main cities. They printed either translations of articles in English
newspapers or the reports of newswriters from up-country. He termed
these news-sheets 'the true native intelligence'. Far from wishing to
impede the flow of written information between Indians, he thought it
good to diffuse among them the small pieces of useful information
which would tend to their general enlightenment.[127]

By the end of the century all was different. Now it was the government's fortnightly reports and political intelligence reports which
were often no more than translations of items in the vernacular
newspapers. The old newswriters of the localities had given way to a
network of correspondents and public men who passed information to
the burgeoning local press, libraries and associations. The key men in
this bottom-up intelligence network combined western and indigenous education. Sometimes they came from similar circles or even
the same families as those which had once provided the newswriters.
The journalistic works of a writer and early nationalist such as Harish
Chandra of Benares, reveal how he assembled many distinct sources
of information. Other literati and public men scattered throughout
north India are among his correspondents. So also were the British
amateur ethnographers and writers who contributed to the ubiquitous
local *Notes and Queries*.[128] But Harish Chandra also drew on family
knowledge, information given by local businessmen, caste elders, the
genealogical priests who kept shop at the great bathing places, and,
sometimes, women's knowledge.[129]

The picture should not be oversimplified. The colonial power could

---

[126] *Benares Recorder*, 30 April 1847.

[127] A. Stirling to Bentinck, encl. in Bentinck's Minute on the press, 6 Jan. 1829, C.
H. Philips (ed.), *The Correspondence of Lord William Cavendish Bentinck* (Oxford, 1977), i,
139, there was a need to 'diffuse knowledge and excit[e] a spirit of enquiry and
reflection among the natives of India'; cf. Metcalfe's minute of 16 May 1835, J. W.
Kaye (ed.), *Selections from the Papers of Lord Metcalfe* (London, 1855), p. 197.

[128] See, e.g., 'Khattriyon ki Utpatti', *Bhartendu Granthavali* (Benares, 1964), iii, 247–
9, where he refers to 'Sherring', 'John Muir', Guru Gobind Singh, Vedic and Muslim
sources all within a few pages.

[129] *Ibid.*, pp. 3–20, 'Agrawalon ki Utpatti' which is based upon oral tradition,
vanshawalis and literary sources British and traditional. Much of his knowledge of the

still muster vast quantities of information: much of it correct and some of it relevant. Some of it even led to action. Conversely, the information available to Indian elites was strikingly incomplete in certain areas. Lines of communication between the Hindu commercial and the Muslim administrative elites were becoming weaker. In the towns, knowledge of peasant and tribal life was minimal, as the novelist Prem Chand insisted. Nevertheless, the Indian 'public man' who emerged after 1860 stood at a critical point where several networks of intelligence stood interconnected. The knowledge of the bazaar, of the bathing festivals of temple and Muslim shrine could be welded into a powerful tool. As the Marathas in the seventeenth and eighteenth century used such an intelligence system to baffle an Emperor without eyes or ears, so their Victorian successors began to put the Viceroys on the defensive.

Curzon's reforms along with the expansion of the Indian Criminal Investigation Department went some way to purging the colonial state's information networks. Fortnightly intelligence reports from civil officers and police abstracts were systematized. Now they at least kept pace with the expansion of the Indian National Congress's information drawn from local newspapers, Congress village organizers and a paraphernalia of reports and enquiries which mirrored the official ones. In the last stages of empire, and with the growing devolution of power to the provinces, the Raj took on some of the appearances of the 'national security state', when its knowledge of events ran ahead of its ability to do anything about them. Yet still the British were very often misinformed. They failed to predict the strength of the Khilafat agitation of 1919, and the Congress election victory of 1937. This was partly because officials were talking to the wrong people. They had good connections with landlords, princes, and secular liberal politicians. Their contacts among Hindu and Muslim religious leaders, village magnates and the vernacular intelligentsia were weak or filtered through the suspect channels of an interested police force. Even when good material came through, political prejudice ensured that intelligence was not acted upon with political foresight. The All-India Congress Committee could not deploy the financial resources open to the colonial state, but its increasing social depth enabled it more accurately to predict the political future—at least among Hindus.

history of Benares and its temples was built up by simply talking to priests, pandas and gosains.

Conclusion

This paper has sought to locate British attempts to generate and
control information for conquest, trade and government in India
within indigenous systems of surveillance and intelligence. This sort
of exercise may help to give greater precision and context to analyses
of 'colonial knowledge' or the role of the 'native informant', both of
which have come to interest historians in the recent past. The information agencies of Indian rulers, both formal and informal, were
particularly well developed. The newswriter system, with its many
checks and balances was reinforced by a flexible system of surveillance and moral suasion which was deployed through local officials of
what has come to be termed 'police'. All these agencies employed a
large number of inferior agents—*harkaras*, *kasids*, and other spies and
runners. Such agents were often members of low castes or tribal
groups, and comprised a substantive service sector in information
skills, the existence of which may require a re-evaluation of the role
and importance of several ritual and occupational groupings whose
functions are usually understood in terms of material production
alone. These agents, in turn, were able to connect with the 'natural'
information-brokers of the localities, barbers, midwives, village
watchmen, astrologers and pilgrims. While these systems were powerful and flexible, they were easily subverted, a factor which may help to
explain the relatively sudden collapse of several apparently stable
Indian polities, including the Mughal Empire and, in 1857, the East
India Company itself.

The British penetrated these Indian information systems very effectively and often quite quickly because they could deploy greater
financial resources than their rivals, and also because they inherited
the authority of the emperors and of the most powerful and well-
informed local rulers in Bengal and Awadh. They significantly
changed the methods by which such information was collated and
diffused, especially through the introduction of the printing press and
the elaboration of the idea of 'treason'. But they were less successful in
controlling and evaluating flows of information within the localities.
This is because they progressively distanced themselves from some of
the most important information brokers of the villages and urban
quarters, indigenous doctors, religious mendicants, tribals and
women. From the point of view of information collection and control,
Company Raj had become a modern state by 1800, but its informa-

EMPIRE AND INFORMATION IN INDIA 43

tion-gathering agencies tended repeatedly to become clogged throughout the nineteenth century, as ideologically-generated 'knowledge panics' about arcane indigenous information set in. In all these events, Indians remained key players in the knowledge bazaar, at times reinforcing British prejudices, at times using their own stores of knowledge against colonial officials, and eventually coming to deploy a successful all-India intelligence system themselves in a printed and easily diffused medium. From this perspective, the study of information, knowledge and communications is an interesting project which might help close the deplorable gap between studies of economic structure, on the one hand, and of orientalism and ideology on the other.[130]

[130] For a recent example of a social study based on the concept of communication see, Ian K. Steele, *The English Atlantic 1675–1740* (New York, 1986). My attention has also been drawn to I. Habib, 'Postal Communications in Mughal India', *Procs Ind. Hist. Congress*, 46th Session, pp. 236–52; M. Z. Siddiqi, 'The Intelligence Service under the Mughals', *Medieval India, a Miscellany*, 2 (London, 1972), pp. 54ff.

[5]

The Prose of Counter-Insurgency[1]

RANAJIT GUHA

When a peasant rose in revolt at any time or place under the Raj, he did so necessarily and explicitly in violation of a series of codes which defined his very existence as a member of that colonial, and still largely semi-feudal society. For his subalternity was materialized by the structure of property, institutionalized by law, sanctified by religion and made tolerable and even desirable—by tradition. To rebel was indeed to destroy many of those familiar signs which he had learned to read and manipulate in order to extract a meaning out of the harsh world around him and live with it. The risk in 'turning things upside down' under these conditions was indeed so great that he could hardly afford to engage in such a project in a state of absent-mindedness.

There is nothing in the primary sources of historical evidence to suggest anything other than this. These give the lie to the myth, retailed so often by careless and impressionistic writing on the subject, of peasant insurrections being purely spontaneous and unpremeditated affairs. The truth is quite to the contrary. It would be difficult to cite an uprising on any significant scale that was not in fact preceded either by less militant types of mobilization when other means had been tried and found wanting or by parley among its principals seriously to weigh the pros and cons of any recourse to arms. In events so very different from each other in context, character and the composition of participants such as the Rangpur *dhing* against Debi Sinha (1783), the Barasat *bidroha* led by Titu Mir (1831), the Santal *hool* (1855) and the 'blue mutiny' of 1860 the

[1] I am grateful to my colleagues of the editorial team for their comments on an initial draft of this essay.

protagonists in each case had tried out petitions, deputations or other forms of supplication before actually declaring war on their oppressors.[2] Again, the revolts of the Kol (1832), the Santal and the Munda (1899-1900) as well as the Rangpur *dhing* and the jacqueries in Allahabad and Ghazipur districts during the Sepoy Rebellion of 1857-8 (to name only two out of many instances in that remarkable series) had all been inaugurated by planned and in some cases protracted consultation among the representatives of the local peasant masses.[3] Indeed there is hardly an instance of the peasantry, whether the cautious and earthy villagers of the plains or the supposedly more volatile *adivasis* of the upland tracts, stumbling or drifting into rebellion. They had far too much at stake and would not launch into it except as a deliberate, even if desperate, way out of an intolerable condition of existence. Insurgency, in other words, was a motivated and conscious undertaking on the part of the rural masses.

Yet this consciousness seems to have received little notice in the literature on the subject. Historiography has been content to deal with the peasant rebel merely as an empirical person or member of a class, but not as an entity whose will and reason constituted the praxis called rebellion. The omission is indeed dyed into most narratives by metaphors assimilating peasant revolts to natural phenomena: they break out like thunder storms, heave like earthquakes, spread like wildfires, infect like epidemics. In other words, when the proverbial clod of earth turns, this is a matter to be explained in terms of natural history. Even when this historiography is pushed to the point of producing an explanation in rather more human terms it will do so by assuming an identity of nature and culture, a hall-mark, presumably, of a very low state of civilization and exemplified in 'those periodical outbursts of crime and lawlessness to which all wild tribes are subject', as the first historian of the Chuar rebellion put it.[4]

---

[2] The instances are far too numerous to cite. For some of these see *MDS*, pp. 46-7, 48-9 on the Rangpur *dhing*; BC 54222: Metcalfe & Blunt to Court of Directors (10 April 1832), paras 14-15 on the Barasat uprising; W. W. Hunter, *Annals of Rural Bengal* (7th edition; London, 1897), pp. 237-8 and JP, 4 Oct. 1855: 'The Thacoor's Perwannah' for the Santal *hool* C. E. Buckland, *Bengal Under the Lieutenant-Governors*, vol. I (Calcutta, 1901), p. 192 for the 'blue mutiny'.

[3] See, for instance, *MDS*, pp. 579-80; *Freedom Struggle in Uttar Pradesh*, vol.IV (Lucknow, 1959), pp. 284-5, 549.

[4] J. C. Price, *The Chuar Rebellion of 1799*, p. cl. The edition of the work used in this essay is the one printed in A. Mitra (ed.), *District Handbooks: Midnapur* (Alipore, 1953), Appendix IV.

The Prose of Counter-Insurgency 47

Alternatively, an explanation will be sought in an enumeration of causes—of, say, factors of economic and political deprivation which do not relate at all to the peasant's consciousness or do so negatively—triggering off rebellion as a sort of reflex action, that is, as an instinctive and almost mindless response to physical suffering of one kind or another (e.g. hunger, torture, forced labour, etc.) or as a passive reaction to some initiative of his superordinate enemy. Either way insurgency is regarded as *external* to the peasant's consciousness and Cause is made to stand in as a phantom surrogate for Reason, the logic of that consciousness.

II

How did historiography come to acquire this particular blind spot and never find a cure? For an answer one could start by having a close look at its constituting elements and examine those cuts, seams and stitches—those cobbling marks—which tell us about the material it is made of and the manner of its absorption into the fabric of writing.

The corpus of historical writings on peasant insurgency in colonial India is made up of three types of discourse. These may be described as *primary*, *secondary* and *tertiary* according to the order of their appearance in time and their filiation. Each of these is differentiated from the other two by the degree of its formal and/or acknowledged (as opposed to real and/or tacit) identification with an official point of view, by the measure of its distance from the event to which it refers, and by the ratio of the distributive and integrative components in its narrative.

To begin with primary discourse, it is almost without exception official in character—official in a broad sense of the term. That is, it originated not only with bureaucrats, soldiers, sleuths and others directly employed by the government, but also with those in the non-official sector who were symbiotically related to the Raj, such as planters, missionaries, traders, technicians and so on among the whites and landlords, moneylenders, etc. among the natives. It was official also in so far as it was meant primarily for administrative use—for the information of government, for action on its part and for the determination of its policy. Even when it incorporated statements emanating from 'the other side', from the insurgents or their allies for instance, as it often did by way of direct or indirect reporting in the body of official correspondence or even more characteristically as 'enclosures' to the latter, this was done only as a part of an argument prompted by administrative concern. In other words, whatever its particular form—and there was indeed an amazing variety ranging from the exordial letter, telegram, despatch and communiqué to the terminal summary, report, judgement and pro-clamation—its production and circulation were both necessarily con-tingent on reasons of State.

Yet another of the distinctive features of this type of discourse is its immediacy. This derived from two conditions: first, that statements of this class were written either concurrently with or soon after the event, and secondly, that this was done by the participants concerned, a 'participant' being defined for this purpose in the broad sense of a contemporary involved in the event either in action or indirectly as an onlooker. This would exclude of course that genre of retrospective writing in which, as in some memoirs, an event and its recall are separated by a considerable hiatus, but would still leave a massive documentation—'primary sources' as it is known in the trade—to speak to the historian with a sort of ancestral voice and make him feel close to his subject.

The two specimens quoted below are fairly representative of this type. One of these relates to the Barasat uprising of 1831 and the other to the Santal rebellion of 1855.

TEXT 1[5]

To the Deputy Adjutant General of the Army

Sir,

Authentic information having reached Government that a body of *Fanatic Insurgents* are now committing *the most daring and wanton atrocities on the Inhabitants* of the Country in the neighbourhood of Tippy in the Magistracy of Baraset and have set at defiance and repulsed the utmost force that the local Civil Authority could assemble for their apprehension, I am directed by the Hon'ble Vice President in Council to request that you will without delay Communicate to the General Officer Commanding the Presidency Division the orders of Government that one Complete Battalion of Native Infantry from Barrackpore and two Six Pounders manned with the necessary compli-ment (sic) of Golundaze from Dum Dum, the whole under the Command of a Field Officer of judgement and decision, be immediately directed to proceed

[5] BC 54222: *JC*, 22 Nov. 1831: 'Extract from the Proceedings of the Honorable the Vice President in Council in the Military Department under date the 10th November 1831'. Emphasis added.

The Prose of Counter-Insurgency 49

and rendezvous at Baraset when they will be joined by 1 Havildar and 12 Troopers of the 3rd Regiment of Light Cavalry now forming the escort of the Hon'ble the Vice President.

2nd. The Magistrate will meet the Officer Commanding the Detachment at Barraset and will afford the necessary information for his guidance relative to the position of the Insurgents; but without having any authority to interfere in such Military operations as the Commanding Officer of the Detachments may deem expedient, for the purpose of routing or seizing or in the event of resistance destroying those who persevere in *defying the authority of the State* and *disturbing the public tranquil[l]ity.*

3rd. It is concluded that the service will not be of such a protracted nature as to require a larger supply of ammunition than may be carried in Pouch and in two Tumbrils for the Guns, and that no difficulties will occur respecting carriage. In the contrary event any aid needed will be furnished.

4th. The Magistrate will be directed to give every assistance regarding supplies and other requisites for the Troops.

Council Chamber   I am & ca

10th November 1831   (Sd.) Wm. Casement Coll.

Secy. to Govt. Mily. Dept.

TEXT

From W. C. Taylor Esqre.

To F. S. Mudge Esqre.

    Dated 7th July 1855

My dear Mudge,

There is a great gathering of Sontals 4 or 5000 men at a place about 8 miles off and I understand that they are all well armed with Bows and arrows, Tulwars, Spears & ca. and that *it is their intention to attack all the Europeans round and plunder and murder them. The cause of all this is that one of their Gods is supposed to have taken the Flesh and to have made his appearance at*

* *JP*, 19 July 1855: Enclosure to letter from the Magistrate of Murshidabad, dated 11 July 1855. Emphasis added.

some place near this, and that it is his intention to reign as a King over all this part of India, and has ordered the Sontals to collect and put to death all the Europeans and influential Natives round. As this is the nearest point to the gathering I suppose it will be first attacked and think it would be best for you to send notice to the authorities at Berhampore and ask for military aid as *it is not at all a nice look out being murdered* and as far as I can make out this is a *rather serious affair.*

Sreecond   Yours & ca

7th July 1855   /Signed/ W. C. Taylor

Nothing could be more immediate than these texts. Written as soon as these events were acknowledged as rebellion by those who had the most to fear from it, they are among the very first records we have on them in the collections of the India Office Library and the West Bengal State Archives. As the evidence on the 1831 *bidroha* shows,[7] it was not until 10 November that the Calcutta authorities came to recognize the violence reported from the Barasat region for what it was—a full-blooded insurrection led by Titu Mir and his men. Colonel Casement's letter identifies for us that moment when the hitherto unknown leader of a local peasantry entered the lists against the Raj and thereby made his way into history. The date of the other document too commemorates a beginning—that of the Santal *hool.* It was on that very day, 7 July 1855, that the assassination of Mahesh daroga following an encounter between his police and peasants gathered at Bhagnadihi detonated the uprising. The report was loud enough to register in that note scribbled in obvious alarm at Sreecond by an European employee of the East India Railway for the benefit of his colleague and the *sarkar.* Again, these are words that convey as directly as possible the impact of a peasant revolt on its enemies in its first sanguinary hours.

III

None of this instantaneousness percolates through to the next level— that of the secondary discourse. The latter draws on primary discourse as *matériel* but transforms it at the same time. To contrast the two types one could think of the first as historiography in a raw, primordial state or as an embryo yet to be articulated into an organism with

[7] Thus, *BC* 54222: *JC*, 3 Apr. 1832: Alexander to Barwell (28 Nov. 1831).

The Prose of Counter-Insurgency 51

discrete limbs, and the second as the processed product, however crude the processing, a duly constituted if infant discourse.

The difference is quite obviously a function of time. In the chronology of this particular corpus the secondary follows the primary at a distance and opens up a perspective to turn an event into history in the perception not only of those outside it but of the participants as well. It was thus that Mark Thornhill, Magistrate of Mathura during the summer of 1857 when a mutiny of the Treasury Guard sparked off jacqueries all over the district, was to reflect on the altered status of his own narrative in which he figured as a protagonist himself. Introducing his well-known memoirs, *The Personal Adventures And Experiences Of A Magistrate During The Rise, Progress, And Suppression Of The Indian Mutiny* (London, 1884) twenty-seven years after the event he wrote:

> After the suppression of the Indian Mutiny, I commenced to write an account of my adventures . . . by the time my narrative was completed, the then interest of the public in the subject was exhausted. Years have since passed, and an interest of another kind has arisen. The events of that time have become history, and to that history my story may prove a contribution . . . I have therefore resolved to publish my narrative . . .

Shorn of contemporaneity a discourse is thus recovered as an element of the past and classified as history. This change, aspectual as well as categorial, sites it at the very intersection of colonialism and historiography, endowing it with a duplex character linked at the same time to a system of power and the particular manner of its representation.

Its authorship is in itself witness to this intersection and Thornhill was by no means the only administrator turned historian. He was indeed one of many officials, civilian and military, who wrote retrospectively on popular disturbances in rural India under the Raj. Their statements, taken together, fall into two classes. First, there were those which were based on the writers' own experience as participants. Memoirs of one kind or another these were written either at a considerable delay after the events narrated or almost concurrently with them but intended, unlike primary discourse, for a public readership. The latter, an important distinction, shows how the colonialist mind managed to serve Clio and counter-insurgency at the same time so that the presumed neutrality of one could have hardly been left unaffected by the passion of the other, a point to which we shall soon return. Reminiscences of both kinds abound in the literature on the Mutiny, which dealt with the violence of the peasantry (especially in the North Western Provinces and central India) no less than with that of the sepoys. Accounts such as Thornhill's written long after the event, were matched by near contemporary ones such as Dunlop's *Service and Adventure with Khakee Ressallah; or Meerut Volunteer Horse during the Mutinies of 1857-58* (London, 1858) and Edwards' *Personal Adventures during the Indian Rebellion in Rohilcund, Futtehghur, and Oudh* (London 1858) to mention only two out of a vast outcrop intended to cater for a public who could not have enough of tales of horror and glory.

The other class of writings to qualify as secondary discourse is also the work of administrators. They too addressed themselves to a predominantly non-official readership but on themes not directly related to their own experience. Their work includes some of the most widely used and highly esteemed accounts of peasant uprisings written either as monographs on particular events, such as Jamini Mohan Ghosh's on the Sannyasi-and-Faqir disturbances and J. C. Price's on the Chuar Rebellion, or as statements included in more comprehensive histories like W. W. Hunter's story of the Santal *hool* in *The Annals of Rural Bengal*. Apart from these there were those distinguished contributions made by some of the best minds in the Civil Service to the historical chapters of the *District Gazetteers*. Altogether they constitute a substantial body of writing which enjoys much authority with all students of the subject and there is hardly any historiography at the next, that is, tertiary level of discourse that does not rely on these for sustenance.

The prestige of this genre is to no mean extent due to the aura of impartiality it has about it. By keeping their narrative firmly beyond the pale of personal involvement these authors managed, if only by implication, to confer on it a semblance of truth. As officials they were carriers of the will of the state no doubt. But since they wrote about a past in which they did not figure as functionaries themselves, their statements are taken to be more authentic and less biased than those of their opposite numbers whose accounts, based on reminiscences, were necessarily contaminated by their intervention in rural disturbances as agents of the Raj. By contrast the former are believed to have approached the narrated events from the outside. As observers separated clinically from the site and subject of diagnosis they are supposed to have found for their discourse a niche in that realm of perfect neutraility—the realm of History—over which the Aorist and the Third Person preside.

IV

How valid is this claim to neutrality? For an answer we may not take any bias for granted in this class of historical work from the mere fact of its origin with authors committed to colonialism. To take that as self-evident would be to deny historiography the possibility of acknowledging its own inadequacies and thus defeat the purpose of the present exercise. As should be clear from what follows, it is precisely by refusing to *prove* what appears as obvious that historians of peasant insurgency remain trapped—in the obvious. Criticism must therefore start not by naming a bias but by examining the components of the discourse, vehicle of all ideology, for the manner in which these might have combined to describe any particular figure of the past.

The components of both types of discourse and their varieties discussed so far are what we shall call segments. Made up of the same linguistic material, that is strings of words of varying lengths, they are of two kinds which may be designated, according to their function, as indicative and interpretative. A gross differentiation, this is meant to assign to them, within a given text, the role respectively of reporting and explaining. This however does not imply their mutual segregation. On the contrary they are often found embedded in each other not merely as a matter of fact but of necessity.

One can see in *Texts 1* and *2* how such imbrication works. In both of them the straight print stands for the indicative segments and the italics for the interpretative. Laid out according to no particular pattern in either of these letters they interpenetrate and sustain each other in order to give the documents their meaning, and in the process endow some of the strings with an ambiguity that is inevitably lost in this particular manner of typographical representation. However, the rough outline of a division of functions between the two classes emerges even from this schema—the indicative stating (that is reporting) the actual and anticipated actions of the rebels and their enemies, and the interpretative commenting on them in order to understand (that is to explain) their significance.

The difference between them corresponds to that between the two

basic components of any historical discourse which, following Roland
Barthes' terminology, we shall call *functions* and *indices*.[*] The former
are segments that make up the linear sequence of a narrative. Conti-
guous, they operate in a relation of solidarity in the sense of mutually
implying each other and add up to increasingly larger strings which
combine to produce the aggregative statement. The latter may thus
be regarded as a sum of micro-sequences to each of which, however
important or otherwise, it should be possible to assign names by a
metalinguistic operation using terms that may or may not belong to
the text under consideration. It is thus that the functions of a folk-tale
have been named by Bremond, after Propp, as *Fraud, Betrayal,
Struggle, Contract,*etc. and those of a triviality such as the offer of a
cigarette in a James Bond story designated by Barthes as *offering,
accepting, lighting,* and *smoking.* One may perhaps take a cue from
this procedure to define a historical statement as a discourse with a
name subsuming a given number of named sequences. Hence it
should be possible to speak of a hypothetical narrative called 'The
Insurrection of Titu Mir' made up of a number of sequences including
Text 1 quoted above.

  Let us give this document a name and call it, say, *Calcutta Council
Acts.* (Alternatives such as *Outbreak of Violence* or *Army Called Up*
should also do and be analysable in terms corresponding to, though
not identical with, those which follow.) In broad terms the message
Calcutta Council Acts (C) in our text can be read as a combination of
two groups of sequences called *alarm* (a) and *intervention* (b), each of
which is made up of a pair of segments—the former of *insurrection
breaks out* (a') and *information received* (a'') and the latter of *decision
to call up army* (b') and *order issued* (b''), one of the constituents in
each pair being represented in its turn by yet another linked series—
(a') by *atrocities committed* (a_1) and *authority defied* (a_2), and (b'') by
infantry to proceed (b_1), *artillery to support* (b_2) and *magistrate to
co-operate* (b_3). In other words the narrative in this document can be
written up in three equivalent steps so that

  [*] My debt to Roland Barthes for many of the analytic terms and procedures used in
this section and generally throughout this essay should be far too obvious to all
familiar with his 'Structural Analysis of Narratives' and 'The Struggle with the Angel'
in Barthes, *Image-Music-Text* (Glasgow, 1977), pp. 79-141, and 'Historical Discourse'
in M. Lane (ed.), *Structuralism, A Reader* (London, 1970), pp. 145-55, to require
detailed reference except where I quote directly from this literature.

The Prose of Counter-Insurgency 55

$$C \equiv (a+b) \dots\dots\dots\dots\dots\dots\dots\dots\dots \text{I}$$
$$\equiv (a'+a'') + (b'+b^{\iota}) \dots\dots\dots\dots\dots \text{II}$$
$$\equiv (a_1+a_2) + a'' + b' + (b_1+b_2+b_3) \dots\dots \text{III}$$

It should be clear from this arrangement that not all the elements of step II can be expressed in micro-sequences of the same order. Hence we are left at step III with a concatenation in which segments drawn from different levels of the discourse are imbricated to constitute a roughly hewn and uneven structure. In so far as functional units of the lowest denomination like these are what a narrative has as its syntagmatic relata its course can never be smooth. The hiatus between the loosely cobbled segments is necessarily charged with uncertainty, with 'moments of risk' and every micro-sequence terminates by opening up alternative possibilities only one of which is picked up by the next sequence as it carries on with the story. 'Du Pont, Bond's future partner, offers him a light from his lighter but Bond refuses; the meaning of this bifurcation is that Bond instinctively fears a booby-trapped gadget.'[*] What Barthes identifies thus as 'bifurcation' in fiction, has its parallels in historical discourse as well. The alleged commitment of atrocities (a_1) in that official despatch of 1831 cancels out the belief in the peaceful propagation of Titu's new doctrine which had already been known to the authorities but ignored so far as inconsequential. The expression, *authority defied* (a_2), which refers to the rebels having 'set at defiance and repulsed the utmost force that the local Civil Authority could assemble for their apprehension', has as its other if unstated term his efforts to persuade the Government by petition and deputation to offer redress for the grievances of his co-religionists. And so on. Each of these elementary functional units thus implies a node which has not quite materialized into an actual development, a sort of zero sign by means of which the narrative affirms its tension. And precisely because history as the verbal representation by man of his own past is by its very nature so full of hazard, so replete indeed with the verisimilitude of sharply differentiated choices, that it never ceases to excite. The historical discourse is the world's oldest thriller.

V

Sequential analysis thus shows a narrative to be a concatenation of

[*] Barthes, *Image-Music-Text*, p. 102.

not so closely aligned functional units. The latter are dissociative in their operation and emphasize the analytic rather than the synthetic aspect of a discourse. As such they are not what, by themselves, generate its meaning. Just as the sense of a word (e.g. 'man') is not fractionally represented in each of the letters (e.g. M, A, N) which make up its graphic image nor of a phrase (e.g. 'once upon a time') in its constituting words taken separately, so also the individual segments of a discourse cannot on their own tell us what it signifies. Meaning in each instance is the work of a process of integration ₒwhich complements that of sequential articulation. As Benveniste has put it, in any language 'it is dissociation which divulges to us its formal constitution and integration its signifying units'.[10]

This is true of the language of history as well. The integrative operation is carried out in its discourse by the other class of basic narrative units, that is, *indices*. A necessary and indispensable correlate of *functions* they are distinguished from the latter in some important respects:

> Indices, because of the vertical nature of their relations are truly semantic units: unlike 'functions' . . . they refer to a signified, not to an 'operation'. The ratification of indices is 'higher up' . . . a paradigmatic ratification. That of functions, by contrast, is always 'further on', is a syntagmatic ratification. *Functions* and *indices* thus overlay another classic distinction: functions involve metonymic relata, indices metaphoric relata; the former correspond to a functionality of doing, the latter to a functionality of being.[11]

The vertical intervention of indices in a discourse is possible because of the disruption of its linearity by a process corresponding to dystaxia in the behaviour of many natural languages. Bally who has studied this phenomenon in much detail finds that one of several conditions of its occurrence in French is 'when parts of the same sign are separated' so that the expression, 'elle a pardonné'taken in the negative, is splintered and re-assembled as 'elle *ne nous a jamais plus pardonné*'.[12]

---

[10] Émile Benveniste, *Problèmes de linguistique générale, I* (Paris, 1966), p. 126. The original, 'la dissociation nous livre la constitution formelle; l'intégration nous livre des unités signifiantes', has been rendered somewhat differently and I feel, less happily, in the English translation of the work, *Problems in General Linguistics* (Florida, 1971), p. 107.

[11] Barthes, *Image-Music-Text*, p. 93.

[12] Charles Bally, *Linguistique Générale et Linguistique Française* (Berne, 1965), p. 144.

The Prose of Counter-Insurgency   **57**

Similarly the simple predictive in Bengali 'shé jābé' can be re-written by the insertion of an interrogative or a string of negative conditionals between the two words to produce respectively 'shé *ki* jābé' and 'shé *nā hoy nā* jābé'.

In a historical narrative too it is a process of 'distension and expansion' of its syntagm which helps paradigmatic elements to infiltrate and reconstitute its discrete segments into a meaningful whole. It is precisely thus that the co-ordination of the metonymic and metaphorical axes is brought about in a statement and the necessary interaction of its functions and indices actualized. However these units are not distributed in equal proportions in all texts: some have a greater incidence of one kind than of the other. As a result a discourse could be either predominantly metonymic or metaphorical depending on whether a significantly larger number of its components are syntagmatically ratified or paradigmatically.[13] Our *Text I* is of the first type. One can see the formidable and apparently impenetrable array of its metonymic relata in step III of the sequential analysis given above. Here at last we have the perfect authentication of the idiot's view of history as one damn'd thing after another: *rising - information - decision - order*. However, a closer look at the text can detect chinks which have allowed 'comment', to worm its way through the plate armour of 'fact'. The italicized expressions are witness to this paradigmatic intervention and indeed its measure. Indices, they play the role of *adjectives* or *epithets* as opposed to verbs which, to speak in terms of homology between sentence and narrative, is the role of functions.[14] Working intimately together with the latter they make the despatch into more than a mere register of happenings and help to inscribe into it a meaning, an interpretation so that the protagonists emerge from it not as peasants but as '*Insurgents*', not as Musalman but as '*fanatic*'; their action not as resistance to the tyranny of the rural elite but as '*the most daring and wanton atrocities on the inhabitants*'; their project not as a revolt against zamindari but as '*defying the authority of the State*', not as a search for an alternative order in which the peace of the countryside would not be violated by the officially condoned anarchy of semi-feudal landlordism but as, '*disturbing the public tranquil[l]ity*'.

If the intervention of indices 'substitutes meaning for the straight-

[13] Barthes, *Elements of Semiology* (London, 1967), p. 60.
[14] Barthes, *Image-Music-Text*, p. 128.

forward copy of the events recounted,[15] in a text so charged with metonymy as the one discussed above, it may be trusted to do so to an even greater degree in discourses which are predominantly metaphorical. This should be evident from *Text 2* where the element of comment, italicized by us, largely outweighs that of report. If the latter is represented as a concatenation of three functional sequences, namely, *armed Santals gathering, authorities to be alerted* and *military aid requested*, it can be seen how the first of these has been separated from the rest by the insertion of a large chunk of explanatory material and how the others too are enveloped and sealed off by comment. The latter is inspired by the fear that Sreecond being '*the nearest point to the gathering . . . will be first attacked*' and of course '*it is not at all a nice look out being murdered*'. Notice, however, that this fear justifies itself *politically*, that is, by imputing to the Santals an '*intention to attack . . . plunder . . . and put to death all the Europeans and influential Natives*' so that '*one of their Gods*' in human form may '*reign as a King over all this part of India*'. Thus, this document is not neutral in its attitude to the events witnessed and put up as 'evidence' before the court of history it can hardly be expected to testify with impartiality. On the contrary it is the voice of committed colonialism. It has already made a choice between the prospect of Santal self-rule in Damin-i-Koh and the continuation of the British Raj and identifies what is allegedly good for the promotion of one as fearsome and catastrophic for the other—as '*a rather serious affair*'. In other words the indices in this discourse—as well as in the one discussed above—introduce us to a particular code so constituted that for each of its signs we have an antonym, a counter-message, in another code. To borrow a binary representation made famous by Mao Tse-tung,[16] the reading, '*It's terrible!*' for any element in one must show up in the other as '*It's fine!*' for a corresponding element and vice versa. To put this clash of codes graphically one can arrange the indices italicized below of *Texts 1* and *2* in a matrix called 'TERRIBLE' (in conformity to the adjectival attribute of units of this class) in such a way as to indicate their mapping into the implied, though unstated terms (given in straight types) of a corresponding matrix 'FINE'.

[15] Ibid., p. 119

[16] *Selected Works of Mao Tse-tung*, vol. I (Peking, 1967), pp. 26-7.

TERRIBLE	FINE
Insurgents	peasants
fanatic	Islamic puritan
daring and wanton atrocities on the Inhabitants	resistance to oppression
defying the authority of the State	revolt against zamindari
disturbing the public tranquil(l)ity	struggle for a better order
intention to attack, etc	intention to punish oppressors
one of their Gods to reign as a King	Santal self-rule

What comes out of the interplay of these mutually implied but opposed matrices is that our texts are not the record of observations uncontaminated by bias, judgement and opinion. On the contrary, they speak of a total complicity. For if the expressions in the right-hand column taken together may be said to stand for insurgency, the code which contains all signifiers of the subaltern practice of 'turning things upside down' and the consciousness that informs it, then the other column must stand for its opposite, that is, counter-insurgency. The antagonism between the two is irreducible and there is nothing in this to leave room for neutrality. Hence these documents make no sense except in terms of a code of pacification which, under the Raj, was a complex of coercive intervention by the State and its protégés, the native elite, with arms and words. Representatives of the primary type of discourse in the historiography of peasant revolts, these are specimens of the prose of counter-insurgency.

VI

How far does secondary discourse too share such commitment? Is it possible for it to speak any other prose than that of a counter-insurgency? Those narratives of this category in which their authors figure among the protagonists are of course suspect almost by definition, and the presence of the grammatical first person in these must be acknowledged as a sign of complicity. The question however is whether the loss of objectivity on this account is adequately made up by the consistent use of the aorist in such writings. For as Benveniste observes, the historical utterance admits of three variations of the past tense—that is, the aorist, the imperfect and the pluperfect, and of course the present is altogether excluded.[17] This condition is

[17] Benveniste, op. cit., p. 239.

indeed satisfied by reminiscences separated by a long enough hiatus from the events concerned. What has to be found out therefore is the extent to which the force of the preterite corrects the bias caused by the absence of the third person.

Mark Thornhill's memoirs of the Mutiny provide us with a text in which the author looks back at a series of events he had experienced twenty-seven years ago. 'The events of that time' had 'turned into history', and he intends, as he says in the extract quoted above, to make a contribution 'to that history', and thus produce what we have defined as a particular kind of secondary discourse. The difference inscribed in it by that interval is perhaps best grasped by comparing it with some samples of primary discourse we have on the same subject from the same author. Two of these[18] may be read together as a record of his perception of what happened at the Mathura sadar station and the surrounding countryside between 14 May and 3 June 1857. Written by him donning the district magistrate's topee and addressed to his superiors—one on 5 June 1857, that is, within forty-eight hours of the terminal date of the period under discussion, and the other on 10 August 1858 when the events were still within vivid recall as a very recent past—these letters coincide in scope with that of the narrative covering the same three weeks in the first ninety pages of his book written nearly three decades later donning the historian's hat.

The letters are both predominantly metonymic in character. Originating as they did almost from within the related experience itself they are necessarily foreshortened and tell the reader in breathless sequences about some of the happenings of that extraordinary summer. The syntagm thus takes on a semblance of factuality with hardly any room in it for comment. Yet here again the welding of the functional units can be seen, on close inspection, to be less solid than at first sight. Embedded in them there are indices revealing the anxieties of the local custodian of law and order ('the state of the district generally is such as to *defy all control*';'the *law* is at a *standstill*'), his fears ('*very alarming* rumours of the approach of the rebel army'), his moral disapprobation of the activities of the armed villagers ('the disturbances in the district . . . increasing . . . in . . . *enormity*'), his appreciation by contrast of the native collaborators hostile to the

---

[18] *Freedom Struggle in Uttar Pradesh*, vol. V, pp. 685-92.

insurgents ('. . . 'the Seths' house . . . *received us most kindly*'). Indices such as these are ideological birth-marks displayed prominently on much of this type of material relating to peasant revolts. Indeed, taken together with some other relevant textual features—e.g. the abrupt mode of address in these documents so revealing of the shock and terror generated by the *émeute*—they accuse all such allegedly 'objective' evidence on the militancy of the rural masses to have been tainted at its source by the prejudice and partisan outlook of their enemies. If historians fail to take notice of these tell-tale signs branded on the staple of their trade, that is a fact which must be explained in terms of the optics of a colonialist historiography rather than construed in favour of the presumed objectivity of their 'primary sources'.

There is nothing immediate or abrupt about the corresponding secondary discourse. On the contrary it has various perspectives built into it to give it a depth in time and following from this temporal determination, its meaning. Compare for instance the narration of events in the two versions for any particular day—for, say, 14 May 1857 at the very beginning of our three-week period. Written up in a very short paragraph of fifty-seven words in Thornhill's letter of 10 August 1858 this can be represented fully in four pithy segments without any significant loss of message: *mutineers approaching; information received from Gurgaon; confirmed by Europeans north of the district; women and non-combattants sent off to Agra*. Since the account starts, for all practical purposes, with this entry, there are no exordia to serve as its context, giving this instant take-off the sense, as we have noticed, of a total surprise. In the book however that same instant is provided with a background spread over four and a half months and three pages (pp. 1-3). All of this time and space is devoted to some carefully chosen details of the author's life and experience in the period preceding the Mutiny. These are truly *significant*. As indices they prepare the reader for what is to come and help him to *understand* the happenings of 14 May and after, when these enter into the narrative at staggered stages. Thus the mysterious circulation of chapatis in January and the silent but expressive concern on the narrator's brother, a high official, over a telegram received at Agra on 12 May conveying the still unconfirmed news of the Meerut uprising, portend the developments two days later at his own district headquarters. Again the trivia about his 'large income and great authority', his house, horses, servants, 'a chest full of silver plate, which stood in the hall and . . . a great store of Cashmere shawls, pearls, and diamonds' all help to index, by contrast, the holocaust which was soon to reduce his authority to nothing, and turn his servants into rebels, his house into a shambles, his property into booty for the plundering poor of town and country. By anticipating the narrated events thus, if only by implication, secondary discourse destroys the entropy of the first, its raw material. Henceforth there will be nothing in the story that can be said to be altogether unexpected.

This effect is the work of the so-called 'organization shifters'[19] which help the author to superimpose a temporality of his own on that of his theme, that is 'to "dechronologize" the historical thread and restore, if only by way of reminiscence or nostalgia, a Time at once complex, parametric, and non-linear . . . braiding the chronology of the subject-matter with that of the language-act which reports it'. In the present instance the 'braiding' consists not only in fitting an evocative context to the bare sequence related in that short paragraph of his letter. The shifters disrupt the syntagm twice to insert in the breach, on both occasions, a moment of authorial time suspended between the two poles of 'waiting', a figure ideally constituted to allow the play of digressions, asides and parentheses forming loops and zigzags in a story-line and adding thereby to its depth. Thus, waiting for news about the movements of the mutineers he reflects on the peace of the early evening at the sadar station and strays from his account to tell us in violation of the historiographical canon of tense and person: 'The scene was simple and full of the repose of Eastern life. In the times that followed it often recurred to my memory.' And, again, waiting later on for transport to take away the evacuees gathered in his drawing room, he withdraws from that particular night for the duration of a few words to comment: 'It was a beautiful room, brightly lighted, gay with flowers. It was the last time I thus saw it, and so it remains impressed on my memory.'

How far does the operation of these shifters help to correct the bias resulting from the writer's intervention in the first person? Not much by this showing. For each of the indices wedged into the narrative represents a principled choice between the terms of a paradigmatic

[19] For Roman Jakobson's exposition of this key concept, see his *Selected Writings, 2: Word and Language* (The Hague and Paris, 1971), pp. 130-47. Barthes develops the notion of organization shifters in his essay 'Historical Discourse', pp. 146-8. All extracts quoted in this paragraph are taken from that essay unless otherwise mentioned.

opposition. Between the authority of the head of the district and its defiance by the armed masses, between the habitual servility of his menials and their assertion of self-respect as rebels, between the insignia of his wealth and power (e.g. gold, horses, shawls, bungalow) and their appropriation or destruction by the subaltern crowds, the author, hardly differentiated from the administrator that he was twenty-seven years ago, consistently chooses the former. Nostalgia makes the choice all the more eloquent—a recall of what is thought to be 'fine' such as a peaceful evening or an elegant room emphasizing by contrast the 'terrible' aspects of popular violence directed against the Raj. Quite clearly there is a logic to this preference. It affirms itself by negating a series of inversions which, combined with other signs of the same order, constitute a code of insurgency. The pattern of the historian's choice, identical with the magistrate's, conforms thus to a counter-code, the code of counter-insurgency.

VII

If the neutralizing effect of the aorist fails thus to prevail over the subjectivity of the protagonist as narrator in this particular genre of secondary discourse, how does the balance of tense and person stand in the other kind of writing within the same category? One can see two distinct idioms at work here, both identified with the standpoint of colonialism but unlike each other in expressing it. The cruder variety is well exemplified in *The Chuar Rebellion of 1799* by J. C. Price. Written long after the event, in 1874, it was obviously meant by the author, Settlement Officer of Midnapur at the time, to serve as a straightforward historical account with no particular administrative end in view. He addressed it to 'the casual reader' as well as to any 'future Collector of Midnapore', hoping to share with both 'that keen interest which I have felt as I have read the old Midnapore records'.[20] But the author's 'delight . . . experienced in pouring over these papers' seems to have produced a text almost indistinguishable from the primary discourse used as its source. The latter is, for one thing, conspicuous by its sheer physical presence. Over a fifth of that half of the book which deals specifically with the events of 1799 is made up of direct quotations from those records and another large part of barely modified extracts. More important for us, however, is the evidence we have of the author's identification of his own senti-

[20] Price, op. cit., p. *clx*.

ments with those of that small group of whites who were reaping the
whirlwind produced by the wind of a violently disruptive change the
Company's Government had sown in the south-western corner of
Bengal. Only the fear of the beleaguered officials at Midnapur station
in 1799 turns seventy-five years later into that genocidal hatred
characteristic of a genre of post-Mutiny British writing. 'The disinclination of the authorities, civil or military, to proceed in person
to help to quell the disturbances is most striking', he writes shaming
his compatriots and then goes on to brag:

> In these days of breech-loaders half a dozen Europeans would have been a
> match for twenty times their number of Chuars. Of course with the
> imperfect nature of the weapons of that day it could not be expected that
> Europeans would fruitlessly rush into danger, but I should have expected
> that the European officers of the station would have in some instances at
> least courted and met an attack in person and repulsed their assailants. I
> wonder that no one European officer, civilian or military, with the
> exception of perhaps Lieutenant Gill, owned to that sensation of joyous
> excitement most young men feel now-a-days in field sports, or in any
> pursuit where there is an element of danger. I think most of us, had we
> lived in 1799, would have counted it better sport had we bagged a
> marauding Chuar reeking with blood and spoils, than the largest bear that
> the Midnapore jungles can produce.[21]

Quite clearly the author's separation from his subject-matter
and the difference between the time of the event and that of its
narration here have done little to inspire objectivity in him. His
passion is apparently of the same order as that of the British soldier
who wrote on the eve of the sack of Delhi in 1857: 'I most
sincerely trust that the order given when we attack Delhi will
be. . ."Kill every one; no quarter is to be given" '.[22] The historian's
attitude to rebels is in this instance indistinguishable from that of
the State—the attitude of the hunter to his quarry. Regarded thus
an insurgent is not a subject of understanding or interpretation but
of extermination, and the discourse of history, far from being
neutral, serves directly to instigate official violence.

There were however other writers working within the same
genre who are known to have expressed themselves in a less

---

[21] Ibid.

[22] Reginald G. Wilberforce, *An Unrecorded Chapter of the Indian Mutiny* (2nd
edition; London, 1894), pp. 76-7.

The Prose of Counter-Insurgency 65

sanguinary idiom. They are perhaps best represented by W. W. Hunter and his account of the Santal insurrection of 1855 in *The Annals of Rural Bengal*. It is, in many respects, a remarkable text. Written within a decade of the Mutiny and twelve years of the *hool*,[23] it has none of that revanchist and racist overtone common to a good deal of Anglo-Indian literature of the period. Indeed the author treats the enemies of the Raj not only with consideration but with respect although they had wiped it off from three eastern districts in a matter of weeks and held out for five months against the combined power of the colonial army and its newly acquired auxiliaries—railways and the 'electric telegraph'. One of the first modern exercises in the historiography of Indian peasant revolts, it situates the uprising in a cultural and socio-economic context, analyses its causes, and draws on local records and contemporary accounts for evidence about its progress and eventual suppression. Here, to all appearances, we have that classic instance of the author's own bias and opinion dissolving under the operation of the past tense and the grammatical third person. Here, perhaps, historical discourse has come to its own and realized that ideal of an 'apersonal . . . mode of narrative . . . designed to wipe out the presence of the speaker'?[24]

This semblance of objectivity, of the want of any obviously demonstrable bias, has however nothing to do with 'facts speaking for themselves' in a state of pure metonymy unsullied by comment. On the contrary the text is packed with comment. One has to compare it with something like the near contemporary article on this subject in *Calcutta Review* (1856) or even K. K. Datta's history of the *hool* written long after its suppression to realize how little there is in it of the details of what actually happened.[25] Indeed the narration of the event occupies in the book only about 7 per cent of the chapter which builds up climactically towards it, and somewhat less than 50 per cent of the print devoted specifically to this topic within that chapter. The syntagm is broken up again and again by dystaxia and interpretation

[23] It appears from a note in this work that parts of it were written in 1866. The dedication bears the date 4 March 1868. All our references to this work in quotation or otherwise are to Chapter IV of the seventh edition (London, 1897) unless otherwise stated.

[24] Barthes, *Image-Music-Text*, p. 112.

[25] Anon., 'The Sonthal Rebellion', *Calcutta Review* (1856), pp. 223-64; K. K. Datta, 'The Santal Insurrection of 1855-57', in *Anti-British Plots and Movements before 1857* (Meerut, 1970), pp. 43-152.

filters through to assemble the segments into a meaningful whole of a primarily metaphorical character. The consequence of this operation that is most relevant for our purpose here is the way in which it distributes the paradigmatic relata along an axis of historical continuity between a 'before' and an 'after', forelengthening it with a context and extending it into a perspective. The representation of insurgency ends up thus by having its moment intercalated between its past and future so that the particular values of one and the other are rubbed into the event to give it the meaning specific to it.

VIII

To turn first to the context, two-thirds of the chapter which culminates in the history of the insurrection is taken up with an inaugural account of what may be called the natural history of its protagonists. An essay in ethnography this deals with the physical traits, language, traditions, myths, religion, rituals, habitat, environment, hunting and agricultural practices, social organization and communal government of the Santals of the Birbhum region. There are many details here which index the coming conflict as one of contraries, as between the noble savage of the hills and mean exploiters from the plains— references to his personal dignity ('He does not abase himself to the ground like the rural Hindu'; the Santal woman is 'ignorant of the shrinking squeamishness of the Hindu female', etc.) implying the contrast his would-be reduction to servitude by Hindu moneylenders, his honesty ('Unlike the Hindu, he never thinks of making money by a stranger, scrupulously avoids all topics of business, and feels pained if payment is pressed upon him for the milk and fruit which his wife brings out'), the greed and fraud of the alien traders and landlords leading eventually to the insurrection, his aloofness ('The Santals live as much apart as possible from the Hindus'), the *diku*'s intrusion into his life and territory and the holocaust which inevitably followed.

These indices give the uprising not only a moral dimension and the values of a just war, but also a depth in time. The latter is realized by the operation of diachronic markers in the text—an imaginary past by creation myths (appropriate for an enterprise taken up on the Thakur's advice) and a real but remote past (befitting a revolt steeped in tradition) by the sherds of prehistory in ritual and speech with the Santals' ceremony of 'Purifying for the Dead' mentioned, for instance, as the trace of 'a faint remembrance of the far-off time when they dwelt beside great rivers' and their language as 'that intangible record on which a nation's past is graven more deeply than on brass tablets or rock inscriptions'.

Moving closer to the event the author provides it with a recent past covering roughly a period of sixty years of 'direct administration' in the area. The moral and temporal aspects of the narrative merge here in the figure of an irreconcilable contradiction. On the one hand there were, according to Hunter, a series of beneficial measures introduced by the government—the Decennial Settlement helping to expand the area under cultivation and induce the Santals, since 1792, to hire themselves out as agricultural labourers; the setting up, in 1832, of an enclosure ringed off by masonry pillars where they could colonize virgin land and jungle without fear of harassment from hostile tribes; the development of 'English enterprise' in Bengal in the form of indigo factories for which 'the Santal immigrants afforded a population of day-labourers'; and last but not the least of bonanzas, their absorption by thousands into labour gangs for the construction of railways across that region in 1854. But there were, on the other hand, two sets of factors which combined to undo all the good resulting from colonial rule, namely, the exploitation and oppression of the Santals by greedy and fraudulent Hindu landlords, money-lenders and traders, and the failure of the local administration, its police and the courts to protect them or redress the wrongs they suffered.

IX

This emphasis on contradiction serves on obviously interpretative purpose for the author. It makes it possible for him to locate the cause of the uprising in a failure of the Raj to make its ameliorative aspects prevail over the still lingering defects and shortcomings in its exercise of authority. The account of the event therefore fits directly into the objective stated at the beginning of the chapter, that is, to interest not only the scholar 'in these lapsed races' but the statesman as well. 'The Indian statesman will discover', he had written there referring euphemistically to the makers of British policy in India, 'that these Children of the Forest are . . . amenable to the same reclaiming influences as other men, and that upon their capacity for civilisation the future extension of English enterprise in Bengal in a large measure depends'. It is this concern for 'reclamation' (shorthand for accelerating the transformation of the tribal peasantry into wage labour and harnessing them to characteristically colonialist projects for the exploitation of Indian resources) which explains the mixture of firmness and 'understanding' in Hunter's attitude to the rebellion. A liberal-imperalist he regarded it both as a menace to the stability of the Raj and as a useful critique of its far from perfect administration. So while he censured the government of the day for not declaring Martial Law soon enough in order to cut down the *hool* at its inception, he was careful to differentiate himself from those of his compatriots who wanted to punish the entire Santal community for the crime of its rebels and deport overseas the population of the districts involved. A genuinely far-sighted imperialist he looked forward to the day when the tribe, like many other aboriginal peoples of the subcontinent, would demonstrate its 'capacity for civilisation' by acting as an inexhaustible source of cheap labour power.

This vision is inscribed into the perspective with which the narration ends. Blaming the outbreak of the *hool* squarely on that 'cheap and practical administration' which paid no heed to the Santals' complaints and concentrated on tax collection alone it goes on to catalogue the somewhat illusory benefits of 'the more exact system that was introduced after the revolt' to keep the power of the usurers over debtors within the limits of the law, check the use of false weights and measures in retail trade, and ensure the right of bonded labourers to choose freedom by desertion or change of employers. But more than administrative reform it was 'English enterprise' again which radically contributed to the welfare of the tribe. The railways 'completely changed the relation of labour to capital' and did away with that 'natural reason for slavery—to wit, the absence of a wage-fund for free workmen'. The demand for plantation labour in the Assam tea-districts 'was destined still further to improve the position of the Santals' and so was the stimulus for indenturing coolies for the Mauritius and the Carribeans. It was thus that the tribal peasant prospered thanks to the development of a vast sub-continental and overseas labour market within the British Empire. In the Assam tea gardens 'his whole family gets employment, and every additional child, instead of being the means of increasing his poverty, becomes a source of wealth', while the coolies returned from Africa or the West Indies 'at the expiry of their contracts with savings averaging £20 sterling, a sum sufficient to set up a Santal as a considerable proprietor in his own village'.

Many of these so-called improvements were, as we know now looking back at them across a century, the result of sheer wishful thinking or so ephemeral as not to have mattered at all. The connection between usury and bonded labour continued all through British rule well into independent India. The freedom of the labour market was seriously restricted by the want of competition between British and indigenous capital. The employment of tribal families on tea plantations became a source of cynical exploitation of the labour of women and children. The advantages of mobility and contractuality were cancelled out by irregularities in the process of recruitment and the manipulation of the contrary factors of economic dependence and social differentiation by *arkatis*. The system of indenturing helped rather less to liberate servile labour than to develop a sort of second serfdom, and so on.

Yet this vision which never materialized offers an insight into the character of this type of discourse. The perspective it inspired amounted in effect to a testament of faith in colonialism. The *hool* was assimilated there to the career of the Raj and the militant enterprise of a tribal peasantry to free themselves from the triple yoke of *sarkari*, *sahukari* and *zamindari* to 'English enterprise'—the infrastructure of Empire. Hence the objective stated at the beginning of the account could be reiterated towards the end with the author saying that he had written at least 'partly for the instruction which their [the Santals'] recent history furnishes as to the proper method of dealing with the aboriginal races'. The suppression of local peasant revolts was a part of this method, but it was incorporated now in a broader strategy designed to tackle the economic problems of the British Government in India as an element of the global problems of imperial politics. 'These are the problems', says Hunter in concluding the chapter, 'which Indian statesmen during the next fifty years will be called upon to solve. Their predecessors have given civilisation to India; it will be their duty to render that civilisation at once beneficial to the natives and safe for ourselves.' In other words this historiography was assigned a role in a political process that would ensure the security of the Raj by a combination of force to crush rebellion when it occurred and reform to pre-empt it by wrenching the tribal peasantry out of their rural bases and distributing them as cheap labour power for British capital to exploit in India and abroad. The overtly aggressive and nervous prose of counter-insurgency born of the worries of the early colonial days came thus to adopt in this genre of historical writing the firm but benign, authoritarian but understanding idiom of a mature and self-assured imperialism.

X

How is it that even the more liberal type of secondary discourse is unable thus to extricate itself from the code of counter-insurgency? With all the advantage he has of writing in the third person and addressing a distinct past the official turned historian is still far from being impartial where official interests are concerned. His sympathies for the peasants' sufferings and his understanding of what goaded them to revolt, do not, when the crunch comes, prevent him from siding with law and order and justifying the transfer of the campaign against the *hool* from civilian to military hands in order to crush it completely and quickly. And as discussed above, his partisanship over the outcome of the rebellion is matched by his commitment to the aims and interests of the regime. The discourse of history, hardly distinguished from policy, ends up by absorbing the concerns and objectives of the latter.

In this affinity with policy historiography reveals its character as a form of *colonialist knowledge*. That is, it derives directly from that knowledge which the bourgeoisie had used in the period of their ascendancy to interpret the world in order to master it and establish their hegemony over Western societies, but turned into an instrument of national oppression as they began to acquire for themselves 'a place in the sun'. It was thus that political science which had defined the ideal of citizenship for European nation-states was used in colonial India to set up institutions and frame laws designed specifically to generate a mitigated and second-class citizenship. Political economy which had developed in Europe as a critique of feudalism was made to promote a neo-feudal landlordism in India. Historiography too adapted itself to the relations of power under the Raj and was harnessed more and more to the service of the state.

It was thanks to this connection and a good deal of talent to back it up that historical writing on themes of the colonial period shaped up as a highly coded discourse. Operating within the framework of a many-sided affirmation of British rule in the subcontinent it assumed the function of representing the recent past of its people as 'England's Work in India'. A discourse of power in its own right it had each of its

The Prose of Counter-Insurgency   71

moments displayed as a triumph, that is, as the most favourable upshot of a number of conflicting possibilities for the regime at any particular time. In its mature form, therefore, as in Hunter's *Annals*, continuity figures as one of its necessary and cardinal aspects. Unlike primary discourse it cannot afford to be foreshortened and without a sequel. The event does not constitute its sole content, but is the middle term between a beginning which serves as a context and an end which is at the same time a perspective linked to the next sequence. The only element that is constant in this ongoing series is the Empire and the policies needed to safeguard and perpetuate it.

Functioning as he does within this code Hunter with all the good-will so solemnly announced in his dedicatory note ('These pages... have little to say touching the governing race. My business is with the people') writes up the history of a popular struggle as one in which the real subject is not the people but, indeed, 'the governing race' institutionalized as the Raj. Like any other narrative of this kind his account of the *hool* too is there to celebrate a continuity—that of British power in India. The statement of causes and reforms is no more than a structural requirement for this continuum providing it respectively with context and perspective. These serve admirably to register the event as a datum in the life-story of the Empire, but do nothing to illuminate that consciousness which is called insurgency. The rebel has no place in this history as the subject of rebellion.

XI

There is nothing in tertiary discourse to make up for this absence. Farthest removed in time from the events which it has for its theme it always looks at them in the third person. It is the work of non-official writers in most cases or of former officials no longer under any professional obligation or constraint to represent the standpoint of the government. If it happens to carry an official view at all this is only because the author has chosen it of his own will rather than because he has been conditioned to do so by any loyalty or allegiance based on administrative involvement. There are indeed some historical works which actually show such a preference and are unable to speak in a voice other than that of the custodians of law and order—an instance of tertiary discourse reverting to that state of crude identifi-cation with the regime so characteristic of primary discourse.

But there are other and very different idioms within this genre ranging from liberal to left. The latter is particularly important as perhaps the most influential and prolific of all the many varieties of tertiary discourse. We owe to it some of the best studies on Indian peasant insurgency and more and more of these are coming out all the time as evidence both of a growing academic interest in the subject and the relevance that the subaltern movements of the past have to contemporary tensions in our part of the world. This literature is distinguished by its effort to break away from the code of counter-insurgency. It adopts the insurgent's point of view and regards, with him, as 'fine' what the other side calls 'terrible', and vice versa. It leaves the reader in no doubt that it wants the rebels and not their enemies to win. Here unlike in secondary discourse of the liberal-imperialist type recognition of the wrongs done to the peasants leads directly to support for their struggle to seek redress by arms.

Yet these two types, so very different from and contrary to each other in ideological orientation, have much else that is common between them. Take for instance that remarkable contribution of radical scholarship, Suprakash Ray's *Bharater Krishak-bidroha O Ganatantrik Samgram*[26] and compare its account of the Santal uprising of 1855 with Hunter's. The texts echo each other as narratives. Ray's being the later work has all the advantage of drawing on more recent research such as Datta's, and thus being more informed. But much of what it has to say about the inauguration and development of the *hool* is taken—in fact, quoted directly—from Hunter's *Annals*.[27] And both the authors rely on the *Calcutta Review* (1856) article for much of their evidence. There is thus little in the description of this particular event which differs significantly between the secondary and the tertiary types of discourse.

Nor is there much to distinguish between the two in terms of their admiration for the courage of the rebels and their abhorrence of the genocidal operations mounted by the counter-insurgency forces. In fact, on both these points Ray reproduces *in extenso* Hunter's testimony, gathered first-hand from officers directly involved in the campaign, that the Santals 'did not understand yielding', while for the army, 'it was not war . . . it was execution'.[28] The sympathy expressed for the enemies of the Raj in the radical tertiary discourse is

[26] Vol.I (Calcutta, 1966), Ch.13.
[27] For these see ibid.,pp. 323, 325, 327, 328.
[28] Ibid., p. 337; Hunter, op. cit., pp. 247-9.

The Prose of Counter-Insurgency   73

matched fully by that in the colonialist secondary discourse. Indeed, for both, the *hool* was an eminently just struggle—an evaluation derived from their mutual concurrence about the factors which had provoked it. Wicked landlords, extortionate usurers, dishonest traders, venal police, irresponsible officials and partisan processes of law—all figure with equal prominence in both the accounts. Both the historians draw on the evidence recorded on this subject in the *Calcutta Review* essay, and for much of his information about Santal indebtedness and bond slavery, about moneylenders' and landlords' oppression and administrative connivance at all this Ray relies heavily again on Hunter, as witness the extracts quoted liberally from the latter's work.[29]

However, causality is used by the two writers to develop entirely different perspectives. The statement of causes has the same part to play in Hunter's account as in any other narrative of the secondary type—that is, as an essential aspect of the discourse of counter-insurgency. In this respect his *Annals* belongs to a tradition of colonialist historiography which, for this particular event, is typically exemplified by that racist and vindicative essay, 'The Sonthal Rebellion'. There the obviously knowledgeable but tough-minded official ascribes the uprising, as Hunter does, to banias' fraud, mahajani transaction, zamindari despotism and sarkari inefficiency. In much the same vein Thornhill's *Personal Adventures* accounts for the rural uprisings of the period of the Mutiny in Uttar Pradesh quite clearly by the breakdown in traditional agrarian relations consequent on the advent of British rule. O'Malley identifies the root of the Pabna *bidroha* of 1873 in rack-renting by landlords, and the Deccan Riots Commission that of the disturbances of 1875 in the exploitation of the Kunbi peasantry by alien moneylenders in Poona and Ahmednagar districts.[30] One could go on adding many other events and texts to this list. The spirit of all these is well represented in the following extract from the *Judicial Department Resolutions* of 22 November 1831 on the subject of the insurrection led by Titu Mir:

[29] Ray, op. cit., pp. 316-19.
[30] Anon., op. cit., pp. 238-41; Thornhill, op. cit., pp. 33-5; L.S.S. O'Malley, *Bengal District Gazetteers:Pabna* (Calcutta, 1923), p. 25; *Report of the Commission Appointed in India to Inquire into the Causes of the Riots which took place in the year 1875 in the Poona and Ahmednagar Districts of the Bombay Presidency* (London, 1878), *passim*.

The serious nature of the late disturbances in the district of Baraset renders it an object of paramount importance that the *cause* which gave rise to them should be fully *investigated* in order that the motives which activated the insurgents may be rightly *understood* and such measures adopted as may be deemed expedient *to prevent a recurrence of similar disorders.*[31]

That sums it up. To know the cause of a phenomenon is already a step taken in the direction of controlling it. To *investigate* and thereby *understand* the cause of rural disturbances is an aid to measures 'deemed expedient *to prevent a recurrence of similar disorders'*. To that end the correspondent of the *Calcutta Review* (1856) recommended 'that condign retribution', namely, 'that they [the Santals] should be surrounded and hunted up everywhere . . . that they should be compelled, by force, if need be, to return to the Damin-i-koh, and to the wasted country in Bhaugulpore and Beerbhoom, to rebuild the ruined villages, restore the desolate fields to cultivation, open roads, and advance general public works; and do this under watch and guard . . . and that this state of things should be continued, until they are completely tranquillized, and reconciled to their allegiance'.[32] The gentler alternative put forward by Hunter was, as we have seen, a combination of Martial Law to suppress an ongoing revolt and measures to follow it up by 'English enterprise' in order (as his compatriot had suggested) to absorb the unruly peasantry as a cheap labour force in agriculture and public works for the benefit respectively of the same *dikus* and railway and roadwork engineers against whom they had taken up arms. With all their variation in tone, however, both the prescriptions to 'make . . . rebellion impossible by the elevation of the Sonthals'[33]—indeed, all colonialist solutions arrived at by the casual explanation of our peasant uprisings—were grist to a historiography committed to assimilating them to the transcendental Destiny of the British Empire.

XII

Causality serves to hitch the *hool* to a rather different kind of Destiny in Ray's account. But the latter goes through the same steps as Hunter's—that is, *context-event-perspective* ranged along a historical continuum—to arrive there. There are some obvious parallelisms in

---

[31] *BC* 54222: *JC*, 22 Nov. 1831 (no.91). Emphasis added.
[32] Anon., op. cit., pp. 263-4.
[33] Ibid., p. 263.

the way the event acquires a context in the two works. Both start off with prehistory (treated more briefly by Ray than Hunter) and follow it up with a survey of the more recent past since 1790 when the tribe first came into contact with the regime. It is there that the cause of the insurrection lies for both—but with a difference. For Hunter the disturbances originated in a local malignance in an otherwise healthy body—the failure of a district administration to act up to the then emerging ideal of the Raj as the *ma-baap* of the peasantry and protect them from the tyranny of wicked elements within the native society itself. For Ray it was the very presence of British power in India which had goaded the Santals to revolt, for their enemies the landlords and moneylenders owed their authority and indeed their existence to the new arrangements in landed property introduced by the colonial government and the accelerated development of a money economy under its impact. The rising constituted, therefore, a critique not only of a local administration but of colonialism itself. Indeed he uses Hunter's own evidence to arrive at that very different, indeed contrary, conclusion:

> It is clearly proved by Hunter's own statement that the responsibility for the extreme misery of the Santals lies with the English administrative system taken as a whole together with the zamindars and mahajans. For it was the English administrative system which had created zamindars and mahajans in order to satisfy its own need for exploitation and government, and helped them directly and indirectly by offering its protection and patronage.[34]

With colonialism, that is, the Raj as a system and in its entirety (rather than any of its local malfunctions) identified thus as the prime cause of rebellion, its outcome acquires radically different values in the two texts. While Hunter is explicit in his preference of a victory in favour of the regime, Ray is equally so in favour of the rebels. And corresponding to this each has a perspective which stands out in sharp contrast to that of the other. It is for Hunter the consolidation of British rule based on a reformed administration which no longer incites jacqueries by its failure to protect *adivasis* from native exploiters, but transforms them into an abundant and mobile labour force readily and profitably employed by Indian landlords and 'English enterprise'. For Ray the event is 'the precursor of the great

[34] Ray, op. cit., p. 318.

rebellion' of 1857 and a vital link in a protracted struggle of the Indian people in general and peasants and workers in particular against foreign as well as indigenous oppressors. The armed insurrection of the Santals, he says, has indicated a way to the Indian people. 'That particular way has, thanks to the great rebellion of 1857, developed into the broad highway of India's struggle for freedom. That highway extends into the twentieth century. The Indian peasantry are on their march along that very highway.'[35] In fitting the *hool* thus to a perspective of continuing struggle of the rural masses the author draws on a well-established tradition of radical historiography as witness, for instance, the following extract from a pamphlet which had a wide readership in left political circles nearly thirty years ago:

> The din of the actual battles of the insurrection has died down. But its echoes have kept on vibrating through the years, growing louder and louder as more peasants joined in the fight. The clarion call that summoned the Santhals to battle . . . was to be heard in other parts of the country at the time of the Indigo Strike of 1860, the Pabna and Bogra Uprising of 1872, the Maratha Peasant Rising in Poona and Ahmednagar in 1875-76. It was finally to merge in the massive demand of the peasantry all over the country for an end to zamindari and moneylending oppression . . . . Glory to the immortal Santhals who . . . showed the path to battle! The banner of militant struggle has since then passed from hand to hand over the length and breadth of India.[36]

The power of such assimilative thinking about the history of peasant insurgency is further illustrated by the concluding words of an essay written by a veteran of the peasant movement and published by the Pashchimbanga Pradeshik Krishak Sabha on the eve of the centenary of the Santal revolt. Thus,

> The flames of the fire kindled by the peasant martyrs of the Santal insurrection a hundred years ago had spread to many regions all over India. Those flames could be seen burning in the indigo cultivators' rebellion in Bengal (1860), in the uprising of the raiyats of Pabna and Bogra (1872), in that of the Maratha peasantry of the Deccan (1875-76). The same fire was kindled again and again in the course of the Moplah peasant revolts of Malabar. That fire has not been extinguished yet, it is still burning in the hearts of the Indian peasants . . .'[37]

[35] Ibid., p. 340.
[36] L. Natarajan, *Peasant Uprisings in India, 1850-1900* (Bombay, 1953), pp. 31-2.
[37] Abdulla Rasul, *Saontal Bidroher Amar Kahini* (Calcutta, 1954), p. 24.

The Prose of Counter-Insurgency   77

The purpose of such tertiary discourse is quite clearly to try and retrieve the history of insurgency from that continuum which is designed to assimilate every jacquerie to 'England's Work in India' and arrange it along the alternative axis of a protracted campaign for freedom and socialism. However, as with colonialist historiography this, too, amounts to an act of appropriation which excludes the rebel as the conscious subject of his own history and incorporates the latter as only a contingent element in another history with another subject. Just as it is not the rebel but the Raj which is the real subject of secondary discourse and the Indian bourgeoisie that of tertiary discourse of the History-of-the-Freedom-Struggle genre, so is an *abstraction* called Worker-and-Peasant, *an ideal rather than the real historical personality of the insurgent,* made to replace him in the type of literature discussed above.

To say this is of course not to deny the political importance of such appropriation. Since every struggle for power by the historically ascendant classes in any epoch involves a bid to acquire a tradition, it is entirely in the fitness of things that the revolutionary movements in India should lay a claim to, among others, the Santal rebellion of 1855 as a part of their heritage. But however noble the cause and instrument of such appropriation, it leads to the mediation of the insurgent's consciousness by the historian's—that is, of a past consciousness by one conditioned by the present. The distortion which follows necessarily and inevitably from this process is a function of that hiatus between event-time and discourse-time which makes the verbal representation of the past less than accurate in the best of cases. And since the discourse is, in this particular instance, one about properties of the mind—about attitudes, beliefs, ideas, etc. rather than about externalities which are easier to identify and describe, the task of representation is made even more complicated than usual.

There is nothing that historiography can do to eliminate such distortion altogether, for the latter is built into its optics. What it can do, however, is to acknowledge such distortion as parametric—as a datum which determines the form of the exercise itself, and to stop pretending that it can *fully* grasp a past consciousness and reconstitute it. Then and only then might the distance between the latter and the historian's perception of it be reduced significantly enough to amount to a close approximation which is the best one could hope for. The gap as it stands at the moment is indeed so wide that there is much more than an irreducible degree of error in the existing literature on this point. Even a brief look at some of the discourses on the 1855 insurrection should bear this out.

XIII

Religiosity was, by all accounts, central to the *hool*. The notion of power which inspired it, was made up of such ideas and expressed in such words and acts as were explicitly religious in character. It was not that power was a content wrapped up in a form external to it called religion. It was a matter of both being inseparably collapsed as the signified and its signifier (*vāgarthāviva samprktau*) in the language of that massive violence. Hence the attribution of the rising to a divine command rather than to any particular grievance; the enactment of rituals both before (e.g. propitiatory ceremonies to ward off the apocalypse of the Primeval Serpents—Lag and Lagini, the distribution of *tel-sindur*, etc.) and during the uprising (e.g. worshipping the goddess Durga, bathing in the Ganges, etc.); the generation and circulation of myth in its characteristic vehicle—rumour (e.g. about the advent of 'the exterminating angel' incarnated as a buffalo, the birth of a prodigious hero to a virgin, etc.).[38] The evidence is both unequivocal and ample on this point. The statements we have from the leading protagonists and their followers are all emphatic and indeed insistent on this aspect of their struggle, as should be obvious even from the few extracts of source material reproduced below in the *Appendix*. In sum, it is not possible to speak of insurgency in this case except as a religious consciousness—except, that is, as a massive demonstration of self-estrangement (to borrow Marx's term for the very essence of religiosity) which made the rebels look upon their project as predicated on a will other than their own: 'Kanoo and Seedoo Manjee are not fighting. The Thacoor himself will fight.'[39]

How authentically has this been represented in historical discourse? It was identified in official correspondence at the time as a case of 'fanaticism'. The insurrection was three months old and still going strong when J. R. Ward, a Special Commissioner and one of the most important administrators in the Birbhum region, wrote in some

---

[38] The instances are far too numerous to cite in an essay of this size, but for some samples see *Mare Hapram Ko Reak Katha*, Ch.79, in A. Mitra (ed.), *District Handbooks: Bankura* (Calcutta, 1953).

[39] *Appendix:* Extract 2.

desperation to his superiors in Calcutta, 'I have been unable to trace the insurrection in Beerbhoom to any thing but *fanaticism.*' The idiom he used to describe the phenomenon was typical of the shocked and culturally arrogant response of nineteenth-century colonialism to any radical movement inspired by a non-Christian doctrine among a subject population: 'These Sonthals have been led to join in the rebellion under a persuasion which is clearly traceable to their brethren in Bhaugulpore, that an Almighty & inspired Being appeared as the redeemer of their Caste & their *ignorance & superstition* was easily worked into a *religious frenzy* which has stopped at nothing.'[40] That idiom occurs also in the *Calcutta Review* article. There the Santal is acknowledged as 'an eminently religious man' and his revolt as a parallel of other historical occasions when '*the fanatical spirit of religious superstition*' had been 'swayed to strengthen and help forward a quarrel already ready to burst and based on other grounds.'[41] However, the author gives this identification a significantly different slant from that in the report quoted above. There an incomprehending Ward, caught in the blast of the *hool*, appears to have been impressed by the spontaneity of 'a religious frenzy which...stopped at nothing'. By contrast the article written after the regime had recovered its self-confidence, thanks to the search-and-burn campaign in the disturbed tracts, interprets religiosity as a propagandist ruse used by the leaders to sustain the morale of the rebels. Referring, for instance, to the messianic rumours in circulation it says, 'All these absurdities were no doubt *devised* to keep up the courage of the numerous rabble.'[42] Nothing could be more elitist. The insurgents are regarded here as a mindless 'rabble' devoid of a will of their own and easily manipulated by their chiefs.

But elitism such as this is not a feature of colonialist historiography alone. Tertiary discourse of the radical variety, too, exhibits the same disdain for the political consciousness of the peasant masses when it is mediated by religiosity. For a sample let us turn to Ray's account of the rising again. He quotes the following lines from the *Calcutta Review* article in a somewhat inaccurate but still clearly recognizable translation:

> Seedoo and Kanoo were at night seated in their home, revolving many things . . . a bit of paper fell on Seedoo's head, and suddenly the Thakoor

[40] *JP*, 8 Nov. 1855: Ward to Government of Bengal (13 Oct. 1855). Emphasis added.
[41] Anon., op. cit., p. 243. Emphasis added.
[42] Ibid., p. 246. Emphasis added.

(god) appeared before the astonished gaze of Seedoo and Kanoo; he was like a white man though dressed in the native style; on each hand he had ten fingers; he held a white book, and wrote therein; the book and with it 20 pieces of paper . . . he presented to the brothers; ascended upwards, and disappeared. Another bit of paper fell on Seedoo's head, and then came two men . . . hinted to them the purport of Thakoor's order, and they likewise vanished. But there was not merely one apparition of the sublime Thakoor; each day in the week for some short period, did he make known his presence to his favourite apostles . . . . In the silvery pages of the book, and upon the white leaves of the single scraps of paper, were words written; these were afterwards deciphered by literate Sonthals, able to read and interpret; but their meaning had already been sufficiently indicated to the two leaders.[43]

With some minor changes of detail (inevitable in a living folklore) this is indeed a fairly authentic account of the visions the two Santal leaders believed they had had. Their statements, reproduced in part in the *Appendix* (Extracts 3 and 4), bear this out. These, incidentally, were not public pronouncements meant to impress their followers. Unlike 'The Thacoor's Perwannah' (*Appendix*: Extract 2) intended to make their views known to the authorities before the uprising, these were the words of captives facing execution. Addressed to hostile interrogators in military encampments they could have little use as propaganda. Uttered by men of a tribe which, according to all accounts had not yet learnt to lie,[44] these represented the truth and nothing but the truth for their speakers. But that is not what Ray would credit them with. What figures as a mere insinuation in the *Calcutta Review* is raised to the status of an elaborate propaganda device in his introductory remarks on the passage cited above. Thus:

> Both Sidu and Kanu knew that the slogan (*dhwani*) which would have the most effect among the *backward* Santals, was one that was religious. Therefore, *in order to inspire* the Santals to struggle they *spread* the word about God's directive in favour of launching such a struggle. The story *invented (kalpita)* by them is as follows.[45]

There is little that is different here from what the colonialist writer had to say about the presumed backwardness of the Santal peasantry,

---

[43] Ibid., pp. 243-4. Ray, op. cit., pp. 321-2.

[44] This is generally accepted. See, for instance, Sherwill's observation about the truth being 'sacred' to the Santals 'offering in this respect a bright example to their lying neighbours, the Bengalis'. *Geographical and Statistical Report of the District Bhaugulpoor* (Calcutta, 1854), p. 32.

[45] Ray, op. cit., p. 321. Emphasis added.

the manipulative designs of their leaders and the uses of religion as the means of such manipulation. Indeed, on each of these points Ray does better and is by far the more explicit of the two authors in attributing a gross lie and downright deception to the rebel chiefs without any evidence at all. The invention is all his own and testifies to the failure of a shallow radicalism to conceptualize insurgent mentality except in terms of an unadulterated secularism. Unable to grasp religiosity as the central modality of peasant consciousness in colonial India he is shy to acknowledge its mediation of the peasant's idea of power and all the resultant contradictions. He is obliged therefore to rationalize the ambiguities of rebel politics by assigning a worldly consciousness to the leaders and an otherworldly one to their followers making of the latter innocent dupes of crafty men armed with all the tricks of a modern Indian politician out to solicit rural votes. Where this lands the historian can be seen even more clearly in the projection of this thesis to a study of the Birsaite *ulgulan* in Ray's subsequent work. He writes,

> In order to propagate this religious doctrine of his Birsa adopted *a new device (kaushal)*—just as Sidu, the Santal leader, had done on the eve of the Santal rebellion of 1885. Birsa knew that the Kol were a *very backward* people and were full of *religious superstition* as a result of Hindu-Brahmanical and Christian missionary propaganda amongst them over a long period. Therefore, it would not do to avoid the question of religion if the Kol people were to be liberated from those wicked religious influences and drawn into the path of rebellion. Rather, in order to overcome the evil influences of Hindu and Christian religions, it would be necessary to spread his new religious faith among them in the name of that very God of theirs, and to introduce new rules. *To this end, recourse had to be had to falsehood, if necessary, in the interests of the people.*
>
> Birsa *spread* the word that he had received this new religion of his from the chief deity of the Mundas, Sing Bonga, himself.[44]

Thus the radical historian is driven by the logic of his own incomprehension to attribute a deliberate falsehood to one of the greatest of our rebels. The ideology of that mighty *ulgulan* is nothing but pure fabrication for him. And he is not alone in his

---

[44] Ray, *Bharater Baiplabik Samgramer Itihas*, vol. I' (Calcutta, 1970), p. 95. Emphasis added. The sentence italicized by us in the quoted passage reads as follows in the Bengali original: '*Eijanyo prayojan hoiley jatir svarthey mithyar asroy grahan karitey hoibey*'.

misreading of insurgent consciousness. Baskay echoes him almost word for word in describing the Santal leader's claim to divine support for the *hool* as propaganda meant 'to inspire the Santals to rise in revolt'.[47] Formulations such as these have their foil in other writings of the same genre which solve the riddle of religious thinking among the Santal rebels by ignoring it altogether. A reader who has Natarajan's and Rasul's once influential essays as his only source of information about the insurrection of 1855, would hardly suspect any religiosity at all in that great event. It is represented there *exclusively* in its secular aspects. This attitude is of course not confined to the authors discussed in this essay. The same mixture of myopia and downright refusal to look at the evidence that is there, characterizes a great deal more of the existing literature on the subject.

XIV

Why is tertiary discourse, even of the radical variety, so reluctant to come to terms with the religious element in rebel consciousness? Because it is still trapped in the paradigm which inspired the ideologically contrary, because colonialist, discourse of the primary and secondary types. It follows, in each case, from a refusal to acknowledge the insurgent as the subject of his own history. For once a peasant rebellion has been assimilated to the career of the Raj, the Nation or the People, it becomes easy for the historian to abdicate the responsibility he has of exploring and describing the consciousness specific to that rebellion and be content to ascribe to it a transcendental consciousness. In operative terms, this means denying a will to the mass of the rebels themselves and representing them merely as instruments of some other will. It is thus that in colonialist historiography insurgency is seen as the articulation of a pure spontaneity pitted against the will of the State as embodied in the Raj. If any consciousness is attributed at all to the rebels, it is only a few of their leaders— more often than not some individual members or small groups of the gentry—who are credited with it. Again, in bourgeois-nationalist historiography it is an elite consciousness which is read into all peasant movements as their motive force. This had led to such grotesqueries as the characterization of the Indigo Rebellion of 1860 as 'the first non-violent mass movement'[48] and generally of all the

[47] Dhirendranath Baskay, *Saontal Ganasamgramer Itihas* (Calcutta, 1976), p. 66.
[48] Jogesh Chandra Bagal (ed.), *Peasant Revolution in Bengal* (Calcutta, 1953), p. 5.

popular struggles in rural India during the first hundred and twenty-five years of British rule as the spiritual harbinger of the Indian National Congress.

In much the same way the specificity of rebel consciousness had eluded radical historiography as well. This has been so because it is impaled on a concept of peasant revolts as a succession of events ranged along a direct line of descent—as a heritage, as it is often called—in which all the constituents have the same pedigree and replicate each other in their commitment to the highest ideals of liberty, equality and fraternity. In this ahistorical view of the history of insurgency all moments of consciousness are assimilated to the ultimate and highest moment of the series—indeed to an Ideal Consciousness. A historiography devoted to its pursuit (even when that is done, regrettably, in the name of Marxism) is ill-equipped to cope with contradictions which are indeed the stuff history is made of. Since the Ideal is suppose to be one hundred per cent secular in character, the devotee tends to look away when confronted with the evidence of religiosity as if the latter did not exist or explain it away as a clever but well-intentioned fraud perpetrated by enlightened leaders on their moronic followers—all done, of course, 'in the interests of the people'! Hence, the rich material of myths, rituals, rumours, hopes for a Golden Age and fears of an imminent End of the World, all of which speaks of the self-alienation of the rebel, is wasted on this abstract and sterile discourse. It can do little to illuminate that combination of sectarianism and militancy which is so important a feature of our rural history. The ambiguity of such phenomena, witnessed during the Tebhaga movement in Dinajpur, as Muslim peasants coming to the Kisan Sabha 'sometimes inscribing a hammer or a sickle on the Muslim League flag' and young maulavis 'reciting melodious verse from the Koran' at village meetings as 'they condemned the jotedari system and the practice of charging high interest rates',[49] will be beyond its grasp. The swift transformation of class struggle into communal strife and vice versa in our countryside evokes from it either some well-contrived apology or a simple gesture of embarrassment, but no real explanation.

However, it is not only the religious element in rebel consciousness which this historiography fails to comprehend. The specificity of a rural insurrection is expressed in terms of many other contradictions

---

[49] Sunil Sen, *Agrarian Struggle in Bengal, 1946–47* (New Delhi, 1972), p. 49.

84   *Selected Subaltern Studies*

as well. These too are missed out. Blinded by the glare of a perfect and immaculate consciousness the historian sees nothing, for instance, but solidarity in rebel behaviour and fails to notice its Other, namely, betrayal. Committed inflexibly to the notion of insurgency as a generalized movement, he underestimates the power of the brakes put on it by localism and territoriality. Convinced that mobilization for a rural uprising flows exclusively from an overall elite authority, he tends to disregard the operation of many other authorities within the primordial relations of a rural community. A prisoner of empty abstractions tertiary discourse, even of the radical kind, has thus distanced itself from the prose of counter-insurgency only by a declaration of sentiment so far. It has still to go a long way before it can prove that the insurgent can rely on its performance to recover his place in history.

Abbreviations

BC:	Board's Collections, India Office Records (London).
JC:	Fort William Judicial Consultations in *BC*.
JP:	Judicial Proceedings, West Bengal State Archives (Calcutta).
MDS:	*Maharaja Deby Sinha* (Nashipur Raj Estate, 1914).

Appendix

Extract 1

I came to plunder . . . Sidoo and Kaloo [Kanhu] declared themselves Rajas & [said] they would plunder the whole country and take possession of it—they said also, no one can stop us for it is the order of Takoor. On this account we have all come with them.

Source: JP, 19 July 1855: Balai Majhi's Statement (14 July 1855).

Extract 2

The Thacoor has descended in the house of Seedoo Manjee, Kanoo Manjee, Bhyrub and Chand, at Bhugnudihee in Pergunnah Kunjeala. The Thakoor in person is conversing with them, he has descended from Heaven, he is conversing with Kanoor and Seedoo, The Sahibs and the white Soldiers will fight. Kanoo and Seedoo Manjee are not fighting. The Thacoor himself will fight. Therefore you Sahibs and Soldiers fight with the Thacoor himself Mother Ganges will come to the Thacoor's (assistance) Fire will rain from Heaven. If you are satisfied with the Thacoor then you must go to the other side of the Ganges. The Thacoor has ordered the Sonthals that for a bulluck plough 1 anna is to be paid for revenue. Buffalo plough 2 annas The reign of Truth has begun True justice will be administered He who does not speak the truth will not be allowed to remain on the Earth. The Mahajuns have committed a great sin The Sahibs and the amlah have made everything bad, in this the Sahibs have sinned greatly.

Those who tell things to the Magistrate and those who investigate cases for him, take 70 or 80 R.s. with great oppression in this the Sahibs have sinned. On this account the Thacoor has ordered me saying that the country is not the Sahibs...

P.S. If you Sahibs agree, then you must remain on the other side of the Ganges, and if you dont agree you cant remain on that side of the river, I will rain fire and all the Sahibs will be killed by the hand of God in person and Sahibs if you fight with muskets the Sonthal will not be hit by the bullets and the Thacoor will give your Elephants and horses of his own accord to the Sonthals . . . if you fight with the Sonthals two days will be as one day and two nights as one night. This is the order of the Thacoor.

Source: JP, 4 October 1855: 'The Thacoor's Perwannah' ('dated 10 Saon 1262').

Extract 3

Then the Manjees & Purgunnaits assembled in my Verandah, & we consulted for 2 months, "that Pontet & Mohesh Dutt don't listen to our complaints & no one acts as our Father & Mother" then a God descended from heaven in the form of a cartwheel & said to me "Kill Pontet & the Darogah & the Mahajuns & then you will have justice & a Father & Mother"; then the Thacoor went back to the heavens; after this 2 men like Bengallees came into my Verhandah; they each had six fingers half a piece of paper fell on my head before the Thacoor came & half fell afterwards. I could not read but Chand & Seheree & a Dhome read it, they said "The Thacoor has written to you to fight the Mahajens & then you will have justice" . . .

Source: JP, 8 November 1855: 'Examination of Sedoo Sonthal late Thacoor'.

Extract 4

In Bysack the God descended in my house I sent a perwannah to the Burra Sahib at Calcutta . . . I wrote that the Thacoor had come to my house & was conversing with me & had told all the Sonthals that they were to be under the charge of me & that I was to pay all the revenue to Government & was to oppress no one & the zamindars & Mahajans were committing great oppression taking 20 pice for one & that I was to place them at a distance from the sonthals & if they do not go away to fight with them.

. . .   .

Ishwar was a white man with only a dootee & chudder he sat on the ground like a Sahib he wrote on this bit of paper. He gave me 4 papers but afterwards presented 16 more. The thacoor had 5 fingers on each hand. I did not see him in the day I saw him only in the night. The sonthals then assembled at my house to see the thacoor.

. . .   .

[At Maheshpur] the troops came & we had a fight . . . afterwards seeing that men on our side were falling we both turned twice on them & once drove them away, then I made poojah . . . & then a great many balls came & Seedoo & I were both wounded. The thacoor had said "water will come out of the muskets" but my troops committed some crime therefore the thacoors prediction[s] were not fulfilled about 80 sonthals were killed.

. . .   .

All the blank papers fell from heaven & the book in which all the pages are blank also fell from heaven.

Source: JP, 20 December 1855: 'Examination of Kanoo Sonthal'.

Part III
Categorical Knowledge

[6]

TWO EUROPEAN IMAGES OF NON-EUROPEAN
RULE
Talal Asad

In order to understand better the relationship between social anthropology and colonialism, it is necessary to go beyond the boundaries of the discipline and of the particular epoch within which that discipline acquired its distinctive character. The descriptive writings of functional anthropology are largely devoted to Africa, are in effect virtually synonymous with African sociology during the twentieth century colonial period. But we need to see anthropology as a holistic discipline nurtured within bourgeois society, having as its object of study a variety of non-European societies which have come under its economic, political and intellectual domination— and therefore as merely one such discipline among several (orientalism, indology, sinology, etc.). All these disciplines are rooted in that complex historical encounter between the West and the Third World which commenced about the 16th century: when capitalist Europe began to emerge out of feudal Christendom; when the conquistadors who expelled the last of the Arabs from Christian Spain went on to colonise the New World and also to bring about the direct confrontation of 'civilised' Europe with 'savage' and 'barbaric' peoples;[1] when the Atlantic maritime states, by dominating the world's major seaways, inaugurated 'the Vasco Da Gama epoch

[1] "The Americas were therefore the scene of the first true empires controlled from Europe, and Western imperial theory originated in sixteenth-century Spain." P. D. Curtin, (ed.) *Imperialism*, London, 1972, p. xiv. For further information on this subject, see J. M. Parry, *The Spanish Theory of Empire in the Sixteenth Century*, Cambridge, 1940.

of Asian history';[2] when the conceptual revolution of modern science and technology helped to consolidate Europe's world hegemony.[3] The bourgeois disciplines which study non-European societies reflect the deep contradictions articulating this unequal historical encounter, for ever since the Renaissance the West has sought both to subordinate and devalue other societies, and at the same time to find in them clues to its own humanity. Although modern colonialism is merely one moment in that long encounter, the way in which the objectified understanding of these modern disciplines has been made possible by and acceptable to that moment needs to be considered far more seriously than it has.

The notes that follow constitute an attempt to examine some of the political conclusions of functional anthropology (African studies) and of orientalism (Islamic studies) in order to explore the ways in which the European historical experience of subordinate non-European peoples has shaped its objectification of the latter. I hope that such a comparison will make somewhat clearer the kind of determination exerted by the structure of imperial power on the understanding of European disciplines which focus on dominated cultures. Such an attempt is not without its dangers for someone who is trained in only one of these disciplines, but it must be made if we are to go beyond simplistic assertions or denials about the relationship between social anthropology and colonialism. I should stress that I am not concerned with all the doctrines or conclusions of functional anthropology—or for that matter of orientalism.

What I propose to do in the rest of the paper is to concentrate on two general images of the institutionalised relationship between rulers and ruled, objectified by the functional anthropologist and the Islamic orientalist. As we shall see, the images are very different, for the first typically stresses *consent* and the other *repression* in the institutionalised relationship between rulers and ruled. After sketching in these two images, I shall go on to indicate significant omissions and simplifications that characterise each of them, and follow this up with some more general theoretical observations concerning what they have in common. I shall then turn to the wider historical location of the two disciplines which, so I shall argue in my conclusion, help us to understand some of the ideological roots and consequences of these images.

[2] Cf. K. M. Panikkar, *Asia and Western Dominance*, London, 1959.
[3] Cf. J. D. Bernal, *Science in History*, London, 1965, especially Part 4.

TALAL ASAD   **105**

II

I begin by characterising what I call the functional anthropologist's view of political domination.

In general, the structure of traditional African states is represented in terms of balance of powers, reciprocal obligations and value consensus—as in the following passage by Fortes and Evans-Pritchard:

> A relatively stable political system in Africa represents a balance between divergent interests. In [centralised political systems] it is a balance between different parts of the administrative organisation. The forces that maintain the supremacy of the paramount ruler are opposed by the forces that act as a check on his powers; [...] A general principle of great importance is contained in these arrangements, which has the effect of giving every section and every major interest of the society direct or indirect representation in the conduct of government [...]
> Looked at from another angle, the government of an African state consists in a balance between power and authority on the one side and obligation and responsibility on the other [...] The structure of an African state implies that kings and chiefs rule by consent.[4]

Echoes of the same view are also found in a comparatively recent paper by P. C. Lloyd, "The Political Structure of African Kingdoms":

> The political elite represent, to a greater or lesser degree, the interest of the mass of the people. In African kingdoms permanent opposition groups within the political elite are not found [...]
> A vote is never taken on any major issue, but all concerned voice their interests and the king, summing up, gives a decision which reflects the general consensus.[5]

This, then is the functional anthropological image of political domination in the so-called tribal world: an emphasis on the integrated character of the body politic, on the reciprocal rights and obligations between rulers and ruled, on the consensual basis of the ruler's political authority and administration, and on the inherent efficiency of the traditional system of government in giving every legitimate interest its due representation.

The orientalist's image of political domination in the historic

---

[4] M. Fortes and E. E. Evans-Pritchard, (eds.), *African Political Systems*, London, 1940, pp. 11-12.
[5] M. Banton, (ed.), *Political Systems and the Distribution of Power*, London, 1965, p. 76 and pp. 79-80.

106   TWO EUROPEAN IMAGES OF NON-EUROPEAN RULE

Islamic world is very different. Here there is a tendency to see the characteristic relationship between rulers and their subjects in terms of force and repression on the one side, and of submission, indifference, even cynicism on the other. The following brief quotation from Gibb's essay "Religion and Politics in Christianity and Islam" illustrates the kind of view I am thinking of:

> ... [the governor's] administrative regulations and exactions on
> land, industry and persons, and the processes resorted to by
> [their] officers were regarded as arbitrary and without authority
> in themselves, and directed only to the furthering of their
> private interests. In the eyes of the governed, official 'justice'
> was no justice. The only authoritative law is that of Islam;
> everything else is merely temporary (and more or less forced)
> accommodating to the whims of a changing constellation of
> political overlords.[6]

A similar kind of image underlies the following remarks by von Grunebaum:

> As an executive officer, the [Islamic] ruler is unrestricted. The
> absoluteness of his power was never challenged. The Muslim
> liked his rulers terror-inspiring, and it seems to have been bon
> ton to profess oneself awestruck when ushered into his
> presence [...] [The medieval Muslim] is frequently impatient
> with his rulers and thinks little of rioting, but on the whole he
> is content to let his princes play their game.[7]

The same author, tracing the political theories of Muslim canonical jurists writes:

> So the requirements of legitimate power had to be redefined with
> ever greater leniency, until the low had been reached and the
> theoretical dream [of a *civitas dei*] abandoned. The believer
> was thought under obligation to obey whosoever held sway, be
> his power *de jure* or merely *de facto*. No matter how evil a
> tyrant the actual ruler, no matter how offensive his conduct,
> the subject was bound to loyal obedience.[8]

He then proceeds, with the aid of further quotations to characterise what he calls "that disillusionment bordering on cynicism with which the Oriental is still inclined to view the political life".

The essential features of this image are to be found in the pion-

[6] J. H. Proctor, (ed.), *Islam and International Relations*, London, 1965, p. 12.
[7] G. E. Von Grunebaum, *Islam, Essays in the Nature and Growth of a Cultural Tradition*, London, 1955, pp. 25-6.
[8] G. E. Von Grunebaum, *Medieval Islam*, Chicago, 1946, p. 168.

eering works of orientalism at the turn of the last century—as in this passage by Snouck Hurgronje:

> The rulers paid no more attention to the edicts of the *fuqaha*, the specialists in law, than suited them; these last in their turn, were less and less obliged to take the requirements of practice into account. So long as they refrained from preaching revolt directly or indirectly against the political rulers, they were allowed to criticise the institutions of state and society as bitterly as they liked. In fact, the works on [religious law] are full of disparaging judgements on conditions of 'the present day'. What is justice in the eyes of princes and judges is but injustice and tyranny...Most taxes which are collected by the government are illegal extortions...; the legally prescribed revenue...is collected in an illegal manner and spent wrongly... Muslim rulers, in the eyes of the *fuqaha*, are not the vice regents of the Prophet as the first four Caliphs had been, but wielders of a material power which should only be submitted to out of fear of still worse to follow, and because even a wrongful order is at least better than complete disorder...[In fact in Islamic history] the people obeyed their rulers as the wielders of power, but they revered the ulama [learned men of religion] as the teachers of truth and in troubled times took their lead from them...In this way, the [religious] law, which in practice had to make ever greater concessions to the use and custom of the people and the arbitrariness of their rulers, nevertheless retained a considerable influence on the intellectual life of the Muslims.[9]

So the orientalist's image may be characterised briefly as follows: an emphasis on the absolute power of the ruler, and the whimsical, generally illegitimate nature of his demands; on the indifference or involuntary submission on the part of the ruled; on a somewhat irrational form of conflict in which sudden, irresponsible urges to riot are met with violent repression; and, finally, an emphasis on the overall inefficiency and corruption of political life.

III

The historical realities, of course, are more complicated than these views. But the remarkable thing in both cases is the direction in which the simplification occurs.

[9]*Selected Works of C. Snouck Hurgronje*, edited by G. H. Bousquet and J. Schacht, Leiden, 1957, pp. 265 and 267.

In Africa, a basic political reality since the end of the nineteenth century was the pervasive presence of a massive colonial power—the military conquest of the continent by European capitalist countries, and the subsequent creation, definition and maintenance of the authority of innumerable African chiefs to facilitate the administration of empire.[10] Everywhere Africans were subordinated, in varying degree, to the authority of European administrators. And although according to functionalist doctrine "Every anthropologist writes of the people he works among as he finds them",[11] the typical description of local African structures totally ignored the political fact of European coercive power and the African chief's ultimate dependence on it.

For example Fortes's *The Dynamics of Clanship among the Tallensi* describes Tale political structure with only a few brief ambiguous references to British rule in the introduction and then again in the final section of the final chapter. Yet in a paper published seven years earlier ("Culture Contact as a Dynamic Process") he had noted that the local District Commissioner among the Tallensi was:

> 6 miles from a police station, and some 30 miles from a perma-
> nent administrative headquarters. The political and legal
> behaviour of the Tallensi, both commoner and chief, is as
> strongly conditioned by the ever-felt presence of the District
> Commissioner as by their own traditions[...] The District
> Commissioner is in direct communication with the chiefs. To
> them he gives his orders and states his opinions. They are the
> organs by which he acts upon the rest of the community, and
> conversely, by which the community reacts to him.[12]

In spite of all this, Fortes had seen the District Commissioner essentially as a "Contact Agent" between European and native cultures, and not as the local representative of an imperial system. It was this non-political perception of a profoundly political fact which led him to assert that the District Commissioner was *not* regarded "as an imposition upon the traditional constitution from without. With all that he stands for, he is a corporate part of native life in this area".

One might suggest that, in spite of methodological statements to

[10] For a summary of these developments with special reference to East Africa (including the southern Sudan) see chapter 11 of L. Mair's *Primitive Government*, London, 1962.
[11] L. Mair, *op. cit.*, p. 31.
[12] *Methods of Study of Culture Contact in Africa*, International African Institute Memorandum XV, London, 1938, pp. 63-4.

the contrary, functional anthropologists were really not analysing existing political systems but writing the ideologically loaded constitutional history of African states prior to the European conquest. This would certainly help to explain the following remarks by the editors of *African Political Systems:* "Several contributors have described the changes in the political systems they investigated which have taken place as a result of European conquest and rule. If we do not emphasise this side of the subject it is because all contributors are more interested in anthropological than in administrative problems".[13] One reason why developments in indigenous political structures due to European conquest and rule were seen as "administrative problems" by European anthropologists was that real political forces in all their complexity formed the primary objects of administrative thinking and manipulation on the part of European colonial officials. Yet the result of identifying the constitutional ideology of 'centralised' African polities with the structural reality meant not analysing the intrinsic contradictions of power and material interest—a form of analysis which could be carried out only by starting from the basic reality of present colonial domination.

Even when later anthropologists began to refer to the colonial presence as part of the local structure they generally did so in such a way as to obscure the systematic character of colonial domination and to mask the fundamental contradictions of interest inherent in the system of Indirect Rule.[14] The role of new political-economic forces brought about by European colonialism (labelled "Social Change") were usually not thought to be directly relevant to an understanding of the dynamic of African political structures operating within the colonial system of Indirect Rule (labelled "Political Anthropology").

With regard to the orientalist's view of typical Islamic political rule there are several negative features I want to point to. The first is that no serious attempt was made until relatively recently[15] to

[13] M. Fortes and E. E. Evans-Pritchard, *op. cit.*, p. 1.
[14] For example L. A. Fallers in his well-known study of the Basoga of Uganda, *Bantu Bureaucracy*, (Cambridge, 1956) focuses on the way in which "co-existence in a society of corporate lineages with political institutions of the state type [introduced by the colonial government] makes for strain and instability" (p. 17)—an essentially Parsonian problem. He is not concerned with the colonial system as such, but with role conflicts inherent in the positions of African headman and civil-servant chief, and European District officers.
[15] An example is I. Lapidus's excellent monograph *Muslim Cities in the Later Middle Ages*, Cambridge, Mass., 1967.

explore in detail the process of mutual accommodation between Islamic rulers and their subjects—as noted, surprisingly enough, by Gibb, who has been so ready elsewhere to project the orientalist's image of Islamic rule:

> We know, in fact, exceedingly little of the inner relations between the government and the people... It can scarcely be doubted that government, in its administrative aspect, was not merely a set of forms imposed upon the people by the will of the conqueror, but an organism intimately associated with the structure of society and the character and ideas of the governed, and that there was a constant interplay between governors and governed. It is necessary to clear the ground of the misconceptions engendered by the abuse of European terms such as despotism and autocracy, and to submit all the traditional organs and usages of government to re-examination, in order to bring out the underlying ideas and relations, and the principles which guided their working.[16]

But something that we do know a little about is the populist tradition in Muslim societies as expressed in the repeated popular revolts[17] deriving their legitimation from Islamic ideology, as well as in the popular distrust of aristocratic institutions[18] (which is by no means the same thing as "oriental cynicism in relation to political life"). Most orientalists have tended to see these revolts as evidence of disorder and decay rather than as the re-affirmation of a populist tradition in Islamic politics.[19] Why, instead of emphasising disorder and repression and explaining this by reference to an intrinsic flaw in Islamic political theory (usually invidiously contrasted with Greek and Christian political theory) did orientalists not attempt to account for the continuing vitality of a populist tradition within changing socio-economic circumstances? More important, why,

[16] H. A. R. Gibb and H. Bowen, *Islamic Society and the West*, Vol. I, Part I, London, 1950, p. 9.

[17] Arab historiography from Tabari to Jabarti is full of information on these revolts. Useful summaries of revolts in the early period of Islam are available in W. Montgomery Watt, *Islam and the Integration of Society*, London, 1961. For a work on working-class organisation and rebellion in medieval urban Islamic society, see C. Cahen, *Mouvement Populaires et Autonomisme Urbain dans l'Asie Musulmane du Moyen Age*, Leiden, 1961. But in both works there is little discussion of the dialectical relationship between political-economic experience and ideological response—although Montgomery Watt makes some attempt in that direction.

[18] This point is interestingly made by M. G. S. Hodgson, "Islam and Image", in *History of Religions*, Vol. II, Winter, 1964.

[19] See E. Abrahamian, "The Crowd in Iranian Politics 1905-1953" (*Past and Present*, no. 41, 1968) for an attempt at describing the active rationality of

when generalising about the essence of Islamic political rule, did orientalists not recognise that their textual sources represented the particular moral stance of a mobile class of religious literati-cum-merchants with a need for political orderliness in particular periods of great social upheaval? Finally, why did orientalists make no attempt to analyse the way in which developing class relations within late medieval Islam were affected by its changing commercial position vis-a-vis Europe and Asia (especially under the impact of European mercantilism) and the significance of such developments for relations between Islamic rulers and their subjects?[20]

IV

Despite the great differences in the images I have been talking about, one pre-disposition that both disciplines appear to have shared is the reluctance to talk explicitly and systematically about the implications of European development for the political systems of non-European societies. There are other parallels also, in the orientation of the two disciplines, to which I now turn.

The functional anthropologist stressed consent and legitimacy as important elements in the political systems of relatively small homogeneous ethnic groups in Africa whose history was assumed in most cases to be inaccessible, and which were seen and represented as integrated systems. In general he equated empirical work with fieldwork, and therefore tended to define the theoretical boundaries of the system under investigation in terms of practical fieldwork. His interest in a-historical, 'traditional' systems (set within an imperial framework which was taken for granted) led him to emphasise the unifying function of common religious values and symbols, and of 'age-old' custom and obligations in the relationship between tribal rulers and ruled. Where the anthropologist was faced with available

---

political crowds in the modern Islamic world. (I am indebted to Peter Worsley for this reference.) "While European journalists have invariably portrayed oriental crowds as 'xenophobic mobs' hurling insults and bricks at Western embassies," observes Abrahamian, "local conservatives have frequently denounced them as 'social scum' in the pay of the foreign hand, and radicals have often stereotyped them as 'the people' in action. For all, the crowd has been an abstraction, whether worthy of abuse, fear, praise, or even of humour, but not a subject of study." (p. 184). It seems that sometimes there is little to distinguish the attitudes of European journalists from that of orientalists.

[20] Social and economic history of the Islamic world is in its infancy (see M. A. Cook (ed.), *Studies in the Economic History of the Middle East*, London, 1970)—an indication of the extent to which idealist explanations in terms of "the religious essence of Islam" have been in vogue among orientalists. This is not unrelated to the fact that orientalists have typically worked on composed literary texts and not in archives. See also R. Owen's

historical evidence relating to conquest—as among the Zulu and Ngoni of southern Africa, or among the Fulani-Hausa of Northern Nigeria—he was of course aware of the importance of force and repression in African political history. But the functionalist perspective made it difficult for him to absorb the full significance of such events into his analysis and so they were generally seen as preludes to the establishment of integrated on-going African political systems which constituted his principal object of enquiry. It is common knowledge that this mode of analysis in social anthropology derives from Durkheimian sociology, which never really developed an adequate framework for understanding historical political processes. The interesting thing is that for a long time the social anthropologist writing about African political systems felt no need to overcome these theoretical limitations. The role of force in the maintenance of African systems of political domination (or of the colonial system of which they were a part) received virtually no systematic attention. The primary focus was usually on the juridical definition of rights and duties between the chief and his subjects.[21]

At this point it should be noted that the orientalist's image of political rule in Islamic society covers a historical span of several hundred years, from the middle ages (the so-called formative period of Islam) until the eighteenth century—a period of economic development and decline, of conquests and dynastic wars, and rule by successive military elites, notably Mamluke and Ottoman. The orientalist, concerned to present a relatively coherent picture of typical rule for such an epoch, could scarcely leave the element of force unmentioned. But the interesting point is that the element of force is not only mentioned, it is made the defining feature of the total political picture, which is then sometimes contrasted with the

---

critical review of *The Cambridge History of Islam* in *The Journal of Interdisciplinary History* (in press).
[21]This is also true of Gluckman, who is usually cited as being one of the first anthropologists to have dealt directly with problems of force and conflict in traditional African societies. Gluckman's view of conflict has typically been a juristic, legalistic one, whence his particular interest in "discrepant and conflicting rules of succession" which he sees as the primary focus of traditional African rebellions" (See his Introduction to *Order and Rebellion in Tribal Africa*, London, 1963). For this reason he fails to make an analytic distinction between *'popular' armed uprisings* and *dynastic rivalries*. The question as to whether a particular internal military challenge against the state's authority is rooted in (actual or potential) class consciousness is more basic than the task of labelling it 'rebellion' or 'revolution'. His failure to appreciate this helps to explain why Gluckman paid no attention to the question of African popular rebellions against European colonial rule.

allegedly different character of political rule in Medieval Christendom. (The suggestion being that since Islamic society lacked a true conception of *political authority*, i.e., of political domination based on general consent, it was inevitable that force should play such a central role in the Islamic political order).[22]

The orientalist concerned to generalise was here faced with a theoretical problem with which the functional anthropologist has not been much troubled. For the anthropologist reared on a-historical Durkheimian sociology, society and polity were usually coterminous. The horizontal links of 'tribal society' were conveniently definable in terms of the vertical links (whether hierarchical or segmentary) of 'tribal political organisation'. But for the orientalist concerned with Islam there was hardly ever such a convergence after the de facto break up of the Abbasid Empire. So in his desire to characterise a distinctive 'Islamic society', on the basis of a considerable body of textual material relating to many eventful centuries, he is led to adopt a partly functionalist perspective: for the emphasis on the integrative role of Islam as a religion is reminiscent of the social anthropologist's treatment of the integrative function of 'tribal' religious values in many African political systems. Islamic history thus collapses into an essentialist synchrony, for much the same reasons as African history does in the hands of the functional anthropologist.

Since the orientalist is concerned by definition with 'a society' of much complexity, he must stress what may be called a form of horizontal integration: the fact that Muslims seemed bound together, despite their subjection to different secular rulers, by their common loyalty to Islam as a religious system—an Islam which was interpreted by, and indeed embodied in, an 'international' community of learned men—the ulama, the sufi shaikhs and so forth. This horizontal religious consensus is then opposed by the orientalist to a vertical political dissensus, in which "everything else is merely temporary and more or less forced accommodation to the whims of a changing constellation of political overlords". This contrast between an integrated Islamic society and a fragmented Islamic polity has encouraged orientalists to oppose the supposedly universal authority of the *sharia* (Islamic law) to the changing constellation of political regimes and practices, often accompanied by

---

[22] See Gibb in Proctor (ed.), *op. cit.*

violence—an opposition with which the medieval Muslim writers
were themselves much preoccupied. In fact it may be argued that
insofar as the modern orientalists can be said to have an explicit
interpretive theory, this is largely quarried from the historically
conditioned writings of the great medieval Muslim theorists—ibn
Khaldun, Mawardi, ibn Taymiyya. The result is a remarkable blur-
ring between historical object and interpreting subject.

My suggestion here is that ultimately the functional anthropologist and the orientalist were concerned with the same theoretical
question: what holds society together? How is order achieved or
destroyed? The former, viewing 'tribal' society as *defined* by (normative) polity, focussed on the consensual relations between African rulers and ruled. The latter, viewing sharia-defined society as
fragmented by (secular) polity, focused on the repressive relations
between Islamic rulers and ruled.

V

I have been trying to argue that both functional anthropology and
orientalism, by selecting certain phenomena, by not asking certain
questions, by approaching history in a certain way, by taking the
problem of social order as their basic theoretical concern, tended to
project characteristic images of the political structure of the non-
European societies they studied. I am now going to suggest that the
historical formation of these European disciplines helps us understand better why the selection and omission occured as they did.

What I want to emphasise here is this: that in contrast to the
modern discipline of Islamic orientalism, functional anthropology
was born *after* the advent of European colonialism in the societies
studied—after, that is, the First World War when the *Pax Britannica*
had made intensive and long-term fieldwork a practicable proposition.

Tribal rulers could be viewed as representative partly because the
anthropologist in the field coming from a crisis-ridden Europe, experienced them as conforming to 'traditional' political norms (as
these had come to be underwritten by a paternalist colonial administration). Colonial ideology generally stressed the essential continuity, and therefore the integrity, of African political cultures
under colonial rule. The anthropologist, it may be argued, was prepared to accept the total colonial system (while quarrelling with
particular colonial policies in relation to 'his tribe') because he was
impressed by its obvious success in maintaining itself and in securing an apparently benign form of local order within the ethnic

group he observed so intimately. He was concerned, as the European administrators for their own reasons were equally concerned, with protecting subordinate African cultures, and was therefore prepared to accept the colonial definition of African polities, and to restate that definition in terms of consent. (Consider to what extent this image has begun to break down with decolonisation in the '60s.)

The point is that unlike nineteenth century anthropology, the objectification of functional anthropologists occured within the context of *routine colonialism*, of an imperial structure of power already established rather than one in process of vigorous expansion in which political force and contradiction are only too obvious.

Orientalism belongs to a different historical moment, and its methods, assumptions and pre-occupations are rooted in the European experience of Islam prior to the advent of Western colonialism in the Middle East. Among the cultural forebears of the modern orientalists were the medieval Christian polemicists who sought to defend the values of Christendom against the threat of Islam.[23] Although modern orientalists rarely engage in overt propaganda, and have adopted a more secular and detached tone, they have still been concerned to contrast Islamic society and civilisation with their own, and to show in what the former has been lacking. In particular, they have been concerned to emphasise the absence of 'liberty', 'progress' and 'humanism' in classic Islamic societies, and in general to relate the reasons for this alleged absence to the religious essence of Islam.[24] Thus in contrast to the social anthropologist whose intention has often been to show that the rationality of African cultures is comprehensible to (and therefore capable of being accommodated by) the West, the orientalist has been far more occupied with emphasising the basic irrationality of Islamic history.

Norman Daniel, in his valuable study *Islam, Europe and Empire*,

[23] See N. Daniel, *Islam and the West, The Making of an Image*, Edinburgh, 1960; and R. W. Southern, *Western Views of Islam in the Middle Ages*, Cambridge, Mass., 1962.
[24] Thus the influential orientalist von Grunebaum: "It is essential to realise that Muslim civilisation is a cultural entity that does not share our primary aspirations. It is not vitally interested in analytical self-understanding, and it is even less interested in the structural study of other cultures, either as an end in itself or as a means toward clearer understanding of its own character and history. If this observation were to be valid merely for contemporary Islam, one might be inclined to connect it with the profoundly disturbed state of Islam, which does not permit it to look beyond itself unless forced to do so. But as it is valid for the past as well, one may perhaps seek to connect it with the basic antihumanism of this civilisation, that is, the determined refusal to accept man to any extent whatever as the arbiter or the measure of things, and the tendency to be satisfied with

116   TWO EUROPEAN IMAGES OF NON-EUROPEAN RULE

(Edinburgh, 1966) has traced the European experience of Islam—
and especially of the aggressive Ottoman Empire of the sixteenth
and seventeenth centuries—which helped to fashion its image of the
tyrannical Islamic polity in the nineteenth century. He suggests that
the three most important elements in this experience were fear of
Turkish power, the absence of a Muslim gentry and the subordinate
position of Muslim women. "To the mind of aristocratic Europe",
Daniel writes, "tyranny was common to all three—to the external
threat, to a polity internally servile and to an enslavement of
women. As time passed, there was increasing communication with
eastern countries and gradually, as the centres of power in the
world shifted, fear gave way to patronage". (p. 11). But the image
of a tyrannical Ottoman structure, as Daniel goes on to show,
remained unquestioned throughout the nineteenth century, and became reinforced through the special notion of Islamic misrule—in
the double sense of inefficient government and fiscal oppression
(both, he might have added, grave sins in the eyes of a self-consciously progressive capitalist Europe).

It was towards the end of the nineteenth century on the eve of
massive imperial expansion, that the foundations of modern orientalism were laid.[25] The literary, philological method of his study
(based on chronicles and treatises acquired from Islamic countries
and deposited in European libraries) meant that the orientalist had
little need for direct contact with the people whose historical culture
he objectified, and no necessary interest in its continuity. In so far
as he addressed himself to the contemporary condition of Islamic
peoples, he saw in it a reflection of his idealist vision of Islamic
history—repression, corruption and political decay.

Most members of the European middle classes before the First
World War viewed the imperialist ambitions of their governments
as natural and desirable.[26] In keeping with these attitudes the opinions that prevailed among them regarding prospective or recent
victims of colonial conquest were usually highly unflattering. This

truth as the description of mental structures, or, in other words, with
psychological truth." *Modern Islam*, Berkeley and Los Angeles, 1962, p. 40.
For an extremely interesting response by a Muslim intellectual see Moham-
med Arkoun, "L'Islam moderne vu par le professeur G. E. von Grunebaum" in *Arabica*, vol. xl, 1964.
[25] Cf. C. J. Adams, "Islamic Religion" (Part I), in *Middle East Studies Association Bulletin*, vol. 4, no. 3, October 15, 1970, p. 3.
[26] Cf. H. Gollwitzer, *Europe in the Age of Imperialism: 1880-1914*, London,
1969. For a study of British public opinion in relation to events preceding
the British occupation of Egypt in 1882, see H. S. Deighton's excellent
article, "The Impact on Egypt on Britain", in P. M. Holt, (ed.), *Political*

TALAL ASAD   **117**

was as true of Asia as it was of Africa in the latter half of the nineteenth century.[27] In this period, influential writers such as Ranke
and Burkehardt, Count Gobineau and Renan, although in disagreement on important matters, were significantly united in their con-
temptuous views of Islam.[28] In this respect, their perspective was
not profoundly different from that of the founders of modern orientalism—e.g. Wellhausen and Nöldeke,[29] Becker and Snouck Hurgronje.[30] It would have been surprising had it been otherwise.
Leone Caetani, an Italian aristocrat, was exceptional among orientalists in condemning European colonial expansion into Islamic
countries.[31] In his commitment to empire and the White Man's
Burden, Snouck Hurgronje was far more typical.[32]

The orientalist's image of repressive relations between Islamic
rulers and their subjects is thus rooted not only in the historic
Christian experience of aggressive Islam (an experience the West
had never had in relation to Africa),[33] but more importantly in the
bourgeois European evaluation of 'unprogressive' and 'fanatical'
Islam that required to be directly controlled for reasons of empire.

As recent rulers of vast Muslim populations, the imperialist rulers
could attempt to legitimise their own governing position with arguments supplied by the orientalists: that Islamic rule has historically
been oppressive rule (colonial rule is by contrast humane), that
Islamic political theory recognises the legitimacy of the effective
de facto ruler (colonial rule is manifestly better than the corruption,
inefficiency and disorder of pre-colonial rule), that political domination in Muslim lands is typically external to the essential articulation of Islamic social and religious life (therefore no radical damage
has been done to Islam by conquering it as its central political
tradition remains unbroken).[34]

It is therefore at this ideological level, I would suggest, that the

and *Social Change in Modern Egypt*, London, 1968.
[27]Cf. V. G. Kiernan, *The Lords of Human Kind*, London, 1969, and the
documentary collection edited by P. D. Curtin, *op. cit.*
[28]Cf. J. W. Fuck, "Islam as an Historical Problem in European Historiography Since 1800" in B. Lewis and P. M. Holt, (eds.), *Historians of the
Middle East*, London, 1962.
[29]J. W. Fück, *op. cit.*
[30]Cf. J.—J. Waardenburg, *L'Islam dans le miroir de l'occident*, The Hague,
1962.
[31]J. W. Fück, *op. cit.* For further details on Prince Caetani, see A. Bausani,
"Islamic Studies in Italy in the XIX-XX cc." in *East and West*, vol. VIII,
1957.
[32]With respect to Holland's colonial role in Indonesia, Snouck Hurgronje
wrote: "Il ne s'agit que d'eveiller une prise de conscience...considerant que
l'independence de la vie spirituelle et la libération de son développment de

two objectifications of political rule again converge. For the orientalist's construct, by focusing on a particular image of the Islamic tradition, and the anthropologist's, by focusing on a particular image of the African tradition, both helped to justify colonial domination at particular moments in the power encounter between the West and the Third World. No doubt, this ideological role was performed by orientalism and by functional anthropology largely unwittingly. But the fact remains that by refusing to discuss the way in which bourgeois Europe had imposed its power and its own conception of the just political order on African and Islamic peoples, both disciplines were basically reassuring to the colonial ruling classes.

de toute pression matérielle est l'une des plus grandes bénédictions de notre civilisation. Nous nous sentons poussés par un zèle missionaire de la meilleure sorte afin de faire participer le monde musulman à cette satisfaction." This was what ultimately justified colonialism: "Notre domination doit se justifier par l'accession des indigènes a une civilisation plus élevée. Ils doivent acquérir parmi les peuples sous notre direction la place que méritent leurs qualités naturelles." Quoted in J.—J. Waardenburg, *op. cit.*, pp. 101 and 102. See also W. F. Wertheim, "Counter-insurgency research at the turn of the century—Snouck Hurgronje and the Acheh War", in *Sociologische Gids*, vol. XIX, September/December 1972. (I am grateful to Ludowik Brunt for this last reference.)

[33] For a discussion about the various elements that went into the making of European views about Africa at the end of the eighteenth century and the first half of the nineteenth, see P. D. Curtin, *The Image of Africa*, London, 1965. According to Curtin this earlier image was on the whole far more favourable than the one prevalent in the latter part of the nineteenth century—i.e. on the eve of the Partition of Africa.

[34] The orientalist's image is still very much alive and still rooted in a structure of sentiments remarkably akin to that displayed by the founders. ("Although there are exceptions," observes C. J. Adams in his survey article, "in the cases of individuals or particular fields of study (Sufism, for example, or Islamic Art and Architecture), to be sure, on the whole one is struck with the negative tone—or if negative be too strong a word, with the tone of personal disenchantment—that runs through the majority of [orientalist] writing about Muslim faith." *Op. cit., p. 3*). I attribute this persistence to the fact that despite profound changes in the world since the late nineteenth century, the power encounter between the West and the Muslim countries continues to express itself typically in the form of hostile confrontations (for reasons too involved to discuss here) and the methods and techniques of orientalism as a discipline, with its basic reliance on philological analysis, remain unaffected. These facts and not mere 'excellence' account for the continuity noted by Adams: "In fact, basic nineteenth-century Islamic scholarship was so competent and exhaustive that it has intimidated many later scholars from attempting re-examinations of fundamental issues. Much of what the pioneers of Islamology wrote has scarcely been improved upon, not to say superseded; it has merely been transmitted and continues to be the most authoritative scholarship we possess in many fields." (*loc. cit.*). Of how many other historical or social science disciplines can such a statement be made?

[7]

The Ideology of 'Tribalism'

by ARCHIE MAFEJE*

FEW authors have been able to write on Africa without making constant reference to 'tribalism'. Could this be the distinguishing feature of the continent? or is it merely a reflection of the system of perceptions of those who write on Africa, and of their African 'converts'? Objective reality is very difficult to disentangle from subjective perception, almost in the same way as concepts in the social sciences are hard to purify of all ideological connotations. Might not African history, written, not by Europeans, but by Africans themselves, have employed different concepts and told a different story? If so, what would have been the theoretical explanation? Are things what they are called, or do they have an existence which is independent of the nomenclature that attaches to them? When it comes to Africa, answers vary independently of whether the observer is a liberal idealist, a Marxist materialist, or an African 'convert'.

It is usually argued that social behaviour in Africa is so diverse, so inconsistent, and so fluid that it is nigh impossible to classify or treat it with any amount of consistency. I am inclined to think that the problem in Africa is not one of empirically diversified behaviour but mainly one of *ideology*, and specifically the ideology of 'tribalism'. European colonialism, like any epoch, brought with it certain ways of reconstructing the African reality. It regarded African societies as particularly tribal. This approach produced certain blinkers or ideological predispositions which made it difficult for those associated with the system to view these societies in any other light. Hence certain modes of thought among European scholars in Africa and their African counterparts have persisted, despite the many important economic and political changes that have occurred in the continent over the last 75–100 years. Therefore, if tribalism is thought of as peculiarly African, then the ideology itself is particularly European in origin.

ANTHROPOLOGICAL MISDIRECTION

In a recent publication P. H. Gulliver, perhaps feeling a little guilty about the continued use of the term 'tribe', explains: 'We do not

* Head of the Department of Sociology, University of Dar es Salaam.

continue to use it in any spirit of defiance, let alone of derogation and disparagement. We use it simply because it continues to be widely used in East Africa itself when English is spoken...among the citizens... there.' The justification is repeated in at least three other places;[1] but it raises several questions. Are things necessarily what they are called? Secondly, to what extent are social scientists bound by the terminology of the natives? Again, is it not significant that the term occurs when English is spoken? In South Africa the indigenous population has no word for 'tribe'; only for 'nation', 'clan', and 'lineage' and, traditionally, people were identified by territory – 'Whose [which Chief's] land do you come from?'

In many instances the colonial authorities helped to create the things called 'tribes', in the sense of political communities; this process coincided with and was helped along by the anthropologists' preoccupation with 'tribes'. This provided the material as well as the ideological base of what is now called 'tribalism'. Is it surprising then that the modern African, who is a product of colonialism, speaks the same language? If that is a great puzzle to the modern social scientist, it was not to Marx, who in 1845 wrote:

The ideas of the ruling class are in every epoch the ruling ideas: i.e. the class which is the ruling *material* force of society, is at the same time its ruling *intellectual* force. The class which has the means of production at its disposal has control at the same time over the means of mental production, so that thereby, generally speaking, the ideas of those who lack the means of mental production are subject to it.[2]

The Anglo-Saxon anthropologists and sociologists in their usual mild manner refer to 'pace-setters' or 'reference groups'.

For some time, and despite the changes that were taking place, most British anthropologists maintained their interest in the study of 'pure' tribes, ignoring any twentieth-century innovations in these societies. At best they regarded these as intrusions, both undesirable and peripheral to the real life of the people. This was in harmony with the theories of indirect rule, as advocated by Lord Lugard and Sir Donald Cameron. As is acknowledged now, indirect rule had very direct economic and political implications. African societies were being drawn into a complex of extractive economic and political relations, the effect of which could not be ignored even by the most tribal-fixated anthropologist. In fact, the liberal sentiment of most anthropologists was touched and

---

[1] P. H. Gulliver (ed.), *Tradition and Transition in East Africa: studies of the tribal element in the modern era* (London, 1969), pp. 2, 7–8, and 24.

[2] K. Marx and F. Engels, *The German Ideology* (London, 1965 edn.), p. 61.

they began to lament the ensuing 'disintegration' of traditional African societies, the loss of their pristine 'equilibrium and cohesion'; they viewed with horror and some concern the 'degradation of the African ethic'.

THE CHANGING PERSPECTIVE

This represented the turning-point for most anthropologists; the situation was not as static as they had supposed. From 1945 onwards a few anthropologists such as the Wilsons, R. Firth, R. Redfield, and Audrey Richards began to talk about 'social change'.[1] By 1959 Max Gluckman could afford to say boldly: 'The tradition of anthropology is still "tribalistic", and with it goes a tendency to make the tribe and the tribesman the starting-point of analysis'.[2] However, as is shown by his later work, Gluckman himself has never abandoned that tradition.[3]

Meanwhile, the basis for the discussion on what we were to mean by 'tribe' or 'tribalism' had been provided in 1956, when J. C. Mitchell published a study, which is now regarded as a classic among anthropologists, of *The Kalela Dance*. This was, according to popular terminology, a tribal dance performed by tribesmen in the Copperbelt. Mitchell, undaunted, came to the startling conclusions that, far from being an expression of tribalism, the Kalela dance was an expression of social differentiation and prestige ranking in town, and that 'tribalism' in town, though not in the rural areas, was merely a 'category of interaction'.[4] This revelation had a dramatic effect on anthropologists, few of whom would thereafter undertake an urban study without repeating the new formula: 'urban is different from rural tribalism'.[5] That continues to be the standard anthropological formula, as is shown by P. H. Gulliver's editorial comments and some of the articles in *Tradition and Transition in East Africa* (London, 1969). A. L. Epstein was one of the

[1] Cf. G. and M. Wilson, *The Analysis of Social Change* (Cambridge, 1945); R. Firth, *Elements of Social Organization* (London, 1951); R. Redfield, *The Primitive World and its Transformation* (Ithaca, 1953); and A. I. Richards, *Economic Development and Tribal Change* (Cambridge, 1954).

[2] Max Gluckman, 'Anthropological Problems arising from the African Industrial Revolution', in A. W. Southall (ed.), *Social Change in Modern Africa* (London, 1961), p. 69.

[3] See Gluckman, *Order and Rebellion in Tribal Africa* (London, 1963), and his contributions to other works: 'The Tribal Areas in South and Central Africa', in Leo Kuper and M. G. Smith (eds.), *Pluralism in Africa* (Berkeley and Los Angeles, 1969); 'Tribalism, Ruralism and Urbanism in Plural Societies', in V. W. Turner (ed.), *Colonialism in Africa, 1870–1960*, vol. III, *Profiles of Change* (Cambridge, 1971); and 'Inter-hierarchical Roles: professional and party ethnics in the tribal areas in South and Central Africa', in M. Swartz (ed.), *Local-level Politics* (Chicago, 1968).

[4] J. C. Mitchell, *The Kalela Dance* (Lusaka, 1956), Rhodes–Livingstone Papers, no. 27.

[5] E.g. in Southall, op. cit. pp. 35 and 67.

very few writers who dared to suggest that Africans in the urban areas could actually reject 'tribalism' as being irrelevant to their problems. He found that the African copper miners of Luanshya refused to accept 'tribal elders' as their representatives or leaders in the struggle against the mine management. At the same time the non-salaried staff among them were suspicious of the leaders from the salaried staff, who tended to act for the benefit of their own group.[1] This was another instance of class formation among Africans.

Whatever the details and the inhibitions, the analysis of social change made it possible for anthropologists to look at the transformation of tribal societies with less jaundiced eyes. 'Winds of change' had come to be accepted as a fact of life; and 'independence', with all that it implied, was fast becoming a reality and no longer a vague idea in the distant future. This caught the attention of the political scientists, who began to move in one by one;[2] sold on the idea of modern nation states, they brought with them a new creed – 'modernisation'. In the drama of 'independence' and under the fervour of this new creed, what was going to be the attitude of the anthropologists? They, being older in the field, were not unduly worried, and remained faithful to their 'tribes'. But this time they were concerned to establish a new truth, namely the 'persistence and resilience' of the tribal systems rather than their 'disintegration' or 'disequilibrium'.[3]

There had already been warnings: for example, W. Watson chose a significant title for his *Tribal Cohesion in a Money Economy* (Manchester, 1958). This has been the theme for the greater part of the past decade. It is an interesting *volte face* on the part of the anthropologists, and represents a shift (not a change) in their ideological perspective. As is illustrated by their admiration for 'go-ahead' tribes such as the Baganda, the Kikuyu, and the Ibo, anthropologists subscribe to the creed of 'modernisation'. But, unlike political scientists and African nationalists, they do not see it as necessarily incompatible with 'tribalism' or 'traditionalism'. All the same, an anthropologist betrays himself when he offers 'tribal institutions and values' as the explanation for the *failure* of Africans to embrance modernity. Here, the anthropologist proves to be a self-contradictory incrementalist, and he cannot argue otherwise

---

[1] A. L. Epstein, *Politics in an Urban African Community* (Manchester, 1958).

[2] Led by David Apter; see his *The Gold Coast in Transition* (Princeton, 1955) and *The Political Kingdom in Uganda* (Princeton, 1961). Cf. also James S. Coleman, *Nigeria: background to nationalism* (Berkeley and Los Angeles, 1958), and K. W. J. Post, *The Nigerian Federal Elections of 1959: politics and administration in a developing political system* (London, 1963).

[3] See I. Lewis, 'Tribalism', in *International Encyclopedia of the Social Sciences* (New York, 1968), vol. XVI, pp. 146–50.

because his organic conception of social structure and institutions commits him irrevocably.

While anthropologists use their tribal ideology to explain both successes and failures in modernisation, political scientists of *all* persuasions use theirs to explain only failures. As a result they talk more consistently and conveniently than anthropologists about problems of 'integration', 'penetration', and 'mobilisation'. However, conceptually, they have greater problems than the anthropologists.

First, despite their 'tribal' language, they know far less about tribes than anthropologists. Secondly, the same 'tribal' language makes it difficult for them to explain similar phenomena elsewhere in the modern world without falling victims to the ethnocentric ideology mentioned in the introduction to this article. The anthropologists can easily escape a similar fate because their professional preoccupation has always been the study of 'tribes' or 'primitive societies'. Of course, even that is not true any more.

THE CONCEPTUAL PROBLEM RESTATED

So far I have merely stated and illustrated my case; I have not proved it. The real basic question is whether it is possible to have 'tribalism' without tribes. But how do we test for the existence of tribes? Classical anthropology depicted tribes as 'self-contained, autonomous communities practising subsistence economy with no or limited external trade'. But in 1940 M. Fortes and E. E. Evans-Pritchard introduced the distinction between 'centralised states' and 'stateless' or 'acephalous' societies;[1] since then, anthropologists have had problems in deciding whether all African polities were tribes, or whether some of them qualified for the more respectable epithet, 'state'. Scale seemed to matter, but anthropologists were satisfied to refer to bigger multi-tribal units such as the Luapula Kingdom of Kazembe in Central Africa, Tshaka's Zulu Empire in South Africa, and the Ashanti Confederacy in West Africa, as 'super-tribes'. In 1956 I. Schapera took it upon himself to clear up some of the confusion and to restate the anthropologist's position. He presented tribes as 'separate "political communities", each claiming exclusive rights to a given territory and managing its affairs independently of external control'.[2]

All said and done, territoriality, primitive government through elders

[1] M. Fortes and E. E. Evans-Pritchard (eds.), *African Political Systems* (London, 1940), passim.

[2] I. Schapera, *Government and Politics in Tribal Societies* (London, 1956), p. 203.

and chiefs, and a primitive subsistence economy emerge as the primary features which distinguish a tribe from other forms of human organisation. 'Culture' was never mentioned as one of these until the arrival of the 'modernisation' crusade in the work of political scientists and pluralist sociologists such as M. G. Smith and J. C. Mitchell.[1] It is therefore very instructive to note that in 1969 Gulliver defines a tribe as 'any group of people which is distinguished, by its members and by others, on the basis of cultural-regional criteria'.[2] We thus see that 'tribe' is now a matter of subjective perception, as if to say: 'That is how the natives see and describe it.'

Although their reasons are suspect, anthropologists may have been right in insisting that traditional or pre-colonial African societies, large or small, were tribes. If we were to restrict the term 'tribe' to specific forms of economic, political, and social organisation that can be fixed in space and time, as I intend to, we would not be wallowing in such utter confusion and incredible inconsistencies. A relatively undifferentiated society, practising a primitive subsistence economy and enjoying local autonomy, can legitimately be designated as a tribe. When such a society strives to maintain its basic structure and local autonomy, even under changed economic and political conditions, perhaps it can be said to exhibit 'tribalism'. But to impose the same concept on societies that have been effectively penetrated by European colonialism, that have been successfully drawn into a capitalist money economy and a world market, is a serious transgression. The new division of labour, the new modes of production, and the system of distribution of material goods and political power give modern African societies a fundamentally different material and social base.[3] It is apparent then that it is not a question of scale, but rather a question of qualitative aspects of social and economic organisation.

This is not to deny the existence of tribal ideology and sentiment in Africa. The argument is that they have to be understood – and conceptualised – differently under modern conditions. There is a real difference between the man who, on behalf of his tribe, strives to maintain its traditional integrity and autonomy, and the man who invokes tribal ideology in order to maintain a power position, not in the tribal area, but in the modern capital city, and whose ultimate aim is to undermine and exploit the supposed tribesmen. The fact that it works,

---

[1] M. G. Smith, *Government in Zazzau* (London, 1960); and J. C. Mitchell, *Tribalism and the Plural Society* (London, 1960).

[2] Gulliver, op. cit. p. 24.

[3] Cf. Marx and Engels, op. cit. pp. 43–4.

THE IDEOLOGY OF 'TRIBALISM' 259

as is often pointed out by tribal ideologists, is no proof that 'tribes' or 'tribalism' exist in any objective sense. If anything, it is a mark of *false consciousness* on the part of the supposed tribesmen, who subscribe to an ideology that is inconsistent with their material base and therefore unwittingly respond to the call for their own exploitation. On the part of the new African élite, it is a ploy or distortion they use to conceal their exploitative role. It is an ideology in the original Marxist sense and they share it with their European fellow-ideologists.

THE THEORETICAL IMPASSE

Aside from their particular ideology – which has been cleverly exposed by John Argyle in a recent study[1] – the anthropologists, sociologists, and political scientists seem to suffer from a common disability in their failure to distinguish sufficiently and consistently between social theory and social action. While it is true that there is a relationship between social classification and social behaviour, it is not true that the two always correspond. Sociologically analysed, things are not necessarily what they are known as socially. The frequent statement by anthropologists who have studied urban societies that 'urban tribalism is different from rural tribalism' is an illustration of how the same classificatory term is employed by the social scientists and the actors to describe entirely different phenomena. C. Lévi-Strauss has suggested that conscious models are poorer than unconscious ones, in that they tell us less about objective reality.[2] Of course, being a member of the club himself, Lévi-Strauss would not extend the same observation to his fellow social scientists.

It is also important to note that classificatory systems are less space-bound than action systems. That is why it is becoming increasingly difficult for the anthropologists to insist on territoriality as being the basis for 'tribalism'. According to their own observations, 'tribalism' has now extended to areas as far removed from the tribal homeland as the cities. Under modern conditions the so-called tribesmen do not live in the same area, though they might still identify with one another in specific contexts. Secondly, even in the rural areas, residence in regions which are known by tribal names is *not* confined to any particular 'tribe', but all the same the inhabitants might still identify very strongly with the region. Certainly, this was the case in the Transkei,

---

[1] W. J. Argyle, 'European Nationalism and African Tribalism', in Gulliver, op. cit. pp. 41–57.

[2] C. Lévi-Strauss, *Structural Anthropology* (New York, 1963), pp. 281–2.

South Africa, where I did field work in 1963.[1] The same tendency was observed among the migrants in Cape Town.[2] Under modern conditions this would emphasise the importance of regionalism at the expense of tribalism.

Closely associated with the above point is the question of cultural identity. Earlier on we observed that 'culture' was not one of the criteria used by British anthropologists to define 'tribe'. This is either because they were unbending structuralists or because they realised that cultural boundaries were more diffuse than political ones. In South Africa the Xhosa-speakers can be said to have shared a common culture over a very wide area, but were divided up into a number of autonomous political units. Like the fictitious 'tribes' that have been mentioned previously in this article, they might use that cultural link in order to secure a more comfortable place in the modern industrial South African society. Would that still constitute 'tribalism'? A typical anthropologist, like the natives affected unfavourably by such a move, would accuse them of 'tribalism'. But their Xhosa-ness in the cultural sense, despite its facilitating effect, would be representative of something entirely different. This point has been made by a number of writers, most of whom however have not been able to overcome their own ideological predispositions. A few examples will suffice:

tribal loyalties and identification are closely linked with appeals...to traditional culture even where the concrete basis for tribalism, for inter-tribal conflict or allegations of unfair participation, is firmly established in contemporary competition for power and economic advantage.[3]

What is basic here is not 'tribal rivalry' so much as a system in which competition is fundamentally important and which provides a multiplicity of sources from which the competitors can draw support.[4]

This leads to the second sense of tribe – namely, as a concept used by townsmen for describing urban divisions and casting blame. As such it is frequently emotive and mythical, and therefore highly flexible, enabling various people to have different explanations of the same issue.[5]

It feels as if everybody is tethered to a chain and cannot move further. R. J. Apthorpe has remarked that 'sociologically analysed, the only thing that is always prior is not the phenomenon of tribalism itself –

---

[1] A. Mafeje, 'Leadership and Change in a Peasant Community'; M.A. thesis, University of Cape Town, 1963.

[2] M. Wilson and A. Mafeje, *Langa: a study of social groups in an African township* (London 1963), pp. 47–9.

[3] P. H. Gulliver, editorial introduction, *Tradition and Transition in East Africa*, p. 12.

[4] R. D. Griller, 'The Tribal Factor in an East African Trade Union', ibid. p. 320.

[5] D. J. Parkin, 'Tribe as Fact and Fiction in an East African City', ibid. p. 295.

whatever precisely that is – but the apparatus of concepts and ideas with which social scientists and others attempt to comprehend this'.[1] To avoid what Marx once called 'idealistic humbug', Apthorpe might have added that the conditions to which the various 'tribalisms' were a response also existed prior to the phenomenon and were, in fact, a result of relative deprivation.[2]

❊　　　❊　　　❊

Apthorpe's main point was to ask if tribalism mattered. The reply is: if 'tribalism' does not matter, the ideology of tribalism, peddled by both expatriate theorists and emergent African middle-class ideologists, matters very much. First, it over-simplifies, mystifies, and obscures the real nature of economic and power relations between Africans themselves, and between Africa and the capitalist world, almost in the same way as the term 'feudalism', applied to Latin America, camouflages the crucial role played by international finance-capital and imperialism in accentuating and perpetuating the existing social formation in that part of the world. Secondly, it draws an invidious and highly suspect distinction between Africans and other peoples of the world. The patronising concession of 'call them the same' is more likely to produce resentment than to facilitate communication. Thirdly, it is an anachronistic misnomer which impedes cross-cultural analysis.

If *regional particularism*, facilitated by the existence of cultural sections within the wider society, and *class formation* were identified as such, instead of ideologising about 'tribes' and 'tribalism', the insights already gained from European, Asian, and American historical experience would be brought to bear more fruitfully upon the African transformation, and with better prospects for further analysis of human societies all over the world. To be able to contribute to that kind of universalism, as social scientists, we need generalisable concepts with high explanatory power – and 'tribalism' is not one of them.

[1] R. J. Apthorpe, 'Does Tribalism Really Matter?', in *Transition* (Kampala), 37, October 1968, p. 22.

[2] For an example, see Gulliver, op. cit. p. 24; I might also cite an M.A. candidate at Makerere University who said that 'tribalism' did not start in Kigeze until 1958.

[8]

Race and the Webs of Empire:
Aryanism from India to the Pacific

Tony Ballantyne

Knowledge, particularly about cultural difference, has emerged as a central theme in recent studies of imperialism. Largely, if not entirely, encouraged by Foucault's work on power/ knowledge and Said's paradigmatic studies of Orientalism, scholars from across the humanities have increasingly highlighted the centrality of the cultural projects of empire building. Studies of colonial disciplines (from cartography to psychology), re-readings of canonical texts, and a new recognition of cultural manifestations of imperial ideologies (from advertisements for soap to the place of Shakespeare in colonial classrooms) have fundamentally reshaped our understandings of the sources, structure and consequences of imperialism.[1] Central to this new scholarship has been a fundamental reappraisal of racial thought: no longer some epiphenomenona of empire, race – a concept that emerged unevenly over time and space – is now seen as being fundamental to the discourses of European imperialism from the sixteenth century on.[2]

This essay re-examines the development of Aryanism within the British empire in the long nineteenth-century. A range of case studies have identified Aryanism – the notion that certain communities shared cultural features as a result of their sharing a common 'Aryan stock' – as one of the most significant racializing discourses in contexts as divergent as India and Nigeria, Ireland and Hawai'i, Argentina and New Zealand.[3] Rather than simply

---

[1]   Some of these developments have recently been reviewed in Tony Ballantyne, 'Archive, State, Discipline: Power and knowledge in South Asian Historiography', *New Zealand Journal of Asian Studies* 3 (2001), 87–105; Dane Kennedy, 'Imperial History and Post-Colonial Theory', *Journal of Imperial and Commonwealth History*, 24 (1996), 345–363; William R. Pinch, 'Same Difference in India and Europe', *History and Theory*, 38 (1999), 389–407; Mrinalini Sinha, 'Britain and the Empire: Toward a New Agenda for Imperial history', *Radical History Review*, 72 (1998), 163–174. Many of the arguments forwarded in this essay are elaborated more fully in Tony Ballantyne, *Orientalism and Race: Aryanism in the British empire* (forthcoming, Palgrave, 2002).

[2]   These arguments remain controversial. The recent *Oxford History of the British Empire* systematically marginalizes the importance of race, while David Cannadine's recent *Ornamentalism: How the British Saw their Empire* (Oxford, 2001) stresses rank and ritual rather than race.

[3]   E.g. Andrew E. Barnes, 'Aryanizing Projects: African Collaborators and Colonial Transcripts', *Comparative studies of South Asia, Africa, and the Middle East*, 17 (1997) 46–68; Edward A. Hagan, 'The Aryan Myth: a Nineteenth-Century Anglo-Irish Will to Power', *Ideology and Ireland in the Nineteenth Century* Tadhg Foley and Sean Ryder eds, (Dublin, 1998), 197–206; K. R. Howe, 'Some Origins and Migrations of Ideas leading to the Aryan Polynesian Theories of Abraham Fornander and

recounting the development of this domain of knowledge narrowly within one colony, this essay argues that a careful examination of Aryanism reveals the profoundly mobile character of racial knowledge and discourses about cultural difference within the British empire, a reality that necessitates a trans-national analysis imperial knowledge production. To achieve this end, this essay reevaluates the place of Aryanism in the historiography of South Asia and the Pacific, revealing the important elisions that can arise from a 'national' history of racial thought. By sketching the conscious transplantation of ethnological models drawn from British India to the New Zealand frontier in the second half of the nineteenth century, I hope to recover the important networks and exchanges that shaped the empire and to underscore the fundamentally intertextual nature of colonial knowledge. Before mapping these 'webs of empire', it is important to begin by sketching the inherited spatial models that order most studies of British imperialism.

I. The spatial imagination of imperial/colonial histories

Over the last decade there have been growing calls for trans-national histories and many historians have insisted that the construction of new analytical models that recover the movement of people, ideas, ideologies, commodities and information across the borders of the nation-states are urgently needed in this global moment. Traditionally, of course, history is conceived of as a temporal discipline in which the fundamental structures of research, analysis, and narrativization are concerned with change over time. But, as we are increasingly aware, history is also a spatial discipline and historical knowledge is also structured by spatial parameters, whether these units are continental, cultural, regional, or, most frequently, national. Calls to fundamentally reorder the spatial basis of historical writing and write histories that look beyond the nation pose a fundamental challenge to history, a discipline that has produced enabling narratives for so many nations and that continues to depend heavily upon state-sponsored archives, institutions, and funding. Breaking this 'narrative contract' – to borrow Sudipta Kaviraj's memorable phrase – between history and the nation-state is difficult, yet this project is pressing as we seek to understand both the complex forces that have framed the asymmetries of our contemporary world and the future shape of the discipline of history itself.[4]

The need to revisit what we might term the 'spatial imagination' of historical writing is particularly vital within the specific context of British imperial and post-colonial history, as the vast majority of historians continue to use one of two models. The first and perhaps dominant historiographical tradition has been the production of metropolitan-focused imperial histories, a tradition revivified by Peter Cain and A. G. Hopkins's model of 'gentlemanly capitalism' and, more recently, by David Hancock's study of the role of London merchants in the integration

---

Edward Tregear', *Pacific Studies*, 11 (1988), 67–81; Mónica Quijada Mauriño, 'Los "Incas Arios": Historia, Lengua y Raza en la Construccion Nacional Hispanoamericana del Siglo XIX', *Histórica* 20 (1996), 243–269.

    [4]   Sudipta Kaviraj, 'The Imaginary Institution of India', *Subaltern Studies VII: Writings on South Asian History and Society* (Delhi, 1993), 1–39

of an eighteenth-century Atlantic world. [5] In viewing the empire and its history from London, these models return indigenous people to the margins of history while foregrounding the powerful financial and mercantile interests of England's southeast. In effect, these models reinscribe London's privileged position as the 'heart' of the empire, the center from where power, people, capital, and ideas flowed out to the colonies in the periphery. The second model neatly inverts this spatial imagination, as many historians working on the 'periphery' – the former colonies of the empire – focus on the severing of the ties to London, charting the progress of the individual colony to independence. These colonial histories typically narrate the birth of the nation in highly teleological narratives that recount the growing maturity of national consciousness and the long and often bloody journey towards the achievement of the nation-state.

Despite increased calls for histories that interrogate the nation-state and recover trans-national exchanges and mobility, these imagined geographies of empire have proven difficult to displace. These two models provide the basic structure for the recent five-volume *Oxford History of the British Empire*, where the empire is repeatedly carved up into national chunks, and even thematic essays often work to reinforce the primacy of the nation-state and the fundamental divide between metropolitan and colonial histories.[6] While this editorial strategy, of course, merely reflects prevailing historical practice, it further legitimates the division between imperial and colonial history. This division of academic labor has been pernicious, disassembling the empire into a series of discrete components, rather than conceiving of it as the product of the 'bundles of relationships' that Eric Wolf identifies as being at the heart of history.[7]

But if the *Oxford History of the British Empire* has reinstantiated this long-established division, it was only able to achieve this by both rejecting the claims of postcolonial discourse analysis and by marginalizing the work of historians of migration, gender and popular culture who have insisted on the profound entanglement of metropolitan and colonial histories. Such work actually has a long lineage that reaches back until the 1980s (if not before), but has become more prominent and theoretically sophisticated over the last ten years.[8] Although grounded in divergent epistemologies and concerns, the work of John MacKenzie and

---

5   David Hancock, *Citizens of the World: London Merchants and the Integration of the British Atlantic Community, 1735–1785* (Cambridge, 1995); P.J. Cain and A.G. Hopkins, *British Imperialism: Innovation and Expansion, 1688–1914* (London, 1993). These arguments are reviewed in Raymond E. Dumett ed., *Gentlemanly Capitalism and British Imperialism: the New Debate on Empire* (London, 1999), Hopkins has articulated a rather different vision in his recent 'Back to the Future: from National History to Imperial History', *Past & Present* 164 (1999), 198–243.

6   E.g. P.J. Cain, 'Economics and Empire: the Metropolitan Context', *Oxford History of the British Empire. Volume 3: the Nineteenth Century* Andrew Porter ed., (Oxford, 1999), 31–52.

7   Eric R. Wolf, *Europe and the People Without History* (Berkeley, 1982), 3.

8   Notable examples include Antoinette Burton, *Burdens of History: British Feminists, Indian Women, and Imperial Culture, 1865–1915* (Chapel Hill, 1994); Catherine Hall, *White, Male and Middle Class: Explorations in Feminist History* (London, 1992); Colin Holmes, *John Bull's Island: Immigration and British Society 1871–1971* (London, 1988); Peter Fryer, *Staying Power: The History of Black People in Britain* (London, 1987); Shompa Lahiri, *Indians in Britain: Anglo-Indian Encounters, Race and Identity, 1880–1930* (London, 2000); Susan Thorne, *Congregational Missions and the Making of an Imperial Culture in Nineteenth-century England* (Stanford CA, 1999).

Catherine Hall in the 1980s played a pivotal rile in underscoring the centrality of empire in metropolitan politics and social life.[9] More recently, Mrinalini Sinha's *Colonial masculinity* (1995) marked a particularly important move towards a history of British imperialism that revealed the complex meshing of metropolitan and colonial histories. Published in the MacKenzie's *Studies in Imperialism* series, *Colonial masculinity* sketched the contours of an 'imperial social formation', a shared (if fundamentally uneven) space of social reform and political debate that transcended national boundaries.[10] In charting the travels of South Asian students, feminists, and social reformers in *fin-de-siecle* Britain, Antoinette Burton has further undercut the division between 'home' and 'away' that structures so much British history, insisting that colonial encounters were staged in London and Oxford as well as in Delhi and Calcutta.[11]

Sinha and Burton have played a key role in bringing the complexities and contradictions of this 'imperial social formation' into focus, highlighting the circulation of both ideas and individuals within the empire. However, their work largely focuses the interweaving of the cultural and political space of a single colony (India in this case) and Britain, rather than what we might term 'horizontal mobility', the forms of movement and cultural traffic that linked colonies in the 'periphery' together. As we shall see, debates over Aryanism reveal that the 'imperial social formation' was more than a dyad, as it did not simply interweave Britain and India, but rather functioned as larger system of mobility and exchange where ideas and ideologies circulated broadly, not only moving between the metropole and its colonies, but also directly between colonies as disparate as India and New Zealand. This essay interrogates a narrow reading of Aryanism's development within colonial New Zealand, reinserting this discursive formation in the complex webs of empire that conditioned intellectual production and cultural forms on the New Zealand frontier.

II. Unraveling a national story

In 1885 Edward Tregear, a leading Pakeha (settler) intellectual published The *Aryan Maori*, a work that drew on European Indology and Orientalist studies of Asian cultures to assert that the Pacific islands had been settled from Asia and that Maori language and culture preserved

---

[9]   E.g. Catherine Hall and Leonore Davidoff, *Family Fortunes: Men and Women of the English Middle Class 1780–1850* (Chicago, 1987); John M. MacKenzie, *Propaganda and Empire: the Manipulation of British Public Opinion, 1880–1960* (Manchester, 1984) and John M. MacKenzie ed., *Imperialism and Popular Culture* (Manchester, 1986). It is important to note that Hall's work on Governor Eyre also anticipated the centrality of mobility in conceptions of imperialism. E.g. Catherine Hall, 'The Economy of Intellectual Prestige: Thomas Carlyle, John Stuart Mill, and the Case of Governor Eyre', *Cultural Critique*, 12 (1989), 167–196 and 'Imperial Man: Edward Eyre in Australia and the West Indies 1833–66', *The Expansion of England: Essays in the Cultural History of Race and Ethnicity Bill Schwarz* ed., (London, 1996).

[10]   Mrinalini Sinha, *Colonial Masculinity: the 'Manly Englishman' and the 'Effeminate Bengali' in the Late Nineteenth Century* (Manchester, 1995).

[11]   Antoinette Burton, *At the Heart of the Empire: Indians and the Colonial Encounter in Late-Victorian Britain* (Berkeley, 1998).

an ancient Aryan heritage 'in an almost inconceivable purity.'[12] Published by New Zealand's Government Printer, Tregear's volume was widely disseminated and elicited considerable attention, both within New Zealand and from an influential international audience. While Tregear's work on Maori origins drew support from authorities such as Horatio Hale and Max Müller, some New Zealand readers doubted Tregear's reliance on comparative philology and comparative mythology – the 'youngest and fairest daughters of Knowledge' – to establish the deep connections that supposedly linked Maori to the other members of the Aryan family. The *New Zealand Herald* castigated Tregear for chasing linguistic 'will-o'-wisps' because, as it asserted, the 'very primitive' Maori language bore no resemblance to the sophisticated Indo-European languages.[13] A year later, the noted lawyer and colonial grandee A. S. Atkinson produced an acerbic dismissal of Tregear's work, relentlessly parodying the search for Maori cognates of Sanskrit terms. Atkinson's essay, published in *The Transactions and Proceedings of the New Zealand Institute*, drew a prompt reply from Tregear, a defensive essay that ceded some ground but restated his central hypothesis: that Maori were Aryans and as such shared profound cultural bounds with Pakeha settlers.[14]

Tregear's work and his exchange with Atkinson have assumed a central place in the intellectual history of colonial New Zealand. In the 1970s and 1980s Keith Sinclair, M. P. K. Sorrenson and Michael Belgrave disregarded Tregear's high standing, both in local scientific circles and on an international stage, to dismiss him as an 'amateur.' Nevertheless, in identifying Tregear as an influential architect of cultural and intellectual imperialism, they all suggested that Tregear's ideas were central in shaping understandings of both Maori history and settler identity.[15] James Belich has recently fortified this argument in an important essay that revisits the construction of the imperial myths and racial ideologies that underpinned colonial New Zealand's cultural and political order. Belich agrees with Sinclair, Sorrenson, and Belgrave, characterizing Tregear's work as a 'joke', but warns that the 'joke was on us, because it obscures the possibility that The *Aryan Maori* became the symbolic bible of

---

[12]   Edward Tregear, *The Aryan Maori* (Wellington, 1885), 1–2, 5–6.

[13]   *New Zealand Herald*, 19 September 1885. This review was critical of Tregear's reliance on etymological rather than structural comparison in *The Aryan Maori*, but this methodological objection was less significant than its rejection of the possibility of any cultural commensurability between Maori and Pakeha. And it was, in any case, only partially accurate as Tregear's work opened with a recognition of the basic divisions between what he termed the 'monosyllabic' languages of East Asia, the 'agglutinated languages' of Central Asia, and the inflected languages of the the 'Semitic and Aryan races.'

[14]   A.S. Atkinson, 'The Aryo-Semitic Maori', *Transactions and Proceedings of the New Zealand Institute* [hereafter *TPNZI*], 9 (1886), 552–576; Tregear, 'The Aryo-Semitic Maori (A reply)', *TPNZI*, 10 (1887), 400–413.

[15]   M.P.K. Sorrenson, *Maori Origins and Migrations. The Genesis of Some Pakeha Myths and Legends* (Auckland, 1979), 22; Michael Belgrave, 'Archipelago of Exiles. A Study in the Imperialism of Ideas: Edward Tregear and John MacMillan Brown', (University of Auckland, M.A. thesis, 1979); Keith Sinclair, *A destiny apart: New Zealand's search for national identity* (Wellington, 1986), 199. This image has been challenged recently in K.R. Howe's biography K.R. Howe, *Singer in a Songless Land. A Life of Edward Tregear 1846–1931* (Auckland, 1991).

Maori-Pakeha relations.'[16] For Belich, Tregear's Aryan theory was 'the apotheosis of the Whitening-Maori myth complex': a cluster of ideas that identified Maori as 'white savages' or a 'sun-tanned Europeans' capable of embracing Christianity, commerce and civilization.[17] Tregear's cherished notion of an Aryan Maori, Belich insists, not only drove the assimilationist direction of government policy but also framed a popular racial folklore that celebrated Maori as warriors and sportsmen, racial tropes that remain powerfully embedded in New Zealand culture today.

Thus, for Belich (and the nationalist historiographical tradition that he embodies), Tregear's work provides powerful insights into the developing cultural program of settler nationalism and marks an important point in the nation's long march towards biculturalism. This is not surprising, given the celebration of nationhood that is an integral part of Belich's work and the very strong investment of New Zealand's liberal historiographical tradition in the nation-state and the prominent role of the state in supporting history in New Zealand.

However to see Tregear's work merely as providing the 'symbolic bible' for the assimilationist vision of settler nationalism is reductive and fundamentally misleading for two reasons. Firstly it presents an anachronistic reading of Aryanism that simply equates the term 'Aryan' with whiteness or the 'Caucasian race', obscuring both the South Asian provenance of nineteenth-century Aryanism and the existence of competing visions of the racial implications of the theory. In identifying Tregear's text as a *foundational* document for settler ethnology and colonial policy-making, Belich abstracts Tregear's work from a much longer tradition of what we might term 'Indocentric ethnology', studies that analyzed Maori culture against the cultural backdrop of South Asia. This tradition not only predated the emergence of settler nationalism by at least a generation but it also militated against a narrow vision of nationhood, insisting that New Zealand's development be framed firmly within broader narratives of racial development and empire-building. Secondly, in locating Tregear's *Aryan Maori* at the head of a genealogy of national intellectual production, Belich systematically excises the broader trans-national and imperial connections that underpinned not only Tregear's work, but also the development of this Indocentric tradition in New Zealand from the 1850s through to the 1920s. It was only in the late 1920s and 1930s – with the rise of a materialist anthropology, the consolidation of a popular settler nationalism, and growing hostility towards the scattered Gujarati and Punjabi migrant communities in New Zealand – that the notion that both Maori and Pakeha could trace their origins back to north India was rejected in favor of a much narrower vision of a national history.

Here I want to explore these two problematics to sketch a very different understanding of the construction of racial ideologies such as Aryanism, one that insists upon the centrality of trans-national networks and imperial discourses in framing the development of Aryanism on the New Zealand frontier. Such an approach does not disregard the nation-state or questions of national culture, but it recognizes that under colonialism nations were themselves constituted out of a broader imperial system characterized by complex forms of mobility and exchange. A trans-national history of Aryanism therefore is grounded in both an appreciation of the significance of the imperial networks that molded the cultural development of individual

---

[16]   James Belich, 'Myth, Race and Identity in New Zealand', *New Zealand Journal of History*, 31 (1997), 17.

[17]   Ibid., 11, 19.

colonies and an insistence that the inter-relationship between the different components of the imperial system is of fundamental importance in the reconstruction of the dynamics of imperialism.

III. A whitening discourse? Aryanism from India to New Zealand

The first step towards constructing a trans-national history of Aryanism is to carefully trace the provenance and cultural freight of this idea. Historians of intellectual production on the New Zealand frontier have generally been concerned with the gradual development of nationalist thought and the development of a national intellectual tradition.[18] Given this heavy investment in the nation, it is hardly surprising that historians have paid limited attention to the origins and development of the Aryan idea in their discussion of Aryan discourses in late nineteenth and early twentieth century New Zealand. The emergence of the Aryan idea and its pivotal role within the empire – especially in colonial India – are treated summarily, reduced to a being the insignificant pre-history of this New Zealand story. Belich, for example, observes: 'Ideas of a shared Indo-European Aryan origin date back to the mid-eighteenth century, and were proselytized by Max Müller in the mid-nineteenth.'[19] In a similar vein M. P. K. Sorrenson noted in his *Maori origins and migrations* (1979) that: 'The late-eighteenth century discovery by the British orientalist, Sir William Jones, of an affinity between Sanscrit and European languages like Greek and Latin, gave a great stimulus to comparative philology.'[20] Even K. R. Howe's 1988 article that sketched intellectual background to the Aryan theories of Tregear and his Hawai'ian correspondent Abraham Fornander paid little attention to the development of the idea in colonial India.[21] These truncated interpretations of the history of the Aryan concept, especially in the case of Belich and Sorrenson, not only deploy terms anachronistically – projecting the terms 'Indo-European' and 'Aryan' back to the mid-1700s when they were not used in English until 1813 and 1839 respectively – but also create an image of a ready-packaged British Aryan discourse which was simply transposed to the study of Maori culture.[22] Reframing the development of Aryanism on the New Zealand frontier as part of an imperial social and intellectual formation, where a multiplicity of connections wove India and New Zealand together, highlights three key features of Aryanism effaced by a simple equation of Aryanism with whiteness: Aryanism's origins in colonial South Asia and its profoundly imperial nature, the multiple valences of the term within both scientific and

---

[18]   Most notably: James Belich, *Making Peoples A History of the New Zealanders from Polynesian Settlement to the End of the Nineteenth Century* (Auckland, 1996); Giselle Byrnes, 'Inventing New Zealand: Surveying, Science, and the Construction of Cultural Space, 1840s–1890s', (University of Auckland, Ph.D. thesis, 1995); Sinclair, *Destiny Apart*; Sorrenson, *Maori Origins and Migrations*.

[19]   Belich, 'Myth, race and identity in New Zealand', 17.

[20]   Sorrenson, *Maori Origins and Migrations*, 18.

[21]   Howe, 'The Aryan Polynesian theories of Abraham Fornander and Edward Tregear.'

[22]   The *OED* records the first use of 'Aryan' in the *Penny Cyclopedia* for 1839, but it was first used in an influential ethnological sense in the 1843 edition of James Cowles Prichard, *The Natural History of Man* (London, 1843), 162, 179–80.

popular racial discourses, and the deep-seated conflicts surrounding the concept's veracity and usefulness.

Firstly, it is important to underline that Aryanism was both the product of what C. A. Bayly terms the 'information order' of colonial South Asia and that its rapid dissemination across the globe was the result of the global reach of British imperial networks.[23] Belich and Sorrenson elide the colonial origins of Aryanism, gesturing towards the significance of Jones and Max Müller, but neglect both the key role that these figures played in framing British imperial mentalities and the centrality of Aryanism in British understandings of India.[24] Although the Aryan concept is based upon the Vedic hymns, which record the incursion of nomadic pastoralists from Central Asia who called themselves 'Arya' (noble) into north India, the birth of Aryanism as an ethnological framework was the direct result of what we might term 'Company Orientalism', the body of knowledge about South Asian languages, cultures, and histories produced by the functionaries of the East India Company.

Despite the cultural weight of 'Arya' as a marker of community in Sanskritic tradition and its embeddedness within a variety of popular cultural discourses and social hierarchies in South Asia, it remained beyond the reach of European Orientalists until the East India Company consolidated its position as a territorial power in South Asia. This notion remained elusive because of the inability of early European experts to access key textual bodies and Brahmanical performative traditions: indeed, in the mid-eighteenth century leading Orientalists doubted whether Europeans would ever decipher Sanskrit. But the deep-seated social and cultural changes accompanying the Company's rise as a territorial power in 1765 enabled a new generation of Company employees to learn Sanskrit and to access Brahmanical tradition. Where the leading Company Orientalist Nathaniel Brassey Halhed found that gaining a solid grounding in Sanskrit in the 1770s was difficult because pandits 'were to a man resolute in rejecting all... solicitations for instruction in this dialect', by the early 1780s Company scholar-administrators was increasingly able to draw upon the expertise of both Hindu and Muslim learned elites.[25] The devastation of the Bengal famines of 1770 and 1783, together with the pressure of the Company's revenue regime, eroded the ability of leading *zamindars* (large land-holders) to provide the generous patronage that had traditionally extended to Bengali Brahmans.[26] Because of the constrained opportunities in rural centers, many pandits moved to rapidly expanding Calcutta, where some found that the Company provided a reliable

---

[23]   C.A. Bayly, *Empire and Information. Intelligence Gathering and Social Communication in India, 1780–1870* (Cambridge, 1996).

[24]   C.f. John Leopold, 'The Aryan Theory of Race', *The Indian Social and Economic History Review*, 7:2 (1970) and 'British Applications of the Aryan Theory of Race to India, 1850–1870', *English Historical Review*, CCCLLII (July 1974), 578–603; Martin Maw, *Visions of India. Fulfillment Theology, the Aryan Race Theory, & the Work of British Protestant Missionaries in Victorian India* (Frankfurt, 1990); Kate Teltscher, *India Inscribed: European and British Writing on India* (Delhi, 1995); Thomas R. Trautmann, *Aryans and British India* (Berkeley, 1997).

[25]   Nathaniel Brassey Halhed, *A Code of Gentoo Laws* (1776) in Marshall ed., *The British Discovery of Hinduism in the Eighteenth Century* (Cambridge, 1970) and P.J. Marshall, 'Introduction', Ibid., 10–12.

[26]   N.K. Sinha, *The Economic History of Bengal* 2 vols. (Calcutta, 1962) II, 147–57.

source of income.[27] This opening up of the 'reserviors of native learning' was such that H. T. Colebrooke observed in 1797 that he could not 'conceive how it came to be ever asserted that the Brahmans were averse to instruct strangers.'[28]

This profound shift in the colonial information order was pivotal in allowing the Company to access both Hindu and Muslim learned traditions and provided the key context for the emergence of a new vision of Asian culture and a new understanding of the very pattern of universal history. Sir William Jones, a leading Company administrator, Enlightenment polymath, and President of the Asiatic Society of Bengal, was the central figure in the project. In effect, Jones's ten 'Anniversary Discourses' delivered to the Asiatic Society from 1784, sketched a new interpretation of both Asian and global history, celebrating the precocious development of the linguistic and literary traditions of India and Persia and identifying Asia as the cradle of humanity. Drawing on both his 'mastery' of Classical and Semitic (Hebrew, Arabic and Persian) languages and his fledgling studies of Sanskrit, Jones asserted that Sanskrit

> is of a wonderful structure; more perfect than the *Greek*, more copious than the *Latin*, and more exquisitely refined than either, yet bearing to both of them a stronger affinity, both in the roots of the verbs and in the forms of the grammar, than could possibly have been produced by accident; so strong indeed, that no philologer could examine them all three, without believing them to have sprung from some common source, which, perhaps, no longer exists...[29]

This argument not only 'elevated' Sanskrit to the level of Latin and Greek, but also undercut long-established traditions of representing South Asian cultures. Where medieval and early modern Europeans underlined the otherness of South Asia, depicting it as an exotic land of marvels and wonders, Jones reimagined it in the language of kinship and affinity.[30] South Asian and European languages were connected, suggesting a fundamental cultural bond in the place of the rigid divisions often drawn between Europe and India. Following on from this, the 'Orient' was no longer a distant and foreign zone but rather was imagined as the very 'birthplace' of civilization from where both modern European and South Asian culture had developed. This connection established by Jones would not only form the basis for the emergence of both the concept of an Indo-European language family in the early nineteenth century, but also provided the foundation for the later work of James Cowles Prichard and F. Max Müller which popularised the notion of 'Aryan' peoples by welding Jones's notion of linguistic affinity to the Vedic accounts of the migration of the 'Aryas.'

If Jones's discovery was a direct result of the translation and textualization of indigenous traditions (a crucial foundation of the Company's colonial authority), his vision of the

---

[27] S.N. Mukherjee, *Calcutta: Myths and History* (Calcutta, 1977), 87–8; Brian A. Hatcher, *Idioms of Improvement: Vidyasagar and Cultural Encounter in Bengal* (Delhi, 1996), 36–7.

[28] H.T. Colebrooke to his father, 3 February 1797, *Sir Thomas Edward Colebrooke, The Life of H.T. Colebrooke* (London, 1873), 89.

[29] William Jones, 'On the Hindu's [sic]', *Asiatick Researches*, 1 (1788), 348–9.

[30] This was an integral part of the elision of 'the exotic, the mysterious, the fantastic' in British depictions of Indian society from the 1770s noted by O.P. Kejariwal: *The Asiatic Society of Bengal and the Discovery of India's Past 1784–1838* (Delhi, 1988), 25.

connections between European and Asian languages quickly became an important element of ethnology throughout the empire, from Ireland to Java. Although, at a general level, Jones's impact can be read as an index of the rising authority of Company Orientalism, more concretely, his influence reflected the complex and increasingly dense systems of cultural communication that integrated the empire. This new ethnological model was communicated throughout the empire thanks to Jones's prominent role in a late Enlightenment republic of letters – his extensive webs of correspondence incorporated leading figures in American, British, and Continental thought (including Edmund Burke, William Robertson, Samuel Johnson, and Benjamin Franklin) – and a thriving print culture that facilitated the rapid dissemination of *Asiatick Researches*, the key forum for the work of Jones and his cohort.[31]

For our purposes here, one of the most striking consequences of these knowledge networks fashioned by Jones was the interweaving of the study of the Pacific and India in Germany. Most intriguingly, it was Georg Forster, a naturalist on Cook's second Pacific voyage, who was central in the popularization of Jones's work in Europe and in the emergence of a German Indological tradition. Just as his account of his voyage with Cook triggered a 'Pacific craze' in Europe, his translation of Jones's Latin rendering of the Sanskrit play *Shakuntala* was central in ushering in an age of 'Indomania' in Germany.[32] In knitting British and German intellectual words together, Forster facilitated the emergence of a significant German tradition of Pacific linguistics, one that viewed the Pacific as an extended frontier of South Asia. Drawing on the 'raw material' produced by British traders, missionaries and ethnographers, Wilhelm von Humboldt suggested that traces of an ancient form of Sanskrit, or 'pre-Sanskrit', could be discerned in the Polynesian languages.[33] Franz Bopp argued that a Malayo-Polynesian language family united most of the Pacific and Southeast Asia. These languages, Bopp believed, had emerged from a degraded form of Sanskrit and this Sanskritic influence was quite evident when Maori and Sanskrit words were compared.[34] This German tradition, like the work of Jones and the pioneering linguistic researches of William Marsden on Malayo-Polynesian languages,[35] imagined the peoples of the Pacific as the descendants of the ancient Sanskrit-speaking peoples of north India: Polynesians were not Caucasians, nor were they Europeans, rather they were one branch of a larger linguistic and cultural family that originated in Asia and now reached from the eastern Pacific to western Europe.

This brings us to the second effect of the truncated visions of the Aryanism in New Zealand historiography. As we have seen, New Zealand historians have generally equated Aryanism with whiteness and, in Belich's case, have asserted that Tregear's theory marked

---

[31]   S.N. Mukherjee, *Sir William Jones. A Study in Eighteenth Century British Attitudes to India* (Cambridge, 1968), 85–8; *Lord Teignmouth, Memoirs of the Life, Writings, and Correspondence of Sir William Jones* (London, 1804).

[32]   See George W. Stocking, Jr, *Victorian Anthropology* (New York, 1987), 23; P.J. Marshall & Glyndwr Williams, *The Great Map of Mankind: British Perceptions of the World in the Age of Enlightenment* (London, 1992), 258.

[33]   Cited in Howe, *Singer*, 49.

[34]   Franz Bopp, *Über die Verwandtschaft der Malayisch-Polynesischen Sprachen: mit den Indisch-europäischen* (Berlin, 1841);

[35]   William Marsden, 'Remarks on the Sumatran languages', *Archaelogia: or, Miscellaneous Tracts Relating to Antiquity* 7 (1782), 154–8.

the 'apotheosis' of the 'Whitening Maori' discourse. This easy equation of Aryanism and whiteness in the New Zealand context is anachronistic, perhaps reflecting a 'common-sense' understanding of Aryanism borne out of Nazi ideologies and the racist programs of the American militias and extreme right. From its emergence in early nineteenth century until the rise of Nazism, however, the term 'Aryan' has carried a range of competing racial connotations. It is important to note, for example, that Sir William Jones's vision of cultural history was quite different from later nineteenth century theories that would equate Aryans (Indians, Europeans and even Polynesians) as the descendants of Noah's son Japhet. In Jones's scheme the Tartars approximated the sons of Japhet, while the more advanced 'Jews and Arabs' were the sons of Shem. The languages of the Semites were fundamentally different from the languages of the final group, the 'Persians and Indians.' This group, the descendants of Noah's son Ham, would conventionally be identified as being black in the nineteenth century. Jones, however, argued that Ham's offspring peopled India, Italy, Greece and perhaps East Asia in addition to Africa. This insistence on the Hamitic origins of what later scholars would call the Indo-European or Aryan family reflected both European and Indian sources. Thomas Trautmann has shown that Jones's theory reworked and extended Jacob Bryant's *Analysis of Ancient Mythology* (1774–6), a work that argued that the Egyptians, Greeks, Romans and Indians were all the descendants of Ham.[36] This identification of Hindus as the sons of Ham was also supported by Indo-Islamic sources. Muhammad Qasim Firishtah's Persian history identified the Indians as the progeny of Ham, while the *Akbarnama* also emphasized the Hamitic origins of the Hindus, while attaching greater value to the Japhetic origins of the Mughals. The currency of these ideas among the learned Indo-Islamic elite simultaneously confirmed the ethnological framework of Genesis and confirmed Jones's vision of India's place in global history.[37] In the nineteenth-century Jones's assertion of the common Hamitic origins of Europeans and Indians was supported by the leading British ethnologist James Cowles Prichard (whose work in turn was a key inspiration for many ethnographers on the New Zealand frontier).[38] Certainly as the nineteenth century progressed some European ethnologists attempted to strip away the South Asian origins of the Aryan term and attempted to reimagine Europe as the home of the Aryan 'race', but such arguments remained marginal within both metropolitan and colonial British science: even at the close of the nineteenth century the Aryan homeland was typically identified as the southern fringes of central Asia or north India.

Thirdly, the common assertion in New Zealand historiography that terms like Anglo-Saxon and Caucasian are synonyms for Aryan not only strips away the South Asian provenance of the Aryan concept but also disregards the central debates over Maori origins in the nineteenth century. From the 1860s through to the 1920s, it was commonly accepted that Maori had indeed migrated into the Pacific from Asia, but the key question was: where exactly in Asia? From the work of Richard Taylor in the 1860s, which identified Maori as displaced Indo-Aryans, to the work of John Turnbull Thomson, who argued that Maori belonged to the 'Barata' race (a widely dispersed group of peoples whose origins could be traced back to the tribal peoples of South India), settler ethnologists fashioned an array of competing

---

[36] Trautmann, *Aryans and British India*, 42–7.

[37] Ibid., 53–4.

[38] James Cowles Prichard, Researches into the Physical History of Man, George W. Stocking Jr. ed., (Chicago, 1973 [1813]), 471; Trautmann, Aryans and British India, 169–171.

ethnological visions.[39] While there was no consensus over the exact origins of Maori in the 1860s or 1870s, no ethnologist of note suggested that Maori were either Caucasian in origin or that they were white. Much was at stake in these debates (and Belich is right to remind us of the great power of racial thought in colonial contexts), as racial origins were not only seen as a litmus-test for an indigenous group's capacity for civilization but also as indicative of their very ability to survive the encounter with Europeans. Where Richard Taylor's assertion of an Aryan brotherhood uniting Maori and Pakeha in his *Our Race and its Origin* (1867) challenged government policy and the racial enmity that fueled the New Zealand wars, Thomson's assertion of Maori's south Indian origins underpinned his belief that Maori were not only destined to die out, but that their extinction was a necessary precondition for the modernization of the colony.[40]

If these debates prior to the publication of Tregear's *Aryan Maori* suggest that racial theories were hotly contested, such debates did not immediately abate with the appearance of Tregear's 'Bible' in 1885. Some critics dissented entirely, disputing the connection between Polynesia and South Asia. Gerald Massey, the important English spiritualist who conducted a lecture tour of New Zealand in the 1880s, elaborated an Afrocentric history of Maori in opposition to the prevailing Indocentrism. He argued that clues to human origins would not be found in the 'degenerated' poetry of the Vedas, but rather in the 'gesture-signs' and 'ideographic' representations of 'the original matter of human thought' which were to be located in ancient Egypt.[41] Massey depicted Africa as the 'Mother' of humanity, asserting it was 'the womb of the human race, with Egypt for the outlet into all the world.'[42] From Egypt different groups radiated outwards, preserving the particular linguistic and cultural traits of the "Motherland" at the time of their departure. He argued that Maori had departed Africa at an early point and in the course of a long migration and subsequent isolation Maori culture deteriorated rapidly: any Maori cultural achievements were a result of their early intercourse with civilization.[43] Scorning the implication of cultural commensurability inherent with an Aryan theory of Maori origins, Massey argued that 'savages' such as Maori and the 'Kaffirs, Hottentots or Bushmen' showed that evolution to be 'undoubtedly a descending as well as an ascending progression.'[44] Other critics, however, supported the notion that Maori did owe a significant cultural debt to South Asia, but that this connection was to the 'primitive' indigenous cultures of South Asia and predated the Aryan invasion. Samuel Peal, an enthusiastic ethnographer on the Assam frontier and a corresponding member of the Polynesian Society, attacked the supposed Aryan

---

[39]   Taylor's work is the focus of Tony Ballantyne, '"Dispersed Jews" or "Southern Aryans"? Missionary Ethnography and the Debate over Maori origins.' North Atlantic Missiology Project, Position Paper 91, University of Cambridge, Harvard University, 1998.

[40]   John Turnbull Thomson, *Rambles with a Philosopher or, Views at the Antipodes by an Otagoian* (Dunedin, 1867), 86–7.

[41]   Gerald Massey, *The Natural Genesis* (2 vols, London, 1883), I, 9.

[42]   Gerald Massey, *A Book of the Beginnings* (2 vols, London, 1881), I, 26. Anne McLintock has recently analyzed some of the relationships between gender, sexuality and colonial geography articulated in passages such as this: *Imperial Leather. Race, gender and Sexuality in the Colonial Contest* (New York, 1995), 1–3, 21–30.

[43]   Massey, *A Book of Beginnings*, II, 597.

[44]   Ibid., II, 537, 596–7.

nature of Maori in order to emphasize differences between Maori and European. Peal was a leading authority on the ethnology of India's north-east frontier and forged an extensive web of correspondents including E. B. Tylor, William Wyatt Gill, Horatio Hale, and Percy Smith and Elsdon Best in New Zealand.[45] On the basis of this extensive network of intellectual exchange, Peal elaborated an Indocentric vision of the Pacific that disputed the authority of Aryanism. Peal argued Maori belonged to a non-Aryan racial community that included the 'Indo-Mongoloids, Dravidians, Malays, Papuans, Polynesians, Formosans, Australians, Massai of east Africa.'[46] The origins of this racial family, Peal suggested, were located in the Gangetic basin among the very tribal peoples, especially the Nagas, who he knew so well.[47] Maori, like the other members of this racial family, were being transformed by 'the missionary and the Trader' and were likely to die out in the face of the racial superiority and cultural sophistication of European settlers.[48]

By the 1890s, however, these competing visions of Maori connections to India were beginning to be woven into an Indocentric synthesis. Rather than serving as the foundational text for this ethnological tradition, Tregear's The *Aryan Maori* was simply one component of this new Indocentric paradigm. As the nineteenth century came to a close, attempts to locate Maori origins within Aryan, Dravidian or tribal communities were no longer of particular concern, as anthropological attention slowly shifted towards the local development of Maori culture and the history of Maori tribal groups. At this stage, the diffusionist model was not entirely supplanted; rather the new Indocentric synthesis provided a general framework for the analysis of Maori culture. In this new synthetic paradigm, various aspects of Thomson's, Peal's and Tregear's research could be drawn upon and reconciled if Maori origins were depicted as more generally Indian. Elsdon Best, a dominant figure in the Polynesian Society and a pioneering anthropologist, was an important advocate of this new synthesis and popularized it not only through his published work, but also through lecture tours and addresses delivered to the Worker's Education Association. The other leading luminary of the Polynesian Society, S. Percy Smith, emphasized Maori debt to a generalized Indian culture in a series of articles and books that spanned over twenty years. The great Maori anthropologist and expert on Polynesian culture, Peter Buck (Te Rangi Hiroa) was a proponent of this theory into the mid-twentieth century as well: his popular *Vikings of the Sunrise* (1938) asserted that his Maori ancestors 'probably did live in some part of India.'[49]

---

[45] For biographical information see Peal's obituary in *The Calcutta Englishman*, 12 August 1897; for Smith's views on Peal's contribution to New Zealand ethnography see his draft obituary Polynesian Society Collection, MS-Papers-1187–226, Alexander Turnbull Library, Wellington [hereafter ATL].

[46] Peal to Smith, 1892 [marked received 16 April], Polynesian Society Collection, MS-Papers-1187–270, ATL.

[47] Peal to Smith, 15 October 1894, Ibid.

[48] Peal to Smith, 17 January 1892 and 25 January 1893, Ibid.

[49] Elsdon Best, 'The Origin of the Maori. The Hidden Homeland of the Maori, and its Probable Location', *Journal of the Polynesian Society* (hereafter JPS), 32, (1923), 10–20; Percy Smith, 'Aryan and Polynesian Points of Contact: the Story of Te Niniko', *JPS*, 19 (1910); 'The Fatherland of the Polynesians: Aryan and Polynesian Points of Contact', *JPS*, 28 (1919); Peter Buck [Te Rangi Hiroa], *Vikings of the Sunrise* (New York, 1938), 35.

By this time, however, the Indocentric synthesis was being marginalized by the emergence of a new materialist anthropology pioneered in the New Zealand context by Raymond Firth. Bearing the clear imprint of Malinowski's functionalism, Firth's *Primitive Economics of the New Zealand Maori* (1929) set a new agenda for the study of Maori culture. Where Tregear, Smith, and Best constructed a genealogy of Polynesian culture and 'excavated' the remnants of Asian practices, Firth foregrounded the material frameworks of indigenous culture and emphasized the importance of internal structures and dynamics.[50] The emergence of this new paradigm, like the earlier debates over the precise location of Maori origins in Asia, reminds us of the dynamic nature of colonial intellectual life. In this shifting and conflicted environment, Tregear's Aryan theory was never hegemonic, but rather was one among many theories of Maori history that framed the development of Maori culture against the backdrop of Asia.

Thus, careful attention to the provenance and dissemination of this theory transforms our understandings of Aryanism on the New Zealand frontier. No longer does it appear simply as a pivotal component within the emergence of a unique national culture, but rather Aryanism is reconceived as an important localized variant of a broader set of imperial discourses that were deeply concerned with the boundaries of race and religion within the empire. Most importantly, this reorientation away from a national history of Aryanism forces upon us a recognition of the centrality of India and India-derived models in framing understandings of global history, of race and religion, and the development of Pacific culture. Aryan theories on the New Zealand frontier were not simply constructed to 'whiten' Maori, rather they were part of imperial discourses that attempted to fashion ethnological taxonomies and reveal the fundamental structures of human history. Within this context, racial thought was increasingly important and Aryanism emerged as one the most powerful, but highly contested, racial discourses within the empire. The two fundamental elements of Aryan theories – that deep connections linked European and Asian culture and that Asia itself was the cradle of humanity – proved highly contentious, whether in South Asia, Britain or on the New Zealand frontier. Belich's work has done much to undercut the older liberal nationalist insistence on the superiority of New Zealand's race relations, but his search for hegemonic racial myths has effaced the intense debates and deep fault-lines engendered by the Aryan theory.

IV. India and the development of colonial New Zealand

In the first part of this paper I highlighted the significance of 'Company Orientalism' in the emergence of Aryanist discourses within the British empire and I have underlined the significance of web of personal correspondence and the importance of print culture in disseminating Jones's new ethnological model. I now will sketch these imperial networks in more detail, mapping the contours of this particular imperial social formation in order to reveal the patterns of exchange that underpinned the emergence of Indocentric interpretations of Maori culture. The existing historiography on racial though in colonial New Zealand has paid limited attention to the sociology of colonial knowledge, focusing narrowly on

---

[50]   Raymond Firth, *Primitive Economics of the New Zealand Maori* (Wellington, 1929). Also see his 'Economic Psychology of the Maori', *Journal of the Royal Anthropological Institute of Great Britain and Ireland*, 55, (1925), 340–362.

representation and exhibiting only limited interest in the social structures, cultural institutions, and knowledge networks that conditioned the production of racial thought, moulded its reception, and determined its material and political outcomes.

A key starting-point for this project is to establish the connections that linked India and New Zealand within the British imperial system. At the start of the twenty-first century, India and New Zealand seems an unlikely pair, linked only by long-established, yet relatively small, Gujarati and Punjabi communities in New Zealand's North Island and, more obviously, a common love of cricket. But such a response reflects the conditioning power of traditions of national history and the systematic erasure of trans-national connections by nationalist projects that imagine the nation as discreet and bounded. On deeper reflection, however, the existence of strong links between India and New Zealand in the long nineteenth century is hardly surprising given the influence of the East India Company in the Pacific Ocean, India's special status within the British empire, and South Asia's profound impact on British 'empires of the mind.'[51]

Before exploring three series of relationships between British India and New Zealand that played a key role in the emergence of Aryanism on the New Zealand frontier, we can note some other domains where British India directly molded the developing cultural pattern of the fledgling New Zealand colony. Indeed, we can note that political institutions developed by the East India Company provided an important range of models for the construction of British colonial authority in New Zealand prior to the signing of the Treaty of Waitangi in 1840 (which formally incorporated New Zealand into the empire). Most notably, the blueprint for colonization developed by Captain William Hobson in 1837 was based upon the 'factory system' of coastal enclaves initially used by the British in India.[52] James Busby, the British Resident in New Zealand, discounted Hobson's plan as he felt the factory model was ill suited to the dispersed nature of New Zealand's settler communities and trading stations. But Busby also drew on South Asian models, suggesting the creation of a protectorate system where an appointee of the Crown would administer the affairs of New Zealand in trust while traditional tribal leaders were tutored in 'good government.' Busby envisaged that this protectorate system would eventually envelope the whole country to arrest 'the miserable condition' of the people through fair and beneficent government.[53]

India-derived models not only played an important role at this key moment when the absorption of Maori into the empire was hotly debated; they re-emerged during the political crisis of the 1860s as well. In December 1868, Governor G. F. Bowen wrote to the Duke of Buckingham to explain the wars that were wracking New Zealand. Bowen believed that three factors caused the conflict: most importantly the 'outbreak of the Hauhau fanaticism', the removal of English forces that elevated 'Hauhau' and Kingitanga confidence and the confiscation of 'rebel' land. Bowen reflected that the intersection of these three causes exactly replicated the 'immediate causes of the Indian rebellion.'[54] Bowen continued:

---

[51]   This phrase is borrowed from Andrew Porter's essay in P.J. Marshall ed., *The Cambridge Illustrated History of the British Empire* (Cambridge, 1996).

[52]   Hobson to Bourke, 8 August 1837, CO 209/2, 30–37, Public Record Office, London.

[53]   Busby to Bourke, GBPP, 1840, no. 238, James Busby, Memoir, CO 209/1, 197–199, Ibid.

[54]   In Bowen's opinion the causes of the Indian rebellion were: '(A.) Religious and national fanaticism. (B.) The recent reduction in the number of English troops employed in India. (C.) The

With regard to the first of these three causes, it may be observed that the religious and national fanaticism of the Hauhaus is analogous to the periodical outbreaks of a similar nature among the Malays (who are probably of kindred race with the Maoris), and among the Hindoos and Mussulmans of India. It may not be altogether impertinent to mention that the 'lily' fills the same place in the mysterious proclamations of the Maori King, as the 'lotus' filled in the missives of some of the native princes in Hindostan.[55]

Bowen, who was writing in the wake of attacks on settlers in Poverty Bay by the prophet Te Kooti and his followers, suggested that the Hauhau forces were carrying out atrocities 'as dreadful as any perpetrated during the great rebellion in India.' Bowen warned against the proposal to withdraw imperial troops from New Zealand, arguing that any withdrawal would be 'naturally similar to the impression which would have been made on the minds of Nana Sahib and the sepoy mutineers by an announcement of the immediate withdrawal of the English troops soon after the massacre at Cawnpore.'[56] Unless the Colonial Office maintained a strong force in New Zealand, the country would face 'a general rising of the disaffected natives' which would lead 'to tragedies as dreadful as Delhi and Cawnpore.'[57] The specters of Nana Sahib and the 'Mutiny' were powerful tools for a colonial administrator who was both required to explain indigenous resistance and desperate to maintain resources in the face of 'native fanaticism.'

   If India profoundly imprinted understandings of cross-cultural relationships in New Zealand, it also had a more general impact on the ways in which the New Zealand landscape was imagined, domesticated and imbued with meaning by Pakeha. Settler surveyors like John Turnbull Thomson, convinced that as a supposedly 'runeless and ruinless land' the New Zealand landscape lacked history, inscribed the land with a new layer of place names, incorporating colony into an imperial matrix of meaning.[58] Wellington, the capital city from the late 1860s, was not only named after the Duke of Wellington Arthur Wellesley, a great military hero in south India as well as the vanquisher of Napoleon, but its suburbs of Khandallah and Berhampore were also testimony to the weaving of India into the local landscape.[59] A cluster of cities and settlements in the Hawkes Bay region, which was settled by Pakeha in the midst of the imperial crises of the 1850s and 1860s, were named after great

---

annexation of the entire territories of the King of Oude.' Governor G.F. Bowen to His Grace the Duke of Buckingham and Chandos, 7 December 1868. *Great Britain Parliamentary Papers*, 1868–9 [307] XLIV, 313.

[55]   Ibid., 314.

[56]   Ibid., 315.

[57]   Ibid.

[58]   Thomson's New Zealand career is sketched in John Hall Jones, *Mr Surveyor Thomson: early Days in Otago and Southland* (Wellington, 1971). On the cultural significance of landscape and naming practices see Hong-key Yoon, *Maori Mind, Maori Land: Essays on the Cultural Geography of the Maori People from an Outsider's Perspective* (Berne, 1986).

[59]   Khandallah's thoroughfares are named after major Indian cities including Agra, Delhi, Karachi, Madras and Shimla. A similar pattern of street-names are to be found at the southern tip of New Zealand in the town of Riverton, which developed in the mid-nineteenth century out of the Jacob's River whaling station.

heroes from British India (Clive, Napier and Hastings) and in the case of Plassey, after the East India Company's famous 1757 victory. Other notable leaders of the East India Company and British military leaders in South Asia were commemorated in the naming of Lawrence, Havelock North, and even Auckland (the prominence of the name Eden in the city's landscape commemorates Lord Auckland's family name).

Beyond these important but general connections, we can note three important constellations of imperial networks that wove the two colonies together and directly contributed to the emergence of Aryanism on the New Zealand frontier. The first of these connections was borne out of the movement of individuals within the empire. Surprisingly strong migration networks linked India and New Zealand in the second-half of the nineteenth century. A large number of the leading figures in the colony's intellectual and political life had strong South Asian connections and many had begun their careers in either the service of the East India Company or, at a later stage, the Indian Civil Service. New Zealand, with its rapidly growing settler population, mild climate, and vaunted class mobility, was an attractive proposition for Britons who has served in South Asia and hoped to advance their career, build families or retire within the empire. The salubrious climate and attractive sea-side setting of Nelson attracted a large number of low ranking 'India-men', while a more prominent cluster were concentrated in two branches of the colonial administration: surveying and forestry.

The East India Company (and subsequently by the Government of India) employed a large number of British surveyors and a significant group of these surveyors subsequently found employment on the New Zealand frontier. While the Joseph Thomas, an influential New Zealand Company surveyor who was subsequently responsibly for surveying the lands of the Canterbury Association, served as an aide-de-camp to Sir John Malcolm in India (in addition to traveling extensively in the Americas), New Zealand's first Surveyor-general John Turnbull Thomson had cut his professional teeth as a Company surveyor in Malaya and Singapore. Thomson's vision of Maori as part of the 'Barata' race was moulded by his extensive experience in the 'East' and was supported by his impressive linguistic skills which were the product of his studies with the renowned *munshi* Abdullah Abdul Kadir in the Straits' Settlements.[60] Another important knot of India-men played a prominent role in making of colonial conservation and molded the shape of colonial forestry in New Zealand. As James Beattie's research is revealing, debates over both topographical and climactic desiccation in the 1870s and 1880s were energized by a series of important networks that linked colonial scientists in India and New Zealand.[61] Captain Inches Campbell Walker, formerly Conservator of the Forests for the Madras Presidency, assumed the position of Conservator of State Forests

---

[60] On 'Munshi Abdullah' and the cosmopolitan world of the Straits see Anthony Milner, *The Invention of Politics in Colonial Malaya: Contesting Nationalism and the Expansion of the Public Sphere* (Cambridge, 1995), 10–30; J.T. Thomson, *Translations from the Hakayit Abdullah* (London, 1874); J.T. Thomson papers, HL, AG-726. The imprint of this Asian experience on his visions of the ethnology of empire are particularly discernible in John Turnbull Thomson, *Rambles with a Philosopher or, Views at the Antipodes by an Otagoian* (Dunedin, 1867), 86–7 and *Some Glimpses into Life in the Far East* (London, 1864), 60, 253–4.

[61] I would like to thank James Beattie for sharing this research with me. Beattie's work upholds the central thrust of Richard Grove's arguments about the significance of inter-colonial exchanges in molding colonial environmentalism. Chapter 4 of Beattie's forthcoming University of Otago thesis

in New Zealand in 1876.[62] This position was created by the 1874 Forest Act authored by Julius Vogel, a piece of legislation grounded in the systematic collection of data from State forestry programs, including India and Ceylon, and supported by another India-man Sir John Cracroft Wilson.[63] Thus, two elite cliques of experienced India hands played a pivotal role in state-sponsored colonial science and were at the very forefront of the colonial project to map and demarcate the land and to police its effective use.

Such forms of migration and mobility were integral to the emergence of Aryanism on the frontier. Strong Indian connections that animated the work of the leading advocates of Indocentric visions of Maori culture. A. S. Thomson, a former military surgeon in the employ of the East India Company and New Zealand's first historian, noted several cultural parallels between Maori and 'Hindoo culture' and suggested that Maori 'had intercourse with men holding the Hindu faith' during their migration to New Zealand.[64] Richard Taylor, who was the first strong advocate of an Indocentric understanding of Maori cultural history, found evidence for this connection while visiting India en route to Britain.[65] Alfred Kingcombe Newman[66], perhaps the most enthusiastic advocate of the newly synthesized Indocentric theory of Maori history in the early twentieth century, also traveled to India to find evidence to support his arguments about Maori origins. For Newman, this trip to Calcutta and Banaras was a journey home: he was born in India and spent his childhood in Madras. It seems that in his adult life India continued to transfix Newman, as he not only traveled in India to further his studies of South Asian cultures but also hatched a scheme to export *ghi* (clarified butter) from New Zealand to India. India retained a similarly strong hold over Tregear's imagination, even long after the debates over The *Aryan Maori* had subsided. In a letter written just before his death in 1931, Edward Tregear, dreamed about voyaging to Punjab and visiting the ancient home of Maori. Again, this unfulfilled quest was more than scholarly: it was personal as well. Tregear's father, who worked for P & O, had died in Bombay, while his uncle was one of the first European soldiers killed during the outbreak of rebellion at Meerut in 1857. For men like

---

traces some of these Indian connections in a detailed discussion of desiccationist discourses in late nineteenth century New Zealand.

[62] Campbell Walker's views of environmental change and the direction of state forestry policy are spelt out in two key publications: 'The Climactic and Financial Aspects of Forestry Conservancy as Applicable to New Zealand', *TPNZI*, 9 (1876), xxvii–xlix and 'State Forestry: its Aim and Object', Ibid., 187–203.

[63] See H5A & B, *Appendices to the Journal of the House of Representatives*, vol. 2, 1874.

[64] A.S. Thomson, *The Story of New Zealand: Past and Present – Savage and Civilized* (2 vols, London, 1859), I, 108–9, 112, 114–6, 120.

[65] Taylor was very impressed by the huge cave temples of Maharashtra and his published work highlighted similarities between Maori art and 'the rock temples of Salsette and Elephanta.' Richard Taylor, *Our Race and its origin* (Auckland, 1867), 24. An undated sketch on a small slip of paper in Taylor's black notebook, which he filled with sketches and notes on his voyage back to England in 1867–71, depicts a top-knotted warrior figure with the caption 'Taken from paintings in the Ajunta Caves 200 miles NE of Bombay.' Taylor Papers, MS-Papers-025–026. A

[66] On Newman see John Stenhouse, '"A Disappearing Race Before We Came Here": Doctor Alfred Kingcombe Newman, the Dying Maori and Victorian Scientific Racism', *New Zealand Journal of History*, 30 (1996), 124–140; Shaun Broadley, 'Science, Race and Politics: an Intellectual Biography of A.K. Newman', (University of Otago, Honours thesis, 1994).

Tregear and Newman, India was invested with deep significance: it was not only a crucial node within the imperial system, but it also stood at the very heart of their family histories and personal lives. Their inclination to identify India as the cradle of civilization and to stress the affinities that connected Indians, Maori, and Pakeha seems more intelligible in light of these connections.

These important ties, embedded both in imperial personnel networks and individual lives shaped by the upheaval of migration, were fortified by increasingly dense bodies of information that provided the crucial raw materials for Indocentric readings of Maori origins. At a fundamental level, the rise of Aryanism and Indocentric theories of Maori origins were the product of an emergent imperial print culture that linked both Maori and Pakeha to the wider world of empire. Although historians of communication such as Harold Innis, Anthony Milner, and, more especially, Benedict Anderson have stressed the centrality of print in the creation of nationalist traditions, C. A. Bayly has highlighted the ways in which print could fashion important networks that transected national boundaries.[67] The rapid development of newspapers on the New Zealand frontier was central in connecting the colony to global systems of information exchange. As Rollo Arnold has emphasized, a striking feature of nineteenth-century newspapers in New Zealand was their relative inattention to national developments. These papers, Arnold demonstrates, were marked by both a strong interest in local affairs and a global orientation: even the smallest provincial newspaper would carry lengthy reports of developments within the empire and the latest news from distant parts of the globe.[68] Similar patterns are discernible in Maori language newspapers, as readers of both state-sponsored and impendent newspapers were kept informed of the latest developments in Sydney, Delhi, London and New York.[69]

Concomitant with the development of this thriving colonial print culture was the emergence of libraries, Athenaeums, and public reading-rooms, institutions that served as crucial nodes for the accumulation and distribution of knowledge within the colony. These repositories of knowledge were fundamental to the construction of Indocentric readings of Maori culture. As we have seen, Aryanism was essentially a comparative approach to the study of cultures and these comparative interpretations depended on assembling large amounts of ethnological material from a wide range of locales. In this regard, libraries on the New Zealand frontier played a vital dual role for comparative ethnologist. Firstly, they made a large amount of recently textualized Maori knowledge available to settlers and, secondly, they provided access to collections of material relating to Asia and especially India. Important Indological texts, such as Mill's *History of British India*, William Robertson's *An Historical Disquisition concerning the knowledge which the ancients had of India*, Max Müller's edition of the *Rg Veda*, and journals such as *Asiatic Researches* and *The Asiatic Journal and Monthly Register*, were easily accessible in University libraries and Athenaeums, while even public libraries in small frontier towns such as Patea (where Tregear began his interest in ethnology) held surprisingly

---

[67] C.A. Bayly, 'Informing Empire and Nation: Publicity, Propaganda and the Press, 1880–1920', *Information, Media and Power Through the Ages*, Hiram Morgan ed., (Dublin, 2001), 179–201.

[68] Rollo Arnold, *New Zealand's Burning: the Settler's World in the Mid-1880s* (Wellington, 1994).

[69] E.g. *Te Karere Maori* 1:5 (1 June 1855) and 5:13 (30 June 1858); *Te Korimako*, 36 (15 January 1885).

rich ethnological collections.[70] Thus, the emergence of Aryanism was underpinned by the simultaneity of the development of these institutions on the New Zealand frontier and the growing authority of Orientalism (in addition to the continued interest of the reading public in travel narratives and popular ethnology).

This brings us to the third and final element of the colonial New Zealand's 'information order' that facilitated Indocentric visions of Maori culture: the emergence of learned institutions with strong and direct connections to India. The first of these of was Theosophy, a movement borne out of the European encounter with South Asian spiritual traditions that stressed public education, an international outlook, and the value of comparative scientific research into religion and culture. Theosophy thrived in New Zealand at the end of the nineteenth century, attracting many freethinkers, feminists, and social reformers. Not surprisingly, Edward Tregear himself was one of the colony's leading Theosophists, contributing many articles to the leading Theosophically-inclined journals *Hestia* and *The Monthly Review*. Tregear was convinced that the 'religions of the East' were crucial sources of 'esoteric knowledge.' Many New Zealanders followed Tregear's lead and embraced the religions of India as a source of spiritual renewal. F. D. Brown, Professor of Chemistry at Auckland University College, simultaneously attacked the materialism of Darwin, Tyndall and Huxley and the conservative nature of the Christian churches. Brown asserted that educated people should break free of the domination of Christianity and look to the "East" for ideas that might "revivify" their spiritual life.[71] Edward Toronto Sturdy, the father of New Zealand Theosophy drew inspiration from witnessing Swami Vivekanada debating with Professor Deuseen, a leading German authority on the Upanishads.[72] Sturdy's faith in India as a source of spiritual truths was confirmed when he acquired 'a very old translation of the Bhagavad Gita made in the time of Warren Hastings.' In 1886 he journeyed to the Theosophical Society's headquarters in Adyar, hoping to study with 'learned Hindus' as he believed that 'in the "Gita" there was teaching I had been seeking for so long.'[73] Before dedicating herself to assisting Annie Besant in India (where she stayed from 1897 to 1938), Lilian Edger argued in 1893 that the authority of the Bible was no stronger than other 'holy books.'[74] These Theosophical connections were a crucial element of

---

[70]   See the *Catalogue of the Library of the Dunedin Athenaeum and Mechanics' Institute*, and the catalogues of the University of Otago Library, the Hocken Library and the Alexander Turnbull Library.

[71]   *TPNZI* 27 (1894) 676. John Stenhouse, 'The "Battle" Between Science and Religion in the Nineteenth Century', (Massey University, PhD Thesis), 1989, 243.

[72]   *Theosophy in New Zealand* 7 n.s. (1946), 59.

[73]   Ibid., 1 n.s. (1940) 17.

[74]   'It has also been said many times that all which stands the test of times is truth and I would point out to you that the Vedas, which was [sic] written as early as 4000 B.C. is still the religious book of Brahminism and having thus stood the test for [sic] time for three times as long as our Gospel narrative may fairly claim to contain some elements of truth.' Lilian Edger, *Religion and Theosophy. A Lecture Delivered in the City Hall, Auckland, New Zealand on Sunday Afternoon, March 26th, 1893* (Auckland, 1893), 7. Edger, the daughter of Reverend Samuel Edger, a well-known liberal Auckland minister, was the first New Zealand woman to receive a M.A. in 1885. In 1891 she joined the Auckland Theosophical Lodge, becoming President in 1896, and general-secretary of the New Zealand section of the Theosophical Society from 1896–7. In 1897 Edger gave the Adyar convention lectures and toured the Theosophical Lodges of India with Olcott in 1898. Later in her career she worked with Annie Besant at the Central Hindu College in Banaras.. Ellwood, *Islands of the Dawn* 106–7. Valuable insight into

the complex tangle of imperial networks that nourished colonial social reform at the close of the nineteenth-century and they reaffirmed the centrality of India in New Zealand's cultural and spiritual life.[75]

While Indocentrism was fostered by this widespread interest in Theosophy and South Asian religious traditions, it was nourished in a more immediate way with the foundation of the Polynesian Society in 1892. Three of the leading advocates of Indocentric visions of Polynesian culture – Elsdon Best, S. Percy Smith and Edward Tregear – were pivotal in the foundation of the Society and in the case of Best and Smith played crucial roles in dictating its intellectual trajectory. The Society (along with the Bishop Museum in Honolulu) was the central node in the development of Pacific ethnology and a key center in the ethnological networks that spanned the empire. It operated both centripetally – drawing in and collecting key materials – and centrifugally, disseminating these materials and new paradigms out into the Pacific and beyond. A cluster of Indian networks was central in these webs of exchange and played a key role in molding the development of Indocentric readings of Maori history. The Society maintained a formal exchange relationship with the Society of Arts of Batavia (which explored Indian influence in Indonesia) and assembled large collections of two Calcutta-based journals, the *Journal of the Buddist Text Society* [sic.] and the *Journal of the Asiatic Society of Bengal*. The Society also directly received a range of important works on Asia, including two works sent to Percy Smith by the Bengali scholar Nobin Chandra Das.[76] Most notably, however, the Assam-based ethnographer Samuel Peal, who argued that Maori belonged to a 'Gangetic race', established a strong relationship with Smith and Best. Between early 1892 and Peal's death in August 1897, these three scholars exchanged ideas about 'primitive' culture, comparative linguistics and racial migrations. Peal was made a corresponding member of the Society and contributed two articles on the origins of Maori to the *Journal of the Polynesian Society*.[77] But Peal's legacy was lasting: on his death Peal bequested his manuscripts, word lists, and a collection of 35 Indian dictionaries and ethnographic works to the Polynesian Society. These works provided an important source for future research on Maori origins and the development of Maori culture. Peal's work and materials encouraged Elsdon Best's search for Maori phallic cults and Alfred Newman, who attempted to provide the definitive case for Indian origins in his *Who are the Maoris?* (c.1912), utilized both the books sent by Nobin Chandra Das and Peal.[78] Thus, these direct connections with India, provided valuable raw

---

Lilian Edger's background can be gained from a collection of her father's essays and sermons, which clearly reveal the influence of Swedenborg. Samuel Edger, *Autobiographical Notes and Lectures,* Kate and Lilian Edger eds., (London, 1886).

[75]   These arguments that stimulated acrimonious debate within the colony. See, for example, James Neil, *Spiritualism and Theosophy Twain Brothers of the Anti-Christ. (Founded on the First Lie, the belief of which brought Death to our Race.) The Origin, Development, and Destruction of These Systems* (Dunedin, n.d.), 54–5; *Christian Outlook*, 4 September 1894, 373; *Weekly Budget* 18 October, 1895.

[76]   These uncataloged works are in the Polynesian Society's closed stack collection at the Alexander Turnbull Library.

[77]   Peal accepted the offer of the position of corresponding member in a letter to Smith, 25 January 1893, Polynesian Society Collection, MS-Papers-1187–270, ATL.

[78]   Although in print Newman advocated a more generalized vision of Maori origins, privately he supported Peal's theory. In a letter to Smith, Peal concluded that the Nagas of Assam 'were the mothers

material – in the form of dictionaries, comparative vocabularies, sketches, and ethnographic essays – that played a central role in the identification of parallels between Maori and Indian culture and location of Maori origins within South Asia.

Conclusion: webs and nodes: rethinking the structure of empire

The existence of a sizable archive of South Asian ethnographic material, in manuscript and published form, in the library of the Polynesian Society in Wellington underscores both the strength of the networks that integrated the British empire and the inherent mobility of colonial knowledge. The development of Aryanism on the New Zealand frontier was not simply the product of local forces nor should it be solely read within the narrative framework of national-history; this essay has made clear that such readings erase the exchanges that wove colonies together into a shared space of intellectual exchange. Mapping the contours of this imperial formation is an important step both towards returning colonial New Zealand to the 'bundles of relationships' that molded the colony's development and, more generally, creating a broader vision of the workings of the British imperial system.

In the place of the long-established traditions of imperial and colonial history, this essay has argued that Mrinalini Sinha's notion of an 'imperial social formation' is a valuable heuristic tool for reconceptualizing the empire. But where Sinha has highlighted the interdependence and mutually constitutive nature of metropolitan and colonial histories, here I have argued that we must also pay close attention to the 'horizontal' connections that linked colonies directly together. Important flows of capital, personnel and ideas between colonies energized colonial development and the function of the larger imperial system. Such exchanges have received only limited attention in the historiography of the British empire because they transgress the analytical boundaries of both metropolitan-focused imperial history (where the empire is viewed from London out) or histories of individual colonies (where the view is from the colony towards London). Recognizing both the strong 'vertical' networks that welded Britain and its colonies together and the importance of 'horizontal' connections between colonies suggests that the web is a useful metaphor for conceiving of the structure of the empire.

The web metaphor has several advantages for the conceptualization of the imperial past. At a general level, it underscores that the empire was a *structure*, a complex fabrication fashioned out of a great number of disparate parts that were brought together into a variety of new relationships. To my mind, the central problem with the 'cultural turn' in imperial history has not the significance attached to representation, but rather the inability of scholars to develop Said's insistence that Orientalism was a system of circulation. Rather than narrowly focus on the rhetorical construction or ideological context of any given text, we need to reconstruct

---

of our Maoris.' Newman to Smith, 5 March 1907, Polynesian Society Collection, MS-Papers-1187–268, ATL. Newman had conducted research at the Polynesian Society Library (see his letter to Smith 13 August 1906 making arrangements for his visit), and in 1907 Smith sent Newman Nobin Chandra Das's work. Smith to Newman 2 March 1907, ibid. On Best, Peal and phallic cults see Best to Peal undated, but in response to Peal's letter dated 31 August 1895, Polynesian Society Collection, MS 80–115–02/02, ATL. Best also sent Peal a newspaper clipping describing a Maori 'phallic cult', Best to Peal May-June 1893, Polynesian Society Collection, MS-Copy-Micro-146, ATL.

the networks that structured the empire and trace the transmission of ideas, ideologies, and identities across space and time. The web captures the integrative nature of this cultural traffic, the ways in imperial institutions and structures connected disparate points in space into a complex mesh of networks. Moreover, the image of the web also conveys something of the double nature of the imperial system. Empires, like webs, were fragile (prone to crises where important threads are broken or structural nodes destroyed), yet also dynamic, being constantly remade and reconfigured through concerted thought and effort: the image of the web reminds us that empire were not just structures, but processes as well.

The inherently relational nature of the empire is also underlined by the image of the web. Where the so much writing on imperial/colonial history reduces the empire to a series of metropole-periphery binaries, the web reinforces the multiple positions that any given colony, city, community or archive might occupy. Calcutta, for example, might be seen as being in a subaltern position in relation to London, but it in turn might be a sub-imperial center where important lines of patronage, accumulation and communication flow out into the South Asian hinterland and beyond to South-east Asia or even the Pacific. And as we have seen archives, libraries, and learned institutions functioned as key nodes within these webs, drawing material together, cataloging and organizing knowledge, and disseminating it throughout the system. These institutions played a key role in the circulation of knowledge that was the very lifeblood of the imperial social formation.

But we might go even further than this. If we conceive of the empire not as a single web, but as a complex agglomeration of overlapping webs, it is possible to envisage that certain locations, individuals or institutions in the supposed periphery, might in fact be the center of complex networks themselves. This was certainly the case with Samuel Peal, whose tireless correspondence from the frontiers of Assam fashioned a complex network of intellectual exchange that reached out not only to Best and Smith in New Zealand, but also to Canada, the United States, the Pacific islands, Australia and incorporated metropolitan figures, including Max Müller himself. In turn, Best and Smith, Peal's correspondents, themselves occupied a central position in a related web of exchange. The Polynesian Society quickly became a leading center for the study of Pacific ethnology and its membership and institutional exchange tapped considerable intellectual resources, allowing Best and Smith to assume a position of great authority in Pacific studies. This intellectual authority exercised from Wellington also reflected New Zealand's gradual emergence as an imperial power in the Pacific: at once a colony and an imperial power, New Zealand fashioned its own webs of influence in the Pacific with limited input from Britain.

While I am suggesting that Calcutta or Wellington could function as imperial centers, I am not advocating an entirely de-centered view of empire. It is crucial to recognize the disparities of power inherent within the empire and that many imperial networks, as well as economic power and imperial authority, were concentrated in Britain itself. Even at the level of intellectual production there is no doubt that the imperial metropole continued to exercise substantial power as metropolitan learned institutions, missionary and reform societies and, of course, the British government had the ability to exercise considerable influence over distant colonies. And, of course, the substantial resources available in London, Oxford or Cambridge allowed for exhibitions, museums and libraries on a scale beyond the reach of the colonies and also facilitated the work of grand theorists such as E. B. Tylor or Max Müller. Yet it is necessary to balance this recognition of Britain's position as an imperial power that was able to fashion a global empire, with an awareness of the ability of administrators, missionaries, settlers and indigenous groups in the colonies to construct bodies of knowledge and meaningful networks of exchange: metropolitan interests might have wished to dominate the empire, but they never enjoyed the hegemony they aspired to.

It is important to underline Sinha's assertion that by its very nature this imperial social formation was uneven: while formerly disparate locations were integrated into a common space, certain groups had greater influence within this domain and the effects of this interweaving of cultures were frequently unequal. This was certainly the case with the imperial webs that linked India and New Zealand. With a few notable exceptions – such as H. H. Risley's embrace of *tapu* as a fundamental element of his racial theory of caste[79] – ethnographic data and analytical models were transplanted from India into the Pacific. Some of these exchanges were via the metropole, whether through Orientalist works published in Britain, the institutional exchanges fashioned by the British scientific establishment, and the webs of correspondence that connected colonial ethnologists such as Tregear to leading British intellectuals such as Max Müller. While these 'vertical connections' to the metropole co-existed with 'horizontal' networks that linked India and New Zealand directly, these direct inter-colonial networks thickened and grew in significance as the nineteenth-century drew to a close.

If these networks had an uneven spatial reach, deep-seated social divisions shaped them as well. Although South Asian intellectuals played a key role in debates over Aryanism within the empire in the nineteenth century, Maori played a limited role in these discursive structures. While it seems that the renowned scribe Te Whatohoro Jury might have encouraged Best and Smith's belief in the Indian origins of Maori and, as we have seen, Peter Buck supported the theory in print, most influential Maori thinkers of the late nineteenth and early twentieth century constructed an alternative and competing vision of their place in history.[80] This counter-narrative was diffusionist as well, but rather than identifying India as the homeland of their ancestors, it identified Maori as Tiu or Hurai: Jews, the direct descendants of the Israelites. This appropriation of Old Testament narratives was a radical challenge to the authority of Pakeha knowledge and the very basis of colonization itself. The Maori prophetic tradition promised that God would directly intervene on the behalf of Maori, his chosen people, and expel Pakeha, restore alienated Maori land and usher in a new age of millennial happiness.[81]

While Maori resisted incorporation into these webs of empire and rejected Indocentric visions of their culture, it was the emergence of both materialist anthropology and a new leftist literary nationalism in the 1930s that undercut the authority of diffusionist theories of cultural development. Although elements of Indocentric interpretations Maori history remain current in 'new age' religious movements in New Zealand and still find some support in South

---

[79]   H.H. Risley, 'The Study of Ethnology in India', *Journal of the Anthropological Institute*, 20 (1891), 259.

[80]   On Whatahoro see Peter Clayworth's forthcoming University of Otago Ph.D. thesis.

[81]   Tony Ballantyne, 'Print, Politics and Protestantism: New Zealand, 1769–1860', *Information, Media & Power through the ages*, 152–179; Bronwyn Elsmore, *Like Them That Dream. The Maori and the Old Testament* (Tauranga, 1985) and *Mana from Heaven: a Century of Maori Prophets in New Zealand* (Tauranga, 1989)

Asia, the new materialist anthropological paradigm fashioned by Raymond Firth reoriented approaches to the study of Maori culture.[82] Cultural analysis was no longer geared towards 'excavating' Aryan remnants or identifying parallels between Maori religion and Hinduism, but instead focused on kinship, resource exploitation, and systems of economic organization. This internalist approach to the study of Maori culture coalesced with a turn to the local in the arts, as New Zealand writers and artists fashioned a stark modernist realism (grounded in an embrace of vernacular language and local landscapes) as the basis for a new vision of national identity. Within such a context, New Zealand's relationship with Britain and its empire was increasingly questioned and the strong ties that linked New Zealand and British India in the late nineteenth century seemed less relevant. These webs, once strong, quickly atrophied and the exchanges that had once nourished settler intellectual life not only perished, but also were disregarded as a result of a new vision of the nation's history. The historical turn to, what Ruth Ross dubbed, the 'autochthonous soil' – beginning with the work of J.C. Beaglehole, popularized by Keith Sinclair and now reinforced by a thriving tradition of bicultural historical writing – has erased many of the connections and exchanges that molded (and continue to mold) New Zealand's development.[83]

There is no doubt that this new national tradition of historical writing has replaced diffusionist speculations on Maori cultural development with a nuanced image of indigenous social structure and fashioned a complex image of the place of race and racial conflict in the nation's development. Yet, the unquestioned use of the nation-state as an analytical frame for historical analysis has had profound implications, as this re-examination of Aryanism on the New Zealand frontier has revealed. Most importantly, it has worked to elide New Zealand's place within the empire and the ways in which imperial ideologies and racial thought were transplanted to New Zealand, contested by a variety of groups, and reworked into novel arguments in response to local pressures. The mold of the 'island story', a story of splendid isolation and internal development, which has had such a powerful purchase in British history, has also provided a popular model for the writing of colonial histories.[84] The need to construct a variety of narratives, to unsettle the naturalness of the nation-state state as an analytical frame, and to map the place of individual colonies within 'imperial social formations' are crucial. In characterizing the empire as a series of dynamic and interlocking webs, this essay has suggested another heuristic tool that may facilitate these projects. The web metaphor draws our attention to the complex interplay between the local, the national, and the imperial and underscores the inherently relational nature of the empire. It furnishes a useful starting-point for mobile imperial histories and histories of imperial mobility, a way for historians to recover the mobility and exchanges that were so central in the constitution of both metropolitan and colonial cultures. Unraveling these webs of empire may provide one way of revealing the trans-national workings of empire and may enable us to recover the

---

[82]   S.M. Gupta, *The Indian Origin of New Zealand's Maori* (New Delhi, 1995); K.R. Howe, 'Maori/Polynesian Origins and the "New Learning"', *Journal of the Polynesian Society*, 108 (1999), 305–325.

[83]   R.M. Ross, 'The Autochthonous New Zealand Soil', *The Feel of Truth: essays in New Zealand and Pacific history* Peter Munz ed., (Wellington, 1960), 49–61; J.C. Beaglehole, 'The New Zealand Scholar, Ibid., 237–54.

[84]   Antoinette Burton, 'Who needs the nation? Interrogating British history', *Journal of Historical Sociology* 10 (1997), 227–248.

centrality of imperialism in the making of the 'satanic geographies' of violence and inequality that characterize our contemporary globalized world.[85]

This article was original published in the *Journal of Colonialism and Colonial History*, **2**(3), (2001) pp. 1–35.

---

[85] Neil Smith, 'The Satanic Geographies of Globalization: Uneven Development in the 1990s', *Public Culture* 10 (1997), 169–189.

Part IV
Measurement and Mapping

[9]
Number in the Colonial Imagination

Arjun Appadurai

In the latter part of 1990, in the last months of the regime of V. P. Singh and in the turbulent transition to the rule of the country by S. Chandra-sekhar, India (especially the Hindi-speaking North) was rocked by two major social explosions. The first, associated with the Mandal Commission Report, pitted members of different castes against each other in a manner that many feared would destroy the polity. The second, associated with the holy city of Ayodhya, pitted Hindus and Muslims against each other over the control of a sacred site. These crosscutting issues, whose interrelationship has been noted and analyzed a great deal in recent months, both involved questions of entitlement (what are your rights?) and of classification (what group do you belong to and where does it fit in the political landscape?). This chapter explores the colonial roots of one dimension of the volatile politics of community and classification in contemporary India. In so doing, it follows the lead of many recent authors who have traced caste and communitarian politics to the politics of group representation in the twentieth century (Kothari 1989a, 1989b; Shah 1989) as well as to the role of the colonial census (Thapar 1989). But the precise and distinctive links between enumeration and classification in colonial India have not been specified, and that is what this essay proposes to do.

Edward Said's famous book (1978) is centrally concerned with the forms of knowledge that constitute what he defined as orientalism, but he does not specify how exactly the orientalist knowledge project and the colonial project of domination and extraction were connected. Nevertheless, in two ways he does set the stage for the argument of this chapter. Discussing the various ways the discourse of orientalism created a vista of exoticism, strangeness, and difference, he says that: "Rhetorically speaking, Orientalism is absolutely anatomical and *enumerative*; to use its vocabulary is to engage in the particularizing and dividing of things Oriental into manageable parts." (Said 1978: 72; emphasis mine). A little later in the book he suggests that in exhuming dead Oriental languages, orientalists were involved in a process in which "reconstructive precision, science, even *imagination* could prepare the way for what armies, administrations, and bureaucracies would later do on the ground, in the Orient " (Said: 123; emphasis mine).

I want in this essay to show that the exercise of bureaucratic power itself involved the colonial imagination and that in this imagination number played a crucial role. My general argument is that exoticization and enumeration were complicated strands of a single colonial project and that in their interaction lies a crucial part of the explanation of group violence and communal terror in contemporary India. In making this argument, it might be noted that I build on Ludden's concern with "orientalist empiricism" (in this volume).

My central question is simple. Is there any special force to the systematic counting of bodies under colonial states in India, Africa, and Southeast Asia, or is it simply a logical extension of the preoccupation with numbers in the metropolis, that is, in Europe in the sixteenth and seventeenth centuries? In asking this question, and in seeking to answer it, I have been inspired by two essays: one by Benedict Anderson (1991) and one by Sudipta Kaviraj (1989), which together suggest an important new agenda for a critique of European colonial rule. Taking the Indian colonial experience as my case, I shall try to elaborate the idea that we have paid a good deal of attention to the classificatory logic of colonial regimes, but less attention to the ways in which they employ quantification, in censuses as well as in various other instruments like maps, agrarian surveys, racial studies, and a variety of other productions of the colonial archive.

Let me briefly anticipate my argument. I believe that the British colonial state did employ quantification in its rule of the Indian subcontinent in a way that was different from its domestic counterpart in the eighteenth century (Brewer 1989) and from its predecessor states in India, including the Mughals, who certainly had elaborate apparatuses for counting, classifying, and controlling the large populations under their control. To make this case, I make two arguments and raise a number of questions for further research. The first, more extensive, argument will seek to identify the place of quantification and enumeration in British classification activities in colonial India. The second, only briefly adumbrated here, will suggest why, contrary to appearance, this variety of "dynamic nominalism" (Hacking 1986) was different from earlier state-supported numerical exercises both in the metropolis and in the colonies.

316   Arjun Appadurai

Enumerative Strategies

Much has been written about the virtual obsession of the British state in India with classifying its Indian population. The *locus classicus* of this literature is Bernard Cohn's essay "The Census and Objectification in South Asia" (1987; original 1984; original manuscript version 1970), where he shows that the Indian census, rather than being a passive instrument of data-gathering, creates, by its practical logic and form, a new sense of category-identity in India, which in turn creates the conditions for new strategies of mobility, status politics, and electoral struggle in India. The classificatory dimension of Cohn's work has been carried forward by many scholars, including Nicholas Dirks (1987), David Ludden (this volume), Gyan Prakash (1990), and several historians of the subaltern school, including Guha (1983), Arnold (1988), and Chakrabarty (1983). It has also recently been resituated in a major study of the orientalist imagination in India (Inden 1990). Cohn's concern with the census has also been carried forth in an important edited collection (Barrier 1981). All these historians have shown, in various ways, that colonial classifications had the effect of redirecting important indigenous practices in new directions, by putting different weights and values on existing conceptions of group-identity, bodily distinctions, and agrarian productivity. But less attention has been paid to the issue of numbers, of measurement, and of quantification in this enterprise.

The vast ocean of numbers, regarding land, fields, crops, forests, castes, tribes, and so forth, collected under colonial rule from very early in the nineteenth century, was not a utilitarian enterprise in a simple, referential manner. Its utilitarianism was part of a complex including informational, justificatory, and pedagogical techniques. Particular functionaries at particular levels of the system filling bureaucratic forms designed to provide raw numerical data did see their tasks as utilitarian in a commonsense, bureaucratic way. State-generated numbers were often put to important pragmatic uses, including setting agrarian tax levels, resolving land disputes, assessing various military options, and, later in the century, trying to adjudicate indigenous claims for political representation and policy change. Numbers surely were useful in all these ways. But the less obvious point is that statistics were generated in amounts that far defeated any unified bureaucratic purpose, and agrarian statistics, for example, were not only filled with classificatory and technical errors; they also encouraged new forms of agrarian practice and self-representation (Smith 1985).

Thus, though early colonial policies of quantification were utilitarian in design, I would suggest that numbers gradually became more importantly part of the illusion of bureaucratic control and a key to a colonial *imaginaire* in which countable abstractions, both of people and of resources, at every imaginable level and for every conceivable purpose, created the sense of a controllable indigenous reality. Numbers were part of the recent historical experience of literacy for the colonial elite (Money 1989; Thomas 1987), who had thus come to believe that quantification was socially useful. There is ample evidence that the significance of these numbers was often either nonexistent or self-fulfilling, rather than principally referential with regard to a complex reality external to the activities of the colonial state. In the long run, these enumerative strategies helped to ignite communitarian and nationalist identities that in fact undermined colonial rule. One must therefore ask how the idea of number as an instrument of colonial control might have entered the imagination of the state?

In regard to England, the answer to this question must go back to the story of numeracy, literacy, state fiscalism, and actuarial thinking in the seventeenth and eighteenth centuries (Hacking 1975; chap. 12; 1982; 1986; Brewer 1989). This is a very complex story indeed, but by the end of the eighteenth century, "number," like "landscape," "heritage," and the "people," had become part of the language of the British political imagination (Ludden: this volume), and the idea had become firmly implanted that a powerful state could not survive without making enumeration a central technique of social control. Thus the census in Britain made rapid technical strides throughout the nineteenth century and doubtless provided the broad scaffolding for the late-nineteenth-century census in India. A recent overview of material on the nineteenth-century census in Britain (Lawton 1978) suggests that, operating as it did within a framework of commonsense classifications, shared by officialdom with ordinary people, the British census did not have the refractive and generative effects that it did in India.

While I cannot decisively show here that the operations of the British census "at home" were different from those in India, there are three sound reasons to suppose that there were important differences. First, the basis of the British census was overwhelmingly territorial and occupational rather than ethnic or racial.[1] Second, insofar as its concerns were sociological in England, the census tended to be directly tied to the politics of representation, as in the issue of "rotten boroughs." Finally, and most important, both British and French census projects (as well as the embryonic social

318   Arjun Appadurai

sciences with which they were associated), tended to reserve their most invasive investigations for their social margins: the poor, the sexually profligate, the lunatic, and the criminal. In the colonies, by contrast, the *entire* population was seen as "different" in problematic ways, this shift lying at the very heart of orientalism (Nigam 1990: 287). Furthermore, in India, this orientalist inclination was preordained to meet its indigenous counterpart in the apparent cardinality of difference in the indigenous ideology of caste, as it appeared to western eyes. The similarities and differences between the British and French colonial projects in this regard have yet to be worked out, but it is clear that the concern with deviance and marginality at home was extended to the management of entire populations in the Orient (Armstrong 1990; Rabinow 1989). While there were clear and important connections between the enterprises of classification, science, photography, criminology, and so on, in the metropolis and in the colonies, it does not appear that enumerative activities had the same cultural form in England and in India, if nothing else because the English did not see themselves as a vast edifice of exotic communities, devoid of a polity worth the name.

In a colonial setting, such as the Indian one, the encounter with a highly differentiated, religiously "other" set of groups must have built on the metropolitan concern with occupation, class, and religion, all of which were a prominent part of the British census in the nineteenth century. This created a situation, part of what David Ludden has, in this volume, called "orientalist empiricism," in which the hunt for information and for archivizing this information took on enormous proportions, and numerical data became crucial to this empiricist drive. By this time, statistical thinking had become allied to the project of civic control, both in England and in France (Canguilheim 1989; Ewald 1986; Hacking 1972, 1982, 1986), in projects of sanitation, urban planning, criminal law, and demography. It would thus have been tempting for European bureaucrats to imagine that good numerical data would make it easier to embark on projects of social control or reform in the colonies.

This argument raises two separate but related issues. Was India a *special* case or a *limiting* case in regard to the role of enumeration, exoticization, and domination in the techniques of the modern nation-state? I would argue that it was a special case, because in India the orientalist gaze encountered an indigenous system of classification that seemed virtually invented by some earlier, indigenous form of orientalism. I do not subscribe to the view that early Hindu texts constitute a simple variation on later orientalist texts, thus justifying the exoticizing tendencies of, for example, the colonial legal digests. Making this case fully would take me too far afield in this context, but let me simply note that essentialism too is a matter of context, and that the relationship between Hindu stereotyping and British essentialism in the matter of caste cannot be considered apart from a thoroughgoing comparison of state formations and religious formations in very different historical contexts.

Nevertheless, it would be foolish to pretend that British orientalism did not encounter in India as indigenous social *imaginaire* that appeared to valorize group difference in a remarkable way. Caste in India, even if it was itself a very complicated part of the Indian social imaginary, and was refracted and reified in many ways through British techniques of observation and control, was nevertheless not a figment of the British political imagination. In this regard, Oriental essentializing in India carried a social force that can come only when two theories of difference share a critical assumption: that the bodies of certain groups are the bearers of social difference and of moral status. This is where India is a *special* case. But looked at from the vantage point of the present, India may also be regarded as a *limiting*[2] case of the tendency of the modern nation-state to draw on existing ideas of linguistic, religious, and territorial difference to "produce the people" (Balibar 1990).

The role of numbers in complex information-gathering apparatuses such as the colonial one in India had two sides that, in retrospect, need to be distinguished. The one side may be described as *justificatory*, the other as *disciplinary*. A very large part of the statistical information gathered by British functionaries in India did not just facilitate *learning or discovery*, in regard to ruling Indian territories. This statistical information also assisted in arguing and teaching, in the context of bureaucratic discourse and practice, first between the East India Company and the English parliament and later between the officials of the Crown in India and their bosses in London (Smith 1985 is a classic statement of the general logic that knits together reports, manuals, and records in nineteenth-century India). Numbers were a critical part of the discourse of the colonial state, because the metropolitan interlocutors of the colonial state had come to depend on numerical data, however dubious their accuracy and relevance, for major social or resource-related policy initiatives. This justificatory dimension of the use of numbers in colonial policy, of course, also relates to the different levels of the British state in India, where numbers were the fuel for a series of nested struggles between Indian officials at the lowest levels of the bureau-

320   Arjun Appadurai

cracy, up the system to the governor-general of India, through a series of crosscutting committees, boards and individual office-holders, who conducted a constant internal debate about the plausibility and relevance of various classifications and the numbers attached to them (Dirks 1987: chap. 10 and 11; Hutchins 1967: 181; Presler 1987: chap. 2).

Numbers regarding castes, villages, religious groups, yields, distances, and wells were part of a language of policy debate, in which their referential status quickly became far less important than their discursive importance in supporting or subverting various classificatory moves and the policy arguments based on them. It is important to note here that numbers permitted comparison between kinds of places and people that were otherwise different, that they were concise ways of conveying large bodies of information, and that they served as a short-form for capturing and appropriating otherwise recalcitrant features of the social and human landscape of India. It is not so much that numbers did not serve a straightforward referential purpose in colonial pragmatics, serving to indicate features of the Indian social world to bureaucrats and politicians, but that this referential purpose was often not so important as the rhetorical purpose. This is in part due to the fact that the sheer vastness of the numbers involved in major policy debates in the nineteenth century often made their strictly referential or "informational" dimension unmanageable.

Yet the justificatory functions of these numerical strategies seem to have been no more important than their pedagogical and disciplinary ones. With regard to this latter function, Foucault's ideas about biopolitics certainly are most relevant, since the colonial state saw itself as part of the Indian body politic while it was simultaneously engaged in reinscribing the politics of the Indian body, especially in its involvement with sati, hook-swinging, possession rites, and other forms of bodymanipulation (Dirks 1989; Mani 1990). I will return to this point later. But the numerical issue complicates matters somewhat. For what is involved here are not simply the logistical needs of the state but also its discursive needs, construed centrally as statistical needs.

What is more, this was not just a matter of providing the numerical grist for a policy apparatus whose discursive form had been constructed through a complex European development involving probabilistic thinking and civic policy. It was also a matter of disciplining the vast officialdom of the colonial state (see also Smith 1985 and Cohn 1987), as well as the population that these officials wished to control and reform, so that numbers could become an indispensable part of its bureaucratic practices and style.

Number and Cadastral Politics

The moment of rupture between the empiricist and disciplinary moments of colonial numerology can be seen in the many technical documents produced in the middle of the nineteenth century. There are many ways in which this shift can be conceptualized, including the one that sees it as a "transformation of the census as an instrument of taxes to an instrument of knowledge," in the words of Richard Smith (1985), who identifies this shift as occurring in the Punjab around 1850. In the discussion that follows, I use a document from roughly the same period, from western India, to illustrate the formation of the new sort of numerical gaze of the colonial state in the middle of the nineteenth century.

This document, published under the title *The Joint Report of 1847*, was actually published as a book in 1975 by the Land Records Department of the state of Maharashtra in western India. Its subtitle is *Measurement and Classification Rules of the Deccan, Gujarat, Konkan and Kanara Surveys*. It belongs to a class of document that shows the East India Company seeking to standardize its land-revenue practices across the full extent of its territories and to rationalize practices generated in the latter part of the eighteenth and in the early part of the nineteenth century, in the heat of conquest. It is, par excellence, a document of bureaucratic rationalization, which seeks to create and standardize revenue rules for all the land under East India Company jurisdiction in the Deccan region. But it also contains a series of letters and reports from the early part of the 1840s, which reveal a serious debate between local and central officialdom about the minutiae of mapping the agricultural terrain of western India, and its larger purposes, such as assessment and dispute-settlement. It is a quintessential document of cadastral politics.

Following Ranajit Guha's characterization of "the prose of counter-insurgency" (Guha 1983), we may call the *Joint Report* a classic example of *the prose of cadastral domination*. This is a prose, composed partly of rules, partly of orders, partly of appendices, and partly of letters and petitions, which must be read together. In this prose, the internal debates of the revenue bureaucracy, the pragmatics of rule-formation, and the rhetoric of utility always accompanied the final recommendations, by authorities at various levels, of new technical practices. These are documents whose manifest rhetoric is technical (i.e., positivist, transparent, and neutral), but whose subtext is contestatory (in regard to superiors) and disciplinary (in regard to inferiors).

The bulk of the document, like most others of its ilk, is truly Borgesian, struggling to find textual methods and representations adequate to capturing both the scope and the minutiae of the Indian agri-terrain. The analogy to Borges's classic story of the map that had to be as large as the domain it iconicized is not fanciful, as is evidenced by the following complaint by one official about an earlier technique of mapping:

> At the time of Mr. Pringle's survey of the Deccan there were some very detailed and intricate records prepared, under the name of kaifiats, which we have also found it expedient to do away with as useless, and tending by their great length and complexity to involve in obscurity, rather than elucidate, the subjects of which they treat, and by their very bulk to render the detection of errors a matter of impossibility (1975 footnote: the kaifiats prepared for many of the villages assessed by Mr. Pringle were upwards of 300 yards in length). (*Joint Report*: 55)

Notwithstanding this complaint in 1840 about the Borgesian absurdities of earlier mapping efforts, the tension between representational economy and detail does not disappear. Throughout the 1840s, a battle continues between the survey authorities of the Deccan and the Board of Revenue, which has somewhat more synoptic and panoptic aspirations for its surveys. There is, *first* of all, the relationship between measurement and classification, which is itself an explicit subject of discussion in many of the letters and reports leading up to the *Joint Report of 1847*, which fixed the basic rules of survey for this region for several subsequent decades. As regards measurement, the British officials directly responsible for the assessment regarded it as a problem of adapting existing trigonometric, topographic, and protraction methods to create maps that they saw as both accurate and functional. They were concerned to "multiply copies of these maps in the most economical and accurate manner, as well as to guard against any future fraudulent attempt at alteration," and therefore these officers suggested that "they should be lithographed" (*Joint Report*: 9–10). The concern for accuracy in measurement already incorporated existing statistical ideas about percentages of error, and of "average error," which they wanted to reduce.

These officers recognized that classification was a much trickier issue than measurement; regarding measurement, however, they were naively positivist ("these results are of an absolute and invariable character, capable of being arrived at with equal certainty by many modes": p. 10). The classification of fields for purposes of a fair assessment posed a host of problems involving the typification of variation for purposes of classification, so that the classification could be general enough to apply to a large region, yet specific enough to accommodate important variations on the ground. The resulting solution was complex and involved a ninefold classification of soils, a complex system of notation for field assessors, and a complex algorithm for translating such qualitative variation into quantitative values relevant to revenue assessment.

Put another way, the detailed disciplines of measurement and classification (the one relying on the iconic practices of trigonometry and surveying in general and the other on numerical and statistical ideas of "average" and of percentage error), were the twin techniques through which an equitable policy of revenue was envisioned, based on principles of the most general applicability that would simultaneously be as sensitive as possible to local variation. This mentality—generality of application and sensitivity to minute variations—was the central tension not just of cadastral surveys but of all the informational aspirations of the colonial state. As I explain below, this mentality is also the crucial link between the cadastral logic of the first half of the century and the human censuses of the latter part of the century, as regards enumeration and exoticization.

The exchanges surrounding the 1847 report also reveal the emergent tension between the varieties of knowledge that constituted "orientalist empiricism." It should not be very surprising that officials more closely concerned with local variation and on-the-ground accuracy and fairness were resentful of the obsessive panoptical needs of the higher levels of the bureaucracy. Illustrating literally the power of the textual "supplement" (in the deconstructionist usage), numerical tables, figures, and charts allowed the contingency, the sheer narrative clutter of prose descriptions of the colonial landscape, to be domesticated into the abstract, precise, complete, and cool idiom of number. Of course, numbers could be fought over, but this battle had a instrumental quality, far removed from the heat of the novel, the light of the camera, and the colonial realism of administrative ethnographies.

These properties were of particular value to those who sought to tame the very diversities of the land and the people that other aspects of the Oriental episteme such as photography, travelogues, engravings, and exhibitions did so much to create. In 1840, Lieutenant Wingate, the official most responsible for translating the assessment needs of the colonial state into locally feasible technical and bureaucratic practices in the Deccan, wrote to the Revenue Commissioner in Poona, his immediate superior, clearly expressing frustration with the changing interests of the central bureaucracy: "The present survey, moreover, was instituted for purely

324   Arjun Appadurai

revenue purposes, and the question of rendering it subservient to those of Geography and Topography is now mooted for the first time. It can hardly therefore be in fairness objected to the plan of operations that it does not include the accomplishment of objects that were not contemplated at the time of its formation" (p. 69).

The official at the next level up in the revenue bureaucracy, though less forthright than Wingate, nevertheless makes it clear that he is puzzled by the relation between the revenue needs and the "scientific" needs of his superiors. He adds, at the conclusion of an important letter, mediating between two important levels of the bureaucracy, that "for every purpose for which a Revenue Officer can desire a map, those already furnished by the late survey under Major Jopp, and those now making out [sic] by the Deccan Revenue Surveys, of which a specimen is annexed, seem to me amply sufficient; and if anything more accurate or detailed be required, it must be, I conclude for some purpose of speculative science, on the necessity or otherwise of which I am not required to express an opinion" (pp. 81–82).

Documents such as the *Joint Report of 1847* were crucial in the disciplining of lower-level, especially native functionaries in the empiricist practices of colonial rule. In the collection of maps, measures, and statistics of every sort, these documents, and the rules contained and debated within them, show that lower-level European officials were critically concerned with making sure that the standards of colonial administrative practice were drilled into the minutest bodily techniques of these measurers. These techniques could be seen as disciplinary techniques applied both to lower-level European officialdom and to their Indian subordinates. But there was an important difference. Whereas the former might not recognize their own subjection to the regime of number in the idioms of science, patriotism, and imperial hegemony (with which they were racially identified), for Indian officialdom, these practices were a direct inscription onto their bodies and minds of practices associated with the power and foreignness of their rulers. In this, as in other aspects of the control of colonial labor and resources, not all subalternities are identical.

The vast apparatus of revenue-assessment was in fact part of a complex apparatus of discipline and surveillance in and through which native functionaries were instilled with a whole series of numerical habits, (tied to other habits of description, iconography, and distinction), in which number played a complex set of roles, including those of classification, ordering, approximation, and identification. The political arithmetic of colonialism was taught, quite literally, on the ground and translated into algorithms that could make future numerical activities habitual and instill bureaucratic description with a numerological infrastructure.

In each of these important ways, the prose of cadastral control set the grounds, and constituted a rehearsal, for later discourse concerning human communities and their enumeration. This rehearsal had three components: it set the stage for the widespread use of standardizing enumerative techniques to control on-the-ground material variations; it treated the physical features of the landscape, as well as its productivity and ecological variability, as separable (to some extent) from the complex social rights involved in its use and meaning for rural Indians; and it constituted a pedagogical preparation for the kind of disciplinary regime that would later be required for human census enumerators and tabulators at all levels.

Number (and the statistical ideology underlying number) was the "ligature" of these cadastral texts and provided the key links between these texts and the debates that they reported and the practices they were designed to discipline. Thus, through a careful reading of these apparently simply technical documents, one can unearth ideological tensions and fractures as well as practices of teaching and of surveillance, in which it is not only the case that "land is to rule" (Neale 1969). Colonial rule had a pedagogical and disciplinary function, so that "land is to teach": the measurement and classification of land was the training ground for the culture of number in which statistics became the authorizing discourse of the appendix (giving indirect weight to the verbal portion of the text) at the same time that it gave higher level officials a pedagogical and disciplinary sense of controlling not just the territory over which they sought to rule, but also the native functionaries through which such rule needed to be effected. As far as the native is concerned, the regime of number, as every page of such documents makes clear, is partly there to counteract the mendacity that is seen as constitutional to most natives, both farmers and "measurers."

We thus have one part of an answer to the question with which we began, namely: what special role does the enumeration of bodies have under colonial rule? I have suggested that numbers were a changing part of the colonial *imaginaire* and function in justificatory and pedagogical ways as well as in more narrowly referential ones. The history of British rule in the nineteenth century may be read in part as a shift from a more functional use of number in what has been called the fiscal militarism of the British state at home (Brewer 1989) to a more pedagogical and disciplinary role. Indian bodies were gradually not only categorized but given quantitative values (Bayly 1988: 88–89), increasingly associated with what Hacking has called "dynamic nominalism" (Hacking 1986), that is, the creation of new kinds of self by officially enforced labeling activities.

Number played a critical role in such dynamic nominalism in the colonial setting, partly because it provided a shared language for information-transfer, disputation, and linguistic commensuration between center and periphery and for debates among a huge army of mediating bureaucrats in India. Number, thus, was part of the enterprise of *translating* the colonial experience into terms graspable in the metropolis, terms that could encompass the ethnological peculiarities that various orientalist discourses provided. Numerical glosses constituted a kind of metalanguage for colonial bureaucratic discourse within which more exotic understandings could be packaged, at a time when the relation between enumerating populations and controlling and reforming society had come together in Europe. These numerical glosses that appear as accompanying data for discursive descriptions and recommendations are best regarded as a normalizing frame for the stranger discursive realities that the verbal portions of many colonial texts needed to construct. This normalizing frame functions at two of the levels discussed by Foucault, those of knowledge and power, text and practice, reading and ruling. Following Richard Smith's distinction (1985) between rule-by-record and rule-by-report, it can be seen that numbers in *records* provided the empirical ballast for the descriptivist thrust of the colonial gaze, whereas numbers in *reports* provided more of a normalizing frame, balancing the contestatory and polyphonic aspects of the narrative portions of these reports, which shared some of the tensions of what Guha has called the "prose of counter-insurgency."

Colonial Body Counts

These enumerative practices, in the setting of a largely agricultural society already to a large degree practically prepared for cadastral control by the Mughal state, had another major consequence. They were not merely a rehearsal for the enumerative practices of the Indian national census after 1870. They also accomplished a major and hitherto largely unnoticed task. The huge apparatus of revenue settlements, land surveys, and legal-bureaucratic changes in the first half of the nineteenth century did something beyond commoditizing land (Cohn 1969); transforming "lords into landlords" and peasants into tenants (Prakash 1990); and changing reciprocal structures of gift and honor into saleable titles, which were semiotically fractured and were rendered saleable, while retaining some of the metonymic force that tied them to named persons. They also unyoked social groups from the complex and localized group-structures and agrarian practices in which they had previously been embedded, whether in the context of the "silent settlement" of *inams* in South India (Frykenberg 1977; Dirks 1987), of *inams* in Maharashtra (Preston 1989), of "bonded" laborers in Bihar (Prakash 1990), or of Julahas in Uttar Pradesh (Pandey 1990). The huge diversity of castes, sects, tribes, and other practical groupings of the Indian landscape were thus rendered into a vast categorial landscape untethered to the specificities of the agrarian landscape.

This unyoking occurs in two major steps, one associated with the period before 1870, in which issues of land settlement and taxation are dominant colonial projects, and the other with the period from 1870 to 1931, the period of the great All-India census, in which the enumeration of human populations is the dominant project. The period from about 1840 to 1870 is the period of transition from one major orientation to the other. The first period sets the stage for the second in that it is dominated by a concern for the physical and ecological basis of land productivity and revenue, and (as I have already suggested) to some extent unyokes this variability from the social and human world associated with it, in the context of efforts to wage a battle of standardization against on-the-ground variation. In the second period, so usefully explored by Rashmi Pant (1987) in the context of the North-West Provinces and Oudh, the reverse move occurs, and human groups (castes) are treated to a considerable extent as abstractable from the regional and territorial contexts in which they function. It is of course important to note that these colonial projects were concurrently plagued by internal contradictions (the urge to specificity and to generalizability in the All-India Census names of castes, for example), by contradictions between different colonial projects, and by, most important, the fact the colonial bureaucratic operations did not necessarily transform practices or mentalities on the ground. I shall return to this issue toward the end of this chapter, in a discussion of the colonial subject.

Pant's seminal essay discusses the way in which caste came to become a crucial "site" for the activities of the national censuses after 1870, against *other* alternative sites. Along with the essay by Smith (1985) referred to already, Pant's argument allows us to see that colonial bureaucratic practice, as a contingent and historically shaped locus of agency in its own right, helped to create a special and powerful relationship between essentialization, discipline, surveillance, objectification, and group-consciousness, by the last decades of the nineteenth century.

Numbers played a crucial role in this conjuncture, and the earlier statistical panopticon was a crucial factor in the gravitation of the census toward caste as a key site of social classification, since caste appeared to be the key at once to Indian social variability as well as to the Indian mentality. Pant, who builds on the earlier work of Smith, points out that the use of caste for "differentiating a stream of data" was first applied in the realm of sex statistics from this region. Specifically, it was argued in the 1872 *Report* of the All-India Census for the North-West Provinces and Oudh that certain hypotheses about sex ratios in relation to female infanticide could only be explained by reference to caste. This concern with explaining and controlling "exotic" behaviors is a crucial piece of evidence that empiricism and exoticization were not disconnected aspects of the colonial imaginary in India. This linkage of empirical statistics and the management of the exotic was the basis for a more general policy orientation to the effect that much of what needed to be known about the Indian population would become intelligible only by the detailed enumeration of the population *in terms of caste*.

Although the subsequent history of the All-India Census shows that, in practice, there were enormous difficulties and anomalies involved with the effort to construct an all-India grid of named and enumerated "castes," the principle was not abandoned until the 1930s. As Pant shows, "by the turn of the century, the epistemological status of caste as a locale for recognizing qualified and socially effective units of the Indian population was well established—as our Census Reports of 1911–1931 confirm" (Pant 1987: 149). But it is also worth noting that since the hunt for data about caste created a huge and unmanageable flow of information, even as early as the 1860s, only "numerical majorities" were given prominence in the census reports. Thus, the concern with numerical majorities emerged as a principle for organizing census information. This apparently innocuous bureaucratic principle, of course, is a logical basis for the ideas of "majority" and "minority" groups that subsequently affected Hindu-Muslim politics in colonial India and caste politics in India during the twentieth century, up to the present.

While it is true that caste as *the* master-trope with which to taxonomize the Indian landscape is a relatively late product of colonial rule (Pant 1987), the more general essentialization of Indian groups goes back at least to the beginnings of the nineteenth century, if not earlier, as Gyan Pandey has shown with regard to the weaving castes of Uttar Pradesh (Pandey 1990). Until the last decades of the nineteenth century, however, the "essentialization" of groups in orientalist and administrative discourse was largely separate from the enumerative practices of the state, except insofar as they were directly linked to localized revenue purposes. A recent analysis of an 1823 colonial census in South India (Ludden 1988) shows that the later nineteenth-century preoccupation with social classification and enumeration is anticipated very early. But this early census seems, on the whole, pragmatic, localistic, and relational in its treatment of groups, rather than abstract, uniformitarian, or encyclopaedic in its aspirations. This was still a census oriented to taxation rather than to knowledge, in Smith's terms.

After 1870, however, not only had numbers become an integral part of the colonial *imaginaire* and of the practical ideologies of its low-level functionaries (as I have suggested), but Indian social groups had become both functionally and discursively unyoked from local agrarian landscapes and set adrift in a vast pan-Indian social encyclopaedia. This unyoking was a function of the growing sense that the social morphology of caste could provide an overall grid, through the census, for organizing knowledge about the Indian population. These are the conditions for the special force of the Indian census after 1870, which was intended to quantify previously set classifications but in fact had just the reverse effect, which was to stimulate the self-mobilization of these groups into a variety of larger translocal political forms.

Here also is the place to note the key difference between the British and their Mughal predecessors: while the Mughals did a great deal to map and measure the land under their control for revenue purposes (Habib 1963), thus generating a large part of the revenue vocabulary alive in India and Pakistan even today, they conducted no known census of persons, a fact noted by Habib as the central reason why it is difficult to estimate the population of Mughal India (Habib 1982: 163). Enumeration of various things was certainly part of the Mughal state *imaginaire* as was the acknowledgment of group identities, *but not the enumeration of group identities*. As for the other major precolonial political formations of the subcontinent, such as the Vijayanagara kingdom, they do not appear to have shared the linear, centralizing, record-keeping modes of the Mughals, and were oriented to number as a far more subtle cosmopolitics of names, territories, honors, shares, and relations (Breckenridge 1983). In this regard, non-Mughal states in the Indian subcontinent before colonial rule (including those like the Marathas who ran elaborately monetized political domains: Perlin 1987) do not seem to have been concerned with number as a direct instrument of social control. Enumerative activities were tied, in these precolonial regimes, to taxation, to accounting, and to land revenue, but the linkage of enumeration to group identity seems very weak indeed. Where it did exist it seems to have been tied to very specific social formations, such as *akharas* (wrestling/gymnastic sodalities), and not to the enumeration of the population at large.[3]

For this last, *totalizing* thrust to enter the *imaginaire* of the state, the crucial intervening step was the essentializing and taxonomizing gaze of early orientalism (of the European variety), followed by the enumerative habit applied to the land in the first half of the nineteenth century, and finally the idea of political representation as tied, not to essentially similar citizens/individuals, but to communities conceived as inherently "special." The essentializing and exoticizing gaze of orientalism in India, in the eighteenth and nineteenth centuries, provides the crucial link between census classifications and "caste and community politics." Here we are finally at the heart of the argument both as regards the differences between the colonial regime in India (and its metropolitan counterparts as well as its indigenous predecessors) and the link between colonial classificatory politics and contemporary democratic politics. The enumeration of the social body, conceived as aggregations of individuals whose bodies were inherently both collective and exotic, sets the ground for group difference to be the central principle of politics. Linking the idea of representation to the idea of "communities" characterized by bio-racial commonalities (internally) and bio-racial differences (externally) seems to be the critical marker of the colonial twist in the politics of the modern nation-state.

What occurred in the colony was a conjuncture that never occurred at home: the idea that techniques of measurement were a crucial way to normalize the variation in soil and land conjoined with the idea that numerical representation was a key to normalizing the pathology of difference through which the Indian social body was represented. Thus, the idea of the "average man" ("l'homme moyen" of Quetelet), smuggled in through statistics (as its epistemological underbelly), was brought into the domain of group difference. This sets up an orientalist extension of the metropolitan idea of the numerical representation of groups (conceived as composed of "average individuals") and the idea of "separate" electorates, which is a natural outgrowth of the sense that India was a land of groups (both for civil and political purposes) *and* that Indian social groupings were inherently "special." Thus, under colonial rule, at least in British India, the numerical dimension of classification carries the seeds of a special contradiction since it was brought to bear on a world conceived as a world of incommensurable *group* differences.

Nationalism, Representation, and Number

The "communitarian" approach, which later (in the first part of the twentieth century) has its most dramatic manifestation in separate electorates for Hindus and Muslims (Hasan 1979; Pandey 1990; Robinson 1974), was by no means restricted to them. It was built on earlier ideas about caste as the critical principal of a general morphology of the Indian population (as known through the census) and still earlier ideas about the powers of enumeration in grasping the variability and the tractability of India's land and resources. This communitarian approach was also crucial in defining the dynamics of ideas of majority and minority as culturally coded terms for dominant and disenfranchised groups in South India (Frykenberg 1987; Saraswathi 1974; Washbrook 1976: chap. 6) and elsewhere. It is thus very plausible to argue, as Rajni Kothari (1989a, 1989b) and others have done, that the very fabric of Indian democracy remains adversely affected by the idea of numerically dominated bloc-voting, as opposed to more classically liberal ideas of the bourgeois individual casting his vote as a democratic citizen.

Although it is beyond the scope of this chapter to show in a detailed way how the cognitive importance of caste in the census of India in the 1870s sets the ground for the communitarian politics of this century, it should be noted that even after 1931, when caste ceased to be a central concern of the Indian census, the idea of politics as the contest of essentialized *and* "enumerated" communities (the latter being a concept I owe to Kaviraj 1989) had already taken firm hold of local and regional politics and thus no longer required the stimulation of the census to maintain its hold on Indian politics. As Shah (1989) has recently noted, there has been a steady (and successful) effort in the last few decades to reverse the post-1931 policy of eliminating caste counts from the census.

Hannah Pitkin (1967) and others have written eloquently about the complex relationships between representation in its moral, aesthetic, and political senses. I need not repeat this western genealogy here, except to note that fairly early in the history of the Enlightenment the idea of democracy became tied to an idea of the representative sovereignty of subjects. Thus, as Frykenberg (1987) has pointed out for the Indian context, electoral politics became both a politics of *representation* (of the people to the people—a game of mirrors in which the state is made virtually invisible) and a politics of *representativeness*, that is, a politics of statistics, in which some bodies could be held to stand for other bodies because of the numerical principle of metonymy rather than the varied cosmopolitical principles of representation that had characterized ideas of divine rule in many premodern polities.

During the nineteenth and early twentieth century, the colonial state found itself in an interesting contradiction in India, as it sought to use ideas of representation and representativeness (numerical at their base) at lower levels of India's political order, with paternalist, monarchic, and qualitative principles at the top. The story of Indian self-government (which was confined to a variety of village and district level bodies during the bulk of the second half of the nineteenth century) became transformed steadily into the logic of Indian nationalism, which co-opted the colonial logic of representativeness and used it to annex the democratic idea of representation as self-representation.

Thus, the counting of bodies that had served the purposes of colonial rule at lower levels in the last half of the nineteenth century turned gradually into the idea of the representation of Indian selves (self-rule) as nationalism became a mass movement. Of course, in hindsight, as Partha Chatterjee has helped us see, nationalism suffered from sharing the basic thematic of colonialist thought and thus could not generate a thoroughgoing critique of it (Chatterjee 1986). So, the politics of numbers, especially in regard to caste and community, is not only the bane of democratic politics in India, but these older identities have become politicized in ways that are radically different from other local conceptions of the relationship between the order of jatis and the logic of the state. The process by which separate Hindu and Muslim identities were constructed at a macro-level, and transformed not just into imagined communities but also into "enumerated communities," is only the most visible pathology of the transfer of the politics of numerical representation to a society in which representation and group-identity had no special *numerical* relationship to the polity.

But it could still be said that colonial rule, either of the British in India, or of other European regimes elsewhere in the world, was not alone in generating enumerated communities. Many large non-European states, including the Ottomans, the Mughals, and various Chinese dynasties, had numerical concerns. Where lies the *colonial* difference? For the mature colonial state, numbers were part of a complex *imaginaire* in which the utilitarian needs of fiscal militarism in the world-system, the classificatory logics of orientalist ethnology, the shadow presence of western democratic ideas of numerical representation, and the general shift from a classificatory to a numerical bio-politics created an evolving logic that reached a critical conjunctural point in the last three decades of the nineteenth century and the first two decades of the twentieth.

The net result was something critically different from all other complex state-apparatuses in regard to the politics of the body and the construction of communities as bodies. Put very simply, other regimes may have had numerical concerns and they may also have had classificatory concerns. But these remained largely separate, and it was only in the complex conjuncture of variables that constituted the project of the mature colonial state that these two forms of "dynamic nominalism" came together, to create a polity centered around self-consciously enumerated communities. When these communities were also embedded in a wider official discourses of space, time, resources, and relations that was also numerical in critical ways, what was generated was a specifically colonial political arithmetic, in which essentializing and enumerating human communities became not only concurrent activities but unimaginable without one another.

This arithmetic is a critical part of colonial bio-politics (at least as regards the British in India) not only because it involved abstractions of number whereas other state regimes had more concrete numerical purposes (such as taxes, corvée labor, and the like). The modern colonial state brings together the exoticizing vision of orientalism with the familiarizing discourse of statistics. In the process, the body of the colonial subject is made simultaneously strange and docile. Its strangeness lies in the fact that it comes to be seen as the site of cruel and unusual practices and bizarre subjectivities. But colonial body-counts create not only types and classes (the first move toward domesticating differences) but also homogeneous bodies (within categories), because number, by its nature, flattens idiosyncrasies and creates boundaries around these homogeneous bodies, since it performatively limits their extent. In this latter regard, statistics are to bodies and social types what maps are to territories: they flatten and enclose. The link between colonialism and orientalism, therefore, is most strongly reinforced not at the loci of classification and typification (as has often been suggested) but at the loci of enumeration, where bodies are counted, homogenized, and bounded in their extent. Thus the unruly body of the colonial subject (fasting, feasting, hook-swinging, abluting, burning, and bleeding) is recuperated through the language of numbers that allows these very bodies to be brought back, now counted and accounted, for the humdrum projects of taxation, sanitation, education, warfare, and loyalty.

My argument thus far might be read as implying that the colonial project of essentializing, enumerating, and appropriating the social landscape was wholly successful. In fact, that is not the case, and there is ample evidence from a variety of sources that the projects of the colonial state were by no means wholly successful, especially in regard to the colonizing of the Indian consciousness. In various kinds of peasant and urban revolt, in various kinds of autobiographic and fictional writing, in many different sorts of domestic formation and expression, and in various kinds of bodily and religious practices Indians of many classes continued practices and reproduced understandings which far predated colonial rule. What is more, Indian men and women deliberately recast their conceptions of body, society, country, and destiny in movements of protest, internal critique, and outright revolt against colonial authorities. It is indeed from these various sources that the energies of local resistance were drawn, energies and spaces (ranging from prayer groups and athletic associations to ascetic orders and mercantile orders) that provided the social basis of the nationalist movement. It was these energies that permitted someone like Gandhi, and many other lesser-known figures, to recapture social and moral ground from the British (and from the discourse of orientalism itself). These reflections bring us back to a problem raised earlier, that of the colonial subject, in relation to the enumerative and classificatory projects of the state.

There is of course no easy generalization to be made about the degree to which the effort to organize the colonial project around the idea of essentialized and enumerated communities made inroads into the practical consciousness of colonial subjects in India. It is easy enough, however, to say that the results must have varied according to various dimensions of the position of the colonial subject: her gender, her closeness to or distance from the colonial gaze, her involvement with or detachment from colonial politics, her participation in or distance from the bureaucratic apparatus itself. It is also true that various Indian persons and groups did remain (in memory if not in empirical reality) tied to locality, whatever the panopticon saw, or said. Also, while certain components of the colonial state were active propagators of the discourses of group identity, others, such as those involved with education, law, and moral reform, were implicated in the creation of what might be called a colonial bourgeois subject, conceived as an "individual." This problem is not resolvable here, but it needs to be remarked as an important issue that any interpretation of enumerated communities will eventually have to engage.

But even if various spaces remained free of the colonial panopticon (whether through the agency of resisting colonial subjects or the incapacities and contradictions of the colonial juggernaut), the fact is that the colonial gaze, and its associated techniques, have left an indelible mark on Indian political consciousness. Part of this indelible heritage is to be seen in the matter of numbers.

It is enumeration, in association with new forms of categorization, that creates the link between the orientalizing thrust of the British state, which saw India as a museum or zoo of difference and of differences, and the project of reform, which involved cleaning up the sleazy, flabby, frail, feminine, obsequious bodies of natives into clean, virile, muscular, moral, and loyal bodies that could be moved into the subjectivities proper to colonialism (Arnold: 1988). With Gandhi, we have a revolt of the Indian body, a reawakening of Indian selves, and a reconstitution of the loyal body into the unruly and sign-ridden body of mass nationalist protest (Amin 1984; Bondurant 1958). But the fact that Gandhi had to die after watching bodies defined as "Hindu" and "Muslim" burn and defile one another reminds us that his success against the colonial project of enumeration, and its idea of the body politic, was not, and is not, complete.

The Postcolonial Heritage

The burning body of Roop Kanwar (associated with the renascent Rajput consciousness of urban males in small-town Rajasthan), the self-immolations of young, middle-class men and women after the Mandal Commission Report was revitalized, and the bodies of the *kar sewaks* in Ayodhya and of Muslims in Lucknow and elsewhere suggest that indigenous ideas of difference have become transformed into a deadly politics of community, a process that has many historical sources. But this cul-

336   Arjun Appadurai

tural and historical tinder would not burn with the intensity we now see, but for contact with the techniques of the modern nation-state, especially those having to do with number. The kinds of subjectivity that Indians owe to the contradictions of colonialism remain both obscure and dangerous.

This essay was conceived and written while the author was a MacArthur Foundation Fellow in the School of Social Sciences, Institute for Advanced Study, Princeton, during 1989–90. I am grateful to the staff of the Institute for all manner of support. This essay was first presented at a panel on "Bodies and States" at the 112th Annual Meeting of the American Ethnological Society, Atlanta, Georgia, April 26–28, 1990. I am grateful for comments and questions from that audience and for the comments of the two discussants, Talal Asad and Roy Porter. This version reflects my debts to suggestions and criticisms from the editors of this volume (Carol A. Breckenridge and Peter van der Veer) as well as from: Dipesh Chakrabarty, Joshua Cole, Nicholas Dirks, Sandria Freitag, David Ludden, and Gyanendra Pandey. I would like to dedicate this essay to my mentor, Bernard Cohn (University of Chicago), who presented me with an early version of his pathbreaking paper on the census when I arrived in his office as a graduate student in 1970. I hope he will treat it as a modest testimony to his stimulation.

Notes

1. Territorial, that is, in its concern with boroughs, counties, and regions. David Ludden: personal communication.

2. I owe this contrast to Dipesh Chakrabarty, to whom I also owe the reminder that this problem is critical to my argument.

3. Sandria Freitag: personal communication.

References

Government of Maharashtra. 1975. Selections from the Records of the Bombay Government of Papers of *The Joint Report of 1847: Measurement and Classification Rules of the Deccan, Gujarat, Konkan and Kanara Surveys*. Nagpur: Government Press.

Amin, Shahid. 1984. "Gandhi as Mahatma: Gorakhpur District, Eastern UP,

1921–2." In Ranajit Guha, ed., *Subaltern Studies: Writings on South Asian History and Society*, III. Delhi/London: Oxford University Press.

Anderson, Benedict R. 1991. "Census, Map, Museum." In *Imagined Communities* (revised edition; original 1983). New York and London: Verso.

Armstrong, Nancy. 1990. "The Occidental Alice." *Differences: A Journal of Feminist Cultural Studies* 2, 2: 3–40.

Arnold, David. 1988. "Touching the Body: Perspectives on the Indian Plague." In Guha and Spivak, *Selected Subaltern Studies*.

Balibar, Étienne. 1990. "The Nation Form: History and Ideology." *Review* (Fernand Braudel Center) 13, 3 (Summer): 329–61.

Barrier, N. Gerald, ed. 1981. *The Census in British India: New Perspectives*. New Delhi: Manohar.

Bayly, Christopher A. 1988. *Indian Society and the Making of the British Empire*. New Cambridge History of India, II, 1. Cambridge: Cambridge University Press.

Bondurant, Joan V. 1958. *Conquest of Violence: The Gandhian Philosophy of Conflict*. Princeton, NJ: Princeton University Press.

Breckenridge, Carol A. 1983. "Number Use in the Vijayanagara Era." Conference on the Kingdom of Vijayanagar, The South Asia Institute, University of Heidelberg, Heidelberg, July 14–17, 1983. Manuscript.

Brewer, John. 1989. *The Sinews of Power: War, Money, and the English State, 1688–1783*. New York: Alfred A. Knopf.

Canguilheim, Georges. 1989. *The Normal and the Pathological*. New York: Zone Books.

Chakrabarty, Dipesh. 1983. "Conditions for Knowledge of Working-Class Conditions: Employers, Government and the Jute Workers of Calcutta, 1890–1940." In Guha and Spivak, *Selected Subaltern Studies*. Oxford.

Chatterjee, Partha. 1986. *Nationalist Thought and the Colonial World: A Derivative Discourse?* London: Zed Books for the United Nations University.

Cohn, Bernard S. 1969. "Structural Change in Indian Rural Society." In Robert E. Frykenberg, ed., *Land Control and Social Structure in Indian History*. Madison: University of Wisconsin Press.

———. 1987. "The Census, Social Structure and Objectification in South Asia." In *An Anthropologist Among the Historians and Other Essays*. Delhi and London: Oxford University Press.

Dirks, Nicholas B. 1987. *The Hollow Crown: Ethnohistory of an Indian Kingdom*. Cambridge: Cambridge University Press.

———. 1989. "The Policing of Tradition in Colonial South India." Presented at the Ethnohistory Workshop, University of Pennsylvania.

Ewald, François. 1986. *L'État Providence*. Paris: B. Grasset.

Frykenberg, Robert E. 1977. "The Silent Settlement in South India, 1793–1853: An Analysis of the Role of Inams in the Rise of the Indian Imperial System." In Robert E. Frykenberg, ed., *Land Tenure and Peasant in South Asia*. New Delhi: Orient Longman.

———. 1987. "The Concept of 'Majority' as a Devilish Force in the Politics of Modern India: A Historiographic Comment." *Journal of the Commonwealth History and Comparative Politics* 25, 3 (November): 267–74.

338   Arjun Appadurai

Guha, Ranajit. 1983. "The Prose of Counter-Insurgency." In Ranajit Guha, ed. *Subaltern Studies: Writings on South Asian History and Society*, II. New Delhi and London: Oxford University Press.

Guha, Ranajit and Gayatri Chakravorty Spivak, eds. 1988. *Selected Subaltern Studies*. New York and Oxford: Oxford University Press.

Habib, Irfan. 1963. *The Agrarian System of Mughal India (1556–1707)*. Bombay and London: published for the Department of History, Aligarh Muslim University by Asia Publishing House.

———. 1982. *An Atlas of the Mughal Empire: Political and Economic Maps*. Centre of Advanced Study in History, Aligarh Muslim University. Delhi and New York: Oxford University Press.

Hacking, Ian. 1975. *The Emergence of Probability: A Philosophical Study of Early Ideas About Probability, Induction and Statistical Inference*. Cambridge and New York: Cambridge University Press.

———. 1982. "Biopower and the Avalanche of Printed Numbers." *Humanities in Society* 5, 3–4 (Summer and Fall): 279–95.

———. 1986. "Making Up People." In Thomas C. Heller, Morton Sosna, and David E. Wellbery, eds., *Reconstructing Individualism: Autonomy, Individuality, and the Self in Western Thought*. Stanford, CA: Stanford University Press.

Hasan, Mushirul. 1979. *Nationalism and Communal Politics in India, 1916–1928*. New Delhi: Manohar.

Hutchins, Francis G. 1967. *The Illusion of Permanence: British Imperialism in India*. Princeton, NJ: Princeton University Press.

Inden, Ronald B. 1990. *Imagining India*. Oxford and Cambridge, MA: Basil Blackwell.

Kaviraj, Sudipta. 1989. "On the Construction of Colonial Power: Structure, Discourse, Hegemony." Presented to a conference on Imperial Hegemony, Berlin. Manuscript.

Kothari, Rajni. 1989a. "Communalism: The New Face of Indian Democracy." In *State Against Democracy: In Search of Humane Governance*. Delhi: Ajanta Publications; New York: New Horizon Press.

———. 1989b. "Ethnicity." In *Rethinking Development: In Search of Humane Alternatives*. Delhi: Ajanta Publications; New York: New Horizon Press.

Lawton, Richard, ed. 1978. *The Census and Social Structure: An Interpretative Guide to Nineteenth Century Censuses for England and Wales*. London and Totowa, NJ: F. Cass.

Ludden, David E. 1988. Caste Landscapes in Southern Tamil Nadu and the 1823 Tirunelveli Census. Forthcoming in Arjun Appadurai, ed., *Caste in Practice*.

Mani, Lata. 1990. "Contentious Traditions: The Debate on *Sati* in Colonial India." In Kumkum Sangari and Sudesh Vaid, eds., *Recasting Women: Essays in Indian Colonial History*. New Brunswick, NJ: Rutgers University Press.

Money, John. 1989. Teaching in the Marketplace, or Caesar Adsum Jam Forte: Pompey Aderat: The Retailing of Knowledge in Provincial England. Clark Library, UCLA, March 4, 1989. Manuscript.

Neale, Walter C. 1969. "Land is to Rule." In Robert E. Frykenberg, ed., *Land*

Control and Social Structure in Indian History. Madison: University of Wisconsin Press.

Nigam, Sanjay. 1990. "Disciplining and Policing the 'Criminals by Birth,' Part 2: The Development of a Disciplinary System, 1871–1900." *Indian Economic and Social History Review* 27, 3 (July–Sept.): 257–87.

Pandey, Gyanendra. 1990. *The Construction of Communalism in Colonial North India*. New Delhi and London: Oxford University Press.

Pant, Rashmi. 1987. "The Cognitive Status of Caste in Colonial Ethnography: A Review of Some Literature of the North West Provinces and Oudh." *Indian Economic and Social History Review* 24, 2: 145–62.

Perlin, Frank. 1987. "Money-Use in Late Pre-Colonial India and the International Trade in Currency Media." In John F. Richards, ed., *The Imperial Monetary System of Mughal India*. Delhi: Oxford University Press.

Pitkin, Hanna F. 1967. *The Concept of Representation*. Berkeley and Los Angeles: University of California Press.

Prakash, Gyan. 1990. *Bonded Histories: Genealogies of Labor Servitude in Colonial India*. South Asian Studies 44. Cambridge and New York: Cambridge University Press.

Presler, Franklin A. 1987. *Religion Under Bureaucracy: Policy and Administration for Hindu Temples in South India*. Cambridge and New York: Cambridge University Press.

Preston, Laurence W. 1989. *The Devs of Cincvad: A Lineage and the State in Maharashtra*. Cambridge/New York: Cambridge University Press.

Rabinow, Paul. 1989. *French Modern: Norms and Forms of the Social Environment*. Cambridge/London: MIT Press.

Robinson, Francis. 1974. *Separatism Among Indian Muslims: The Politics of the United Provinces' Muslims, 1860–1923*. London and New York: Cambridge University Press.

Said, Edward W. 1978. *Orientalism*. New York: Vintage Books.

Saraswathi, S. 1974. *Minorities in Madras State: Group Interest in Modern Politics*. Delhi: Impex India.

Shah, Arvind M. 1989. "Caste and the Intelligentsia." *Hindustan Times*. March 24.

Smith, Richard S. 1985. "Rule-By-Records and Rule-By-Reports: Complementary Aspects of the British Imperial Rule of Law." *Contributions to Indian Sociology* 19, 1: 153–76.

Thapar, Romila. "Imagined Religious Communities? Ancient History and the Modern Search for a Hindu Identity." *Modern Asian Studies* 23(1989): 209–32.

Thomas, K. 1987. "Numeracy in Early Modern England." *Transactions of the Royal Historical Society* 5th series 37: 103–32.

Washbrook, David A. 1976. *The Emergence of Provincial Politics: The Madras Presidency, 1870–1920*. Cambridge and New York: Cambridge University Press.

[10]

'KAFIR TIME': PREINDUSTRIAL TEMPORAL CONCEPTS AND LABOUR DISCIPLINE IN NINETEENTH-CENTURY COLONIAL NATAL*

BY KELETSO E. ATKINS

APART from a very few exceptions, South African labour history presents an angle of vision that only allows us to see how external factors – ecological disasters or social controls (devised by capital and the colonial state) – drove labour into the market; or alternatively, they show how the absence of such factors permitted a temporary escape from wage employment. Most students of the period, attribute the self-direction and relative freedom of Natal's African population to the availability of land which ensured an independent subsistence, as well as to the inability of the small settler community to agree on an effective 'native labour policy'. Important as these economic and political factors were, such explanations fall short of assessing the rich cultural nuances surrounding the problem, a failing that can only distort our efforts to comprehend the substance of black proletarianization.

What is really remarkable is how precious little we know about the preindustrial African (in this case, northern Nguni) work ethic, about the ways in which such an 'inner compulsion' or ethos shaped the African response to the wage economy, determined his work choices and affected his on the job behaviour. A key place in which we might begin to correct this deficiency is by probing more deeply into the changes we can identify in the temporal consciousness of African workers.

As in E. P. Thompson's article on the temporal reorientation of the English working class,[1] so this piece seeks to examine basic cultural phenomena ordering and coordinating the daily activities of Natal Zulus; it aims to explore changes in time perceptions – the shift from peasant to industrial time – as they were experienced by these northern Nguni-speakers on coming into contact with a society undergoing early stages of capitalist growth; and it concretely demonstrates how Christianity aided the transitional process. This analysis however must be understood in the context of a settler-based colonial regime, in which the master and servant represented totally different social worlds and operated from systems of logic that mutually eluded comprehension. The friction caused by this state of affairs was considerable and may be seen as one of the potent factors blocking Natal's advancement along industrial lines.

I

Natal was declared a British colony in 1843. Gradually, labour intensive sugar production and shipping came to form the major industries in the economy.

* I am indebted to Steven Feierman, Victoria Coifman, Allen Isaacman and Shula Marks for their comments on an earlier version of this paper.

[1] E. P. Thompson, 'Time, work-discipline, and industrial capitalism', *Past and Present*, XXXVIII (1967), 56–97.

While scarcity of manpower was a dominant problem throughout the colonial period, it is noteworthy that initially labour was touted as one of the colony's chief assets; a view shaped as much to the overwhelming numbers of Africans in the District, as by the fact that the indigenous population had from the outset demonstrated their value as peasant producers and, even more significantly, had displayed a willingness to engage in rural and urban wage employment. Thus one of the phenomena that needs to be explained is why the early reports of reliable, diligent workers were by the mid-1850s almost uniformly supplanted with accounts of incorrigible contract breakers who refused to work fully the year round. The concurrent development of Africans insisting on selling their labour on the briefest terms – that is, by the day (or some fraction of that time unit) – was critical in both shaping and reinforcing negative attitudes held by whites of African workers. The matter of concern to us here, however, is not so much to set out the combined causes that made it possible for Africans to sustain this behaviour as to discover the factors which produced it in the first place. Therefore the arguments alluded to above are not strictly relevant to our present theme.

To properly interpret the African response to capital's demands on their labour, archival and ethnographic sources on northern Nguni society have been analysed for pertinent material regarding internalized, entrenched everyday values, especially temporal constraints, not easily assimilable to the new economic needs of the colony. On these issues, direct African testimony for the period is sketchy at best and for this reason settlers' descriptions of local labour have been used. Although this latter body of evidence is largely negative, it was nonetheless found, when checked against the other data, that these records often reflected concrete and surprisingly detailed information about the attitudes of black labourers. Taken together, our sources have enabled us to work up a profile of the peasant worker and to broaden our understanding of black/white colonial labour relations. We begin this discussion with comments made in 1846 by the planter, 'H. W. L.'. His remarks are important because they put the problem into immediate perspective.

I am not one of those, who, when they arrive in a settlement, because they see a number of blacks infer that they have a right to the labour of those persons, and that if they will not work for them they are set down as lazy scoundrels. But I am one of those who maintain that *if a number of Kaffers come voluntarily and offer their service, and accept service at a given rate of money wages, and for a specified time, that I have a right to the services of those persons, until the time expires.* (emphasis added).[2]

Time was at the nexus of the 'kafir labour problem'. No sooner was a work agreement made than confusion arose from the disparate notions of the white employer and his African employee regarding the computation of time. Otherwise said, the record of persistent desertions from service was in very many instances related to the fact that the terms of master–servant contracts, which were based on European units of measure, did not accord with the African mode of temporal reckoning.

Like most preindustrial people, the Zulu used the moon and stars to keep track of time. The season of cultivation was announced by the *isiLimela*, the star-cluster called the Pleiades. Early star-gazers observed also that the

---

[2] 'Labour', *Natal Witness* (hereafter, *NW*), 11 December 1846.

evening star, *isiCelankobe*, appeared when men were asking for boiled maize, their evening meal; and that *iNdosa* rose before the morning star, *Ikwezi*, when night was advanced.[3]

Inyanga, the word for 'moon', was also the name by which the Zulu called their 'moon period' or lunar month. They computed time by the phases of the moon and the annual cycle was divided into thirteen 'moons',[4] each associated with ecological changes and social activities that represented time indicators for holidays and seasons. As, for example, *uNcwaba* was the new grass moon, the month in which the land took on a rich, dark green hue; *uMasingana*, the moon of the new season's food, was the time of the annual rites of the First Fruits; and during *uNtlaba* the red flower of the aloe came forth, hence 'moon of the aloes'.

The circuit of the *inyanga* was about twenty-eight days. *Inyanga file* (the 'moon is dead'), that is the interlunary period, 'the moonless day when everyone paid respect to the darkness', was traditionally observed as an unlucky or sacred day of abstinence from work and pleasure seeking.[5] 'We had no Sundays in Zululand', recalled Mpatshana ka Sodondo, 'what we went by was the waning of the moon'.[6] When the new moon made her appearance important undertakings were commenced with confidence of success.

Coming as they did from a culture that had adopted and adapted precision instruments and other convenient methods of timekeeping – watches, clocks, solar calendars, etc., the last named containing time units (months) of irregular and capricious lengths (e.g. 28, 29, 30 and 31 days) – whites contemptuously referred to the lunar reckonings as the 'kafir month'. The complications arising from the two systems of time notations were enormous, as this agitated correspondence from 'C.P.', dated (and this is the pivotal clue) 29 October 1846, attest.

This afternoon, because I would not pay a kafir *whose month is up on the last day of the month, I was abused like a thief*. He shook his stick at me, and was so violent that if I could have got assistance, I would have sent him to the tronk [gaol]...[emphasis added].[7]

The following observations made in 1855 by the missionary Alfred Rivett carry more evidentiary weight.

The month of service (their wages are paid monthly) begins with the new moon, but often before it is quite completed, they will come to their master, asking for their money, and although the month is not ended they will declare it is by an appeal to the fact that the moon 'inyanga file' is dead. *They cannot understand there being more than 28 days in a month. It is impossible to make them believe there are 31*...[emphasis added].[8]

[3] Henry Callaway, *The Religious System of the AmaZulu* (Cape Town, 1970), 397; A. T. Bryant, *The Zulu People As They Were Before the White Man Came* (Pietermaritzburg, 1949), 251–2.

[4] David Leslie, *Among the Zulu and the AmaTongas* (New York, 1969), 394–6; Bryant, *The Zulu People*, 254–6; Eileen Krige, *The Social System of the Zulus* (Pietermaritzburg, 1962), 412.

[5] Bryant, *The Zulu People*, 254–6; Callaway, *The Religious System*, 393–9; R. Č. À. Samuelson, *Long, Long Ago* (Durban, 1929), 304.

[6] Testimony of Mpatshana ka Sodondo, in C. Webb and J. Wright (eds), *The James Stuart Archives* (Pietermaritzburg, 1982), III, 301.

[7] 'Contracts with Native Labourers', *NW*, 6 November 1846.

[8] Alfred Rivett, *Ten Years Work in Natal* (London, 1890), 22.

Confusion surrounding this issue led to notable incidents such as the 1858 'Strike among kafir mail carriers'. This involved ten men who had been hired for six months (from 2 July to 2 January) to carry mail between Durban and Maritzburg. Evidently, 'by some process of their own', the postmen 'arrived at the conclusion that their engagement expired on the 28th December'. The situation was made all the worse because of the strikers stubborn insistence on their 'unwritten and ignorant system of computing time in opposition to the statements of the Postmaster and the interpreter'. To ensure the incident would have no imitators severe punishments rather than fines and light jail sentences were recommended.[9]

What stands forth most clearly is that resorting to summary punishments (including such draconian measures as floggings and extended stretches in the gaol) to discipline preindustrial workers around the question of time, had the effect of driving labour from the market. Yet employers seemed astonishingly slow to learn lessons from this, and were slower still in taking constructive steps to rectify what would prove to be a long-standing problem. Years later, in 1894, a colonist was prompted to suggest that provision be made for 'the boys in town [for] a lecturer or teacher who would, say, once a week, impart free instructions on the European method of computation of time'. This perceptive individual pointed out that,

If it could be explained to them that they are not engaged by the lunar month, it would save much difficulty.... *At present in very many cases, either the master or mistress must give way to the ignorance of the monthly servant, or the native thinks he has been cheated of his time*... Many a score of good, hardworking boys found themselves landed in the gaol in consequence of disagreements with their employers, caused in the first instance by their inability to reckon their own time, *and then the case is frequently aggravated by the employer being unable to explain matters in the native language*... [emphasis added].[10]

Several details arising from this passage merit attention. First, it makes clear the attitude of workers regarding efforts to impose a system foreign to their basic pattern of thought – it was viewed as an attempt to cheat them of their time; secondly, to mollify servants, employers had either to submit to indigenous usages or risk the former's precipitate withdrawal from the market; another point made explicit was the quality of labour – 'Many a score of good, hardworking boys' – alienated from wage employment in consequence of such disputes; and finally, the last raised issue, recognition that mutual inability to communicate needs was a major factor aggravating master–servant relations, we want to examine in depth.

Reverend C. W. Posselt's prefatory comments in his Zulu–English phrase-book published in 1850 'to facilitate intercourse with the natives', catch the blatant mood of cultural chauvinism prevailing in the settlement. Posselt's conviction was that 'mistresses and masters [did] not want to know the barbaric dialect of their servants beyond the small circle of subjects which [had] an immediate reference to the kind of labour wherein natives were employed...'[11] The sentiments evoked by these words no doubt helped

---

[9] 'Strike Among the Kafir Mail Carriers', *Natal Mercury* (hereafter, *NM*), 14 January 1858.

[10] 'Monthly Native Servants', *NM*, 25 April 1896.

[11] C. W. Posselt, *The Zulu Companion Offered to the Natal Colonist to Facilitate Intercourse with the Natives* (Pietermaritzburg, 1850), 3.

perpetuate a general contempt for Zulu culture. Particularly noticeable was the almost total ignorance of Zulu and the indifference as to acquiring it exhibited by the emigrants.[12] Settlers deigned only to acquire a hybrid version (Fanagalo) of the language.[13] Rarely was the effort made to learn proper Zulu so as to obtain a clear sense of Zulu terms and phrases. The word 'inyanga', for instance, was translated to conform with European time units; it was not seen as expressive of the lunar-seasonal phenomena of the Zulu *inyanga*. Yet such deliberate perversions or 'mis-translations', as Carl Faye an interpreter in the Native Affairs Department noted, led to most serious consequences and he cautioned that:

It is not advisable, when interpreting, to give the name of an English calendar month as the equivalent of a Zulu lunar month; the two do not begin together, nor do they end together, and besides the Zulu name is expressive in a way peculiar all to itself: then again the seasons themselves are not always identically the same each year, and a mistake in interpreting may have a very important bearing on some question or other and lead to serious consequences. *It is advisable therefore to give the original Zulu name given by a Native, and if the meaning of it be required, to ask the Native himself for it and then give it up in that way* [emphasis added].[14]

Problems also arose owing to the absence of a concept in Zulu to denote our 'year'. Take the word *uNyaka* or *umNyaka*. A. T. Bryant tells us that Europeans 'quite mistakenly' assumed this term signified 'year'. However, to the traditional Zulu the word had quite another meaning. Their annual cycle was divided into two seasons of which both had approximately six 'moons'; *uNyaka*, the rainy or field work season; and *ubuSika*, the dry or winter season. The point is *the two were entirely separate and distinct*.[15]

Two things seem fairly evident: first, it was no accident that the word denoting the time of greatest activity and importance in the Zulu work schedule was redefined to correspond with the western calendar; and secondly, few individuals were better suited to systematically undertake to corrupt the language than were missionaries who pioneered publishing works in the vernacular, including Zulu phrasebooks, dictionaries and grammars.

Religion is a vehicle for disseminating culture and in carrying forth their civilizing mission the 'soldiers of Christianity' sought, among other things, to inculcate industry, the moral of steady work. 'Our natives will not be anything', the missionary Charles Kilbon observed, 'if they do not feel the propriety and necessity of forming habits of industry and frugality, as their easy going ways do not furnish favourable soil for the Gospel'. Thus we early find individuals such as Reverend Henry Callaway resolving 'to make the Kafirs around [his mission station] feel as much as possible the value of time, labour and skill'.[16] With this plainly being a directed objective, it must have seemed entirely appropriate to stretch the bounds of the preindustrial *uNyaka* to incorporate the notion of a more stable, continuous duration of labour.

[12] Charles Barter, *The Dorp and the Veld* (London, 1852), 223–4.
[13] D. T. Cole, 'Fanagalo and the Bantu languages in South Africa', *African Studies*, XII, 1 (March 1953), 1–9.
[14] Carl Faye, *Zulu References for Interpreters and Students* (Pietermaritzburg, 1923), 52.
[15] Bryant, *The Zulu People*, 249–51.
[16] American Board of Commissioners for Foreign Mission (hereafter, ABC): 15.4, V. 10. Charles Kilbon to Judson Smith, 21 July 1884; Extracts from the Journal of Rev. Dr Henry Callaway, *Mission Field* (1 October 1859), 37.

How did this exercise in cultural engineering work itself out in practice? Consider a work-seeker being told by a settler–farmer, '*Ngiya kukutola umnyaka wonke*'.[17] Such verbal contracts in fact were constantly entered into if found mutually agreeable. A translation of the arrangement, however, reveals the rub: 'I will hire you for the whole year (twelve 'moons')', was the farmer's version of the contract. But, and this is an important 'but', to the traditional Zulu the above sentence, loosely rendered, translates: 'I will hire you for the whole of the field work season (six 'moons').' This explanation makes more meaningful the following statement (1868) by the magistrate of Alexandra: 'The period of six months continues here to be the maximum term of service, and it seems as if the kafir was [*sic*] unable to [perceive] the idea of a longer unbroken term of exertion.'[18]

In other words, often they would be at cross-purposes without their being aware of it. But sensible employers requiring a year round workforce managed to avoid labour difficulties by adopting the relay method. This involved a private arrangement between a colonist and the head of a homestead, the latter agreeing to provide a continuous, circulating supply of labour.

II

A further point of serious contention was the length of the working day. The crisis was most noticeable in commercial agriculture where 'kafir time' had a profoundly adverse effect on the development of sugar plantations.

Aside from the daily passage of the sun (*ilanga*) across the sky and the natural rotation of the seasons, the fundamental tempo and rhythms of life are dictated by, Edward Hall argues, a foundation of unspoken assumptions (primary level culture) accepted as unquestioned reality and which controls everything we do.[19] Hall's very fascinating discussion of this 'other dimension of time', leads us to a wider consideration of northern Nguni cosmography.

Zulu society provides an apt setting for this kind of analysis because their universe was filled with frightening phenomena over which they exercised little control. Intensely real and universally prevalent among the people was the belief in unseen and evil influences. They were habitually occupied with fear of being attacked by *abatakati* (witches or 'evil doers') who went about at dead of night accompanied by familiars, causing sickness and death.[20] To avoid meeting these dreaded objects the Zulu conducted their affairs in the safe light of day and refrained from going abroad at night which, we are told, was a great consolation to the small settler community that lived among them.[21]

---

[17] Posselt, *The Zulu Companion*, 8. J. L. Dohne translates umNyaka as 'Literally – a space of a year; = civil year, a period of a year': *A Zulu–Kafir Dictionary* (Cape Town, 1857), 251.

[18] Secretary for Native Affairs, Natal, File 1/3/18. Annual Report for the County of Alexandra, 14 January 1868; George Russell, *The History of Old Durban and Reminiscences of an Emigrant of 1850* (Durban, 1899), 104.

[19] Edward Hall, *The Dance of Life: The Other Dimension of Time* (New York, 1984), 3–4.

[20] C. L. S. Nyembezi, *Zulu Proverbs* (Johannesburg, 1963), 113.

[21] Axel-Ivar Berglund, *Zulu Thought-Patterns and Symbolism* (Sweden, 1976), 276–8, 286 and 364; Thomas B. Jenkinson, *AmaZulu: The Zulus Their Past History, Manners, Customs, and Language* (New York, 1969), 30; ABC: 15.4, v. 5, Josiah Tyler to Rufus Anderson, 14 February 1853.

Along with sinister spirits, natural hazards in the physical environment posed added constraints on traditional societies. In times past, to secure immunity from fever the Zulu retired to their huts before sundown, emerging in the morning when the dew was off the grass.[22] This adaptive response most probably originated in regions where malaria was endemic. Force of habit and continued belief in the efficacy of the custom may account for its eventual spread outside Zululand. But notwithstanding similar preventive strategies, homesteads in the more tropical colonial districts continued to suffer from sicknesses thought to be environmentally related.

It is important to appreciate some of this background because it helps us greatly to understand how the conventions or protective measures taken to deal with these natural and superhuman forces may have operated outside the traditional context and may have ultimately come to interfere with the industrial work regime on commercial sugar estates. Starting in 1849, the whole coastline of Natal was taken up in cane production. The plantation economy during its formative years was essentially a decentralized system which incorporated two productive processes within the ownership of one unit. One such operation was agricultural, based on the cultivation and harvesting of cane. The other was industrial involving the crushing of cane and the boiling and treatment of juice in the mill.[23]

Observations made by the successful planter Edmund Morewood raise an important point about the availability of local labour that should not be lost to view. Except at 'crop-time', Morewood asserts, the cultivation of sugar required very little hard labour, and then, as it happened, the best time for taking off the crop fell in the slack season (*ubuSika*) of the Zulu calendar when hands were most plentiful.[24] Another point well worth record and attention is that, insofar as the agricultural side of the operations was concerned, no substantial readjustments were required in the temporal bearings or the labour rhythms of the workforce. Where difficulty materialized was around the industrial aspects of the plantation which introduced a time routine that ran counter to indigenous conventions. These are facts not lightly to be minimized. For the pressing concern of Natal planters and other early employers of African labour was *not*, as commonly assumed, 'will the Kafirs work?'; rather, the big question was: *could Africans be persuaded to submit to an extension of work 'hours' beyond their customary active work day?*[25]

It seems few cane growers understood the rationale behind the peasant notion of a 'fair day's work', yet most agreed that the African's diurnal pattern of 'late' rising and 'early' retirement had a ruinous effect on the nascent industry. Roberts Babbs, proprietor of the Umlass Plantation and an individual reputedly possessing 'extraordinary skill in managing kafirs',[26] provides invaluable details regarding the peasant's disinclination to discard their traditional chronology.

---

[22] Captain Walter R. Ludlow, *Zululand and Cetewayo* (London, 1882), 99.

[23] Peter Richardson, 'The Natal sugar industry in the nineteenth century', in W. Beinart *et al.*, *Putting a Plough to the Ground* (Johannesburg, 1986), 136–7.

[24] 'A description of the farm Compensation', by Edmund Morewood, Durban, 1853, in Alan Hattersley (ed.), *The Natalians* (Pietermaritzburg, 1940), 89–91.

[25] 'Labour', *NM*, 13 June 1856.

[26] 'Mr Babbs's letter', *NM*, 5 October 1855.

It is generally known that the Kafir looks to the sun's course to regulate his hours of labour; that 'puma langa' with him, commences about an hour after sunrise, and that 'shuna langa' begins with the same time before sunset. It is difficult either to induce or compel him to work either before or after those periods of the day, which have received his arbitrary definition of sunrise and sunset.[27]

Essentially the difficulty was this. The value of time fluctuated as the cycle of sugar production passed from summer to winter season. In summer there were sufficient working hours (14 hours of daylight) to perform routine operations such as weeding, and, etc. All the heavy work however came at one time of the year – in winter with the harvesting and crushing. Once the cane was cut it was important to convey it to the mill as rapidly as possible, and then carry out the crushing immediately. Neglect at this stage could ruin the quality of the sugar.[28] At the height of the manufacturing process, from June through September when the bulk of the crop would be attempted to be secured, the average of the sun's course was ten and a half hours. Allowing the peasant's definition of a work day (as between sunrise and sunset) meant the loss of two precious daylight hours. According to Babbs, ten hours of 'good efficient labour without including meal times' were needed to perform only 'a moderate day's work'; were labourers left to persist in their habits a day's work could not be performed and a great amount of produce would be jeopardized, if not spoiled. Nor, he contended, was it unreasonable to demand ten working hours per day for in Mauritius fourteen and fifteen hours were not unfrequent, and similar working hours were customary in the West Indies.[29]

Sobering lessons were drawn from the experience of the Springfield Estate. Writing of the problems plaguing that new operation, the *Natal Mercury* reported that:

The proprietors have secured for the present a sufficient number of Kafirs for *day work*; but *it is essential to the perfect success of sugar manufacture that the operations during the season, should proceed night and day, without interruptions*; and for this purpose, it will be absolutely necessary to obtain labour of a more settled and suitable character. *The aversion of our natives to night work*, and to any work in cold weather, *as well as their peculiar social habits will for a lengthened period render it impossible to rely on their labour alone* [emphasis added].[30]

Three months later in September 1855, the *Mercury*'s lead article announced 'The Springfield Sugar Mill [had] been closed for more than a fortnight for want of labour...'[31] Babbs, in offering a counterview of Springfield's misfortunes and the problems confronting commercial farming in general, emphasized strongly that 'want of labour' was not the only nor the most important factor hampering tropical agriculture. That the industry was undercapitalized (i.e. without up-to-date machinery) and lacked the necessary organizational and managerial skills to cope with the cultural idiosyncrasies of the workforce, were all potent elements in its early failures.[32]

---

[27] 'Labour', *NM*, 13 June 1856.
[28] Hugh Tinker, *A New System of Slavery: The Export of Indian Labour Overseas, 1830–1920* (New York, 1974), 27.
[29] 'Labour', *NM*, 13 June 1856.
[30] 'A visit to Springfield', *NM*, 27 June 1855.
[31] Lead Article, *NM*, 21 September 1855.
[32] 'The Labour question', *NM*, 5 October 1855.

Here we should acknowledge their attempts to impose an industrial discipline by apportioning 'piece work'. As early as 1852 hiring by the job rather than for stated periods of service was recommended for cane cultivation. The chief argument employed for advocating such an arrangement was that parties undertaking tasks worked more satisfactorily and got through much more in less time than the usual day labour. 'It was no uncommon sight', recorded the Inanda magistrate, 'to see the labourers under this system returning from the fields by noon, or shortly after, having completed their tasks for the day'.[33] Despite such efforts to increase efficiency and attract labour onto the market, the response of Natal Africans was negligible.

The preceding discussion shows most clearly how crucial the struggle over time was for sugar plantations where the time between removing and manufacturing the crop was very short and the sheer drudgery of the tasks put an enormous strain on workers. But what also needs to be kept in view is that an independent workforce was incompatible with sugar, a crop almost invariably associated with repressive labour systems. This is why it became imperative for Natal cane growers to introduce, beginning in 1860, indentured labourers from India.

III

The situation developed somewhat differently in the urban areas. This should not, however, be taken to mean that migrant workers completely discarded their temporal identity or that no traces of it survived in the town milieu. Even in the major European centres Africans 'succeeded in their usual stolid fashion of establishing the custom of a day's work as between "sun up" and "sun down"'. Wrote Russell in 1895, 'Our initial difficulties in regulating their hours of labour have not yet been overcome, notwithstanding a half a century of experience acquired in prisons, garrisons, railways and mining camps.'[34] Throughout this period the 'kafir month' also continued to be problematic, forcing government belatedly to seek a legislative remedy. Hence for the purposes of Act 40 of 1894, the Master and Native Servant Law, a new calendar was devised wherein the twelve months were officially given an equal number of units of thirty days.[35] The reform however had only a limited impact on the diminution of time disputes. What was especially at issue was the question of cultural conversion.

Several town mission schools had by 1862 informally included in their curricula matters of common knowledge and scientific explanations of natural phenomena. At Lewis Grout's mission formal examinations in basic astronomy were conducted; and, as already noted, Reverend Callaway had determined 'to teach the value of time, labour and skill'.[36] But the conversion process was slow. This was partly owing to the migratory nature of the

[33] 'Sugar planting in Natal', *Natal Times and Mercantile and Agricultural Gazette*, 5 November 1852; Resident Magistrate Report Inanda Division, 1880, in *Blue Book for the Colony of Natal* (Pietermaritzburg, 1880), Section JJ, 101.

[34] Russell, *The History of Old Durban*, 128–9.

[35] Robert L. Hutchins (ed.), *Statutes of Natal, 1845–1899*, II (Pietermaritzburg, 1901).

[36] G. H. Mason, *Zululand: A Mission Tour* (London, 1862), 24; J. W. Colenso, *Ten Weeks in Natal* (Cambridge, 1855), 256–7; Henry Callaway's Journal, 37.

workforce; and partly because, as Hall explains, 'one of the principal characteristics of PL [primary level culture] is that it is particularly resistant to manipulative attempts to change it from the outside...Unlike the law or religious or political dogma, these rules cannot be changed by fiat, nor can they be imposed on others against their will, because they are already internalized.'[37] As a rule, then, Natal employers learned either to give way to traditional usages such as the lunar month, or do without local labour altogether.

One should not infer from this that the reaction of town workers to the new set of temporal boundaries was uniform. Quite rightly you would expect attitudes to vary from period to period and from one group to another. Hence in centres like Durban and Maritzburg it is possible to discern, one and at the same time, strenuous resistance and quite remarkable adaptive responses as well.

On coming to town the fluctuating workforce found itself caught in (to borrow Le Goff's phrase) 'a chronological net',[38] a complex fabric of merchant time, church time, leisure time controls, and so on. Along with new work routines, for example, came the regimentation of organic functions: monthly workers were obliged to alter their meal patterns to authorized intervals of breakfast, lunch and supper, a practice contrary to the traditional custom of eating twice a day, that is around 11 a.m. and 6 p.m. or dusk. Yet they did not readily yield to these efforts by management to co-ordinate job schedules. Strong attachment continued to be shown for the custom of taking meals in common. Labourers steadfastly opposed attempts to rotate meal-times, refusing to eat till all their workmates assembled 'to share in the pot'.[39]

Mornings in Zululand were ushered in by the rising of the *Ikwezi* star, around 4 a.m. But it was the music of beasts, birds and insects that engaged the immediate attention for the singing or calling was kept up the whole twenty-four hours constituting a day, by various animals, in turn, as their *time* for performing came round. Zulu folktales turned the singing and calling of birds into language. Thus the large black owl, called uMandubulu, was said to say, '*Vuka, vuka, sekusile*', 'Get up, get up, it has dawned'. About the same time the iNkovana owl would be heard to say, '*Woza, woza, woza ngikubone*', 'Come, come, come that I may see you'. And at Zulu homesteads the common cock entered the vocal competition shouting, '*Woza la! Si lapha!*', 'Come over here! This is where we are!' The first cockcrow announced the small hours of the night; the second crowing saluted the dawn.[40]

Man-made signals replaced this natural performance and aided town workers in determining their temporal bearings. Though public clock-time was established at Durban in 1860,[41] it is valid to say that many years would pass before the migrant population developed clock consciousness. Rather devices of a more utilitarian character, the most familiar being the 'time bell', regulated work and various aspects of nineteenth century urban life.

'True local time' was first recognized in 1854 when the mayor semi-officially

---

[37] Hall, *The Dance of Life*, 7.

[38] Jacques Le Goff, *Time, Work and Culture in the Middle Ages* (Chicago, 1980), 48.

[39] Russell, *The History of Old Durban*, 130.

[40] Samuelson, *Long, Long Ago*, 45–6 and 413–19; testimony of Lunguza ka Mpukane, in *Stuart Archives*, I, 322; Nyembezi, *Zulu Proverbs*, 60.

[41] Russell, *The History of Old Durban*, 495.

commenced the practice of hoisting a flag on his tall flagstaff at five minutes before nine every morning and lowering it at nine in the evening. But owing to burgessess questioning the accuracy of the time-flag led to it being given up. Under alternative arrangements the Corporation undertook to ring St Paul's cathedral bell every morning, 'precisely at nine o'clock solar time'. The bell began to chime at the hour and continued for two minutes.[42]

The practice at Maritzburg, the administrative centre of the colony and headquarters of the military, was to discharge a cannon at eight o'clock every morning – the hour when all African servants and labourers were expected to be at their work. Presently, the hour of gunfire was altered to nine but, as local lore has it, workers experienced difficulty phasing their 'inner timing mechanisms' with the new starting hour of labour. In recounting (1881) the familiar tale Bertram Mitford wrote,

[he] still persisted in sticking to the old hour, and from sheer force of habit would go to his master for his daily task. The 'baas', however, would put him off: 'Don't bother me now, come by-and-by when the gun fires!' 'What does he say?' would be the inquiry of an expectant group when their spokesman returned. 'He says "come by-and-by".' Directly the expected detonation was heard nearly every native throughout the city would exclaim 'Haow! Ubain-bai!', and betake himself to his work. The expression stuck, and forthwith the gun became ubain-bai! among the native population of Natal, extending thence to Zululand.[43]

From Russell's historical ruminations one learns further that, 'all good niggers were supposed to go to their respective places when the camp bugles recalled the military to their quarters at 9 pm'.[44]

Decisive progress towards an industrial regimen came with the imposition of the seven-day work/rest rhythm,[45] a custom transmitted throughout a large part of the world by Christianity. Sabbath-day observances therefore made it incumbent upon mistresses and masters to teach such useful notions as the 'week', the 'weekend' and the proper time sequence of 'workdays' (euphemistically termed 'weekdays'), for which there were no words in Zulu. Hence Monday came to be appropriately known to servants as 'the turning out to work-day' (*umSombuluko*); Tuesday, as 'work-day the second' (*um-Sombuluko wesibili* or *Olwesibili*); and so on till Saturday, which became 'the filling up or completing day' (*umGqibelo*). Sunday or 'church day' was *iSonto*.[46]

Influences of the weekly rhythm ran shallowest in remote country districts. Employed labour on small white farms often took advantage of the Sunday proscription to earn a few additional pence working on land occupied by Indians.[47] One group of sabbath-breakers, reproved for not keeping the Lord's Day, summed up their sentiments with the query: 'Why did not the Lord

[42] 'Time', *NM*, 7 February 1854; 'Uniformity of time', *NM*, 17 March 1853; Russell, *The History of Old Durban*, 436.

[43] Bertram Mitford, *Through the Zulu Country : Its Battlefields and Its People* (London, 1883), 148.

[44] Russell, *The History of Old Durban*, 495.

[45] For a wider discussion of the 'week' see Eviatar Zerubavel, *The Seven Day Circle : The History and Meaning of the Week* (New York, 1985).

[46] Bryant, *The Zulu People*, 256.

[47] 'Coolie masters and Kafir servants', *Natal Colonists*, 7 January 1873.

command the monkeys to keep holy the Sabbath and not on that day to rob our gardens?'[48]

The reverse of this can be seen in the towns where the growing experience was towards an outward conformity to these new points of temporal references. There are of course notable reasons for this. The urban centres presented stimulating environments, challenged traditional assumptions, and fostered change. But perhaps of even more permanent significance was the complex nature of the urban economy and the conditions of urban labour. To generalize broadly, a number of practical advantages were to be gained in recognizing the established work-week pattern, the public holidays and other structured time intervals encountered during their town sojourn. All of this and more is indicated in the fact that by 1881,[49] but the cumulative evidence suggests well before that date, segments of the cities' black labouring population were perceiving time in discrete market as well as non-economic terms – namely, regular work time, over time and leisure time.

People in the urban areas were encouraged to explore a variety of choices. In this connection it is noteworthy that not a few young men could be found who had learned to 'mark time' spent on chores so as to attend with master's permission or at their own insistence, the one hour's school each evening in the week. At Maritzburg, St. Mary's seven o'clock bell tolled the start of classes; and a 'native' service was generally held twice on Sunday – one in the afternoon at three o'clock and the other in the evening at seven.[50] Attendance however fluctuated very considerably owing to various causes, a leading one being the migratory character of the workforce which was a bar to early mission churches having any real lasting influence.

Observance of traditional holidays regularly interrupted the flow of labour; and natural rhythms continued to have an impact on work patterns and social customs. The 'moon of the new season's fruits' (*uMasingana*) was widely celebrated among Natal Zulus. While this annual festival officially opened the season of plenty, the actual abundance of foodstuffs came with the gathering in of the ripe grain from the fields, about March and April. Therefore the common practice during the first four months of the year was for large numbers of Africans to withdraw to their kraals to help with the harvest and eat green mealies. This practice lessened the amount of labour in the towns and threw extra work on those who remained.[51]

Before the advent of electricity for general consumption,[52] seasonal differences in the duration of daylight affected the length of the work day and other

[48] Methodist Missionary Society: File 317. Extracts from the Journal of Reverend Joseph Jackson, 7 January 1861. As Lunguza ka Mpukane stated, 'There was no such thing as Sunday or a day of rest in Zululand. We worked any and every day. We knew nothing of Sunday, Monday, Tuesday, etc. We heard of all this in Natal. It was incumbent on every man to work every day. Should he not work he would be asked who told him not to work'; in *Stuart Archives*, I, 339.

[49] See, for example, 'Togt Kafirs again', *NM*, 11 June 1881.

[50] United Society for the Propagation of the Gospel (hereafter, USPG): Walter Baugh to E. Hawkins, 8 May 1859.

[51] USPG: Report of D. E. Robinson, Missionary at Durban, 30 June 1873.

[52] Apart from a small electrical plant laid down in the Market Square in 1886, oil continued to be the universal method of lighting until the late 'nineties. See for example, John McIntyre, 'From settlement to city', in Allister Macmillan (ed.), *Durban Past and Present* (Durban, 1936), 51.

areas of social life. Missionaries frequently remarked that school attendance fell off with the brightening of days in summer when the general practice with householders was to put off their tea an hour or more to take a walk, or engage in some outdoor occupation while the daylight continued, a custom that kept servants on the job until between eight or nine o'clock. With the return of the colder season school attendance increased.[53]

Another factor directly contributing to irregular trends in colonial commerce was the weather. Labour demands at Durban and Maritzburg, for example, fluctuated with the overberg trade. Year after year, prior to the coming of the railways, trade with the interior during the winter came practically to a standstill. Drought, frost and grass fires destroyed the pasturage, making it impossible to work the oxen along the dusty roads. Moreover the business of the merchant middleman was subject to the accidents of wagon transport often caused by heavy rains which rendered roads impassable, thus preventing delivery of goods into the towns. Notwithstanding the erratic nature of these occupations, we are told, in slack spells 'time was by no means frittered away'. One wholesale firm managed to maintain discipline by occupying 'boys' with the job of 'wheeling sand from the billowy heaps in Smith Street to fill up the hollow at the back of the store'.[54]

Port employment was especially at the mercy of the seasons. Violent winter gales caused numerous wrecks on Durban's back-beach and frequently vessels were left riding at anchor in the roadstead because shifting bars and sandbanks blocked the entrance to the harbour. But a busy day at Port Natal usually commenced at 7 a.m. and ended at 5 or 6 p.m. From the 'eighties, and with improved shipping facilities, the industry grew more labour-intensive. During periods of increased trade, operations proceeded round the clock and on Sundays. By 1895 tiers of electric globes illuminated the wharves and permitted workers to carry on with their tasks after dark.[55] Such conditions not unexpectedly gave rise to labour unrest. That dissatisfaction is vividly seen in the rich record of industrial protest among dockhands of which time disputes were a major grievance. Most of all, the sources convey that it was through the process of defining this as well as other concerns central to their daily existence and in the course of struggling around these issues, Africans gained not only a new time sense but a greater understanding of their role in the workplace. Specifically, the disputes to which we allude were centred on demands for both the 'weekend' and Sabbath rest days.

A usage that crystallized into town custom was the Saturday half-holiday. It came to flourish in full favour at Durban in 1856 when wholesale merchants agreed they would close their places of business at two o'clock on Saturday afternoon.[56] Subsequently the hour was pushed back to one o'clock. With the early cessation of weekend business activities came the separate social timing of organized entertainment. As, for example, the whole of Maritzburg, men, women and children, black and white, turned out for the great weekly festival conducted by the military band in front of Government House; similar

---

[53] USPG: Walter Baugh to E. Hawkins, 10 October 1860.

[54] Russell, *The History of Old Durban*, 128–9; John Robinson, *A Life in South Africa* (London, 1900), 188–9.

[55] J. Forsyth Ingram, *The Colony of Natal* (London, 1895), 91; McIntyre, 'From settlement to city', 51.

[56] Russell, *The History of Old Durban*, 286.

Saturday concerts were offered by Durban's Volunteer Band on the Market Square.[57] African workers also made use of the leisure period tending to personal needs or simply relaxing in the company of friends. Of course, it would become a source of provocation when deprived of this, their 'rightful season of rest'. 'Togt' men, that is the day labourers who were heavily employed on the wharves and who frequently were compelled to work through the weekends including on Sundays, raised the loudest protest. From 1881 onwards, it is common to come upon references such as the following:

Employers of Kafir labour experience great inconvenience frequently on account of togt natives refusing to work after certain hours. They seem to be impressed with the idea that they ought not to work after one o'clock on Saturday, six o'clock during the remainder of the week, and not on Sundays at all. Masters are placed at a great disadvantage by the refusal of togt natives to work at these specified times...[58]

Since the laws regulating daily workers did not state what number of hours constituted a day's work – especially with regard to Saturday, how much labourers were entitled to for Sunday work, etc., – strike action around these questions was significant. Although generally conducted on a small scale, several major strikes did occur during this period. Such as in 1895 when 'about 200 natives, led by one over 6 ft high, in the employ of the Union Co.,... marched in a body on Saturday afternoon to the residence of Mr T. S. Alston, the Company's Durban Agent', demanding over-time pay.[59] Four years later, nine Africans appealed against the magistrate's ruling which forced them to work after one o'clock. A higher court deciding for the appellants concluded that as the 'Togt Regulations' were silent with regard to the hours of Saturday labour, daily workers were entitled to follow town custom.[60] Clearly this was an important victory for labour – employers were now obliged to pay black workers for half-holiday overtime.

One remaining observation must be added to the arguments and illustrations presented here. But first it is helpful to recall how the Zulu was deterred by fear of the *abatakati* from participating in labour and other affairs after sunset. Consistent with this aversion was their resistance to night work on sugar estates. It is therefore intriguing, given the imposing magnitude of this belief, that unlike their custom-abiding rural counterparts, town workers appear to have overcome their terror of the powers loosed in the night. What special set of circumstances or modifying influences justified the risks implied in breaching this proscription? How did urban labourers reinterpret the ancient norms to suit their altered behaviour?

Two broad categories of night-time engagements were recognized in the municipalities – that which was considered socially permissible and that which was characterized as anti-social. Subsumed under the former was night shift job work made necessary to accommodate periods of increased shipping at the Point. Large monetary inducements tempted servants, monthly employed and working daily, to hire out nightly on the docks. From these efforts by blacks to maximize their earnings, we get complaints from masters that, 'some of

---

[57] *Life at Natal a Hundred Years Ago, by a Lady* (Cape Town, 1972), 78 and 127.
[58] *Natal Advertiser* (hereafter, *NA*), 9 May 1893.
[59] 'Labour demands', *NW*, 26 November 1895.
[60] 'Native work on Saturday: Lower Court decision quashed', *NA*, 15 April 1899.

their boys after working in town till 5 o'clock went to the Point and worked till 9 o'clock or 10 o'clock, receiving something like 4 or 5s. for the night and, thus, instead of having a full blown native in the morning they had a half dead one'.[61]

In other respects the enlargement of the day to encompass late night activities constituted a problem of growing proportion. Whereas an early Durbanite could write that initially curfews were unnecessary for 'as a rule superstition and custom operated favourably in restraining Africans from being abroad after dark',[62] before the opening of the 1860s the migrant population had summoned the courage to engage not only in 'legitimate' but also 'questionable' nocturnal pursuits. Recurring throughout the documentation, decade after decade, are reports of loiterers and vagrants who nightly roamed about the towns' residential areas and suburbs. The one huge irony in all this is that the conditions creating this situation were largely of the towns' own making.

Beyond the wages earned for their day's exertion, jobbers could expect no support for their day-to-day sustenance or upkeep. Masters were neither legally committed to the extra expense of supplying rations nor were they bound to provide shelter. And in the early decades of the colonial period, except for the modest efforts of mission churches, there were no eating facilities to speak of, no public resthouses or other accommodations where, say, for a small sum, Africans could refresh themselves and find a hot meal. This was an extraordinary situation for a people accustomed to the idea of *ubuntu* (hospitality), the social quality of neighbourliness which made a *muntu* (a human being). Yet these were the dismal facts of town existence. To satisfy the basic human requirements day workers were forced to deviate from custom and to modify their ideology in a way that allowed them to retain familiar institutions while adjusting to a starkly new experience.[63]

We do not as yet possess direct African testimony regarding these matters for this period; but it may quite possibly be, as Philip Mayer found much later in his East London study, that migrants rationalized away ancient fears with the explanation that the evil power of witches was largely associated with the community at home, that in the European centres they were safe from the witch's pursuit.[64]

Whatever the combination of circumstances that 'let loose' these men upon the towns, the municipal response was to pass legislation which in effect attempted to colonize the worker's leisure time. The 9 o'clock curfew bell sounded in Maritzburg officially for the first time in 1871; three years later similar measures were instituted at Durban. These laws remain in effect today.

---

[61] 'Native labour: employers taking action', *NM*, 11 July 1902.

[62] Russell, *The History of Old Durban*, 495.

[63] For a broader discussion of this problem see Keletso E. Atkins, 'The cultural origins of an African work ethic and practices', unpublished Ph.D., University of Wisconsin-Madison, 1986, ch. 6.

[64] Philip Mayer, *Townsmen or Tribesmen : Conservatism and the Process of Urbanization in a South African City* (Cape Town, 1971), 160 and 163–4.

244   KELETSO E. ATKINS

SUMMARY

This article attempts to understand in substantive terms the nature of black proletarianization in Natal, South Africa. This is undertaken by moving beyond arid explanations of outside agencies to focus on some of the underlying cultural premises that ordered the day-to-day activities of northern Nguni communities. This article examines their temporal perceptions, exploring within the colonial context the shift from peasant to industrial time, and showing the central role mission churches played in the transition process.

Two important disclosures emerge as a result of this study. First, it conclusively demonstrates the existence of a rich history of nineteenth century African labour action (where until now the overwhelming assumption among historians has been that no such activity existed), much of which was related to the struggle over the definition of time. Secondly, it presents a more balanced picture of the migrant worker. One finds groups of labourers who continued to adhere to old attachments, while others adapted in a rather remarkable fashion to the conditions of the industrial workplace. Most striking of all, is that both were capable of dictating the terms of labour, whether they involved demands for the lunar month or the half-holiday and Sabbath rest day.

[11]

Mapping an Empire: Cartographic and Colonial Rivalry in Seventeenth-Century Dutch and English North America

Benjamin Schmidt

HOW do maps influence empires? How do the signs and symbols of geography shape the contours and circumstances of colonial expansion? Consider the case of the Netherlands—cartographers extraordinaire of early modern Europe—and England and their respective pursuits of New World ambitions.

For the better part of the seventeenth century, the Dutch Republic and England waged an inconspicuous yet nonetheless vigorous struggle over that section of America situated between the thirty-eighth and forty-second parallels, extending westward from the Atlantic coast, and referred to, variously, as New Netherland, New England, and ultimately New York. The contested land lay beyond the range of the common Hapsburg enemy and therefore invited a rivalry on terms somewhat different from others theretofore conducted in America. For much of this period, in fact, the Anglo-Dutch antagonists in the New World remained nominal allies in the Old, united in their struggle against Spanish imperialism ("universal monarchy") and reformed Catholicism ("Romish popery"). Indeed, both maritime powers plundered the Caribbean waters to their mutual profit, and both prosecuted colonial strategies at the expense of the Iberian powers in South America. Both sought easy profits in the south, while pursuing more elusive empires in the north.

Elusive, that is, for a variety of reasons, not least of which was the intensifying friction between the Dutch and English at their various points of colonial contact. Whatever the ultimate outcome of the rivalry (and the present state of colonial historiography tends to demote the role of the eventual loser), the process of colonial positioning and imperial asserting turned out to be a lively one, especially during the middle decades of the seventeenth century. The two nations had in fact never been equally balanced in the

Benjamin Schmidt is an assistant professor of history at the University of Washington. He would like to acknowledge the helpful comments received when versions of this article were presented at the annual conference on New York State History (1995) and at symposiums held at Hofstra University and the Internationales Forschungszentrum Kulturwissenschaften, Vienna. He especially thanks David Buisseret, Susan Danforth, Charles Gehring, Richard Kagan, Thomas DaCosta Kaufmann, Ineke Phaf-Rheinberger, Stuart Semmel, Pamela Smith, and Louise Townsend for their criticisms. He gratefully acknowledges the generous support of the H. F. Guggenheim Foundation and the Committee on Degrees in History and Literature at Harvard University.

New World. Though the republic's navy compared favorably with its competitor's, the English easily outnumbered the Dutch in numbers of settlers abroad. From the start, moreover, the growing population of the English majority quickly spilled onto those lands claimed by the Dutch minority. Throughout the 1630s and 1640s, hostilities flared along the southern and northern borders of the Dutch settlement, occasioning repeated demands from both parties for more clearly—and more ambitiously—enunciated expressions of sovereignty. Meanwhile in Europe, matters heated up dangerously around the middle of the century, by which time Parliament had passed the first Navigation Act (1651), deliberately designed to challenge Dutch shipping. Antagonisms erupted into full-blown war the following year, commencing the first of three major conflicts between the leading Protestant powers of seventeenth-century Europe.

It was around this time, too, that the newly instated governor of New Netherland dispatched a lengthy memoir to the States General in The Hague meant to articulate, as forthrightly as possible, the Dutch position in North America. Peter Stuyvesant, the presumed author of that memoir, was certainly no stranger to the challenges of empire, having served the Dutch West India Company for most of his adult life, first as supercargo in the West Indies (where he famously sacrificed a leg for his patrons' ambitions) and later as director general of New Netherland. Shortly after assuming the latter post in 1647, Stuyvesant drew up his "Description of the Boundaries of New Netherland"—really a position paper of sorts—concerning the extent and limits of Dutch sovereignty in North America. He aimed to set the record straight on Dutch prerogatives abroad and to preempt any further English "usurpations," as he called them, or larger-scale conflicts. For, whatever the imbalances in America, the Dutch enjoyed the right of prior possession (*jus primae occupationis*) by their governor's estimation, in recognition of their pioneering efforts in the early years of the century. From as early as the 1610s, Stuyvesant argued, the States General had chartered commercial companies to explore and settle these "uninhabited" lands, and the Dutch West India Company, founded in 1621, had taken great pains to compensate the Indians for the rights to the same. Any English claim to Dutch lands could be justifiably ignored.[1]

But where, precisely, did these lands lie and how could the governor actually prove the primacy of Dutch claims? To establish exactly that, Stuyvesant referred their "High Mightinesses" of the States—who in turn referred the English ambassador—to the oldest maps of the colonies, which clearly outlined the Dutch possessions and plainly demonstrated (so the director general maintained) the legality of the States' dominion:

---

[1] [Peter Stuyvesant], "Description of the Boundaries of New Netherland," in E. B. O'Callaghan and B. Fernow, eds. and trans., *Documents Relative to the Colonial History of the State of New York* (hereafter cited as *N.Y. Col. Docs.*), 15 vols. (Albany, 1853-1887), 1:542–46. The document was read at The Hague on Nov. 6, 1653, signed "last of February, 1651," and apparently drawn up sometime in 1649 by the governor or his officers (see ibid., 546 n. 1). It thus coincides precisely with the mid-century Anglo-Dutch hostilities.

We shall now state how long and how wide the limits of New Netherland can be asserted along the coast, inasmuch as it has been discovered and frequented by the Dutch nation, in virtue of the above mentioned [West India Company] charter, long before any of the English visited that coast, *as can be demonstrated by old maps whereon the islands, bays and rivers stand recorded by Dutch names.*[2]

These old maps—presumably attached to the memoir and ceremoniously unfurled for the regents' perusal—were intended to clinch the case by offering irrefutable geographic evidence of the Dutch-ness of New Netherland.[3] If the lands possessed Dutch names, then they must, of course, be of Dutch possession. And the maps demarcated a province unmistakably labeled New Netherland, consisting of numerous recognizably Dutch place-names: New Holland for the distinctive hook-shaped cape located along the forty-second parallel, Vlieland and Texel for the sizable islands just south of that cape, New Amsterdam for the bustling commercial port at the colony's center, Fort Nassau for the outpost situated along the colony's southern river, and so forth. Geography, in other words, and most particularly cartographic nomenclature, supported Dutch claims. A few years later, another official memoir of *"English Encroachments"* made much the same point when it confidently declared that New Netherland "was first discovered and found, in the year 1609, by the Netherlanders, as its name imports." "That this country was first of all discovered and found out by Netherlanders," the document continued, "appears also from the fact that all islands, bays, harbors, rivers and places . . . *have Dutch names.*"[4] Once again, the Dutch offered a neat, if somewhat syllogistic, argument of inherent geographic affinity and cartographic superiority. With a wave of Dutch maps—maps produced in the Netherlands yet published in multiple languages and circulated throughout Europe—Stuyvesant and the States hoped to stave off the challenge of English arms.

To those interested in creating a New World empire, maps surely mattered. Together with other tools of the geographic trade—globes, atlases, prints, paintings, travel narratives—maps provided the means to construct, no less than project, an image of power and possession abroad. No mere semblance of empire, maps furnished monarchs and merchants the very materials out of which distant empires could be fashioned. "Mapmaking," conclude J. B. Harley and David Woodward in their multivolume *History of Cartography,* "was one of the specialized intellectual weapons by which power

---

[2] [Stuyvesant], "Description of the Boundaries of New Netherland," 544 (emphasis added).

[3] Such "cartographic petitions," had been used some 35 years earlier when the Block and Hendricksz. maps arrived at The Hague (1614 and 1616, respectively; see pp. 557, 572 below) attached to requests for trading privileges in the outlined regions.

[4] "Memoir of the English Encroachments on New Netherland," in O'Callaghan and Fernow, eds., *N.Y.Col. Docs.,* 1:564 (emphasis added). The memoir was "drawn up from divers letters, papers and documents comprising the situation of New Netherland" and received by the States General on Jan. 2, 1656.

could be gained, administered, given legitimacy, and codified."[5] By means of cartography, lands could be sketched, sovereignty staked, and ambitions articulated. "Give me a map, then, let me see how much / Is left for me to conquer all the world," proclaimed Marlowe's imperial Tamburlaine. [6] All of which is not to suggest that maps alone made the empire—that the Spanish, to cite one example, could not have conquered and colonized America without cartographers to demonstrate these developments on paper. Columbus reached a world utterly new and ultimately profitable to Castile, whether he mapped it or not. Yet cartography did serve the Castilians, as it did other Europeans engaged in the drive to colonize abroad and simultaneously convince rivals at home of the legitimacy, feasibility, and enforceability of their imperial claims.

Compare, in this regard, the purpose and effect of the earliest European representations of America, the "La Cosa" and "Cantino" maps, both produced around 1500.[7] Lavishly designed and richly colored, the monumental *mappamundi* of Juan de La Cosa summarized nearly a decade of astonishing discoveries in an expanding western hemisphere. With notable cartographic daring, La Cosa's work demonstrated evidence of Columbus's Caribbean explorations, John Cabot's reconnaissance of Newfoundland, and the voyages of Alonso de Hojeda, Amerigo Vespucci, and Vicente Yáñez Pinzón along a Brazilian coast that juts dramatically eastward on the map toward Africa. Appearing some half dozen years after the Treaty of Tordesillas (1494), La Cosa's map might have been expected accurately to illustrate the agreed-upon division of the New World arranged between the kings of Spain and Portugal. Not so. Commissioned, presumably, by Castilian patrons, the La Cosa map shows a series of Spanish flags all along the southern portions, together with a smattering of English flags in the north. Place-names, by and large, celebrate Spanish princes and Italian navigators under their employ—

---

[5] Harley and Woodward, "Concluding Remarks," in Harley and Woodward, eds., *History of Cartography*, vol. 1: *Cartography in Prehistoric, Ancient, and Medieval Europe and the Mediterranean* (Chicago, 1987), 506. Mapmaking and political ideology have been the focus of Harley's considerable research into historical cartography. See, among his numerous publications, "Silences and Secrecy: The Hidden Agenda of Cartography in Early Modern Europe," *Imago Mundi*, 40 (1988), 57–76; "Maps, Knowledge, and Power," in Denis Cosgrove and Stephen Daniels, eds., *The Iconography of Landscape: Essays on the Symbolic Representations, Design and Use of Past Environments* (Cambridge, 1988), 277–312; and, esp. "Deconstructing the Map," *Cartographica*, 26, No. 2 (1989), 1–20. Theoretical issues related to what Harley calls "the cartographic discourse" are treated in R. A. Rundstrum, ed., "Introducing Cultural and Social Cartography," *Cartographica*, 30, No. 1 (1993), and a special issue on "Maps and Mapping," *Word and Image*, 4 (1988). On the topic of colonial cartography in particular see Walter D. Mignolo, *The Darker Side of the Renaissance: Literacy, Territoriality, and Colonization* (Ann Arbor, 1995), and Barbara E. Mundy, *The Mapping of New Spain: Indigenous Cartography and the Maps of the Relaciones Geograficas* (Chicago, 1996). For the 16th and 17th centuries more generally see David Buisseret, ed., *Monarchs, Ministers, and Maps: The Emergence of Cartography as a Tool of Government in Early Modern Europe* (Chicago, 1992).

[6] Christopher Marlowe, *Tamburlaine the Great, Part II*, 5.3.123–24.

[7] Both images are excellently reproduced in Jay A. Levenson, *Circa 1492: Art in the Age of Exploration* (Washington, D. C., 1991), 86–87 (Cantino), 230–32 (La Cosa).

yet exclude, as far as possible, any indication or recognition of Portuguese labors.[8]

The Cantino map, in contrast, offers the perspective of Castile's chief rival, Manuel I. Named for the Ferrarese envoy who illicitly obtained sketches for the map from the Portuguese court, this 1502 planisphere is no less elaborate than its Spanish counterpart and no less enthusiastic in its portrait of the New World. The overall effect, though, gives a distinctly different impression of the discoveries that favors the Lusitanians' deeds at the expense of Castile. Thus, although the Caribbean is recognized as "*Las antilhas del Rey de castella*," pride of place is given to Brazil—"discovered by Pedro Alvares, a nobleman of the house of the King of Portugal," as the caption reads—and to other lands placed optimistically under the banner "*del Rey de portuguall*." Portuguese flags triumphantly claim most of the enormous landmass of South America as well as the coasts of Africa and the scattered islands of the "*Mare Oceanus*." A prominent line drawn down the middle of the map does indicate how these lands, by agreement of the Iberian monarchs, rightfully belong to the Portuguese. Yet a convenient cartographic adjustment of the line and the lay of the land it demarcates allows Newfoundland and all of Greenland to fall (erroneously) within the domain of Manuel I.[9]

Imperial geography of this sort originated well before the colonial rivalries of the Renaissance, of course. We take for granted the ideological component of traditional T-O maps and the "moralized geography" that so permeated European mapmaking of the Middle Ages.[10] However inadequate their knowledge of the world, medieval Christian cartographers had reasons other than ignorance to illustrate Jerusalem as the physical as well as spiritual center of the universe. The Hereford Cathedral's mappamundi of circa 1300 represented a tripartite world as aesthetically pleasing as it was spiritually soothing. A typically circular orbis, it portrayed the three continents (Asia, Africa, and Europe) divided by three waters (the Don, the Nile, and the Mediterranean) and inhabited by descendants of the three Noahides (Shem, Ham, and Japheth). In the thirteenth-century Ebstorf mappamundi

---

[8] Kenneth Nebenzahl, *Atlas of Columbus and the Great Discoveries* (Chicago, 1990), 30–33; Harley, *Maps and the Columbian Encounter* (Milwaukee, 1990), 60–62; E. Roukema, "Some Remarks on the La Cosa Map," *Imago Mundi*, 14 (1959), 38–54.

[9] Nebenzahl, *Atlas of Columbus*, 34–37; Harley, *Maps and the Columbian Encounter*, 63–65; E. L. Stevenson, *Marine World Chart of Nicolò de Canerio Januensis, 1502 (circa): A Critical Study with a Facsimile* (New York, 1907–1908).

[10] The conventional T-O configuration portrayed the world as a floating disk engulfed by a circular (O-shaped) body of water. Through this landmass intersected three major "lines" of water running from the periphery to the center—the Mediterranean from the bottom, the Nile from the right, and the Don from the left—in the shape of the letter T. On medieval cartography see Woodward, "Medieval Mappaemundi," in Harley and Woodward, eds., *Cartography . . . in Europe*, 286–370. For a thoughtful consideration of the cartographic semiotics of this period see Marcia Kupfer, "Medieval World Maps: Embedded Images, Interpretive Frames," *Word and Image*, 10, No. 3 (1994), 262–88. "Moralized geography" is treated by Juergen Schultz, "Jacopo de' Barbari's View of Venice: Map Making, City Views, and Moralized Geography Before the Year 1500," *Art Bulletin*, 60 (1978), 425–74.

(circa 1240), Christian ideology encompasses the map just as the figure of Christ literally embraces the imagined Christian world, his face gazing serenely from Eden in the east, his arms clasping the antipodes north and south, and his feet protruding near the Pillars of Hercules to the west.[11] Ideology—religious, political, or otherwise—can be read from scores of such maps produced throughout the Middle Ages and into the Renaissance.

The advent of scientific cartography in the early modern period in no way diminished the ideological function of maps. The rediscovery of Ptolemaic charting, the development of Mercator's projection, the broadening empirical knowledge of non-European lands, as well as the improvements in printing, binding, and coloring techniques, all contributed to the stunning progress of the cartographer's craft during the sixteenth and seventeenth centuries. Yet the same overseas voyages that stimulated the advancement of geographic learning also encouraged the sort of cartographic chicanery evinced by the Cantino and La Cosa maps. Early modern mapmakers, no less than their medieval predecessors (or, for that matter, their modern successors), deftly directed their cartographic discourse to express a culturally specific geographic *Weltanschauung*. By the seventeenth century, cartographers enjoyed, if anything, better and more sophisticated means to make their case. Maps assumed an even more potent purpose in the age of empire.[12]

Nowhere is this sense of purpose more apparent than in the maps of the New World, on which European geographers celebrated the "discoveries" and empires of their patrons. And no maps of the New World, in turn, were more celebrated than those produced in the Netherlands. Dutch cartography flourished in the early modern period and especially in the seventeenth century, when the republic attained a preeminent position among European geographers. From the firms of Blaeu, Hondius, and Janssonius came the highest quality printed maps, globes, and atlases. Off the presses of Amsterdam, Leiden, and The Hague rolled a steady stream of travel narratives, exotic prints, and overseas histories. Much of this material was produced in multiple languages (including Latin) and distributed throughout Europe. In many instances, publishers outside the Netherlands crudely pirated, brazenly copied, or otherwise relied on Dutch originals to satisfy

[11] Both maps are reproduced in Woodward, "Medieval Mappaemundi," 310 (Ebstorf), 311 (Hereford).

[12] Traditional histories of mapmaking that make the whiggish case for a so-called scientific cartography—for the development, during the early modern period, of more mathematically advanced and therefore more objectively posited systems of charting—include Lloyd A. Brown, *The Story of Maps* (Boston, 1949); G. R. Crone, *Maps and Their Makers: An Introduction to the History of Cartography* (London, 1953); and Leo Bagrow, *History of Cartography*, ed. R. A. Skelton (Cambridge, Mass., 1964). For a revisionist perspective of Dutch cartography see Kees Zandvliet, *De groote waereld in 't kleen geschildert: Nederlandse kartographie tussen de Middeleeuwen en de Industriële Revolutie* (Alphen aan den Rijn, Neth., 1985), and the programmatic call to action of Harley and Zandvliet, "Art, Science, and Power in Sixteenth-Century Dutch Cartography," *Cartographica*, 29, No. 2 (1992), 10–19. Both of these latter studies take care to distinguish between the increasingly sophisticated descriptive abilities of cartographers, on the one hand, and the continued ideological function of maps, on the other hand. For revisionist approaches to the question of science and maps more generally see note 5.

local demand. The overall effect placed the republic in the enviable position of setting the geographic agenda for the rest of Europe. Dutch cartography simply dominated the field. It is no wonder, then, that Stuyvesant turned with such confidence to maps in his colonial gambit with the English.

Despite their remarkable early modern prominence, Dutch maps of America have managed largely to escape the gaze of latter-day historians. Perhaps owing to the relatively modest Dutch legacy in the West or perhaps (from the other historiographic perspective) owing to the relatively minor western presence in the republic's overseas empire, Dutch representations of North America have received surprisingly little attention, especially as they relate to the subject of European expansion and colonialism. There exist, certainly, specialized studies of individual maps and the more famous seventeenth-century Dutch atlases.[13] But most of the sources, and especially the rich cartographic materials related to New Netherland, have been typically overlooked in studies of early American history in general and the Anglo-Dutch rivalry in particular.

Overlooked, though not entirely for lack of trying. The mapping of New Netherland represents, in many ways, the high point of seventeenth-century European cartography and has drawn a degree of notice from both connoisseurs and specialists. I. N. Phelps Stokes's monumental *Iconography of Manhattan Island* offers a superb corpus of sources, carefully annotated and lovingly presented in six thick and beautifully illustrated volumes. Yet the author-collector's self-proclaimed purpose to "arrange all of the available material in strictly chronological order, and to allow the facts . . . to speak for themselves" wants much by way of cultural analysis.[14] Tony Campbell revisited some of the most important of these materials some thirty years ago in a masterly piece of carto-bibliography, although his illumination of this crucial series of maps follows Stokes's essentially Rankean vision of presenting rather than interpreting the evidence.[15] Both Campbell and Stokes

---

[13] Much of the recent work on Dutch maps has been the labor of Gunther Schilder (see especially his *Monumenta Cartographica Nederlandica* [Alphen aan den Rijn, Neth., 1986–]). Schilder has dedicated most of his efforts to the genre of world maps—large and lavish wall maps that had relatively less exposure than the smaller and cheaper maps that featured New Netherland—and to the compilation of carto-bibliographies. He has eschewed any attempt to locate the political and cultural meanings of these sources. Work on the Blaeus (father and son) has focused primarily on the business side of their cartographic enterprise. See, for example, J. Keuning, *Willem Jansz. Blaeu: A Biography and History of his Work as a Cartographer and Publisher* (Amsterdam, [1973]), and Cornelis Koeman, *Joan Blaeu and his "Grand Atlas"* (Amsterdam, 1970).

[14] Stokes, *The Iconography of Manhattan Island, 1498–1909*, 6 vols. (New York, 1915–1928), 4:ix. Compare G. M. Asher's pioneering bibliography and map list for New Netherland, *A bibliographical and historical essay on the Dutch books and pamphlets relating to New Netherland and the Dutch West India Company* (Amsterdam, 1854–1867).

[15] Campbell, "New Light on the Jansson-Visscher Maps of New England," *Map Collectors' Series*, 24 (1965). Compare William P. Cumming, *The Southeast in Early Maps . . . during the Colonial Period* (Princeton, 1958), and "The Colonial Charting of the Massachusetts Coast," in *Seafaring in Colonial Massachusetts*, Publications of the Colonial Society of Massachusetts, 52 (1980), 67–118. For a more innovative approach, which considers Indian along with European

demonstrated an overriding concern with dating the maps and arranging them as accurately as the minute distinctions between various states allowed. Both scrutinized, but only hesitatingly analyzed, their materials. Helpful as the organization of these sources may be, it hardly begins to account for their broader purpose or local influence in the seventeenth century.[16]

Yet the Jansson-Visscher series of maps, which justifiably occupied so much of these scholars' energies, performed a political, no less than a carto-graphic, role precisely in the critical period of colonial competition. They, along with other Dutch representations of America, emerge as the most broadly dispersed and, consequently, most widely recognized documents asso-ciated with the region. The Jansson prototype map—the standard carto-graphic source for New Netherland derived from the earlier maps of the Amsterdam publisher Willem Blaeu, the Leiden geographer Joannes de Laet, and, ultimately, the unheralded navigator Adriaen Block—formed the basis for the next half century's charting of New Netherland and New England. Variants of the map were printed repeatedly in the Netherlands, disseminated in countless European atlases, geographies, and mariners' guides, and revived in England, of all places, where the reworked plates served well into the eigh-teenth century. The all-important Jansson-Visscher series set the terms for the way seventeenth-century Europe illustrated, visualized, and disputed the region variously called New Netherland, New England, and New York.[17]

place-names, see Peter Benes, ed., *New England Prospect: Maps, Place Names, and the Historical Landscape,* Dublin Seminar for New England Folklife (Boston, 1980).

[16] More recently, a number of self-consciously revisionist studies have placed Dutch maps in the context of (New) Netherlandish culture—though with mixed results. The sources of 17th-century geography are perceived by Svetlana Alpers, *The Art of Describing: Dutch Art in the Seventeenth Century* (Chicago, 1983), 119–68, as reflecting typically Dutch patterns of representa-tion and thus indicative of a "mapping impulse" in early modern Dutch culture. Yet Alpers regards cartography mainly as an exercise in meticulous observation, contending that Dutch maps of the New World offered "a detached or perhaps even a culturally unbiased view of what [was] to be known in the world" (p. 163). Rather than read these sources for evidence of colo-nial ideology, Alpers discerns only a peculiar "realism"—virtuoso feats of description and verisimilitude—that she considers an ideological end in and of itself. Donna Merwick makes maps central to her innovative study of colonial New York, *Possessing Albany, 1630–1710: The Dutch and English Experiences* (Cambridge, 1990), identifying a number of important manu-script maps to elucidate a crucial chapter of Albany's history. Yet Merwick directs her carto-graphic gaze only toward intra-Dutch conflicts of the early 17th century and—surprisingly, given the comparative aims of her study—leaves out all discussion of English maps or even Dutch maps produced at the height of their colonial rivalry. Merwick contends, moreover, that the English controlled the "interpretation of the land" (p. 286), a conclusion that could only be reached by ignoring the crucial cartographic sources of the mid-17th century. Patricia Seed rightly emphasizes the Dutch use of maps in claiming possession of their New World territo-ries, in *Ceremonies of Possession in Europe's Conquest of the New World, 1492–1640* (Cambridge, 1995). Yet Seed pays relatively less attention to maps—as source material and evidence—than to cartographic nomenclature appearing in written accounts, and she does not discuss any of the major mid-17th-century maps (e.g., of Blaeu, Janssonius, or Visscher). She may also underesti-mate the degree to which the English cared about the signs and symbols of geography—a point discussed below.

[17] The southern reaches of the region under consideration received briefly the name "Nya Swerige" (New Sweden) during Chancellor Axel Oxenstierna's short-lived colonization in America (1638–1655). The name never enjoyed much cartographic notice, however, appearing

These terms, there can be no doubt, were distinctly Dutch—the Netherlandish nomenclature established on the old maps to which Stuyvesant referred and to which the English (as will become apparent) strongly objected. The Jansson prototype dates from roughly the same period as Stuyvesant's memoir, though it started to take shape three or four decades earlier, when the Dutch first began to visit—and chart—the region. Block's figurative map of 1614 (Figure I) established the outlines of the region and the major points of geographic reference. The name "Nieu Nederlandt" appears here for the first time and designates the entire region from the fortieth to the forty-fifth parallel (from present-day New Jersey to northern Maine) and from the Atlantic coast to the appositely named Great River of New Netherland ("Groote Riviere van Nieu Nederlandt").[18] The river to the south and west receives the name of the then-stadholder, Prince Maurits ("Mauritius Rivier"), while the hooked peninsula in the center of the map pays tribute to the States General with the title "Staten Hoeck" (compare, too, "Staten Bay" for present-day Cape Cod Bay). With these and other names, Block dutchified the landscape much the way his rival, Captain John Smith, later sought to anglicize the area he had baptized New England. It was in the preface to his 1616 map of New England, after all, that Smith famously invited his royal patron "to change [the] Barbarous names, for such English, as Posterity may say, Prince Charles was their Godfather."[19]

In this colonial name game, however, the Dutch surely enjoyed greater success than the English. The process of patriotic cartography begun by Block continued over the ensuing years, primarily through the voluminous output of Blaeu. Blaeu's popular *Paskaart van Guinea, Brasilien en West Indien* (circa 1617; see Figure II) retains much of the nomenclature of Block's chart, though on it Mauritius Rivier and Staten Hoeck frame a flamboyant coat of arms of the United Provinces that decorates an expansive "New Netherland." Blaeu, moreover, spread the name and the news of the Dutch colony in numerous reprints of the map, included in the printer's vast stock of maritime atlases and in copies by his competitors for their own atlases. Nearly identical maps appeared at the address of Jacob Arentsz. Colom and Anthonie Jacobsz., two of Amsterdam's leading publishers of sea charts in the middle decades of the seventeenth century.[20] Blaeu's workshop also put

most famously on a Swedish map published, after the fact, in Thomas Campanius Holm, *Kort beskrifning om provincien Nya Swerige uti America som nu förtjden af the Engelske kallas Pensylvania* . . . (Stockholm, 1702).

[18] This was the extent of the area for which a cartel of Amsterdam merchants—those who had originally commissioned Block's expedition and map—had petitioned the States General for the exclusive right to trade. Compare "Resolution of the States General on the Report of the Discovery of New Netherland," in O'Callaghan and Fernow, eds., *N.Y.Col. Docs.*, 1:10, and Simon Hart, *The Prehistory of the New Netherland Company* (Amsterdam, 1959). Block's "Groote Riviere van Nieu Nederlandt" designated, approximately, the St. Lawrence and Ottawa Rivers.

[19] Smith, *A Description of New England* . . . (London, 1616), in Philip L. Barbour, ed., *The Complete Works of Captain John Smith (1580–1631)*, 3 vols. (Chapel Hill, 1986), 1:309, and compare 1:319–20.

[20] Colom, *Pascaert van Guinea, Brasilien en West Indien* (1631); Theunis (Anthonie) Jacobsz. *Pascaert van Guinea, Brasilien en West Indie* (c. 1650). For a complete list of derivative

FIGURE I

Adriaen Block, *Figurative Map of New Netherland*, 1614. This map may represent a contemporary copy of Block's original manuscript map, which was submitted to the directors of the Dutch West Indian Company in 1614. Courtesy of the Algemeen Rijksarchief, The Hague, Netherlands.

MAPPING AN EMPIRE   559

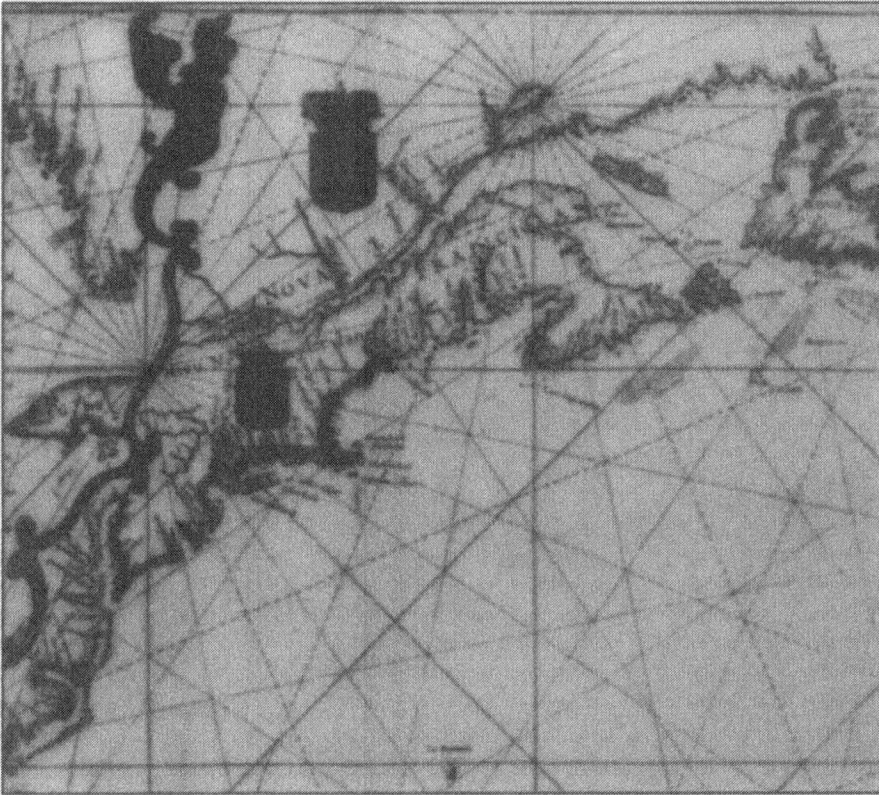

FIGURE II

Willem Jansz. Blaeu, *Paskaart van Guinea, Brasilien en West Indien,* circa 1617
(detail). The larger *paskaart* (or nautical chart) from which this detail derives
shows the eastern coastline of North and South America to Rio Plata, together
with a section of the coasts of Peru, Guinea, and northwest Africa above the
equator. Note the (darkened) arms of the United Provinces covering present-
day New England. Courtesy of the I. N. Phelps Stokes Collection, Miriam and
Ira D. Wallach Division of Art, Prints, and Photographs, New York Public
Library, Astor, Lenox, and Tilden Foundations.

out globes that, from 1622, bore the name New Netherland, and these too
were reproduced by other geographers and circulated around the staterooms
and studies of Europe. Finally, Blaeu's *Paskaart van Guinea* served as the
basis for a more elaborate, decorative map dedicated exclusively to the region

maps see Stokes, *Iconography of Manhattan Island,* 2:138. For more on Colom, Jacobsz., and their
enormous stock of maps see Koeman, comp. and ed., *Atlantes Neerlandici. Bibliography of
Terrestrial, Maritime and Celestial Atlases and Pilot Books, Published in the Netherlands up to 1880.*
6 vols. (Amsterdam, 1967–1985), 4:119–51 (Colom), 223–65 (Jacobsz.).

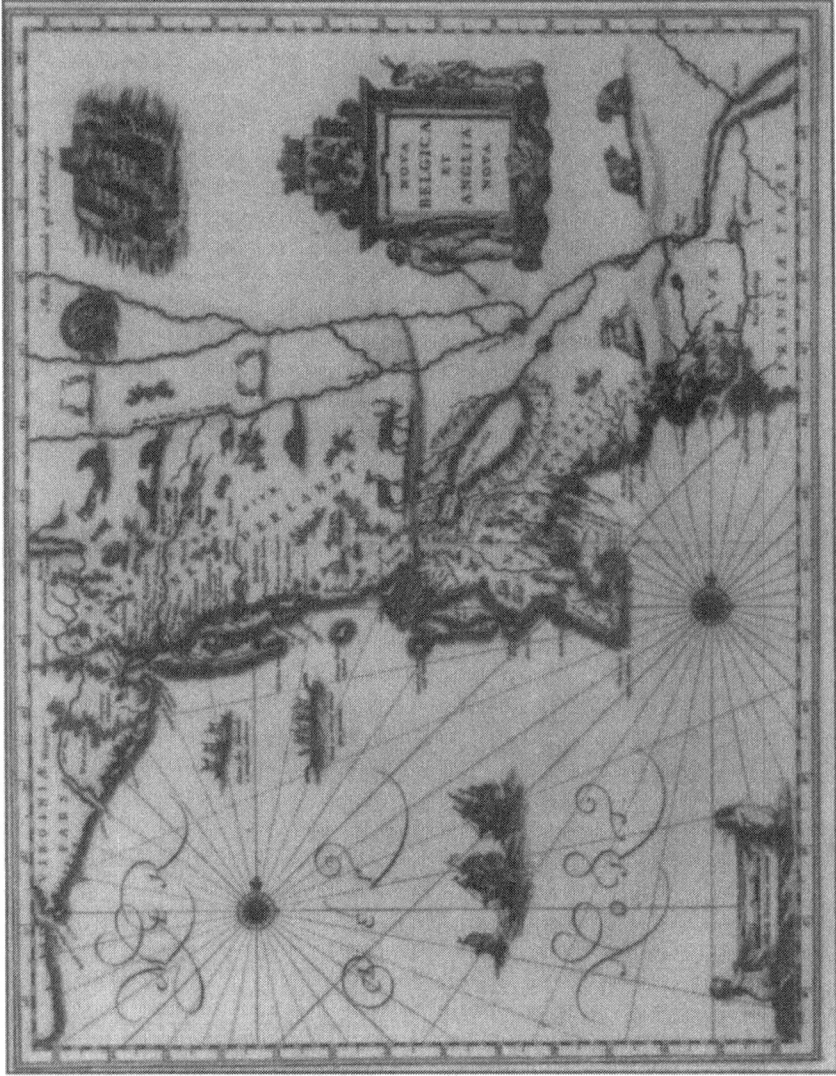

FIGURE III

Willem Blaeu, *Nova Belgica et Anglia Nova*, 1635. The map is oriented east-west (the top of the map is west), a practice not uncommon in premodern cartography. Courtesy of the John Carter Brown Library at Brown University.

of New Netherland—the first such published source of its kind (Figure III). By 1635, when this work first appeared in print, Blaeu could hardly ignore "New England"—by now much more populous and extensive than New Netherland—and his map accordingly carries the title, *Nova Belgica et Anglia Nova*. Belgica gets priority, however—a distinction emphasized by the crowned arms of the United Provinces perched above the cartouche. Ships in the Atlantic bear tricolor Dutch flags (these are engraved with three stripes and would have been tinted red, white, and blue by a colorist), and three Indian canoes approach the Dutch port, here labeled New Amsterdam.[21] By now, the fame of New Netherland had spread: "a beautiful country on Florida adjoined / Is with the sweet name of *Netherland* coined," wrote the Dutch humanist, diplomat, and jurist Hugo Grotius.[22] Blaeu made that "sweet name" yet further known by publishing his map repeatedly throughout the century, on its own and in the multiple and multilingual editions of his renowned *Grand Atlas*.[23]

These maps and that of the Leiden geographer de Laet—included in his authoritative *Nieuwe Wereldt* (1630) and in the Latin and French editions that soon followed—set the stage for the appearance of Joannes Jansson's much copied prototype.[24] Once again, and perhaps still more emphatically, New Netherland is cast in the spotlight. In the first state of the map, dated 1651, a modest cartouche in the lower right corner displays a simple Dutch coat of arms (Figure IV). In the second version, by Nicolas Visscher (1655), an elaborate vignette features a view of New Amsterdam (inset) with a Dutch flag raised proudly above the fort (Figures V, VI). The province "New Netherland" is positioned prominently on the map; the viewer's eye follows the compass lines and the scattered vessels on a direct course to the

---

[21] Blaeu's image of harmonious Dutch-Indian commerce—from the European perspective, the meeting of ships and canoes added up to trade—resembles a similar image in the so-called Hartgers View. Published originally by Joost Hartgers in his *Beschryvinghe van Virginia, Nieuw Nederlandt, Nieuw Engelandt, en d'Eylanden Bermudes, en S. Christoffel* (Amsterdam, 1651), though depicting an earlier scene of c. 1626–1628, the Hartgers engraving portrays the fort and settlement of New Amsterdam with 4 Indian canoes and an equal number of Dutch-flagged ships (plus an indeterminate rowboat) off the shore of lower Manhattan. By implying a relaxed and mutually beneficial relationship—the number and location of the vessels are very carefully balanced—the Blaeu map and the Hartgers engraving suggested, rightly or not, an easy alliance between the Dutch and the Indians. In the context of early Americana, these images also insinuated a distinction between the Dutch experience in the New World and that of other colonial powers—notably England and Spain—who suffered notoriously from their poisoned relations with the Indians. The Hartgers View appears in Stokes, *Iconography of Manhattan Island*, 1: plate 1.

[22] Grotius, *Bewys van den waren godsdienst* (n.p., 1622), "*Waervan een schoon landouw met Florida belend / Werd met den soeten naem van Nederland bekend.*"

[23] On the *Grand Atlas*, its dissemination, and the larger publication project of the Blaeu family see Keuning, *Willem Jansz. Blaeu*, and Koeman, *Joan Blaeu*.

[24] De Laet, *Nieuwe wereldt oft Beschrijvinghe van West Indien* (Leiden, 1630). The Latin edition appeared in 1633 and the French followed in 1640, thereby assuring the widest possible European audience for de Laet's map as well as the determinedly Dutch nomenclature that distinguishes the text. De Laet, who was himself a director of the WIC, patroon of New Netherland, and proprietor of "De Laetsburg" on the Hudson, gave what can best be characterized as the company line in his various works of geography that dealt with New Netherland.

heart of the Dutch settlement. This lies on what the cartographer now labels the Great River, offering the alternatives of Manhattan, North, Montaigne, and Maurits River.[25] What the English insisted on calling the "De la War[e] Bay" appears on this map as the "South River"—south, that is, of New Netherland, though obviously north from the perspective of Virginia. At the mouth of this river can be found "Fort Nassau."[26] "Staten Hoeck" refers to the tip of the cape now dubbed New Holland, beneath which are those islands of famously Dutch names: Vlieland, Texel, Hendrick Christiansz., and Block.[27] Even the engraver's typography colludes in emphasizing the Dutch domains. Bold roman letters in the middle of the map announce the Dutch colony; New England, meanwhile, is spelled out in italic and marginalized, literally, to the upper right corner. (Much the same happens to "Virginia," in the lower left corner, though "Nova Francia" is placed somewhat more visibly beneath the town of Quebec.) The Jansson-Visscher map, perhaps better than any diplomatic mission, made a persuasive—not to mention propagandistic—case for the place of the Netherlands in North America. A none-too-subtle attempt at cartographic coercion, it bestowed New Netherland, graphically, on the Dutch.

To this cartographic offensive, the English responded defensively at best. Much to their chagrin, they had little success in mapping the region or propagating their geographic views. It was not quite that the English lacked altogether a cartographic tradition. Edward Wright's "improved" Mercator projection had famously inspired Shakespeare's sense of physiognomy: "He does smile his face into more lynes then are in the new Mappe with the augmentation of the Indies."[28] Nonetheless, England's relatively limited experi-

[25] "Groote Rivier of Manhattans R.[,] Noort Rivier[,] Montaigne Ri.[,] Maurits Rivier"—also known today as the Hudson River.

[26] An alternative Dutch name for the Delaware, the "Wilhelmus Rivier," after William of Orange, appears on a manuscript map of c. 1640 by the Utrecht antiquarian Aernout van Buchel (who had a financial interest in the WIC) and again in David de Vries, *Korte historiael ende journaels aenteyckeninge van verscheyden voyagiens in de vier deelen des weereldts-ronde, als Europa, Africa, Asia, end America gedaen* (Hoorn, 1655); compare Stokes, *Iconography of Manhattan Island,* 2:111. Thus the two major rivers of the Dutch colony went by the names "South" and "North" or by the more princely titles "Wilhelmus" and "Mauritius." It is not altogether clear if these alternatives represented rival republican and royalist nomenclature—to parallel, perhaps, Statist and Orangist political rivalries in the United Provinces. In all cases, the names were decidedly Dutch. Van Buchel, it is worth adding, referred to New Netherland on a separate occasion as "Colonia Batavica," using a name otherwise associated with the major Dutch fort in the East Indies, Batavia, now known as Djakarta (see Stokes, *Iconography of Manhattan Island,* 4:944).

[27] Nantucket, Naushon, Martha's Vineyard, and Block Island, respectively, though the size and location of these islands is rather inaccurate and conjectural.

[28] Shakespeare, *Twelfth Night,* 3.2.78–80. Note, however, that Wright's *Certaine errors in navigation* (London, 1599), which posed a direct challenge to Mercator, does not actually carry maps. The so-called Wright map did come out eventually in Richard Hakluyt, *Principal Navigations, Voyages, Traffiques, and Discoveries of the English Nation* (London, 1598–1600), yet it was engraved by the Dutch cartographer Hondius, who had published a version of the map one year earlier in Amsterdam.

FIGURE IV

Joannes Jansson, *Belgii Novi[,] Angliæ Novae, et Partis Virginiæ Novissima Delineatio*, circa 1651. Though engraved with far greater topographic detail than Blaeu's *Nova Belgica*, Jansson's map relied heavily on many of the decorative features of the earlier work—most notably, the flora and fauna and the vignettes of native life. Courtesy of the John Carter Brown Library at Brown University.

ence in engraving, printing, and disseminating maps meant that it could hardly compete with the thriving cartographic trade of Amsterdam.[29] By comparison, English printed maps of America were inadequate: limited, derivative, or just plain inferior. Smith's maps prevailed for much of the cen-

[29] The literature on Dutch cartography is voluminous. Excellent surveys include Koeman, *Geschiedenis van de kartografie van Nederland: Zes eeuwen land- en zeekaarten en stadsplattegronden* (Alphen aan den Rijn, Neth., 1983), and Zandvliet, *De groote waereld*. See also two outstanding works of reference: Peter van der Krogt, Marc Hameleers, and Paul van den Brink, *Bibliografie van de geschiedenis van de kartografie van de Nederlanden* (Utrecht, 1993), and Koeman, *Atlantes Neerlandici*. On English efforts see Sarah Tyacke, ed., *English Map-Making, 1500–1650: Historical Essays* (London, 1983); Norman J. W. Thrower, ed. *The Compleat Plattmaker: Essays on Chart, Map, and Globe Making in England in the Seventeenth and Eighteenth Centuries* (Berkeley, 1978); and P.D.A. Harvey, *Maps in Tudor England* (London, 1993).

FIGURE V

Nicolas Jansz. Visscher, *Novi Belgii Novæque Angliæ nec non Partis Virginiæ Tabula,* circa 1655. This exceedingly rare first state of Visscher's map copies many of the features of the Jansson map, inverting in the process some of the distinctive decorative detail (e.g., the prominent turkey strutting in the vicinity of what would become Worcester, Massachusetts). Courtesy of the John Carter Brown Library at Brown University.

tury, shaping most Britons' perception of their chief American colonies. Yet his map of New England (1616), despite its author's unbridled ambition, limited itself to the area north of Cape Cod (Figure VII). Likewise, the widely publicized map of Virginia (1612) kept cautiously to the south of the Chesapeake (Figure VIII).[30] Samuel Purchas, perhaps the greatest geographer of seventeenth-century England and no friend of the Dutch, had to rely almost exclusively on Amsterdam cartographers to illustrate his epic

[30] The map of New England inserted into Smith's *Description of New England* was drawn and perhaps engraved by Simon van de Passe (son of the well-known Dutch engraver Crispijn van de Passe) and based on sketches made in situ by Smith. *The Map of Virginia* (Oxford, 1612) is the work of William Hole based on cartographic materials provided by Smith and decorative figures taken from the Flemish engraver Theodor de Bry and published originally in Thomas Hariot, *A briefe and true report of the new found land of Virginia* (Frankfurt am Main, 1590).

FIGURE VI

Detail of Figure V. This early view of New Amsterdam dates from 1650–1653.
Note the tri-striped Dutch flags on the ship and raised above the settlement's
fort. Courtesy of the John Carter Brown Library at Brown University.

Hakluytus Posthumus, or, Purchas his Pilgrimes.[31] A notable exception is *The
North Part of America* (Figure IX), attributed to Henry Brigges yet copied, in
all likelihood, from an anonymous map printed in a Dutch volume of the
previous year.[32] John Speed's 1626 atlas, *A prospect of the most famous parts of
the world,* carried maps by Amsterdam engravers and other prints simply
lifted or copied from Abraham Ortelius and Blaeu. For the map of America,
Blaeu's lines were retraced by Abraham Goos, an Amsterdammer, who
replaced Dutch nomenclature with English to the best of his ability. The
results are neither terribly convincing nor compelling.[33]

None of these maps considered directly the area encompassed, and the
problem posed, by "New Netherland." That took until the 1670s, by which
time the English controlled both the colony itself and the engravers' plates to

[31] Purchas, *Haklytus Posthumus* (London, 1625). For the editor's antagonisms toward the
republic see the scurrilous "Note Touching the Dutch" (addressing the "terrible tragedie of
Amboyna") that follows the wildly patriotic "Epistle Dedicatorie," devoted to the theme of
England's imperial ascendance.

[32] The Purchas map is signed "R: Elstracke sculpsit" and derives almost certainly from a
map published in Athanasius Inga's Dutch-language *West Indische Spieghel* (Amsterdam, 1624)
or, perhaps, from an unidentified third map on which the other two are based. The second map
of America included by Purchas is Hondius's "Americae descrip[tio]." It was printed in its original, somewhat outdated form—dating from the early 17th century, well before either the
English or the Dutch began seriously to settle North America—and it noncommittally calls the
region nearest New England "Norumbega." The vessels that decorate the seas surrounding
America fly Dutch flags, however, lending a distinctly Netherlandish flavor to the map.

[33] Speed's "world" atlas, the first ever to bear an English name on the title page, followed
the atlases of Ortelius and Mercator by over a half century. "Thus," writes Skelton, "the substantial demand for printed maps in England in the late 16th and early 17th centuries was
mainly supplied by the great cartographic industry of the Netherlands." See the
"Bibliographical note" in the facsimile edition of Speed's *A prospect of the most famous parts of
the world,* ed. Skelton (Amsterdam, 1966), v.

FIGURE VII

John Smith, *New England,* 1616/7. This is the fourth state of a map that first appeared early in 1617 (New Style), right after Smith (b. 1580) had turned thirty-seven and just before the close of the year 1616 (Old Style), which ends in March (thus "*Ætatis* 37, *Anno* 1616"). It is based on Smith's own sketches, though the printer, George Low, availed himself of the services of the Dutch engraver Simon van de Passe for the actual drawing of the map (see bottom left). Courtesy of the John Carter Brown Library at Brown University.

portray it. The 1676 edition of Speed's *Prospect* included, for the first time, *A Map of New England and New York,* very similar in appearance to the Jansson prototype (Figure X). The Stuart arms now crown the cartouche, and most of the nomenclature is likewise adjusted in deference to the new regime. The leading Restoration geographer, John Seller, brought out a *Mapp of New Jarsey* following the grant of that province to the staunch royalist Sir George Carteret (Figure XI). Neither a cartographer nor an engraver of much skill, Seller later published his maritime atlas, *The English Pilot,* "from old worn Dutch plates," as Samuel Pepys reproachfully put it.[34] The map of New

34 Another 17th-century English atlas, Peter Heylyn, *Cosmographie* (London, 1652), contains a confusing map, "Americae. Descriptio nova," that sandwiches "No: Belgeum" between

FIGURE VIII

John Smith, *Virginia,* 1612. This represents the ninth state of a map engraved originally by William Hole. It corresponds to the region depicted in the lower left corner of the Jansson prototype. Courtesy of the John Carter Brown Library at Brown University.

Jersey, too, derives from Dutch models, its decorative elements borrowed directly from the Jansson-Visscher series. An inset in the upper right corner depicts the former town of New Amsterdam, now relabeled New York.

Published sometime during the early years of English control (circa 1664–1674), Seller's map represents one of the quickest and most direct

---

Maryland and Virginia, slightly to the west of the Chesapeake. In the text describing "Novum Belgium," the author popularized the tale of Hudson's English commission—of the navigator exploring the North American coast originally under orders of the English crown. It further implies that the Dutch colony, in its earliest years, recognized this fact (and English claims to the region) by submitting to Capt. Samuel Argall, "Governor of Virginia," in 1614. A later Dutch official, according to Heylyn's version of events, went ahead and violated English sovereignty by "[giving] unto the country the name *New Netherland,* conferr[ing] new names on all the Bays and Rivers of it." In attacking the "new names" of the Dutch, the author thus indicates a prior state of more legitimate English (or, conceivably, Indian) geographic nomenclature. See Heylyn, *Cosmographie,* III, as well as Beauchamp Plantagenet, *A Description of the Province of New Albion* ([London], 1648), 17, which similarly recounts the Argall adventure and speaks of the role of "[Dutch] Maps and printed Cards, calling this part *New Netherland.*"

FIGURE IX

Henry Brigges (attrib.), *The North Part of America,* 1625. Note this very early usage of "Hudsons R[iver]" in print for what Block and Blaeu had already dubbed "Mauritius Rivier." Courtesy of the John Carter Brown Library at Brown University.

responses of London cartographers to the capture of New Netherland.[35] It pales, though, in comparison to the brilliantly triumphant and fabulously presumptuous *Totius Neobelgii Nova et Accuratissima Tabula,* which appeared at the Amsterdam address of Hugo Allard shortly after the recapture of the colony by the Dutch in 1673 (Figure XII). The map's baroque cartouche, coupled with the famous "Restitutio" view of New Amsterdam (Figure XIII), declare grandiloquently the restoration of Dutch power—however brief—to the province. A victorious Athena (goddess of war and peace, guardian of

---

[35] The map is dated 1664 by Stokes—the year of Charles's royal grant (*Iconography of Manhattan Island,* 1: 213–16). Jeannette D. Black questions this dating, however, based on the map's resemblance to Augustine Heerman's *Virginia and Maryland* (1673), which Seller offered for sale in 1674 (William Blathwayt, *The Blathwayt Atlas: A Collection of 48 Manuscript and Printed Maps of the 17th Century Relating to the British Overseas Empire . . . ,* 2 vols., ed. Black, [Providence, R. I., 1970–1975], 2: 88–92.) Black's dating of c. 1674 is not entirely convincing either, though, and the best that can be said is that the map dates from the first decade of English control—probably between 1664 and 1673—making it, in any event, one of the first published responses by English mapmakers to the Dutch cartographic claims to the region.

FIGURE X

John Speed, *A Map of New England and New York*, 1676. Though much of the Dutch nomenclature from the earlier maps has been deleted by the English engraver, Francis Lamb, certain names persist, especially along the upper Hudson. Note also how Charles II's arms crown a cartouche remarkably similar in form to that of the circa 1651 Jansson map. Courtesy of the John Carter Brown Library at Brown University.

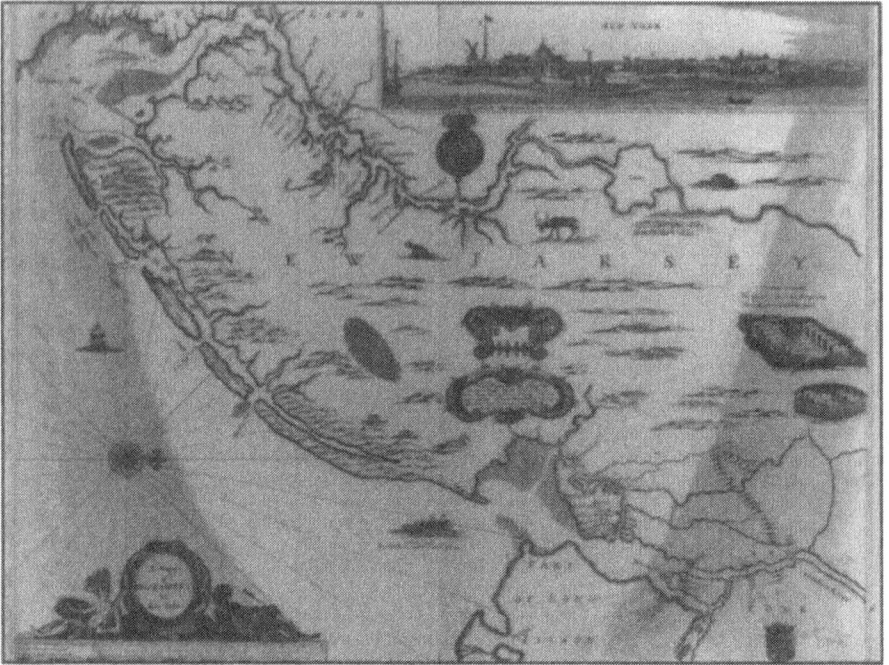

FIGURE XI

John Seller, *Mapp of New Jarsey*, circa 1664–1674. The view of what is now called New York comes from the Visscher map, and many of the decorative details are taken directly from the Jansson prototype. Courtesy of Yale Center for British Art, Paul Mellon Collection.

cities) stands amid her supplicants, Indian and European, with a laurel wreath in her outstretched hand. Meanwhile, Hermes, god of commerce and messenger to the Olympians, tilts his caduceus in the direction of tribute-bearing Indians. Much of the rest of the map resembles the more elaborate later states of the Jansson-Visscher series. Yet added to the "Mar del Nort" and placed conspicuously above the heads of the gods (and the female figure on the left, who appears to represent the iconic Maiden of Holland), one can make out the fleet of Cornelis Evertsen, speeding decisively toward victory off the shores of New Amsterdam. One of the finest examples of seventeenth-century cartographic art, the Allard map demonstrates just how effortlessly the Dutch could outmap the English.[36]

---

[36] Seller, *The English Pilot, The First Book* (London, 1671), represented, according to Coolie Verner, "the first major sea-atlas produced in England" after decades of dependence on Dutch products. The success of this work relied, nonetheless, on a royal privilege granted in 1671 that protected the "hydrographer to the King" for a period of 30 years from all continental—read Dutch—competitors. See the "Bibliographical note" to the facsimile edition; Seller, *The English Pilot, The Fourth Book*, ed. Verner (Amsterdam, 1967), v.

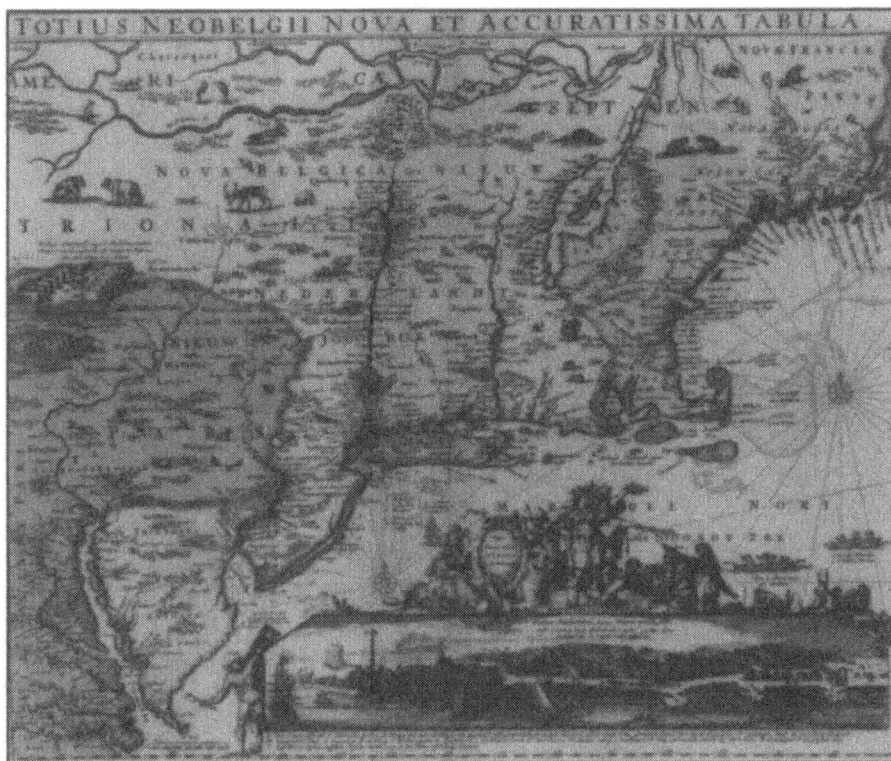

FIGURE XII

Hugo Allard [J. Ottens], *Totius Neobelgii Nova et Accuratissima Tabula*, after 1682. This sixth state of the Allard map (fifth to show the "Restitutio" view) carries the imprint of Joachim Ottens and appeared after the Dutch colony had reverted to the English. Note, among the half dozen changes made by Ottens, the addition of Philadelphia on what Allard (circa 1673) had called the "Zuydt Rivier of [or] Delaware." Courtesy of the John Carter Brown Library at Brown University.

Did any of this matter? Did it bother the English that their Dutch rivals consistently outmaneuvered them in the imperial contest of geography? In a very practical sense, it mattered quite a bit, because maps played an important part in colonial diplomacy, employed in the settlement of border disputes, the negotiation of treaties, and the like. Stuyvesant, recall, referred to "old maps" of the colony—perhaps those of Block or his fellow navigator Cornelis Hendricksz.—when he filed his memorandum to the States General around the middle of the century.[37] Another document from the States'

---

[37] An equivalent English response to such cartographic bombast came only decades after the fact. Sometime in the second quarter of the 18th century, well after the Anglo-Dutch wars, Matthias Seutter produced a "Recens edita" of the by then much outdated Jansson-Allard map with a new

FIGURE XIII

Detail of Figure XII. The "Restitutio" view of Lower Manhattan ("New Amsterdam, recently named New York," as the updated caption reads) dates presumably from sometime between August 1673 and November 1674, during which time the Dutch recaptured the colony. Courtesy of the John Carter Brown Library at Brown University.

records indicates that maps changed hands between English and Dutch ambassadors seeking to settle a boundary dispute in the vicinity of Hartford.[38] In yet another diplomatic encounter of 1659, when the Dutch envoy Augustine Heermans paid a visit to Philip Calvert, secretary to the governor of Maryland, maps were laid out between the two men as they held an after-dinner discussion regarding "our South River, called of old Nassau river," as Heermans put it.

> After the cloth was removed, [we] talked about his charts or maps of the country, of which he laid on the table two that were engraved and one in manuscript. One was printed in Amsterdam, by direction of Captain Smith, the first discoverer of the Great bay of Chesapeake, or Virginia; the second appeared also to be printed at Amsterdam, at the time of Lord Balthamoor's patent; we knew not by whom or where the manuscript was drawn. All differed, one from the other.

In this instance, negotiations proved fruitless: the Dutch matched the English argument for argument, map for map. Heermans reported that Calvert came close to losing his temper, at one point insisting on English priority in the Delaware "for it obtained its name from them." "And we answered, No," Heermans assured his superiors, convinced as he apparently was that in this case English names could be ignored.[39]

The English could not as easily ignore the products of Dutch geography, much as they tried. Well-publicized Dutch maps and nomenclature, it seems, annoyed the English, occasioning outbursts of frustration and petulant complaint. Sir Dudley Carleton, the irascible English ambassador to The Hague, alerted his patrons on the Privy Council in 1621 that the Dutch had "entered upon some partes" of what the English called Virginia "and given new names to the severall portes appertaining to that part of the countrie." "After their manner they gave their own names of New Netherlands [and] a south & a north sea, a Texel, a Vlieland, & the like," wrote Carleton indignantly.[40] In a later

---

cartouche (c. 1725–1730). It depicts a long queue of Indians and gods presenting their tribute to a seated monarch, presumably George I or II. Because Seutter signed his cartouche "Geographer to the Holy Roman Emperor" ("Sac. Caes. Maj. Geographi"), his efforts might be seen as a pro-Hanoverian gesture to the German-speaking elector rather than an unambiguously English one.

[38] Hendricksz. was among the first Dutch navigators in the region and a commander of an early settlement on the upper Hudson. He is credited with a figurative map dated 1616, reproduced in Stokes, *Iconography of Manhattan Island*, 2: plate 24.

[39] Heermans, "Journal of the Dutch Embassy to Maryland," in O'Callaghan and Fernow, eds., *N.Y.Col. Docs.*, 2:93. Heermans reported back to Stuyvesant on the meeting and actually recommended that the Dutch governor see to it that still better maps be made; the English ones (in this case) were "utterly imperfect and prejudicial to us" (A. Heermans and R. Waldron to Stuyvesant, Oct. 21/11, 1659, ibid., 99). Heermans's reference must be to the English "manuscript" map rather than to the Smith or "Amsterdam" maps. In all cases, the incident well illustrates the attention paid to cartography and the considerable efforts vested in setting the geographic terms in border disputes.

[40] Privy Council to Carleton, Dec. 15, 1621, in O'Callaghan and Fernow, eds., *N.Y.Col. Docs.*, 3:6-7; Carleton to Lords of the Council, Feb. 5, 1621, ibid., 7–8. When they did use the

report, this time directed to the secretary of state, another observer complained that the Dutch had squeezed themselves "as Interlopers" between English settlements in Virginia and New England. "At their returne of their voyage," this report continued, "certaine Hollanders" had arrogantly "published a Mapp in ye Low Countries of ye sayd sea coaste comp[re]hended betwixt Virginia and Cape Codd, undr ye tytle of New Netherlands, giving ye name of the Prince of Aurange to the countrie and river of Manahata, where the Dutch are now planted . . . and giveing other Dutch names to other places."[41]

Just as the Dutch took great care to "baptize" the landscape, in Carleton's mocking expression, the English took pains to avoid virtually all reference to their rival's names. English printed and manuscript maps, to be sure, employed English nomenclature wherever practical. When that proved absolutely impractical, though—in referring, for example, to the Dutch settlement otherwise called "New Amsterdam"—native names filled the gap. It was the "town of the Manadoes" or the "governor of Manahatan" in most English documents, official communications, and works of geography.[42] This policy allowed John Ogilby, in his translation of Arnoldus Montanus's Dutch-language *America,* to refrain from practically all mention of New Netherland. The single instance where Ogilby mustered the courage to call the Dutch colony by its Netherlandish name occurred when he described the English effacement of the same:

> Now [1664] begins *New Netherland* to lose the Name, for his Majesty having conferr'd by Patent upon his Royal Highness the Duke of *York* and *Albany,* all the Acquisitions made upon Foraigners . . . it was by him [Colonel Richard Nicolls, in the service of York] thought fit to change some principal denominations of places, viz. *New Netherland* into *York-shire; New Amsterdam* into *New York;* Fort-*Amstel* into *Fort-James; Fort-Orange* into *Albany.*[43]

---

name, the English consistently referred to "New Netherlands," though the name appears as "New Netherland" in virtually all Dutch sources.

[41] John Mason to [John Coke], Apr. 2, 1632, ibid., 16–17, and referring back to the situation of "1621 or thereabouts." In much the same vein, John Pory informed Virginia officials, in 1622, of Dutch activities to the north of the English colony and of the geographic presumptions of the Dutch: "And by the way that yow may know how stronghe the Flemmings make title from 40 to 44 degrees, they call Hudson his river Prince Maurits his river; Cape-Cod the Stakes [States] Hooke; Sagadahoc or thereabouts Prince Henricks river and the great bay . . . Grave William Bay." In the specific names to which he draws attention, Pory seems remarkably attuned to the politics of geography and nomenclature. The passage is cited in Stokes, *Iconography of Manhattan Island,* 4:50–51. (And *nota bene* the Swedish complaints, as in the "Further Memorial delivered by his Swedish Majesty's Resident, to their High Mightinesses," in O'Callaghan and Fernow, eds., *N.Y.Col. Docs.,* 2: 241, regarding Dutch pretensions expressed "by the published maps of New Netherland.")

[42] Instances abound. See, for example, Oliver Cromwell to the governors of New England (concerning matters of the "Manhattoes"), Feb. 17, 1654 (Old Style), cited in John Thurloe, comp., *A Collection of the State Papers of John Thurloe . . . ,* 7 vols. (London, 1742), 1:722.

[43] Ogilby, *America: being the latest and most accurate description of the New World* (London, 1671), 169, and compare 168–82 for the entire section on the former colony of New Netherland. The Dutch original came out in Amsterdam; Montanus, *De nieuwe en onbekende Weereld: of Beschryving van America en 't Zuid-land* (1671). The section on New Netherland, derived largely

Charles II naturally privileged English nomenclature in his official grant of the region to his brother, James. More impressive is the Stuart monarch's ability to desist completely from alluding to Dutch names or even presence in the region. Equally impressive is the speed with which Governor Richard Nicolls "erased" (the word is George Downing's) Dutch nomenclature from all records within hours of winning the colony. Though Dutch documents persisted for some years in using the old names—or such new ones as "New Orange," invented in 1673 when the republic briefly reclaimed the colony—council minutes of the English sign off from "Fort James in New York" from the outset.[44] This was unprecedented. Spain, for example, had used the name Mexico for years following its conquest of that land, and the United States had no qualms in adopting the Spanish name Florida or the French (and plainly imperialist) Louisiana when it assumed control of those territories many years later.

The seventeenth-century English, however, focused considerable energy, attention, and anxiety on the whole issue of names, maps, and geography. It was not simply that they avoided the Dutch designations; they also called into question the very process of Dutch naming, as if it were, in and of itself, an illegitimate undertaking on the part of the upstart republic. The text accompanying the "Description of the Towne of Mannadens"—a topographical view of New Amsterdam known as the "Duke's Plan"—identified a certain "Peter Stanzan" (Stuyvesant) as the governor of "Manados and New Netherland (so called by the Hollanders)": so called, since the name itself lacked authenticity.[45] Sir George Downing, English ambassador to The Hague and nephew of Massachusetts governor John Winthrop, made use of the same expression in an audacious speech to the States General in 1664. His sneer almost audible, Downing coolly dismissed "the business of the New-Netherlands (so called)" by asserting his monarch's "natural" rights of sovereignty to the region of "New-England."[46] Downing's official memorial on the colony's surrender reported more strongly how "the Duke of York hath . . . finally, by means of his soldiery" reduced the Dutch enemy and succeeded

---

from de Laet and Adriaen van der Donck, is on 123–34. Both editions carry identical maps (based on Visscher's) with Dutch nomenclature. There is also an engraving of "Novum Amsterdam" with a discernibly Dutch flag flying over what by then was an English fort (Fort James). Ogilby's work thus illustrates excellently the perils for the English of depending on the skills of the Dutch in geography, cartography, and engraving.

[44] See, for example, the very early letter of Nicolls to John Young dated Sept. 8 at "N: Yorke" and the other early documents cited in Stokes, *Iconography of Manhattan Island*, 4:244 ff., and compare *N.Y. Col. Docs.*, 3:68 ff. Also relevant is the WIC report that details the Dutch capitulation and notes how the Duke of York had caused the colony to be "reduced, captured and subjected to the English authority . . . and in addition . . . immediately called . . . by the name New York"; Michiel Ten Hove to States General, Oct. 24, 1664, ibid., 272.

[45] "Description of the Towne of Mannadens in New Netherland as it was in Sept: 1661," in J. Franklin Jameson, ed., *Narratives of New Netherland, 1609–1664* (New York, 1909), 424. The view itself is beautifully reproduced in Stokes, *Iconography of Manhattan Island*, 1: plate 10.

[46] Downing to States General, Dec. 20, 1664, in O'Callaghan and Fernow, eds., *N.Y. Col. Docs.*, 2:302. This report was twice published in London for its propaganda value, first in 1664 as *A discourse: vindicating His Royal Master from the insolencies of a scandalous libel* and then in 1672, on the occasion of the third Anglo-Dutch War, as *A discourse written by Sir George Downing, the King of Great Britain's envoy extraordinary to the States of the United Provinces*.

thereby "to erase the name of New Netherland from the map."[47] These were fighting words indeed, and if the English and Dutch did not ultimately wage their battles over the maps themselves, geography and the potent symbols on which it was based remained much on the minds of those who orchestrated the diplomatic wars and formulated the terms of surrender.

It would be difficult to contend that cartography, in the final analysis, instigated imperial expansion and motivated colonial wars. Maps naturally were not the sole or even preeminent cause of the Anglo-Dutch conflicts. Fierce economic rivalries, stubborn colonial jealousies, and irreconcilable ideological differences all contributed to the steadily worsening relations between Europe's leading Protestant powers. And Dutch maps, it should also be stressed, were not designed solely to antagonize the English. Both Blaeu's *Nova Belgica* (1635) and Jansson's prototype map (1651) paid prominent enough attention to Indians—depicted in canoes that navigate the Atlantic, in the vivid vignettes that fill the hinterland, and in the decorative borders of the cartouche—to suggest a somewhat different, though not necessarily contradictory, semiotic subtext. These favorable and frankly optimistic renderings of the native population followed a long history of republican propaganda predicated on the idea of a Dutch-American alliance to challenge the hegemony of Spain. Maps, together with scores of political pamphlets, promoted an image of eager Indian partners in the New World.[48] Finally, the products of Dutch cartography also had an obvious decorative function. Engraved maps, commonly colored and framed, hung prominently in well-to-do burgers' homes. Maps, like books, do furnish a room.[49]

Yet none of these other purposes in any way diminishes the obvious political—anti-English—purpose of seventeenth-century Dutch cartography. Again and again, maps appeared in official records, Dutch as well as English, as points of colonial contention. Time after time, geographic nomenclature and cartographic configuration provoked sharp disagreement. Maps exercised Ambassador Downing no less than Governor Stuyvesant, if for entirely opposing agenda.

In the end, the Dutch and English very nearly did come to blows over issues of what might be called geographic protocol. The incident took place late in 1663, when New England's Captain John Scott moved his troops brazenly into the western part of Long Island, from where he dispatched a challenging note to Director Stuyvesant. Scott's letter concerned the much-disputed matter of sovereignty and insisted, in no uncertain terms, on England's rights to Long Island. Striking a menacing tone, Scott called for a noon meeting the following day in Flatbush (which the Dutch called

[47] Ten Hove to States General, Oct. 6, 1664, in O'Callaghan and Fernow, eds., *N.Y.Col. Docs.*, 2:255–56.

[48] For representations of America during the Dutch Revolt see Benjamin Schmidt, "Tyranny Abroad: The Dutch Revolt and the Invention of America," *Zeventiende Eeuw*, 11 (1995), 161–74, which details the strenuous propaganda campaign waged over the image of the New World.

[49] On the decorative function of Dutch maps see the catalogue, *Kunst in Kaart* (Amsterdam, 1991), and James A. Welu, "Vermeer and Cartography" (Ph. D. diss., Boston University, 1977).

Midwout). He addressed his letter "To the Honble Peter Stuyvesant, General of the Dutch on the Manhattans," and, whatever the English captain's other affronts (reputedly many), it was the perceived inadequacy of this salutation that ultimately became the focus of contention. For "it [was] the opinion of his Honour, the Councillors present and the Burgomasters of this city [New Amsterdam], both from the address and some conversation with the bearer, that the name of General or Director of *New Netherland* was omitted, and the address simply 'Petrus Stuyvesant' through studied slight."[50]

This was not the first time such a "slight" had occurred. Just two months earlier, the English had committed a similar act of impertinence with a Dutch delegation attending the Connecticut General Assembly at Hartford. Brought together to settle yet another boundary dispute, the assembly had taken a typically hard-line position and stated so in a document drafted and addressed to Stuyvesant. This it then submitted to the Dutch party, one of whom recorded how "in the evening [of October 15, 1663] a letter was delivered to us with this superscription: *These for the Right honnourable Peter Stuyvesant, d' Generael at the Manados.* We said to the secretary who brought it, that it ought to be, Director-General of *New Netherland.* He answered, that it was at our option to receive it or not."[51]

While the delegates to the assembly balked at this challenge and accepted the letter, Stuyvesant, two months later, refused to tolerate such English posturing. The director "resolved to return the messenger the letter unopened, saying that there was no other Petrus Stuyvesant here than the Director-General of New Netherland; if Captain Schott [sic] meant him, then his Honor must be acknowledged in that quality." At this point, the English messenger strongly advised the Dutch to open the letter, sensing the disaster that might otherwise ensue. Stuyvesant would not budge, and, in the end, the courier opened the letter himself and read its contents aloud to the assembled officials of New Netherland. "Whereupon 'tis resolved to send some persons"—though, significantly, not Stuyvesant himself—"to Midwout to see and hear what [the] said Captain Schott should propose," noted the Dutch scribe, careful to use the Netherlandish, rather than English, name for the proposed location of the Long Island showdown.[52]

We conclude, thus, where we started, with Peter Stuyvesant standing on geographic ceremony: insisting, that is, on deference to Dutch names, maps, and geographic proprieties, to the great irritation of his English rivals. The Dutch and their governor made much of these nettlesome symbols of geography, using their strength to their best advantage in pursuit of an American

---

[50] Schott, "Extract from the Record of what passed between Captain John Schot . . . ," in O'Callaghan and Fernow, eds., *N.Y.Col. Docs.,* 2:393 (emphasis added).

[51] Cornelius van Ruyven et al., "Journal kept . . . in the month of October, 1663," ibid., 392. Compare Stuyvesant's complaint to the States around this time that the Hartford council "declared absolutely, That *they knew no New Netherland;* refusing the Director General and Council even the title now, for forty years, set forth in your High Mightinesses commission," in Ten Hove to States General, Jan. 21, 1664, ibid., 224.

[52] Schott, "Extract from the Record," 393.

empire—even as late as 1663. Matters, to be sure, did not always work out to Dutch satisfaction in this regard. When the States General's arms were affixed to a certain tree in the vicinity of Hartford, the English not only yanked down this symbol of Dutch sovereignty but also carved "a fool's face in the place thereof, to the gross disparagement of their High Mightinesses."[53] By and large, however, the Dutch won the battle of symbols even as they lost the war of dominion. Whatever the outcome in New Netherland, symbols plainly mattered, and the Dutch controlled those symbols most uniquely suited to empire: maps and other devices of geography. The Dutch dictated the cartographic discourse, and this palpably frustrated their English rivals. Maps on their own did not the empire make, yet they surely enlivened the colonial rivalry, giving powerful expression to the ideological agenda of their makers.

[53] "Deduction, or Brief and clear account of the Situation of New Netherland," in O'Callaghan and Fernow, eds., *N.Y. Col. Docs.,* 2:135, and compare the Dutch interrogations conducted on this matter in the "Examination of the divers Englishmen taken on Long Island," 146–49.

[12]

Scientific Exploration and Empire

ROBERT A. STAFFORD

Throughout the nineteenth century Britain sustained a programme of scientific exploration linked directly with her Imperial and trading interests. It played an important role both in shaping and expressing her culture. Although official commitment to exploration remained sporadic and efforts were rarely systematic, the continuity of British exploration is striking, and its purpose and style remained remarkably consistent. Britain maintained a higher level of exploratory activity than any other Great Power, making the promotion and popularity of exploration a powerful indicator of the strength of Britain's expansionist drive from the 1790s to the First World War.

Exploration can be defined as goal-directed research that creates knowledge in the laboratory of the wilderness. The explorer plays the same role in this regard as the scientist or inventor, increasing the capital of whatever group gains access to the new information. Exploration is an act of intervention that alters perspectives, probabilities, and processes in its parent culture and those that become its objects. People on the receiving end usually felt this most acutely, but Europeans were also aware of their intrusive impact on alien environments and cultures and realized that they themselves were being ineluctably altered by contact. The explorer was the catalyst that started the reaction, the agent of Europe's inevitable confrontation with peripheral lands.

Since the fifteenth century European exploration and imperialism had developed in the same cultural milieu as science, technology, the extractive industries, and the arts, all of which expressed the drive for wealth, control, and knowledge of the natural world. By the late eighteenth century exploration was a self-imposed expectation of the Great Powers. Particularly after Cook's voyages, the Enlightenment's voracious appetite for facts provided a powerful stimulus to discovery.[1] The comprehensive researches of Alexander von Humboldt added new rigour to this scientific enterprise by demonstrating that discrete data from different disciplines could be correlated to construct theoretical models with wide predictive

---

[1] In Vol. II, see chap. by Glyndwr Williams.

value regarding natural processes and patterns of distribution. The power and confidence bequeathed to Britain by industrialization, grafted on to the scientific curiosity sanctioned by the Reformation, combined in the nineteenth century to intensify the nation's expansionist tendencies until they dominated most aspects of culture.[2]

The Organization of Exploration: Metropole and Periphery

The Royal Navy played a major role in managing British exploration during the first half of the century, controlling the world-wide marine charting effort, formalized with the foundation of the Admiralty's Hydrographic Department in 1795, that became one of the outstanding cartographic accomplishments of the Victorian age.[3] The great explorations that characterized the period from 1790 to 1830 were largely maritime coastal reconnaissances. During this era the Admiralty organized voyages of discovery that served a subsidiary training function during lulls in the hostilities with the French, whose achievement in hydrography Britain surpassed only in 1850. Like the Ordnance Survey maps of Britain, the celebrated Admiralty charts codified scientific, strategic, and commercial intelligence, constituting a significant investment in national expansion. For the premier naval, colonial, and maritime trading power, they were a necessity: they made the seas safe to travel. Because of the tradition begun by Joseph Banks[4] of assigning naturalists to naval surveying expeditions, a great deal of scientific research was accomplished during the course of the hydrographic endeavour. Such posts enabled Charles Darwin, Joseph Hooker (later Director of Kew Gardens), Joseph Jukes (later Director of the Geological Survey of Ireland), and Thomas Huxley (later Professor at the Royal School of Mines) to establish their reputations. The amateur tradition and decentralized structure of British science thus linked with official initiatives and resources in the cause of exploration.

In 1830 the Royal Geographical Society (RGS) was founded in London by a small group of enthusiasts led by John Barrow, Second Secretary of the Admiralty from 1804 to 1845. Its goals and membership were based on those of the African Association, established by Banks in 1788 to promote exploration in Africa and elsewhere, and the Raleigh Club, formed by supporters of exploration who seceded from the Travellers Club in 1826. Like earlier geographical societies set up in Paris (1821) and Berlin (1828), the RGS sought to promote scientific exploration over-

---

[2] Stephen Kern, *The Culture of Time and Space, 1880–1918* (Cambridge, Mass., 1983); Edward W. Said, *Culture and Imperialism* (London, 1993).

[3] G. S. Ritchie, *The Admiralty Chart: British Naval Hydrography in the Nineteenth Century* (London, 1967).

[4] In Vol. II, see pp. 247, 249; 566–67; 573–74.

seas, presenting the results as maps and memoirs in its *Journal* and *Proceedings*.[5] From its inception, the cartographers, military officers, colonial administrators, scientists, politicians, diplomats, and travellers who managed the RGS explicitly linked the Society's activities with Imperial affairs.[6] Most of the early papers were contributed by the Admiralty and the Colonial, Foreign, and Indian Offices. The annual addresses of RGS Presidents, like the memoirs, were replete with the language of national expansion, assumptions of moral and technological superiority over other races, expressions of a natural theology that saw design in human settlement patterns and environmental adaptation, and assertions of Britain's right and duty to act at will around the world. Geography at the RGS was conceived and practised in an ideological and institutional matrix that enmeshed the goals of science and the nation in the practicalities of Imperial rule.[7] In the widest context, the initiatives of the RGS represented an overseas extension of the wave of quantification, classification, and improvement that transformed Europe as a corollary of industrialization.

The RGS managed to secure partial government sponsorship for several early expeditions, such as Robert Schomburgk's to British Guiana in 1831–35 and William Ainsworth's to Armenia and Kurdistan in 1838–40. Disappointing results, however, soon forced the Society to shift to a secondary role in co-ordinating rather than funding explorations. Naval officers, meanwhile, played a key part in Arctic exploration from 1820 to 1850, an endeavour driven as much by the urge to redeem the quest's chief martyr, Sir John Franklin, who perished in 1847, as to conclude the search for a North-west Passage. In roughly the same period, naval officers took part in steamship explorations of the Niger and Zambezi rivers in Africa that were driven by humanitarian pressure to encourage legitimate commerce and supplant the slave trade. The Niger voyages culminated the series of explorations inspired by Mungo Park, another geographical martyr patronized by Banks's African Association. The Zambezi initiative arose from the celebrity of the missionary David Livingstone. The Admiralty's Hydrographic Department played a central role in these undertakings, the line of succession running from Banks through Barrow to Francis Beaufort and John Washington, official Hydrographers in the periods 1829–55 and 1855–63. Barrow dominated naval exploration and most

---

[5] Hugh Robert Mill, *The Record of the Royal Geographical Society* (London, 1930), remains a more informative source than Ian Cameron, *To the Farthest Ends of the Earth: The History of the Royal Geographical Society, 1830–1980* (London, 1980).

[6] D. R. Stoddart, 'The R. G. S. and the "New Geography": Changing Aims and Roles in Nineteenth-Century Science', *Geographical Journal*, CXLVI (1980), pp. 190–202.

[7] David N. Livingstone, 'The History of Science and the History of Geography: Interactions and Implications', *History of Science*, XXII (1984), pp. 271–302; in this volume, see above, pp. 285, 286–88.

of Britain's terrestrial exploratory effort from Banks's death in 1820 until his own retirement in 1845.[8] These scientific officers wielded great power in Britain's geographical community. Holding posts in the RGS, Royal Society, British Association for the Advancement of Science, and other learned organizations, they ensured that the Senior Service's interests were attended to on most expeditions. As the great rivers were charted, however, and exploration of continental interiors became the only way to reduce the *terra incognita* further, the Admiralty lost its paramount geographical influence. The way was open for another institution to fill the void: the RGS only required determined leadership to enable it to realize the hopes of its founders.

At the RGS, the naval retreat was largely completed by 1850, when Sir Roderick Murchison, building on the work of other reformers, took firm control of Britain's specialist geographical institution and transformed it into the nation's—indeed, the world's—undisputed directorate of exploration. Murchison had already had three careers before he focused on geography: as a soldier, a fox-hunter, and a geologist who defined the Silurian, Devonian, and Permian stratigraphic systems. Like Humboldt, Murchison believed geology and geography were sister sciences, and his military and hunting background rendered him particularly interested in landforms and geography. Murchison not only saw the data provided by geography as critical to the advancement of all sciences, but as crucial to the commercial, military, and philanthropic endeavours of Europe, and Britain in particular. The key to his passionate interest in geography, as that of Victorians in general, was the map. As a spatial science of relationships, geography not only provided topographical base maps upon which scientific data could be recorded, but it codified information of immense value to everyone involved in managing outcomes based on interaction with the physical world. Maps provide a symbolic language that can legitimize the political power and territorial imperatives of those who deploy it. While Murchison and his colleagues understood the significance of maps as intellectual weapons, they spoke of them publicly as objective, value-neutral tools produced for the common good.[9]

Murchison was an ardent patriot who saw his geological tours as military campaigns, relied on imperial metaphors to describe the spread of his stratigraphic designations around the world, and supported the expansion of Britain's Empire throughout his career as a pillar of the scientific establishment. Murchison believed that the natural sciences played an important role in furthering British interests and that the nation had an obligation to support her scientists. His

[8] Christopher Lloyd, *Mr. Barrow of the Admiralty: A Life of Sir John Barrow, 1764–1848* (London, 1970).

[9] J. B. Harley, 'Maps, Knowledge and Power', in D. Cosgrove and S. Daniels, eds., *The Iconography of Time* (Cambridge, 1988), pp. 277–312.

forceful character, indefatigable zeal, extensive social connections, and Imperial proclivities went far to ensure that the relationship between British science and Britain's Empire was mutually advantageous.

Murchison, perhaps more keenly than any contemporary savant, felt the connection between science and Empire. While his work to establish this connection found occasional expression through his offices in the Royal Society, Geological Society, and British Association, his most concerted efforts were channelled through the RGS. As his stratigraphic career flagged for want of continental masses to subdue in the early 1850s, he moved to align the RGS more closely with national needs. Many other public figures recorded similar feelings, but several first-rank scientists, including Darwin, Lyell, Huxley, Joseph Hooker, and Alfred Wallace, shunned Murchison's reconstituted RGS as a promotional farce insulting genuine science. Still, even these critics, as well as other proponents of exploration who did not advocate Empire, willingly used the influence of the RGS to raise funds for research. Conflicting agendas were thus subsumed under a blend of Imperial, humanitarian, and scientific rhetoric: Murchison's genius was to package proposals in language that balanced the factions. In part, he sought to popularize exploration in order to secure official funding for a series of expeditions that satisfied the public's thirst for adventure, the scientists' demand for data, the merchants' desire for details about new markets and sources of supply, and the government's need for objective information upon which to base diplomatic and Imperial decisions. At the same time, the RGS provided Murchison with a new vehicle for his insatiable ambition to win social rank through national service. His assumption of command at the RGS also coincided with his engineering of the British Association's recognition of geography as an independent science—again, the motive was to feed and tap public interest in geography for the benefit of all sciences.

Having set geography's house in order and installed himself as its presiding presence, Murchison completed a complementary manœuvre in geology that cemented his position as the unassailable leader of the mid-Victorian exploration drive. In 1855 he was appointed Director-General of the Geological Survey of Great Britain. The first Director-General, Sir Henry De la Beche, acting in the manner of his counterpart Sir William Hooker, Director of Kew Gardens, had established the Survey in 1835 to delineate the kingdom's geological structure and mineral deposits on Ordnance Survey maps. De la Beche had performed a good deal of Imperial work, employing the Survey's Museum of Practical Geology to evaluate colonial ore samples, testing overseas coals to facilitate the navy's global deployment of steamships, and founding geological surveys in overseas dependencies. As with the RGS, the Survey gave Murchison a foundation, and again he erected an edifice of decidedly Imperial style. Not only did he accomplish far more colonial geology than his predecessor, partly because the mid-century gold rushes dramatically raised expectations of mineral wealth, but he used the Survey's Royal School of Mines to supply geologists for RGS-sponsored expeditions. These forays provided valuable geographical information while allowing Murchison, by proxy, to map the strata of new regions and test his own geological theories. The colonial surveys enabled Murchison to promote the extension of topographical and geological mapping throughout the Empire. Colonial geologists and botanists also accomplished much original exploration in the course of research largely directed from London. Their results were fed back to the 'centres of calculation', contributing to Europe's preponderant knowledge of peripheral regions,[10] though important theories as well as data issued from the colonial frontier where scientific principles were constantly honed against exotic phenomena. In geology, botany, biology, ethnography, and astronomy, colonial and expeditionary access conferred substantial advantage on British scientists. Indeed, so adept were British scientific leaders, such as Banks and Murchison, at exploiting the research opportunities created by Empire that they can be thought of as 'sub-imperialists' who transformed the physiology of the Imperial state in the manner of symbiotic parasites that create niches for themselves in return for services to their host.

Through institutional power and social prestige, Murchison dominated British exploration from the early 1850s until his death in 1871, standing forth unquestionably as the key figure between the death of Banks and the First World War. Murchison's career spanned the transition between gentlemanly amateurs who worked through informal networks based on the scientific societies, and trained professionals employed by specialized government departments. The influence of learned societies linking officialdom and science in support of exploration outlasted Murchison, and new Empire-wide networks developed around the geological surveys, botanical gardens, natural history museums, and universities that were gradually installed in the colonies. Yet Murchison's leadership coincided with the high noon of Victorian prosperity, so that he was able to engineer a brilliant burst of exploration on the basis of the interest in overseas opportunities generated by the cycle of great gold rushes, the success of free trade, and the anti-slavery movement.[11] Following Murchison's death, other presidents with direct links to the Empire led the RGS into the twentieth century, but none approached his success in promoting exploration. Though rising Imperial sentiment swelled RGS membership and the Society briefly experimented with direct support of

---

[10] Bruno Latour, *Science in Action: How to Follow Scientists and Engineers Through Society* (Milton Keynes, 1987), chap. 6.

[11] D. H. Hall, *History of the Earth Sciences during the Scientific and Industrial Revolutions* (Oxford, 1976), pp. 160–90, correlates exploratory activity with economic fluctuations.

imperialistic ventures in Africa,[12] the era of primary exploration was ending by the 1880s, Britain's capacity for action was increasingly constrained, and the RGS itself, under the pressure of geography's evolution into a rigorously defined discipline, was transformed into a specialist scientific society. As a result, it was purged of its fashionable, political, and military factions and the attendant ideologies of imperialism, racism, and environmental determinism that had helped express the social utility of this heterogeneous science during its infancy.[13] Thus, while an appreciation of the RGS is critical to understanding the motives and mechanisms behind nineteenth-century British exploration, the Society's Imperial role actually lessened in proportion to the rise of overt imperialism. Except for the poles, the explorers had nearly worked themselves out of a job by the late 1880s, an eventuality Gladstone foresaw as early as 1864, when he remarked to the RGS: 'Gentlemen, you have done so much that you are like Alexander, you have no more worlds to conquer.'[14] The four main regions in which British exploration focused during the century were the Arctic, Australia (Map 14.2), Africa (Map 14.1), and Central Asia. The rest was essentially a piecemeal mopping-up operation.

Official explorers invariably carried detailed instructions drawn up by their sponsors. Until the 1840s such instructions for maritime or riverine Imperial expeditions were usually written by Barrow at the Admiralty. The Colonial Office wrote its own directives, providing general desiderata to be modified by specific local instructions for colonial explorations. For expeditions beyond the Empire, the Colonial Office issued detailed orders direct from London. Again, because of his connection with the African Association, the ubiquitous Barrow wrote the instructions for the expeditions to the Niger hinterland that completed Park's work. Explorers on official service were given the full support of the Imperial government, including naval passages, diplomatic and consular back-up, and aid from colonial and Indian administrations. In the colonies, unclaimed territories, and poorly explored sovereign nations, a good deal of discovery was also accomplished by unofficial British explorers who usually enjoyed the sanction, if not the financial support, of the Imperial or colonial governments. Scientists such as Alfred Wallace likewise received official help while working in remote regions like the Dutch East Indies.

As the RGS gained effective control of British Imperial exploration in the late 1840s it became the chief authority for drafting expeditionary instructions. To ensure co-ordination among all interest groups, the RGS solicited research suggestions from the Colonial or Foreign Office, the Royal Society, and government

---

[12] R. C. Bridges, 'The R.G.S. and the African Exploration Fund, 1876–80', *Geographical Journal*, CXXIX (1963), pp. 25–35.

[13] Stoddart, 'R.G.S. and the "New Geography"'; Livingstone, 'History of Science'.

[14] *Proceedings of the Royal Geographical Society*, XIV (1869–70), pp. 214.

Algiers
Tripoli
Ghadames
Cairo
In Salah
Ⓐ
Murzuk
Ghat
Aswan
Nile
Ⓒ
Suakin
Shendi
Massawa
R. Senegal
Timbuktu
Ⓖ
R. Gambia
Segu
Sokoto
Ⓑ
Lake Chad
White Nile
Sennar
Bamako
R. Niger
Bauchi
Kano
Kukawa
Blue Nile
Harar
Freetown
Badagry
R. Benue
Yola
Lake Rudolf
Stanley Falls
Mt. Kenya
Tana R.
Stanley
R. Congo
Lake Victoria
Mt. Kilimanjaro
Mombasa
L. Tanganyika
Zanzibar
Indian Ocean
Luanda
Livingstone
Ⓓ
Benguela
L. Nyasa
R. Zambezi
Shesheke
Victoria Falls
Quelimane
Beira
MADAGASCAR
Walvis Bay
Ⓕ
Limpopo R.
Kuruman
Orange R.
Lourenço Marques
Atlantic Ocean
Ⓔ
Durban
Cape Town

Ⓐ 1770-1856
Barth; **Clapperton; Denham;**
Hornemann; **Laing; Oudney**

Ⓑ 1770-1890
Barth; Baikie; **Clapperton;**
Denham
Hornemann; **Lander bros;**
Oudney; Thomson

Ⓒ 1768-1814
Bruce; Burckhard

Ⓓ 1856-1890
Baker; **Burton** & Speke; Cameron;
Livingstone; Thomson

Ⓔ 1813-1820
Campbell; Moffat

Ⓕ 1851   Ⓖ 1795-1806
Galton   Laing; Park

Bold name denotes explorer
mentioned in chapter

0   miles   1000
0   km   1000

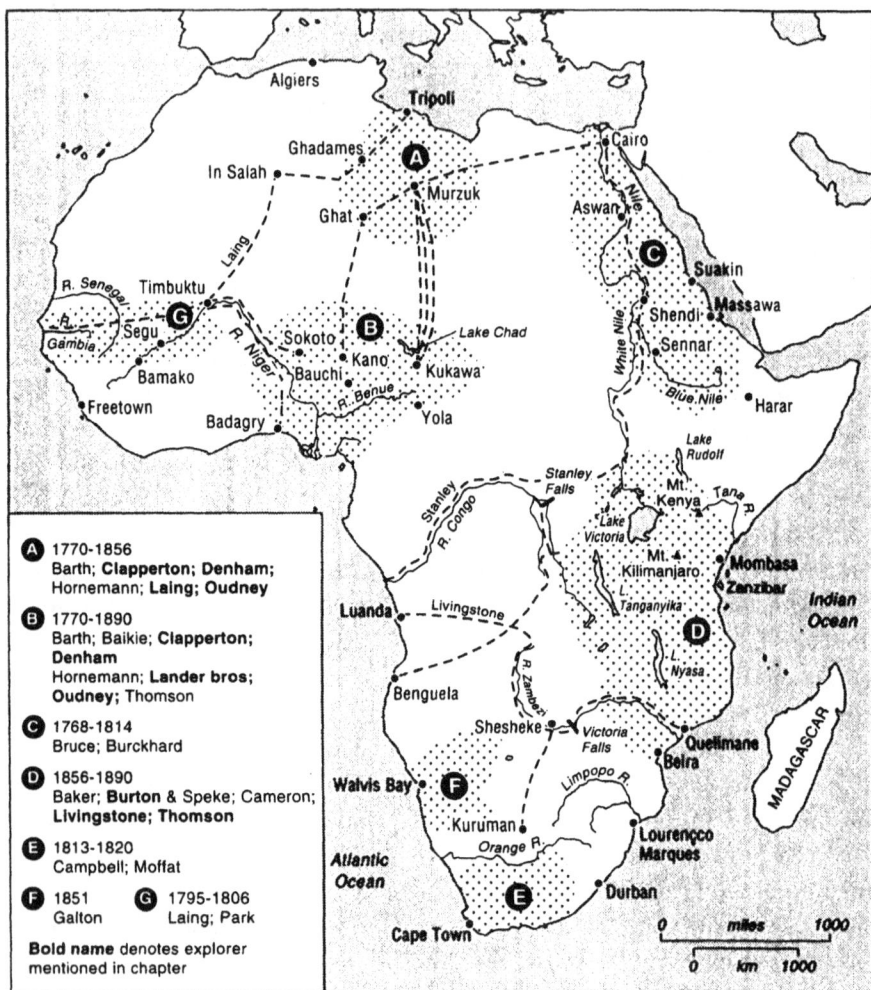

MAP 14.1. British Exploration in Africa

scientists such as the naval Hydrographer, the Directors of Kew Gardens and the Geological Survey, and Sir Edward Sabine, a specialist in terrestrial magnetism.[15] Emphases in instructions varied with the region and objective, but they generally called for methodical instrumental observation, map-making, written narrative, collection of botanical, geological, zoological, and ethnological specimens, weather recording (temperature and barometric pressure), and inquiry into native languages, customs, population distribution, productions, and trade patterns. Explorers were directed to update their journals daily, trusting nothing to memory. Those travelling outside the British sphere were instructed to send out frequent dispatches, including tracings of maps, to preserve their work from accidents such as Alexander Gordon Laing's murder near Timbuktu in 1826.[16] Explorers were also enjoined to respect native mores, avoid violence, distribute gifts, trade fairly, and cultivate a good name for whites.

Even at this level exploration was profoundly exploitative, for it took hostages in the form of data used to inform decisions about territories made without the knowledge or consent of their inhabitants. The concentration of scientific and commercial data in Europe helped tip the balance of power against the indigenous peoples of other continents, whose control over their destinies could be eroded as surely by map coordinates and museum specimens as by steamships, bullets, and treaties of cession. Natives themselves understood something of this, as was demonstrated by instructions to Dixon Denham, Walter Oudney, and Hugh Clapperton on their mission to the Niger interior in 1822–25 (Map 14.2), to avoid shocking the Africans by blatantly collecting natural history specimens,[17] and the concealment by Richard and John Lander of their interest in the course of the Niger from suspicious local rulers.[18]

Changes in the metropolitan context in which exploration evolved were variously expressed in peripheral regions. In Australia the voyages of Cook, Flinders, Vancouver, and the French had surveyed most of the coastline by 1805 (Map 14.2). While charting continued under captains such as Philip Parker King and John Lort Stokes until the 1850s, few mysteries remained except possible river discoveries. The focus of activity moved inland once the Blue Mountains of New South Wales were crossed in 1813. The two expeditions of 1817–18 led by John Oxley, that colony's Surveyor-General, started a series of explorations by army officers such as Charles Sturt, surveyors like Thomas Mitchell, and bushmen such as Edward

---

[15] John Cawood, 'The Magnetic Crusade: Science and Politics in Early Victorian Britain', *Isis*, LXX (1979), pp. 493–518.

[16] 'The Letters of Major Alexander Gordon Laing, 1824–26', in E. W. Bovill, ed., *Missions to the Niger*, 4 vols. (Cambridge, 1964–66), I, pp. 123–390.

[17] 'The Bornu Mission, 1822–25', in Bovill, ed., *Missions to the Niger*, II, pp. 20–21.

[18] Robin Hallett, ed., *The Niger Journal of Richard and John Lander* (London, 1965), p. 118.

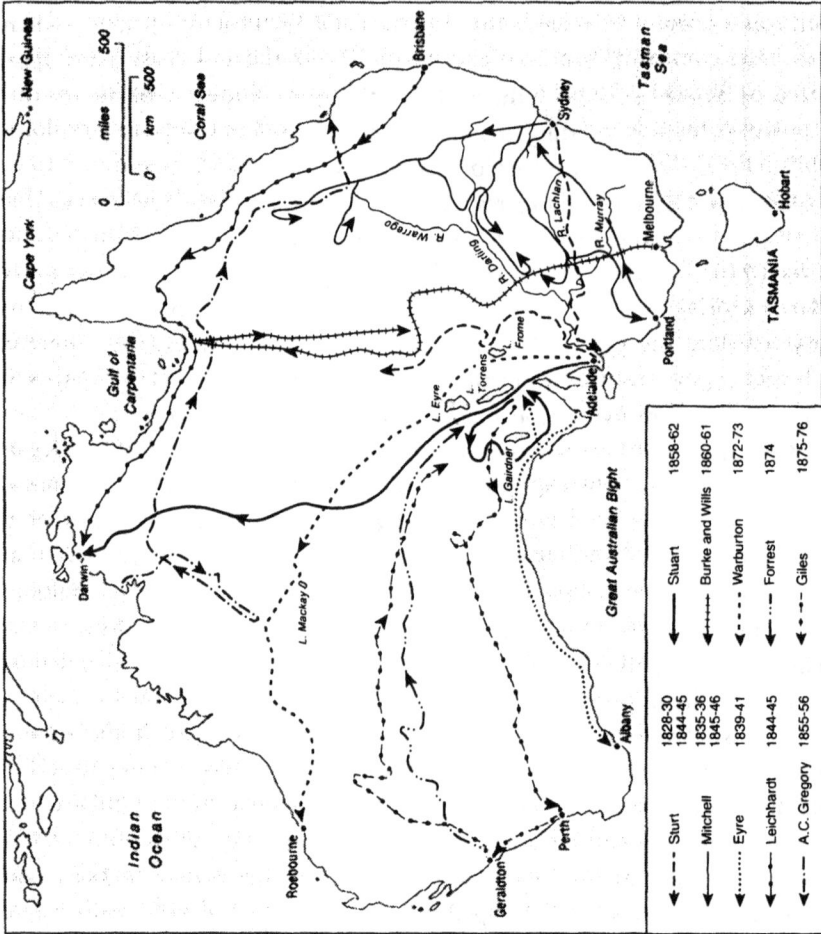

MAP 14.2. The Exploration of Australia

Eyre that revealed the broad outline of the interior by the 1860s. These expeditions were usually the initiative of individual colonies seeking to discover new areas for settlement and to understand the continent's topography. The Colonial Office sanctioned the expenditures and wrote the general instructions, including guidelines about interaction with Aborigines. This remained the pattern until the 1860s, when exploratory management as well as initiative shifted to the colonies in parallel with their assumption of responsible government. In this period open competition broke out between South Australia and Victoria for the glory of first traversing the continent from south to north. The Burke and Wills Expedition, organized by Victoria's Royal Society, illustrates how colonial scientific institutions took over the role of their metropolitan progenitors in sponsoring exploration within the British voluntarist tradition.[19] The Imperial factor continued to be felt in Australian exploration, though it was increasingly mediated by the RGS. The North Australian Exploring Expedition of 1855–56, for example, was promoted and organized by the RGS, funded by the Colonial Office, supported by the Admiralty (aided by Victoria) which seconded its Government Botanist, and led by Augustus Gregory, Assistant Surveyor-General of Western Australia.[20] The strategic interests of the Imperial government centred on ascertaining the north coast's resources to promote settlement as well as trade and communications with Asia.

In Canada and Cape Colony, settler enterprise, even more than the initiative of colonial governments, drove exploration in the first half of the century. In Canada, Colonial Office control again gave way to local management except when Imperial issues that transcended individual colonies or affected global strategy were at stake. Examples are the Palliser Expedition of 1857–60, which surveyed a railroad route to British Columbia to knit together Britain's North American possessions, and the North-West American Boundary Commission of 1858–63, which delimited the international border west of the Rockies. Since the British took the Cape in 1795, southern African exploration was left largely to missionaries, hunters, trekkers, and prospectors operating from Cape Colony and later the Boer republics without government assistance. Yet the Imperial government threw its full support behind Livingstone's Zambezi Expedition of 1857–63 because of its objectives to undermine the East African slave trade while developing new markets and resources for British industry. The government was careful, however, to dissociate itself from Livingstone's colonizing schemes.[21] In New Zealand, missionaries and surveyors of Wakefield's company led the way before sheep graziers, prospectors,

---

[19] Alan Moorehead, *Cooper's Creek* (1963; Melbourne, 1985).

[20] A. C. and F. T. Gregory, *Journals of Australian Explorations*, 2nd edn. (1884; Victoria Park, Western Australia, 1981); J. H. L. Cumpston, *Augustus Gregory and the Inland Sea* (Canberra, 1972).

[21] Tim Jeal, *Livingstone* (New York, 1973), pp. 184–94; Robert A. Stafford, *Scientist of Empire: Sir Roderick Murchison, Scientific Exploration, and Victorian Imperialism* (Cambridge, 1989), pp. 172–82.

and government geologists took the initiative. The motives of colonial epicentres in sponsoring exploration were more parochial than those of London. Expansion and political consolidation were key considerations; scientific research was less important than development, extraction, and trade. Colonial exploration focused on agricultural and pastoral lands, timber, minerals, and routes for stock droving, river navigation, and railways. After the rushes in California and Victoria, gold became a prime goal because of its capacity to initiate self-sustaining economic growth.

India, typically, went its own way about exploration. The Great Trigonometrical Survey, permanently founded in 1818, remained the main vehicle for Indian initiatives, accomplishing much external exploration in the Himalayas as well as mapping British possessions in the subcontinent. The topographical maps produced by the Survey constituted an important aid to British rule, comparable to the railway or telegraph in their elaboration of a space-time grid that enabled the marshalling of the information, troops, and resources necessary to subdue and govern the vast territory. As in Britain and the colonies, these maps were also used by India's Geological Survey, permanently established in 1851, to lay down the territory's structure and mineral resources. The explorations beyond the frontiers provided valuable intelligence about tribal areas, mountain passes, and the shrinking No Man's Land between the British and Russian spheres of influence. They also enabled the Indian authorities to try to funnel the trade of Central Asia. Much of this work was done by the 'pundits', native officers of the Survey who carried out a breathtaking series of covert explorations between 1865 and 1875. India, too, developed voluntarist associations such as the Asiatic Society of Bengal (1784) that sponsored and rewarded scientific activity, complementing the initial botanical (1786–Calcutta Botanical Gardens), geological, and forestry (1847–Bombay Forest Department) establishments of the East India Company.

The Indian Navy also performed a great deal of primary exploration, completing hydrographic surveys from the East African coast to the Straits of Malacca between 1770 and the mid-nineteenth century. The Company's policy of introducing steamboats on the Indus and Ganges and deploying them in punitive campaigns throughout its sphere[22] also necessitated the charting of the major rivers of southern Asia. Valuable palaeontological and zoological collections made on these missions were transmitted to the metropolitan scientific societies, providing important data for the debate on the progression of life. Perhaps the best example of such steam-powered exploratory work was the survey of the Tigris–Euphrates river system carried out by Captain Francis Chesney, RA, during

---

[22] Daniel R. Headrick, *The Tools of Empire: Technology and European Imperialism in the Nineteenth Century* (Oxford, 1981).

1835–37 to ascertain its suitability as a new route to India. The scheme proved a failure, largely due to technological advances favouring ocean-going steamships, but a wealth of political, commercial, and scientific data was gleaned and an enduring British presence established. Expressing the logic by which exploration often led to intervention, Chesney advocated the establishment of trade depots as 'points of support' for British efforts to increase the region's commerce.[23] Chesney's work, like that of other British expeditions in Ottoman territory and the trans-Himalayan zone, highlights the political and military value of geographical information about sensitive zones, and how exploration often blended into espionage.

Britain took the lead in opening 'the Dark Continent', focusing successively on the Niger, the interior of southern Africa, the Central Lakes, and the Nile. Except the series of West African explorations conducted by the Colonial Office between 1818 and the 1830s and several Niger voyages organized by the Admiralty, much of Britain's African exploration was overseen by the Foreign Office in conjunction with the RGS. Murchison's close relationship with Lord Clarendon during the 1850s was instrumental in this regard. In the case of Macgregor Laird's steam exploration of the Niger in 1832–34, which sought to capitalize on the trade potential revealed by Richard and John Lander, attacking the slave trade and spreading Christianity were adduced as additional benefits from the introduction of British commerce. The Admiralty provided this private expedition with a naval lieutenant to survey the river; Laird, in turn, extracted a pledge that no information from the chart produced would be divulged without his company's permission.[24] Twenty years later the navy returned the favour, allowing Laird's trading agent to accompany William Balfour Baikie's government-funded Niger expedition.[25] By the 1850s the lesson of quinine as a malarial prophylactic had been learned: Baikie's voyage proved Europeans could maintain their health in tropical Africa. By the 1890s female explorers such as Mary Kingsley were also adding laurels to Britain's record of African discovery,[26] though women were not admitted as RGS Fellows until 1904. As noted, southern Africa was largely explored as a result of local colonial initiative. The Central Lakes and the Nile tributaries were explored to solve the mystery of the Nile's source, but as the scale of Arab slaving operations in East Africa was revealed, humanitarianism and the promotion of

---

[23] Francis R. Chesney, *The Expedition for the Survey of the Euphrates and Tigris*, 2 vols. (London, 1850), II, pp. 601–02.

[24] MacGregor Laird and R. A. K. Oldfield, *Narrative of an Expedition into the Interior of Africa by the River Niger*, 2nd edn., 2 vols. (1837; London, 1971), I, p. 11.

[25] William Balfour Baikie, *Narrative of an Exploring Voyage up the Rivers Kwora and Binue*, 2nd edn. (1856; London, 1966), p. 5.

[26] Dea Birkett, *Mary Kingsley: Imperial Adventuress* (Basingstoke, 1992).

legitimate commerce were again deployed to encourage further activity that created the preconditions for annexation. International rivalry for discoveries remained muted before the 1880s, when the quickening pace of annexation in Africa and the shrinking size of untracked regions created friction between European powers.

The Explorers: Styles, Methods, Impacts

While for the most part untiring in following their instructions, explorers interpreted their marching orders according to their own lights. Such ambitious, often flamboyant men were relatively unlikely to be restrained by official dictates once their quests led them beyond Europe's reach. The personalities and motives of explorers were as varied as one might expect in such a broad-based, long-term cultural activity, but discernible patterns emerge. The most significant was the shift during the mid-nineteenth century from the old model of the explorer as self-effacing, duty-driven national servant to a larger-than-life celebrity whose sensational exploits acted out both personal obsessions and public fantasies. George Vancouver exemplifies the first type, Richard Burton the second. Most explorers were serving or former military officers; a few were professional scientists. Many built careers as colonial administrators or diplomats on the foundation of their service in the cause of discovery. Their ability to move between professions by seizing opportunities created by Britain's overseas activities illustrates the larger cultural context of expansionism in which both exploration and empire flourished.

The explorer in the field had to be a man or woman of many parts to accomplish his or her goals—leader, emissary, pathfinder, hunter, observer, collector, recorder, cartographer, and often artist. Unlike their naval counterparts, overland explorers were immersed in alien environments for months or years, having no choice but to get along with indigenous peoples. Sturt believed success came by 'steady perseverance and unceasing attention, by due precaution and a mild discipline'.[27] Eyre admitted that the leader was always lonely and anxious, since one false step or bad judgement might endanger the party or ruin its chances of success.[28] Rarely was the explorer alone: in colonial settings he was accompanied by assistants, native guides, and scientific collectors. Explorers in tropical Africa required bearers because of the susceptibility of draft animals to sleeping sickness and the necessity of carrying trade goods, gifts, and supplies. Many complained of their

[27] Charles Sturt, *Narrative of an Expedition into Central Australia*, 2nd edn., 2 vols. (1849; Adelaide, 1965), I, p. 148.

[28] Edward John Eyre, *Journals of Expeditions of Discovery into Central Australia*, 2nd edn., 2 vols. (1845; Adelaide, 1964), I, p. 24.

impedimenta, Joseph Thomson lamenting 'the dreadful incubus of a caravan'.[29] There was also the strain of maintaining one's dignity amidst crowds of curious natives who had often never seen a European before.

Much of the explorer's energy was dedicated to the day-to-day logistics of moving through the country and dealing with subordinates, animals, equipment, and natives. Terrain and climate were constant issues, as were, depending upon circumstances, disease, water supply, food for man and beast, shelter, and steam fuel. But getting there and back were not enough: concerted scientific work was required to bring new regions within Europe's ken and ambit. The pattern of scientific expectation evolved from eighteenth-century precedents, and the explorer's equipment reflected these requirements. His standard gear—essentially the means for land navigation—included a telescope, a compass for travel and mapping, a sextant for making astronomical observations to determine latitude, chronometers to determine longitude, an artificial horizon, used in conjunction with the sextant for taking altitudes, a barometer to determine altitude by atmospheric pressure, and thermometers to record temperature and determine altitude by boiling point. Other equipment might include surveying chains to measure actual distances travelled, a pedometer to measure approximate distances, a theodolite to measure horizontal angles for triangulation and mapping, sounding lines for determining river and lake depths, and a hygrometer to measure humidity. More specialized research might demand a microscope, blowpiping apparatus for chemical analysis of minerals, or instruments to record terrestrial magnetism and compass deviation due to a ship's iron hull.

Explorers were beset with endless problems maintaining their instruments. Compasses were lost, barometers were broken, chronometers changed rates or stopped, instruments split from heat, their glasses were sandblasted by ferocious winds, thermometers calibrated for English temperatures burst in desert climes, and natives begged precious mercury that was, in Clapperton's words, 'like asking me to part with my heart's blood'.[30] In perhaps the most humourous juxtaposition of scientific order and wilderness recalcitrance, W. B. Baikie had his African crewmen trample the grass at an observation site in order to clear a space for his instruments, only to find he had chosen a hippo track whose owner nearly bowled him over lumbering back to the Niger.[31]

Ever resourceful, explorers improvised and endured, completing an astonishing range of research under the most trying conditions. Accurately fixing positions remained the *sine qua non*. Some colonial explorers went further as they entered

---

[29] Joseph Thomson, *To the Central Africa Lakes and Back*, 2nd edn., 2 vols. (1881; London, 1968), I, p. ix.

[30] Bovill, *Missions to the Niger*, IV, p. 630.

[31] Baikie, *Narrative of an Exploring Voyage*, pp. 136–37.

the void beyond mapped districts, surveying baselines and triangulating to determine co-ordinates that were then measured by chaining and checked by celestial observation. Similarly, altitudes taken by instruments were verified by geometric calculation. Explorers were guided in such activities by procedures as well as instructions, the Admiralty publishing its *Manual of Scientific Enquiry* in 1849 and *Instructions for Hydrographic Surveyors* the following year.[32] Paralleling the shift of power in expeditionary organization, the navy's manual was superseded in 1854 by the RGS's *Hints to Travellers*, which soon achieved world-wide fame.[33]

Not all explorers found science stimulating. The more individualistic tired of the daily round of observations, preferring to engage directly with the landscape and people, and revert to subjective, circumstantial reportage. Differences in approach were sometimes striking even between colleagues. On the Bornu Mission, the leader Denham spent his time hunting, recording impressions, commenting on African women, and even accompanying an Arab slave-raiding party, while Oudney, one of the Scottish naval surgeons so conspicuous in Victorian exploration, made comprehensive scientific observations and collections that constituted the chief results of the mission.[34] Similarly, on the Palliser Expedition across British North America, it was the geologist James Hector, another Scottish doctor, rather than John Palliser, a wealthy big-game hunter turned explorer, who accomplished the most significant discoveries.[35] Some explorers, like Charles Sturt, managed to balance their leadership and scientific roles, while others, such as McDouall Stuart, minimized observations to push through to their goals. Scientific leaders, however, could become so engrossed by fieldwork that expedition management suffered. After the Scottish naval surgeon W. B. Baikie assumed command of the Niger expedition of 1854 when its leader died, he busied himself collecting specimens while a serious confrontation with his sailing master was brewing.[36] Joseph Thomson, on the other hand, who had been trained in geology and made substantial contributions to several disciplines, admitted that 'scientific cares' spoiled the charm of new scenery.[37] When life itself was at stake, even exacting observers sometimes had to jettison instruments, collections, and journals.

The highly processed data gathered by the explorers were introduced into Imperial culture through scientific societies, newspapers, and museums,

---

[32] John Herschel, ed., *A Manual of Scientific Enquiry* (London, 1849); Ritchie, *Admiralty Chart*, p. 198.

[33] Royal Geographical Society, *Hints to Travellers* (London, 1854).

[34] Bovill, 'Bornu Mission'.

[35] Irene M. Spry, *The Palliser Expedition: An Account of John Palliser's British North American Expedition, 1857–1860* (Toronto, 1963).

[36] Baikie, *Narrative of an Exploring Voyage*, pp. 47–53, 92.

[37] Joseph Thomson, *Through Masai Land*, 3rd edn. (1885; London, 1968), p. 203.

influencing attitudes towards distant territories and peoples. The RGS remained the key institution in this process, shaping the make-up and agendas of outbound expeditions and mediating inbound results. Exploration and its narration, which represented new lands by word, map, and illustration, taught Britons to think about, act in, and finally absorb these areas into their consciousness. Exploration thus became an important part of the process of imperialism, for even when it did not lead directly to annexation, it enclosed vast tracts of the periphery, including their inhabitants and resources, within Europe's purview.

Nineteenth-century exploration favoured the taxonomic, spatially oriented field sciences such as geology and botany because their data could be easily and profitably collected. It was no coincidence that these were the very disciplines required to sustain colonization and commerical penetration of new territories, in that they listed resources and suggested use patterns. Indeed, the rise during the heyday of free-trade expansion of bio-geography, the study of the distribution of organisms,[38] prefigured the development of formal imperialism's characteristic socio-political science—geopolitics.[39] The times called forth the appropriate sciences, which in turn supported the culture that nurtured them.

Exploration literature, a stream of growing significance in national culture, expressed the initiatives of the field sciences and contributed to the vision of Empire that was a major component of Britain's will to rule abroad. While the novel and the historical narrative opened history to the Victorian middle-class, exploration and travel literature made geography available, so that the British public learned the entire world, in both time and space, was accessible for objectification, appropriation, and use. The explorer's text was authoritative and highly subjective, but what and how he chose to describe were constrained by the expectations of his own culture. By reshaping the periphery through the conventions of European representation, science, like literature, helped create what Edward Said terms 'structures of feeling',[40] sets of attitudes that sustained Empire by incorporating its exotic lands and inhabitants into metropolitan consciousness. While Said's theory remains controversial because of its assumed dependence on fictional interpretation, first-hand evidence supports it, not least from the scientists, who were frequently active proponents of Empire for ideological as well as professional reasons.[41] On a practical level, scientific exploration helped British

---

[38] Janet Browne, *The Secular Ark: Studies in the History of Biogeography* (London, 1983); Robert A. Stafford, 'Annexing the Landscapes of the Past: British Imperial Geology in the Nineteenth Century', in John M. MacKenzie, ed., *Imperialism and the Natural World* (Manchester, 1990), pp. 67–89.

[39] Kern, *Culture of Time and Space*, pp. 223, 239.

[40] Said, *Culture and Imperialism*, p. 14.

[41] Stafford, 'Annexing the Landscapes'; Adrian Desmond, 'The Making of Institutional Zoology in London, 1822–36', *History of Science*, XXIII (1985), pp. 153–85, 223–50; Livingstone, 'History of Science'.

colonists feel at home in their 'neo-Europes'[42] by providing dimensions and explanations for alien environments, as well as strategies for exploiting them. Exploration literature, like the novel, thus portrayed colonial and unannexed territories as 'realms of possibility'[43] and, by maintaining a tradition of British engagement, became a key element of the 'official mind' of imperialism.[44] The narratives, as much as the explorations they chronicled, constituted acts of possession that legitimized and encouraged territorial control.

The logic of geographical discovery undertaken in an atmosphere of utilitarian improvement or redemption often led explorers to propose schemes to develop the territories revealed. The meaning and use of travel literature had already evolved during the Enlightenment from an emphasis on gathering and disseminating information to interpreting and applying it.[45] By 1850 this process had so accelerated that the Christian belief that natural resources exist to be employed for man's improvement had been overtaken by dramatic growth, through technology, in Europeans' power to remake the world. The two traditions fused in the conviction that man was destined to master nature. This drive, in turn, encouraged the development of the civilizing mission, which sought to improve native societies along rational lines.[46] Most explorers and scientists worked within a framework of environmental determinism that allowed them to lament the passing of native peoples before the European advance while justifying the process by analogy to the struggle for survival between species. Explorers and policy-makers were therefore predisposed to continue dialogue with particular places. Explorers usually eschewed outright annexation, but many advocated trading, settler, and missionary activities that made intervention more likely. Baikie, for example, while stating 'I am no advocate for endeavouring to acquire new territory' on the Niger, followed Chesney in encouraging the establishment of permanent depots to facilitate commerce and realign regional trade patterns in Britain's favour.[47] Thomson noted that his exploration of Masai Land led almost inevitably to its coming within Britain's sphere of influence.[48]

---

[42] Alfred W. Crosby, *Ecological Imperialism: The Biological Expansion of Europe, 900–1900* (Cambridge, 1986).

[43] Said, *Culture and Imperialism*, p. 75.

[44] Ronald Robinson and John Gallagher, with Alice Denny, *Africa and the Victorians: The Official Mind of Imperialism* (London, 1961; new edn., 1981).

[45] Barbara Stafford, *Voyage into Substance: Art, Science, Nature, and the Illustrated Travel Account, 1760–1840* (Cambridge, Mass., 1984).

[46] Michael Adas, *Machines as the Measure of Men: Science, Technology, and Ideologies of Western Dominance* (Ithaca, NY, 1989), pp. 70, 212.

[47] Compare Baikie, *Narrative of an Exploring Voyage*, pp. 394, 456, and Alexander Nzemeke, *British Imperialism and African Response: The Niger Valley, 1851–1905* (Paderborn, 1982), pp. 47–135.

[48] Thomson, *Through Masai Land*, pp. ix, 8.

Wherever they penetrated, explorers carried a British yardstick of scenery. As Said remarks, 'English places have a kind of export value':[49] the same was true of English stratigraphic sections which, like English manufactured goods, became recognized as patterns world-wide.[50] Explorers filled their descriptions of new landscapes with comparisons to those of the British Isles and the language of Romanticism, even seeing 'ruinous cathedrals and castles' in African dunes[51] and regretting Australia's want of 'bold or fantastic features, by which the imagination is excited and curiosity enhanced'.[52] Park-like scenery remained the ideal because it combined the beautiful with the tame and useful. The more perceptive explorers were sensitive to the interplay of landscape and emotion and the aesthetic dialogue between nature and civilization, waste and verdure. Similarly, their comments about space evinced a value system based on European concepts of size, regularity, and control. Hugh Clapperton described the plantations of Sokoto as being 'as neatly fenced as if they were the property of Englishmen', while the Landers pined for neat English cottages, complaining that African mud huts 'banish every favorable impression'.[53]

Because of homesickness, outraged sensibilities, or the imperative to convey intelligible images of outlandish places, the explorers thus projected a vision of the home islands on to new lands abroad, conquering them by an act of comparative imagination that began the process of reshaping them into something familiar enough to accept and enjoy. The explorers also carried a full battery of literary reference, so peripheral territories could be storied by analogy to stock scenes from literature—itself a canon often shaped by expansion and Empire. Illustrating this two-way trade in images that supplanted or expropriated native cultures, thereby embedding stereotypes facilitating European domination, the Landers compared an African ceremony to restore the eclipsed moon to a scene from *Robinson Crusoe*, noting that it only wanted a cannibal vignette to complete it.[54] Reversing the comparison between reality and art fifty years later, H. Rider Haggard recycled the physical features from Joseph Thomson's *Through Masai Land* to create a fictitious African topography for *King Solomon's Mines*.[55] The European imagination learned to encompass the world's diversity through the literature of exploration, which presented the periphery as a frontier for acting out both old and new challenges.

[49] Said, *Culture and Imperialism*, p. 94.

[50] Stafford, *Scientist of Empire*, p. 19.

[51] Walter Oudney's words: Bovill, *Missions to the Niger*, II, 188.

[52] Paul Edmund De Strzelecki, *Physical Description of New South Wales and Van Diemen's Land*, 2nd edn. (1845; Adelaide, 1967), p. 55.

[53] Bovill, *Missions to the Niger*, IV, p. 774; Hallett, *Niger Journal*, p. 184.

[54] Hallett, *Niger Journal*, p. 168.

[55] Thomson, *Through Masai Land*, p. xii.

While explorers generally saw what they were conditioned to see, many found the wilderness frightening and oppressive. Laird noted that the stillness of the forest of Sierra Leone 'chills the heart, and imparts a feeling of loneliness which can be shaken off only by a strong effort'.[56] Thomson, on the other hand, described his 'perfect ecstasy' in the forests of East Africa—the 'ideal of my dreams', where 'everything was strange, and grand, and colossal!'[57] Again, their differing reactions may be attributable to the half-century between them, though individual sensibilities play a part. Laird, writing in the mid-1830s, inhabited a world replete with ancient forests, in which nature still held sway over much of the planet, settlement frontiers were opening, and the maps of several continents still labelled vast areas *terra incognita*. His outlook—essentially a holdover from eighteenth-century sensibility—only saw nature as beautiful where it was tamed and useful. Thomson, in the early 1880s, lived in a world of closing frontiers, shrinking blank spots, and wild nature retreating everywhere before triumphant technological man. He had the luxury and (perhaps unconscious) sensibility to celebrate the value of something disappearing as rapidly as indigenous peoples—primeval wilderness capable of awing humans.

The numinous, dream-like quality of Thomson's experience suggests two further linkages. First, the new appreciation for wild nature and empty space coincided with the discovery of the unconscious and exploration of the irrational or intuitive as alternatives to inductive reasoning. As world-wide exploration dispelled the 'glowing hues of fantasy' that had beckoned Thomson to Africa,[58] the quest for untracked territory moved to the inner *terra incognita* of the human mind. The ritual baptisms in which several explorers indulged upon reaching their goals, such as MacDouall Stuart at the Timor Sea or Thomson at Lake Nyasa,[59] suggest that exploration represented a journey of discovery into the self, a plunge into the wellsprings of the soul, as much as geographical research. Secondly, absorption in overseas wilderness represented a form of time travel: the experience had not been available in western Europe for centuries. Conrad captured all of these themes in *Heart of Darkness*, with its focus on emptiness, timelessness, and implacable nature. The similarity between his description of the tropical forest and Thomson's is striking.[60] By the 1880s it was only in remote regions like the Congo or the East African highlands that such themes could still be acted out.

---

[56] Laird and Oldfield, *Narrative of an Expedition*, I, p. 181.

[57] Thomson, *To the Central African Lakes*, I, pp. 51–52.

[58] Thomson, *Through Masai Land*, p. 7.

[59] J. MacDouall Stuart, *Explorations Across the Continent of Australia*, 2nd edn. (1863; Adelaide, 1963), p. 57; Thomson, *To the Central African Lakes*, I, pp. 259–61.

[60] Compare Thomson, ref. 57, with Joseph Conrad, *Heart of Darkness* (1902; Harmondsworth, 1973), p. 48.

In the final decades of the century, therefore, the periphery came to represent an alternative to the confusing, suffocating restraints of modernist Europe, where urbanization and technology had transformed the very dimensions of life and thought. The cultural reactions to this trend—geopolitics, preservation of wilderness, exploration of the unconscious, fascination with the primitive—were paralleled by the politics of imperialism, the impulse to claim more space.[61] Yet British Imperialism went further in its acquisitiveness than expropriating land to commandeer the future. It also sought, through the willing aid of geology, to lay claim to the earth in depth, adding the lower portion of the third dimension to this grand Cartesian plan for enclosure. Similarly, Britain's upsurge of enthusiasm for mountaineering during the second half of the century, another activity closely linked to geography and Empire, represented the conquest of height, complementing geology's annexation of the subterranean world. The process of cultural appropriation reached backward within the fourth dimension as well, where stratigraphy and palaeontology helped annex 'deep time', beyond the past revealed by history and archaeology.[62] The British mind, therefore, balanced in dynamic tension between the dual concepts of the periphery as a primitive playground for the imagination and another locus for development. Imperialism was compatible with both these ideas, for it appropriated territories and their potentialities in order that Britons might transform them, thereby reliving the European experience in new settings that provided opportunities to avoid past mistakes. The role colonies played in the growth of European environmental consciousness and the vehemence of ideological debates about colonial development index the profound psychological ambivalence that lay behind this dialectic.[63]

The intoxication with space found expression not only in Imperialism, but in public interest in exploration, the mania for maps, emigration, and an outpouring of novels of Empire that chronicled the claustrophobia of the home islands and the reaction—greed for land and a longing for freedom to act in an unregulated landscape.[64] The explorer was the archetype of this fantasy of escape on to a larger stage where the ego could assert itself on an heroic scale. Exploration, like Empire, offered renewal for the race and the individual in reliving the immemorial saga of conquering nature, aided by the science and technology that proved the superiority of Europeans and their right to rule. Just as the rising curve of British

---

[61] Kern, *Culture of Time and Space*, pp. 4, 92.

[62] Stafford, 'Annexing the Landscapes'.

[63] Richard H. Grove, *Green Imperialism: Colonial Expansion, Tropical Island Edens and the Origins of Environmentalism, 600–1860* (Cambridge, 1995); John M. Mackenzie, *The Empire of Nature: Hunting, Conservation and British Imperialism* (Manchester, 1988).

[64] Kern, *Culture of Time and Space*, p. 166. Novels of Empire are thoroughly treated in Susanne Howe, *Novels of Empire* (New York, 1949) and Patrick Brantlinger, *Rule of Darkness: British Literature and Imperialism, 1830–1914* (Ithaca, NY, 1988).

exploration during this century charts Britain's economic, technological, and military dominance, it also indicates the rise to power of the middle classes. While the landowning classes supported exploration because it generated strategic, scientific, and prestige dividends, the middle classes provided the real impetus behind the nation's investment in overseas discovery. Middle-class scientists, military officers, merchants, and financiers, working through institutions like the RGS and the British Association that represented the community of interest between the traditional élites and rising economic groups, pushed the hardest for exploration and stood to gain the most from it.

While its material goals were obvious, the middle class also needed mental space that was unavailable in Britain's constricted landscape, where every acre was locked into the pattern of control that expressed the hegemony of the traditional élite. Through the technology, science, and organizational abilities that symbolized its ascendancy, the middle class seized on the overseas wilderness as its own fiefdom, calling new worlds into being to redress the balance of the old. Exploration, like the missionary movement, colonization, and the growth of commerce, was largely an assertion of middle-class goals, methods, and values through horizontal expansion. Leaving the finite fields of the occupied home islands, the explorers forged into the seemingly infinite jungles, deserts, forests, and prairies overseas. There they discovered room to create new Britains, built from scratch to middle-class design. They painted a picture of unbounded scope for improvements of every kind, from exploiting virgin resources to civilizing savage natives.

As their treatment of scenery suggests, explorers were often tense and despondent. They fought back by naming things, symbolically claiming alien territories by representing them with English terms. This act of supreme ego—a demonstration of control that had nothing to do with actual sovereignty—stamped new lands with the image of Europe, beginning the process of wresting them from the control of indigenous peoples.[65] Naming was at once an act of cultural imposition and of despoliation. It connected previously unknown places with European history, notifying other powers that Britain had some claim upon them by right of discovery. British explorers generally named geographical features and dedicated their narratives according to the Imperial social hierarchy: royalty first, followed by Cabinet-level sponsors, metropolitan department heads, colonial Governors or patrons, officers of the explorer's own service or institution, admired scientists or authors, mentors, friends, and relatives. Literary characters and places were also commemorated, and European place-names freely reused. For some, naming was an opportunity to remember and repay; for others, it was an act of

[65] Paul Carter, *The Road to Botany Bay: An Exploration of Landscape and History* (Chicago, 1987).

vengeance against hostile environments.[66] For Thomson, replacing 'uncouth' African names with English ones was simply a relief.[67]

Thomson and many other explorers saw discovery as conquest.[68] Claiming ceremonies, like naming, expressed this scientific equivalent of Imperial expansion. Maritime explorers had long claimed uncharted islands and coasts, but as the discovery frontier moved inland, policy changed to acquisition only where required, and explorers limited themselves to reaffirming British ownership of unvisited portions of recognized claims. In this respect exploration evolved from actual into symbolic conquest, though its cultural significance remained as high. As harbingers of European civilization, explorers developed an entire set of triumphal rituals: naming, claiming, self-baptism, flag-raising, toast-drinking, observing holidays, carving or burying records of achievement, recovering the possessions of martyred predecessors, and partaking of European foods upon their return. Ceremonial etiquette even evolved for meeting other whites in outlandish locations. James Stewart of the Livingstonia Mission introduced himself to Joseph Thomson at Lake Tanganyika 'according to the African salutation *à la mode*—"Mr. Thomson, I presume?" '[69] Such incidents became tropes in exploration literature that merged into mainstream culture, reflexively reinforcing the commitment to expansion. The behaviours ratified by the explorers, as well as their activities, overlaid a web of European association on new lands.

Explorers lost no opportunity to impress indigenous peoples with the superior power of Europeans. Much of this display centred on demonstrations of science and technology, which in the industrial era supplanted religion as key criteria for measuring human capacity. This transformation in attitudes also expressed the rise to power of the middle class, as well as its growing dominance of exploration. While the middle class was neither uniform nor unique in its scientific outlook— explorers continued to be recruited from the gentry—bourgeois intermediaries like John Barrow were instrumental in propagating the new doctrine that material achievement offered the most accurate gauge of civilization. Barrow served as an editor for John Murray, the premier English publisher of geographical narratives who, like Barrow, was a founder and Council member of the RGS. Through many articles in Murray's influential *Quarterly Review*, Barrow also tutored the public in interpreting exploration. Parvenus who made their careers by understanding science and technology thus drew upon and shaped the work of explorers, redefining the relativities between cultures to reflect their own values.

---

[66] e.g. John Oxley, *Journals of Two Expeditions into the Interior of New South Wales*, 2nd edn. (1820; Adelaide, 1964), pp. 91, 257.

[67] Thomson, *To the Central African Lakes*, I, pp. 148–49.

[68] Ibid., I, p. 211.

[69] Ibid., II, p. 4.

It was natural, therefore, that explorers exhibit the technical means that enabled their travels, including complex technics such as steamboats, guns, and scientific instruments, and objects as mundane as fireworks and magnets deployed simply to awe and entertain. Their mapping and observational activities were particularly stark demonstrations of cultural superiority, for native peoples often could not understand them. As with primeval environments, explorers often felt that in visiting indigenous cultures they were travelling millennia into the past, confronting ancestral stages of their own culture. The shock of peering into this ancient mirror forced Europeans to question industrial progress, but the disparities revealed easily confirmed the validity of Britain's choices. The decompression required to enter cultures with neither a clock-based sense of time nor a time-based work ethic usually produced frustration equivalent to a mental attack of the bends. Non-European spatial perceptions were similarly rejected.[70] Because quantification was central to industrialism and science, explorers not only used it to evaluate other cultures, but became uneasy when failed instruments left them in the same state of helpless inaccuracy as indigenes. One reason for the phenomenal popularity of the explorer in this era was that he 'voyaged at or beyond the frontiers of technology', demonstrating that the few remaining places not accessible to steam and telegraph could nevertheless be penetrated with a minimum of modern equipment.[71] Explorers were among the élite few who could take full advantage of the global transport systems;[72] for their place-bound audience, much of the excitement of their adventures lay in the disjunction between racing out to the jumping-off point backed by all the logistical might of Britain, and then slowing to the crawl of horse, camel, or safari as they entered unknown lands where Europe's writ did not yet run.

The explorers functioned as living projections of Europe, fired into the void of the peripheral wilderness like modern scientific probes into deep space. They delivered a sharp sense of what the new worlds overseas felt like, reimporting into Britain the colours, sights, sounds, smells, variety, and uninhibited behaviours conspicuously lacking in the culture of physiological denial codified in industrialism's Gospel of Work. The lands revealed by exploration offered an enticing antidote to the cult of the machine—a return to nature and the primitive. At the same time, they offered the lure of new worlds to conquer. This bifocal vision goes far to explain the great vogue of exploration narratives in the nineteenth century: they offered both escape into alternative worlds that were *real*, and psychological respite from the repression of Victorian mores. Audiences allowed themselves to

---

[70] Adas, *Machines as the Measure of Men*, pp. 177–97, 245–49, 259–64.

[71] E. J. Hobsbawm, *The Age of Capital, 1848–1875* (1975; New York, 1979), p. 62.

[72] R. A. Buchanan, *The Power of the Machine: The Impact of Technology from 1700 to the Present*, 2nd edn. (1992; Harmondsworth, 1994), p. 123.

enjoy explorers' escapades because they were conducted as scientific exercises with the full panoply of brass instruments, assumptions of white superiority, moral high-mindedness, and commercial perspective. Audiences did not respond to the work of scholars like Burton who, chameleon-like, shifted into the worlds they discovered. They favoured instead bluff authors like Lander or Thomson, who told an adventure story as straightforwardly as they accomplished their goals. The public's favourite, however, remained Livingstone, the martyr who suffered more, and seemed to enjoy it more, than any other explorer.

Victorian British culture was pervaded by geographical knowledge and metaphors that reflected the nation's powerful expansionist urge. While Britain's literate middle class demonstrated a seemingly insatiable appetite for exploration narratives,[73] the teaching of geography languished before the Devonshire Commission of 1870–75 recommended the establishment of a national curriculum, long the pattern on the continent. Yet by 1886, when the RGS published the Keltie Report on geographical education in Britain, no evidence of a general improvement in standards could be detected.[74] Britons' appetite for geography sprang not from schooling, but from direct engagement with commercial, Imperial, and philanthropic endeavours overseas, and more especially from identification with national heroes who were enlarging Britain's sphere in the world. Exploration exemplified the cultural importance of geography more clearly than any other contemporary activity. In the actions of the explorer in the field, in the style and workings of the Royal Geographical Society, in the content and texture of the narratives, maps, and art that conveyed the results of exploration, the emphasis on control of space is paramount. Exploration and Empire sprang from the same motives and mutually supported each other in defining, exploiting, and acquiring territory. Mapping the world and subjecting it to scientific inventory were principle accomplishments of nineteenth-century European civilization. These activities resulted from the same drive for expansion, power, and global connectivity that fuelled imperialism, free trade, emigration, the missionary movement, and the construction of world-wide transport and communications networks. Science operates within the same paradigm of control as technology. In Victorian Britain, they fused with exploration and Empire in support of an aggressive culture that sought to export its achievements for the betterment of Greater Britain. Scientific exploration led this movement, feeding information into metropolitan culture that facilitated the creation, maintenance, and expansion of Empire. Gladstone was more prescient than he knew: exploration and the cultural power of geogra-

[73] e.g. David Livingstone's *Missionary Travels* (London, 1857) sold 70,000 copies in eighteen months.
[74] Stoddart, 'R.G.S. and the "New Geography"'.

phy waned precisely as Empire reached its zenith. The once-actual realms of fantasy—mapped, annexed, and bureaucratized into banality—were then internalized in art and other symbolic forms. Yet during the Victorian heyday of British expansion, science and Empire reached their most perfect congruence in the activity of exploration, an acquisitive quest for knowledge that conferred power over new territories while sculpting metropolitan culture to support its use.

Select Bibliography

J. N. L. BAKER, *History of Geographical Discovery and Exploration* (New York, rept. of 2nd edn. of 1937, 1967).

MORAG BELL and others, eds., *Geography and Imperialism, 1820–1940* (Manchester, 1995).

IAN CAMERON, *To the Farthest Ends of the Earth: The History of the Royal Geographical Society, 1830–1980* (London, 1980).

PAUL CARTER, *The Road to Botany Bay: An Exploration of Landscape and History* (Chicago, 1987).

ALFRED FRIENDLY, *Beaufort of the Admiralty The Life and Times of Sir Francis Beaufort, 1774–1857* (London, 1977).

ROBIN HALLETT, ed., *Records of the African Association, 1788–1831* (London, 1964).

CHRISTOPHER HIBBERT, *Africa Explored: Europeans in the Dark Continent, 1769–1889* (London, 1982).

PETER HOPKIRK, *The Great Game* (London, 1990).

JOHN KEAY, ed., *The Royal Geographical Society History of World Exploration* (London, 1991).

CLEMENTS MARKHAM, *Memoir of the Indian Surveys* (London, 1871).

—— *The Fifty Years' Work of the Royal Geographical Society* (London, 1881).

HUGH ROBERT MILL, *The Record of the Royal Geographical Society* (London, 1930).

G. S. RITCHIE, *The Admiralty Chart: British Naval Hydrography in the Nineteenth Century* (London, 1967).

JANE ROBINSON, *Wayward Women: A Guide to Women Travellers* (Oxford, 1990).

ROBERT ROTBERG, ed., *Africa and its Explorers* (Cambridge, Mass., 1970).

DONALD SIMPSON, *Dark Companions* (London, 1975).

ROBERT A. STAFFORD, *Scientist of Empire: Sir Roderick Murchison, Scientific Exploration, and Victorian Imperialism* (Cambridge, 1989).

R. V. TOOLEY, *The Mapping of Australia* (London, 1979).

DEREK WALLER, *The Pundits: British Exploration of Tibet and Central Asia* (Louisville, Ky., 1990).

Part V
Indigenous Knowledge:
Environment, Medicine, Landscape

[13]

Introduction:
disease, medicine and empire

David Arnold

'Historians of Africa', wrote K. David Patterson and Gerald W. Hartwig in their introduction to *Disease in African History* published in 1978, 'have generally neglected the study of past health conditions – as well as the role of disease, health care and medicine in history – despite the obvious importance of the disease burden on the African continent.'[1] That statement (partly through Hartwig and Patterson's own labours) seems significantly less accurate today than a decade ago. The history of disease and medicine in general is not now as neglected as it once was and though much of that scholarly attention has focused on the role and impact of disease and medicine in European and North American societies, the rest of the world has come increasingly under scrutiny as well. Some areas have been more extensively investigated than others: the literature on Africa is now impressively varied and wide-ranging;[2] that on South and Southeast Asia remains relatively impoverished, while the Pacific region and Australasia can boast a rapidly growing literature of its own.[3] Much more, doubtless, can and will be done, but it is at least clear that many historians are now aware of the richness of the medical archive and its value for the study of social, political, and economic history.

Perhaps not surprisingly in view of the novelty of the field, there exists little agreement as to what are the central issues in the history of medicine and disease in the extra-European context. There is certainly no consensus over the approach to be adopted. Much of the existing literature has been frankly exploratory in character, doing little more than identifying episodes or trends that appear to be of wider significance or to represent historical turning points in their own right. As in Europe, some writers have confined themselves to the study of a single epidemic, aiming thereby to expose the conflicts and tensions revealed by a society in crisis;[4] others have framed their enquiry in

2   **IMPERIAL MEDICINE**

terms of a 'political economy' of health and disease and sought to relate the incidence of disease and the allocation of health care resources to the political and economic structures of colonial rule.[5] A few, even more ambitiously, have described the global dissemination of disease over the past five centuries.[6] Historical demography is one area of rapidly growing interest, while the emerging discipline of medical anthropology has also begun to open up new historical approaches to the study of disease and medicine in indigenous societies in Africa, Asia, Oceania and the Americas.[7] Given such a diversity of approaches and given, too, the continuing division between those who see the history of medicine as an unfolding story of scientific discovery and declining death rates and those who see medicine in a more interpretive light as a 'cultural artifact' and a 'reflection of a society's total being',[8] it is unlikely that any agreed overall picture will emerge in the near future. It would anyway be rash to assume that any kind of natural or automatic congruence exists between the historical experiences of the geographically, politically and culturally diverse lands that formed the western colonial world in recent centuries.

But while this volume cannot lay claim to any such comprehensiveness or universality, it does at least suggest the importance of certain emerging themes and issues in the history of medicine and disease and their role within the context of the colonial encounter. By focusing upon the nineteenth and twentieth centuries, a time of momentous change in the history of western medicine as in the lives of most non-European peoples, by identifying disease and medicine as a site of contact, conflict and possible eventual convergence between western rulers and indigenous peoples, by illustrating the contradictions and rivalries within the imperial order itself, by identifying the importance of medicine and disease to the ideological and political framework of empire, and by drawing attention to the role of medical agencies and practices in shaping the impact and identity of colonial regimes, the contributors demonstrate the centrality of disease and medicine to any understanding of imperial rule.

The main concern here is not so much with disease and medicine as such as with their instrumentality – what they reveal about the nature and preoccupations, the ambitions and the methods of an encompassing imperialism. At the same time the authors do not see western medical ideas and institutions as operating in a cultural void or as structures that could be imposed willy-nilly on compliant indigenous societies. Rather they see medicine and disease as describing a relationship of power and authority between rulers and ruled and between colonialism's constituent parts. These relationships are neither static nor necessarily uncontested: they are subject to influences emanating from the West (not least through developments in medical science during the period) as well as changes arising from within the territories themselves. This complex and shifting relationship is at the core of the case studies that follow, and it is hoped that through their examination of disease and medicine they will help to contribute to a fresh appraisal of the nature and consequences of imperialism itself.

Disease

For many nineteenth and early twentieth century European administrators, reformers and physicians the hazards and depredations of disease were an established part of a hostile and as yet untamed tropical environment. Africa, Asia, the Americas, were all seen to have their fatal and incapacitating diseases, and only through the superior knowledge and skill of European medicine was it thought possible to bring them under effective control. In this view European medical intervention represented progress towards a more 'civilised' social and environmental order. Thus Florence Nightingale, no insignificant figure in the history of Britain's colonial medical policies, saw the creation of a public health department for India as part of a mission to 'bring a higher civilisation into India'. Introducing health care to the subcontinent, she believed, was not only itself 'a noble task': it was nothing less than 'creating India anew'.[9] Similarly for the missionary and explorer David Livingstone medicine offered a way to rescue Africa from its suffering state, 'civilise' it, and prepare it for the blessings of Christianity.[10]

Although the negative health consequences of a European presence were sometimes recognised (as in the case of venereal disease), medicine was taken as a prime exemplar of the constructive and beneficial effects of European rule, and thus, to the imperial mind, as one of its most indisputable claims to legitimacy. Hubert Lyautey, the leading exponent of military medicine as an aid to the establishment of French power in Africa, went so far as to proclaim that 'La seule excuse de la colonisation c'est le médecin'.[11] In a speech made in 1926, towards the end of his active career, Lyautey confessed that colonialism had its 'harsh aspects' and was neither 'beyond reproach' nor 'without blemish'. But, he insisted, if there was one thing that 'enobles it and justifies it, it is the action of the doctor'.[12] Historians, too, have sometimes come close to endorsing this judgement. Writing in terms that echo Lyautey, Lewis Gann and Peter Duignan claimed, in discussing falling mortality rates and surging population growth in colonial West Africa, that 'whatever political disadvantages

4   IMPERIAL MEDICINE

colonialism might possess, from the biological standpoint its record is one of the greatest success stories of modern history'.[13]

But most recent writers have taken a far more critical view, highlighting the disastrous demographic and social consequences of initial European contact and seeing colonialism itself as a major health hazard for indigenous peoples. The 'successes' of western medicine, if apparent at all, are seen to have arrived late in the colonial era or as benefiting only a fraction of the total population.[14] One line of argument has centred on the often devastating effects of epidemic diseases unwittingly introduced by Europeans and unleashed on societies without prior experience of their ravages and with pitifully little immunity against them. Among the most spectacular examples of this were the smallpox, measles and other epidemics which accompanied the Spanish conquests of Mexico and Peru in the early sixteenth century. These 'virgin soil epidemics' are now believed to have done at least as much as Spanish arms and audacity in toppling the Aztec and Inca empires, decimating the indigenous population with infections to which the conquerors themselves were largely immune.[15] This pattern of bacteriological invasion was repeated in many other parts of the non-European world in later centuries – among the Khoikhoi of southern Africa in the eighteenth century, for example, or among the Australian aborigines, the New Zealand Maori and the Pacific islanders in the eighteenth and nineteenth centuries. Half of the aboriginal population around Port Jackson was thought to have perished from smallpox in 1789: in 1875 a measles epidemic killed nearly a third of the indigenous Fijians[16]. In many parts of the globe, therefore, Europeans had, quite literally, a 'fatal impact' on indigenous society. As Charles Darwin put it, 'Wherever the European has trod death seems to pursue the aboriginal. We may look to the wide extent of the Americas, Polynesia, the Cape of Good Hope and Australia, and we find the same result.'[17] So obvious was the association – in the indigenous perception as well as Darwin's – between disease and the whiteman's arrival by sea that Cook Islanders in the 1830s used the phrase 'I am shippy' when they fell prey to a foreign illness.[18] While to historians of the West the period 1300 to 1600 might appear to be the age of greatest epidemiological onslaught,[19] to historians of large parts of Africa, Oceania, and possibly of South and Southeast Asia as well, the eighteenth and nineteenth centuries, the age of European conquest and colonisation, was an era when epidemic mortality reached proportions almost on the scale of the Amerindian deaths in the sixteenth century.[20] Patterson and Hartwig concluded that, with the possible exception of West Africa, 'the unhealthiest period in all African history was undoubtedly between 1890 and 1930'.[21]

DISEASE, MEDICINE AND EMPIRE   5

Such assertions are, of course, extremely difficult to substantiate. We know as yet too little about the nature and extent of disease (and other causes of mortality) among the inhabitants of the Americas, Black Africa or Polynesia before the Europeans' arrival, even about cholera and smallpox in India before the establishment of British rule, to make such claims with confidence. It is probably a mistake to assume that pre-colonial societies, even those that existed in virtual isolation from the rest of the world, enjoyed an idyllic existence free from endemic disease and the periodic suffering caused by famine, warfare and pestilence.[22] It may be that the spate of epidemics which afflicted many societies following the white man's arrival have assumed significance simply because Europeans were on hand to record them. Many earlier epidemiological and ecological catastrophes may have preceded them without finding their way into any surviving historical account. It seems improbable, for example, that the ancient trading links between India and East Africa had not brought epidemics of smallpox in their wake long before the nineteenth century, or that pilgrimage routes to and from Mecca had not for centuries blazed epidemic trails across North Africa, the Middle East and western Asia.

But, even with that important caveat in mind, it still seems likely that the scale and intensity of European intervention in the period from the late eighteenth to the early twentieth centuries had a massive, and possibly unprecedented, epidemiological and environmental impact on the peoples of Africa, Asia and Oceania. The reasons are worth summarising.

Europeans forged new epidemiological links, either by relaying diseases (like smallpox and measles) long present in Europe or by establishing ties between parts of the world that had previously had few (if any) such connections with each other. The manner in which plague travelled from Hong Kong in 1894 to Bombay in 1896, to Cape Town in 1900 and Nairobi in 1902, and then to West Africa a decade or so later is indicative of the new facility of disease transmission opened up by modern trade, transport and imperial ties: and the pattern was repeated, in even more rapid and devastating form, in the influenza pandemic of 1918–19. As well as the diseases themselves, European trade and transportation helped the spread of disease vectors, the mosquitoes, fleas and lice by which epidemics were communicated.[23] Even where some contact had existed before 1800 along the African and Asian littorals, nineteenth-century European commercial and political penetration and the creation of colonial infrastructures – roads, railways, systems of labour migration, military recruitment and civilian administration – broke through the coastal barriers and destroyed the quarantining effects that distance and slow land transportation had for-

6   **IMPERIAL MEDICINE**

merly had on the dissemination of imported diseases. The way in which the 1918–19 influenza pandemic spread along these interior lines of contact and communication in Africa – through soldiers and mineworkers, through markets and railway stations – was a striking demonstration of the degree of European commercial and administrative penetration by the end of the First World War.[24]

Some diseases were transmitted directly by Europeans themselves. The spread of syphilis – known to sixteenth and seventeenth-century India as *firangi roga*, the European disease – was closely associated with European sexual contact.[25] White soldiers, along with local auxiliaries, porters and camp-followers, were potent disseminators of disease. Colonial wars of conquest, the crushing of local rebellions, and the military campaigning of two world wars, brought epidemiological disaster to civilian populations as well as creating high rates of disease mortality among the soldiers themselves.[26] Colonial labour recruitment policies also had serious health consequences both for the workers and for the communities from which they were drawn. Crowded and insanitary conditions in mine compounds and on plantations created micro-environments favourable to the spread of disease among the work force, aided by venereal disease contracted through prostitution, by alcoholism and by industrial pollution. The diseases of the mine, the factory and the city were, in turn, carried back by returning migrant workers to their own families and villages.[27]

On an even larger scale, the nature of the colonial economy and the ecological changes brought about (or hastened) under colonialism, could have far-reaching and enduring effects on public health. The expansion of irrigation canals and the construction of railway embankments created favourable habitats for malaria-carrying mosquitoes in India.[28] In East Africa the spread of uncultivated bush in the wake of the rinderpest, smallpox and famine that hit the region in the early colonial period are thought to have been responsible for the rapid dissemination of tsetse-borne sleeping sickness. In John Ford's damning phrase, the advent of colonialism in Africa marked 'an outbreak of biological warfare on a vast scale'.[29]

In time a colonial regime might provide a health care system that went some way towards meeting the needs of the indigenous population, but this might only partly compensate for the health problems which colonial land and labour policies had themselves helped to create.[30]

But critical though the demographic and social impact of disease undoubtedly is, it does not exhaust the importance of the disease factor in the history of European imperialism and of indigenous experience and response. The history of disease is more than just a history of

DISEASE, MEDICINE AND EMPIRE   7

microbes, mortality and medicine. Inevitably 'man clothes his cosmos in a moral cloak',[31] and in every society, present as well as past, disease, especially epidemic disease, takes on a wider social, political, and cultural significance. The current AIDS epidemic is but the latest reminder of an enduring human disposition to read meaning into collective affliction – to attribute blame and find scapegoats, to see the hand of God or the Devil in the otherwise enigmatic distribution of sickness and suffering. As Terence Ranger's essay in this volume reminds us, different sections of society can derive starkly different messages from a single catastrophe. In a colonial situation, where the cultural and political gulf between rulers and ruled was likely to be peculiarly acute, epidemics might variously be seen as a divine judgement on a benighted people or as a colonial malevolence unleashed against a troublesome race. The concurrence of epidemic catastrophe with European conquest deepened the bewilderment and trauma of conquest itself. The greater the white man's immunity, the greater the suspicion that he must be in some way complicit in the indigenes' misery and sickness.[32]

Disease was a potent factor in the European conceptualisation of indigenous society. This was especially so by the close of the nineteenth century when Europeans began to pride themselves on their scientific understanding of disease causation and mocked what they saw as the fatalism, superstition and barbarity of indigenous responses to disease. Le Roy Ladurie writes (in a borrowed phrase) of the 'unification of the globe by disease' in the period after 1300.[33] In a pathogenic sense there is much truth in this; but perceptually, in the imperial age, disease was one of the great dividers. The emergent discipline of 'tropical medicine' gave scientific credence to the idea of a tropical world as a primitive and dangerous environment in contradistinction to an increasingly safe and sanitised temperate world. As Europe began to free itself from its own epidemiological past, it was forgotten that diseases like cholera, malaria, smallpox and plague, though increasingly banished to the tropics, were part of Europe's own recent experience. Disease became part of the wider condemnation of African and Asian 'backwardness' just as medicine became a hallmark of the racial pride and technological assurance that underpinned the 'new imperialism' of the late nineteenth century.

Beneath the language of medical objectivity and the talk of 'sanitary science', European medical attitudes often remained highly subjective, embodying the social and cultural prejudices of the age. For Christian missionaries in Africa disease was tangible proof of a moral and social sickness it was their religious duty to dispel. The readiness with which endemic yaws in Uganda was mistaken for sexually-transmitted

8   IMPERIAL MEDICINE

syphilis was arguably not just a case of medical misdiagnosis or even
a consequence of current research interests in Europe but also a revelation of missionary doctors' presumptions about African promis-
cuity.[34] Likewise, cholera in India was more than a dreaded disease. It
was associated with much that European medical officers and administrators found outlandish and repugnant in Hindu pilgrimage and ritual
– so much so that the attack on cholera concealed a barely disguised
assault on Hinduism itself.[35]

The association of diseases like smallpox, plague, cholera and
malaria with the indigenous population – a development fostered by
the growing understanding of disease aetiology and transmission in the
late nineteenth century – deepened European suspicions of the indigenous population as a whole and of those servants, subordinates and
fellow town-dwellers with whom they lived in epidemiologically close
proximity. Science – and the fear of catching 'native' diseases – provided a pretext for withdrawing from closer social contact and for
locating European residential areas well away from 'native reservoirs'
of disease in the bazaars, townships, slums and coolie lines. In the
extreme case of South Africa medically-inspired social segregation
hastened the move towards the racial segregation of an incipient
apartheid; but it had its counterparts elsewhere, especially in British
West Africa around the turn of the century, and for a while racial segregation became 'a general rubric of sanitary administration set by the
Imperial government for all [its] tropical colonies'.[36]

Ill-health among indigenous peoples fostered Europeans' growing
sense of their innate racial and physical superiority. In the Darwinian
age, little regret was felt over indigenes who fell sick or perished at
the mere sight of a white man. It was easy to believe in the superiority
of the biologically 'fittest'. Debilitating and incapacitating illness like
sleeping sickness – the 'negro lethargy' of the West African slave
traders – and malaria fostered ideas of weakness, indolence and
inferiority, and contributed powerfully to the development of racial
stereotyping by Europeans.[37] The converse of this (as Waltraud Ernst's
essay reminds us for the British in India) was that those Europeans
who fell physically or mentally sick were quickly institutionalised or
sent back to Europe before the image of white superiority could become
tarnished.

Disease environments and perceptions of disease exercised a critical
influence on the very character of the emerging imperial order. In some
regions of the world, the epidemic invasions that accompanied the
Europeans' arrival helped to clear the white man's path, brushing aside
military resistance and emptying lands suited to white farming and
settlement. This pattern, set in the Americas in the sixteenth century,

DISEASE, MEDICINE AND EMPIRE   9

was replicated in later centuries, albeit on a smaller scale, in Australia and New Zealand, at the Cape and in the highlands of Kenya. As A. W. Crosby has argued, European expansionism into the 'neo-Europes' of the temperate regions of the globe, was aided by the operation of a 'biological imperialism' which enabled the establishment of European crops, animals and diseases at the expense of native flora, fauna and peoples. On the other hand, European control was likely to be costly and precarious in areas where the disease factor worked in the opposite direction.[38]

Crosby's biological determinism has much to commend it, but it overlooks the Europeans' capacity to devise structures of exploitation and control that would turn even environmentally hostile lands to their own advantage and profit. Although European mortality on the coast of West Africa was so staggeringly high as to earn it the epithet 'the white man's grave', Europe continued to conduct a highly profitable trade in slaves and gold using African traders, chiefs and other local intermediaries to supplement a minimal and transient European presence. In the West Indies, increasingly a disease environment costly of white men's lives (largely because of diseases imported through the slave trade), African slave labour was used to produce the sugar Europe craved, the slaves being either immune to such diseases or considered cheap enough to be expendable in the pursuit of greater profits. In eighteenth-century India, too, although it was conventional wisdom that new arrivals seldom lasted more than two monsoons, there was no question of abandoning valuable trade and possessions because of high European mortality. It should anyway be remembered that before the mid-nineteenth century Europeans were by no means in agreement as to the cause of high mortality in the tropics. Moreover, Europe's own death rates were still extremely high. A man might as easily die of smallpox (or drink) in eighteenth-century London as in Calcutta, but he might have fewer opportunities to 'shake the pagoda tree' and make the fortune that would set him up for life.[39]

The disease factor could be further mediated through the recruitment of local military and administrative auxiliaries. The recruitment of two West Indian regiments in 1794 was one of the ways in which the British countered the recent devastation caused to European armies in the region by yellow fever.[40] Even after western medicine had become more knowledgeable, British and French colonial expansion and control in Africa and Asia continued to rely heavily on indigenous soldiers, supplemented by smaller numbers of 'seasoned' Europeans.[41] And, in similar fashion, the disease burden in African mines or on tropical plantations was largely shifted from whites onto black or brown migrant workers.[42] Disease before 1900 might discourage white settlement and the use of white labour but it was certainly not an insurmountable barrier to European manipulation and control.

Medicine

Much as Crosby presents an argument for biological determinism in the history of European expansion, so Daniel R. Headrick has recently made a case for technological determinism in opening the flood-gates of nineteenth-century empire. He lists medicine among the several 'tools of empire' that enabled or facilitated western penetration and domination of the non-European world and cites quinine prophylaxis as a specific and critical illustration. Whereas for centuries Europeans, whether would-be conquerors, traders, explorers or missionaries, had persistently fallen prey to tropical fevers, the successful use of quinine by Dr William Baikie's Niger expedition of 1854 proved, Headrick argues, that disease need no longer be a barrier to European exploration and control.[43] As Oliver Ransford succinctly puts much the same point, quinine became 'the prime factor in allowing the whiteman's conquest of Black Africa.'[44]

Headrick's rather selective reading of the evidence leaves several considerations out of account. Forty years after the Niger expedition, a large percentage of European traders, missionaries and officials in West Africa were still dying (or becoming seriously ill) from malaria and yellow fever. Although European mortality in tropical Africa began to decline significantly from the 1890s, this appears to have been due more to the sanitary measures that followed Ronald Ross's discovery of the role of mosquitoes in malaria transmission than to quinine prophylaxis.[45] The use of quinine as a prophylactic was by no means as common in the second half of the nineteenth century as Headrick's account would seem to imply, and although Livingstone was an influential advocate of its use, there was no agreement about the dosage required. Quite apart from the difficulties of obtaining supplies adequate in quality as well as quantity, and the dauntingly unpleasant side-effects quinine could have, insufficient or inconsistent dosage could result in attacks of blackwater fever, which killed or incapacitated many Europeans, such as the missionaries around the shores of Lake Nyasa (Malawi) in the 1890s.[46] It would, therefore, be erroneous to over-estimate the importance of medicine in general and quinine in particular as a weapon in the armoury of nineteenth-century empire. Some medical authorities, like L. J. and J. M. Bruce-Chwatt, prefer to date the most significant advances in tropical medicine to the 1940s rather than the 1850s: only then, they claim, on the very eve of the

DISEASE, MEDICINE AND EMPIRE   11

white man's *departure* from Black Africa, was the 'menace of disease and death' at last 'largely dispelled . . . from the European penetration of tropical Africa'.[47]

Nonetheless, Headrick's argument, even if it exaggerates the specific importance of quinine, does direct attention to a major issue: what part did medicine play in the European imperialism of the late nineteenth and early twentieth centuries? Did it facilitate European expansion? Or did it contribute in other ways to the establishment and consolidation of imperial power? Was its influence confined only to the Europeans themselves or did it have a direct impact on the lives and attitudes of their new-found subjects?

In the long history of European expansion medicine was not a factor of consistent moment. Arguably, and it is a point supported by several of the contributions to this volume, western medicine attained its greatest importance in imperial ideology and practice between 1880 and 1930, the period when European empires were at their most expansive and assertive.

In earlier centuries, and especially before 1800, western medicine was far less domineering in its relationship with indigenous societies, and indeed was largely confined to the Europeans themselves. The Dutch and English East India companies, for example, had shipboard and shorebased physicians and surgeons to minister to the needs of their traders, officials, sailors and soldiers. The first hospitals established at places like Cape Town and Batavia (Djakarta) nestled close to the forts whose occupants they were designed to serve. Only rarely did European physicians offer their services to local rulers – as when the English company's William Hamilton treated the Mughal emperor Farruksiyar in 1714–15 – and even then commercial rather than medical objectives were likely to be uppermost.[48]

Before 1800 (in striking contrast with the late nineteenth century) Europeans commonly sought the help of local physicians, partly because so few of their own were available, partly from a conviction that they were likely to be better acquainted with the diseases (and the remedies) of the place. The Spanish in the Americas, despite their general disregard for the indigenous cultures, adopted a number of local medicines, including the use of cinchona ('Peruvian bark') as a febrifuge; and, until the Inquisition intervened, the Portuguese in western India used Brahmin 'panditos', practitioners of Hindu Ayurvedic medicine, as their physicians.[49] The English East India Company encouraged its servants to rely on local rather than expensively imported medicines, arguing in 1622 that 'the Indies hath drugs in far greater plenty and perfection than here'.[50] In an age when folk medicine still thrived in Europe, white settlers overseas often devised their own medicines making use of locally avalable plants and animals.[51]

During the course of the nineteenth century, however, Europe took a radical step away from medical pluralism. A growing conviction of the unique rationality and superior efficacy of western medicine began to possess European doctors and lay men alike. One factor in this was the momentous discovery by Edward Jenner in the 1790s of cowpox vaccination: this was the first clear demonstration that man could master a major disease and it was a European innovation that was rapidly and confidently exported to the non-European world.[52] Important, too, in changing European attitudes was the growing professionalism of doctors trained and qualified by European medical schools, such as Edinburgh, and dispatched in significant numbers to the expanding outposts of empire. Late in the century the status and authority of western medical practitioners was further enhanced by the development of the specialist sciences of modern medicine. Bacteriology, pioneered by Louis Pasteur and Robert Koch between the 1860s and 1880s, was particularly significant in ushering scientific medicine into an age of 'curative confidence'.[53] The creation of the London and Liverpool schools of tropical medicine in 1899 and the introduction of courses in the subject at the universities of Edinburgh, Durham, Aberdeen and Queen's Belfast (along with parallel developments on the continent and in the United States) raised tropical medicine to a pinnacle of importance in an already prestigious profession.[54]

Nor was this new-found confidence and influence restricted to the laboratory, the surgery and the hospital ward. Recourse to state power to enforce sanitary and health measures (as in Victorian Britain) gave the medical profession unprecedented authority in public life and affairs of state, and this was quickly reflected in Europe's overseas possessions too. One of the characteristics of the period of imperial administration between 1880 and 1930 was the spate of laws, proclamations and decrees giving state sanction to health measures of various kinds. The plague epidemics of the late nineteenth and early twentieth centuries provoked some of the most drastic legislative responses; but smallpox, sleeping sickness and malaria also called forth many of the colonial state's most sweeping enactments (even if, in practice, such laws proved singularly difficult to enforce).[55]

As Malcolm Nicolson's account illustrates for the case of New Zealand, where there were few other educated and trained professional men to hand, doctors became all-purpose 'experts', authorities on matters as diverse as 'native affairs' and town planning. They were recruited as military advisers and impromptu diplomats, as geologists and pioneer anthropologists. If David Livingstone represents an early

DISEASE, MEDICINE AND EMPIRE 13

archetype of the medical missionary and explorer in the mid-nineteenth century, Leander Starr Jameson, associate of Cecil Rhodes and leader of the 'Jameson Raid' into the Transvaal in 1895, epitomises the medical man turned adventurer and politician in the high noon of empire half a century later.[56]

Modern medicine forged new and powerful links between the imperial capitals and distant colonial domains. The turn of the century witnessed the emergence of peripatetic medical specialists, men of the eminence of Britain's Ronald Ross and Germany's Robert Koch, who visited colonial territories from West Africa to New Guinea hoping to bring the benefit of their metropolitan expertise to the service of embattled colonial administrations. The special commission appointed by the British government to investigate plague in India in the 1890s (discussed here by Ian Catanach) was one of the first of many such enquiries – into sleeping sickness in Uganda in 1902, for example, or malaria in Nyasaland (Malawi) a decade later.[57] By this date, whole societies (and not just small colonies of European soldiers, traders and settlers) were being brought under western medical scrutiny. Indeed, the purview of tropical medicine was as wide as imperialism itself, reaching even beyond the formal bounds of empire into regions like Central America where the United States' strategic interests in the contruction of the Panama canal led to a massive campaign to eradicate yellow fever between 1905 and 1913.[58]

All this stood in abrupt contrast with less than a century earlier when European medicine had felt itself competent to deal with only that limited range of afflictions – smallpox, leprosy, lunacy – with which Europeans were long acquainted or which they felt were too dangerous to be ignored.[59] Vaccination, as I argue in the Indian context, made smallpox uniquely subject to western medical intervention at a comparatively early date in the history of colonialism. In many territories, even in the second half of the nineteenth century, vaccination and the segregation of lepers and lunatics were among the few 'medical' services provided. Not only could European medicine at the time offer few other solutions: it lacked even a basic knowledge of the state of health among the great majority of the population, and, indeed, colonial administrations recognised no pressing responsibility for their wellbeing.[60]

The causes and consequences of this rapid transition from white man's medicine to public health during the latter decades of the nineteenth and early years of the twentieth centuries are touched upon in several of the essays in this volume and have received some discussion elsewhere as well. But some of the more salient features of this transformation and of its relationship with a burgeoning imperialism

14   **IMPERIAL MEDICINE**

might usefully be outlined here.

There were several imperatives behind increasing western medical intervention. One was the growing realisation, which first gained recognition in India during the course of the nineteenth century, that the health of European soldiers and civilians could not be secured through measures directed at their health alone. As Bengal's newly created Sanitary Commissioner observed in 1865: 'Even if we look no further than the protection of the health of the European soldiers, it will be evidently insufficient if we endeavour to improve the condition of our cantonments alone, and ignore the existence of the masses of the native population by which our troops are surrounded.'[61] It followed, therefore, that the protection of European health could only be attained by measures that took western medicine into the 'black towns' and bustees. Military losses to disease were particularly persuasive in forcing the British (and other colonial powers) to take responsibility for indigenous health. With casualties often heavier from disease than from battle, and given the military's importance to the maintenance of imperial control, the health of soldiers (especially white soldiers) was a high priority of the colonial state. But medical investigations, whether into venereal disease, or cholera, or (as John Farley shows) bilharzia, repeatedly demonstrated that the sanitary and medical security of the military could not end at the barrack gates, but had to extend into adjacent urban and rural areas and even to the indigenous population as a whole.

European self-interest was at work in other ways, too. In an age of expanding world-wide trade and communications, Europe was well aware of its own increased vulnerability to 'tropical' diseases. The cholera epidemics that reached Europe from India several times between the 1830s and 1890s were a persistent and worrying reminder: so were occasional importations of yellow fever from West Africa and the West Indies.[62] In order to counter this threat a series of international (in practice European) sanitary conferences were held from 1851 onwards. In addition to seeking to introduce measures to intercept diseases like cholera before they reached Europe, the conferences also put pressure on individual powers to tackle the more serious epidemic diseases in their own colonies. As the 'factory of cholera', British India was subject to repeated international censure, and the advent of plague there in 1896 put further pressure on the British administration.[63] In an era of competitive imperialism persistently high levels of epidemic mortality were seen as a mark of poor colonial management. King Leopold's requests in 1903 and 1906 for international assistance in combating sleeping sickness in the Congo were partly an attempt to improve the highly unfavourable reputation his regime had already acquired.[64]

Capitalism's internal contradiction between the pursuit of labour efficiency (and thus of workers' health) and the pursuit of profit impelled European colonial regimes and the commercial and industrial enterprises that worked under them towards greater involvement in indigenous health care. There were several interlocking considerations here. Ill-health, especially the circulation of epidemic disease, among African and Asian workers, posed a hazard for white employees and their families. High morbidity and mortality rates interfered with the efficiency and profitability of production in mines, plantations and factories, and discouraged further labour recruitment. In areas where agricultural productivity was adversely affected, as in late nineteenth-century India, by recurrent epidemics and famine, state revenues were directly threatened; while in Africa military recruitment for the First World War highlighted (as it had in Britain at the time of the Boer War) the political disadvantages of an undernourished and unhealthy population.[65] Careless, therefore, though early European dominion often was of the health of its subjects, there was a growing appreciation of the practical returns of investing in the health of the workforce. Given the critical importance of indigenous labour to the realisation of wealth from the colonies, *some* degree of medical intervention was clearly in the colonial interest, providing it did not eat too substantially into the profitability of empire and individual enterprise. The development of tropical medicine and the enthusiasm with which it was taken up by Joseph Chamberlain during his term as Britain's Colonial Secretary between 1895 and 1903 was motivated above all by a desire to protect the lives of the growing number of Europeans living and working in the tropics. But, in an age in which the imperial powers were anxious to unlock the mineral and agricultural wealth of their 'undeveloped estates', the health of indigenous labour was too important to be entirely overlooked. Disease, in the parlance of the 1920s and 1930s, was an obstacle to 'development'.[66] But, because of the self-interested reasons for colonial concern, medical intervention was piecemeal and selective, with scant resources concentrated in areas vital to the operation of the colonial economic and adminstrative system. Thus, while the mine compounds, the plantations, the barracks and the main urban centres were favoured, there was a general neglect of the rural population and of the health of women and children. There was an emphasis on epidemic rather than endemic disease, and upon curative rather than preventive medicine.

The value of medicine as an aid to economic imperialism was most fully realised by the emissaries of North American capitalism. Having undertaken an extensive anti-hookworm campaign in the southern

16   **IMPERIAL MEDICINE**

United States as a way of improving labour efficiency and integrating
the neglected South more fully into the expanding industrial economy
of the North, the Rockefeller Foundation turned its attention overseas
at a time when the United States was embarked on its own expansionist drives. In addition to promoting campaigns against hookworm
and later against bilharzia and other diseases of the tropics and funding
research on tropical medicine in general, the Rockefeller Foundation,
under the guidance of Frederick T. Gates, saw medicine as a superior
form of propaganda for the benefits of western civilisation and
capitalism and as a way of opening up Asia to American commercial
and industrial penetration.[67]

But increasing western medical intervention cannot be explained in
terms of immediate material self-interest alone. Medicine was a part
of the ideology as well as the accountancy of empire. D. Schoute once
argued that when the British occupied the Dutch East Indies early in
the nineteenth century they replaced the Dutch company's narrowly
'commercial' medical outlook (aimed solely at keeping its European
employees alive) with an 'idealist' vision of medicine in the service of
the entire population, Indonesian and European alike. As Schoute himself made clear, the practical outcome of these medical initiatives was
small, but the idea of a medicine for the people had, he claimed, a
lasting influence on the subsequent medical policy of the restored
Dutch administration.[68] The case of the Dutch East Indies, like that
of smallpox vaccination in India, and of attempts to take western
medicine to the indigenous peoples of New Zealand and South Africa
at a slightly later date, all point to the way in which medicine was
coming to be seen as having a wider utility in the service of empire.[69]
Even before the scientific breakthroughs of the late nineteenth century,
imperial powers were beginning to use medicine as a demonstration
of their benevolent and paternalistic intentions, as a way of winning
support from a newly subject population, of balancing out the coercive
features of colonial rule, and of establishing a wider imperial hegemony
than could be derived from conquest alone. Given the limited military
and administrative resources at the disposal of the early colonial
regimes, this was a potentially important weapon in the consolidation
of imperial rule, though experience sometimes showed that it might
have the reverse effect of deepening mistrust of European motives.
While many of these early initiatives lost their way, falling victim to
administrative neglect or financial stringency, they paved the way for
a return in the late nineteenth century to ideas of wholesale medical
intervention.

It was not only colonial administrations and imperial powers that
saw in medicine a wider utility. With Livingstone as their mentor, late

nineteenth-century missionaries in Africa appreciated the unique opportunity medicine offered to establish contact with the indigenous population and hopefully to gain an influence over them. As Bishop Smythies of the Universities Mission to Central Africa testified in 1893:

> there are some mission fields in which only doctors seem to be able to gain any great influence. There is a fantastic hatred to [sic] Christianity, which can only be broken down by sympathy shown for the sufferings of the body. . . together with the power to alleviate them. It seems as if it is only through medical work. . . that an opening to the hearts of these people can be found.[70]

Missionaries were accordingly recruited specifically for their medical training, and hospitals and dispensaries became central elements in missionary strategy. Missionaries identified themselves with western medicine's 'empirical and rational approach' and through it sought to counter the authority of their rivals, the 'witchdoctors'.[71] Medical work brought missionaries some conversions, though not a few of those they tended and cured took the missionaries' medicine without surrendering their own religious beliefs and their theories of disease causation.[72]

Empire

In the closing years of the nineteenth century medicine became a demonstration of the superior political, technical and military power of the West, and hence a celebration of imperialism itself. It gave expression to Europe's faith in its own innate superiority, its mastery over man as well as nature. Medicine registered the imperial determination to reorder the environment and to refashion indigenous societies and economies in the light of its own precepts and priorities.

As imperial economies and administrative systems expanded and sought a more comprehensive hold over the lives and labour of the people, medicine developed as a central agency for the acquisition of knowledge and the extension of control. Medicine was one of the ways in which imperialism sought to 'know' the people and establish its authority over them – through the vast quantities of information about diseases and health that began to be amassed in statistical and scientific form and through the development of medical agencies, themselves often branches of the state structure itself, that began to reach out into the countryside as well as the towns. The process was not everywhere the same. Sometimes it was slow and faltering: it pro-

18   IMPERIAL MEDICINE

gressed more quickly in some territories and under some colonial powers than others. But it seemed to reach a general crescendo between the 1890s and the First World War with major campaigns against sleeping sickness, plague, cholera, yellow fever and malaria. In many regions this sudden proliferation of medical power was central to the development of a colonial state and often to the development of the colonial economy as well. Campaigns like those against sleeping sickness in the Congo or against cholera in the Philippines were (as Maryinez Lyons and Reynaldo Ileto both demonstrate) massive exercises in state intervention and social manipulation.[73] Medical intervention impinged directly upon the lives of the people, assuming an unprecedented right (in the name of medical science) over the health and over the bodies of its subjects. Whereas in the pre-colonial past health and medical care were matters for individual initiative or at most communal effort, under imperial rule they became part of a wider process of state regulation and centralised control. Rudolph Virchow, the pioneer of cellular pathology, once claimed that politics was 'nothing but medicine on a grand scale'.[74] In the light of the imperialism of the 1890s and 1900s one is tempted to revise that statement and contend that the imperial medicine of the period was nothing less than politics on a mass scale.

The very nature of late nineteenth-century medicine contributed to this far-reaching medical interventionism. Seeing itself as rational, scientific and universalistic, western medicine defined itself in opposition to the presumed irrationality and superstition of indigenous medicine. The customs and beliefs of the people were treated as obstacles to be overcome, obscurantism to be brushed aside by the new scientific age. They had to be replaced, as one writer put it in 1950, by 'genuine knowledge'.[75] Because the bacteriology of Pasteur and Koch understood disease in terms of microbal invasions, which it was the task of medicine to uncover and counter through the use of specific therapeutics, the social, cultural and economic context of disease was largely ignored.[76] Imperial regimes were encouraged to believe that they could resolve their most pressing health problems by tackling them scientifically, and by showing sufficient resolution to carry them through regardless of local opposition and dissent. The medicine of the late nineteenth and early twentieth centuries was thus of a peculiarly confident and determined kind, believing that it was acting in the best interest of the people. It was confidently assumed that there could be self-contained technical solutions to what were in reality complex social, economic and environmental problems.

DISEASE, MEDICINE AND EMPIRE 19

The involvement of the military in the medical interventionism of the imperial period is one of its most striking and significant features. In part it reflected the prominence of the army in the establishment and maintenance of the imperial regimes in general, as well as the extent to which the health of the military remained one of the prime incentives behind wider medical action. Governments were prepared to commit resources to the protection of the army's health and sanitation to an extent unthinkable for civilian populations. Apart from missionaries, army medical corps were often the sole agencies involved in research into tropical medicine and constituted the only reservoirs of medical expertise that could be called on in an emergency. In some areas – like Morocco under French rule, or the Sudan under the British, the military monopolised the provision of western medical care until after the First World War.[77] But no less significant was the disposition to see (and speak of) medical intervention in military terms: the French, in particular, 'tackled the battle for health as a military operation', setting up mobile army medical teams to combat sleeping sickness, leprosy and malaria in rural Africa,[78] and the Americans and Belgians showed a similar reliance. It was often felt that the military had the resolution (as well as the manpower) that the civilian administration lacked and was less likely to be constricted by red tape and local opposition. But the military was also likely to ride roughshod over civilian dissent. To civilian eyes, the army's medical operations looked little different from its more familiar military role and the governments were perhaps not unwilling for them to be reminded of imperial might in this way. But one of the consequences of this medical and military assertiveness was that it was likely, as in the Philippines, to alienate the people still further rather than eliciting gratitude and obedience.

The role of the army is a reminder, too, of the importance of considering the manner and the means of European intervention. Attention so far has mainly focused on medical ideas and policies to the neglect of the institutions and agencies through which western ideas and practices were actually relayed to the indigenous peoples. The doctor's race, sex and demeanour could matter as much as the therapies he proffered. Physical contact between doctor and patient could be one of the most direct and traumatic aspects of the colonial encounter.[79] Nor should the importance of indigenous agencies be overlooked. To supplement its own limited manpower and to carry out the more menial medical roles of dressers and vaccinators, colonial medicine looked for local recruits. Initially such subordinates were generally despised and subject to the European prejudices of the day. 'Technical knowledge is easily acquired by the African', the head of colonial Kenya's medical service pronounced in 1926 of African medical assistants, 'but a sense of responsibility, pertinacity, honesty and general trustworthiness are woefully lacking'.[80] But once, for reasons of political pressure or administrative necessity, Asians and Africans began to be given specialist training and professional responsibility the earlier visible foreignness of western medicine became diluted, there could be greater freedom of communication between doctor and patient and rather more sensitivity might be shown than formerly to local sentiment and custom. The Africanisation or Indianisation of medical personnel probably facilitated the eventual acceptance and assimilation of what had once been exclusively the white man's medicine.

The medical interventionism of the late nineteenth and early twentieth centuries threw up its own internal conflicts and contradictions. Western medicine was not moving into a therapeutic and cultural void. Western medical measures threatened many deeply-held beliefs, many long-established social practices. Not surprisingly, they were often greeted with wild rumours, profound suspicion, evasion and resistance. There was violence and rioting as homes and property were destroyed, people were searched, and medical suspects were carted off, like convicts, to hospitals, segregation camps and lazarets. The scale and intensity of these reactions, though by no means universal, raised doubts among colonial administrators about the medical efficacy, the political expediency, and the financial desirability of such massive undertakings. In some cases compromise was preferred to confrontation, even if it meant sacrificing medical objectives and allowing indigenous spokesmen and medical practitioners some part in the conduct of public health campaigns.[81] There was, besides, little agreement among the medical specialists themselves as to how major epidemics like sleeping sickness or plague should be brought under control, and these divisions of expert opinion often inhibited the development of effective and consistent disease-control strategies.[82] Again, as Ian Catanach reminds us for India's plague years, civil administrators were often unwilling to abdicate responsibility to medical officers and experts and insisted that the direction of such far-reaching and politically-sensitive matters must remain firmly under administrative control. The more established colonial power became (or the more it fell back upon the support of 'traditional' elites and social groups in the face of mounting nationalist opposition) the more reluctant it was to undertake a wholesale medical interventionism that might undermine an already precarious status quo.

DISEASE, MEDICINE AND EMPIRE 21

By the 1920s the administrative and technological limits of western medicine were becoming apparent, as the 1918 influenza pandemic served to remind both the colonisers and the colonised. Although the war and the pandemic acted as a stimulus to the expansion of rural public health in some parts of Africa, the onset of the Depression barely a decade later imposed fresh curbs on public health expenditure. The 'heroic' age of medical intervention was over. A number of major epidemic diseases had by that stage either been curbed or, for reasons independent of western medical action, had ceased to be matters of major colonial concern. There was a growing realisation, too, that disease admitted of few easy solutions, and that much of the ill-health of the colonial world was almost intractably bound up with problems of poverty and nutrition.[83] As Michael Worboys shows, the interwar years brought some recognition that deficient nutrition, rather than major epidemic diseases, now stood in the way of colonial 'development'. But since, as Audrey Richards demonstrated in her pioneering study of the Bemba,[84] diet was largely inseparable from culture, this presented an even larger and more problematic site for state intervention. Although there was some shift from curative to preventive medicine, from epidemic disease to endemic ill-health and undernutrition in the inter-war period, the scale of the problem revealed was too great (and too costly in terms of colonial money and manpower) for most colonial administrations to contemplate tackling in any comprehensive way.

Perhaps the final contradiction of western medical intervention lay in its legacy for the unravelling of empire. The position of western medicine during the Afro-Asian struggles for independence was often ambiguous. On the one hand some nationalists looked to a revival of indigenous medicine as part of a rediscovery of their own cultural roots and rejected the West's alien therapeutics. On the other hand, indigenous practitioners of western medicine were often influential members of the nationalist middle class and colonialism was condemned for its stinginess in bestowing the benefits of western medicine.[85] Perhaps this very ambivalence was an indication of the strength of the impact imperial medicine had made upon indigenous societies.

Notes

I am indebted to John MacKenzie and Terence Ranger for their helpful comments on an earlier draft of this introduction. But neither of those good doctors bears responsibility for any ailments that continue to afflict it.
1 K. D. Patterson and G. W. Hartwig, 'The disease factor: an introductory overview', in G. W. Hartwig and K. D. Patterson (eds.), *Disease in African History: An Introduc-*

22   **IMPERIAL MEDICINE**

tory Survey and Case Studies, Durham, N. C., 1978, p. 3.

2 See K. D. Patterson, 'Disease and medicine in African history: a bibliographical essay', *History in Africa*, I, 1974, pp. 141–8; D. Patterson (comp.), *Infectious Diseases in Twentieth-Century Africa: A Bibliography of their Distribution and Consequences*, Waltham, Mass., 1979; S. Feierman (comp.), *Health and Society in Africa: A Working Bibliography*, Waltham, Mass., 1979; S. Feierman, 'Struggles for control: the social roots of health and healing in modern Africa', *African Studies Review*, 28, 1985, pp. 73-147.

3 R. MacLeod and M. Lewis (eds.), *Disease, Medicine and Empire*, London, forthcoming; N. G. Owen (ed.), *Death and Disease in Southeast Asia: Explorations in Social, Medical and Demographic History*, Singapore, 1987.

4 The 1918 influenza pandemic has been a particularly rewarding example of this approach. See Terence Ranger's chapter and the references cited there; also H. Philips, 'The local state and public health reform in South Africa: Bloemfontein and the consequences of the Spanish 'flu epidemic of 1918', *Journal of Southern African Studies*, 13, 1987, pp. 210-33; G. Rice, 'Christchurch in the 1918 influenza pandemic', *New Zealand Journal of History*, 13, 1979, pp. 109-37.

5 L. Doyal, *The Political Economy of Health*, London, 1979; M. Turshen, *The Political Ecology of Disease in Tanzania*, New Brunswick, 1984.

6 A. W. Crosby, *The Columbian Exchange: The Biological and Cultural Consequences of 1492*, Westport, Conn., 1974; W. H. McNeill, *Plagues and Peoples*, Harmondsworth, 1979.

7 For some Indian examples see, I. D. Mills, 'The 1918–19 influenza pandemic: the Indian experience', *Indian Economic and Social History Review*, 23, 1986, pp. 1-40; T. Dyson (ed.), *India's Historical Demography: Studies in Famine, Disease and Society*, London, forthcoming. A useful collection of papers on medical anthropology is D. Landy (ed.), *Culture, Disease, and Healing: Studies in Medical Anthropology*, New York, 1977.

8 C. E. Rosenberg, 'George Rosen and the social history of medicine', in C. E. Rosenberg (ed.), *Healing and History*, Folkestone, 1979, p. 3. Cf., F. F. Cartwright, *A Social History of Medicine*, London, 1977, p. 1: 'The primary purpose of a social history of medicine must be to describe how the practice of medicine has affected the health and development of people.'

9 Quoted in E. Cook, *The Life of Florence Nightingale*, II, London, 1914, p. 1.

10 J. J. McKelvey, *Man against Tsetse: Struggle for Africa*, Ithaca, 1973, pp. 19-21. See, too, the discussion of western medical missions as a 'reconstructive force' in late nineteenth-century China in R. H. Graves, *Forty Years in China*, Baltimore, 1895, chapter 14.

11 Quoted in C. D. Langen's introduction to D. Schoute, *Occidental Therapeutics in the Netherlands East Indies during Three Centuries of Netherlands Settlement (1600–1900)*, Batavia, 1937, p. iii.

12 Quoted in J. Paul 'Medicine and imperialism in Morocco', *MERIP Reports*, 60, 1977, p. 7.

13 Quoted in Patterson, 'Disease and medicine', p. 148.

14 E.g., J. Suret-Canale, *French Colonialism in Tropical Africa, 1900–1945*, London, 1971, pp. 395-416.

15 D. Joralemon, 'New World depopulation and the case of disease', *Journal of Anthropological Research*, 38, 1982, pp. 108-27; Crosby, *Columbian Exchange*, chapter 2.

16 R. Elphick and H. Giliomee (eds.), *The Shaping of South African Society, 1652–1820*, London, 1979, pp. 22-3; A. W. Crosby, *Ecological Imperialism: The Biological Expansion of Europe, 900-1900*, Cambridge, 1986, chapters 9 and 10; D. Morley, 'Severe measles', and M. Kamien, 'The Aboriginal Australian experience', in N. F. Stanley and R. A. Joske (eds.), *Changing Disease Patterns and Human Behaviour*, London, 1980, pp. 117, 256.

17 Quoted in A. Moorehead, *The Fatal Impact: An Account of the Invasion of the South Pacific, 1767–1840*, Harmondsworth, 1966, p. 212.

DISEASE, MEDICINE AND EMPIRE 23

18 R. Lange, 'Plagues and pestilences in Polynesia: the nineteenth-century Cook Islands experience', *Bulletin of the History of Medicine*, 58, 1984, p. 332.

19 'The sacrifice of human lives resulting from the global spread of pathogenic agents during these three centuries [1300–1600] has had no parallel before or since': E. Le Roy Ladurie, *The Mind and Method of the Historian*, Brighton, 1981, p. 30.

20 E.g., in Equatorial Africa and the Congo: Suret-Canale, *French Colonialism*, pp. 36-7; O. Ransford, *'Bid the Sickness Cease': Disease in the History of Black Africa*, London, 1983, p. 76. Disease was not the only cause of the massive population decreases recorded, but equally military conquest, coercive labour policies, and the disruption of agricultural production also contributed to the depopulation of early Spanish America.

21 Patterson and Hartwig, 'The disease factor', p. 4. India, too, may have reached a peak of mortality at about this time: see I. Klein, 'Death in India, 1871–1921', *Journal of Asian Studies*, 32, 1973, pp. 639-59.

22 Lange, 'Plagues and pestilence', pp. 326-9.

23 E.g., the jigger-flea from South America to Africa: see H. Kjekshus, *Ecology Control and Economic Development in East African History: The Case of Tanganyika, 1850–1950*, London, 1977, pp. 134-6.

24 I. R. Phimister, 'The "Spanish" influenza pandemic of 1918 and its impact on the Southern Rhodesian mining industry', *Central African Journal of Medicine*, 19, 1973, pp. 143-6; J. W. Brown, 'Increased intercommunication and epidemic disease in early colonial Ashanti', in Hartwig and Patterson, *Disease in African History*, p. 191.

25 J. M. de Figueiredo, 'Ayurvedic medicine in Goa according to European sources in the sixteenth and seventeenth centuries', *Bulletin of the History of Medicine*, 58, 1984, p. 227; M. J. Azevedo, 'Epidemic disease among the Sara of Southern Chad, 1890–1940', in Hartwig and Patterson, *Disease in African History*, p. 134.

26 Notably in East Africa during the First World War: A. Beck, *A History of the British Medical Administration of East Africa, 1900–1950*, Cambridge, Mass., 1970, p. 59-64.

27 M. W. De Lancey, 'Health and disease on the plantations of Cameroon, 1884–1939', in Hartwig and Patterson, *Disease in African History*, pp. 153-79; I. R. Phimister, 'African labour conditions and health in the Southern Rhodesian mining industry, 1898–1953', in I. R. Phimister and C. van Onselen, *Studies in the History of African Mine Labour in Colonial Zimbabwe*, Gwelo, 1987; R. M. Packard, 'Tuberculosis and the development of industrial health policies on the Witwatersrand, 1902–1932', *Journal of Southern African Studies*, 13, 1987, p. 186.

28 I. Klein, 'Malaria and mortality in Bengal, 1840–1921', *Indian Economic and Social History Review*, 9, 1972, pp. 132-60.

29 J. Ford, *The Role of Trypanosomiases in African Ecology: A Study of the Tsetse Fly Problem*, Oxford, 1971, p. 489. See also Kjekshus, *Ecology Control*.

30 T. O. Pearce, 'Political and economic changes in Nigeria and the organisation of medical care', *Social Science and Medicine*, 14, 1980, p. 95.

31 B. D. Paul, 'The role of beliefs and customs in sanitation programmes', in Landy, *Culture, Disease, and Healing*, p. 235.

32 N. Wachtel, *The Vision of the Vanquished: The Spanish Conquest through Indian Eyes, 1530–1570*, New York, 1977; D. Arnold, 'Cholera and colonialism in British India', *Past and Present*, 113, 1986, pp. 128-31.

33 Le Roy Ladurie, *Mind and Method of the Historian*, p. 29.

34 J. Orley, 'Indigenous concepts of disease and their interaction with scientific medicine', in E. E. Sabben-Clare, D. J. Bradley and K. Kirkwood (eds.), *Health in Tropical Africa during the Colonial Period*, Oxford, 1980, pp. 127-37.

35 Arnold, 'Cholera', pp. 140-2. Mental illness also occasioned extreme views of the 'native' mind and character: M. Vaughan, 'Idioms of madness: Zomba lunatic asylum, Nyasaland, in the colonial period', *Journal of Southern African Studies*, 9, 1983, pp. 218-38.

36 R. E. Dumett, 'The campaign against malaria and the expansion of scientific, medicial, and sanitary services in British West Africa, 1898–1910', *African Historical*

24   **IMPERIAL MEDICINE**

Studies, 1, 1968, p. 71; L. Spitzer, 'The mosquito and segregation in Sierra Leone', *Canadian Journal of African Studies*, 2, 1968, pp. 49-61; M. W. Swanson, 'The sanitation syndrome: bubonic plague and urban native policy in the Cape colony, 1900–1909', *Journal of African History*, 18, 1977, pp. 387-410.

37 McKelvey, *Man against Tsetse*, pp. 7-8; cf., Ronald Ross, *Memoirs*, London, 1923, p. 43, for malaria as a cause of Indians' 'great timidity', 'habit of unquestioning obedience' and 'amazingly deliciate physique'.

38 Crosby, *Ecological Imperialism*.

39 P. D. Curtin, '"The White Man's Grave": image and reality, 1780-1850', *Journal of British Studies*, 1, 1961, pp. 94-110; T. Wilkinson, *Two Monsoons*, London, 1976; H. Furber, *Rival Empires of Trade in the Orient, 1600–1800*, Minneapolis, 1976, p. 6.

40 F. Guerra, 'The influence of disease on race, logistics and colonisation in the Antilles', *Journal of Tropical Medicine and Hygiene*, 69, 1966, p. 34.

41 W. B. Cohen, 'Malaria and French imperialism', *Journal of African History*, 24, 1983, pp. 23-36.

42 G. Burke and P. Richardson, 'The profits of death: a comparative study of miners' phthisis in Cornwall and the Transvaal, 1876–1918', *Journal of Southern African Studies*, 4, 1978, p. 169. In Fiji indentured Indian labourers were brought in to work the sugar estates when the native Fijians were hit by the 1875 measles epidemic: Morley, 'Severe measles', p. 117.

43 D. R. Headrick, *Tools of Empire: Technology and European Imperialism in the Nineteenth Century*, New York, 1981, chapter 3.

44 Ransford, *'Bid the Sickness Cease'*, p. 71, though significantly the reference here is to the period from the 1880s.

45 Dumett, 'Campaign against malaria', pp. 155-7.

46 Cohen, 'Malaria', pp. 25-8; M. Gelfand, *Lakeside Pioneers: Socio-medical Study of Nyasaland (1850–1920)*, Oxford, 1964, pp. 11-14.

47 L. J. and J. M. Bruce-Chwatt, 'Malaria and yellow fever', in Sabben-Clare, *Health in Tropical Africa*, p. 58.

48 D. G. Crawford, *A History of the Indian Medical Service, 1600–1913*, I, London, 1914, pp. 113-28; for early Dutch medicine and hospitals at Batavia and the Cape, see Schoute, *Occidental Therapeutics*, and E. H. Burrows. *A History of Medicine in South Africa up to the End of the Nineteenth Century*, Cape Town, 1958, chapters 1 to 5.

49 C. S. Kidwell, 'Aztec and European medicine in the New World, 1521–1600', in L. Romanucci-Ross, D. E. Moerman, and L. R. Tancredi (eds,), *The Anthropology of Medicine: From Culture to Method*, New York, 1983, pp. 20-31; de Figueiredo, 'Ayurvedic medicine'. The Portuguese physician Garcia d'Orta at Goa in the sixteenth century and the Dutch Jacobus Bontius in Java in the seventeenth both studied and wrote major works about local drugs and medical practices.

50 Crawford, *Indian Medical Service*, I, p. 22.

51 E.g., among the Boers: Burrows, *Medicine in South Africa*, pp. 190-4.

52 J. Z. Bowers, 'The odyssey of smallpox vaccination', *Bulletin of the History of Medicine*, 55, 1981, pp. 17-33.

53 O. Temkin, *The Double Face of Janus*, Baltimore, 1977, p. 48.

54 Dumett, 'Campaign against malaria', p. 163; Michael Worboys, 'The emergence of tropical medicine: a study in the establishment of a scientific speciality', in G. Lemaine, R. MacLeod, M. Mulkay and P. Weingart (eds.), *Perspectives on the Emergence of Scientific Disciplines*, Hague, 1976, pp. 75-98. For the professionalisation of medicine in the United States during this period and its relationship with industrial capitalism, see E. R. Brown, *Rockefeller Medicine Men: Medicine and Capitalism in America*, Berkeley, 1979, pp. 74 f.

55 Swanson, 'Sanitation syndrome', and my chapter below; for developments in state medicine in Britain in this period, see J. L. Brand, *Doctors and the State: The British Medical Profession and Government Action in Public Health, 1870–1912*, Baltimore, 1965.

56 See Burrows, *Medicine in South Africa*, for the involvement of Dr W. G. Atherstone

DISEASE, MEDICINE AND EMPIRE 25

in various aspects of South African public life; and T. Ranger, 'The mobilisation of labour and the production of knowledge: the antiquarian tradition in Rhodesia', *Journal of African History*, 20, 1979, pp. 507-24, for the doctor, oral historian and ethnologist J. Blake-Thompson; and, more generally, Paul, 'Medicine and imperialism'.

57 McKelvey, *Man against Tsetse*, pp. 71-84; A. J. Duggan, 'Sleeping sickness epidemics', in Sabben-Clare, *Health in Tropical Africa*, pp. 19-29.

58 G. M. Gibson, *Physician to the World: The Life of General William Crawford Gorgas*, New York, 1950; A. J. Ornstein and J. Le Prince, *Mosquito Control in Panama*, New York, 1916. See also Reynaldo Ileto's chapter in this volume.

59 Schoute, *Occidental Therapeutics*, pp. 41, 165-7; Burrows, *Medicine in South Africa*, pp. 64-6.

60 W. Nitisastro, *Population Trends in Indonesia*, Ithaca, 1970, p. 41; Burrows, *Medicine in South. Africa*, pp. 102-3, 121-2. As late as 1892, one West African Governor professed himself 'in perfect ignorance of sickness and mortality among tribes of the interior': Dumett, 'Campaign against malaria', p. 154.

61 Quoted in J. W. Cell, 'Anglo-Indian medical theory and the origins of segregation in West Africa', *American Historical Review*, 91, 1986, p. 321. As both Waltraud Ernst and John Farley show, 'poor whites' were also a major source of colonial concern if only for reasons of racial prestige.

62 W. Coleman, 'Epidemiological method in the 1860s: yellow fever at Saint-Nazaire', *Bulletin of the History of Medicine*, 58, 1984, pp. 161-3. As the work of Koch and Haffkine on cholera and its prophylaxis indicate, Europe used overseas territories like Egypt and India as laboratories for the investigation of diseases that still threatened Europe itself. The French (notably under Laveran) similarly used Algeria for research into a malaria that still menaced Mediterranean Europe, and yellow fever was a cause of concern in the United States long before the Havana and Panama campaigns at the turn of the century. In 1892, the year Haffkine presented his initial work on cholera prophylaxis in Paris, the disease was raging in the city. It was only because he was barred from conducting further tests in his native Russia that Haffkine turned to India instead in 1893–6 and so became involved in 'tropical' medicine: G. H. Bornside, 'Waldemar Haffkine's cholera vaccines and the Ferran-Haffkine priority dispute', *Journal of the History of Medicine*, 37, 1982, pp. 404-5.

63 N. Howard-Jones, *The Scientific Background of the International Sanitary Conferences, 1851–1938*, Geneva, 1975, pp. 74, 78-9.

64 McKelvey, *Man against Tsetse*, pp. 40-2; H. G. Soff, 'Sleeping sickness in the Lake Victoria region of British East Africa, 1900–1915', *African Historical Studies*, 2, 1969, p. 261; and Maryinez Lyons' chapter below.

65 Doyal, *Political Economy*, chapter 7; M. Gelfand, *A Service to the Sick: A History of the Health Services for Africans in Southern Rhodesia (1890–1953)*, Gwelo, 1976, pp. 17-18, 28, 36, 40; Beck, *British Medical Administration*, p. 73.

66 'The ravages of the tsetse-fly are the greatest menace to the development of tropical Africa', reported the East African Commission of 1925: Ford, *Role of Trypanosomiases*, p. 1; Worboys, 'Tropical medicine', p. 83-5; Dumett, 'Campaign against malaria', pp. 167-84. See, too, Michael Worboys' discussion of nutrition below.

67 Brown, *Rockefeller Medicine Men*, pp. 105-29. 'The Rockefeller programmes did not concern themselves with worker's physical productivity alone. They were also intended to reduce the cultural resistance of "backward" and "uncivilised" peoples to the domination of their lives and societies by industrial capitalism.' E. R. Brown, 'Public health in imperialism: early Rockefeller programs at home and abroad', *American Journal of Public Health*, 66, 1976, p. 900.

68 Schoute, *Occidental Therapeutics*, p. 189.

69 See my essay on smallpox vaccination below; Burrows, *Medicine in South Africa*, pp. 180-2 for the 'conquest by civilisation' policy in New Zealand and South Africa.

70 Quoted in Gelfand, *Lakeside Pioneers*, p. 8. The evangelical value of medical work had been appreciated in India and China at a slightly earlier date than in tropical

26   **IMPERIAL MEDICINE**

Africa – between the 1830s and 1850s. See I. H. Hacker, *A Hundred Years in Travan-core, 1806–1906*, London, 1908, chapter 6; E. V. Gulick, *Peter Parker and the Opening of China*, Cambridge, Mass., 1973.

71 Gelfand, *Lakeside Pioneers*, p. 307; Burrows, *Medicine in South Africa*, p. 181. T. O. Ranger, 'Godly medicine: the ambiguities of medical mission in southeast Tanzania', *Social Science and Medicine*, 15, 1981, p. 262.

72 Ranger, 'Godly medicine'; P. C. G. Adams, 'Disease concepts among Africans in the Protectorate of Northern Rhodesia', *Rhodes-Livingstone Journal*, 10, 1950, pp. 14-50.

73 See also Duggan, 'Sleeping sickness', pp. 21-3; D. Arnold, 'Touching the body: perspectives on the Indian plague, 1896–1900', in R. Guha (ed.), *Subaltern Studies*, V, Delhi, 1987, pp. 55-90.

74 Quoted by R. W. Lieban, 'The field of medical anthropology', in Landy, *Culture, Disease, and Healing*, p. 14.

75 G. Maclean, 'Medical administration in the tropics', *British Medical Journal*, 1, 1950, p. 759.

76 Brown, *Rockefeller Medicine Men*, p. 75; Temkin, *Double Face of Janus*, pp. 435-6; Turshen, *Political Ecology*, pp. 11-16.

77 Paul, 'Medicine and imperialism', p. 8; G. W. Hartwig, 'Smallpox in the Sudan', *International Journal of African Historical Studies*, 14, 1981, pp. 15-16.

78 S. Ofusu-Amaah, 'The African experience', in Stanley and Joske, *Changing Disease Patterns*, p. 312; J. H. Ricosse, 'French West and Equatorial Africa', in Sabben-Clare, *Health in Tropical Africa*, pp. 228-38; McKelvey, *Man against Tsetse*, pp. 126 f.

79 F. Fanon, *A Dying Colonialism*, Harmondsworth, 1970, pp. 104-9.

80 Quoted in Beck, *British Medical Administration*, p. 84; cf., my chapter below.

81 I. J. Catanach, 'Plague and the Indian village, 1896–1914', in P. Robb (ed.), *Rural India: Land, Power and Society under British Rule*, London, 1983, pp. 216-43, and his essay in this volume; Arnold, 'Touching the body'. Two other inhibiting factors were important. One was the many technical difficulties that confronted western medicine in the tropics, even in such relatively simple matters as vaccination: Brown, 'Increased intercommunication', p. 189, and my chapter. Another critical factor was the unwillingness of most imperial governments to fund large-scale preventive campaigns. To his lasting chagrin, Ross was never allowed to conduct an imperial campaign against malaria-carrying mosquitoes with the kind of resources used by the Americans in Cuba and Panama: Dumett, 'Campaign against malaria', pp. 166-7, 189-90.

82 Beck, *British Medical Administration*, pp. 24-35; Worboys, 'Tropical medicine', pp. 90-1.

83 Beck, *British Medical Administration*, pp. 105 f.

84 A. Richards, *Land, Labour and Diet in Northern Rhodesia: An Economic Study of the Bemba Tribe*, Oxford, 1939, especially the introduction and chapter 3, 'Native views on food'. See, too, the special issue on 'African native diet', in *Africa*, 11, 1936.

85 E.g., Roger Jeffrey, 'Doctors and Congress: the role of medical men and medical politics in Indian nationalism', in M. Shepperdson and C. Simmons (eds.), *The Indian National Congress and the Political Economy of India 1885–1985*, Aldershot, 1988, pp. 160-73.

[14]

Natural Sciences

Patrick Harries

And out of the ground the Lord God formed every living beast of the field, and every fowl of
the air; and brought them unto Adam to see what he would call them: and whatsoever Adam
called every living creature, that was the name thereof.
(Genesis 2:19)

When Henri-Alexandre Junod left Southampton for Lourenço Marques on 16 June
1889, his mind was occupied by thoughts of his first posting as a missionary. His
excitement rose noticeably as he neared Africa. When the 'Tartar' docked at Lisbon,
the exotic plants found in the city's botanical gardens captivated him.[1] Three weeks
later the ship stopped at Durban for two days where he greatly appreciated the 'luxu-
riant winter vegetation'. It 'would be impossible to describe', he exclaimed, 'the pleasure
we experienced in the presence of this new nature: flowers, butterflies, all unknown
until that moment!'[2] Three months after his arrival in Mozambique Junod had to
reassure the mission council in Lausanne that the passion with which he pursued
natural history in his spare time had not dented his evangelical zeal. The biological
and theological sciences were organically tied, he reminded his superiors, for 'nature
is the work of God and merits attention and calls for study'.[3]

The glorification of God through the examination of his handiwork was only one
of the reasons for Junod's interest in the natural sciences. By ordering the world of
plants and animals, Junod seemed to bring an element of domestication to the amor-
phous and chaotic world that surrounded the mission. Through his entomological and
botanical studies, he was able to explain the local environment in terms of a system
of understanding that he and others qualified as universal. But this understanding
was built on a hierarchy of knowledge that, as this chapter will reveal, created and
encouraged imperialism. Local people were excellent observers and collectors of data,
had their own ideas about classification and contributed in important ways to 'scientific' knowledge; but ultimately Junod felt that they were unaware of the true system
underlying the organization and understanding of nature.

This chapter suggests that the division of scientific knowledge into racial categories
helped portray the seizure of other peoples' lands as a natural process, even a benevolent
duty. In this chapter I attempt to show how research in the natural sciences rested on
an unequal encounter between different ways of naming, organizing and understand-

ing nature. The racialized concept of 'science', I believe, accompanied and informed the deliberate, rational decisions, taken on the basis of political and economic criteria that informed the logic of imperialism. But science also supplied individuals such as Junod with the methodology needed to study society and, at the same time, provided indigenous scholars with some of the intellectual capital needed to secure their position as a political élite.

Collecting in Switzerland

The role of churchmen as agents of Christianity and civilization has a long history in Switzerland. In the late eighteenth century roving evangelists and educated clergymen stranded in rural outposts found in the study of nature both an intellectual challenge and a diversion from a humdrum existence.[4] Sharp differences of soil, temperature, rainfall, vegetation and animal life, often on the same mountain, provided the collector in Switzerland with a rich environment in which to practise his pastime. Pastors confined by their profession to one small district gained national renown by supplying urban experts with a range of rare specimens. They formed the backbone of the learned associations that provided a forum for discussion cutting across regional, linguistic and religious differences.[5] Stern Calvinist ministers promulgated the disciplined collecting of plants, insects and rocks as an edifying way of displacing frivolous, even pagan village pastimes. Collecting also took the pastor into the fields where his knowledge of science allowed him to act as the secular as well as spiritual advisor to his parishioners. But the overriding reason for this clerical enthusiasm for collecting and classifying was the glorification of God's handiwork: the demonstration that the rich diversity of nature could be reduced to visible patterns and systems that could only be explained in terms of divine inspiration. In this sense, collecting was like poetry or painting, a means of celebrating both the landscape and its maker.[6]

By uncovering the natural order of the earth and the living objects that inhabited it, learned individuals were able to exercise a symbolic dominance over the environment. They (re)ordered the perception of nature in a way that made it entirely familiar to their generation. By cataloguing and classifying plants, animals and minerals according to 'modern' criteria, or by collecting meteorological statistics, they convinced themselves of their ability to understand their world and exercise some control over its development. This confidence was supported by the many learned societies, established in the early nineteenth century, that gave a new professionalism to the study of nature. These popularized findings through small and large meetings as well as through the media of scientific journals and monographs, museum exhibitions, botanical gardens and herbaria.[7] Members of learned societies in Switzerland constructed scientific truth when they tested their findings in open debate and corroborated their evidence by drawing on the work of colleagues elsewhere. For the Swiss, these societies stressed the regional or federal basis of intellectual life in the country, and they provided an important forum in which men of ability could advertise talents appreciated by the growing commercial and industrial bourgeoisie. This activity gave men of science and letters a new source of intellectual and social capital and a very personal stake in the identification of science with progress.[8]

The intellectual filing system developed by men of science and letters tamed the chaos of the world and reduced the terror of the unknown. This heroic role was one of the principal attractions of natural science. While botanizing in the High Alps, Jean-Jacques Rousseau thought himself 'almost another Columbus'.[9] Other collectors were perhaps more modest in their musings, but they shared with Rousseau the self-imagery of the intrepid explorer as they 'discovered' and 'penetrated' 'lost valleys' and 'new worlds'.[10] Romanticism compounded the heroic imagery of these explorers who, like Alexander von Humboldt, tested their vigour and masculinity in the Alps before journeying to unexplored parts of the world. In the mid-nineteenth century, a climber such as Emile Javelle imagined the conquest of an alpine peak to be the equivalent of crossing an unexplored Australian desert.[11] The peasants in this wilderness were as ignorant as they were close to God.[12] The locals might be naturally hospitable, but they were still *hommes sauvages*, 'children burned by the sun' whose ideas showed a 'mixture of reason and superstition'.[13] They were good observers of nature but were unable to classify or explain the data they collected with such vigour.[14]

Men of science and letters took their idea of knowledge into the Alps with missionary zeal, for they believed their studies would lead the popular classes from the bondage of ignorance into a universal, objective and egalitarian system of understanding. In the nineteenth century, the light of civilization brought by books and libraries to dark mountain huts and villages became an important literary motif in Switzerland.[15] This new way of thinking relegated local ideas to the position of 'folk beliefs' that would disappear under the swell of modernity, together with linguistic dialects and pagan customs. Men of science and letters substituted the tyranny of knowledge for the tyranny of superstition in Switzerland, and in less than a generation, they would take these ideas and practices to Africa.

Science in Support of Religion

Henri-Alexandre Junod was raised in this intellectual climate. When his father Henri left the small village of Lignières to study in Neuchâtel, the cantonal capital had developed into an international centre of scientific research. The polymath Frédéric de Rougemont was one of the earliest to return from the Prussian capital where he had studied under the geographer Karl Ritter. But most famous was Louis Agassiz who, after his move to the newly-established Neuchâtel Academy in 1832, became the moving force behind the recently formed natural history society. He quickly provided this institution with its own scientific journal and turned the town's museum into one of the best regional repositories of natural history specimens in Europe. Grants from the Prussian king and local wealthy amateurs paid for these and other institutions in Neuchâtel; their generosity also funded field expeditions that allowed Agassiz to send Johan von Tschudi to Peru in the footsteps of von Humboldt in 1838.

During his stay in Neuchâtel, Agassiz built up an internationally renowned research team. Its members included Arnold Guyot, who had studied under Ritter and von Humboldt in Berlin. In 1848 Guyot would follow Agassiz to the United States where he started a long and distinguished career six years later, as professor of physical geography and geology at Princeton, then called the College of New Jersey.[16] Carl Vogt would become a well-known figure in political and scientific life in Germany and Switzerland. After leaving Neuchâtel, he became a leading materialist thinker, a member of the cantonal and federal parliaments and rector of the University of Geneva towards the end of his life. Like Vogt, Edouard Desor was a political refugee from Giessen in the Grand Duchy of Hesse. He was the only member of Agassiz's team to remain in Neuchâtel, where he became professor of geology at the Academy and a leading intellectual and political figure in the canton.[17] In 1846 Agassiz moved to the United States where, in the words of Stephan Jay Gould, he became 'the most powerful and imperious biologist' in the country. 'Without doubt,' writes Gould (who admittedly stood in Agassiz's line of descent at Harvard), he was 'the greatest and most influential naturalist of nineteenth-century America.'[18] It should be stressed that, on his departure from Switzerland, Agassiz endowed his small town with an important physical and intellectual heritage that served as an inspiration to later generations of aspirant natural scientists in Neuchâtel.

Part of the renown of Agassiz and his colleagues came from their willingness to spend extended periods of time in the Alps where they recovered the fossil remains of marine and other animals, and measured the structure and movement of glaciers. Through his field studies, Agassiz came to punctuate the long history of the world with a series of catastrophes followed by distinct, special creations. At least partly for religious reasons, Agassiz refused to recognize any connection between these 'epochs of creation'. Like Cuvier, he refuted Lamarck's explanation of the resemblance between the fossilized plants and animals found in different geological strata: that living organisms were able to adapt themselves physically, over generations, to their changing environment. Instead, Agassiz saw the will of God behind the evolution of life on earth. His findings and those of his colleagues pushed back the age of the world and filled it with a startling diversity. But they quickly divided into two schools. While Guyot and de Rougemont reassessed the Biblical narrative of Creation in the light of recent geological discoveries, Vogt developed a purely materialist approach to the subject.[19] Agassiz's work said little about the origins of humanity, which he left dangling on the edge of a monstrous gap bordered on the one side by the act of creation and on the other by Biblical and classical scholarship. To fill this void, Desor and Frédéric de Rougement threw themselves into the study of primitive societies.[20]

During the 1850s interest in this work increased palpably as engineers cut the first railways through the mountains of Switzerland. When they drilled through different geological strata, they uncovered a series of fossils that allowed a far closer reading of the prehistoric past. At the same time, the discovery of Stone Age villages along the shores of several Swiss lakes merely heightened the passion with which people searched for their origins. Henri Junod's generation obsessively gathered evidence on the beginnings and development of the physical world and the place occupied by humanity in its long history. This deep concern with the relationship between geology, society and history was transmitted to his son's generation, many of whom, as missionary explorers trained in Greek and Latin, would see in Africa a reflection of Europe's prehistory and, more distantly, the primitive origins of humanity.

While pastor of Chezard-Saint-Martin, Henri Junod taught natural history, particularly geology and ornithology, in the village school. One of the young people who fell under the spell of this charismatic clergyman was a young primary school teacher named Fritz Tripet. Self-taught and from a humble background, Tripet, with Junod and others, became in 1873 a founder member of the Independent Church of

Neuchâtel. A decade later, equally under the influence of Junod, he was appointed the professor of botany at the town academy.[21]

When Henri Junod and his family moved to the cantonal capital in 1867, he introduced his children to the botanical diversity found in the Collégiale's garden and encouraged them to collect and classify plants. This led Henri-Alexandre to assemble his first formal register of dried plants with the help of his elder sister Elizabeth.[22] The boy's love for natural history blossomed when he entered Neuchâtel's classical *collège latin*, a building housing the town's library and the outstanding natural history museum built up by Agassiz and his colleagues. The school's teaching staff included Paul Godet (1836-1911), a Berlin-trained expert in the taxonomy of regional molluscs, a field that lent itself both to the collection of fossils and the careful observation of minute detail. Paul formed part of the intellectual aristocracy of the town. His father, Charles-Henri Godet (1797-1879), was an internationally-renowned botanist whose friends and acquaintances stretched from Alexandre von Humboldt to Agassiz, Shuttleworth and Jacob Burckhardt (who lodged with the family as a young man).[23] Paul's uncles, Frédéric and Georges Godet, were the town's two outstanding theologians and his cousin Philippe Godet was an important literary and intellectual figure who later became an influential Liberal politician and eventually rector of the university. Henri-Alexandre Junod would later remark on the profound impact on his life of this family of eminent humanists.[24]

While at school in Neuchâtel, Henri-Alexandre Junod also benefited from the patronage of Fritz Tripet, at this time secretary of the natural history society founded by Agassiz. As the editor of its journal for almost 30 years and professor of botany at the academy, he was a locally influential figure. Throughout his long career, Tripet organized outings aimed at introducing students to the glorious detail of uncorrupted nature, and encouraged his charges to find a patriotic pride in the discovery of plants which he duly named and classified. In general, Tripet emphasized what we might today call 'fieldwork' over and above the more abstract questions raised by plant anatomy.[25] He also managed to publish the work of promising young scientists; in the late 1870s–80s, he was able to place Henri-Alexandre Junod's first articles on zoological and botanical topics in *Le Rameau de Sapin*, the journal of the junior branch of the canton's natural history society.[26]

At college Junod was strongly influenced by Paul Godet's uncle Georges, the professor of theology who introduced him to the work of Kant. He particularly fell under the spell of Georges' brother Frédéric, the professor of exegesis and criticism who, through his lectures, tutorials and publications, kept before his students the unique elements of Christianity: Christ's virgin birth, the incarnation of God in man, the crucifixion and resurrection. In an intellectual climate shaken by the recent discoveries of Darwin and others, these pious Calvinists and their *émigré* friends in America and elsewhere battled against conservatives who saw science solely as a breeding-ground for the scepticism and rationalism undermining Biblical revelation. The contemplation of nature embraced by the Godets and their friends provided hope to lives weighed down by original sin and the fear evoked by the doctrine of predestination. Their faith was confirmed rather than shaken by the extended size of the heavens discovered by astronomers, the wealth of detail revealed by the microscope and, particularly in Neuchâtel, the series of preordained, divine creations uncovered by geology and palaeontology. God's power and benevolence were visible to them in the intricate design and wonderful harmony of nature. For these deeply religious men, Psalm 104 rang with new meaning as they read it in the light of scientific discovery: 'How manifold are thy works, O Lord! In wisdom hast thou made them all!' Rather than undermine belief, science served to increase the patent glory of God.

From America, their friend Louis Agassiz saw the diversity in the natural world as the product of a 'superior intelligence' that was also responsible for the physical resemblances between species of different epochs. The species 'manifested in the animal and vegetable kingdoms', he wrote, were produced by 'the thoughts of the Creator of the Universe'.[27] But Agassiz left the Biblical tradition when he abandoned the Mosaic version of creation and refuted the idea that species originated in single pairs. Instead, he ascribed life on earth to a series of special creations when he asserted that, after the destruction of species during catastrophes, they were repeatedly created again in new forms and in large numbers, in habitats intended for them by God.[28]

The influential works of Arnold Guyot and his close friend Frédéric Godet conformed more closely to the Biblical narrative. Like Buffon and Cuvier, they reinterpreted the seven days of Biblical creation as seven stages or geological epochs in the cosmic history of the world.[29] Like Schleiermacher, they believed human reason as much as personal revelation demonstrated the existence of God. For Godet, science was 'a sister, a powerful ally of faith'.[30] 'The light of religious revelation and science shines from different origins', he wrote in the manner of Francis Bacon, 'one comes from the sky and the other from the earth, but in meeting they combine to produce perfect clarity.'[31] For Guyot, 'the book of Nature' was as much the work of God as the Bible: both were a source of divine knowledge. 'Coming from the same Author, [they] complement one another, forming together the whole revelation of God to man.' By revealing nature's intricacy of design, its regularities and laws, scholars provided 'innumerable proofs of the almighty power and wisdom of its author'.[32] The glimpse of the 'Celestial Pilot' provided by nature was even clearer when viewed from the pulpit. There, Henri-Alexandre's father thundered against 'the obscurantists, the stiflers, the gagging priesthood', who questioned the material and social benefits brought by science. Like his friends Frédéric Godet and Arnold Guyot, Henri believed that a thorough knowledge of science would reinforce the doctrines of Christianity and draw to it 'the noblest of thirsting souls'.[33]

These Christians found their religious beliefs confirmed as they came to view the act of creation as less the product of a single divine *fiat* somewhere in a remote past and more as an ongoing process, linking the past with the present and the future. In this way God was not, as St Augustine had first speculated, a transcendental figure beyond the stars who had created the world and then left it to its own devices; nor was he a watchmaker who had merely set the mechanism ticking. God was rather an all-pervading presence whose immanence and omniscience could be read in the series of creations that constituted the world in both time and space. This way of perceiving nature, as the harmonious handiwork of God, infused earnestly severe men like Henri Junod and Frédéric Godet with a sensibility that could move them to tears when reading a weighty scientific tome such as Oswald Heer's *The Primeval World of Switzerland*. In the canton of Vaud, it led pastor Henri Berthoud to write a treatise on the relationship between the science of geology and the Biblical notion of creation.[34] The dogged earnestness of the collector appealed strongly to the evangelical temperament, as did the wondrous detail produced by God's creative powers through time and space. For this reason, many eminent Christians in the Swiss Romande, particularly those associated with the missionary movement, devoted themselves to collecting and systematizing elements of nature that revealed the existence of a benevolent creator.[35]

For these men the study of nature was associated with the thrill of discovery, conquest and pride, but it was also a mark of virtue and good taste, a source of consolation for those weighed down by the consequences of sin and an emotional release from an otherwise rigorous lifestyle. The naturalist drew his energy in different measure from this stew of concerns, a situation quickly reflected in the divisions within natural theology. Not all evangelicals ranked reason above mystery or valued logic more than emotion. Many pietists continued to follow the Biblical narrative of creation, and criticized the attempts of Agassiz and others to establish natural laws that were not the direct product of divine ordination.[36]

In Neuchâtel this perspective produced the sort of natural history undertaken by Samuel Robert (1853–1934) who saw lepidoptera purely as an expression and proof of God's glory. Through purchase and exchange, Robert assembled a magnificent collection of 23,000 butterfly species from all over the world. But while Robert was only interested in the remarkable beauty and diversity of these insects, a collector such as Frédéric de Rougemont's son Frédéric (a pastor in the Independent Church) sought to discern the divine laws behind the ordering of the diversity of nature. To achieve this, he hunted and raised butterflies, investigated their habitats, and attempted, within the narrow confines of one specific region, to uncover a classificatory 'system' based on the Linnaean model.[37] He also sought to infuse the young with his enthusiasm. When his brother, the professor of natural history at the academy, died unexpectedly, de Rougemont and Tripet arranged for Henri-Alexandre to continue his research into microlepidoptera. In 1884 the twenty-one-year-old Junod published his findings on the anatomy, habitat and customs of a tiny butterfly in the scientific journal founded by Louis Agassiz some forty years earlier.[38]

During his first year at college, Henri-Alexandre joined the Société de Belles-Lettres, the intellectually and socially important student association presided over by Edouard Jacottet, future missionary-linguist in Lesotho. In the close world of the faculty of theology Junod counted Henry Appia, the son of one of the founders of the Red Cross, among his closest friends.[39] Junod finished his four years at university as head student of the faculty and president of the local chapter of the Société de Belles-Lettres. In the society's *Revue* he published poetry and articles on regional history and literature from a romantic perspective. But as a student he was particularly renowned for natural history essays, strongly derivative of Lamartine, that personified nature. Through a combination of sentimentality, information and moral philosophy, these works spoke of a lofty spirituality in God's handiwork. His readings could hold an auditorium of *belletriens* spellbound. An admirer wrote of a young man

> whose gaze knows how to penetrate the mysteries of nature and discover movement and life where the greatest scientists have seen only inertia and immobility, Junod, who recognizes a soul under the icy exterior of a drop of frozen rain and who believes he is able to perceive religious and moral instincts in the soul of a small tree frog and a yearning for perfectibility.[40]

Inevitably, Agassiz stood out as an exemplary figure for the young theology student who, as president of the society, commissioned a bust of the great man. On his return from his studies in Berlin in 1885, Junod took up the position of pastor at Môtiers, a small town in the Val-de-Travers from which, exactly 120 years earlier, Jean-Jacques Rousseau had been expelled by the local clergyman and his followers after a stay of two years. The botanizing philosopher had then moved to the neighbouring village of Couvet, where he was fêted as a hero, before moving to a safer abode on a small island in the nearby Lake Bienne. In 1885 Rousseau's spirit and his reflections on the plants and people of the upper stretches of the Val-de-Travers, were still felt in Couvet, the seat of the Dubieds, Henri-Alexandre's mother's family, and in Môtiers, the site of his church. At the foot of the valley the spirit of Agassiz was recalled when the bust of the great man, ordered by Junod and his friends, was eventually unveiled in the Neuchâtel Academy in 1887.[41]

When Junod left for Lourenço Marques in 1889, he carried with him a love of the natural and theological sciences typical of the dominant male figures in his life. He saw the post to which he had been sent by his vocation as not only an opportunity to convert the heathen and revivify his church at home but a chance to uncover new botanical and zoological species.[42] This was a good time for an energetic young man to seek his fortune overseas, for there was little left to discover in Switzerland; collectors had been reduced to discovering sub-species or at best filling in gaps in previous studies.

Perhaps Junod was aware that, as early as the middle of the century, an ambitious botanist such as Pierre-Edmond Boissier (1810–85) had been obliged to look to Spain, then later the Middle East and the edges of India, to discover new plants. Boissier's willingness to move to the edges of Europe and beyond had paid handsomely. In a manner that set a shining example for younger botanists, he had described (alone or with the aid of collaborators) a phenomenal 131 new genera of plants and 5,990 new species. William Barbey (1842–1914) continued this tradition when he established the Boissier Herbarium in Geneva in honour of his father-in-law. This institution pursued a policy of purchasing botanical collections, sponsoring expeditions, and publishing the findings of men on the spot worldwide.[43] The long depression at the end of the nineteenth century restricted costly periods of fieldwork or extended them into a permanent expatriation, causing several naturalists from the Swiss Romande to became pioneering figures in the fields of entomology and botany in places as far removed as Russia, Cuba, Costa Rica and Venezuela.[44] Perhaps most importantly for Henri-Alexandre Junod, Paul Berthoud had sent several new species of ants from the Transvaal; and when his sister married the widowed missionary, she too started to send insects back to Neuchâtel. Her packages included a particularly large and rare collection of butterflies that arrived on Godet's desk at the museum just as Junod discovered that his microlepidoptera did not represent a new species.[45] As Junod left Switzerland, it seemed fame could only be won by collectors in those rare parts of the world little touched by European enterprise.

The natural sciences were also being rapidly transformed at the end of the nineteenth century. For decades the *homme de cabinet* or armchair expert and the amateur collector in the field had existed in an easy symbiosis. In Neuchâtel the growth of the Natural History Museum had traditionally depended on the generosity of the town's many traders, missionaries, soldiers and travellers living abroad. In a way that reinforced their ties with home, these men sent 'curiosities' to their compatriots in the museum. But the gap between the collector and the classifier widened into something of a generational gap following the spectacular achievements of Darwin, when botanical and zoological excursions lost ground to theory and the rise of the 'new biology' in the German universities. In the last third of the century, innovators in the field shifted from collecting and documenting the majestic diversity of nature to revealing its causes and consequences. In England this tension was captured by George Eliot in *Middlemarch*, where the old order of science and the new are represented by the figures of Mr. Farebrother and Lydgate: the one concerned with collecting and systematizing, the other with embryology and connective tissues.

Technological developments also encouraged the move from the field to the laboratory as increasingly powerful microscopes allowed professionals to pierce below the surface and specialize in morphology, embryology and physiology. In some cases this led them to reclassify plants and insects according to minutiae previously not visible to the human eye. The sheer volume of species discovered rendered the old, encyclopedic museum collections impracticable and forced experts to specialize in narrow fields. As prestige and status passed to the professional scientist, the thrill of discovery shifted away from the painstaking but plodding 'antiquarian' work of collectors such as Tripet and de Rougement.[46] Even Boissier, an internationally renowned botanist, came under fire for his unwillingness to ask more general and abstract questions of his material.[47]

Religion underlay much of this shift in thinking. If conservatives had seen the work of Agassiz and his colleagues as leading towards an unsavoury deism, the direction taken by science at the end of the nineteenth century pointed towards a far less savoury atheism. The social and economic instability accompanying industrialization was compounded as biologists and geologists reformulated species and dissolved the clear distinctions between the sexes, the animal and plant kingdoms and even the existence of humanity as a separate species. For many Darwinians, evolutionism publicized the arbitrary nature of classification by contradicting the idea that anatomical characteristics of living organisms were fixed and constant through time. As science challenged established ideas on the fixity of species and the place of humanity in the universe, it inevitably cast doubt on the story of creation and even the existence of God. It promoted the secularization of science as clergymen lost their leading role in the study of nature.[48] As a believer by temperament and an amateur with a broad appreciation of the natural sciences, Junod was better suited to be in the field in Africa than in the laboratory in Europe.

African Adventures in Taxonomy

For many years only the most intrepid naturalists had visited Lourenço Marques, a backward corner of a shabby colony.[49] But when Junod arrived, the town was entering a period of sudden and unprecedented prosperity. As the natural port for the newly discovered Witwatersrand gold fields, it attracted a diverse, cosmopolitan population – figures such as Rose Monteiro, who earned an income by selling zoological and botanical specimens to collectors in Europe, or the young soldier, Captain Freire de Andrade, who produced a valuable book on the tree flowers of Mozambique.[50] Junod arrived in Africa from a country where nature was being divided, demarcated and domesticated, where wild animals lived increasingly on sufferance. At Rikatla he felt that he had been transported into 'an entirely new world' where nature was in an almost pristine condition.[51]

Three months after coming to Rikatla, Junod wrote to William Barbey for the first time. Although he specialized in the Near and Middle East, Barbey had purchased several important southern African herbaria and was prepared to subsidize the work of collectors living on the edges of the European world.[52] He was keen to expand his institute's African holdings and viewed missionary societies as a means of achieving this end.[53]

In October 1889 Junod offered to send Barbey both dried plants and the seeds of species suitable for cultivation in hot houses or gardens where they would 'flourish … beneath the sky of the fatherland'.[54] Ambitious and energetic, he took just sixteen months to gather over 300 different plant species. Starting from the hill above Lourenço Marques, he explored the 23-kilometre stretch of land between the town and Rikatla, to the north. He spent his spare time from his mission investigating the groves of palm trees and marshy hollows lying behind the coastal dunes. There, he found new plants soon to be named *Striga junodii* Schinz and *Triumfetta junodii* Schinz (see plate 5). Evangelical itineration allowed him to scour the plant life of five distinct geographical areas. These included the Manununu forest covering the bend in the Nkomati valley, the sandy dunes along the coast, the wet depressions behind the coastal hills, the clayey patches of black, *nyaka* soil and the rocky Libombo mountains on the border with the Transvaal.[55] In the Makororo forest on the route from Rikatla to Antioka, he discovered the *Empogona junodii* Schinz. However, it was the Morakwene forest that received his full attention, an area covering the south bank of the Nkomati estuary from the coast to the drift, as well as two small islands in the river. With its dense underbrush and thick creepers, this impenetrable forest was an 'eldorado' for the naturalist. Junod was particularly attracted by the striking burgundy-coloured flowers that appeared after the first summer rains on a tree orchid and he quickly gave his name to this plant, *Monodora junodii* (family name Annonaceae). The Makandja forest on the left bank of the Nkomati estuary also impressed him, with its rich and varied flora supported by a dark clay soil.[56]

One of Junod's first steps at his mission station was to establish what he called, with a touch of irony, 'a museum'. In this centre he dried plants that he dispatched for the first time, in January 1891, to Geneva, where Barbey undertook to have them named, classified and described in an article tentatively called 'Plantae Junodiae'.[57] The missionary was 'very proud' when told that his first consignment contained at least one unknown species that would thenceforth bear the name *Melhania junodii* Schinz.[58] As further encouragement Barbey supplied Junod with the equipment needed to establish a herbarium, with information on how to dry plants, particularly during the sub-tropical wet season, and how to ensure their safe delivery to Europe.[59] He also offered to act as an agent for the sale to museums and collectors in Europe of any of Junod's plants not required by his herbarium. In response, Junod assembled collections holding 100 different species of lichen, fruit, flowers and roots. With the money earned from the sale of these plants he offered sixpence to guides to take him into inaccessible swamplands where rare plants were to be found, and hired the services of others prepared to journey up the Nkomati river in search of other plantlife. He also trained and employed an assistant to dry and press specimens and prepare them for dispatch to Europe.[60] When Junod left Mozambique for Switzerland in 1896 he had inscribed 500 different plant species in his botanical register.

Three years later he returned to Africa to take up a post at the school for evangelists at Shiluvane in the Eastern Transvaal. The flora of the Delagoa Bay area paled in comparison with that of Junod's new home.[61] Shiluvane was at the heart of a rich botanical area encompassing the Drakensberg and adjoining plateau, the thick forests on the eastern slope of the mountain, the foothills in which the mission was situated and the hot Lowveld folding into the coastal plain. Shiluvane occupied a central position in the Swiss mission field and on his various trips to Pietersburg, via the Woodbush and Haenertsberg, and to the Spelonken and Komatipoort, Junod was able to enlarge and diversify his botanical collection. At the height of the malarial summer, he and his family spent several weeks every year in the highlands, at Howick in Natal or in Lesotho. In 1903 alone, he gathered over 200 plant species while holidaying in the mountainous terrain of Witzieshoek and Thababosigo. As he combed the area around the Paris mission stations with his friend Edouard Jacottet, he looked with envy at the unexplored flora of the Maluti mountains. By the time Junod left Shiluvane for Rikatla in 1906, he had added over 2300 plant species to the original 500 in his collection.[62]

During the ten years that Junod had spent in Switzerland and the Transvaal, the Delagoa Bay region had been thoroughly botanized. The Portuguese had sent an official to collect plants, and a renowned collector and future professor of botany in Berlin, Rudolf Schlechter, had also spent four months scouring the area.[63] Sadly for botany but happily for anthropology, this competition encouraged Junod to specialize in the study of human beings. Over the next decade, he inscribed fewer than 100 plants in his register. But once he had established his reputation in the field of anthropology, he returned with relish to botanize in his free time. In the three years before Junod returned definitively to Switzerland in 1920, he collected examples of 1,550 different plant species drawn from many parts of southern Mozambique as well as the Zoutpansberg, the Spelonken, Johannesburg, Witzieshoek, and Pinetown in Natal.[64]

Henri-Alexandre Junod discovered many new plants during his years in Southern Africa and is today recognized as one of the pioneer botanical explorers of the region. Apart from Barbey, he corresponded with various botanists to whom he sent material. These included John Briquet, the director of the Delessert Conservatory in Geneva, a botanical institute housing numerous South African collections;[65] Fritz Tripet and Paul Godet in Neuchâtel; J. M. Wood, the director of the botanical gardens in Durban; Joseph Burtt Davy, the government botanist in Pretoria; and Thomas Durand, the director of the botanical gardens in Brussels.[66] The plants he gathered in the Delagoa Bay region were described in 1899 in two articles co-authored with Hans Schinz.[67] The celebrated Swiss botanist continued to publish articles on Junod's collection over the next thirty years and, with perhaps some exaggeration, placed him amongst the greatest collectors of African flora of his generation.[68] Junod's memory was perpetuated by the genus *Junodia paxis* of the family Euphorbiaceae (later synonymized with *Epinetrum delagoense*) and by some thirty different plant species, including the *Gladiolus junodi* pictured on plate 4. Today his plant specimens are housed in herbaria throughout the world.[69]

Despite this success in the field of botany, Junod found the Delagoa Bay region a richer field for entomology and it was in this area that he initially invested most of his energy.[70] Although Lourenço Marques lay on the edge of the tropics, the hill above the town was arid and the meagre vegetation produced few flowers. But on this bush, he wrote with pleasure in 1891, 'live an astonishing and surprising collection of fauna', particularly the caterpillars that serve as the larval form of several species of butterflies and moths.[71] At Rikatla he found it more difficult to trace rare species;

5.1 Henri-Alexandre Junod hunting butterflies on the escarpment near Shiluvane.
(© Swiss Mission Archive, Lausanne)

but within two years he had trained 'intelligent natives' to recognize exotic insects and uncover their habitat. In the Morakwene forest he found rare caterpillars and large numbers of wood-boring beetles called longicorns or Cerambycidae. The wide diversity of trees and bushes in the forest provided a home for a large range of *Papilio* in spring and summer and several varieties of African *Charaxes* in autumn and winter. In a field of cashew trees hosting rare bushes and tropical vines lived a world of exotic Swallowtail, Swordtail and Dawn butterflies.

Junod sometimes raised butterflies and moths from their form as caterpillars, but more frequently he resorted to employing assistants to chase these insects from their habitat by beating the bush at specific times of day or night. His assiduousness brought quick results. In November 1890 he discovered a butterfly (*Teracolus calais*) in the Lower Nkomati valley that had only been associated with tropical areas previously. In the same year he found a new species of wattle bagworm, the larval form of the moth *Acanthopsyche junodi*, now *Kotochalia (Chaliopsis) junodi* (Heylaerts), at Howick in Natal, as well as five examples of the lovely *Precis cuama*. Later, he discovered the first example of this species in the Delagoa Bay area. In 1891 one of his assistants brought him a magnificent butterfly belonging to the large, fast-flying *Papilio* group, a genus first established by Linneaus in 1758. The man had caught the butterfly in the Morakwene forest and Junod quickly sent it for identification to Roland Trimen, the entomologist who served as director of the South African Museum in Cape Town.

In 1893 Trimen described the butterfly, pictured in plate 6, as a new species and gave it the name *Papilio junodi*, commonly known today as 'Junod's swordtail'. It took Junod just seven years to assemble some 200 different species of moths and 184 species of butterfly. This came close to half the butterflies thought to exist in the entire subcontinent at that time.[72]

From his 'museum', Junod tirelessly sought out and studied crickets, grasshoppers, ants, spiders, wasps, bees, moths, molluscs, lizards, frogs and especially caterpillars, beetles, bugs and butterflies. He sold rare butterflies to the museum in Neuchâtel and to collectors such as Roland Trimen.[73] He also sold entomological collections, including a wide spectrum of Coleoptera (beetles) from Shiluvane, to the newly opened Rothschild Museum of natural history in Tring, England.[74] He later assembled a beautiful collection of butterflies and coleoptera for the natural history museum in Lourenço Marques.[75] His 'baboon' spider, or tarantula, remains a prize for any arachnophile (see plate 8).[76] In an attempt to identify and name his specimens Junod corresponded with experts in Lausanne, Geneva, Zurich, Berlin, Bucharest, Turin, Paris, Caen, London and Cape Town. Lepidoptera (butterflies and moths) were sent to Frédéric de Rougemont, Trimen, and A. G. Butler at the British Museum. In Lourenço Marques he met and later corresponded with the distinguished entomologist, W. L. Distant. Coleoptera went to Dr Bugnion in Lausanne and especially Louis Péringuey at the museum in Cape Town; Tenebrionidae (darkling beetles) to Mr Fairmaire in Paris; Orthoptera (crickets, grasshoppers and cockroaches) and Hymenoptera (wasps, bees and ants) to Dr von Schulthess-Rechberg in Zurich (where some were classified by Auguste Forel); Hemiptera (including the bugs of which he was particularly fond) were sent to Prof. Montandon in Bucharest; and caterpillars to Mr Heylaerts, a Dutch specialist.[77]

Henri-Alexandre Junod won an international reputation as an entomologist. Like Roger Hamley in Elizabeth Gaskell's *Wives and Daughters* (1866), who was received as a 'fashionable lion' after his return home following a tour of exploration sponsored by the Geographical Society, Junod was admired for his scientific achievements. During his first furlough in Switzerland (1896–9) he worked through his collections and co-authored a series of articles with European experts. In a work on the beetles of the Delagoa Bay region, written with Bugnion, he listed 479 species, including eight new species of darkling beetles (amongst which a 'toktokkie' beetle, *Psammodes junodi*), about 80 species of long-horned, wood-boring beetles (Cerambycidae), as well as seven new species of locusts and mantids (together with a new genus, *Junodia amoena*). This led Bugnion to compare the wealth of beetles to be found in the Delagoa Bay area with the vaunted fields of Brazil and India.[78] In other articles published in 1899 Junod noted hundreds of different species of Orthoptera, Hemiptera and Hymenoptera, of which several dozen were new discoveries.[79] His collection of Hydrophilidae was analysed and described in articles by Dr Achille Griffini of Turin and Dr Maurice Regimbart of Evreux.[80] In 1904, W. F. Purcell published an article on the numerous scorpions and spiders found by Junod at Shiluvane, and Forel determined the ants found by the industrious missionary and his colleagues Paul Berthoud and Georges Liengme. Louis Péringuey was full of praise for Junod's work on Coleoptera, especially those found around Rikatla, and also published an article on the missionary's findings at Shiluvane.[81] Junod hoped that his many scientific articles would one day be assembled in a single volume, tentatively entitled *The Natural History of Delagoa* or *The Flora and Entomological Fauna of Delagoa* and, as late as 1914, he displayed his rich botanical and zoological collections at the Swiss National Exhibition.[82]

5.2 African collectors provided Junod with a range of plants and insects. In this
photograph a 'botanist' and a 'coleopterist', both unnamed, flank Spoon Libombo,
Junod's butterfly collector and one of his major informants in the field of ethnography.
All three men hold the equipment needed to undertake their various tasks.
(© Swiss Mission Archive, Lausanne)

Although Junod's interest in natural science was overtaken by his new passion for anthropology, he left an indelible mark on the entomological map of south-east Africa. Scores of insects and plants today bear his name, or that of his wife, or the many stations of the Swiss Mission.[83] The missionary doctor Georges Liengme also scoured nature for new species and passed his name to beetles, and like Paul Berthoud, to ants found in Gazaland.[84] This system of naming, using Latin binomials, was an integral part of the process of taking hold of the land, for it embraced and assimilated the local in a way that made the foreign familiar and domesticated the disorderly for the European scientist.

Throughout his stay in Southern Africa Junod supplied the Natural History Museum in Neuchâtel with a wide range of animals and insects. The museum supplied him with flasks, dissecting cases, cyanide and nets and frequently paid for the items collected or for their delivery. This policy paid handsome dividends. The Museum register records receiving from Junod in 1911 'a precious collection' of Hemiptera and in 1912, 187 Orthoptera and Hymenoptera. His molluscs were also considered 'extremely interesting' and were accompanied by a steady stream of sea shells, bird skins, eggs and nests, sea urchins, snakes and lizards, several frogs, a crocodile and various (unidentified) mammals.[85] By appealing to men on the spot such as Junod, as well as to other Neuchâtelois resident overseas, the museum built up a mass of objects

Natural Sciences 137

that could later be sifted through by the experts.[86] Junod concurred with this ethos. 'In collecting all these facts,' he remarked, 'we accomplish a sort of highly dignified ministry and, perhaps, we furnish those who will systematize them one day with the key to many problems.'[87]

Just as biology and theology overlapped, botany and zoology frequently imbricated. This happened when Junod stumbled upon a little-known bush housing several new species of longicornes or when he found an unusual caterpillar lodged on the underleaves of a plant that he was drying for his herbarium. Biology and sociology met up when Junod used his considerable linguistic skills to question informants about local plants and animals. His strong interest in landsnails, for example, moved in an ethnographic direction when informants told him that they used the animals' shells as containers in which to deposit money earned in South Africa. The uninspiring moth *Acanthopsyche junodi* (Heylaerts) took on a new allure when it was noted that its larval form (as the wattle bagworm) produced a cocoon, often found hanging on thorn trees, that proved useful as a penis-sheath. He developed a deep respect for indigenous powers of observation and an admiration for the indigenous system of classification. He also had a high regard for the way in which local people exploited plants for qualities that were at once medicinal, magical, sartorial and nutritional in edible or liquid form. He was intrigued by the way trees were associated with deities and spirits, and plants and animals were employed in rituals as talismans, objects of taboo, or as a means of divination.[88]

At a time when biologists seldom mentioned the names and achievements of their native assistants, Junod made a point of drawing attention to the work of these individuals and on one occasion he photographed his three major collectors.[89] Elias Libombo or 'Spoon', a local diviner who sold thatching grass, and whose wife had joined the mission, proved a particularly adept butterfly collector. As a young boy looking after his father's goats, 'Spoon' had chased after birds, mice, lizards and rabbits and he had observed the habits and movements of a wide range of animals. This proved a useful training for a naturalist and contributed to Spoon's skill as a butterfly collector.

To succeed in this field, a collector has to be aware of the short life span of the butterfly, its selective feeding habits and its sensitivity to ecological and climatological change. An expert like Elias Libombo had to catch the high-flying, swooping charaxes as well as skippers flitting from plant to plant. He needed to recognize the larval host plants of different species of butterfly and he had to know where on these plants the female would lay her eggs. He needed to identify when, and for how long, adults would emerge and fly, the places favoured by males searching for mates, and the kind of food preferred by both male and female adults. To achieve these ends he had to be able to distinguish in particular the coloration, shape and design according to which butterflies were situated in genera, species and varieties. Because of his abilities as a collector, Junod entrusted Spoon with a net, bottles, ether, and numerous paper cones in which to capture, kill and store his specimens. He was frequently sent on expeditions to the butterfly collectors' 'Eldorado' on the lower Nkomati. On at least one occasion Junod sent Spoon on an extended trip of several days to the *terra incognita* on the bend in the Nkomati.[90]

It did not take long before the missionary's attention was drawn to the way in which locals made sense of their environment. He was intrigued by the names often given by children to beetles because of their shape, colour, taste or design; or because certain species, like the weevil (*Curculionidae Brachycerus*), were considered a sign of good fortune. Perhaps most importantly, he discerned a 'notion of *order*' in the natives' classification of Mammalia.[91] Although the locals did not group animals into large classes resembling genera and species, they placed animals in small groups, if only because some were considered taboo or physically disgusting.[92] They also speculated on the place of humanity in this system of classification when they saw apes as a degenerate form of humankind.[93] More broadly, he noted that the Thonga had a 'rather pantheistic notion' of creation that they shared with 'many very educated scientists of our age'.[94]

Junod was particularly impressed by the locals' ability to name plants and situate them in groups that broadly resembled genera and even species. Natives recognized the visible relationship between various forms of Lobeliae that they grouped together under the term *Shilawana*. The same sense of classification caused them to give the name *Shitshinyambita* to all the Strigae, a genus of the Scrophulariaceae family. Ferns were also placed in a common 'genus' when they were labelled *Tsuna*. Locals not only distinguished between different genera; they also broke these large categories into 'species' through the use of diminutive terms or by attaching the generic name of a plant to the habitat in which it was found. So the *Muhlu* (a tree of the Asclepiadaceae family) was called a *Muhlu wa ntlhaba* when found in dry bushland, and a *Muhlu-tjobo* when located in the wet marshlands along the coast. In a similar way, the *Ntjhesi* (*Hibiscus*) was divided into the *Ntjhesi* of the *ntlhaba* (*Hibiscus surratensis*, etc.), the *Ntjhesi* of the *nyaka* (dark soil), and the little *Ntjhesi* of the *ntlhaba* (the *shitjhesi sha ntlhaba* or *Sida cordifolia* of the *Hibiscus* genus of the Malvaceae family). Natives also sometimes distinguished male and female forms within their plant categories. In this way the 'genus' *Munywane* was divided into male and female forms that European scientists would recognize as *Epaltes gariepina* and *Blumea aurita*.[95]

Junod came to realize that the botanical knowledge of the natives was the product of 'a true and, in a certain sense, scientific observation on their part'. It was certainly 'more general' than that of the European peasantry, he speculated, perhaps comparable to 'that of our forefathers of two or three hundred years ago, before Botany became a true science'. Even children, he observed, could point out roots used for medicinal purposes.[96] This practical outcome was fortunate, for he was coming under increasing pressure from the mission to demonstrate the utility, explanatory value and didactic benefits of his entomological and botanical studies.[97]

Junod found the indigenous people had a great deal to teach European scientists about the utility of plants. On several occasions he invited natives to his museum where they supplied him with the local names and uses of plants in exchange for a shilling. He never seemed to consider that this source of commercial gain might inspire informants to exaggerate or embellish their accounts. Junod recognized that diviners (who predicted the future) and *gobelas* (skilled in exorcizing unwelcome spirits) possessed an intricate knowledge of the animals and plants used in the pursuance of their professions. He particularly admired old women and *nangas*, or specialist medicine-men, whose knowledge of the medicinal, nutritional and magic properties of plants constituted a rough form of classification. The *nanga* were familiar with 'real, powerful drugs' which they administered in conjunction with therapeutic practices.[98] In a way that indicates a genuine desire to coax medicinal cures from local plants, Junod assembled a 'Ronga pharmacopoeia' in the ethnographic museum in Neuchâtel and sent plants to Geneva for analysis.[99] He also attempted, with little success it seems, to commercialize the pith of a local palm (probably *Corchons junodi*)

5.3 Butterfly and insect trays. Insect collections captured the intricacy and beauty of God's world. But they also encouraged missionary entomologists to study the reproduction of species and to confront the process of natural selection.
(© Swiss Mission Archive, Lausanne)

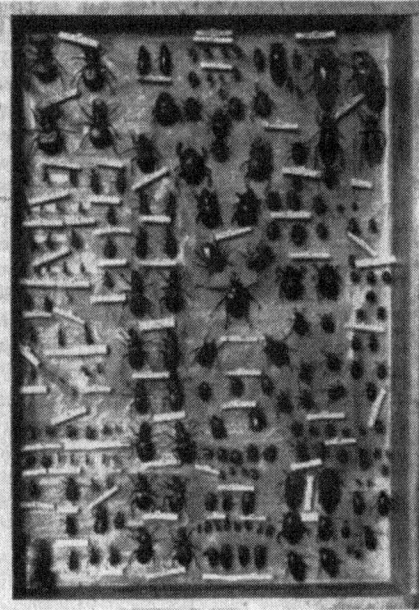

as a substitute for cork. In general, Junod valued the religious utility of the study of nature over and above the commercial benefits to which it could be applied.[100]

In 1893 Junod saw 'God's infinite wisdom' behind the diversity of nature. 'Nature is a book, in Africa as in Europe', he wrote, and a means of praising 'the beauty and power of the Creator'.[101] Four years later he drew the attention of an audience in Neuchâtel to natural history as a means 'to admire the magnificent work of the Creator on the marvellous planet that we inhabit'.[102] In his retirement he carved this belief on the two large cupboards, filled with butterflies and beetles, that occupied a central place in his home in Geneva. 'The earth is full of Your riches' read the inscription, from the Psalms.[103] Junod was thrilled by the discovery of new animal and plant species and delighted in their infinite range of detail, colour, shape, design and texture. The blue and green *Chrysomilidae* shone 'like saphyrs and emeralds', while the ground beetle of this family, called *Euschizomerus junodi* (Pér) was 'a charming little insect with a triangular thorax'. He thought the *Amaurodes passerini* Westwood a 'magnificent species' of the scarab group (of dung beetles).[104] He was also enthralled by the way in which insects communicated with one another, protected themselves against predators and reproduced their species. Very quickly, he came to tie the classification of insects to customs and habits that were shaped by environmental factors rather than divine design. By emphasizing natural processes as well as taxonomic structures, Junod gave more immediate agency to nature and history than to God. This meant that, as the missionary-scientist reiterated his belief in the powers of the creator, he was also disengaging the hand of God from the order of nature.

Social Evolution and Natural Imperialism

By the end of the century Junod stressed (if only to scientists) that as a collector he was no longer just concerned with classification and anatomy. His major interest had become the place of plants and animals in the human and natural environment. This shift in interest was largely motivated by his growing engagement with the theory of evolution through natural selection.[105] In Cape Town Roland Trimen was at the centre of a circle of collectors who sought to explain the existence and reproduction of animal and plant species in terms of natural selection. He quickly introduced Junod to the works of evolutionists such as A. R. Wallace and H. W. Bates. Another important influence at this time was James Bryce, who Junod met in Lourenço Marques in 1895 and with whom he shared an interest in botany. Bryce portrayed Africa as both a menagerie for fauna extinct elsewhere in the world and as an endlessly sprawling, unkempt botanical garden. He attributed this abundance of nature to 'the fact that the country was occupied only by savages, who did little or nothing to extinguish any species nature had planted'. He went on to speculate that this 'may have caused many weak species to survive when equally weak ones were perishing in Asia at the hands of more advanced races of humankind'.[106]

For Bryce and many other Europeans, Africa was a privileged site from which to view the process of natural selection: what had transformed Europe during prehistoric times was taking place before their eyes. The Cape lion had been exterminated in the mid-1860s, the last quagga had died in the Amsterdam zoo in 1883 and the white rhinoceros teetered on the brink of extinction. By the end of the century, the last remnants of vast herds of migrating springbok, gnu and hartebeest were being gathered into game reserves.[107]

Africa's early stage of evolution was particularly visible to entomologists. In many parts of Europe, they watched nervously as the butterflies' original floral habitat was replaced by commercial crops, plantations and forests, or by the new and hardy plant species that followed in the wake of population movements. In sharp contrast, the natural vegetation of Africa and the fauna it hosted seemed to have undergone little change. W.L. Distant believed that, because the vegetation of south-east Africa had been little disturbed by human agency, it harboured species of butterfly that had been destroyed by more industrious races elsewhere in the world. Hence more species of butterfly were found in Southern Africa than in the entire European continent; Britain's sixty-six species were the meagre vestiges of a far richer age. Distant believed that lepidoptery would provide, like paleontology or philology, a window into prehistoric times. 'These pleasant Durban glades were no longer only emporiums to supply museum drawers with specimens, but were full of nature's record of the past – like hieroglyphic writings, but unlike them, most at present we cannot read.' Similarly, a cabinet of butterflies 'now not only exhibits what used simply to be called the "works of nature", but absolutely in many cases shows how nature works'.[108]

Under the influence of Trimen, Distant, Bryce and others, Junod soon started to see natural selection at work, particularly in the fields of Lepidoptera and Hemiptera. In order to distinguish and classify butterflies more clearly, he focused on the reproductive cycle of the insects, particularly the various stages of their metamorphosis. He quickly noted the relationship between insects and a changing rather than pristine environment. In many areas the butterfly *Papilio corinneus* had been decimated because the bush on which it laid its eggs was an important source of indigenous medicines. But the same butterfly proliferated in the Morakwene forest where the underbrush proved impenetrable to human agency. He noted that only the fittest butterflies and moths survived, as spiders, birds, rodents, mantises, lizards and frogs preyed upon them incessantly. Their caterpillars were parasitized by wasps and flies or eaten by human beings.[109] Junod realized that, in order to preserve themselves in such a way as to reproduce their species, insects had evolved various protective mechanisms. To repel their enemies, insects would sting and bite, adopt threatening postures, or emit discharges that were venomous, painful, irritating or malodorous. They had also developed camouflage into a fine art. This was clearly visible when the immature larval form of the Swallowtail butterfly curled itself in such a way as to resemble the droppings of a bird, or when the wattle bagworm hid itself in a sheath of twigs or leaves.

Most startling was the mimicry practised by butterflies and moths. Junod came to see that the survival of egg-laying female butterflies depended on how closely their coloration and design conformed to butterflies considered by predators to be malodorous, bitter-tasting or even toxic. Through this natural selection the animals seemed to practise an involuntary form of deceptive mimicry. Other butterflies developed a protective camouflage when the only survivors over generations were those whose design and colour conformed to elements of the local environment. Through a close comparison of the spectrum of variation in a species, Junod was able to document the degree to which these insects adapted physically to changing floral and faunal kingdoms. When a species of butterfly left its home area and moved to an area to which it was not adapted, he noticed that the butterflies declined in number, strength and size, or were made extinct. He saw how in one area a female butterfly would 'mimic' the colour of a local, poisonous butterfly in such a way as to protect itself against predatory birds. Yet in a neighbouring area, where the birds did not exist, members of this species of butterfly would keep their original colouring and design as they had no need to participate in this 'mimicry'. The same process was observable when the clearing of vegetation caused a poisonous or malodorous butterfly to emigrate or die and render the mimicking species unprotected. Similarly, when a change in climate caused the dark lichen on the pale bark of a tree to die, dark butterflies lost their 'natural' camouflage and became an easy prey to predators.

Through these entomological observations Junod noted the effect of rapid changes in the physical world upon the involuntary mutation, or evolution, of what he started to call 'Darwinian species'. He came to recognize that the process of 'natural selection' in the animal world was the product of many centuries of 'pitiless' struggle.[110] While he could accept Darwinian ideas about the evolution of plants and animals, Junod was, perhaps understandably, only able to apply these ideas to humankind in a selective manner.

For Mary Barber, one of Trimen's circle, the theory of natural selection had fundamentally challenged the idea of divine providence, the Christian tenets of humility, love and compassion and the special place of humanity in the order of the world.[111] For Darwin, natural selection was a purely mechanical phenomenon; devoid of all purpose, it was marked by callous indifference to the human condition. These were the starkly materialist ideas that Carl Vogt had carried to Neuchâtel in the winter of 1862-63 and that Agassiz, Godet and Guyot had so stridently opposed. Agassiz had hammered away at the rivets of Biblical truth that no longer seemed plausible in the light of scientific explanation. But like the geologists who had peopled the Alps with dragons a generation earlier, he refused to remove those rivets and combined his strictly scientific work with an unshakable belief in God's plan. For example, Agassiz's careful observation of the movement of glaciers led him to discover the ice age, but it also led him to see these huge blocks of frozen water functioning as God's ploughs in prehistoric times. In a similar way, he thought God's creation of each individual species of flora and fauna served to magnify his majesty through deep time.[112]

Junod had been raised with this conception of the world. But the view of his father's generation, that the organic world was the product of successive divine creations, was challenged by Junod's entomological observations in Africa and by a new intellectual climate. Within the space of twenty years, the young student who had erected the bust to Agassiz at the Academy in Neuchâtel had come to adopt Darwin's ideas on the dominant role of the environment in natural selection.[113] But although Junod could accept the random and 'pitiless' way in which natural selection affected the animal and plant kingdoms, he found it far more difficult to apply these ideas to laws of human development. If eternal salvation was the aim of life on earth, the process of evolution had to be influenced by individual choice, reason and morality – ultimately by order, progress, and divine purpose. Under the influence of the popular Free Church of Scotland natural scientist and African traveller, Henry Drummond, Junod focused on God's role as an 'Invisible' or 'Spiritual' Environment that encompassed the evolution of organic material. The comparative study of humanity in Africa and Europe showed how mankind had evolved with God's help from a primitive stage, still visible in Africa, to a more advanced phase in Europe. The path of progress was far from smooth but it gave a purpose to the present and instilled the future with the prospect of perfectibility.[114] Through this compromise with Darwinism, Junod was able to retain both his belief in the basic tenets of Christian humanism and his faith in science.

Over time, Junod came to view Africa's isolation from the centres of world enlightenment as both the cause of the continent's retarded material development and its means of protection from the vices of industrial civilization. At the end of the nineteenth century these vices threatened to engulf Africans who, unlike butterflies or beetles, had not been hardened by an extended struggle against invasive marauders. The indigenous Bushmen, Hottentots and Vaalpens were clearly dying out.[115] In a way that echoed Darwin's views in *The Descent of Man*, Junod feared that the black man 'has not been moulded by a civilization where the struggle for survival is pursued without truce or respite'.[116] This was a defenceless world into which a corrupt European civilization had suddenly inserted slavery, alcoholism and greed. Gonorrhea, syphilis, TB, as well as the acquired habits of prostitution, homosexuality and onanism, threatened to curtail the reproduction of indigenous society. Money was eating at the ligaments of tribal controls. Without the ability to defend itself, primitive society was increasingly threatened by a retrograde movement in the process of evolution toward simplification, degeneration and, finally, extinction, like certain entomological and botanical species.[117] In 1898 Junod still vacillated about the physical threat to native peoples brought by the vices of industrialization.[118] As medical evidence pointed towards the possibility of racial extinction, he wrote in 1912 that the situation in South Africa was 'very serious'. Fifteen years later he thought 'the extinction of the race is possible in the long run'.[119]

This threat of extinction was particularly visible to Junod (as it was to Darwin) when 'primitive people' were removed from their natural homes to industrial cities. As an entomologist interested in the geographical distribution of forms, Junod had supplied de Rougement with butterflies for comparison with members of the same species found in Switzerland. Just as the small size of the African variants indicated an incomplete adaptation to the local environment, the physical infirmities of tribesmen in the towns and their degenerate and imitative culture underlined the unnatural nature of this urbanization.[120] In the insalubrious, impersonal environment of the towns, primitive people were exposed to all the vices of European civilization and could deteriorate in strength or even suffer extinction, like the humble butterfly.[121]

Many Social Darwinists regarded this environmental threat to humanity as a natural process, even a form of progress, through which society purified and strengthened itself. For the distinguished hunter and naturalist, F. C. Selous, the unequal 'struggle for survival' between indolent natives and vigorous Europeans seemed to legitimate the seizure of a continent.[122] For men like A. R. Wallace and particularly Ernst Haeckel, civilization seemed to stand in the way of the progress accompanying natural selection. They believed that the extinction of weaker races was inevitable and that the process of natural selection, if left to its true course, would bring about an improvement in the racial stock of humankind.[123] By the end of the century Auguste Forel started to advocate chilling ways of intervening in what Herbert Spencer had called 'the natural process of elimination by which society continually purifies itself'. Forel came to believe that the composition of humanity could be improved by a 'rational selection' and 'a bit by bit ... elimination ... of those who were of limited use to the development of humanity'.[124] In South Africa, the anthropologist Dudley Kidd became an early and influential proponent of eugenics.

Junod refused to explain society in these strictly materialist terms. In a way that conformed more closely to Lamarck's notion of evolution, he believed that a weak or inferior society could change, adapt and fortify itself through rivalry and competition. Like Henry Drummond, Junod was convinced that human beings, particularly missionaries, had a moral duty to intervene on the side of the weak in the unequal struggle for survival. By exercising their superior qualities of compassion and self-sacrifice, human beings could shape and direct the course of evolution in a way that converged with Christian principles. Junod argued that the onus on society to defend the weak was imperative, even in terms of natural selection, because the weak provided the strong with the continuing competition that ultimately ensured their strength and the reproduction of the species.[125]

Slipping again from Darwin's notion of natural selection to Lamarck's concept of adapted evolution, Junod believed that Africans could fortify themselves as a race if they adopted the work habits of their white employers and, particularly, if they took on the beliefs and practices of Christianity.[126] But they needed equally to adopt the scientific rationality and logic brought to Africa by Europeans.[127] The eradication of superstition 'will only be possible under a twofold influence, the increase of the scientific spirit, which will conquer and destroy the absurdities of the animistic magical conceptions involved in these practices, and the Christian Religion'.[128] For Junod, as for a scientist like Edward O. Wilson today, the idea of science divided the world into two unequal camps. 'The fundamental difference between the European and the Bantu mind' was that Europeans have the '*scientific spirit* and the Bantus the *magic conception of Nature*'.[129] For the natives, nature was not governed by impersonal forces that could be observed in an objective and scientific manner; nature was rather linked to spiritual forces that had continually to be propitiated. From this perspective, science and enlightenment were ranged on the side of Europe against the superstition and darkness that pervaded life in Africa.

In the final sermon delivered to his congregation in Môtiers before leaving for Edinburgh and Africa, Junod referred to Immanuel Kant as 'the greatest philosopher of our time'.[130] In a famous essay on the Enlightenment, still the starting point for any university option on the subject, Kant described how society emancipated itself from an immature stage of ignorance and error through the attainment of Reason.[131] This way of thinking was rooted in the ideas of Diderot and Condorcet who equated reason with truth and saw in the Enlightenment a superior stage in the development of humanity. For these *esprits de lumière*, the movement of humanity towards a common, enlightened adulthood held out the possibility of universal equality; but in the process they also tied social difference to distinct, hierarchical stages in the evolution of civilization.[132] Many of these ideas took a racial hue that became stronger as the nineteenth century advanced. In some circles they still hold currency today.[133]

Junod ascribed to this view of science as a touchstone of civilization for, although the natives' concept of science was 'extremely interesting', in the final instance they exhibited 'the want of an enlightened botanical sense'. This was partly because their botanical knowledge was overly utilitarian. In practice, unless related species served as food or medicine, or were known to attract good fortune or ward off evil, they were given only the most generic titles.[134] Thus while Junod was able to distinguish between over twenty types of lichen, the locals merely called these *bulele*. They used the same generic classification when they referred to all ferns indiscriminately as *tsonna*, while Junod assiduously detailed and sorted this order of Filicopsida into different species.[135] Perhaps most importantly, the natives grouped plants according to their external characteristics alone. Because they had never dissected a flower and showed no interest in the morphology of plants or how they lived and reproduced, locals were unable to see or explain the respiratory function of leaves or generalize about the male and female characteristics of plants. This meant that they were unable 'correctly and universally' to recognize the relationship between species and that their broad categorization of plants seldom conformed to the genera defined by 'modern science'. For example, three different kinds of Vernonia were given different names under the local system of classification, although belonging to the same genus, that is, *Ntshontshongori* (*V. cinerea*), *Nkukulashibuya* (*V. perotteti*) and *Hlunguhlungu* (*V. tigna*). On the other hand, plants belonging to entirely different genera could be grouped together in local categories. Hence the *Ndjiba* (*Apalatoa delagoensis*) was grouped with the little Ndjiba, or *Shindjibana*, in a way that obscured its membership (as *Synaptolepis oliveriana* Thymeleaceae) of a completely different plant family.[136]

The zoological knowledge of the indigenous people was, Junod believed, still at a 'very primitive stage'. It was perhaps equal to that of Leviticus, the Old Testament figure associated with taboos.[137] As most insects were not eaten, they were called by only the most general names. All butterflies bore the title *phaphalati* and all the black beetles living in sandy areas were named *shifoufounounou*. Although women of the Nkuna clan distinguished between animals with hoofs and those with paws, they did so merely because the latter were wild beasts whose meat was fit only for men. While it was rare to find a native who could trace a species of moth or butterfly to a particular type of pupa or chrysalis, insect pests or those associated with local 'superstitions' were named, as were all edible insects.[138] Wizards could introduce copridae beetles (*gadlen*) into the bodies of their victims. The long-legged *shitshinyariendo* bird foretold misfortune on the road. The *buwumati* snake and the *nkangu* bird also served to warn of danger. Owls were seen as dangerous familiars, the agents used by witches in the pursuit of evil. Witches employed a range of animal familiars; apparently sent to harm individuals and their families, locals regarded such creatures with a level of suspicion that amounted to a rudimentary form of classification.[139]

Junod believed that the natives' knowledge of botany and zoology exhibited an appreciation of systematics and logic and that it showed a capacity for improvement. But their naming practices differed from one area to another, changed over time and their meaning was infused with superstition and magic. The universal principles of description and organization brought to Africa by Europe were clearly superior to a vision of the environment still dominated by despotic chiefs and mindless customs. Natural selection would run its course as the 'strange, unscientific ideas' of the natives locked in an unequal struggle with the 'scientific knowledge' of the Europeans.[140] 'Let the great modern principle of experimental science be instilled into their minds', advised Junod, 'and all that scaffolding of superstitions, which appear to them most reasonable now, will tumble down at once.'[141] He believed that these 'superstitions will not withstand the test of science and will pass away'.[142]

Imperialism had a strong effect on this binary, hierarchical and racialised arrangement of knowledge. During a furlough in Switzerland in January 1897, Junod presented a paper on 'The Climate of Delagoa Bay' before the Natural History Society of Neuchâtel.[143] The paper was an interesting mixture of themes reminiscent of his student essays. In a way that combined scientific observation with morality and meteorological statistics with political commentary, he spoke of the tripartite conquest that formed the essence of colonialism. The first was the military conquest of Africa. Speaking in the aftermath of the Luso–Gaza war of 1894–95 that had resulted in the burning of Rikatla and his removal from the Portuguese colony, Junod expressed bitterness at the way imperial armies ignored the social and spiritual well-being of indigenous peoples and trampled on their rights. Small wars brought in their wake the unrestricted sale of alcohol and the social degradation of the population. Fortunately, evangelical Christianity counter-balanced the wars of conquest with its 'second crusade'. 'But there is a third conquest that is taking place today from one end of the world to the other':

> it is that of science, that goes out across the continents, gathering its rich harvest of facts, studying geographical and climatic phenomena, collecting new animal forms, observing the customs and languages of primitive races, all in order to one day reconstruct the admirable set of facts, to understand if not the reason behind, at least the way in which humans and things are arranged on our marvelous planet.[144]

This portrayed science as a closed system of knowledge capable of transforming the world into a single, ordered and comprehensible universe dominated by Europe. Mary-Louise Pratt has remarked that taking possession of the world in this manner, without violence and destruction, was part of the utopian, innocent vision of European global authority.[145] It rested on the enlightened reformers' notion of rational knowledge as a liberating, politically neutral force, a way of understanding the world that was as noble, but ultimately as authoritarian, as religion. There was a closed finality in the faith Junod attached to both creeds, ranging light against darkness and reason against ignorance. The contribution of his representation of science to the constitution of power became clear when he described the 'temple of science' as the home to the 'scientific truth' that 'rules the whole of the civilized world'.[146] Or when he wrote that 'the light of knowledge will certainly, in the course of a long time, dissipate all those shadows of animism from the native soul'.[147] In an age preceding mechanized and atomic warfare, industrial genocide, HIV/AIDS and the destruction of the environment, Junod felt that 'to work for science is noble, science has never opposed the betterment and ennoblement of humanity'.[148] At times, he personified science as a living thing.[149] Junod's faith in science led him to believe, like Buxton and Livingstone, that enlightened thought and religion were the keys to progress and the means to regenerate Africa's 'intellectual energies and inventive faculties'.[150]

This path had been visibly trodden in Europe where the remnants of pagan practices provided tangible proof of the need for men of science and letters to complete the modernization of society. 'In all civilized countries, the peasantry or the less cultivated portion of the town population' still adhered to the vestiges of an age of magic and animism.[151] The culture of reason and religion carried by 'the enlightened classes' had yet to conquer the final redoubts of ignorance in Switzerland.[152] Junod saw the incomplete nature of this struggle in the botanical knowledge of European peasants, which he considered less thorough than that of Thonga tribesmen.[153] Even in places like La Chaux-de-Fonds, one of the industrial centres of modern Switzerland, witch-craft was still to be found. In this watchmaking centre in the canton of Neuchâtel, Junod had seen the heart of a goat or sheep pierced by a woman with at least fifty big pins in an attempt to injure her enemy.[154] Animistic beliefs were still current in other parts of western Switzerland where peasants talked to their bees in the same manner as Thonga tribesmen talked to their pigeons.[155] In both Africa and the Alps progress was held in check by customs that few dared to challenge for fear of disturbing the equilibrium of small, isolated communities.[156]

Junod found a common humanity when he compared 'the popular ideas, the superstitions of the less educated classes of our own countries with those of the black Africans'. But there was little equality in his vision of the struggle between a popular culture, based on superstition and mindless custom, and an elite culture built on the body of knowledge associated with modern science and enlightened religion. These 'superstitions' and 'animistic conceptions' were the product of inviolable customs 'transmitted from prehistoric times'. In those parts of Europe 'where education is thinly spread ... they still form the very basis of the mentality'.[157] The form of enlightenment pursued by church and school was based on a combination of religion and science, spirituality and materialism. With the help of this blend of reason and religion, the ruling class had delivered most of Europe from the tutelage of superstition and magic. In Africa, it promised to do the same.[158]

Many Africans must have been perplexed by the manner Junod learned from their ways of examining and organizing nature, and yet dismissed them as 'superstitions'. At the same time his ranking of animals into a hierarchy of species seemed to undermine their utility. By distinguishing between higher and lower species, he found the small animals, such as caterpillars, coleoptera, larvae, termites and locusts 'hideous' and 'nauseating' while locals considered them tasty and nutritious.[159] The obsession with which Junod gathered individual plants and insects must have seemed particularly frivolous to people pitted against nature and concerned to draw from it a raw practicality. They could neither understand his disdain for the prophetic significance of certain animals and plants, nor his reckless insouciance in the face of their supernatural powers.

It did not take much ingenuity to see that the story of creation featured in Junod's textbook on elementary science, published in Thonga in 1904, contradicted that found in the entire existing repertoire of literature in that language. In *Butibi*, Junod sought to provide Thonga scholars with a scientific understanding of the world, but his chapters on geological history and palaeontology inevitably recast as 'superstition' the Mosaic interpretation of creation found in the *buku* and Old Testament publications in Thonga.[160] Despite these contradictions, some young people started to see Junod's way of making sense of nature as a source of power to be harnessed. In 1909 one of Mozambique's earliest nationalist figures, Francisco Albasini's son João, publicly repudiated the old Gaza king Gungunyana and advocated rule by 'the civilized, serious, thoughtful men who truly possess scientific knowledge'.[161] An influential *assimilado* like Raúl Honwana thought his teacher Henri-Alexandre Junod 'a great man of learning' with an impressive 'science laboratory in his house'. In the same way as his teacher, or Albasini and many others like him, Honwana built the fortunes of his powerful family on the enlightenment of science and the revelation of religion.[162]

This notion of science as a closed system of knowledge regulated by precise rules, gave little recognition to the collection of data by Africans and ignored the systems and arrangements through which they ordered knowledge and infused it with meaning. In the process it portrayed modern science as the product of a civilization diffused from Europe to a grateful world. Yet, as I have tried to show in this chapter, one root of modern science has to be located in the messy, everyday encounters between men on the spot such as missionaries, diviners, *nangas*, *gobelas*, rain-makers and Christian converts. Like similar processes in many corners of a world increasingly dominated by

Europe, these African encounters contributed to the triumph of the Linnean model as a 'universal' way of understanding nature. At the same time, this way of seeing contributed to the authority of a 'modern' elite equipped with the skills and energy needed to push both metropole and colony in new and exciting directions.

A web of intellectual, social and institutional forces associated with Western learning and literacy held this idea of 'progress' in place. But in the 1890s the community of readers fed by the Swiss mission was limited in size. The following two chapters examine the historical role of the missionaries in the transcription of the local language and in the spread of literacy. Reading and writing were closely associated with the dissemination of science and Christianity, but the role of literacy was contested and (re)constituted, as was the meaning attributed to these ideas and practices.

Notes

1   *Bulletin de la Mission romande (BMR)* (1889) 85,7, August, p. 285.
2   Swiss Mission Archives (SMA), Lausanne. 503. Junod to mission council, 5 July 1889.
3   SMA 503. Junod to mission council, 30 October 1889.
4   As did doctors obliged to live in rural villages by their calling or by their interest in the healing properties of plants. C. Secrétan, 'Savants et chercheurs' in Daniel Baud-Bovy, Paul Bessire, Charly Clerc (eds), *La Vie Romantique au Pays Romand* (Lausanne, 1930), pp. 199, 200; Marc Weidemann, 'Un pasteur-naturaliste du XVIIIᵉ siècle: Elie Bertrand (1713–1797), *Revue Historique Vaudoise* (1986), pp. 63–108. For the same process in Britain, cf. Charles J. Withers, 'Geography, Natural History and the Eighteenth-century Enlightenment: putting the world in place', *History Workshop Journal* (1995) no. 39, spring, p. 154.
5   L. Vulliemin, *Le Doyen Bridel: essai biographique* (Lausanne, 1855), pp. 120–3. On these learned associations, see note 7, below.
6   Benjamin Grivel, 'Alpinisme et Romantisme: le goût de la montagne' in Baud-Bovy et al., *La Vie Romantique*, p. 181.
7   The Société helvétique was founded in 1767 and the Société helvétique de sciences naturelles in 1815. In western Switzerland, the Société de physique et d'histoire naturelle was founded in Geneva in 1790 and the Conservatoire botanique in 1824. In Lausanne, the Société vaudoise de sciences naturelles was established in 1815 as a section of the Société helvétique. A natural history museum was built in 1817 and a scientific journal established in 1841.
8   Eugène Rambert, *La Société vaudoise des sciences naturelles: sa fondation et son développement* (Lausanne, 1876), pp. 8–9.
9   J-J. Rousseau, *Rêveries du promeneur solitaire* (Paris, [1782] 1933), p. 725.
10 Charles Secrétan, 'Albert de Haller' in *Galerie Suisse: Biographies Nationales* (Lausanne, 1876), p. 604; M. Murith, *Le guide du botaniste qui voyage dans le Valais* (Lausanne, 1810), p. 31; Marc Théodore Bourrit (1776) cited in C. Reichler and R. Ruffieux (eds), *Le Voyage en Suisse: anthologie des voyageurs français et européens de la Renaissance au XXe siècle* (Paris, 1998), p. 284. See also 'Introduction,' p. 8.
11 Emile Javelle, *Souvenirs d'un alpiniste* (Lausanne, Paris, [1886] 1920), p. 295.
12 On these ambivalences, see Eugène Rambert, 'Les plantes alpines' (pp. 84, 87, 123) and 'Le chevrier de Praz-de-Fort' [1865] in his *Récits et Croquis* (Lausanne, 1889); Javelle, *Souvenirs d'un alpiniste*, pp. 30, 42; Juste Olivier, *Le Canton de Vaud* (Lausanne, 1837) 1, p. 34.
13 André Bordier, *Voyage pitoresque aux glacières de Savoye* (Geneva, 1773) cited in Reichler and Ruffieux, *Le Voyage en Suisse*, p. 342; Horace-Benedicte de Saussure, *Premières ascensions au Mont-Blanc* (Geneva, 1834), p. 129; Rambert, 'Les plantes alpines' pp. 84, 87.
14 For an expansion of these ideas, and much of this section, see P. Harries, 'From the Alps to Africa: Swiss missionaries and the rise of anthropology' in Hellen Tilley and Robert Gordon (eds), *Anthropology, European Imperialism, and the Ordering of Africa* (Manchester, 2007).
15 Marc Théodore Bourrit (1776) cited in *Le Voyage en Suisse*, p. 333; Vuillemin, *Doyen Bridel*, p. 198; Secrétan, 'Savants et Chercheurs' in Baud-Bovy et al. (eds), *La Vie Romantique*, p. 200; Rambert, 'Une bibliothèque à la montagne' in *Récits et Croquis*.
16 Guyot remained at Princeton until his death in 1884. See L. C. Jones, *Arnold Guyot et Princeton* (Neuchâtel, 1929). For Guyot's ideas on Creation, see Ronald L. Numbers, *Creation by Natural Law: Laplace's Nebular Hypothesis in American Thought* (Seattle, WA, and London, 1977), pp. 91–100; David N. Livingstone, *Darwin's Forgotten Defenders: The Encounter between Evangelical Theology and Evolutionary Thought* (Edinburgh, 1987),

pp. 2–23, 77–80.

[17] Vogt remained with Agassiz from 1839 to 1844. He then mixed with radical figures in Paris and Geneva before returning to Giessen. The political upheavals of 1848 in Germany caused him to return to Switzerland where he became professor of geology and paleontology in Geneva in 1853 and of comparative anatomy in 1872. See F. Gregory, *Scientific Materialism in Nineteenth Century Germany* (Dordrecht and Boston, MA, 1977), pp. 51–79, 175–8, 197–204. On Desor, see Karl Vogt, *Eduard Desor. Lebensbild eines Naturforschers* (Breslau, 1883); Marc-Antoine Kaeser, *L'Univers du Préhistorien: science, foi et politique dans l'oeuvre et la vie d'Edouard Desor (1811–1882)* (Paris, 2004)

[18] S. J. Gould, *Bully for Brontosaurus* (London, 1991), p. 312; Gould, *Hen's Teeth and Horses' Toes* (London, [1983] 1990), p. 108; R. L. Numbers, *The Creationists* (New York, 1992), p. 7. But note that Adam Kuper refers to Agassiz as 'the eccentric Lamarckian biologist of Harvard' in his *The Invention of Primitive Society* (London, 1988), p. 44. Another member of Agassiz's team, the botanist Léo Lesquereux, also moved to an important career in the United States.

[19] Frédéric de Rougemont published his lectures on this theme, given at the Neuchâtel Academy in the winter of 1841, as *Fragments d'une histoire de la terre, d'après la Bible, les traditions païennes et la géologie* (Neuchâtel, 1841). See also his *Histoire de la terre d'après la Bible et la géologie* (Paris, 1856). On Guyot, see p. 128 above. Vogt translated Robert Chambers' *Vestiges of Creation* and, following the publication of *The Origin of Species*, became a vigorous Darwinian propagandist, see p. 24 above.

[20] Cf. Frédéric de Rougemont, *Le Peuple primitif: sa religion, son histoire et sa civilisation* (Geneva and Paris, 1855–57) 3 vols; also his *L'Homme primitif* (Neuchâtel, 1870). On Desor, see Kaeser, *L'Univers du Préhistorien*, pp. 265–356.

[21] M. de Tribolet 'Fritz Tripet: professeur de botanique à l'académie: 1843–1907' in *Bulletin de la société neuchâteloise des sciences naturelles (BSNSN)* (1909), pp. 35, 92, 99; Henri Junod [père], *Sermons* (Neuchâtel, 1884), p. ix.

[22] Botanical Conservatory, Geneva; Boissier Herbarium (henceforth BCG. BH), Junod to W. Barbey, 2 January 1892.

[23] Charles–Henri Godet collected twelve thousand plant species and in 1852 published the classic *Flore du Jura*, a work supplemented by new findings in 1869. Lionel Gossman, *Basel in the Age of Burckhardt: A Study in Unseasonable Ideas* (Chicago, 2000), pp. 207–8.

[24] In a letter to the secretary of the Swiss Mission, dated 30 October 1889, Junod recalled Paul Godet's profound influence on him as both collector and teacher (SMA 503). In a later letter to Philippe Godet, dated 15 October 1912, he mentioned Frédéric, Georges and Philippe as the greatest influences on his life, apart from his father. University and Cantonal Library of Neuchâtel, Philippe Godet papers MS 3164.131. On Paul Godet, see G. Dubois, *Naturalistes Neuchâtelois du XXe siècle* (Neuchâtel, 1976), pp. 49–51. Paul Godet's most famous doctoral student was Jean Piaget, an expert in molluscs who would go on to revolutionize the world of child psychology, see J.-M. Barrelet and A.-N. Perret-Clermont (eds), *Jean Piaget et Neuchâtel: l'apprentie et le savant* (Lausanne, 1996), pp. 35, 57, 97–9; F. Vidal, *Piaget before Piaget* (Cambridge, MA, 1994), pp. 23–33, 116. The role of the Godets in the intellectual life of fin-de-siècle Neuchâtel is remembered in Guy de Pourtalès, *Chaque mouche a son ombre 1881–1919* (Paris, 1980) vol. I, pp. 70–8. In the context of this tightly-woven intellectual world, it is interesting to note that Jean Piaget's father, the historian Arthur Piaget, was a contemporary of Henri-Alexandre Junod and that the two families mixed socially. Jean's parish pastor was Henri-Alexandre's brother, the amateur palaentologist and temperance activist, Charles-Daniel Junod. Archives of the Société de Belles-Lettres, Neuchâtel, Henri-Philippe Junod to Comité des anciens Belleletriens, 23 February 1982.

[25] The stress on direct observation as a method of teaching went back to Rousseau and the Vaudois pedagogue, H. Pestalozzi. De Tribolet, 'Fritz Tripet,' p. 94. See also the narrative of Louis Favre's popular novel, *Robinson de la Tène* (Neuchâtel, 1875) in which he combined instructive tours through the countryside with lessons on geography, natural history and prehistory.

[26] H.-A. Junod, 'Le triton lobé' in *Le Rameau de Sapin* (1879) 13, August, pp. 31–2, 35–6; 'L'Erythronium dens canis. Linné' in *Le Rameau de Sapin* (1882) 16, November, pp. 41–2.

[27] Elizabeth Cory Agassiz, *Louis Agassiz: his Life & Correspondence* (Boston, MA, 1885) vol. I, p. 244; L. Agassiz, *Contributions to the Natural History of the United States of America* (1859) vol. I, p. 135, cited in Ernst Mayr, *Evolution and the Diversity of Life* (Cambridge, MA, 1976), p. 256.

[28] Ronald L. Numbers, 'Creating Creationism: Meanings and Uses since the Age of Agassiz' in D. N. Livingstone, D. G. Hart and M. A. Noll (eds), *Evangelicals and Science in Historical Perspective* (New York, 1999), p. 235. E. Lurie, 'Louis Agassiz and the idea of evolution', *Victorian Studies* (1959) 3.

[29] Frédéric Godet, 'Les six jours de la création' in his *Etudes bibliques* (Neuchâtel and Paris, 1889); Guyot's ideas on Creation are treated in Numbers, *Creation by Natural Law*, note 16 above. One of the pioneers of this 'day-age theory' was Hugh Miller (1802–56) of the Free Church of Scotland, an institution with close links to evangelicals in western Switzerland. See his *The Two Records: Mosaic and Geological* (n. p. , 1854) and *The Testimony of the Rocks* (Edinburgh, 1857). On the tenacity of the 'day-age' theory of Creation, see Numbers, *The Creationists*, pp. 7, 9, 12, 67, 107.

[30] V. Rossel, *Histoire littéraire de la Suisse romande* (Neuchâtel, 1903), p. 606.

[31] Godet, 'Les six jours', p. 88.

[32] Arnold Guyot, *Creation, or, the Biblical Cosmogony in the Light of Modern Science* (New York, 1884), pp. 3–4, 7.

[33] 'Les obscurantistes, les éteignoirs, la prêtraille,' in H. Junod, *Du manque de pasteurs et des moyens d'y remédier* (Neuchâtel, 1864), pp. 17, 23–4, 29, 40. See also Junod, *Sermons*, p. 186, and Jones, *Arnold Guyot et Princeton*, p. 92 and passim.

[34] Junod, *Sermons*, p. ix. See also P. Godet, *Frédéric Godet: 1812–1900* (Neuchâtel, 1913), pp. 82, 334. Henri Berthoud (sen.), *Etude sur les rapports de la cosmogonie mosaïque avec la géologie: précédée de quelques considérations générales sur la Bible et les sciences* (Lausanne, 1859).

[35] These included the professor of geology at the Lausanne Academy, Eugène Renevier, who served on the major governing bodies of the mission for almost forty years, and as its president from 1883 to 1906; the naturalist and former missionary in India, Auguste Glardon (a member of the mission council, 1869–73 and 1881–89) and the famous botanist William Barbey (council member from 1891 to 1908). Henri-Alexandre's brother, the future pastor Charles-Daniel Junod, would in his turn become a noteworthy palaeontologist. A. Grandjean, *La Mission romande* (Lausanne, 1917), pp. 268–9, 311–12; Dubois, *Naturalistes Neuchâtelois*, p. 108. For a parallel situation with comparable outcomes, see J. Clifford, *Person and Myth: Maurice Leenhardt in the Melanesian World* (Berkeley and Los Angeles, 1982), pp. 13–15.

[36] Cf. Jules Marcou, *Life, Letters and Works of Louis Agassiz* (New York, 1896), pp. 192–3, 218. Numbers distinguishes between 'progressive creationists' and 'strict creationists', see his 'The Creationists' in David N. Lindberg and Ronald L. Numbers (eds), *God and Nature: Historical Essays on the encounter between Christianity and Science* (Berkeley and Los Angeles, 1984), pp. 391–3. See also J. R. Topham, 'Science, natural theology and evangelicalism in early nineteenth century Scotland' in David. N. Livingstone, D. G. Hart and M. A. Noll (eds), *Evangelicals and Science in Historical Perspective*, (New York, 1999), pp. 142–3.

[37] C. Dufour and J-P. Haenni, *Musée d'histoire naturelle de Neuchâtel* (Hauterive, Neuchâtel, 1985), p. 46; Dubois, *Naturalistes Neuchâtelois*, p. 51.

[38] H–A. Junod (étudiant) 'Les états de larve et de nymphe de l'hyponomeuta stannellus (Thunberg)' in *BSNSN* (1884) 14, pp. 1–9.

[39] Cf. Anon., *Henry Appia: sa jeunesse – son activité: souvenirs receuillis* (Geneva, 1905), p. 118. This work provides a sympathetic picture of student life in Neuchâtel's Faculty of Theology in the early 1880s.

[40] The essays were published between 1880 and 1887. The praise came from 'J. C. ' [James Chepard], 'Chronique de Neuchâtel' in *Revue de Belles-Lettres* (1883) 11:6, p. 219.

[41] See the *Souvenir de l'inauguration du buste élevé à L. Agassiz par la Société de Belles-Lettres dans le bâtiment académique de Neuchâtel, le 12 mai 1887* (Neuchâtel, 1887).

[42] Junod, 'Sur quelques larves inédites de Rhopalocères', *BSNSN* (1891–92) 20, p. 18; Junod, 'La faune entomologique de Delagoa – Lèpidoptères', *BSNSN* (1898–99) 27, p. 10; Junod, 'La faune entomologique du Delagoa – coléoptères' *Bulletin de la société vaudoise des sciences naturelles* (henceforth *BSVSN*) (1899) 35, p. 162.

[43] Jacques Naef, 'La botanique' in J. Trembley (ed.), *Les savants genevois dans l'Europe intellectuelle: du XVIIe au milieu du XIXe siècle* (Geneva, 1987), pp. 360–7. New plants were still discovered in the Alps de Bex and the Pays d'Enhaut in the early 1880s, see T. Durand and H. Pittier, *Catalogue de la flore vaudoise* (Lausanne, 1882), p. 395. Entomologists like Auguste Forel were also obliged to look beyond Switzerland in their search for new species. Cf. A. Forel, *Mémoires* (Neuchâtel, 1941), pp. 63, 164, 183ff.

[44] Cf. P. L. Gorchakovsky, C. Favarger and P. Küpfer, 'Onésime Clerc (1845–1920), naturaliste: un Neuchâtelois en Russie', *Bulletin de la société neuchâteloise des sciences naturelles* (1995), p. 118; Jordí Martí-Henneberg and Anne Radeff, *Henri-François Pittier, 1857–1950* (Lausanne, 1986); Paul Biolley, *Costa Rica et son avenir* (Paris, 1889).

[45] Cf. *Formica Berthoudi, Camponotus Eugeniae* and *C. Valdeziae.* Auguste Forel, 'Etudes Myrmécologiques en 1875', *BSVSN* (1876) 14, pp. 33–8; 'Etudes Myrmécologiques en 1879', *BSVSN* (1879) 16, pp. 108–10. Museum of Natural History, Neuchâtel, annual reports for 1884, 1886, 1889; *Nouvelles de nos missionnaires* (1886) 1:9, 9.

[46] Rambert, *La Société vaudoise*, pp. 25–6. See also W.-L. Distant, *A Naturalist in the Transvaal* (London, 1892), p. 124; D. E. Allen, *The Naturalist in Britain: a Social History* (London, 1976), pp. 179–93.

[47] Naef, 'La botanique', p. 364.

[48] J. H. Brooke, *Science and Religion: some historical perspectives* (London, 1991), p. 50.

[49] G. Bertoloni, 'Illustratio rerum naturalium Mozambici' in *Novi Commentari Academiae Scientiarum Instituti Bononiensis* (Bologna) (1849) X; W. C. H. Peters, *Naturwissenchaftliche Reise nach Mossambique in den Jahre 1842–1848* (Berlin, 1861, 1864, 1868), 3 vols.

[50] Rose Monteiro had lived and worked with her husband in west-central Africa. See Joachim John Monteiro, *Angola and the River Congo* (London, [1875] new edn 1968). She helped Joachim send dried plants collected in the Lourenço Marques area to Kew Gardens in 1876–78 when he served as the Cape's labour agent in the town. She returned in the late 1880s to Lourenço Marques where she lived on the Polana bluffs, to complete

her husband's work and collect saleable insects. Junod felt that her *Delagoa Bay, its Natives and Natural History* (London, 1891) contained 'much interesting information', although 'without claiming any great scientific accuracy', see *Life of a South African Tribe* (London, 1927) (*LSAT*) II, pp. 147–8, n1. He was more critical of her work in a private letter to Eugène Autran, the conservator of the Boissier Herbarium, 19 May 1892 in BCG.BH. On Rose Monteiro, see Jeanne Penvenne, *African Workers and Colonial Racism: Mozambican Strategies and Struggles in Lourenço Marques, 1877–1962* (Portsmouth, NH, London, 1995), pp. 58–9. On Freire de Andrade as botanist, see Henri-Philippe Junod, *Henri-A. Junod: Missionnaire et Savant, 1863–1934* (Lausanne, 1934), p. 43.

51 See chapter four, p. 107.

52 These included the collections of Boivin, Gueinzius and Krauss, as well as the herbarium of Pierre Verreaux (1807–1873). An associate of Andrew Smith at the Cape, Verreaux became a celebrated dealer in natural history specimens on his return to Paris. H. M. Burdet and A. Chapin, 'Les herbiers de Genève', *Webbia* (1993) 48, pp. 238–9.

53 Cf. his letter to Harry Bolus, February 1890 in University of Cape Town, Bolus Collection, p. 234. Barbey had asked Paul Berthoud to collect plants in the Northern Transvaal just as the region was being scoured by the German botanist R. Rehmann. See his *Polypetalae Rehmannianae* (1887–8).

54 BCG.BH, Junod to Barbey, 30 October 1889; SMA 503 Junod to secretary, 30 October 1889.

55 SMA 503, Junod to secretary, mission council, 30 October, 1889; Junod, 'Correspondences: de Rikatla à Marakouène' *BSNG* (1891) 6, p. 320; Hans Schinz and H.-A. Junod, 'Zur Kenntnis der Pflanzenwelt der Delago–Bay' in *Bulletin de l'Herbier Boissier* (1899) 7, 2. BCG.BH, 'A propos de l'herbier de Shiluvane, apporté en 1893 [sic. 1903] par Mr Henri-Alexandre Junod.'

56 Junod, 'La faune entomologique du Delagoa – lepidoptères', *BSNSN* (1898–99) 27, pp. 186, 189; *Nouvelles de nos missionnaires* (1892) 15,1, p. 11.

57 BCG.BH, Junod to Barbey, 1 September 1891; *Nouvelles de nos missionnaires* (1892) 15,1.

58 BCG.BH, Junod to Barbey, 25 July and 4 October 1891. I have been unable to find this species as it does not conform to the rules of the International Code for Botanical Nomenclature.

59 BCG.BH, Junod to E. Autran, 15 February and 5 September 1892. Junod had in fact learned to press and dry plants from a Paris Geographical Society publication for travellers.

60 Junod, 'Correspondances', Rikatla, 23 November 1891, *BSNG* (1892–93) vii, p. 531; BCG.BH, Junod to Autran 19 May and 5 September 1892; note entitled 'Collections Junod à vendre', 15 March 1904.

61 BCG.BH, Junod, 'A propos de l'herbier de Shilouvâne'; Junod, *LSAT*, II, p. 238.

62 BCG.BH, Junod to Barbey, 15 January 1903 and 24 May 1906; Junod to Schinz, 20 October 1903; Junod to Beauverd, 2 March 1910.

63 BCG.BH, Junod to Barbey, 25 February 1898. In 1891 F. R. R. Schlechter (1872–1925) embarked on extensive botanical voyages in Southern Africa, including Mozambique. F. A. Mendonça, 'Botanical collectors in Mozambique' in A. Fernandes (ed.), *Comptes rendus de la IVe réunion plénière de l'association pour l'étude taxonomique de la flore d'Afrique tropicale à Lisbone et Coimbra* (Lisbon, 1962).

64 BCG.BH, Junod to Maurice Barbey, 25 April 1919; CBG.HB, 'Compte des plantes de l'herbier sudafricain de H. A. Junod expédié à l'herbier Boissier', annexure III attached to Junod to Prof. Chodat, 3 January 1921. See also Junod's original botanical register, lodged in the Boissier Herbarium.

65 Cf. J. Thunberg and N. L. Burman, Allioni, Houttuyn, Van Royen and others.

66 Junod, *LSAT* II, p. 147 n. 1.

67 Schinz and Junod, 'Zur Kenntnis der Pflanzenwelt', continued in *Mémoire de l'herbier Boissier* (1900) 10.

68 Cf. Hans Schinz, 'Beiträge zur Kenntnis der Afrikanischen Flora', *Bulletin de l'herbier Boissier* (1896) 4; (1896) 5 and (1899) 7. J. Burtt-Davy was less glowing in his praise. Although he recognized the pioneering work of Junod around Shiluvane, Burtt-Davy found his plant specimens 'often scrappy and unfit for determination'. J. Burtt-Davy, 'First annotated catalogue of the vascular plants of the Transvaal and Swaziland' in *Report of South African Association for the Advancement of Science* (*RSAAAS*) (1908), p. 232.

69 See the *Index Kewensis*. Also the entry on Junod in M. Gunn and L. E. Codd (eds), *Botanical Exploration of Southern Africa: an Illustrated History* (Cape Town, 1981), p. 203.

70 Junod, *LSAT* I, p. 1.

71 Junod, 'Correspondence: de Rikatla à Marakouène', p. 322.

72 Trimen described *Papilio junodi* in the *Transactions of the Entomological Society of London* (1893), p. 138. The genus was later changed from *Papilio* to *Graphium* and the butterfly is now known as *Graphium junodi*, a Swordtail (Trimen, 1893). Junod, 'La faune entomologique', pp. 180, 184, 200, 219, 224, 240. E. L. L. Pringle, G. A. Hening and J. B. Ball (eds), *Pennington's Butterflies of Southern Africa* (Cape Town, 1978, 2nd edn, 1994), pp. 301, 306.

73 In December 1891 Junod claimed to have amassed a collection of beetles and butterflies worth almost £200, CBG. HB, Junod to Barbey, 2 December 1891. On his sales to Trimen, see South African Museum, Trimen letterbooks, 31 July 1890 to 17 February 1892. Junod's gifts and sales of butterflies were noted in the Annual Reports of the Natural History Museum, Neuchâtel for 1892, 1894 (SF50 for 'insects') and 1911. Anon., *Le musée d'histoire naturelle* (Neuchâtel, 1899), p. 40, mentions receiving a 'rich collection' of butterflies from Junod at Rikatla.

152   Natural Sciences

74 This collection was bought by the Hon. Walter Rothschild who opened the museum in 1889. Today it is in the
    Natural History Museum, London. W.-L. Distant, *Insecta Transvaaliensia: a contribution to the entomology of
    South Africa* (London, 1924), p. 99 and plate xvi.
75 SMA 303/11C, P. Loze to mission secretary, 5 June 1934.
76 In 2002 Richard Gallon discerned a new tarantula genus, *Harpactirinae*, in which he grouped the species
    Augacephalus junodi. This species had earlier been named *Pterinochilus junodi* (Simon 1904). *Bulletin of the
    British Arachanological Society* (2002) 12, 5.
77 Junod, 'La faune entomologique – coléoptères', pp. 132, 163, 177; Junod, 'Rikatla à Marakouène', p. 323.
78 E. Bugnion, 'Remarques supplémentaires' following Junod, 'La faune entomologique – coléoptères', p. 189.
79 Junod and O. de Schulthess-Schindler, 'La faune entomologique du Delagoa – *orthoptères*', *BSVSN* (1899) 132;
    Junod and A. L. Montandon, 'La faune entomologique du Delagoa – *hémiptères*', *BSVSN* (1899) 132; Junod
    and A. de Schulthess-Schindler, 'La faune entomologique du Delagoa – *hyménoptères*', *BSVSN* (1899) 133.
80 Dr Griffini, 'Sui Cybiser raccolti dal Rev. Junod a Delagoa', *Boll. dei Musei di Turino* XIII (1898) N° 325;
    Dr Regimbart, 'Monogr. Gyrinidae', *Ann. Soc. Entomologique de France* (1893); Regimbart, *Dytiscidae et
    Gyrinidae d'Afrique et de Madagascar* (Brussels, 1895).
81 L. Péringuey, 'A descriptive catalogue of the coleoptera of South Africa. Pt II', *Transactions of the South
    African Philosophical Society* (henceforth *TSAPS*) (1896) 7, pp. 113–480; Péringuey, 'Descriptive catalogue of
    the coleoptera of South Africa – part III', *TSAPS* (1897) 10, 1, p. 23; Péringuey, 'Fourth contribution to the
    South African coleopterous fauna,' *TSAPS* (1892) 6, 2, pp. 95–6. Péringuey, 'Some new coleoptera collected
    by Rev Henri A. Junod at Shiluvane, near Leydsdorp, in the Transvaal', in *Trans. Novitat Zoologicae* (1904)
    11, pp. 448–50. W. F. Purcell, 'On the scorpions, Solifugae and a trapdoor spider collected by the Rev. Henry
    A. Junod at Shiluvane near Leydsdorp in the Transvaal', *Trans. Novitat Zoologicae* (1903) 10, 2. For the ants,
    cf. Carebara junodi Forel (1904) and *Monomorium junodi* Forel (1910). In 1894 Forel determined *Monomorium
    delagoense, Tetramorium delagoense, Camponotus delagoensis, Crematogaster transvaalensis, Crematogaster
    delagoensis* and *Opthalmopone Berthoudi*.
82 He envisaged reworking published articles into chapters on the region's climate, flora, butterflies, coleoptera,
    orthoptera and hemiptera. CBG.HB, Junod to Autran, 19 February 1900. On the National exhibition, see H.
    Büchler, *Drei Sweizerische Landesausstellungen: Zurich 1883, Genf 1896, Bern 1914* (Zurich, 1970).
83 The beetles included *Eudema Rikatlense* (found in the small lake behind the hill on which the mission was
    built) and *Graphopterus antiokanus*. The butterflies, *Papilio junodi* (Trimen), *Paralethe dendrophilus junodi* (Van
    Son), *Acrae nohara junodi* (Oberthür). He raised an emperor moth, *Gonimbrasia belina junodi* (Oberthür),
    from the *mopane* worm; another moth, *Eumeta Junodi*, from the larval form while on holiday at Howick. He
    named another moth after his wife Emilie (*Chalia Emiliae*). E. L. L. Pringle, G. A. Henning and J. B. Ball
    (eds), *Pennington's Butterflies of Southern Africa* (2nd edn, Cape Town, 1994) p. 33. E. C. G. Pinhay, *Moths of
    Southern Africa* (Cape Town, 1975), pp. 39, 114. For some of the other insects, including ants, rove beetles,
    assassin bugs and owlflies, see *Bulletin of the American Museum of Natural History* (1921–2) XLV; Péringuey,
    'Fifth contribution to the South African coleopterous fauna', *TSAPS* (1892) 6:2, pp. 248, 326–7, 479; Distant,
    'Descriptions of new species of Hemiptera-Heteroptera' *Annals and Magazine of Natural History* (1898) 2;
    Junod, 'La faune entomologique – lépidoptères', p. 233.
84 *Crematogaster liengmei, Pheidole liengmei* and *Tetraponera liengmei*. Peringuey gave the name *Bostrichophorus
    liengmei* Pér. to a beetle found by Liengme on the banks of the Limpopo. Junod, 'La faune entomologique
    – coléoptères', p. 165.
85 The molluscs were mainly giant land snails (Achatina). See also the species *Lentorbis junodi* (Connolly, 1922),
    Ferrissia junodi (Connolly, 1925), *Hippeutis junodi* (Connolly, 1922) and *Haloschizopera junodi* (Monard,
    1935).
86 In this way, for instance, it was discovered that two of the reptiles sent from Lesotho in 1907 by Mlle Jacot
    represented new species.
87 Junod, 'Le climat de la baie', p. 78. He was correct here, for scientists are turning increasingly to old museum
    collections to study the variation in species and to gauge historical changes in the ecological balance. See also
    the reference to Mlle Jacot in the previous footnote.
88 Junod, *LSAT* I, pp. 65–6; II, p. 332.
89 Steven Shapin, 'The invisible technician' in *American Scientist* (1989) 77, November-December.
90 University of South Africa (UNISA), Junod Collection (JC) 3. 3 'Elias, un ancien de l'église africaine'; Junod,
    'La faune entomologique – lèpidoptères', pp. 179, 223.
91 Emphasis in the original. Junod, 'Les Ba-Ronga: étude ethnographique sur les indigènes de la baie de Delagoa',
    BSNG (1898) 10, 21, p. 419; Junod, 'La faune entomologique – coleoptères', pp. 170, 176, 177, 184; Junod,
    LSAT II, pp. 344–45.
92 Junod, *LSAT* II, pp. 81–3, 344.
93 Junod, *LSAT* II, p. 344.
94 Junod, *LSAT* II, p. 302.
95 Junod, *LSAT* II, pp. 329–30. This form of classification is still employed today, see C. A. Liengme, 'Plants

used by the Tsonga people of Gazankulu' in *Bothalia* (1981) 13, 3 and 4, pp. 513–14.

[96] Junod, 'Rikatla à Marakouène,' p. 320; Junod, *LSAT* II, pp. 332, 345, 589; Junod, 'Les Ba-Ronga', p. 22. For a good introduction to the disordered history of European plant taxonomy, see Anna Pavord, *The Naming of Names: The Search for Order in the World of Plants* (London, 2005).

[97] BCG.BH, Junod to Barbey, 2 January 1892.

[98] BCG.BH, 'Botanique indigène', attached to Junod to Barbey, 16 October 1891. Junod, *LSAT* II, pp. 328, 435ff, 482, 657; Junod, 'The best means of preserving the traditions and customs of the various SA native races', *Report of the South Africa Association for the Advancement of Science* (1907), p. 149.

[99] BCG.BH, Junod to Autran, 1 December 1896. He sent plants known to supply antidotes against migraines, gonorrhoea and other maladies to Mr Chodat in Geneva for medical analysis. See the archives of the Ethnographic Museum of Neuchâtel for lists of plants making up the 'pharmacy of the Ba-Ronga' and a 'collection of native medicinal roots'.

[100] Junod declined, for instance, to take up Barbey's suggestion that coffee could be established as a cash crop in the Delagoa Bay area, see BCG.BH, Junod to Barbey, 5 July 1893.

[101] Junod, 'Une promenade aux environs de Rikatla' in Anon., *Chez les Gouamba: glanures dans le champ de la Mission romande* (Lausanne, n.d., approx 1893), p. 11.

[102] UNISA.JC: 6. Conférences: à Neuchâtel, 1897.

[103] Henri-Philippe Junod, *Henri-A Junod: Missionnaire et Savant 1863–1934* (Lausanne, 1934), p. 64.

[104] Junod, 'La faune entomologique – coleoptères', pp. 172, 175, 186.

[105] Ibid., p. 178.

[106] J. Bryce, *Impressions of South Africa* (3rd edn, London, 1899), p. 17.

[107] Cf. A. H. Keane's entry on 'South Africa' in the *Encyclopaedia Britannica* (1902) XXXII, p. 711.

[108] Distant, *Naturalist in the Transvaal*, pp. 41, 124–5.

[109] Junod 'La faune entomologique – lèpidoptères', pp. 228, 242; Junod, *LSAT* II, pp. 80–1; Junod, 'Promenade aux environs de Rikatla'.

[110] Junod, 'La faune entomologique – lèpidoptères', p. 232; Junod, *LSAT* I, p. 65.

[111] Compare M. E. Barber on 'a divine guardianship, a Protecting Power, which cares and provides for all' in her 'On the structure and fertilization of Liaris Bowkeri', *Journal of the Linnean Society* (1869), 5, pp. 470–1, with her starkly Darwinian approach in 'On the peculiar colours of animals in relation to habits of life', *Transactions of the South African Philosophical Association* (1877–78), 1:4, pp. 27ff. On Barber, see William Beinart, 'Men, Science, Travel and Nature in the Eighteenth and Nineteenth-century Cape,' *Journal of Southern African Studies* (1998) 24, 4, pp. 792–9.

[112] S. J. Gould, *Hen's Teeth*, p. 81.

[113] Agassiz held these views until his death in 1873. In 1908, on receipt of Mrs Barbey's translation of a work by A. R. Wallace, Junod acknowledged that he found the theory of evolution to be 'true and fruitful' ('juste et féconde'). BCG.BH, Junod to Barbey, 9 October 1908.

[114] Junod, 'God's Ways in the Bantu Soul', *International Review of Missions* (1914) 111, pp. 96–7. On Henry Drummond's fusion of science and religion, see James R. Moore, 'Evangelicals and Evolution', *Scottish Journal of Theology* (1985) 38. Drummond's most influential work, which sold 70,000 copies in five years and was published in multiple editions, was *Natural Law in the Spiritual World* (London, [1883] 29th edn, 1890).

[115] On the extinction of the Bushmen and the Vaalpens, see A. C. Haddon, Presidential address to Section H – Anthropology – of the British Association for the Advancement of Science, *Report of the 75th meeting*, 1905, pp. 521, 525.

[116] Junod, 'Les Ba-Ronga', p. 114. See the section of chapter seven entitled 'On the extinction of the races of men' in Darwin, *The Descent of Man* (London, 1874). These ideas anteceded Darwin, cf. A. M. Kass and E. H. Kass, *Perfecting the World: The life and times of Dr. Thomas Hodgkin, 1798–1866* (New York, 1988), p. 392. In 1865 Tiyo Soga criticized the notion of social and physical degeneration in 'What is the destiny of the Kaffir race?' in D. Williams (ed.), *The Journal and Selected Writings of the Rev. Tiyo Soga* (Cape Town, 1983), p. 178.

[117] Junod, *LSAT* I, p. 10; Junod, *LSAT* II, pp. 96–7, 111, 166.

[118] See the contradictory passages in 'Les Ba-Ronga,' pp. 7 and 486.

[119] Junod, *LSAT* II, pp. 541, 629–30. On the medical evidence, see J. Bruce–Bays, 'The injurious effects of civilisation upon the physical condition of the native races of South Africa' and J. A. Mitchell, 'The growth of the native races of the Cape Colony and some factors affecting it', both in *Report of the South African Association for the Advancement of Science* (1908). Junod was a vice–president of section F of this association.

[120] F. de Rougemont, 'Catalogue des lépidoptères du Jura neuchâtelois' in *BSNSN* (1900–1901) 29, pp. 291, 307.

[121] Junod, *LSAT* I, p. 10.

[122] F. C. Selous, *Sunshine and Storm in Rhodesia* (New York, [1896] 1969), p. 67, cited in Brooke, *Science and Religion*, p. 295.

[123] Jacques Roger, 'L'Eugénisme, 1850–1950' in his *Pour une histoire des sciences à part entière* (Paris, 1995), pp. 411–12.

154   Natural Sciences

[124] Auguste Forel, *Mémoires* (Neuchâtel, 1941), p. 167. The quote from Spencer is in Karl Degler, *In Search of Human Nature: the decline and revival of Darwinism in American social thought* (New York, 1991), p. 11. Until recently, August Forel was regarded as a sufficiently neutral public figure for the SF1000 note to carry his image.

[125] Junod, 'Les Ba-Ronga', p. 116; Junod, *LSAT* I, p. 11; *LSAT* II, p. 632. For Henry Drummond's views on this issue, see his *The Ascent of Man* (London, 1894) and Brooke, *Science and Religion*, pp. 16–17, 311.

[126] See p. 82.

[127] Junod, 'Les Ba-Ronga', pp. 115–16.

[128] Junod, *LSAT* II, p. 536.

[129] Junod, 'The Magic conception of nature amongst Bantus', *South African Journal of Science* (1920) 17, p. 79. Italics in the original.

[130] UNISA. Junod Collection. Seven Sermons. Sermon given at Môtiers ,1 January 1887 and Couvet, 25 January 1887. See also Cantonal and Public Library, Neuchâtel, Philippe Godet Collection MS 3164.131, Junod to P. Godet, 15 October 1912. On the wider influence of Kant's teachings on aspirant missionaries in Neuchâtel, see H. Perregaux, *Edmond Perregaux missionnaire: d'après sa correspondance 1868–1905* (Neuchâtel, 1906), p. 70.

[131] Immanuel Kant, 'What is Enlightenment?' in Peter Gay (ed.), *The Enlightenment: A Comprehensive Anthology* (New York, 1973), p. 385. On the racial tenor of Kant's approach, see Wolbert Schmidt, *Afrika im Schatten der Aufklärung. Das Afrikabild bei Immanuel Kant und Gottfried Herder* (Bonn, 2000).

[132] Jacques Roger, 'La lumière et les lumières' in his *Pour une histoire des sciences.*

[133] Cf. David Elliston Allen, who writes, 'a taste for nature, in fact, seems to arise of its own accord at a certain point in the maturing of civilizations'. *The Naturalist in Britain: a Social History* (London, 1976), p. 27.

[134] Cf. Junod, 'Les Ba-Ronga', p. 16; BCG.BH, Junod, 'Botanique indigène'.

[135] Junod, 'Rikatla à Marakouène', p. 320; BCG.BH, Junod, 'Botanique indigène'; Schinz and Junod, 'Zur Kenntnis der Pflanzenwelt', p. 888.

[136] Cf. Junod, *LSAT* II, pp. 328–32.

[137] Junod, *LSAT* II pp. 344–5.

[138] Junod, 'La Faune entomologique – coléoptères', p. 184; Junod, 'Les Ba-Ronga', pp. 419–20; Junod, *LSAT* I, p. 65; Junod, *LSAT* II, pp. 80, 83, 341–2.

[139] Junod, *LSAT* II, pp. 336, 512, 515.

[140] Junod, *LSAT* I, pp. 9, 166, 521. .

[141] Junod, 'The best means', p. 143.

[142] Junod, *LSAT* I, pp. 9, 521.

[143] Later published as Junod, 'Le climat de la baie de Delagoa', *BSNSN* (1896–97) 25.

[144] 'Le climat de la baie de Delagoa', p. 77. See also LSAT I, pp. 541–2.

[145] Mary Louise Pratt, *Imperial Eyes: travel writing and transculturation* (London, 1992), pp. 39, 57.

[146] Junod, 'The best means of preserving', p. 142; Junod, 'La faune entomologique' *BSNSN* p. 178; Junod, *LSAT* I, p. 7.

[147] Junod, 'The best means of preserving', p. 143.

[148] Junod, *LSAT* I, pp. 10–11.

[149] Junod, *LSAT* II, p. 301.

[150] Junod, 'Les Ba-Ronga', p. 248. See also J. M. MacKenzie (ed.), *Imperialism and the Natural World* (Manchester, 1990), pp. 6–7.

[151] Junod, 'Best means of preserving', p. 143.

[152] Junod, 'Sorcellerie d'Afrique et sorcellerie d'Europe: étude d'ethnographie comparée', *Foi et Vie* (1910) 13, p. 622.

[153] Junod, *LSAT* II, p. 332.

[154] Junod, 'The Magic conception of nature', p. 84.

[155] Junod, *LSAT* II, pp. 336n1, 345–6n1.

[156] Junod, 'Les Ba-Ronga,' p. 246; Junod, *LSAT* II, p. 150.

[157] Junod, 'Les Ba-Ronga,' p. 246; Junod, 'Sorcellerie d'Afrique', p. 622.

[158] Junod, 'The Magic conception of nature', p. 84.

[159] Junod, *LSAT* I, p. 65; *LSAT* II, pp. 80–2.

[160] H. A. Junod, *Butibi: Notions of Elementar[y] Science; Noçoes de Sciencia Elementár* (Lausanne, 1904). An enlarged edition appeared in Ronga in 1928, *Vutivi: Notions of Elementary Science* (Lausanne, 1928). The New Testament was translated into Gwamba in 1894 and the full Bible into Thonga in 1907.

[161] João Albasini, editorial in *O Africano*, 22 May 1909, cited by J. Penvenne, 'Principles and passions: capturing the legacy of João dos Santos Albasini', paper presented to the African Studies Centre, Boston University, 1991.

[162] Allen Isaacman (ed.), *The Life History of Raúl Honwana: an inside view of Mozambique from colonialism to independence, 1905–1975* (Boulder, CO and London, 1988), p. 58.

[15]

Colonial conservation, ecological hegemony and popular resistance: towards a global synthesis

Richard H. Grove

In most historical analyses of the colonial impact on indigenous rural societies there has been until recently an almost exclusive preoccupation with arable systems. The startling neglect of the non-arable landscape has been unfortunate since, in many societies, the ability to exploit marginal, non-arable land and forest has been critical to survival and the capacity to do so has become steadily more constrained as resources have been devoted to commodity production. Colonial rule has been particularly important in this respect. Colonialism and its successor states have brought about a transformation in the nature of the tenurial relationships between people, forest and other non-arable land. This has involved, in essence, a transition away from locally evolved man – land relations towards direct private property status or to direct state control. These changes have often involved a growing exploitation of the landscape for commodity production and a corresponding erosion in customary controls and common property rights or conventions.[1] The ecological transition has largely, although by no means exclusively, followed upon the spread of a European capitalist system over the globe with the corresponding penetration of a Western economic process beyond as well as within the colonial context.[2]

This chapter is primarily concerned with the political economy of Western ecological systems, and the consequences of their extension to the colonial periphery, particularly in forms of forest conservation. However, it also seeks to underline the importance to the latter task of understanding the evolution of new forms of ecological control, particularly at state level, at much earlier stages in the development of the mercantile maritime states, at a time before the growing resource demands of these states were exported from Europe. While the main emphasis is here upon the political economy of colonial forest and soil controls the societal response to other major forms of ecological intervention also

IMPERIALISM AND THE NATURAL WORLD

deserves a more thorough examination than is possible here. In particular, the gazetting of game reserves, the enclosure of common grazing lands, the draining of marshlands, the destruction of indigenous irrigation systems and the creation of new ones have all interacted in a significant way with social change, social exclusion and the dynamics of popular protest. Until recently however too little has been known about the minutiae of the relations between people and their environment to address historical problems in this fashion. Indeed, even in arable or non-forest contexts the ecological details of direct colonial intervention in the production process have received remarkably little attention.[3]

However, there is little doubt that it was in the imposition of new forms of land-designation, as between private and public and in the interruption of customary methodologies of interaction with forest, pasture and soil that colonial states (and post-colonial states effectively modelled on them) have exercised the most intimate and often oppressive impact on the daily lives and ways of production of the rural majority throughout much of the (especially tropical) world. This has been implicitly borne out by the apparent frequency of episodes of resistance to this species of colonial impact that have taken place throughout the period of the expansion of the capitalist forms of economic and political control. It is the forms of colonial ecological control, particularly 'conservation' structures and the circumstances of resistance to such control, that are the focus of this chapter.[4] The complexities of their political role, I argue, have been very much underplayed.[5] Recent studies of episodes of 'resistance', particularly by the 'Subaltern School' of Indian historians, have emphasised a largely autonomous notion of peasant resistance quite separate from the mainstream of the political economy of elitist resistance.[6] It would be easy to offer a critique of this view, in advocating a 'rounded history' that integrates elitist and subaltern approaches. Instead the dynamic I wish to draw attention to relates to the critical importance of ecological constraints in stimulating and guiding both phases of acquiescence and phases of 'resistance' to the developing interventions of capital and the colonial state in the lives of a variety of different classes of indigenous rural people and, in some instances among colonial settlers themselves. To date, because of the lack of consideration of the ecological context the significant linkages and synchroneities, on a global scale, between these forms of resistance have been neglected.[7] This task has now been given an added incentive and feasibility both by the current environmental crisis in much of the tropics and by an emerging body of work on and understanding about the history and mechanisms of colonial ecological change and control. Until recently much studies have been

[16]

COLONIAL CONSERVATION AND POPULAR RESISTANCE

compartmentalised by sub-continent, state or colony, particularly in the work of Stebbing, Brascamp (the pioneer in the field),[8] Tucker, Gadgil and Guha in South Asia and Stebbing and Beinart in southern Africa.[9] In my own work I have recently attempted to stress the global common denominators of methodologies of colonial ecological control as they have developed over the three centuries since about 1640 and the synchroneity in the emergence of scientific rationales for control. It has become clear that the technical and colonial discourses of conservation have operated for much longer than is often realised, throughout the imperial context. This phenomenon alone, I think, helps and in fact demands an equivalent inspection of modes of popular response to the effects of that discourse.[10] One can now begin to expose the extraordinary vigour with which conservation programmes, in particular, were pursued after the early nineteenth century and to understand the technical agendas and powerful motivations behind these programmes. Principal among these motives was a deep insecurity about the prospects for the long-term survival of the colonial state and a deep anxiety about the consequences of climatic change and environmental deterioration.

Both these concerns were particularly prevalent in India and southern Africa between about 1835 and 1880. From a present-day viewpoint the latter anxiety, now very familiar, but whose antecedents go back to the mid-seventeenth century, might be thought to have had its merits, particularly in view of current preoccupations with notions of sustainable development.[11] Significantly, however, the conservation structures which evolved from early notions of the limitability of resources were frequently just as destructive or oppressive in their effects on indigenous societies as direct ecological destruction and appropriation of environments and common rights by private capital. The vigour and extent of the resistance movements which rose to these new forms of ecological control both deserve their own narrative and may serve as an object lesson for more contemporary advocates of conservationist prescriptions to global environmental problems.

Colonial ecological interventions, especially in deforestation and subsequently in forest conservation, irrigation and soil 'protection', exercised a far more profound influence over most people than the more conspicuous and dramatic aspects of colonial rule that have traditionally preoccupied historians. Over the period 1670 to 1950, very approximately, a pattern of ecological power relations emerged in which the expanding European states acquired a global reach over natural resources in terms of consumption and then, too, in terms of political and ecological control.[12] It is tempting to conceptualise this process in terms of the European system' set out by Immanuel Wallerstein.[13] However,

[17]

IMPERIALISM AND THE NATURAL WORLD

in some respects, the notion of a European-centred system fails as an explanatory device, particularly in Western India and West Africa where several indigenous states are now known to have developed extensive systems of ecological control and state resource monopoly.[14] Instead it is possible to postulate a periodised model which is relatively simple in structure and which, between 1670 and 1935, resulted in the incorporation of much of the forest and non-arable land of the world under two main control systems. These were developed first on tropical islands and then in India (largely in forest control) and South Africa and the southern United States (largely in soil conservation). By the beginning of the twentieth century the Indian model had become dominant, and was challenged only completely in Anglophone Africa by North American notions of soil control and a game-reserve ideology. In French Africa and South-East Asia a forest system very close to the Indian model prevailed. In maintaining this dominant pattern a coterie of highly mobile scientific experts, again dominated by Indian colonial expertise, steadily grew in influence.

At least three essential kinds of motivation in the construction of colonial agendas for conservation need to be considered. Firstly, one is dealing with notions of control and with the wish to appropriate resources first for private capital and then for the needs of the state. These last two have not always constituted identical interests. In fact, in the long term the environmental concerns of the state have tended to be at variance with short-term capital interests. In this way ecological constraints have thus had an exceptional impact on what one is accustomed to think of as the economic priorities of the colonial state. Secondly, one is concerned with the emerging interest of states in preventing or localising environmental degradation or climatic change that would threaten their economic or political viability, either directly through threatening production in drought periods or indirectly through the social disorder which drought and famine might incur.[15] A third motivation, and by no means an insignificant one, relates to motives of aesthetic or ritual concern. Particularly during the period 1660–1860 at least part of the early development of colonial environmental concern was connected with the mental location of 'Edens' and 'Paradises' within various parts of the tropical landscape. At first this imposition of desired environment was limited to paradisal or utopian perceptions of tropical island environments. Later, however, such idealist and, indeed, 'orientalist', notions became bound up closely with perceptions of the 'tropical' in general and with taxonomies of natural history and concerns about species rarity in particular. During the nineteenth century the emergence of an ambiguous philosophy of game reservation combined such 'Edenic' constructions with a more blatantly class-orientated

COLONIAL CONSERVATION AND POPULAR RESISTANCE

interest in retaining large animal species for exclusive European delectation, for commercial profit or for recreational hunting purposes.[16] The overarching process, however, was characterised by a process of drawing lines and boundaries. These both articulated the new assertion of control and arrogated the ecological realm to the state. In the case of the forest reserve, the case for state control was very significantly strengthened by the co-option of the arguments of scientists and early conservationists. Without massive state intervention, these arguments ran, climatic and environmental cataclysm might result. Effectively then, the increased credibility accorded to state science gave the colonial state *carte blanche* and a vast new role in claiming control and justifying its stewardship over non-arable land. By the 1890s in India this new role reached an extraordinary degree of development, with up to 30 per cent of the area of some provinces coming under forest department control. A broad sociological analysis of the impact of this process is long overdue, although not within the scope of this chapter. This kind of state intervention was highly contradictory in nature. In particular it was relatively hostile to the profit-maximising activities of private capital in timber production and to expansion in the area of arable land. Instead the state and science collaborated in re-shaping the landscape according to a particular new set of 'scientific' agendas.

However, not all the motivations involved were scientific or even immediately economic. For example, it is now becoming clear that the origins of the colonial game or forest 'reserve' and the concept of the 'native reserve' were functionally and politically interrelated, particularly in southern Africa, central India and the Western United States.[17] Given the great expansion in the land-control ambition of the European empires during the colonial period it is surprising that scholars who have explored the symbolism of boundary-making have tended to neglect the influence of forest and land boundaries on the pre-colonial patterns of social life in forest, pasture or arable land. A part of the explanation for this may lie in the general absence of much significant research upon pre-existing systems of environmental knowledge and indigenous environmental religion as well the general failure, by historians at least, to investigate the dynamics of the social relations between pre-industrial man and his ecological constraints. Some recent micro-studies, mainly in Africa, are notable exceptions to this general rule. These are beginning to show that Golden Age notions of pre-colonial 'common rights' and 'common property resources' are largely mythical. Instead, highly complex ecological power relations often subsisted by which those in authority sought to retain or reinforce their power in terms of their claims to particular parts of nature. These were sometimes sanctioned by particular environmental cosmologies and religious beliefs.[18] Only

[19]

IMPERIALISM AND THE NATURAL WORLD

when this area of neglect begins to be substantially filled will one really be able to expect a thorough understanding of the social effects of the confrontation between emergent colonial ecological or conservationist systems and the social lives of the people upon whom they were imposed. Until that time, it may be suggested, discussions will normally be confined to defining the nature of colonial discourses of science, nature and conservation and to the fairly empirical reporting of episodes of resistance or non-resistance to the practical impact of colonial ecological intervention in local society.[19]

The evolution of systems of ecological control and conservationism, 1200–1960

The major shift from common property to private or state control was not exclusively confined to the colonial context after 1600. The beginnings of this process can be identified very much earlier, particularly in the internal colonialisms of Britain, France and Japan. Significantly, it was in the process of conquest that the Normans imposed new notions of feudal control in England, marking off great tracts of land for the king. This imposition involved the re-inventing or fabrication of a tradition of royal tutelage over forest and waste land which had never existed in Saxon England or had only done so in the very loosest and relatively non-controversial terms.[20] Despite high rates of deforestation in sixteenth-century England, it was not until the reign of Charles I that the state attempted to intervene again so extensively in forest control. Even then attempts made by the king to secure firmer control over forests took place more for the sake of his own business interests than on behalf of state needs. Nevertheless, the increased interest shown by the state at this period in carving up and improving marshland and forest reflects a more generalised development taking place in Europe at the period in which increased appropriation of organisms, parts of the environment, society and even the individual person were signalled by a whole variety of methodologies of boundary-making and classification. In the Fenlands of eastern England large-scale capital-intensive drainage projects were embarked upon, while new ideas about formalised and efficient ways of laying out land after drainage were developed.[21] As far as English forests were concerned the fall of Charles I marked at least a temporary end to such projects, many of which had provoked extensive political opposition at a variety of levels. In essence, the availability of capital and new market demands for raw materials meant that such programmes had to be transferred elsewhere. It meant, for example, that the failure of the Commonwealth and then the Restoration state to develop a forest

[20]

COLONIAL CONSERVATION AND POPULAR RESISTANCE

policy internally in England (although there was a different and more colonial deforestation story in Scotland) led to the development of a huge and rigidly defined forest reserve system in New England after 1691 organised under a Surveyor-General.[22] When this system broke down after 1776 the same concept was transferred, very loosely at first, to western India.[23] In France, in contrast, where the state was faced with the same problem of strategic naval timber supply, a form of internal forest colonialism developed first under Colbert in the framework of the Forest Ordinance of 1669 with the creation of Départements de L'Eaux et Forêts.[24]

Until about 1770, then, the objectives of the continental systems of ecological control were strictly related to naval timber requirements and the other lesser raw material needs of the imperial despotisms. A similar rationale dictated the forest policies of the expanding Maratha system after about 1710.[25] While these objectives remained important until about 1850, other quite different and innovatory forest management considerations were also emerging in the early eighteenth century, although at first only in the early oceanic island colonies. These originated in a kind of environmental concern which had not been important in Europe.[26] The experience of introducing European plantation systems on islands such as Barbados and St Helena quickly gave rise to the realisation that rapid environmental degradation was taking place. This soon led, in turn, to the idea of preventative control, so that formal forest reservation and soil erosion prevention measures became a part of the role of the colonial state in Barbados and other West Indian islands after 1670 and on St Helena in 1709. Similar developments took place in Japan in the late seventeenth century.[27] Here too, forest protection was begun with the express purpose of preventing soil erosion. Allied to this new notion was the re-emergence among European natural philosophers and colonial settlers of a 'desiccation' theory linking deforestation with rainfall change and generalised climatic change.[28] This theory, which had lain dormant since its first formulation by Theophrastus in Classical Greece, was revived between about 1590 and 1700. It has now been confirmed as a valid theory, to some extent, by recent findings about the nature of the carbon dioxide cycle and by micro-climate studies in the Amazon basin.

After 1767 the desiccation theory provided the main motivation behind the introduction of a forest reservation system in Mauritius under the new Physiocratic regime which had been installed on the island as the behest of the Duc de Choiseul, after the collapse of the Compagnie des Indes. It was thus in Mauritius that a new kind of rationale for state forest control was first elaborated and put into practice as the earliest example of a system that was to become global

IMPERIALISM AND THE NATURAL WORLD

in application. The system developed on St Helena also played an important linking role in this development. The East India Company first became aware of the desiccation theory in about 1784 and embarked on a deliberate programme of tree planting in St Helena to counter the climatic threat that was believed to exist. By 1836 it was thought that this programme had been successful in reversing a decline in rainfall. The observations on this subject made by Dr J. D. Hooker, later Director of Kew Gardens, became a major factor in promoting the introduction of forest conservancy in India after 1847.[29]

The environmental consequences of a colonial agrarian system first made themselves clearly felt on islands where the notion of widespread desiccation provided a very compelling argument for state intervention. However the logic of the desiccation argument was not applied in Africa or India until the 1840s. The relative delay in the diffusion of the technical notion of desiccation can be partly explained by the initial shortage of ecological information and by the fact that even where deforestation was very rapid, as it was in Western India between 1815 and 1840, the consequences only gradually became apparent. Instead an indirect consequences of deforestation, the silting of major river estuaries and ports, provided the first hard evidence to which scientists could point in attempts to gain state intervention.

From as early as the 1770s one can also start to trace the involvement of professional scientists with their own agendas, and with an increasingly powerful technocratic hold over the colonial state, unparalleled in Europe. Indeed, the very concept of a 'state scientist' was one that first emerged in the conditions of the colonial periphery, rather than in the European metropolitan context.[30] The combination of unpredictable physical conditions and a powerful state apparatus intimidated by the thought of social unrest meant that a relatively small number of scientists were able to wield a great deal of practical control over colonial land-use policy, although much earlier in French than British territories. This culminated, during the period 1837–47, in a process by which a handful of scientists in the East India Company medical service were able to propagandise connections between deforestation, drought and the threat of economic and social breakdown. These ideas were based largely on the writings of Alexander von Humboldt, whose work at this period was becoming frequently quoted in the new Indian scientific journals. They proved sufficiently convincing to coerce the East India Company into initiating a rigid forest conservation policy of a kind which it had, until that time, consistently resisted. An essential element of this new policy consisted in the systematic exclusion of private timber interests from the state forest reserves.[31] Furthermore, a growing alliance between navy and medical lobbies, with their own

[22]

COLONIAL CONSERVATION AND POPULAR RESISTANCE

priorities, made the case for state forest control irresistible. The mind-set of the critical decade between 1837 and 1847 deserves close attention since the programme evolved at that time became a model for forest conservation throughout most of the rest of the imperial context. It was a policy which served as a cover for a complex agenda. This included aesthetic notions, species depletion concerns, public health worries, fear of famine, fear of timber shortage, fear of drought and above all fear of catastrophic regional and continental climatic change.[32] It was the ability to convincingly articulate the latter possibility (with all it meant, to borrow the terminology of Mary Douglas, in terms of death, money and time) that was most important in policy terms even though at later stages the desirability of the colonial state being able to guarantee a sustainable supply of timber for itself became more frequently voiced as a motive for monolithic forest reservation.[33] Moreover, the colonial social critique of tribal forest peoples was already becoming extensive in the 1840s.[34] When environmental damage started to be seen as a product of the agrarian systems of the forest dwellers, the environmental critique helped to reinforce existing social prejudice, and vice versa. It is no coincidence that political pressure for serious ecological controls in forest areas in India built up at the same time, in the late 1830s, as early 'tribal' anthropology began,[35] and as pioneering attempts were made to curb female infanticide and prevent *Meria* sacrifice. The development of scientific rationales for forest protection helped, too, to justify the drive to gather information on the tribes. Moreover, forest policy and tribal policy were both seen at this time as necessarily involving the geographical demarcation of 'reserves' both to exclude unwanted elements and economic activities, and to control others.

One early result of this mixed social agenda, which developed alongside simpler environmental fears, was an early preoccupation with critiques of shifting cultivators and their agronomies during the 1840s, a critique which quickly developed into an obsession. In part, shifting cultivation was an inherently autonomous activity whose participants were not easily amenable to social control. Local terminologies for the activity, such as *jhum* or *koomri*, were soon adopted to colonial categories. They could easily (and, from scientific hindsight, generally wrongly) be faulted in environmental terms.[36] Furthermore, particularly in the first two decades of the Bombay Conservancy in 1847–67, the activities of shifting cultivators presented a much softer political target than the far more damaging activities of timber operators with their allies in high places.[37] Even so, in these first two decades the basic needs of villagers in and near forests were taken into account far more sympathetically than was later the case. Hugh Cleghorn in particular (a medical surgeon appointed Inspector-General to the Madras Forest Service in 1856)

[23]

IMPERIALISM AND THE NATURAL WORLD

developed a striking change of heart in his attitudes to shifting cultivation during the 1850s; so that during this period he tended to overlook or permit extant shifting cultivation, transferring his critique instead to the depredations of illegal commercial fellers, plantation owners and railway builders.[38] In general the powers of the Bombay Forest Department, which the state attempted to legitimate on Maratha precedents, were far too weak to prevent continuing and rapid deforestation.[39] It was this realisation that helped to bring about the far more oppressive regimes of the post-1865 period, when German forestry 'science' replaced the Maratha, Scottish and French methods which had been favoured earlier and which continued to be important in the Madras Presidency. The basic infrastructure for forest conservation was in place, however, well before 1865.[40] Similar developments took place at the Cape, where the notion of the forest reserve had become a very convenient vehicle for state social control.[41] Early conservation programmes at the Cape failed when state conservationists started to promulgate the unpopular view that the activities of European farmers were as important in explaining environmental deterioration as the activities of African farmers.[42] This was a point made too by Cleghorn in connection with the activities of European planters who were, however, a much weaker lobby in India than were settler farmers at the Cape.[43]

From 1872 methods of forest conservation developed in Mauritius, the Cape and India on the one hand and Algeria on the other were taken on in one colony after another, as well as outside the colonial empires. As a result of their pioneering work in France and Algeria scientists of the French forest service were invited to advise on the forest administration of the Ottoman Empire. These experts visited and reported on Cyprus, for example, in 1872.[44] This transfer of the colonial forest control system from regional sub-bases to a global context was achieved mainly during the period 1870–1920. Some individual scientists stand out as having played a disproportionately influential part in this process: Hugh Cleghorn, D. E. Hutchins and H. H. Thompson being cases in point. Between them, they set up or reorganised the forest conservation systems of dozens of colonial territories. As early technical or 'development' consultants employed on a world-wide basis, they encouraged the imposition of a relatively homogeneous ecological ideology that lasted until the end of the colonial period, particularly in South-East Asia, throughout sub-Saharan Africa and in Central America.[45] Even the United States Forest Department owed much to the Indian model prior to the era of progressivist conservation.[46] However, although the French and Indian models of management became dominant, other colonial technical models also emerged. In southern Africa the more locally derived conservationist ideology of Dr John Croumbie Brown with his

COLONIAL CONSERVATION AND POPULAR RESISTANCE

technical emphasis on grass-burning prevention and irrigation development became influential, especially in South Africa and Rhodesia.[47] After the 1920s the influence of the American dustbowl philosophy became more widespread among colonial officials, a development that can be related in part to the increased intervention of Whitehall in ecological matters, the waning influence of Indian expertise in Africa and the lack of emphasis in Indian colonial conservation thinking on pastoral and soil erosion problems.[48] However the didactic manner in which soil conservation policies were pursued in the period 1930–55 in Anglophone Africa led, as had happened in India, to the imposition of land control policies which often involved a forced-labour component and other less direct forms of coercion, and policies which in political terms were even more provocative.[49]

The social response to colonial conservation and other ecological interventions

'Famine always lies at the bottom of an insurrection,' Louis Madelin wrote of rural France in 1789. Behind most rural resistance movements in the colonial context has lain a threat to a margin of ecological survival, a margin nurtured through years of custom and experience. However, ecological controls imposed in the metropolitan as well as the colonial states have often caused discontent among a whole variety of classes and groups and not simply among 'tribals' or 'peasants'. Indeed Sumit Sarkar's notion of a 'primitive rebellion' is very difficult to sustain in this context.[50]

Instead, many low-level movements responding to ecological trauma have, on the contrary, been highly complex in the sensitivity of their response and in the shifting nature of their allegiances. Such resistance movements have not been confined to particular classes. Rather, they have frequently involved 'baronial', bourgeois or land-owning resisters as well as subsistence resisters; and occasionally, as in Wynaad, Kerala, in 1805, or the Bombay Presidency in the 1870s, strategic alliances between the two. The connections between notions of ecological survival and threats to spiritual and cultural order or well-being have often been very significant.[51] Partly for this reason the involvement of millenial, religious or totemic movements has often provided a central uniting influence and motivating force behind ecological resistance movements. This has long been the case. For example, in some of the earliest recorded resistance movements to imperial ecological dispositions, in the Roman Empire, the dispossession of pastoralist and peasant farmers in Tunisia by colonial plantation settlers produced its own vigorous

IMPERIALISM AND THE NATURAL WORLD

counter-movement, inspired by a 'Donatist' cult of Christianity.[52] The material on such early movements is limited. Far more is known, however, about the social context of peasant resistance to feudal notions of forest control in medieval Europe and particularly medieval England, where population growth increased pressure on marginal common property resources. Furthermore the 'baronial' classes also found post-Conquest forest policies oppressive. In this connection, the forest Charter of 1217 which followed Magna Carta was important in the sense that it started ¡a process whereby the ability of the state in England to curtail customary forest rights became significantly constrained in comparison to other parts of Europe or the early colonial empires.[53] In 1215 King John was compelled to agree, by one of the articles of Magna Carta, to the 'disafforesting' of all the lands of country which had been 'made forest' during his reign. By the Charter of 1217 it was provided that all the forests which Henry II had afforested should be 'viewed by good and lawful men' and that all that had been made forest, other than his own royal demesne, was forthwith to be deforested. In accordance with this Charter special perambulations were ordered to be made before 1224–25 by twelve knights elected for the purpose to ensure compliance with the Charter.

Widespread deforestation in connection with rises in population, state-sponsored colonisation, state-building and urbanisation in many parts of the world in the early 'medieval' period after about AD1200 has frequently involved the progressive over-running of 'forest tribes' in places as far apart as eastern Germany or the Gangetic plain. For example, many of the wars between the Hindu and non-Hindu groups in India were specifically framed in terms of disputes about political control of forest regions, where expanding and disforesting states have encountered resistance from groups trying to prevent encroachment. In England, the early phase of resistance to the growing ecological dominance of the state and major landowners which had subsequently diminished in the wake of the population decline caused by the Black Death, only really recommenced with the abrupt liquidity of the land market occasioned by the dissolution of the monasteries. This *de facto* privatisation threatened common rights in many areas. In Huntingdonshire in 1569, for example, the extinction of woodland rights by a new owner led to several violent clashes and the subsequent intervention of the Chancellor in the dispute on the side of the common-right holders and against the landowner.[54] Such popular opposition to state intervention intensified during the period between 1580 and 1660, particularly as the richer gentry sought to impose closer control over woodlands in western England. Increases in availability of floating capital and the simultaneous emergence of the early joint-stock companies gave rise, after about

COLONIAL CONSERVATION AND POPULAR RESISTANCE

1600, to extensive land-development projects both domestically, in Eastern England, as well as in the West Indies and as part of East India Company plantation activity, all of which involved large-scale ecological and social impacts and which quickly provoked local resistance.[55] In the Fenland prolonged local resistance to the Merchant Venturers' drainage projects was a natural consequence of the considerable trauma which such schemes implied to long-established grazing regimes and common rights.[56] Indeed this opposition was so effective and prolonged, particularly in areas such as the Isle of Axholme, that it constituted a major factor in the distribution of support for the Parliamentary interest during the civil war, while the 'projectors' themselves generally supported the Royalist cause. Furthermore on several occasions Cromwell himself went so far as to actively and specifically champion the cause of the commoners in the Fens. At another level, Lilburne, Wildman, and other Levellers became involved at various stages with the 'anti-projector' fen drainage resisters. Large-scale enclosure of previously commonable fens fell into the same category as ship money and other expedients which undermined property rights and demonstrated absolutist tendencies in central government. Considerations of social justice and harmony swiftly evaporated if they conflicted with fiscal imperatives.[57] The problem did not end, of course, with the fall of the King. Instead, the seizure of Royalist land during the Commonwealth period provoked an early excursion into planning for state naval timber reserves alongside major rivers in the late 1640s. However, these efforts as well as related attempts to acquire closer state control over naval timber in the Forest of Dean quickly sparked disturbances among the very commoners who constituted such an essential part of the political constituency of the Commonwealth. Even the Restoration state could not politically afford to ride roughshod over this interest group. In this way, by about 1685, effective large-scale state intervention in forest control came to be abandoned domestically by the English state.[58]

Ironically, then, it was the relative success of sectional and low-level opposition to the growing ambitions of the state for internal ecological control and for land-use 'planning' that led directly to the very precocious and geographically very extensive colonial forest policy embarked on in New England by the English after 1691.[59] The fact that the French were not compelled by successful popular protest to seek such fresh resource fields at such an early date may explain much of the later superiority in British hold over global forest resources as a dynamic strategic factor. However, colonial forest policy in New England also led directly to the loss of those colonies. It stoked the fires of settler opposition and nascent separatist tendencies in direct and non-direct ways. A whole sub-culture of civil disobedience was created from about

IMPERIALISM AND THE NATURAL WORLD

1710 right through to 1776, in which forest regulations were continually broken by individual settler and timber interests alike, with the critical and growing connivance of the colonial courts and much of the colonial establishments.[60] In this way, grievances over oppressive imperial forest policy became, effectively, as important as any other more short-term factors in the development of the American Revolution, particularly in the way in which an entire subversion of imperial legitimacy was generated by the connivance of the legislative arm. Law-breaking, at an insidious level, had been the norm for sixty years by 1776. The revolution was thus very much stimulated by the collusion and collaboration of a variety of class and commercial interests resisting colonial forest policy.[61] British assertion of control over forests at the Cape, and then in Malabar and Burma, was a direct result of the loss of the North American source of timber supply and the consequent strategic crisis in naval demand for raw materials in the context of the wars with the French between 1793 and 1815.[62]

The French Revolution itself, in its rural and agrarian aspects, was also dynamically connected with the growing and vice-like grip of the state and its rural allies over the common ecological rights of the peasantry. However, the class dynamics of this conflict were rather different from the American situation although the context was arguably equally colonial, a matter of the urban class interest extending a resource search out into the countryside. The effects of this process were much exacerbated by the monolithic character of Colbert's 1669 Forest Ordinance and the apparatus of control that went with it. This apparatus grew steadily in power during the eighteenth century, assisted by the growing crisis over ship timber.

The steady erosion of the element of marginal land flexibility in France during the eighteenth century dramatically increased the vulnerability of the peasantry to economic and climatic pressures. Regional fuelwood shortages became acute, while the crop failures of the early 1780s became especially significant. Both before and during the revolution incendiarism and illegal wood-gathering became widespread weapons against the growing controls and shortages.[63] In some villages in rural south-west France long-running battles over common access to marshes, woodlands and fishing rights were fought out between peasants and landlords in the second half of the eighteenth century. R. B. Rose, in his recent study of Davenescourt has shown how the originally relatively weak position of the peasantry in the *guerres des arbres* was critically redressed in the years after 1790.[64] In the long term, the degree to which the majority of the population gained in these terms from the Revolution is questionable. Initially relieved by the events of 1789–92 the Revolution eventually betrayed the ecological basic needs of the

COLONIAL CONSERVATION AND POPULAR RESISTANCE

rural peasantry, particularly as urban elements used the fluidity of the new situation to further bolster their control over the countryside. Nevertheless, overall access to resources did improve, even if it was at the expense of long-term ecological balance. In fact, the evidence seems to indicate that by about 1798 the net ecological result of the Revolution consisted in an uncontrolled ransacking of forest land and mountain slopes, particularly in southern France. Soil erosion in the south-east and Basses-Alpes, already bad, became catastrophic.[65] Indeed, in the course of trying to cope with the hydraulic consequences of deforestation at this period, a whole generation of French engineers specialising in soil-erosion prevention emerged, whose writings became influential among later colonial scientists.[66]

The two revolutionary phases in North America and in France were distinctly different in context from the phases of resistance against the systems of 'scientific conservation' that were emerging in the early island colonies of Britain and France. These were based on new conceptualisations of catastrophic resource depletion, where the establishment's commitment against environmental 'crime', especially against illegal tree-cutting and over-grazing, was becoming quite marked. Thus on St Helena, as early as the 1745, transgressions against forest rules by settler common-right holders had already started to preoccupy the local government to an unprecedented extent. The government even threatened to treat such offences as illegal goat-grazing as 'capital' crimes, but was prevented from doing so by the intervention of the East India Company Directorate which at this stage did not see the logic in enforcing anti-soil erosion legislation as strongly as the St Helena government precociously did. The resulting conflicts mirrored to some extent the basic conflicts among commoners, the state and private capital which were going on in England. In the colony, however, the emerging environmental issues underlying the conflict were quite different. In October 1745 Thomas and Henry Greentree *(sic)* were arraigned for refusing to impound their goats when ordered to do so. The official record stated:

> to deter others from daring to offer the least contempt for the future ordered that each of the Greentrees should be fined Ten pounds. . . we told them that they ought to look upon this fine as a very mild punishment for so great a crime . . . that disobeying lawful authority was much the same as resisting it and resisting authority was the beginning of a Rebellion which was a capital crime.

When the Directors heard of this exaction they took a critical view of the Governor's action and the island Council had to backtrack, blandly reporting to the Directors that 'we have repaid the Messrs Greentrees their fines according to your orders, as you're of opinion that the Goats are more use than Ebony they shall not be destroyed in future'.[67]

Initially, then, the metropolitan authorities themselves resisted the

[29]

IMPERIALISM AND THE NATURAL WORLD

operation of early conservation laws in some limited contexts against the wishes of local government, if they perceived short-term profit to be thereby put at risk. At another kind of level, a comparable antagonism developed when Pierre Poivre introduced a set of new and draconian forest protection rules on the Ile de France (Mauritius), after 1767, based both on 1669 French Forest Ordinance precepts and on a coherent desiccationist philosophy. These measures encountered stiff opposition from settler landowners as well as iron foundry interests. Later, sugar plantation owners vigorously resisted state laws against forest clearance until as late as the 1850s under British rule.[68] The general point here is that, having espoused the role of environmental arbiter, the colonial state immediately found itself confronting a whole variety of classes and economic factions with varying interests in either resisting any check on resource depletion or resisting imposed methods of control in so far as they threatened customary management. While the state in Britain was, in general, not able to embark on the kinds of forest controls that evoked such bitter opposition in France and New England the vigour of the enclosure and emparking movement which it sanctioned for private landowners during the eighteenth century had analogous, although far more fragmented, effects. Enclosures of commons and parks tended to affect rights to game more than woodland rights.[69]

Such measures helped to criminalise a growing sector of the population, although without evoking the kinds of intensified resistance that could actually threaten the security of the state.[70] Moreover, for the state itself, opposition to ecological control was now only significant outside Britain, where colonial sources of timber were acquiring increasing importance.

At the outset of British territorial expansion in the west of India the rapid extension of political control immediately raised the issue of forest management, ownership and the social control of forest dwellers. Some early attempts at resisting colonial forest control in this context occurred shortly after the assumption of East India Company rule. However such episodes were not entirely new since the Company had inherited a dynamic situation in which the successor states to the Mogul empire, with their growing resource and political ambitions, were already in constant conflict with forest 'tribes'.[71] More importantly, some of the successor states to Mogul rule had been quick to embark on monopolist policies towards timber resources. After annexation the intensification of imperial timber demands with the onset of the Napoleonic wars exacerbated these tensions; particularly as the British were disposed, after 1792, to allocate forests to private or to state control, ignoring any kind of customary right. While in so doing they differed little from their indigenous state predecessors, East India Company

[30]

COLONIAL CONSERVATION AND POPULAR RESISTANCE

occupation quickly provoked the emergence of alliances between ruling and 'tribal' groups.[72] Thus between 1796 and 1805 Kurichians and other shifting cultivators found themselves uniting to fight a war against the new occupiers alongside the forces of, for example, Kerala Varma, Rajah of Kottayam.[73] Between 1815 and 1842 the developing East India Company state on the west coast found itself continually in conflict with the Bhil tribes from Sind in the north to North Canara in the south. Control of forests thus became synonymous with the political control of dissent, leaving aside notions of resource control or conservation.[74]

Throughout the west coast of India, where the forests played a critical part in the early formulation of the scientific conservation ideology of the East India Company, programmes for resource control and conservation were increasingly frequently used to justify political controls for which no other easy rationale could easily be found. Attaching blame to forest tribes for ecological as well as political trouble-making was a logical development at this stage and one that could be used to justify far more oppressive controls than might otherwise have developed, and in particular to allow any customary land-rights to be ignored. The political 'bargain' struck by the East India Company with the Dangs Rajah can be seen in this light: Alexander Gibson, the first Forest Conservator of the Bombay Presidency, commented that 'the annual payment made to the chiefs is the ...most satisfactory outcome that could be devised to keep the peace in that wild country'.

Despite the political advantages endowed by forest control, the upper echelons of the Company were eager to contest such notions of state intervention. This helps to explain why, when the Bombay Forest Department was founded in 1847, it was explicitly justified by the Company Directors on the basis of the climatic threat posed by deforestation, rather than on the timber-need arguments which it had consistently rejected.[75] What was more, the British fell back upon Maratha methods of forest reservation and state rights over particular timbers as part of the legal rationale for wresting control of forest lands back out of the landowning hands to which they had been formally granted in the opening years of the century.

During this period developments closely parallel to those in western India were taking place in southern Africa and in Algeria. To account for this simultaneity, and for the extraordinary haste with which the British and French colonial states took on their new conservation and control role in the 1840s and 1850s requires an appreciation of the way in which environmental anxieties (which were certainly a concern of the state) also provided a heaven-sent opportunity to deal with more generalised resource demands, crises of indigenous resistance and fears of loss of control.[76] Both in India and, to a much greater extent, in South Africa

[31]

IMPERIALISM AND THE NATURAL WORLD

these fears stemmed partly from an awareness of population pressures and fear of famine. Apart from the case of Sind, all the first forest reserves in western India and the Cape were founded in close association with popular unrest and military confrontation.[77] It was also at this period, during the European crisis of 1848, that grievances against new systems of 'scientific' forest controls became part of the agenda of rural 'jacqueries' in south-west Germany where peasants and some townspeople were united by common attempts to reappropriate the wealth of forests.[78] There had been other more isolated and short-lived instances of the revival of popular opposition to state forest ambitions in England in 1830–31 in association with the Captain Swing riots[79] and in France against the new Forest Code of 1827. In the latter case opposition to the Code built up particularly in the Midi and in Corsica. In the Ariège region of south-western France peasants waged the long drawn-out War of the Demoiselles, so named because men dressed as women to avoid recognition. Such movements can be treated as continuing and striking instances of resistance to the impact of internal colonialism.[80]

These European rebellions were a clue to what would happen a little later in India where a German-influenced system supplanted less formalised forest-management models after 1878.[81] There are other, more direct, connections to be made between the historical development of revolutionary political philosophy and the alienation of peasants from forests during this period. In particular, Marx's first political essays and the self-confessed stimulant to his first attempts at serious analysis of social process stem from his concern with the criminalisation of the peasant by new forest laws in the 1840s. The young Marx objected, above all, to the new development of forced labour in the forest as a punishment for forest crime.[82] It may come as no surprise, therefore, to find that the beginnings of organised resistance to the new, monolithic kinds of forest control can be traced to the same period, both in central Europe and in India. Early murmurings of resistance specifically against formal forest controls in India began as early as 1842 when the first timber contracts with the Dangs chiefs, in Northern Gujerat, were made. From that time onwards it is probably fair to say that almost all the major episodes of coordinated popular resistance to colonial rule in India especially in 1856–57, in 1920–21 and the early 1930s were, almost barometrically, preceded by phases of vigorous resistance to colonial forest control. Some of these episodes were directly linked with the more urban-based protest episodes, while others were not.[83]

In 1851, only three years after the Bombay Forest Department was established in 1847 on a 'climatic anxiety' basis, more organised forms of resistance started to appear in direct response to the imposition of timber fees which could not be related by any stretch of the imagination

COLONIAL CONSERVATION AND POPULAR RESISTANCE

to any customary system. The negotiating skills of Surgeon Alexander Gibson, the first Forest Conservator of the Bombay Presidency, successfully defused this early confrontation and it should be noted that, by and large, the forest departments founded by the Company in their brief span between 1842 (when the first reserves were founded in Sind) and 1865 were more sensitive to the possibilities of rebellion and more willing to recognise and discriminate between the different kinds of social forces causing deforestation. In the 1851 confrontation forest landowners in the Thana district of the Presidency formed a convenient 'alliance' with the Varli tribal group and actually persuaded them to march in protest into Bombay as well as stimulating agitation within the forest itself.[84] The Indian forest department system at this stage was, as yet, by no means monolithic and was able to adjust pragmatically to what was, as Alexander Gibson saw it, legitimate protest. This was at a time long before an oppressive bureaucratic framework had armed itself with a more inflexible scientific ideology of forestry. The fact that the early Forest departments in the Bombay and Madras Presidencies were run by officers of the Medical Service helps to account for this. In the Madras Forest Department, for example, founded in 1856 by Hugh Cleghorn, the senior officers of the service were all Indians until 1865, as was Chatur Menon, the planner of the pioneering Nilumbur teak plantations. The indigenous element was still significant. Furthermore, in Madras the early hostility to shifting cultivators became diluted in a significant way between 1856 and 1870 by Hugh Cleghorn's recognition that the depredations of invading lowland cultivators, timber interests and railway builders were far more destructive than the recurrent effects of *koomri* or shifting cultivation. Instead, the principal problem in the Nilgiri hills, as Cleghorn identified it in 1866, was that 'capital' was flowing into the area, largely in the form of plantation investment. This was, he thought, an inherently destructive process.

Nevertheless, in spite of this element of flexibility, the early nationalist movement in the Bombay area was able to use grievances against the forest department to motivate rural support. From about 1870 onwards the Bombay Association and the Poona People's Association actively sought out a broader constituency among the forest users and dwellers of Thana district. This meant that by the end of the decade the Poona People's Association and the new Thana Forest Association were able to act as the main spokesmen for protests against increasingly restrictive forest rules, deriving a considerable political constituency thereby. The strength of these new movements eventually impelled the authorities to set up the Bombay Forest Commission to investigate and report (in 1887) on forest grievances in a comprehensive, although ultimately ineffectual, fashion.

[33]

IMPERIALISM AND THE NATURAL WORLD

The steadily growing restrictions on forest rights and dispossession of customary rights particularly after the passing of the 1878 Forest Act had, in fact, ended any notions of flexibility. The rebellions in Bastar in 1876 and the Rampa rebellion in the Godavari conveniently mark the beginning of this period.[85] The incorporation of pre-colonial forced labour practices, such as *begari*, in which labour was traded simply for the right of residence, served to legitimate forest control by the re-inventing of a tradition in a surprisingly insidious fashion. The history of indigenous rebellions and forest *satyagraha* against the Indian Forest Department after 1878 has been extensively documented elsewhere.[86] Existing accounts, however, have largely ignored the scarcity of forest rebellions before 1878 while simultaneously neglecting the growing complexity of these resistance movements *after* Indian independence, since when the Indian government has pursued a forest policy little different (indeed) from that of the colonial period. The two most potent forces in generating resistance after independence, it may be said, were the continuing and increasing restrictions placed on shifting cultivation and the sale of forest produce coupled with the alienation of tribal people from their land as a result of debt transactions. The period after 1940 seems to represent a new phase in this development, and a date far more significant than 1947. Rates of eviction increased dramatically after that time with the large-scale transfer of villages to absentee landlords.[87] Then began what one may term the 'disillusion phase'. This started when peasants and tribals realised that *zamindari* abolition would generally not benefit them and that indigenous rule did not imply any freedom in the forests.[88] The illicit peasant invasion of *zamindari* forests in north Bihar in 1946 was an important precursor of this phase.[89] In Madya Pradesh the kinds of resistance movements which first appeared during the 1920s reappeared with redoubled vigour in the late 1950s, especially under the leadership of Kangha Manjhi in 1959–62. This insurgency was quickly succeeded by the movements in Andhra Pradesh in 1960-64. The latter were significant in so far as they provided a fertile ground for Naxalite agitation in the period up to 1970. With recent research it is becoming clear that the Naxalite movement itself would not have acquired momentum had it not been successful in finding deep roots in grievances against the Forest Department and its restriction on shifting cultivation in northern West Bengal, in the Darjeeling area and in the Srikukulam region of Orissa.[90] In this respect the ecological origins and rural constituency of the Naxalite movement, in terms of the way it drew upon grievances against state agricultural and forest policies, have mirrored the character of both the embryonic nationalist movement in Zimbawe and the Mau Mau rebellion in Kenya.[91]

The development of the Bhil movement around Dhulia in 1972–74,

COLONIAL CONSERVATION AND POPULAR RESISTANCE

led by Ambarsing Suratwanti, once again related to large transfers of
land out of tribal hands and the growth in what were effectively forced
labour or *begari* regimes exploiting dispossessed tribal people.[92] Over a
much longer period, in Chotanagpur, the Jharkhand movement has
always been closely associated with, if not entirely reliant on, forest
resistance movements. In 1978-79 parts of the movement found a
particular focus in resistance to the planting of teak.[93] This became
central to the resistance movement and to opposition to the activities
of a local Forest Development corporation typical of the kind that
sprouted all over India during the period 1969–80. The concessions
achieved by these last movements have generally been trivial. Their
character and their agendas need to be carefully distinguished from the
development of the Chipko movement.[94] Even so the central issue of
local control over land and vital common property resources has been a
critical common denominator.[95] Overall it is striking to observe how the
Indian forestry establishment, in terms of practical policies as distinct
from the politics of White Papers, has steadily strengthened the forces
alienating people from their forest resources, in a forest estate being
gradually whittled away by the unleashing of often blatantly corrupt
commercial forces in the forest sector.[96] The real ecological priorities of
the post-independence Indian government are perhaps best summarised
by the killing of sixteen peasants in early 1984, slaughtered as they led
their cattle on to pasture the rights over which they disputed with the
management of the Bharatpur Wildlife Sanctuary. More recently Baiga
tribespeople have continued to be evicted in large numbers from the new
national parks and game (tiger) reservations in Madhya Pradesh.[97] Thus
the continuing human cost of wildlife conservation in India, let alone
forest conservation, has been a high one.

Forest resistance movements in India were and are largely autonomous in origin and mobilisation. However, they were harnessable by
more elite nationalist formations and, more recently, by contemporary
radical leftist movements. Most significantly, they have provided much
of the impetus behind separatist movements in India in the post-
independence period. This impetus has depended, however, on the existence of dynamic links between the rural protest movements and radical
urban-based groupings. Even in predominantly arable parts of rural
India, it is difficult to underestimate the critical part played by 'ecological grievances', particularly those relating to wood supply, access to
grazing and local irrigation, in provoking the kind of widespread rural
discontent upon which 'national' political movements have depended
for their constituency. In Bihar, for instance, during the 1920s and 1930s,
peasants were caught between, on the one hand, the increasingly
awkward administrative obstacles placed by the state on access to forest

[35]

IMPERIALISM AND THE NATURAL WORLD

reserves, and on the other by the steadily more rapacious depredations of landlords encroaching on grazing lands and common rights. The striking irony is that, far from assisting the poorer peasants in their struggle to loosen this ecological stranglehold, the Congress governments newly elected to power after 1937 and again in 1946 actually connived with the landlords, at least in Bihar, in enabling the continuing erosion of common property resources.[98] This kind of political betrayal by the nationalist movement helps to explain the intensity of ecological resistance movements in the post-independence era in India.

The ecological controls originated in colonial India, particularly those developed in the name of forest conservation, have evoked similar patterns of response in most of the other territories in which they have been applied. Thus the British annexation of Cyprus in 1878 was soon followed, in 1879, by the passing of a forest law based directly on the Indian Forest Act of 1878. Indian colonial 'experts' such H. Cleghorn, B. Madan and D. E. Hutchins regularly advised on management of the Cyprus forests.[99] Australian species were imported and active reafforestation commenced. Incendiarism, which had taken place almost every year until 1965, became a regular feature of the rural response to forest reservation and planting. Forest reservation presented a strong impediment to rural pasture needs, especially for those herding goats. Repeated floods of propaganda failed to ameliorate the problem. As in India a phase of disillusion after independence about the absence of change in state forest policies sparked renewed incendiarism. To add to the problem, communal struggles between Turkish and Greek Cypriots were also characterised by the use of incendiarism as a familiar weapon of protest and conflict. One conservator, Chapman, was led to ask in 1966, 'how much longer, one wonders, will it be before the forest can be dissociated from political disturbances and before forest incendiarism ceases to be a stick to beat the government?'[100]

A remarkably similar pattern of response to forest reserve control developed in Algeria, another ex-Ottoman territory, during the colonial period. In this case the French Forest Code of 1827 was imposed almost unaltered. Here too, resistance generally took the form of incendiarism. The conflagrations of 1859, 1863, 1870, 1876, 1881, and 1892 'became literally engraved on the collective colonial memory, that is, they comprised an element of colonial political culture then in the process of formation'.[101] In Algeria, the new forest controls effectively interrupted a long-established pattern of indigenous transhumance, land use and trading patterns in forest products long established in the Beni Salah and Edough mountains. Initially Arab lands were seized and sold to trading companies, many of them English,[102] before the process was bolstered by a forest reserve system. Annual firing was already practised by the Beni

COLONIAL CONSERVATION AND POPULAR RESISTANCE

Salah farmers in the course of *Kusar* agriculture and was easily adapted to more active incendiarism. The most destructive fires occurred in 1881, the turn of the Islamic century and the year of the Sudanese Mahdi. An investigative commission pointed to the influence of a revolt in the city of Oran and the French invasion of Tunisia in the same year as factors encouraging the incendiarists. The great fear of the French on this occasion, however, was that the real force behind the fires was the resurgence of Sufi agitation and Pan-Islamic propaganda. A millenarian and Mahdist influence was almost certainly involved. Behind it all, however, remained the economic attack on the Algerian way of life. As one Algerian author commented in 1881, 'the fires in our canton must be attributed to the motive of revenge against the forest companies'.[103]

Simultaneously, at the other end of Africa, serious resistance to colonial forest policy began in Natal after 1882, where, once again, a version of the Indian Forest Act was put in place under the tutelage of D. E. Hutchins.[104] Under this Act the Africans were progressively criminalised and 'forest crime' rose every year until 1898. Hutchins wrote that he believed that

> Forest property [*sic*] is similar to game, it is widely dispersed and difficult of protection. It is easy for a Kaffir to slip into a forest, cut a sapling and sell it as a pole at the nearest canteen, as for a poacher to knock over a pheasant... forest policy should be pursued...against forest destruction as firmly as other moral evils are faced.[105]

Between 1858 and 1888 game reservation policies were being pioneered in the Transvaal and then in Natal, Southern Rhodesia and Nyasaland. In essence, these policies were aimed at excluding all Africans from game reserves and banning African hunting.[106] It has recently been argued that the first game reserves and national parks in South Africa effectively took on a role as symbolic vehicles for Afrikaner nationalism.[107] As a corollary of this the discriminatory effects of the reserves and their extraordinary claims over land can also be firmly be linked to nascent African nationalism. Even where this symbolism was less clear-cut, as in Nyasaland, the new hunting regulations played a prominent part in evoking the kinds of grievances articulated in the first nationalist developments north of the Zambezi, and particularly in the Chilembwe rising in 1915.[108]

The increasingly political response to colonial land-use policies in Africa did not take place in a theoretical or comparative vacuum. By the early 1920s, for instance, the example of the Russian Revolution began to seep on to the political agendas of early anti-colonial struggles. Here, too, it should be remembered that actual peasant involvement in pre-1917 rebellions was primarily motivated and constrained by ecological marginality. Thus during the massive agrarian unrest of 1905–07 the

[37]

IMPERIALISM AND THE NATURAL WORLD

illicit cutting of wood constituted the main part of mass actions against landowners.[109] Lenin had written, 'the lumber industry leaves all the old patriarchal way of life practically intact, enmeshing in the worst forms of bondage the workers who are left to toil in the remote forest depths'.[110] In fact truck payments and extra-economic forms of bondage had prevailed in Russia not as mere remnants from a pre-capitalist social formation but as terms of exploitation guaranteeing stability to capitalist accumulation.[111] The analogy with colonial forest policy, especially in central India and Southern Rhodesia, was a close one. In both, erstwhile shifting cultivators and pastoralists were co-opted as 'forest serfs', and permitted to reside in forest areas only on condition they provided part of a permanent labour pool for the reserve system. In southern Africa too, as in Algeria, incendiarism became a major ecological weapon, although not one employed exclusively by African farmers. In Southern Rhodesia active incendiarism of grasslands in Matabeleland accompanied the annexation of land by European farmers and the effective agricultural and ecological marginalisation of the Ndebele. Much of the firing, however, as local officials discovered, was in fact carried out by European farmers anxious to pin blame on Africans and thereby to secure their eviction to reserves.[112] The religious importance of particular parts of the tree cover and landscape played a role, too.[113] Much opposition had been sparked in south-west India to forest policy when sacred woods were transgressed upon.[114] So too, opposition to the Matopos National Park in Southern Rhodesia focused on the religious significance of particular parts of the Matopo hills. Later, during the late 1940s, the Ndebele pursued their case against their exclusion from the national park through legislative means. The details of this legal battle, which are copiously documented, highlight the confrontation which had developed between the confident and exclusionist claims of 'scientific ecology' and the basic political and religious claims of an indigenous people.[115]

After 1918 renewed fears of the consequences of drought throughout southern Africa, encouraged particularly by the report of the South African drought commission in 1922, led to a spurt of forest reserve declarations in Nyasaland and the Rhodesias designed ostensibly to protect watersheds, avoid regional climatic change and prevent soil erosion. Large-scale removal of villages from new forest reserves such as that on Dzalanyama mountain in central Nyasaland were one result.[116] At first these evoked little in the way of organised resistance. In contrast, the response to similar efforts at introducing Indian forest policies in Anglophone west Africa, and particularly to the Gold Coast and Nigeria, promoted a vigorous protest.[117] First attempts were made to install a forest department and forest legislation on the Indian model in the Gold

COLONIAL CONSERVATION AND POPULAR RESISTANCE

Coast in 1909.[118] The project was an immediate failure. Most of the affected chiefs objected strongly, legally armed, as they were, by the fact of their holding far more freehold rights than did their indigenous contemporaries in East and southern Africa.[119] Only in 1928 were forest reserves established in the Gold Coast. Even then, establishment took place only after a long propaganda campaign and process of negotiation between chiefs and the state. When the Forest Department was resuscitated in 1928 wholesale concessions were made to indigenous rights, involving a strong element of local self-management. Most of the imported Indian foresters were sent home during the 1920s, appalled by the almost entirely successful efforts of the Gold Coast chiefs to torpedo their plans. They were succeeded by far more pragmatically minded and flexible military officers who were quite happy to make the desired concessions. Of course, the element of white settler agriculture was largely absent in the Gold Coast so that political pressures to bolster conservation policies as a mask for discriminatory land policies were far less.[120] The same could hardly be said of conservation policies further south in Africa.[121] In Kenya, the introduction of a forest policy on the Indian model after the turn of the century provoked a gradually intensifying conflict between the colonial authorities and peasant farmers and pastoralists over access to lands and woods that were essential to survival in drought periods, particularly as competition from European landowners increased. The Tugen people, in particular, had become largely successful, by the early 1950s, in sabotaging many of the programmes of the Forest Department.[122] Resistance to post-1940 compulsory soil conservation and terracing in East Africa proved an even more explosive political issue since these schemes are inherently more socially invasive and geographically ambitious in conception than forest policy. Early soil conservation concepts developed in the Cape Colony in the 1860s were reinforced by North American precedents in 1920s and 1930s and then imported into Rhodesia, Nyasaland and Kenya between 1930 and 1955.[123] In each of these territories, from about 1942 onwards, compulsory soil conservation programmes, often involving forced labour and other legal sanctions, sparked determined resistance movements, both violent and non-violent, many of which were enlisted to support the emergent nationalist movements.[124] In each case, then, resentment against conservation controls fed directly into the embryonic nationalist movements, probably far more potently than had been the case in India. Indeed, Vail and White have recently shown how, in Nyasaland, in the political turmoil that surrounded the creation of the new Federation (of Rhodesia and Nyasaland), no other issue generated such mass resentment as compulsory soil conservation terracing.[125]

In Southern Rhodesia soil and forest conservation measures became

IMPERIALISM AND THE NATURAL WORLD

inextricably bound up with peasant resistance and with the rise of the
nationalist movement over a much longer time-scale than in neighbouring territories. Evictions and resettlement under the Land Apportion-
ment Act in the 1940s laid the foundation for a radical peasant nationalism, which was to come fully into the open only with the guerrilla war
after 1965.[126] Coming on top of resentment already aroused, the effects
of the Native Land Husbandry Act, introduced in 1951, were nothing
less than calamitous. The measure had been introduced in response to
alarmist estimates of soil erosion losses, the result of the systematic
over-populating of the native reserves. The Act demanded reallocation
of holdings on an 'economic' basis, often involving wholesale movements and resettlement of population, with little regard to ancestral
ties. These movements were literally carried out with the rigour of a
military exercise, using army transport and personnel. Heightened
regulations for destocking and conservation were vigorously imposed.
The suffering and hostility to which the scheme gave rise were accen-
tuated by a five-year plan for its acceleration, launched in 1955. It had
been anticipated that those who could not be allocated land would find
employment in urban areas. The threatened break-up of the Central African Federation, however, resulted in heightened unemployment,
exacerbating resentment both in towns and on the land. The report of
the Mangwende Commission in 1961, which had enquired into the
unrest, confirmed the fierce resistance which had been mounted to 'land
husbandry measures' inside one reserve. The commission found that
unrest was related directly to landlessness resulting from the 1951 Act,
which in some areas, because of the workings of the Act, had reached
50–60 per cent. Widespread arson and other destruction had been
provoked. The report of the Mangwende Commission led to some
lessening in the rigour with which the Act was applied.[127] Despite this
response Martin and Johnson, in their chronicle of the Zimbabwe
African National Union (ZANU), have confirmed that the Land Husbandry Act provided the final catalyst for concerted nationalist resistance.[128] Moreover, during the period 1957–72 resistance to Rhodesian
forest policy grew steadily in the Eastern Highlands, manifested mainly
in incendiarism and resistance to the vagaries of a colonial soil conservation policy, the technical agendas of which were constantly changing.[129] The deeply destabilising effect of these policies on the tenants-at-
will of the Forest Department helped to provide a fertile ground for the
progress of insurgency from Mozambique in the early 1970s.

A series of attempts were made after 1945 to introduce the kinds of
soil conservation programmes which had been developed in southern
Africa into both Anglophone and Francophone West Africa, and especially to Nigeria.[130] Once again the contrast with the course of policy in

[40]

COLONIAL CONSERVATION AND POPULAR RESISTANCE

the white settler states was striking. Efficient activity by urban nationalist workers sent out to village areas in Northern Nigeria, particularly during 1948, quickly quelled any hopes the Colonial Office may have had for soil conservation and most programmes were abandoned by the end of the year.[131] As one Nigerian Geological Survey officer remarked when reporting his survey of Oko village in Awa division, 'Measuring the land aroused suspicion so that only rapid survey methods could be used and attempts made to elicit information from individuals were hampered by the interference of irresponsible elements from outside the village.'[132] An additional reason why, arguably, imposed soil and forest conservation strategies were pursued less determinedly in the colonial Gold Coast and Nigeria than in other parts of Anglophone Africa was the growing awareness developed by the younger post-war generation of experts that indigenous land-use methods actually possessed merit in conservation terms. The protection afforded by sacred groves in Eastern Nigeria to otherwise highly erodable water catchments was noted on at least one occasion as meritorious.[133]

Such a developing sensitivity to indigenous land-use practices stands, in fact, in stark contrast to the monolithic dam-building and irrigation projects pursued, under the tutelage of ex-patriate engineers by, for example, the independent Nigerian government during the 1960s and 1970s. These projects have often involved the large-scale eviction of local farmers and their compulsory resettlement in unsuitable areas. Such schemes have themselves, not surprisingly, evoked strong local resistance in recent times by farmers who clearly understood the local ecological constraints better than state-employed 'experts'.[134] Indeed peasant communities, particularly in the colonial context, have often been made painfully aware of the superiority of their own knowledge by the sheer degree of vacillation over time in the kinds of 'scientific advice' offered for colonial and post-colonial land-use prescriptions. Pelzer records the tale of an off-duty Dutch official who fell into conversation with a *tani* working his ricefield. When the Netherlander asked the Javanese how he liked the local Dutch administrators, the peasant good-humouredly voiced his irritation at their constant interference; 'One week they come and tell us to hoe with our backsides towards the sun and the next week they tell us we should be hoeing with our backsides away from the sun.' In Java, in particular, such attitudes helped to explain indigenous hostility to government-sponsored migration schemes. However, a more general lesson can be drawn about the nature of indigenous resistance to imposed notions of land management based on 'expertise'.[135] Some of the more recent ecologically damaging and capital-intensive 'resource conservation' and 'development' projects actually owe their original concept and inception to late colonial 'development'

[41]

IMPERIALISM AND THE NATURAL WORLD

schemes, many of which were actually put forward as sops to deflect nascent nationalist protests about low levels of local investment. The Shire Valley Project in Malawi and the Jonglei canal scheme in the Sudan have been examples of this phenomenon. In Ethiopia, the Awash Valley Development Project actually helped to bring to life the separatist movements in Tigre and Eritrea, as local pastoral regimes were dangerously interrupted.[136] While ostensibly 'conservationist', all these schemes have proved ecologically unwieldy and highly invasive to local, evolved relationships between subsistence farmers and pastoralists and their respective environments. All have evoked bitter conflicts between local people and the state.[137]

In recent years the media have accustomed us to the spectacle of indigenous peoples vigorously resisting the depredations of state forest concerns, timber developers or dam-builders on lands vital for subsistence. However, as the above account should make clear, historically resistance to other more controlled forms of ecological transition has been opposed equally strongly. Since the mid-eighteenth century the emerging discourses of natural science have played a major part in this dynamic. As they have been adopted by states in the course of the diffusion of capitalism, especially in the context of colonial rule, such discourses have been utilised to justify and promote unprecedented acquisitions of control over large parts of the landscape, above all in south-east Asia and Africa. In these regions forest reserves, game reserves and soil protection schemes have served to erode indigenous 'rights' and access to previously loosely defined or 'common property' resources. To some extent it may be possible to argue, for example in the case of India, that colonial forest conservation, as an early form of 'sustainable management', prevented what might have been an even more disastrous transition under an unbridled capitalist regime of resource extraction. However, since the systems of knowledge and even the more idealistic conservationist agendas used to justify colonial ecological control were almost entirely externally derived, their impact on indigenous peoples has been almost entirely negative. Ignoring often long-evolved relationships between people and nature, the effects of 'conservation' have tended to profoundly threaten traditional mechanisms of subsistence and thereby to threaten and alienate whole cultures from their environmental contexts. One should not be surprised, then, to find that attempts to oppose the forces of capitalist ecological manipulation have been frequent, although rarely effective in terms of restoring traditional ecological relationships. Equally, it is clear that the more closely one investigates episodes of rural resistance to capitalist or monolithic state ambitions, the more one is likely to uncover the political significance of the ecological element in the motivation of the resister.

[42]

COLONIAL CONSERVATION AND POPULAR RESISTANCE

Notes

1 See Garret Hardin, 'The tragedy of the commons', *Science*, 162 (1968), pp. 1243–48.
2 For a broad analysis of the kinds of environmental changes that have followed the spread of Western industrial culture see T. Weiskel, 'The ecological lessons of the past: an anthropology of environmental decline', *The Ecologist*, 19 (1989), pp. 98-103. Weiskel does not consider the history or impact of colonial conservation.
3 There are some significant pioneers in this field, however, mainly among Africanist historians. See especially Christopher U. Hill, 'Santhal bataidars in Purnia district: ecological evolution of a sharecropping system', and *Political Weekly*, 22 August 1987. For eastern Africa see H. Kjekjus, *Ecology Control and Economic Development in East African History: The Case of Tanganyika 1850-1950*, London, 1977. For a valuable micro-study see E. C. Mandala, 'Capitalism, ecology and society: the Lower Shire valley of Malawi, 1860-1960', unpublished Ph.D. thesis, University of Minnesota, 1983.
4 This chapter is necessarily limited in geographical scope. The emphasis here is on the British colonial context. Ideally comparable developments in Lusophone and Francophone Africa and in South America would need to be considered more extensively.
5 However, see P. Blaikie, *The Political Economy of Soil Erosion in Developing Countries*, London, 1985, for a contemporary approach.
6 E.g., Ranajit Guha, *Elementary Aspects of Peasant Insurgency in Colonial India*, Delhi, 1983; and papers in the *Subaltern Studies* volumes, 1-5, Delhi 1983–88.
7 See J. C. Scott, *Weapons of the Weak: Everyday Forms of Peasant Resistance*, New Haven, Conn., 1985; and his *The Moral Economy of the Peasant*. Surprisingly, in both these major works Scott skirts the critical part played by ecological pressures in guiding peasant action. While M. Gadgil and R. Guha, in 'State forestry and social conflict in British India', *Past and Present* (May 1989), have attempted a pioneering India-wide analysis of the ecological bases of social conflict, their conclusions have been distorted by an over-narrow geographical and temporal concentration. At another level, they have not understood the nature of the environmental anxieties and political motivations behind early colonial conservation policies.
8 See Brascamp's articles in *Tijdschrift voor Indische Taal, Land en Volkekunde*, all issues 1921–31.
9 E. P. Stebbing, *The Forests of India*, 3 vols., London, 1921; E. P. Stebbing, *The Forests of West Africa and the Sahara: The Struggle for Modern Conditions*, London, 1935; M. Gadgil and R. Guha, 'State policy and social conflict in British India', *Past and Present* (May 1989); R. Tucker, 'The depletion of India's forests under British imperialism: planters, foresters and peasants in Assam and Kerala, pp. 118-41 in D. Worster (ed.), *The Ends of the Earth: Essays in Environmental History*, Cambridge, 1988. See also papers in D. Anderson and R. Grove, *Conservation in Africa: People, Policies and Practice*, Cambridge, 1987.
10 R. Grove, 'Conservation and colonial expansion; a study of the development of environmental attitudes and conservation policies on St Helena, Mauritius and in Western India, 1660-1860', unpublished Ph.D. thesis, Cambridge University, 1988; R. H. Grove, 'Scottish missionaries, evangelical discourses and the origins of conservation thinking in southern Africa, 1820-1900', *Journal of Southern African Studies*, 2 (1989), pp. 163-88; R. H. Grove, 'Early themes in African conservation: the Cape Colony in the nineteenth century', in D. Anderson and R. Grove, *Conservation in Africa*.
11 For a global approach to the history of ideas about climate and artificially induced climatic change and risk see C. Glacken, *Traces on the Rhodian Shore: Attitudes to Nature From Classical Times to 1800*, Berkeley, 1967.
12 For some details of this see R. Tucker and J. F. Richards, *Global Deforestation and the World Economy*, Durham, NC, 1983; and D. Albion, *Forests and British Seapower*, Harvard, 1926.
13 I. Wallerstein, *The Modern World System: Capitalist Agriculture and the Origins of the European World Economy in the 16th Century*, New York, 1972.

IMPERIALISM AND THE NATURAL WORLD

14 For details of pre-colonial afforestation and control see K. Pelzer, *Pioneer Settlement in the Asiatic Tropics: Studies in Land-use and Agricultural Colonisation in Southeast Asia*, New York, 1948. The forest management systems of the Maratha state and the Travancore, Cochin and Malabar rajas are still a largely uninvestigated field. In Yorubaland a major transition in state forest control took place during the 1830s when the Ibadan state decreed that the forest belts that traditionally surrounded cities were no longer required; Dr Toyin Falola, University of Ife, pers. comm.

15 See R. H. Grove, 'Surgeons, forests and famine: the emergence of the conservation debate in India 1788-1854', *Indian Economic and Social History Review*, 1990.

16 See Grove, 'Conservation and colonial expansion'; and J. Prest, *The Garden of Eden: The Recreation of Paradise in the Botanic Garden*, New Haven, Conn., 1981 for discussion of Edenic constructions of nature; for an analysis of the history and ideology of colonial game preservation see J. MacKenzie, *The Empire of Nature: Hunting, Conservation and British Imperialism*, Manchester, 1989.

17 See Grove, 'Scottish missionaries, evangelical discourses', for the working of this functional connection.

18 E.g., Jack Stauder, *The Majangir: Ecology and Society of a Southwest Ethiopian People*, Cambridge, 1971. An important recent attempt to investigate 'indigenous conservation' and its connections with environmental aspects of religious belief in detail is B. B. Mukamuri, 'Rural environmental conservation strategies in south-central Zimbabwe; an attempt to describe Karanga thought patterns, perceptions and environmental control', paper presented to African Studies Association of the UK conference, Cambridge, September 1988. See also A. H. Pike, 'Soil conservation among the Matenge tribe', *Tanzania Notes and Records* No. 6 (1938), pp. 79-81.

19 See A. L. Stoler, 'Rethinking colonial categories: European communities in Sumatra and the boundaries of rule', *Comparative Studies in Society and History*, 1 (1989), pp. 134-61. In this connection, Stoler notes, quoting Memmi, that 'colonialism creates both the coloniser and the colonised'. In forest terms, this can certainly be applied. The rigidity of colonialist land-use categories was not to be found in contemporary England.

20 J. C. Fox, *The Royal Forests of England*, London, 1905.

21 R. H. Grove, 'Cressey Dymock and the draining of the Fens', *The Geographical Journal* (March 1981), pp. 27-38.

22 J. J. Malone, *Pine Trees and Politics: The Naval Stores and Forest Policy in Colonial New England, 1691-1775*, Oxford, 1966. A parallel development took place in the Dutch context. The first formal colonial forest reserve system was set up in Java in the mid seventeenth century. In this sense, the need to find alternate sources of timber for the growing Dutch economy was even more urgent than in England or France. See P. Boomgard, 'The Dutch colonial forest system in Java after 1650' in J. Dargavel(ed.), *Changing Tropical Forests*, Canberra, 1989.

23 Grove, 'Conservation and colonial expansion'.

24 J. C. Brown, *The French Forest Ordinance of 1669*, London, 1879.

25 For details of this see *Report of the Bombay Forest Commission*, vol. 1 (1887), Bombay, pp 22-30.

26 Grove, 'Conservation and colonial expansion'. The critical importance of the colonial island periphery in promoting notions of environmental anxiety is an idea signally omitted by Keith Thomas in his survey of the development of environmental ideas at this period in *Man and the Natural World*, Oxford, 1983.

27 R. S. Troup, *Colonial Forest Administration*, Oxford, 1940, p. 446.

28 Grove, 'Conservation and colonial expansion'.

29 *Ibid.*

30 *Ibid.*

31 Grove, 'Surgeons, forests and famine'.

32 *Ibid.*

33 M. Douglas, 'Environments at risk', in *Essays in the Sociology of Perception*, London, 1973.

34 E.g., see John Wilson, *An Anthropology of the Tribes of Western India*, Bombay, 1846.

[44]

COLONIAL CONSERVATION AND POPULAR RESISTANCE

35 *Ibid.*; and F. Padel, 'The evolution of the colonial discourse on the tribes of India, 1800-1947', unpublished D. Phil. thesis, Oxford University, 1988.

36 For a useful survey of the effects of shifting cultivation see P. Vitebsky, 'Policy dilemmas for unirrigated agriculture in Sri Lanka: a social anthropological report on shifting and semi-permanent agriculture in an area of Maneragala district', Report to the ODA, London, 1984.

37 Alexander Gibson, appointed the first Conservator of the Bombay Forest Service in 1847, soon discovered that the opposition of timber merchants and landowners to forest conservation was so effective that he had to restrict himself to seeking controls on probably the least damaging set of forest-clearers, the shifting cultivators. However, he also pioneered the official concept of the 'village forest', a Forest Department categorisation significantly abandoned later in the century.

38 H. Cleghorn, *The Forests and Gardens of South India*, Edinburgh, 1861.

39 *Report of the Bombay Forest Commission*, pp. 22-30.

40 The first two decades of state forest conservation policy have been set aside in the analysis by M. Gadgil and R. Guha, in 'State forestry and social conflict'. One reason for this is that the climatic risk rationale for the precocious foundation of the Bombay Forest Department cannot easily be adapted to the simplistic nationalist critique of state forest control which these authors adopt. A more rigorous history would reveal the need for a less doctrinaire analysis than that set out by Gadgil and Guha.

41 Grove, 'Scottish missionaries, evangelical discourses'.

42 Grove, 'Early themes in African conservation'.

43 Cleghorn, *Forests and Gardens of South India*.

44 J. W. Thirgood, *Man and the Mediterranean forest*, London, 1981. See also articles in all issues of *Revue des eaux et forêts*, of 1877.

45 One of the first exports of Indian forest service expertise was represented by the enlistment of G. Storr-Lister in the Cape Forest Department in 1875. Cleghorn visited and gave advice about Cyprus during the 1870s. D. E. Hutchins, formerly of the Madras Forest Department, was taken on by the Eastern Cape Conservancy in 1881 and also reported on the Cyprus forests in 1889. Indian and Cape forest officials were employed to advise on policy in the following territories: Cyprus (1879, 1909, 1930); Mauritius (1880, 1903); Jamaica (1886); British Honduras (1886); Tobago (1887); Trinidad (1887); Leeward Islands (1887); Antigua (1888); Malaya (1900); Southern Rhodesia (1896), 1902); Gold Coast, 1908; Uganda (1912); Kenya (1922); Northern Rhodesia (1927); Tanganyika (1930). Forest officers from India were seconded in British Honduras, Ceylon, Gold Coast, Kenya, Malaya, Nigeria, Sierra Leone, Trinidad, Uganda and Burma among other territories (R. S. Troup, *Colonial Forest Administration*; this is by no means an exhaustive list).

46 See Grove, 'Conservation and colonial expansion'; F. B. Hough (ed.), Report of the Committee on the Preservation of Forests: House Report no 259, 1st Session, 43rd Congress, Washington DC, 1874. Hough makes specific reference to the precedent set by the Madras Forest Service. Similarly, Hugh Cleghorn was influential on the work of George Perkins Marsh, an early ideologue of American conservationism.

47 The 'Forest and Herbage Protection' Acts of the Cape Colony were simply transferred without alteration to Southern Rhodesia, much as Indian Forest Law was transferred directly to Natal and the Gold Coast. T. R. Sim, conservator of the Eastern Cape and a disciple of John Croumbie Brown, conducted one of the first surveys of and reported on policy for the Rhodesian forests in 1902.

48 For an analysis of the impact of American 'dustbowl' conservation ideologies in southern Africa see W. Beinart, 'Soil conservationism'.

49 There is as yet no satisfactory overall history of forest and soil conservation policy for either colonial Africa or India.

50 Sumit Sarkar, 'Primitive rebellion and modern nationalism: a note on forest satyagraha in the non-cooperation and civil disobedience movements', in K. N. Panikkar (ed.), *National and Left Movements in India*, New Delhi, 1986.

51 Similarly, post-Second World environmental movements in Europe, India and North America have involved a whole range of peasant/working-class/middle-class/intelli-

IMPERIALISM AND THE NATURAL WORLD

gentsia alliances as well as alliances between notions of physical and 'spiritual' survival.

52 B. N. Wood, 'African peasant terrorism and Augustine's political thought', in F. Krantz (ed.) *History from Below*.

53 J. C. Cox, *Royal Forests*, p. 6.

54 C. Marsh, Churchill College, Cambridge. This material emerged in the course of Dr Marsh's work on the 'Family of Love' communities in Huntingdonshire.

55 B. Sharp, *In Contempt of all Authority: Rural Artisans and Riots in the West of England*, 1586-1660, Berkeley, 1980.

56 The 'resistance' here consisted mainly in bank-breaking and widespread crop burning, as at Epworth, Lincolnshire, in 1645; K. Lindley, *Fenland Riots and the English Revolution*, London, 1982.

57 Lindley, *Fenland Riots and the English Revolution*. Camden in *Britain* (1637) asserted that the fenmen were 'a kind of people according to the nature of the place where they dwell, rude, uncivil, and envious to all others, whom they call Uplandmen'. Another writer in 1629 noted that the 'generality of the fen people were very poor, lazy, given to much fishing and idleness...very much against the draining because they found their conditions should be worse, which thing was about impossible' (Lindley, p. 2). Such a belittling discourse paved the way for the drainage developers to ignore the interests of the fenmen, a type of use of 'ethnological' discourse which later capitalist manipulators of landscape in the colonial context were also quick to adopt.

58 J. Thirsk (ed.), *Agricultural History of England and Wales*, 5 (1985), p. 376. Riots broke out in 1680 and 1688 in the Forest of Dean even though far more parliamentary time was spent discussing the Forest of Dean than any other royal forest; Hart, *Commoners of Dean Forest*, pp. 52-71, 74-5. The problem did not end there, however. A century later renewed pressure to enclose Dean for the state both for timber and coal led to episodes of active resistance culminating in the involvement of the Forest of Dean in the Captain Swing Revolt in 1831. The critical role played by this region in the Chartist agitations (for which several forest men were tried at Monmouth in 1841) can be traced back to forest grievances too. See R. Anstis, *Warren James and the Dean Forest Riots*, Coalway, Glos., 1986.

59 Malone, *Pine Trees and Politics*.

60 Malone, *Pine Trees and Politics*.

61 For a later account of rural American resistance to state control see J.Garentin, *Power and Powerlessness: Quiescence and Resistance in an Appalachian Valley*, Oxford, 1980.

62 See Grove, 'Conservation and colonial expansion'.

63 Cobban, *The Social Interpretation of the French Revolution*, pp. 100-1. See also the allusions made to illegal woodgathering in the 1830s by Honoré de Balzac in *Les paysans* and in his letter to P. S. B. Gavault, quoted in J. Scott, *Weapons of the Weak*: 'The rights of pasturing their cows, the abuse of gleaning grapes, had gotten established little by little in this fashion. By the time the Tonsards and the other lazy peasants of the valley had tasted the benefits of these four rights acquired by the poor in the countryside, rights pushed to the point of pillage, one can imagine that they were unlikely to renounce them unless compelled by a force stronger than their audacity.'

64 R. B. Rose, 'Jacqueries at Davenescourt in 1791: a peasant riot in the French revolution', in F. Krantz (ed.), *History from Below: Studies in Popular Protest and Popular Ideology in Honour of George Rudé*, Montreal, 1985.

65 See chapter on soil erosion in France in P. Blaikie and H. Brookfield, *Land Degradation and Society*, London, 1987, esp. pp. 129-36.

66 See especially J. A.Fabre, *Essai sur la théorie des torrents et des rivières*, Paris, 1797.

67 St Helena Records; Government Diary, October 1745, p. 83. Govt. Archives, St H.

68 R. Brouard, *The Woods and Forest of Mauritius*, Port Louis, 1963.

69 G. Shaw-Lefevre, *The Game Laws*, London, 1874.

70 D. Hay, 'Poaching and the game laws in Cannock chase', in D. Hay and E. P. Thompson (eds.), *Albion's Fatal Tree: Crime and Society in Eighteenth Century England*, Harmondsworth, 1977; E. P. Thompson (ed.), *Whigs and Hunters: The Origins of the Black*

COLONIAL CONSERVATION AND POPULAR RESISTANCE

Act, Harmondsworth, 1977; J. Broad, 'Whigs and deer stealers in other guises; a return to the origins of the Black Act', *Past and Present* (1988).

71 Chetan Singh, 'Conformity and conflict: tribes and the "agrarian system" of Mughal India', *Indian Economic and Social History Review*, 23, 3 (1988) pp. 320-40.

72 It should be pointed out that the onset of British rule in India was not always initially to the disadvantage of 'tribal' groups. After the massive de-populaton of West Bengal occasioned by the 1770 famine, for example, the Santhals were able to spread out to occupy areas where they had never previously been known. How far the conditions of British rule allowed this it is hard to say.

73 P. R. G. Mathur, 'Political awakening among the tribes of Wynaad', in Singh, *Tribal Movements*.

74 For the strategic aspects of this policy see K. Ballhatchet, *Social Policy and Social Change in Western India, 1817-1830*, London, 1957.

75 Although it should be said that between 1837 and 1845 forest reserves were frequently advocated by local and naval timber agents to gain control of the forests in northern Gujerat in the Dangs and Panch Mahals districts.

76 See Grove, 'Scottish missionaries, evangelical discourses'.

77 The Sind (Scinde) case is somewhat different. Here, between 1842 and 1848, forest reserves were established on the sites of hunting reserves long established by the Sindhi Rajahs. In this case formal establishment was welcomed by local farmers since they immediately gained access to pastures and arable land from which they had previously been excluded. See Capt. J. Scott, *Report on the Canals and Forests of Sind*, Bombay, 1853.

78 P. Linebaugh, 'Karl Marx, the theft of wood and working-class composition', pp. 85-110 in T. Platt and P. Takagi (eds.), *Crime and Social Justice*, London, 1981.

79 R. Anstis, *Warren James and the Dean Forest Riots*, Coalway, Glos., 1986. The most deep-seated and extensive part of the Captain Swing movement took place in the Forest of Dean, building on long-held resentments against the enclosure activities of naval timber interests. So too, the Forest contributed the greatest single number of transportees to Tasmania.

80 See Eugen Weber, *Peasants into Frenchmen*, Stanford, Calif., 1976; especially pp. 485-92, where he applies Frantz Fanon to nineteenth-century France. For a case study of cork workers who took over and ran their own enterprises as producers' co-operatives during the Second French Republic see Maurice Agulhon, *La République au village*, Paris, 1970, pp. 126-45, 305-60.

81 See Gadgil and Guha, 'State forestry and social conflict'.

82 K. Marx (1847), Proceedings of the Sixth Rhine Province Assembly, Third Article; *Debates on the Law of the Theft of Wood*; K Marx and F. Engels, *Collected Works*, vol. 1, New York, 1975.

83 For a useful recent discussion of the connections between 'Gandhian hegemony' and rural forest protest movements see Atluri Murali, 'Civil disobedience movements in Andhra, 1920-1921; the nature of peasant protest and the methods of Congress political mobilisation', in Kapil Kuman (ed.), *Congress and Classes*, New Delhi, 1987. Murali asserts that, while Congress may have gained from the forest movements, their origins were relatively autonomous. While accepting the 'Gandhian hegemony' the local Congress leaders often took the lead from the autonomous articulation of local forest grievances rather than the other way about.

84 *See Bombay Forest Commission*, pp. 22-40.

85 See D. Arnold, 'Rebellious hillmen; the Gudem Rampa uprisings, 1839-1922', in Ranjit Guha (ed.), *Subaltern Studies*, 11, Delhi, 1982.

86 See Gadgil and Guha, 'State forestry and social conflict'. See also R. Guha, *The Unquiet Woods: Ecological Change and Peasant Resistance*, Delhi, 1989.

87 K. S. Singh, 'The Gond movements', in *Tribal Movements in India*, pp. 177-83.

88 *Ibid.*, p. 181.

89 See V. Damodaran, 'Popular protest, the Congress and the National movement: Bihar 1938-1948, unpublished Ph. D. thesis, University of Cambridge, 1989, chapter 5.

90 P. K. M. Rao and P. C. P. Rao, 'Tribal movements in Andhra Pradesh', in K. S. Singh,

IMPERIALISM AND THE NATURAL WORLD

Tribal Movements in India, pp. 354-72. See also Samanta Banerjee, *In the Wake of Naxalbari: A History of the Naxalite Movement in India*, Calcutta, 1980; Sohail Jawaid; *The Naxalite Movement in India: Origins and Failure of the Naxalite Revolutionary Strategy in West Bengal, 1967-1971*, New Delhi, 1979.

91 For the ecological basis of these movements see (on Southern Rhodesia) G. Passmore, 'The native land husbandry policy', chapter 5 of unpublished Ph.D. thesis, University of Rhodesia, 1979; G. Passmore, 'Rhodesia: a documentary record of policy failure', unpublished MS paper; and (on Kenya) D. Throup, *Economic and Social Origins of the Mau Mau*, London, 1988.

92 D. S. Kulkarni, 'The Bhil movement in the Dhulia district, 1972-1974', in K. S. Singh, *Tribal Movements in India*.

93 K. S. Singh, 'Tribal secessionist movements in Chotanagpur', in his *Tribal Movements in India*.

94 Although Chipko has also concerned itself with distinguishing the relative demerits of teak as against other tree species, especially 'sal'. The much greater involvement of women in prominent positions in Chipko is a further distinguishing feature.

95 Anil Agarwal, 'Ecological destruction and the emerging patterns of policy and popular protest in rural India', *Social Action*, 1 (1985), pp. 54-80.

96 For an account of the effects of the expansion of these commercial forces see W. Fernandes and Geeta Menon, *Tribal Movements and Forest Economy: Deforestation, Exploitation and Status Change*, New Delhi, 1984.

97 BBC World Service, Interview with Jocasta Shakespeare of Jersey Wildlife Trust, 28 May 1989.

98 See V. Damodaran, 'Betraying the people: popular protest, the Congress and the National movement in Bihar, 1938-1948', chapter 2. Damodaran's conclusions are similar to those espoused by Murali in Andhra, namely that the institutional connections between the Congress and much more radical local protest movements prevented disillusion with the Congress (in actually dealing with ecological grievances) escalating into a complete break. Even the Kisan Sabha in Bihar was unable to bring itself to make such a break before independence. Political co-option therefore, allowed ecological impoverishment to continue unhindered in large parts of India.

99 Thirgood, *Man and the Mediterranean Forest*, London, 1977.

100 *Ibid.*

101 David Prochaska, 'Fire on the mountain: resisting colonialism in Algeria', in D. Crummey (ed.), *Banditry, Rebellion and Social Protest in Africa*, London, 1986.

102 For example, the London and Lisbon Cork Wood Company which purchased concessions in 1865.

103 Prochaska, 'Resisting colonialism in Algeria', p. 243. Resistance to French colonial forest policy was not confined to Algeria. In Madagascar, too, the installation of forest reserves after 1896 was stiffly resisted. The full history of these episodes remains to be written. I am indebted to Professor Maurice Bloch of the London School of Economics for this information.

104 T. R. Sim, *Forests and Forest Flora of the Cape Colony*, Cape Town, 1907. D. E. Hutchins had originally been employed in the Madras Forest Service.

105 *Report of the Conservator of Forests*, Cape Town, 1889, p. 303.

106 J. Carruthers, 'Game protection in the Transvaal, 1846-1921', unpublished Ph.D. thesis, University of Cape Town, 1988.

107 J. Carruthers, 'Creating a national park, 1910-1926', *Journal of Southern African Studies*, 2 (1989) pp. 188-217.

108 G. Shepperson, *Independent African: John Chilembwe and the Origins, Setting and Significance of the Nyasaland Rising of 1915*, Edinburgh, 1958.

109 See Linebaugh, 'Karl Marx, the theft of wood'.

110 V. I. Lenin, *The Development of Capitalism in Russia*, Moscow, 1899.

111 See M. Perrie, 'The Russian peasant movement of 1905-1907, its social composition and revolutionary significance', *Past and Present*, 57 (1972).

112 National Archives of Zimbabwe, GF files on 'grassfires' 1912–20; see also R. H. Grove, Introduction to *Conservation and People in Zimbabwe, 1890-1980*, forthcoming.

COLONIAL CONSERVATION AND POPULAR RESISTANCE

113 Mukamuri, 'Rural environmental conservation'.

114 See M. Gadgil and V. D. Vatala, 'Sacred groves of Maharashtra; an inventory', in S. K. Jain (ed.), *Glimpses of the Ethnobotany of Bombay*, Oxford 1981; P. C. Hembram, 'Return to the sacred grove', in Singh (ed.), *Tribal movements in India*, pp. 87-91.

115 See T. Ranger, 'Whose heritage? The case of the Matobo National Park', *Journal of Southern African Studies*, 2 (1989), pp. 217-49.

116 Malawi National Archives, Zomba, Malawi; Forest Department files, 1920-40.

117 For references to resistance to forest policy initiatives in Nigeria in 1900-20 see E. E. Enabor, 'The future of forestry in Nigeria', in *The challenge of deforestation in Nigeria*, Ibadan, 1986; and A. H. Unwin, *West African Forests and Forestry*, London 1920.

118 Troup, *Colonial Forest Administration*, pp. 323-7.

119 J. Brown Wills, *Agriculture and Land Use in Ghana*, Oxford and Accra, 1962, pp. 229-36.

120 The contrast with developments in Malaysia in the same year, 1928, is remarkable. In the Trengannu rebellion of that year, sparked by new forest and land tax laws, Lebai abdul Rahman led a force of 1,000 rebels. The revolt was put down savagely after a few weeks by the colonial authorities, with many casualties resulting. This revolt marked the final stage in acquisition of full control of the Malay states by the British. For details of the rebellion see Dato Seri Lela di-Raja, 'The Ulu Trengannu disturbance, May 1928', *Malaysia in History*, vol. 12, no. 1 1968. The brutal tradition of state suppression of forest-dwellers has, of course, been consistently reinforced in the post-independence era, particularly in Sarawak.

121 Government of the Gold Coast; Annual Reports of the Forest Department, 1909-40.

122 D. Anderson, 'Managing the forest: the conservation history of Lembus, Kenya. 1904-1963', in Anderson and Grove, *Conservation in Africa*, pp. 249-65.

123 Beinart, 'Soil conservationism', and 'Introduction: the politics of colonial conservation', *Journal of Southern African Studies*, 2 (1989), pp. 143-63; Throup, 'Economic and social origins of Mau Mau'; A. Thurston, *Smallholder Agriculture in Colonial Kenya: The Official Mind and the Swynnerton Plan*, Cambridge, 1987.

124 There is as yet no useful published history of the colonial forest and soil protection programmes of Africa. An early attempt to survey the field in Africa is D. Anderson and A. C. Millington, 'Political economy of soil erosion in Anglophone Africa', in A. C. Millington, S. K,. Mutiso and J. A. Binns (eds.), *African Resources*, vol., 2, *Management*, Reading, 1990.

125 L. Vail and Landeg White, 'Tribalism in the political history of Malawi', in L. Vail (ed.) *The Creation of Tribes in southern Africa*, London, 1989. For details of resistance to soil terracing policies in Nyasaland and associated mass actions and riots in the wider context of the 1959 emergency in Nyasaland see *Report of the Nyasaland Commission of Inquiry*, Colonial Office, London, 1959; and W. Beinart, 'Agricultural planning and the late colonial technical imagination; the Lower Shire valley in Malawi, 1940-1960', in *Malawi: An Alternative Pattern of Development*, Edinburgh, 1984. According to E. C. Mandala ('Capitalism, ecology and society'), the soil terracing policies were not universally unpopular; some farmers voluntarily continued the practice after independence. See also R. I. Rotberg, *The Rise of Nationalism in Central Africa: The Making of Malawi and Zambia*, 1873-1964, Cambridge, Mass., 1966, pp. 171-99.

126 G. C. Passmore, 'Rhodesia, a documentary record of policy failure', MS of forthcoming article, pp. 3-5.

127 *Ibid.*, pp.5-7.

128 D. Martin and P. Johnson, *The Struggle for Zimbabwe: The Chimurenga War*, London, 1981.

129 J. Mtisi, 'Population control and management; a case study of Nyamukwara Valley tenants at Stapleford Forest Reserve, 1929-1971', paper presented to session on Conservation and rural People in Zimbabwe at African Studies Association of the UK conference, Cambridge, September 1988.

130 The diffusion of ideas between the colonial powers on conservation policies by this period was rapid; for a complete survey see A. Harroy, *Afrique, terre qui meurt*, Brussels, 1949.

IMPERIALISM AND THE NATURAL WORLD

131 To date there is no survey of popular resistance to colonial forest policy in West Africa; however, A. H. Unwin, *West African forests and forestry*, London, 1920, is a useful basic guide to the development of forest conservation in West Africa, providing some perhaps unwitting insights into indigenous responses.

132 A. T. Grove, *Land Use and Soil Conservation in Parts of Onitsha and Owerri Provinces*, Geological Survey of Nigeria, Zaria, 1951.

133 *Ibid.*

134 Probably the most violent episode of resistance to a 'development' project in Nigeria was that at the Bakolori Dam site in 1980. This is described in an important case by W. A. Adams; 'Rural protest, land policy and the planning process on the Bakolori Project, Nigeria', *Africa*, 58 (1988), pp. 315-36.

135 K. L. Pelzer, *Pioneer Settlement in the Asiatic Tropics: Studies in Land Utilisation and Agricultural Colonisation in Southeastern Asia*, New York, 1948, p. 233.

136 M. Gamaleddin, 'State policy and famine in the Awash valley of Ethiopia', in Anderson and Grove (eds.), *Conservation in Africa*, pp. 327-44.

137 It should not be thought, however, that colonial conservation ideologies have had a total monopoly in the stimulation of resistance to overbearing attempts at managing the landscape. There is a growing body of evidence to indicate that a whole series of soil conservation initiatives in Communist China have been abandoned since the early 1960s in direct response to widespread popular opposition.

[50]

[16]

Beyond the Colonial Paradigm

*African History and Environmental History
in Large-Scale Perspective*

WILLIAM BEINART

Human beings are, before anything else, biological entities. Their interactions with other species and with the natural environment, and their appropriation of the natural resources without which life is impossible, must be central elements in human history. Significant sorties have been made into this terrain in a variety of historical writing, and perhaps more in other disciplines. Some earlier Western intellectual traditions evinced a strong environmental determinism to explain different forms of society, racial characteristics, and social division. This tendency has now largely been jettisoned by historians. A simultaneous concern, however, evident at least since the Enlightenment, has been analysis of human effects on the natural world. This strand, fueled by an anxious environmentalism and by the reaction to concrete modernism, has been dominant in recent environmental history, especially in writing about the consequences of European imperialism.

Alfred Crosby placed the earth-shattering environmental consequences of European expansion over the last five hundred years at the heart of world history. Eurasian diseases and immunities, together with the technology gap and ruthless conquest, facilitated the devastating depopulation of the Americas and their repopulation by invaders—human, animal, and plant.[1] The taming of nature and indigenous peoples emerges as the central motif for Crosby and those influenced by him.[2] Such approaches offer striking insights into both rapid environmental change and global race relations, because they help to explain how particular demographic balances were established in various parts of the colonized world.

The new environmental history has provided a useful stimulus to Africanists because it shares many of their well-established moral concerns and perspectives. In the roughly fifty years since African countries began to shake off colonial control, major advances have been made in revealing the African past, and a vast volume of literature has been produced that will remain an enduring legacy. The subdiscipline of African history has initially been informed by a set of assumptions that might broadly be conceived as corrective. Research has dwelled on the achievements of precolonial states and societies, on the exploitation and colonial conquest of Africa, and on the repressive nature of colonial rule and racial segregation. In fulfillment of the stirring 1960s call by Terence Ranger, historians demonstrated African agency, African initiative, and the salience and legitimacy of African resistance.[3] This broad approach survived the disillusionment with African nationalism in the 1970s and has been extended into the subsequent attention to peasants, workers, women, and popular politics and religion.

Environmental issues, long of interest to historians and social scientists working on Africa, slipped easily into the anticolonial framework and also in important respects extended it. These issues have provided additional scope for interdisciplinary interaction with geographers and archaeologists as well as natural and medical scientists, whose fields contain deep wells of accumulated research. Environmental concerns have necessitated moving away from well-thumbed administrative files to explore new archival sources. They have opened the way to consideration of fascinating nonhuman agents in history, such as fire and water, animals, insects, and plant invaders. They have raised further questions for oral fieldwork on themes strongly familiar to the majority of Africans who, until recently, lived in rural settings. Both African people and the settlers and colonists who came to the continent debated environmental issues intensely; nature and landscape have also been evoked in many different modes of cultural expression. An environmental approach facilitates the mining of rich but still-neglected seams of intellectual and cultural history, from African fables and ecoreligions to the colonial fascination with botany and wildlife.

This chapter, focused on areas of Africa that came under British control, is divided into two sections. I illustrate briefly six interlinked lines of analysis in recent African environmental history; all bear considerable import for understanding the relationship between colonizer and colonized, white and black. Such approaches are beginning to assume the status of a new paradigm and have successfully inverted colonial stereotypes that celebrated Western knowledge and bemoaned Africans as environmentally profligate. I then raise questions about this new paradigm and offer some alternative propositions that might move the debate beyond inversions of colonial narratives.

First, the environmental consequences of colonial incursions have been explored, including appropriation by companies and settlers of natural resources such as wildlife, forests, minerals, and land. This process was at the heart of European expansion from its very inception: a core myth of the foundation of Madeira, one of the first islands colonized outside Europe, was a seven-year fire by which this densely wooded landscape was cleared for settlement.[4] Spanish conquistadors claimed tracts of the Americas not only by reading proclamations and by warfare, but also by symbolically striking trees or lopping branches with their swords.[5]

Some Africanist writing shared what John MacKenzie calls the apocalyptic vision of global environmental history, based on the profoundly disruptive colonial encounters in the Americas and Australia.[6] Helge Kjekshus's *Ecology Control and Economic Development in East Africa* (1977) is a somber account of early colonial rule in Tanzania, sketching the impact of war and diseases such as smallpox and chiggers. Critically, he argued that colonialism spread the endemic tsetse fly and trypanosomiasis, causing sleeping sickness in humans and effectively excluding cattle from large areas.[7] Ecological catastrophe was reflected in a period of demographic halt or decline, perhaps comparable to the period of the slave trade in parts of West Africa.[8] In *The Empire of Nature,* MacKenzie himself vividly illustrates the predatory character of settler and imperial hunting in southern Africa, which catastrophically reduced wildlife and was responsible for the extinction of a couple of species.[9] Environmental decay is discussed in many studies of partial displacement, or compression of African societies into smaller areas of land, as a result of settler colonialism from South Africa to Kenya.

Second, it has been recognized that colonial states in Africa became concerned about environmental regulation, including forest protection, wildlife preservation, soil erosion, and water conservation. They also attempted to eradicate, through environmental management, human and animal diseases, such as malaria, trypanosomiasis, and tick-borne maladies, whose complex ecological etiology was becoming apparent. But colonial environmental management has been characterized as highly intrusive.[10] Approaches to forestry, it has been argued, were drawn from the scientific and commercial models of Europe and India that excluded rural people.[11] Similarly, purity in conceptions of wilderness resulted in the depopulation of national parks.[12] "Fortress conservation," excluding African people from reserves (while allowing access to tourists and scientists), came to characterize wildlife management before and after independence.[13]

Conservationist interventions, linked with other imperatives of agricultural development and social control, also fed into wholesale attempts to change African patterns of land use. Such interventions, whether attempts to sedentarize transhumant pastoralists, or villagize societies with scattered settlement, have been seen in themselves as a major cause of rural degradation, both social and environmental.[14] Colonial development and conservation projects, rooted in a scientific and modernizing logic, have been subjected to particularly critical scrutiny because they outlived the colonial era and remained central in the development strategies of independent African states and international agencies.

Third, the inadequacy of colonial and Western science has frequently been stressed, an argument strengthened by the failure of many major schemes even after independence. Although political resistance and bureaucratic incapacity played a part in the mishaps of planning, nevertheless lack of research, misunderstanding, scientific hubris, and technical weakness have all been demonstrated by researchers. Interventions designed to control trypanosomiasis by the slaughter of game or removal of people in the early decades of this century may instead have facilitated its spread. Kate Showers argues that faulty colonial contour-bank construction in lowland Lesotho, one of the most eroded landscapes on the continent, resulted in stormwater welling up, breaking through, and forming new gullies.[15]

A striking example, which rapidly achieved paradigmatic status in the literature, is Fairhead and Leach's West African research in *Misreading the African Landscape*. They illustrate how, over many years in Guinea, French colonial officials and subsequent experts interpreted the patches of forest to be found in the savannah zone as evidence of deforestation, and framed their interventions with this assumption in mind. By contrast, Fairhead and Leach found that "elders and others living behind the forest walls provide quite different readings of their landscape and its making. At their most contrasting, they bluntly reverse policy orthodoxy, representing their landscape as half-filled and filling with forest, not half-emptied and emptying of it. Forest islands, some villagers suggested, are not relics of destruction, but were formed by themselves or their ancestors in the savanna."[16] In this analysis, settlement brought forests. Scientific understanding and interventions were flawed by their lack of social understanding, or their subservience to colonial political and cultural agendas.

Fourth, as a corollary, the validity and salience of local knowledge about the environment, and means of living in it, have become an increasingly rich area of research as well as a powerful ideological factor in the debate over the right to manage resources. It is a point made with equal force in respect of Australian aboriginal people or Native Americans, although the argument has potentially greater policy import in Africa and Asia, where so many indigenous peoples were comprehensively disposessed.

Perhaps it is not coincidental that some of the most trenchant statements have come from West African contexts, in that this region was least affected by settler colonialism and maintained particularly innovative forms of agricultural production. In his influential book *Indigenous Agricultural Revolution,* Paul Richards explored the capacity of West African smallholders to make "the best of natural conditions, ... capitalizing on local diversity."[17] "This ecological knowledge" he argued, was "one of the most significant of rural Africa's resources" and was by no means simply a "hangover from the past." He focused on food-crop strategies, especially low-technology, wetland rice cultivation in Sierra Leone, where "people's science" was at work in the deployment of locally evolved seed varieties to cater for small variations in natural conditions.[18] Any outside aid, he argued, should work flexibly with local knowledge and techniques. His research feeds into concerns articulated by Calestous Juma in *The Gene Hunters* about the intellectual property rights of local people everywhere over both wild and cultivated species in the face of a new international "scramble for seeds."[19]

Local knowledge has also been addressed in debates about the thorny question of the environmental vulnerability of common-property regimes. Most Africanists have rejected simple renditions of the "tragedy of the commons," in which individuals maximize exploitation of a free common resource at the cost of the resource itself.[20] Counterarguments have noted that private landholding has been no guarantee against environmental degradation: freeholders have frequently mined the land and moved on.[21] Moreover, people have gained access to commons as members of communities, with traditions of socially circumscribed usage; local authorities, customs, and religious ideas often reinforced constraints on exploitation.

In a key article on overgrazing controversies, Homewood and Rodgers argued further that common management systems show limited evidence of serious degradation. They questioned calculations of fixed carrying capacities for East African pastures and suggested that overgrazing is frequently invoked but not botanically demonstrated. Referring to Baringo District in Kenya, they maintained that "the history of the area is more suggestive of a series of oscillations in stock numbers and vegetation conditions precipitated by . . . climatic fluctuations governing this semiarid area, rather than a long-term trend of anthropogenic environmental destruction."[22] An avalanche of studies in range ecology has developed such findings.[23] In sum, they suggest that the economic and social benefits, especially for poor people, of access to common grazing for animals, vital for multiple uses such as draft, milk, meat, and exchange, are not generally outweighed by the environmental costs.[24]

South Asian and Latin American literature about the "environmentalism of the poor" provides a parallel.[25] Poor people, especially in rural areas, who are immediately dependent on natural resources have an overwhelming interest in retaining them in usable form as well as maintaining equitable access. Appreciation of local knowledge has been accompanied by sensitivity to gender relations and recognition of the role of African women, as the continent's main cultivators, on the front line of managing nature.

Fifth, scholars have systematically illustrated the centrality of conflicts over natural resources and environmental issues in rural anticolonial movements and rebellions. Following the Second World War, developmental strategies overlaid trusteeship as a guiding philosophy of empire in what has been called the second colonial occupation in Africa. State intervention helped both to trigger protest and to drive peasants into the arms of nationalists. My own research in African history began nearly twenty-five years ago with an attempt to investigate the Pondoland revolt in South Africa in 1960—perhaps the country's most serious rural rebellion of the twentieth century. It was too difficult to research at the time, but with new material and fresh perspectives gathered in the last few years, I have become more aware of its environmental origins.[26] Rural people were disturbed about the government's conservation-driven rehabilitation program; anger seethed over denial of access to reserved forests; and conflict also simmered over a succession dispute, prompted many years before by the state's dismissing a chief for failing to cooperate in locust eradication. Chieftaincy was a lightning rod for such conflicts both because of the intermediary role of traditional authorities and their responsibility for many aspects of environmental management.

Last, the fortunes of African societies have long been enmeshed in global economic and social forces and have thus been increasingly susceptible to environmental calamity. Elias Mandala's investigations of rural economy and ecological management in the lower Tchiri Valley in Malawi demonstrate how global and regional processes shaped its people's options in responding to floods in the 1930s.[27] Drawing on Amartya Sen's idea of entitlements to food, rather than drought, as the major factor behind famine, Megan Vaughan and others have explained the centrality of markets and economic and gender differentiation in mapping susceptibility to hunger.[28] The far-reaching environmental and social repercussions of African civil conflicts bred in the Cold War have also been investigated. Warring parties shot elephants for their ivory in Angola and Mozambique; millions of involuntary refugees placed intense pressure on resources in receiving areas. Debt and structural adjustment have prompted the stripping of natural resources for export and compounded environmental losses.

In summarizing and juxtaposing a range of arguments, I have inevitably simplified individual studies and connections between them. This increasingly wide-ranging literature is now a valuable resource in a number of disciplines. It captures not only the recent mood of Africanist scholarship but also certain striking features of both the colonial relationship and postcolonial states. Academic research is by no means the only vehicle for such ideas. Nevertheless, inverting colonial ideas about environmental degradation has been part of a far-reaching critique of asymmetrical power relations, both within particular countries and between the global North and South. Fundamental assumptions about knowledge, consumption, and rights to resources, as well as about inequality, have been challenged. At least at the level of development rhetoric, if not always in its practice, sensitivity to local knowledge and participatory planning, rather than root-and-branch intervention, are widely advocated. Development strategies designed to be both pro-peasant and gender-sensitive, such as dispersed agroforestry or social forestry rather than afforestation in plantations, have reflected these new directions.

These analytical and policy gains must not be lost. However, these lines of analysis are now sufficiently robust to withstand examination and extension. Arguments rooted in an anticolonial and sometimes populist discourse can present us with too neat an inversion and analytical closure, which is not always appropriate in a postcolonial world and might obscure important lines of research. We need to find routes forward without losing sight of issues of equity or the imperative to combat racial assumptions in respect of resource use and management.

Other branches of African studies, where the recent political travails of the continent have helped to provoke uneasiness, offer guidance. Historians of the slave trade and slavery, long a touchstone for developments in African history, have evolved a more complex sense of responsibility and morality. Their view recognizes the slave trade not only as a European-controlled system of exploitation but also as a trade with African participation and with many complex outcomes.[29] The rise of great West African empires, notably Asante, Dahomey, and Oyo, was intimately linked with slave capture, trade, militarization, and intensified forms of internal slavery. Similarly, although analysts of contemporary African governance differ in their explanations, some are forging a historically informed vision integrating the legacy of colonialism with a critique of African political practice and

African modes of authority.[30] This literature opens up questions of responsibility and agency that we need to address in environmental history.

One route forward may be to consider a longer time span and a comparative approach. The environmental history of the Americas has provided one model by which to explore the African case. But, as Crosby notes, the two continents' experiences differ fundamentally. Unlike most indigenous peoples in the Americas and Australasia, Africans weathered the storm of colonialism, demographically speaking. Certainly, important new human diseases were introduced during the early colonial period, as well as the epizootic rinderpest in the 1890s, which devastated cattle herds. But Africans in many regions had the immunities, and the demographic and political weight, to withstand disease and displacement. (The Khoisan peoples of southern Africa were an exception in this respect.) In the longer term, the demographic explosion of the twentieth century (and earlier in some places) is far more notable than any temporary halt. African populations increased eightfold, perhaps more in some countries, during the twentieth century. Moreover, it is now commonplace to argue that direct colonial control was a relatively brief episode in much of Africa, lasting less than a century in most places and little more than sixty years in some. This observation applies even in parts of southern Africa, where settlers gained the strongest foothold; and European agrarian settlement has been decisively driven back in most of the subcontinent during the past few decades. Environmentally and demographically, colonialism was less cataclysmic than in North and South America, the Caribbean, Australia, and New Zealand.

This is not to suggest that African societies were unconnected to the extraordinary global interchange of species and techniques that accompanied imperial expansion over the past half-millennium. Some crops, including species of palm, sorghum, millet, yams, rice, teff, and coffee were domesticated in Africa, or, like bananas, came very early from farther east. But Africans absorbed many new species through the European maritime empires because plants domesticated elsewhere offered enhanced food security, productivity, variety, labor savings, or cash-crop opportunities—notably, but by no means only, American crops and fruits such as maize, cassava, tomatoes, beans, chilies, potatoes, tobacco, cocoa, prickly pear, and avocados. A strand in the literature sees the introduction of maize, the most important of these crops, in some areas as a colonial imposition. But as James McCann shows, maize came early to Africa: it was widely reported in the seventeenth century, well before any direct colonization, and traveled along African routes. The crop was, for example, "part of the historical conjuncture that resulted in Asante's historical prosperity and hegemonic growth."[31] The Asante kingdom became perhaps the most populous and powerful in West Africa during the eighteenth and nineteenth centuries. The spread of such plants was a testament to agricultural innovation rather than to colonial imposition. In turn, new species fundamentally altered the range and balance of edible plants in the continent, helping to shape demography, farming systems, and environmental impact over the long term. This impact was not predictable. Although a valuable food source, maize also probably helped to spread malaria and exhausted the soils in areas where it was cultivated intensively and continuously.

We need also to understand that Africans, and especially Bantu-speaking black Africans, were migrants and colonizers in the continent. In his overview, *Africans,* John Iliffe places environmental control consequent on such migration at center stage: "Africans have been and are the frontiersmen who have colonized an especially hostile region of the world on behalf of the entire human race. That has been their chief contribution to history. It is why they deserve admiration, support, and careful study."[32] Some may be uneasy about according environmental control quite so central a role in the contributions of Africans to world history, and clearly women as well as men were at the cutting edge of these frontiers. Nevertheless, there is evidence that precolonial land settlement and subsequent demographic and economic growth could involve exhaustion of resources as well as beneficial use.

The spread of Bantu-speaking people from West Africa through much of the rest of sub-Saharan Africa, about two to three thousand years ago, together with the techniques, livestock, and crops which they were developing, necessarily involved unsustainable demographic expansion in local areas.[33] Interpretations of the decline of Great Zimbabwe in the fifteenth century have invoked the exhaustion of soils, firewood, and pastures. "Without fundamental changes in technology and agricultural system," Graham Connah concludes, "it was fated to destroy itself."[34] Robert Harms compares the Nunu of the Congo Basin to the New England settlers at much the same time, concerned primarily with taming the land and maximizing their take of fish.[35] Sutton discusses sophisticated East African irrigation and terracing systems capable of supporting dense settlement, which broke down by the early nineteenth century, probably because of declining yields under intensive exploitation.[36] The Bemba practice of *citimene,* or ashbed cultivation, involving the lopping and burning of trees, helped transform this part of Zambia, even if it was relatively containable in times of land plenty.[37] The Bemba symbol of masculinity was the ax.

All human survival disturbs nature, itself a dynamic set of forces, and this is a condition of development. Clearly, the impact of hunter-gatherers is of a different order from that of industrial society, but, as now seems to be accepted, the earliest aboriginal settlers in the Americas and Australia, even without iron tools or livestock, contributed to the extermination of animal species. Critically, historians must allow for changes within societies at particular phases of their encounters with nature. Trade, markets, and technological change, both international and local, have given specific natural resources value as commodities. The ivory trade is a case in point, and it is worth stressing that for any agrarian African society elephants were among the most dangerous animals, trampling and eating crops. Commercialization of palm oil in nineteenth-century coastal West Africa led to removal of some forest cover and the establishment of new plantations. Fairhead and Leach's illustration of African capacities to afforest land around their settlements does not prove that deforestation is a myth. Their work is a valuable corrective to overarching narratives of degradation, and we must be cautious about generalizations. But the dominant trend over the twentieth century in many African countries is more likely to have been deforestation, and satellite imagery for the last couple of decades suggests this trend is accelerating in some areas.

Everywhere, new techniques of hunting by firearms, fishing with nets, and cultivating with plows could alter relationships between people and nature. In her discussion of soil erosion in Lesotho, Showers focuses on colonial interventions and responsibility, but the Sotho themselves transformed their agrarian, military, and transport systems in the nineteenth century. They adopted horses and sheep, as well as ox-drawn wagons and sledges; they intensified plow cultivation of the lowlands with new crops of wheat and maize; and they colonized mountain zones.[38]

This argument does not preclude periods of relative stability in particular locales, nor do I suggest that all environmental transformation is best conceived as degradation. Moreover, it certainly allows for a dynamic view of local knowledge; and we still have a great deal to learn about the accommodations reached between people and nature, the way these were interpreted in different societies, and the way they were policed. Environmental regulation could be expressed in part through customary and religious practices, and, as David Maxwell and Terence Ranger have argued, the eco-religious elements in Zimbabwean territorial cults did not disappear in the twentieth century.[39] They may in fact have been reinforced as an explanation of agro-ecological stress and as a popular critique of state intervention.

The same logic might apply to management of common property resources. Although Africanists are correctly wary of simplified models depicting a tragedy of the commons, we should not, conversely, assume that common-property regimes are environmentally beneficial. When control and accountability do break down, degradation can occur under the pressure of social change, urbanization, markets, war, and drought.[40] Examples can be found from the West African Sahel to the Eastern Cape in South Africa. Where land boundaries are tightening, continued transhumance can be a recipe for conflict. In some peri-urban contexts with very rapid population growth, uncertainty over land rights has exacerbated difficulties in providing urban services and developing urban environmental controls. Mary Tiffen, Michael Mortimore, and Francis Gichuki demonstrate in their book *More People, Less Erosion* that peasants greened their land in Machakos district, Kenya, over a period of fifty years from an environmental low point in the 1930s, despite increases in population. In many respects, the study echoes others in praise of local knowledge. But they also suggest that a key factor in the transition from "badlands to farmlands" was the landholders' ability to secure effectively private rights over, and to invest in, both arable and grazing land.[41] In other cases, such as in the Eastern Cape, common property together with lack of resources have inhibited investment, improvement, and effective land management. We have to allow for variable outcomes.

More-complex readings of the history of science and knowledge, an exciting area of academic enterprise, may also be valuable. First, scientific developments, research agendas, and institutions, even when government-funded, were rooted in far broader intellectual networks than could be shaped by any particular state; the relative autonomy of scientific investigation, debates within disciplines, and battles between scientists and officials are all evident. Second, the dichotomy between Western science and local knowledge also requires modification. Although some encounters were characterized by mutual incomprehension, systems of knowledge have often been porous and plural over a long period. On the one hand, for example, Steven Feierman argues that African medical ideas were open to many new influences.[42] On the other, even at the height of colonial control, there was a significant sprinkling of sensitive scientists, not least in ecological, agricultural, and medical fields, as well as innumerable anthropologists whose record of local knowledge and techniques is now a baseline for research.[43] Transmission of ideas and practices was clearly mediated by relationships of power, but that imbalance did not in itself halt the process.

Third, scientific work, past and present, shapes our very capacity to think about environmental change, about the history of relevant disciplines that must be part of environmental history, and about ecological interactions that are far beyond the powers of historians and social scientists to research. Richards, often cited as a key advocate of African knowledge, also insists that social scientists listen to natural scientists. He has celebrated John Ford's analysis of the history of trypanosomiasis in Africa precisely because it required the understanding of a natural scientist to unravel complex issues of habitat, vectors, and immunities. He distances himself from those social scientists who wish "to mine the natural sciences" very largely "for material that might lend itself to cultural critique" and to examine only "the marginal cases, where the bioscientific problem was framed in an unprofitable way," as in the "excesses of colonial agricultural planning."[44]

Failures in planning have perhaps been better rehearsed by historians than the rapidity with which scientists in Africa grappled with, and sometimes understood, complex diseases, ecologies, and natural phenomena. Historians must remain critical and identify instances where the intersection of scientific practice and state power has disadvantaged poor people or women, but they must also remain humble in recognition of the limits of our discipline. Local knowledge also has its limitations, sometimes tragically, in respect of diseases such as AIDS. All knowledge exists to be tested, rejected, and built upon. Where local communities have limited capacity for many types of environmental and disease management, it may be wise to bring sensitive science and the state back in.[45] Not all experts are outsiders, and such debates are increasingly generated within African countries.

Science and the state remain potentially powerful allies for poor people. Elizabeth Colson's study of the consequences of building the Kariba Dam on the Zambezi River helped initiate valuable anthropological research into the social and environment costs of big dams.[46] In South Africa and Zimbabwe, the unequal distribution of reservoir water to commercial farms and white suburbs was a fundamental aspect of discrimination and apartheid. But not all big dams are bad dams. Leaving aside the vexed question of irrigation, African countries are urbanizing rapidly and irrevocably. Social justice, urban health, and environmental improvement demand clean water. Dams, diversion of water, flooding of dam catchments in rural areas, and water processing may all be a necessary consequence. The environmentalism of the poor in the urban areas increasingly focuses on the demand for such services at an affordable rate; in South Africa, at least, the same needs are evident in dense rural settlements.[47]

Moreover, ecological outcomes, whether in zones managed by local communities or by national states, are unpredictable, as both history and the natural sciences tell us. So may folklore. I suggested at the outset that one of the most exciting areas opened up by an environmental focus lies in cultural history—well explored in the British historiography of landscape and literature, attitudes, and art, but less so in African studies.[48] Fables were one sphere of African culture that explored encounters with the natural world. Such stories are sometimes good to think with.

Many fables illustrated perceived animal characteristics and abounded with metaphors and observations drawn from nature, but they also offered a mirror on human society. They could be moral tales, explanatory myths, or more open-ended narratives. They clearly changed through time and, like other local knowledge, incorporated new influences. In Khoisan and African stories of South Africa, for example, the jackal and hare were usually tricksters. Khoisan jackal fables collected in the mid-nineteenth century wove wagons, farmers, and sheep into their narratives.[49] Settlers not only brought with them parallel folklore but also recorded and reworked indigenous fables that had meaning for them. The imbrication of these traditions, reflecting also social and agrarian change, is a fascinating topic in itself.

Destruction of species and even conservationist interventions have often produced unexpected consequences. The partial eradication of jackals in early twentieth-century South Africa, supported by conservationists who wished to stop the daily driving and kraaling (corralling) of livestock, contributed to a rapid rise in the number of sheep and thus to South Africa's equivalent of the Dust Bowl in the early 1930s.[50] Unpredictability can also work in the opposite direction. In the late nineteenth century, the future for wildlife in much of southern Africa seemed bleak. Some wild animals were, however, protected in enclaves, and the system of parks and reserves was gradually extended throughout the region. From the 1950s, these efforts were supplemented by game farming on private land, partly as a source of meat and trophies and partly as an alternative to pastoral farming, from which returns were declining. Initiatives such as the Campfire Program in Zimbabwe have attempted to extend this trend into communal areas. In the vast area that encompasses South Africa, Botswana, Zimbabwe, and Namibia, wildlife numbers have increased in the past couple of decades to their highest level since 1900. The state, by reserving land; capitalist farmers, by switching land use rapidly; and science, in the shape of veterinary medicine and zoology, have all contributed to this outcome. Biodiversity has benefited, but the recovery of wildlife has not yet produced a more equitable division of rural resources.

Although the bulk of academic writing sees wildlife conservation as a product of the colonial state, serving white and Western interests, new studies are beginning to reveal African agency in this sphere. The origins of the Moremi National Park in Botswana, now at the heart of the valuable Okavango delta reserve, can be traced to the enthusiasm of African advisers to the local BaTawana chieftaincy in the 1950s and 1960s. They worked with white adventurers and sometimes in the face of opposition from the colonial Bechuanaland protectorate.[51] The history of African ideas and practices regarding animals, which in many parts of the continent shaped the rhythms of everyday life, has been less well researched. From a rich base of anthropological material it is patent that certain species, at least, were sometimes protected. Similar exciting but neglected fields are the history of landscape and the built environment—not least because relatively few structures were made by specialists. As in the case of environmental history as a whole, their study demands a multifaceted, totalizing approach that draws on analysis of production, technology, environmental change, and style.

I have sought to test contrasting narratives written about African environmental history. Time scales, disciplines, and ideological vantage points all inform the interpretations offered. Although I emphasize human capacities to shape the environment, other themes, notably vulnerability and the all-pervasive environmental constraints on human activity, deserve attention. But I do not believe that these views need always be mutually exclusive, and indeed a number of the texts discussed demonstrate that they are not. Mahmood Mamdani, who sees the primary divide in African studies as between communitarians and modernists, argues not only for an awareness of the roots of these positions but also for a synthesis.[52] Achieving it may not be easy. A profound ambivalence can be detected in recent Africanist writing, by scholars both in Africa and outside, which, while emphasizing the asymmetry of global relations and the history of racist assumptions, struggles to free historiography and social studies from narratives of dependency, victimhood, and romanticism. We must continue to explore not only African creativity and resistance but also other forms of African agency, not least the shared human capacity to wield power for ill as well as good, over nature as well as people.

NOTES

1. Alfred W. Crosby, *The Columbian Exchange: Biological and Cultural Consequences of 1492* (Westport, CT: Greenwood Press, 1972) and *Ecological Imperialism: The Biological Expansion of Europe, 900–1900* (Cambridge: Cambridge University Press, 1986); William Cronon, *Changes in the Land: Indians, Colonists, and the Ecology of New England* (New York: Hill and Wang, 1983).

2. William Beinart and Peter Coates, *Environment and History: The Taming of Nature in the USA and South Africa* (London: Routledge, 1995).

3. T. O. Ranger, *The Recovery of African Initiative in Tanzanian History* (Dar es Salaam: University College, 1969) and *Rhodes, Oxford, and the Study of Race Relations* (Oxford: Clarendon Press, 1989); John McCracken, "Terry Ranger: A Personal Appreciation," *Journal of Southern African Studies* 23 (1997): 175–85.

4. Crosby, *Ecological Imperialism*, 76.

5. Stephen Greenblatt, *Marvelous Possessions: The Wonder of the New World* (Chicago: University of Chicago Press, 1991), 56.

6. John MacKenzie, "Empire and the Ecological Apocalypse: The Historiography of the Imperial Environment," in *Ecology and Empire: Environmental History of Settler Societies,* ed. Tom Griffiths and Libby Robin (Edinburgh: Keele University Press, 1997), 215–28.

7. Helge Kjekshus, *Ecology Control and Economic Development in East African History* (London: Heinemann, 1977); Leroy Vail, "Ecology and History: The Example of Eastern Zambia," *Journal of Southern African Studies* 3 (1977): 129–55.

8. Kjekshus, *Ecology Control,* 25. He notes that this must be a speculative conclusion. For a discussion, see Juhani Koponen, *People and Production in Late Precolonial Tanzania: History and Structures* (Helsinki: Finnish Society for Development Studies, 1988), 362 ff.

9. John MacKenzie, *The Empire of Nature: Hunting, Conservation and British Imperialism* (Manchester: Manchester University Press, 1988).

10. William Beinart, "Soil Erosion, Conservationism and Ideas about Development," *Journal of Southern African Studies* 11 (1984): 52–83; David Anderson and Richard Grove, eds., *Conservation in Africa: People, Policies and Practice* (Cambridge: Cambridge University Press, 1987).

11. Ravi Rajan, "Imperial Environmentalism or Environmental Imperialism? European Forestry, Colonial Foresters and the Agendas of Forest Management in British India, 1800–1900," in *Nature and the Orient: The Environmental History of South and Southeast Asia,* ed. Richard H. Grove, Vinita Damodaran, and Satpal Sangwan (Delhi: Oxford University Press, 1998): 324–71.

12. Jane Carruthers, *The Kruger National Park: A Social and Political History* (Pietermaritzburg: Natal University Press, 1995); Terence Ranger, "Whose Heritage? The Case of the Matobo National Park," *Journal of Southern African Studies* 15 (1989): 217–249, and *Voices from the Rocks: Nature, Culture and History in the Matopos Hills of Zimbabwe* (Oxford: James Currey, 1999).

13. Dan Brockington, *Fortress Conservation: The Preservation of the Mkomazi Game Reserve, Tanzania* (Oxford: James Currey, 2002).

14. Anderson and Grove, *Conservation in Africa;* F. Wilson and M. Ramphele, *Uprooting Poverty: The South African Challenge* (Cape Town: David Philip, 1989); Pat McAllister, "Resistance to 'Betterment' in the Transkei: A Case Study from Willowvale District," *Journal of Southern African Studies* 15 (1989): 346–68; Nancy Jacobs, *Environment, Power, and Injustice: A South African History* (Cambridge: Cambridge University Press, 2003).

15. Kate B. Showers, "Soil Erosion in the Kingdom of Lesotho: Origins and Colonial Response," *Journal of Southern African Studies* 15, no. 2 (1989): 263–86, and *Imperial Gullies: Soil Erosion and Conservation in Lesotho* (Athens: Ohio University Press, 2005).

16. James Fairhead and Melissa Leach, *Misreading the African Landscape: Society and Ecology in a Forest-Savannah Mosaic* (Cambridge: Cambridge University Press, 1996), 2–3, and *Reframing Deforestation: Global Analysis and Local Realities: Studies in West Africa* (London: Routledge, 1998); Melissa Leach and Robin Mearns, eds., *The Lie of the Land: Challenging Received Wisdom on the African Environment* (Oxford: James Currey, 1996).

17. Paul Richards, *Indigenous Agricultural Revolution: Ecology and Food Production in West Africa* (London: Unwin, 1985), 41; Paul Richards, "Ecological Change and the Politics of African Land Use," *African Studies Review* 26 (1983): 1–72.

18. Richards, *Indigenous Agricultural Revolution*, 142.

19. Calestous Juma, *The Gene Hunters: Biotechnology and the Scramble for Seeds* (London: Zed Books, 1989); Amos Kiriro and Calestous Juma, eds., *Gaining Ground: Institutional Innovations in Land-Use Management in Kenya* (Nairobi: Acts Press, 1989).

20. Graham Hardin, "The Tragedy of the Commons," *Science* 162 (December 1968): 1243–48.

21. Gavin Williams, "Introduction: Farmers, Herders and the State," *Rural Africana* 25–26 (1986): 1–23.

22. Katherine Homewood and W. A. Rodgers, "Pastoralism, Conservation and the Overgrazing Controversy," in Anderson and Grove, *Conservation in Africa*, 123.

23. Roy Behnke, Ian Scoones, and Carol Kerven, *Range Ecology at Disequilibrium* (London: Overseas Development Institute, 1993); Ian Scoones, ed., *Living with Uncertainty: New Directions in Pastoral Development in Africa* (London: Intermediate Technology Publications, 1995).

24. Ben Cousins, "Livestock Production and Common Property Struggles in South Africa's Agrarian Reform," *Journal of Peasant Studies* 23, nos. 2–3 (1996), special issue on "The Agrarian Question in South Africa," ed. Henry Bernstein, 166–208.

25. Ramachandra Guha and Joan Martínez-Alier, *Varieties of Environmentalism: Essays North and South* (London: Earthscan, 1997).

26. William Beinart, "Environmental Origins of the Pondoland Revolt," in *South Africa's Environmental History: Cases and Comparisons,* ed. Stephen Dovers, Ruth Edgecombe and Bill Guest (Cape Town: David Philip, 2002), 76–89.

27. Elias C. Mandala, *Work and Control in a Peasant Economy: A History of the Lower Tchiri Valley in Malawi, 1859–1960* (Madison: University of Wisconsin Press, 1990).

28. Megan Vaughan, *The Story of an African Famine: Gender and Famine in Twentieth-Century Malawi* (Cambridge: Cambridge University Press, 1987); Alex de Waal, *Famine That Kills: Darfur, Sudan, 1984–5* (Oxford: Clarendon Press, 1989) and *Famine Crimes: Politics and the Disaster Relief Industry in Africa* (Oxford: James Currey, 1997).

29. Paul E. Lovejoy, *Transformations in Slavery: A History of Slavery in Africa* (Cambridge: Cambridge University Press, 1983); Patrick Manning, *Slavery and African Life: Occidental, Oriental and African Slave Trades* (Cambridge: Cambridge University Press, 1990).

30. Jean-François Bayart, *The State in Africa: The Politics of the Belly* (London: Longman, 1993); Jean-François Bayart, Stephen Ellis, and Beatrice Hibou, *The Criminalization of the State in Africa* (Oxford: James Currey, 1999); Patrick Chabal, *Power in Africa: An Essay in Political Interpretation* (Basingstoke: Macmillan, 1994); P. Chabal and Jean-Pascal Daloz, *Africa Works: Disorder as Political Instrument* (Oxford: James Currey, 1999); Mahmood Mamdani, *Citizen and Subject: Contemporary Africa and the Legacy of Late Colonialism* (London: James Currey, 1996); George B. N. Ayittey, *Africa Betrayed* (New York: St. Martin's Press, 1992).

31. James McCann, *Maize and Grace: Africa's Encounter with a New World Crop, 1500–2000* (Cambridge, MA: Harvard University Press, 2005), 43.

32. John Iliffe, *Africans: The History of a Continent* (Cambridge: Cambridge University Press, 1995), 1.

33. Jan Vansina, in *Paths in the Rainforests: Toward a History of Political Tradition in Equatorial Africa* (London: James Currey, 1990), does not see exhaustion of resources as a necessary part of the process.

34. Graham Connah, *African Civilizations: Precolonial Cities and States in Tropical Africa: An Archaeological Perspective* (Cambridge: Cambridge University Press, 1987), 209.

35. See Robert Harms, *Games against Nature: An Eco-cultural History of the Nunu of Equatorial Africa* (Cambridge: Cambridge University Press, 1987), 245—although he probably pushes the analogy too far.

36. J. E. G. Sutton, "Irrigation and Soil-Conservation in African Agricultural History," *Journal of African History* 25, no. 1 (1984): 25–42.

37. Audrey Richards, *Land, Labour and Diet in Northern Rhodesia: An Economic Study of the Bemba Tribe* (London: International Africa Institute, 1939); Henrietta Moore and Megan Vaughan, *Cutting Down Trees: Gender, Nutrition, and Agricultural Change in the Northern Province of Zambia, 1890–1990* (London: James Currey, 1994).

38. Showers, *Imperial Gullies.*

39. David Maxwell, *Christians and Chiefs in Zimbabwe: A Social History of the Hwesa People, c. 1870s–1990s* (Edinburgh: Edinburgh University Press, 1999), 53 ff.; Terence Ranger, *Voices from the Rocks: Nature, Culture, and History from the Matopos Hills of Zimbabwe* (Bloomington: University of Indiana Press, 1999).

40. Cousins, "Livestock Production and Common Property Struggles," 171; he notes especially Trond Vedeld, "Local Institution-Building and Resource Management in the West African Sahel," Pastoral Development Network, Overseas Development Institute, Network Paper 33c (1992), and Trond Vedeld, *Village Politics: Heterogeneity, Leadership, and Collective Action among the Fulani of Mali* (Ås: Agricultural University of Norway, 1997).

41. Mary Tiffen, Michael Mortimore, and Francis Gichuki, *More People, Less Erosion: Environmental Recovery in Kenya* (Chichester: John Wiley, 1994), 5.

42. Steven Feierman, "Struggles for Control: The Social Roots of Health and Healing in Modern Africa," *African Studies Review* 28 (1985): 73–147; Steven Feierman and John M. Janzen, eds., *The Social Basis of Health and Healing in Africa* (Berkeley: University of California Press, 1992).

43. Helen Tilley, "African Environments and Environmental Sciences," in *Social History and African Environments,* ed. William Beinart and JoAnn McGregor (Oxford: James Currey, 2003), 109–30.

44. M. Priscilla Stone and Paul Richards, "The Integration of the Social and Natural Sciences: The View from the Program on African Studies," unpublished paper.

45. Ben Fine and Colin Stoneman, "Introduction: State and Development," *Journal of Southern African Studies* 22, no. 1 (1996): 5–26, quoting Peter B. Evans, et al., *Bringing the State Back In* (Cambridge: Cambridge University Press, 1985).

46. Elizabeth Colson, *The Social Consequences of Resettlement* (Manchester: Manchester University Press, 1971).

47. David A. McDonald, ed., *Environmental Justice in South Africa* (Athens: Ohio University Press, 2002); David A. McDonald and Greg Ruiters, eds., *The Age of Commodity: Water Privatization in Southern Africa* (Sterling, VA: Earthscan, 2006).

48. Keith Thomas, *Man and the Natural World: Changing Attitudes in England, 1500–1800* (London: Penguin, 1984); Simon Schama, *Landscape and Memory* (London: Fontana, 1996). But see Ute Luig and Achim von Oppen, eds., "The Making of African Landscapes," special issue of *Paideuma: Mitteilungen zur Kulturkunde* 43 (1997).

49. W.H.I. Bleek, *Reynard the Fox in Africa; Or Hottentot Fables and Tales* (London: Trüber and Co., 1864).

50. William Beinart, *The Rise of Conservation in South Africa: Settlers, Livestock, and the Environment, 1770–1950* (Oxford: Oxford University Press, 2003).

51. Maitseo Bolaane, "Chiefs, Hunters and Adventurers; The Foundation of the Okavango/Moremi National Park, Botswana," *Journal of Historical Geography* 31 (2005): 241–59.

52. Mamdani, *Citizen and Subject.*

[17]

Cars Out of Place:
Vampires, Technology, and Labor
in East and Central Africa

LUISE WHITE

THIS ESSAY IS ABOUT things that never happened. The African vampires discussed here are not the undead but men and occasionally women specifically employed—as firemen in East Africa and game rangers in Central Africa—to capture Africans and extract their blood.[1] Such vampires were said to exist throughout much of East and Central Africa; they were a specifically colonial phenomenon and were first noted in the late 1910s and early 1920s. In the colonial versions of these stories, most vampires were black men supervised on the job by white men, but in postcolonial versions who works for whom has become unclear. Although it seems plausible that these stories originated in botched medical procedures done in too great haste during World War I,[2] establishing their source does not account for their meaning thirty years later, or their power, or the passion with which they were retold and withheld. Stories in which colonial employees drained Africans of their blood may reveal more than the vivid imagination of their narrators; they disclose the concerns and anxieties of people at a specific time and place.

Vampires and Colonial
Historiography

The problem of how to interpret the imaginary has haunted the historiography of colonialism like no other issue. "Believe me," wrote Frantz Fanon, "the zombies are more terrifying than the settlers; and in consequence the problem is no longer that of keeping oneself right with the colonial world . . . but of considering three times before urinating, spitting, or going out into the night." He envisioned a day when,

after centuries of unreality, after having wallowed in the most outlandish phantoms, at long last the native, gun in hand, stands face to face with the only forces that contend for his life—the forces of colonialism. And the youth of the colonized country, growing up in an atmosphere of shot and fire . . . does not hesitate to pour scorn on the zombies of his ancestors, the horses with two heads, the djinns who rush into your body while you yawn.[3]

But the opposite appeared to have happened. Survivors of a famine in Malawi recalled that the goats they sold to buy food turned into snakes when their new owners took them home;[4] Africans in colonial Northern Rhodesia who opposed federation with white-dominated Southern Rhodesia believed that sugar had been poisoned by the English "House of Laws" to sap their will;[5] guerrillas in Zimbabwe's war of liberation not only believed in spirit mediums, they claimed to have been supplied with goods by their ancestors' spirits.[6]

How do we account for this? Michael Taussig offers two extremes, that academic representations of superstition are "blind belief in blind belief" and that such explanations reflect another level of reality, "in which faith and skepticism easily coexist."[7] I want to suggest that both analyses are unsatisfactory; they treat imaginary events as make-believe, locating them firmly in the gaze of the observer, not that of the people whom they terrify and fascinate. We must ask instead what things that never happened meant to the people for whom they were real—people who, in many cases, claimed these things happened to them. Rewriting colonial histories means asking how the colonial experience created what Ann Stoler has called "hierarchies of credibility."[8] Dismantling those hierarchies so that phantoms and fantasies can be reinserted into colonial historiography requires linking the revisionist histories themselves with the methodologies on which they are built.

Although postcolonial discourses have provided an undifferentiated account of colonialism,[9] recent research has shown colonialism to be far more fragmented than earlier studies revealed. The colonialism that was, in Frederick Cooper's words, "acceptable in polite company," policed itself, while the colonized struggled to control their own lives.[10] The meaning of ethnicity now seems to have been refashioned under colonial rule,[11] and white power has been deconstructed from a monolith to a fractured group whose cohesion came from the class-based critique of continually redefining who was white and the privileges being white entailed.[12] Making the colonized a disciplined, exploitable labor force, or westernized in any way, was not easy: ex-slaves, for example, struggled to maintain their customary rights to land and crops rather than work as free labor, while casual labor—the work men could do a few days a week or a month to eke out a living—might have been exploited, but it was beyond employers' control.[13] Every shantytown, beggar, and runaway wife was an affront to the ability of colonialists to control the cities they designed.[14] Where labor performed to imperial expectations, it nevertheless produced a cycle of official violence and reform: colonial terrorism had its own aesthetic that made its victims dangerous and primitive, innocent and in need of protection.[15] All this suggests that the dichotomized categories of rulers and ruled are obsolete, and that colonial situations might best be studied for their ambiguities as much as for their injustices.[16]

We know that colonialists understood this—their documents were obsessed with poor whites and the dangers of Africans in European clothing[17]—but how did Africans express the contradictions of their oppression? In African history, the search for African voices with which to write has been an academic obsession for almost thirty years. While the formal study of oral tradition was to provide a concrete methodology with which historians might study a precolonial past filled with mythical heroes and landscapes,[18] colonial historians were not supposed to have such images to interpret. Oral histories were by definition about things that were within a living memory; facts could be checked by interviewing a number of informants. The emphasis was on how to verify, not how to interpret.[19] Even a long overdue feminist critique of oral history addressed the politics of the collection of oral materials, not their interpretation.[20] As ethnography and anthropological objects have been decentered in the last decade,[21] academic attentions have subtly shifted to the individual; methodological debates in oral history have concentrated, like those in literature, on establishing the authority and authenticity of the voice of the colonized.[22] Life histories have come to be considered more authentic than simple interviews; letting African voices speak for themselves has not only become a methodology, it has become a minor publishing enterprise.[23] But concerns about validity, authenticity, and letting Africans speak for themselves are concerns about how scholars may best represent African experiences, concerns that emerged from the very academic processes by which colonial history has been what Gyan Prakesh calls "Third Worlded"—made into an object of study in the First World and given new and powerful meanings by subordinated groups there.[24] But in many cases, establishing the authenticity of the voice—or cacophony of voices—has left it disembodied and decontextualized. Colonial subjects have been enframed as they have been represented. Techniques of authenticating, as Timothy Mitchell has shown, position the observer: "The world is set up before the observing subjects as though it were a picture of something."[25]

The study of colonial vampires may reverse this trend. These vampires are described in a wide variety of oral accounts, and, as descriptions of things that never happened, should begin to subvert some of our ideas about what constitutes authenticity. The study of colonial vampires is authentic not because of any particular legitimacy of the voices I quote, but because it involves writing about the colonial world with the images and idioms produced by the subjects themselves. Like postcolonial rainmaking or the hybrid beasts of modern bride-wealth payments, vampires are an epistemological category with which Africans described their world.[26] I argue that these vampires are not simply generalized metaphors of extraction and oppression but that these images are, like other orally transmitted information, told at specific times to specific people for specific reasons.[27] They describe not only the extraction of blood but how it occurs, who performs it, and under what conditions and inducements. I argue that it is possible to read—or more precisely, to hear—specific vampire accusations as a debate among working men about the nature of work: not its material conditions or remuneration, but how the experience of skilled or semi-skilled labor and involvement with machines could change the men who were so engaged. This is not the only interpretation of vampire accusations that is possible, of course, but it is the one that conforms most closely to the details and the emplotment of working men's accounts. The men quoted here were colonial policemen, firemen, health inspectors, tailors, and railway workers who passed from unskilled apprenticeship to engine drivers. All described these vampires in similar terms, noting the secrecy of the work, the intensity with which it was supervised, and the impossibility of knowing who exactly did it, so that the vampires known to laboring men had definite characteristics. Interpreting vampires from working men's accounts does not tell us more about these vampires than other sources might, but it allows us to examine differentiation in the labor process and within the labor force in the words and categories of laboring men.

Most of the data presented here comes primarily from interviews with former laborers and artisans—men who were not specialized storytellers at all—conducted in rural western Kenya in 1986 and in and around Kampala, Uganda, in 1990. Although many women told these stories with passion and graphic detail as well,[28] this article is based on oral data that was presented to me as men's stories. Many of the returned migrants I interviewed in rural western Kenya claimed that once home they never told their wives these stories because "my wives were adults and could get the stories from other sources,"[29] or "none of my wives could realize the seriousness of these stories, but"—turning to my male research assistant—"a man like you can realize the value and seriousness of any story."[30] Men who claimed to have done the work of capture themselves said "they could not tell anyone, not even my wife" about it, even after they had told my assistant,[31] but a man who narrowly escaped the clutches of Nairobi firemen from a "town toilet" in 1923 told everyone about it: "Why not? I am lucky to have escaped and therefore must talk freely about it."[32] What kind of stories were these, that were so contested, and so gendered, and that were withheld or broadcast according to individual experience, not the story?

These stories were about blood, but they were also about occupations. If blood is taken to be universal, then its power to terrify comes from that; if blood is taken to be a gendered bodily fluid, then the loss of blood is far more alarming to adult men than to adult women.[33] But in either case, blood is the most ambiguous of bodily fluids; according to context it can signify life or death. Other bodily fluids, semen or breast milk, do not. It is possible that stories about blood, and specific forms of its removal, articulate and point out ambiguities. When the systematic removal of blood is associated with a specific occupational group, it suggests that the ambiguities have to do with certain kinds of labor.[34] Read as stories about blood, vampiric firemen represent certain reservations about specific skills, and the alliances made through on-the-job training, hierarchy, and an extended working day.

While published accounts of these stories were not uncommon, most of the data presented in this article are personal narratives. In many ways, these stories fit the format of urban legends—most people believed that it was a well-established fact that firemen captured people for their blood—but the use of folkloric categories does not adequately describe the extent to which these stories were debated and contested by their narrators. Many of my informants insisted that these stories were false because they never met anyone who knew a victim. A few others explained that these stories arose when Africans were unwilling to participate in colonial medical experiments. According to one man, "when the Europeans were here we had a lot of diseases. . . . They were doing research . . . and it was not easy to convince somebody that they were going to do research on them so what they did was to kidnap those people."[35] Another said he was "convinced that these people came from hospitals because nowadays people are required to donate blood for their sick relatives."[36] As late as 1972, a Tanzanian newspaper ran a half-page article explaining that firemen did not kill people.[37] One month later, "Nearly Victim" wrote to the editor refuting the article: "Where did hospitals get their supply of blood in those grim days, before Independence? People used to disappear mysteriously in those days . . . or didn't you know that the blood was used to treat the white man only?"[38] But some people were aware of the ambiguity of these stories: "It seems these stories were true, first of all considering that they existed as stories and those who lost their relatives . . . can prove it. However, those people whose relatives were not taken can say these ·stories were false."[39]

Vehicles and Vampires

Stories about blood-sucking firemen, known in East Africa by variants of the Kiswahili term *wazimamoto*, the men who extinguish the fire (or heat, or light, as in brightness but not as in lamp), and in Central Africa as *banyama*, the men of the meat, or animals, as in game rangers or possibly hunters, cover a wide geographic range, from the East African coast to eastern Zaire to at least as far south as the Limpopo.[40] Many of these narratives contain generic fire brigade vehicles; more often than not, captured people were put into a vehicle and taken away, sometimes to be kept in a pit in the local fire station, "the property of the government."[41] Although there is an obvious association to be made of the red of fire engines and the red of blood—in the unimaginative words of one man, firemen's "equipment is always red and so is blood, therefore any African in the olden days could easily conclude that they were involved in blood-sucking"[42]—it should be noted that this was an association most of my informants generally did not make. In the late 1950s and 1960s Europeans had their own set of rumors about the dangers of driving red cars,[43] but my informants were more concerned with describing "cars which bore a cross"[44] or "a grey Land Rover with a shiny metal back,"[45] than they were with pointing out the dangers of the color red. Indeed, the vehicles they described had no lights and often no windows.

Vehicles in *wazimamoto* stories were not only dangerous, they were found in the most unlikely places and relationships. A sixty-year-old man in Kampala claimed that in the days when "the only departments with cars were the police and fire brigade," the yellow fever department captured people; "but since they had no motor vehicles of their own, they had to use the fire brigade department's motor cars," which was how this rumor began.[46] In rural Tanganyika during World War II a blood drive to supply plasma to troops overseas failed because a fire engine was always stationed by the small airstrip and Africans assumed the blood was to be drunk by Europeans. Years later, it was said that the blood of unconscious Africans was collected in buckets and then rushed to Dar es Salaam in fire engines.[47] In Dar es Salaam in 1947, according to a former superintendent of police, a blood transfusion service was established but had no transport of its own, and so fire engines carried blood donors to the hospital, giving rise to the rumor "that the vehicles, usually with a European volunteer in charge, were collecting African males for their blood and that it was a plot by Europeans to render them impotent."[48] Officials' folklore about the fear of fire engines had it that during Christmas 1959, police in Mbale, Uganda, patrolled the African townships in the local fire engine, to keep even the criminals inside their homes.[49]

Trucks and cars were out of bounds as well. Early in 1939 when the governor of Northern Rhodesia visited the liberal settler Gore-Browne in his unlikely estate in Northern Province, his car was followed by a vanette. This caused great suspicion; it was said that Gore-Browne and the new governor "were concocting plans for kidnapping on a large scale."[50] In Lamu, Kenya, in the mid 1940s, Medical Department trucks patrolled the streets "and, should it come upon a straggler, draws from his veins all his blood with a rubber pump, leaving his body in the gutter."[51] A dozen years later in western Kenya, "motor vehicles painted red" drained the blood from lone pedestrians captured along the Kisumu to Busia highway; the blood was then taken to blood banks in hospitals.[52] In eastern Zambia in 1948 children were lured to trucks on the road at nighttime, made helpless and invisible with the *banyama*'s wands, and taken to towns across the border in Malawi where they were fattened on special foods while the European employers of *banyama* drank their blood; they returned home "very emaciated."[53] The domestic relations of Europeans, when enclosed in vehicles, were extremely suspicious. In rural Tanganyika in the late 1950s a white geologist was attacked; he aroused local suspicions because there were curtains on the windows of his truck.[54] In 1959 in what was then Salisbury, Rhodesia, a "courting couple" in a parked car in an isolated spot were attacked because of "an almost firm belief" that Africans were being captured and drugged and loaded onto a Sabena aircraft on which their bodies were "cut up and canned during the flight" to the Belgian Congo.[55] Automobiles could be made to perform dreadful tasks. In western Kenya in 1968, travelers feared accepting rides because the *wazimamoto* had cars with specially designed backseats that could automatically drain the blood of whoever sat there.[56]

Representing Bureaucracy

What are these stories about? They are about vehicles in unexpected places, used for unintended purposes; these are stories about borrowed transport. But was this borrowing symbolic or literal? Did it represent permeable administrative boundaries or simple lapses in colonial funding and vehicle allocations? Were the signs and symbols of bureaucratic authority being contested in a popular discourse or were official cars being appropriated by underfunded bureaucrats? While I doubt that the Ugandan yellow fever department took blood samples using fire brigade vehicles—Kampala did not have a fire engine until after 1932—everywhere but Nairobi fire-fighting equipment was routinely used, by all accounts badly, by police. Dar es Salaam did not have a fire brigade until 1939; Mombasa until 1940; and Kampala until 1953. Until then untrained police forces were usually unable to contain fires in those cities: "The manipulation of the fire appliances in the event of emergency is left to the unskilled, untrained, and undrilled efforts of a few African constables."[57] In many towns, "we only heard about *wazimamoto* but never saw any."[58] But where there was a formal and well-organized fire brigade, it did not do much better. Nairobi's fire brigade had its own quarters, a fire master, and two fire engines, but in 1926 there was a commission of inquiry to investigate why it was so incompetent, and nine years later it received only forty-two fire calls.[59] After World War II, fire stations became powerful images in some places. In 1947, a riot at the Mombasa Fire Station badly damaged a fire engine.[60] In Dar es Salaam in 1959, "one could observe an occasional African crossing the street to get as far away from the fire station as possible and running when in front of the station."[61] Elsewhere, fire stations did not carry the same meanings.[62] Indeed, the men and women in Kampala who named different departments in Entebbe which received the blood—the welfare department, the yellow fever department, the veterinary department—may not have been confused, they may have been stating the problem of these stories: How do you locate extraction in bureaucracy when bureaucracy seems so fluid?

Indeed, suppose our own academic questions were anticipated, or even essential, to how these stories were narrated? What if the confusion of services and terrors was in fact the emplotment? What if "What were fire engines doing in the places they did not belong?" meant "What sort of society puts fire engines on runways, and blood-draining vehicles on the streets at night?" The account of the blood-draining truck from Lamu, for example, puts the blame firmly on its intent, not its construction. Africans did not misrepresent ambulances—vans with tubes and pumps inside them—but they misrepresented their motives: the trucks did not cure sick people but attacked those unlucky enough to be walking alone at night. These stories may be a colonial, African version of a complaint one now hears daily in Africa: that officials have failed to keep the streets safe. These narratives make access, mobility, and safety into issues for debate and reflection. They make the concrete and the mechanical into problematics.

But it is unlikely that this is all they mean. The presentation of cars in stories, even stories about vampires, reveal popular ideas about the interaction between culture and technology, between bodies and machines.[63] Automobiles generate their own folklore in industrial societies,[64] where they literally become the vehicles for older symbols and associations, and where their material value is at least equal to their symbolic value.[65] That vehicles could be controlled, modified, and transformed may have reflected the imagined powers of their manufacturers or the real needs of their owners.[66] Cars can take people away; motoring and roads are, by definition, ways of erasing boundaries and reclassifying space:[67] roads are someone's order and someone else's disorder. The vanette behind the governor's car, the fire engines on the runway, and the courting couple's darkened car implied the contradiction of orderly relations: they were parked in confusing spaces that blurred boundaries.[68] But the blurred boundaries may not have been those between the yellow fever department and the fire brigade; they may be those between certain kinds of employment and machines: someone's blurred boundaries was someone else's identity. Uniforms, drills, daily polishings of equipment[69]—men "dressed in fire brigade uniforms in the daylight . . . doing this job for Europeans who were at that time their supreme commanders"[70]—all these things made some jobs appear categorically different from the casual labor a man could take up and abandon with ease.

Concealing Men

These stories do not tell us anything about the living African men inside the vehicles.[71] Cars without windows cannot reveal the men inside; so either they were not an important part of these stories, or they were known to be hidden, or they were at least undetectable. One man said he could not be sure of the race of *bazimyomwoto* in Kampala because they always did their work at night.[72] Another claimed that they were chosen for their jobs with great secrecy and caution. "It was not an open job for anybody, you had to be a friend of somebody in the government, and it was top secret, so it was not easy to recruit anybody to begin there, although it was well paid."[73]

If vehicles without windows or lights concealed their occupants, they also hid the work of fighting fires, and the labor process of capturing people: "I only heard that *wazimamoto* sucked blood from people, but I never heard how they got those people."[74] "The act was confidential."[75] The relationship of vehicles—and their specific sounds—to work obscured the work. In Nairobi in the 1940s, "Their actual job was not known to us. All we were told was that they were supposed to put out burning fires. Whenever there was a burning fire we would hear bell noises, and we were told that the *wazimamoto* were on their way to put it out."[76] In general, the *wazimamoto* "ambushed people and threw them in a waiting vehicle,"[77] and "the victims used to call out for help when they were being taken in the vehicle,"[78] but even men and women who narrowly escaped capture did not know much more. In western Kenya late one night in 1959 a woman "found a group of men hiding behind a vehicle that had no lights of any sort." She ran and hid, but they looked for her until "the first cock crowed and one of them said, 'Oh oh oh the time is over.'"[79] In rural Buganda that same year—across eastern Africa, 1959 was a year of widespread blood accusations[80]—a man was awakened by villagers "saying that the place had been invaded by *bazimyomwoto*." He hid behind a large tree and "narrowly evaded capture." In the full moon's light he could see their car and their clothes—"black trousers and white coats"—but could not describe what they did: "Afterwards I heard that several people had lost their blood."[81]

Even men who claimed to have done this work, either as firemen or policemen, described a labor process that had more to do with hierarchies and automobiles than with co-workers. One such man said that capturing Africans was essential to discipline, rank, and on-the-job seniority, but he described the organization of work as a relationship to a white man and a waiting vehicle.

When one joined the police force [in Kampala] in those olden days he would undergo the initial training of bloodsucking. . . . When he qualified there, he was then absorbed into the police force as a constable. This particular training was designed to give the would-be policeman overwhelming guts and courage to execute his duties effectively. . . . During the day we were police recruits. Immediately after sunset we started the job of man-hunting. . . . We would leave the station in a group of four and one white man who was in charge. Once in town we would leave the vehicle and walk around in pairs. When we saw a person, we would lie down and ambush him. We would then take the captured person back to the waiting vehicle. . . . We used to hide vehicles by parking them behind buildings or parking a reasonable distance from our manhunt. . . . The precautions we took were to switch off the engine and the lights.[82]

Here, knowledge of the vehicle is described in much greater detail than is knowledge of the white man. Moreover, the extension of the working day is taken for granted in this account. What does it mean when people describe technology, equipment, and modified vehicles in ways that obscure descriptions of work and the time the work takes? The absence of light and useful windows, the "shiny metal back" made these vehicles closed, protected, and opaque. Their insides were not known. Men who could describe the insides of pits could not describe the insides of trucks.[83] Dangerous vehicles and the modifications specific to them made the men who performed the work of capture safe, secluded, and anonymous; even they could not describe what they did. But veiling labor with different mechanisms—curtains, no lights, shiny metal backs—kept it secret and indicated that something the public should not see was going on inside. Veiling labor focused attention on it, and on the need to maintain secrecy, and made it the object of scrutiny and speculation.[84] Making certain jobs hidden located them in the realm of the imagination; while certain kinds of workers might complain about a lack of public awareness of their jobs, that lack of awareness gave the public enormous control: their description of what went on in the hidden vehicle went unchallenged by the men in the cars.[85] Where Africans could describe the inside of vehicles, it was as a site of fiendish production—the Sabena aircraft on which Africans recently turned into pigs were canned. To counter the fears of what was inside a curtained van a Tanganyikan district officer (and mystery writer) gave villagers a tour of the inside of a white geologist's van; he thought that if they saw what the curtains actually hid—a bed, a table and chairs, and a photograph of a fiancee—he could guarantee the young man's safety.[86]

Technology and Narrative

The veiling of labor was frequently done with metal and electrical equipment. In Kampala it was commonplace to explain that the term *bazimyomwoto* referred to the use of automotive equipment, not to fire fighting. "These people did their job at night, so when they approached somebody they would switch off the lights, and in Kiswahili to switch off is *kuzima* and the light is *moto*."[87] This translation of Kiswahili into Luganda is wrong; *kuzima taa* means "to put out the light"; *kuzima moto* means "to put out the fire." But it is a mistranslation that reflects the importance of automobile equipment in Ugandan vampire stories.

And what is that importance? It seems to be a knowledge of the mechanics of engine sounds and electrical systems. Such technical knowledge is not only specialized and privileged, it conceals a labor process. But such a labor process, that "hidden abode of production," discernible only when one leaves the noise of the factory,[88] may have been kept secret by laborers themselves. Work routines learned on the job may have produced an unexpected camaraderie. A man who was a railway fireman in Nairobi from 1936 to 1958 described a fantastic subterranean system of technical sophistication.

Pipes were installed all over the town. People never used to know the exact place where the pipes were, but us, we used to know. Whites were very clever. They used to cover the pipes and taps with some form of iron sheets. When a fire was burning anywhere we would go locate the tap and fix our hoses up. . . . Running water was there throughout the year, therefore we never experienced any shortage of water at any time of the year.[89]

This account praises informal knowledge, which could only be learned on the job, or from co-workers' conversations and anecdotes, especially in places where recruits were hired off the street and did not graduate from training programs.[90] Nairobi in the mid 1930s had two fire engines and 508 hydrants, and virtually no funds for hydrant or water distribution system repair.[91] In this account the informal expertise of fire fighting—passed from white man to black man—was knowing where the pipes were hidden, not putting out fires. But in Kampala,

they kept victims in big pits. Those pits were made in such a way that no one would notice them. Whites are very bad people. They are so cunning and clever. . . . The job of police recruits was to get victims and nothing else. Occasionally we went down the pits and if we were lucky saw bloodsucking in progress but nothing more. . . . Those pits were really hidden, and even those working within the police station could not notice them.[92]

My point is not that the knowledge of technology was more important than the work itself, but that the knowledge that was otherwise secret bonded a few select Africans to specialized procedures. In 1958 in eastern Zambia, prison warders overheard rumors that the local station of the Society of Missionaries for Africa, everywhere called the White Fathers, were about to kidnap Africans and had already marked their victims with "the Sign of the Cross which was not visible to the intended victim or to his fellows but only to the Europeans and their African henchmen."[93] The invisible signs, the secrets of the pipes and the pits, reveal another dimension to workers' own and popular perceptions of the advantages—technological and social—of skilled labor.

Occupational folklorists have described how technical expertise is parodied by those so skilled—the pilots who board a plane with a white cane and dark glasses—as a challenge to managerial authority.[94] Bolivian tin miners performed ceremonies that denied the importance of skill, "to make the tools help us in our work."[95] African historians who have been able to compare oral and written accounts of the same skilled labor have shown how specialized, skilled labor portrays itself and is portrayed in words of privilege and superiority. Mine managers' views of Basotho shaft sinkers in South Africa, for example, encouraged their sense of superiority but also praised their camaraderie; Basotho shaft sinkers spoke of their favored status in the mine compounds and of the high wages their specialization offered.[96] Workers' narratives may reveal the tensions and conflicts within the workplace that managerial accounts omit. Workers' oral narratives about technology, however imprecise and inaccurate they are, might be a way to foreground the ambiguities and conflicts about the work itself. The man who boasted of the knowledge of hidden pipes he shared with "clever whites" was proud of his on-the-job training. He insisted that in his twenty-two years as a railway fireman he never saw anyone captured, although he admitted that "on seeing us people used to run in all directions."[97] But other men saw certain kinds of skills as inviting danger. A Ugandan man of about the same age said that *bazi-myomwoto* "operated in villages during the night. A bell would be tied up to an electricity pole and when it was rung, immediately a vehicle would drive by to pick victims. Once a man was captured near my home. He was one of the Uganda Electricity Board workers."[98] African concerns about mechanization, about the technological nature of skilled jobs, may have been expressed in vampire stories. These concerns do not seem to have been about the societal impact of mechanization, but were about a gendered boundary between men and machines that could refashion potency and performance.[99] People in Dar es Salaam, for example, feared that the men who went to give blood in fire engines would become impotent, or that firemen had injections that could make men "lazy and unable to do anything."[100] Blood accusations were most public in the mines of colonial Katanga after mechanized shovels were timed and tested against a team of pick and shovel men.[101]

Vampire stories were most private when occupations were neither challenged nor explained. The return home leveled the distinctiveness of the most extraordinary careers: "All policemen in those olden days were the agents of *wazimamoto*." But "when someone was a policeman he remains so even after leaving his job. Policemen are always careful what they leave out. Retired policemen cannot tell you what they were doing during their working time."[102] The same man who described how best to park a car when capturing unwary Africans said he could not tell anyone about it. "How could I do that after swearing to keep secrets? The works of policemen were very hard and involved so many awful things some of which cannot be revealed to anyone. Because of the nature of my work I could not tell anyone even my wife. . . . Even my brothers I could not tell."[103] Storytelling both presents personal identity and allows it to be negotiated and redefined by the audience; withholding stories may permit personal and professional identity to be rigidly maintained.[104] These stories were not explanations; they were accusations: they did not explain misfortune, but imputed work, identity, and loyalty.[105]

Tools of Empire

When studying narratives about vampiric firemen in Africa, it is important that we identify what was weird and unnatural in these stories to their tellers, and not become overly concerned with what seems weird and unnatural to ourselves. It is easy for Western scholars to get bogged down in the issue of blood-drinking Europeans, but that is in fact the most natural part of the story, demonstrated over and over by community and common sense: "Of course the stories were true. . . . People used to warn each other not to walk at night."[106] But what was unnatural and weird to the people who told these stories may well have been those things that were rare and unnatural in their daily lives—cars and electricity.

But these stories are not simple condemnations of technological change and motor transport; medical technology and cars and electrical equipment were, in narrative and in daily life, mediated through a very African medium—working men. Specialized equipment was used by small specialized occupational groups, and for these men, technology had an intense meaning: they talked about it in interviews more than they talked about work. For the most part, technical knowledge was apportioned so sparingly and so slowly that it seemed to defy natural laws, so that railway firemen could claim that they had water even in the dry season. In reality, the allocation of specialized tools and tasks to a few skilled laborers kept most people in ignorance of how automobiles or electricity poles actually worked; on a symbolic level, this kept technology from becoming naturalized in any way.

The very peculiarity of cars, lights, and mirrors made the men who could use them a little peculiar as well. The new tools not only bonded men to machines in odd ways—whatever went on inside the curtained truck—but bound men to mechanization. Marxist theorists of the labor aristocracy have described how the work rhythms required by the technological demands of new industries identified skilled workers with management in nineteenth-century England;[107] although the same processes did not take place in nonindustrialized Africa, it is likely that their specialized tools and techniques placed skilled labor under their employers' control in ways that unskilled labor had never been managed. These men might know where "the clever whites" hid their pipes, or pits, or signs, or have had the on-the-job training "to execute his duties effectively," but they were, in the process, never insulated from their employers' supervision and command.

Tools and technology have recently been studied as one of the ways Europeans dominated the colonized world; they were supposed to overpower Africans or to mystify them.[108] But the contradictory meanings of tools in these stories is too complex, and too layered, to be explained in any single way. The tools in these stories have been assimilated; to some extent, they were already familiar objects, whatever their origin.[109] What made them fearsome was how and why they were used—both in narrative and as narrative. On the Northern Rhodesian Copperbelt there was *mupila*, "white balls of drugs" thrown into the path of a lone traveler to whom the *banyama* then spoke. "If he answered all his power left him, his clothes fell off, and he no longer had a memory or a will."[110] In southeastern Zaire in the 1940s, rubber tubes and flashlights had the same effect.[111] In Dar es Salaam thirty years later, "They use many things to catch people. Sometimes they use a mirror. . . . Your mind changes and you just follow to any place they go."[112] Tools themselves, properly used, could disempower ordinary Africans. Those who were skilled enough to use them lost something too, not direction, but their identity: they became invisible.

Cars Out of Place   39

In these narratives, technology reveals unnatural acts—not blood-sucking, which is weird only to us, or even odd behavior in the backseats of parked cars, but the regimented labor process required by technology: on-the-job training, rank, time discipline, and intense supervision, even after hours. The cars and lights and mirrors in these stories were not the only Western, specialized tools introduced into colonial Africa, but they were the only equipment that regularly featured in vampire stories over a wide geographic and cultural area. These technologies aroused accusations about the forcible removal of blood not because they were foreign or even because they were associated with a dominant power; these technologies featured in these stories because they aroused the greatest anxieties.[113] But they did not arouse anxieties because they were imperfectly understood or imperfectly assimilated or because automobile lights could never become a "natural" African symbol; these were technologies that exposed other kinds of relationships. The presence of bells or cars without lights in so many personal narratives about vampires revealed the extent to which these new tools and technologies meant something terrifying to individual Africans. They were not terrifying in and of themselves but because of how they were used and by whom. In Edwardian England the stirrups became an important symbol of the abuses of gynecology and vivisection; at the same time stirrups figured in the era's pornography.[114] This is not because there was anything incomprehensible about the stirrup, but because stirrups could be used to represent domination, not mobility or sportsmanship, in a variety of contexts. In Eastern Africa, the relationships revealed by the new technologies of cars and bells and lights were those of hard control: intrusive to the point of extracting blood, intensive to the point of supervising skilled labor on the job or after hours. Men and women in Uganda who translated *bazimyomwoto* as "the men who turn off the light" had a powerful, mechanical term to describe the work that extracted blood, the skilled Africans who carried it out, and the whites who supervised them. Naming the vampires after what they did to a car pronounced their work unnatural; it made it clear that these tasks were performed at night, well beyond the standards and the norms of the working day. Thus the term captured the distinctions between the skilled workers, the European overseers, and the population their job it was to abduct.[115]

But how are we to make sense of these particular arrangements of metal and electric lights and blood? Which was most horrible, the draining of blood or the use and abuse of familiar tools and trucks? Certainly the way that vehicles without lights, rubber pumps, or bells became compelling images in these stories made statements about the nature of modernity and progress,[116] but these images were always activated by employed Africans. In Kampala the *bazimyomwoto* "employed agents who lived among the people and had cars."[117] But was it the owners, the drivers, or the cars that took the blood? Such a question may make distinctions that these narratives studiously avoided. While my informants were crystal clear that the *bazimyomwoto* were humans, most described the technological aspects of human agency. They did not make a clear-cut boundary between man and machine, and if we attempt to impose such a line, we may lose sight of their questions and anxieties: If someone works with specific tools in a specific mechanized space, or even when he is taken to donate blood in a fire engine, how can he retain his masculinity, his humanity? What kind of being lives in a truck with curtained windows, and what kind of beings reproduce in the backseat of parked cars?[118]

Conclusions

Why vampires? Why did African men represent the conflicts and problematics of the new economic order in stories about public employees who suck blood? The simplest answer is perhaps best: no other idea could carry the weight of the complications of work, identities, and machines. First, it is a metaphor of colonial origin; despite official attempts to link it to "traditional" practices, *banyama* or *bazimyomwoto* emerged in the late 1910s and early 1920s.[119] Secondly, witchcraft accusations—which do not have the same meaning in the areas under discussion—blame misfortune on individuals; they seek to redress, or at least explain, wrongs. Vampire accusations do not have the same kind of specificity. Although individuals are named and blamed and sometimes even attacked, they were identified as agents, as part of a chain of command: they were not identified in order to get them to reverse their actions; they were identified in order to assess responsibility. Vampires were new symbols for new times.[120] And this made them uniquely well suited to represent the conflicts and ambiguities of labor, because vampiric firemen were not an established fact: many people doubted their existence, and insisted that the rumors began when Africans misconstrued European actions. The debate was not merely about whether or not colonial vampires existed, but about the nature and the attributes of certain kinds of labor. The disputable character of *wazimamoto* was precisely its importance; such disagreements continually posed the questions, Did an identifiably separate group of skilled laborers exist? and, if they did, What was their impact on the wider society?

Notes

Research for this essay was supported by the Division of Humanities at Rice University, the Graduate School at the University of Minnesota, the Institute for the Humanities at the University of Michigan, the American Philosophical Society, and the National Endowment for the Humanities. I would like to thank my research assistants, Odhiambo Opiyo in Siaya, Kenya, and Fred Bukulu, Remigius Kigongo,

Godfrey Kigozi, and William Wagaba in Kampala, Uganda. Mark Auslander, Misty Bastian, William Beinart, Jeanne Bergman, Frederick Cooper, Susan Geiger, Gillian Feeley-Harnik, Ivan Karp, Randall Packard, Stuart Schwartz, and Ann Laura Stoler commented on earlier drafts.

1. I am using the term *vampire* with some hesitation. On the one hand I do not want to submerge an autonomous African category—blood sucker or blood drinker—in a European one, but on the other I would like this work to make sense outside of Africa, and to access the confusions about gender embodied in blood accusations that is a hallmark of *Dracula* scholarship: the removal of blood by the penetration of subcutaneous fluids queries conventional ideas about penetration, orifices, and men and women. See Christopher Craft, "'Kiss Me with Those Red Lips': Gender and Inversion in Bram Stoker's *Dracula*," *Representations* 8 (1984): 107–33; Phyllis A. Roth, "Suddenly Sexual Women in Bram Stoker's *Dracula*," *Literature and Psychology* 27, no. 3 (1977): 113–21; and Stephanie Demetrakopoulos, "Feminism, Sex Role Exchanges, and Other Subliminal Fantasies in Bram Stoker's *Dracula*," *Frontiers: A Journal of Women's Studies* 11, no. 3 (1977): 104–13. Moreover, *Dracula* is a story about racial differences: vampires are not simply undead humans, but a separate group with a distinctive method of feeding and reproduction; see John Allen Stevenson, "A Vampire in the Mirror: The Sexuality of Dracula," *Proceedings of the Modern Language Association* 103, no. 2 (1988): 139–49; and Stephen D. Arata, "The Occidental Tourist: *Dracula* and the Anxiety of Reverse Colonization," *Victorian Studies* 33, no. 4 (1990): 621–45.

2. See Geoffrey Hodges, *The Carrier Corps: Military Labor in the East African Campaign* (Westport, Conn., 1986), 120–39, 206–10.

3. Frantz Fanon, *The Wretched of the Earth*, trans. Constance Farrington (New York, 1963), 56, 58.

4. Megan Vaughan, *The Story of an African Famine: Gender and Famine in Twentieth-Century Malawi* (Cambridge, 1987), vii.

5. Hortense Powdermaker, *Copper Town: Changing Africa* (New York, 1962), 62; Peter Fraenkel, *Wayaleshi* (London, 1959), 196–200; Arnold Leonard Epstein, "Unconscious Factors in the Response to Social Crisis: A Case Study from Central Africa," *Psychoanalytic Study of Society* 8 (1979): 3–39.

6. David Lan, *Guns and Rain: Guerrillas and Spirit Mediums in Zimbabwe* (London, 1985), xv–xvii.

7. Michael T. Taussig, *The Devil and Commodity Fetishism in South America* (Chapel Hill, N.C., 1980), 230.

8. See Ann Laura Stoler, "'In Cold Blood': Hierarchies of Credibility and the Politics of Colonial Narratives," *Representations* 37 (1992): 151–89.

9. See Bill Ashcroft, Gareth Griffiths, and Helen Tiffin, *The Empire Writes Back: Theory and Practice in Postcolonial Literatures* (London, 1989); Kwame Anthony Appiah, "Is the Post- in Postmodernism the Post- in Postcolonial?" *Critical Inquiry* 17, no. 2 (1991): 336–57; Ian Baucom, "Dreams of Home: Colonialism and Postmodernism," *Research in African Literatures* 22, no. 4 (1991), 5–27.

10. Frederick Cooper, "From Free Labor to Family Allowances: Labor and African Society in Colonial Discourse," *American Ethnologist* 16, no. 4 (1989): 745–65; Kristin Mann, *Marrying Well: Marriage, Status, and Social Change Among the Educated Elite in Colonial Lagos* (Cambridge, 1985); William Beinart and Colin Bundy, *Hidden Struggles in Rural South Africa* (London, 1987).

11. John Iliffe, *A Modern History of Tanganyika* (Cambridge, 1979), 314–38; Charles H.

Ambler, *Kenyan Communities in the Age of Imperialism* (New Haven, 1987); Ian Goldin, "The Reconstitution of Coloured Identity in the Western Cape," in Shula Marks and Stanley Trapido, eds., *The Politics of Race, Class, and Nationalism in Twentieth-Century South Africa* (London, 1987), 156–81; David William Cohen and E.S. Atieno Odhiambo, *Siaya: The Historical Anthropology of an African Landscape* (London, 1989), 25–35; Leroy Vail, ed., *The Creation of Tribalism in Southern Africa* (Berkeley, 1989).

12. David Arnold, "European Orphans and Vagrants in India in the Nineteenth Century," *Journal of Imperial and Commonwealth History* 7, no. 2 (1979), 104–27; Dane Kennedy, *Islands of White: Settler Society and Culture in Kenya and Southern Rhodesia, 1890–1939* (Durham, N.C., 1987); Waltraud Ernst, "The European Insane in British India, 1800–1858: A Case Study in Psychiatry and Colonial Rule," in David Arnold, ed., *Imperial Medicine and Indigenous Societies* (Manchester, Eng., 1988), 27–44; Ann Laura Stoler, "Rethinking Colonial Categories: European Communities and the Boundaries of Rule," *Comparative Studies in Society and History* 31, no. 1 (1989): 134–61.

13. Frederick Cooper, *From Slaves to Squatters: Plantation Labor in Zanzibar and Coastal Kenya, 1890–1925* (New Haven, 1980); and *On the African Waterfront: Urban Disorder and the Transformation of Work in Colonial Mombasa* (New Haven, 1987); Louise Lennihan, "Rights in Men and Rights in Land: Slavery, Labor, and Smallholder Agriculture in Northern Nigeria," *Slavery and Abolition* 3, no. 2 (1982): 111–39; Suzanne Miers and Richard Roberts, eds., *The End of Slavery in Africa* (Madison, Wisc., 1988); Dipesh Chakrabarty, "Conditions for Knowledge of Working-Class Conditions: Employers, Government, and the Jute Workers of Calcutta, 1890–1940," *Subaltern Studies* 2 (1983): 259–310.

14. Marjorie Mbilinyi, "Runaway Wives in Colonial Tanganyika: Forced Labour and Forced Marriage in Rungwe District, 1919–1961," *International Journal of the Sociology of Law* 16 (1988): 1–29; and "'This Is Unforgettable Business': Colonial State Intervention in Urban Tanzania," in Jane L. Parpart and Kathleen A. Staudt, *Women and the State in Africa* (Boulder, Colo., 1989), 111–29; Philip L. Bonner, "Family, Crime, and Political Consciousness on the East Rand, 1939–1955," *Journal of Southern African Studies* 14, no. 3 (1988): 393–420; Luise White, *The Comforts of Home: Prostitution in Colonial Nairobi* (Chicago, 1990), 65–72, 126–46, 212–17, 221–28.

15. Ranajit Guha, "The Prose of Counter-Insurgency," *Subaltern Studies* 2 (1983): 1–42; Michael T. Taussig, *Shamanism, Colonialism, and the Wild Man: A Study in Terror and Healing* (Chicago, 1987), 2–134; Frederick Cooper, "Mau Mau and the Discourses of Decolonization," *Journal of African History* 29, no. 2 (1988): 313–20. For gendered critiques, see Lata Mani, "Contentious Traditions: The Debate on SATI in Colonial India," *Cultural Critique* 7 (1987): 119–56; and Luise White, "Separating the Men from the Boys: The Construction of Sexuality, Gender, and Terrorism in Central Kenya, 1939–59," *International Journal of African Historical Studies* 25, no. 1 (1990): 1–25.

16. Homi K. Bhabha, "Signs Taken for Wonders: Questions of Ambivalence and Authority Under a Tree Outside Delhi, May 1817," *Critical Inquiry* 12 (1985): 144–65; David Arnold, "Touching the Body: Perspectives on the Indian Plague, 1896–1900," *Subaltern Studies* 5 (1987): 55–90; Achille Mbembe, "Domaines de la nuit et autorité onirique dans les Maquis du Sud-Cameroun, 1955–1958," *Journal of African History* 32, no. 1 (1991): 89–121; and Gayatri Spivak, quoted in Henry Louis Gates, Jr., "Critical Fanonism," *Critical Inquiry* 17 (1991): 466.

17. Arnold, "European Orphans," 104–27; Randall M. Packard, "The 'Healthy Reserve' and the 'Dressed Native': Discourses on Black Health and the Language of Legiti-

Cars Out of Place   **43**

mation in South Africa," *American Ethnologist* 16, no. 4 (1989): 686–703; Ann Laura Stoler, "Carnal Knowledge and Imperial Power: Gender, Race, and Morality in Colonial Asia," in Micaela di Leonardo, ed., *Gender at the Crossroads of Knowledge: Feminist Anthropology in the Postmodern Era* (Berkeley, 1991), 51–101.

18. Jan Vansina, *Oral Tradition* (Chicago, 1967); and Vansina, *Oral Tradition as History* (Madison, 1985); David Henige, *The Chronology of Oral Tradition: Quest for a Chimera* (Oxford, 1974); Joseph C. Miller, ed., *The African Past Speaks: Essays on Oral Tradition and History* (Folkstone, Eng., 1980); Luc de Heusch, *The Drunken King; or, The Origin of the State*, trans. Roy Willis (Bloomington, Ind., 1982); V. Y. Mudimbe, *Parables and Fables: Exegesis, Textuality, and Politics in Central Africa* (Madison, Wisc., 1991), 86–138.

19. Vansina, *Oral Tradition as History*, 12–13; White, *Comforts of Home*, 21–28. In this way, the study of witchcraft or of men who turned into lions became primarily the domain of anthropologists, not historians.

20. Claire C. Robertson, "In Pursuit of Life Histories: The Problem of Bias," *Frontiers* 7, no. 2 (1983): 63–69; Susan N. G. Geiger, "Women's Life Histories: Content and Method," *Signs: Journal of Women in Culture and Society* 11, no. 2 (1986): 334–51; and "What's So Feminist About Women's Oral History," *Journal of Women's History* 2, no. 1 (1990): 169–82; Marjorie Mbilinyi, "'I'd Have Been a Man': Politics and the Labor Process in Producing Personal Narratives," and Marjorie Shostak, "'What the Wind Won't Take Away': The Genesis of *Nisa—the Life and Words of a !Kung Woman*," in Personal Narratives Group, *Interpreting Women's Lives: Feminist Theory and Personal Narratives* (Bloomington, Ind., 1989), 204–27, 228–40.

21. Johannes Fabian, *Time and the Other: How Anthropology Makes Its Object* (New York, 1983); and James Clifford and George E. Marcus, eds., *Writing Culture: The Poetics and Politics of Ethnography* (Berkeley, 1986). In African history, the disaffection with the ethnographic object was as much a product of the researches of nationalist historiography as it was of debates in anthropology; see Steven Feierman, *Peasant Intellectuals: Anthropology and History in Tanzania* (Madison, Wisc., 1990), 13–17.

22. There is a useful summary of literary debates in Gates, "Critical Fanonism," 457–70; but see Gayatri Chakrovarty Spivak, "Can the Subaltern Speak?," in Cary Nelson and Lawrence Grossberg, eds., *Marxism and the Interpretation of Culture* (Urbana, Ill., 1988), 127–57. For debates within oral history and anthropology, see also Vansina, *Oral Tradition as History*, 18–21; Sidney W. Mintz, "The Sensation of Moving, While Standing Still," *American Ethnologist* 16, no. 4 (1989): 786–96; and J. B. Peires, "Suicide or Genocide?: Xhosa Perceptions of the Nongqawuse Catastrophe," *Radical History Review* 46, no. 7 (1990): 47–57.

23. See Mary Smith, *Baba of Karo: A Woman of the Muslim Hausa* (London, 1954; new ed., New Haven, 1981); Marjorie Shostak, *Nisa: The Life and Words of a !Kung Woman* (New York, 1983); Jean Davison with the women of Mutira, *Voices from Mutira: Lives of Rural Gikuyu Women* (Boulder, Colo., 1989); Margaret Strobel and Sarah Mirza, *Three Swahili Women: Life Histories from Mombasa, Kenya* (Bloomington, Ind., 1989); and the U.S.-produced Swahili edition, *Wanawake watatu wa Kiswahili: Hadithi za maisha kutoka Mombasa, Kenya* (Bloomington, Ind., 1991); Belinda Bozzoli with the assistance of Mmantho Nkotsoe, *Women of Phokeng: Consciousness, Life Strategy, and Migrancy in South Africa* (Portsmouth, N.H., 1991). The Swahili version of *Three Swahili Women* was published in the United States because no Kenyan publisher was interested; see Geiger, "Women's Life Histories," 182n. The life histories of women tend to proclaim their authenticity; see Domitila Barrios de Chungara and Moema Viezzer, *Let Me Speak!: Testimony of Domitila, a Woman of the Bolivian Mines* (New York, 1978), while those of

men are often summarized by scholars, without apology; see Hoyt Alverson, *Mind in the Heart of Darkness: Value and Self-Identity Among the Tswana of Southern Africa* (New Haven, 1978); Tim Keegan, *Facing the Storm: Portraits of Black Lives in Rural South Africa* (London, 1988); and Paul Lubeck, "Petroleum and Proletarianization: The Life History of a Muslim Nigerian Worker," *African Economic History* 18 (1989): 99–112. For a notable exception, see Allen Isaacman, ed., *The Life History of Roul Honwana: An Inside View of Colonialism to Independence, 1905–75* (Boulder, Colo., 1988).

24. Gyan Prakash, "Writing Post-Orientalist Histories of the Third World: Perspectives from Indian Historiography," *Comparative Studies in Society and History* 32, no. 2 (1990): 383–408; see also Gates, "Critical Fanonism," 457–60.

25. Timothy Mitchell, *Colonizing Egypt* (Berkeley, 1991), 60.

26. See Feierman, *Peasant Intellectuals*, 245–64; and Jean and John L. Comaroff, "Goodly Beasts, Beastly Goods: Cattle and Commodities in a South African Context," *American Ethnologist* 17, no. 2 (1990): 195–216; Sharon Hutchinson, "The Cattle of Money and the Cattle of Girls Among the Neur, 1930–83," *American Ethnologist* 19, no. 2 (1992): 294–316.

27. See for example the freewheeling discussion of *Dracula* in Franco Moretti, *Signs Taken for Wonders: Essays in the Sociology of Literary Forms* (New York, 1983), 90–104; and Taussig's account of the Nakaq, the fat-extracting phantasm of the southern highlands of Peru, *Devil and Commodity Fetishism*, 238.

28. For urban women's stories, see Luise White, "Bodily Fluids and Usufruct: Controlling Property in Nairobi, 1919–39," *Canadian Journal of African Studies* 24, no. 3 (1990): 418–38.

29. Peter Hayombe, Uhunyi Village, Alego, Siaya District, Kenya, 20 August 1986; see also Menya Mauwa, Uchonga Village, Alego, Siaya District, Kenya, 19 August 1986.

30. Zebede Oyoyo, Goma Village, Yimbo, Siaya District, Kenya, 13 August 1986.

31. Anyango Mahondo, Sigoma Village, Alego, Siaya District, Kenya, 15 August 1986. Throughout the interview Mahondo insisted that my assistant, Odhiambo Opiyo, not tell me about his days as a policeman, despite the fact that I was sitting between them and Opiyo and I were conferring in English during the interview.

32. Zebede Oyoyo.

33. Rodney Needham, "Blood, Thunder, and the Mockery of Animals," *Sociologus* 14, no. 2 (1964): 136–49; Victor Turner, *The Forest of Symbols: Aspects of Ndembu Ritual* (Ithaca, N.Y., 1967), 41–42, 59–81, 249–51; Luc de Heusch, *The Drunken King; or, The Origin of the State* (Bloomington, Ind., 1982), 168–73.

34. In Kenya in 1939 there was a spate of rumors about blankets saturated with a medicine that would make men impotent: this was a semen story, to be sure, and it involved Europeans, technology, and commodities, but it did not involve labor; *Nairobi District Annual Report, 1939*, p. 3, Kenya National Archives (KNA) /CP4/4/1.

35. George Ggingo, Kasubi, Uganda, 15 August 1990.

36. Ofwete Muriar, Uchonga Village, Alego, Siaya District, Kenya, 11 August 1986; see also Kersau Ntale Mwene, Kasubi, Uganda, 12 August 1990; Joseph Nsubuga, Kisati, Uganda, 22 August 1990; letter to the editor, *The Standard* (Tanzania), 2 February 1972, 6.

37. S. Lolila, "Firemen Are Not 'Chinja-Chinja,'" *The Standard*, 10 January 1972, 3. *Chinja-chinja* is the intensive form of the word for "slaughterer" and is sometimes used interchangeably with the local term for vampire in East Africa.

38. Letter, *The Standard*, 2 February 1972, 6.

39. Gregory Sseruwagi, Lubya, Uganda, 28 August 1990.

Cars Out of Place **45**

40. Rik Ceyssens, "Mutumbula: Mythe de l'opprime," *Cultures et développement* 7, nos. 3–4 (1975): 485–550; Mwelwa C. Musambachime, "The Impact of Rumor: The Case of Banyama (Vampire-Men) Scare in Northern Rhodesia, 1930–1964," *International Journal of African Historical Studies* 21, no. 2 (1988): 201–15.

41. Anyango Mahondo.

42. Ibid.

43. V. W. Brelsford, "The 'Banyama' Myth," *NADA* (Ministry of Internal Affairs, Salisbury, Rhodesia) 9, no. 4 (1967): 54–56; J. A. K. Leslie, personal communication, 13 March 1990; Graham Thompson, personal communication, 28 August 1990; Atieno Odhiambo, personal communication, 31 December 1990.

44. Abdullah Sonsomola, Kisenyi, Uganda, 28 August 1990.

45. Peter Fraenkel, *Wayaleshi* (London, 1959), 201.

46. Samuel Mubiru, Lubya, Uganda, 28 August 1990. But according to E. E. Hutchins, district officer in Morogoro with many years' experience in Tanganyika,

> The old story that certain Europeans wandered about the country seeking human blood for the purpose of making medicine was revived, I believe, some years ago in the Kiloga District, where officers of the Veterinary Department collected blood in test tubes from numbers of natives for the purpose of finding out whether yellow fever had ever been endemic in the Territory.

Morogoro District, vol. 1, part A, sheets 25–26, August 1931, film no. MF15, Tanzanian National Archives (TNA).

47. W. Arens, *The Man-Eating Myth: Anthropology and Anthropophagy* (Oxford, 1979), 12–13.

48. Michael Macoun, personal communication, 13 March 1990.

49. Brelsford, "The 'Banyama' Myth," 54.

50. Thomas Fox-Pitt, District Commissioner, Mpika, to Provincial Commissioner, Northern Province, Kasama, 6 March 1939, National Archives of Zambia (NAZ)/SEC2/429, Native Affairs: Banyama.

51. Elspeth Huxley, *The Sorcerer's Apprentice: A Journey Through East Africa* (London, 1948), 23.

52. E. S. Atieno Odhiambo, "The Movement of Ideas: A Case Study of the Intellectual Responses to Colonialism Among the Liganua Peasants," in Bethwell A. Ogot, ed., *Hadith 6: History and Social Change in East Africa* (Nairobi, 1976), 172.

53. John Barnes, Fort Jameson, Northern Rhodesia, to J. Clyde Mitchell, Rhodes-Livingstone Institute, Lusaka, 10 October 1948, J. C. Mitchell Papers, Rhodes House, Oxford, MSS. Afr. s. 1998/4/1.

54. Darrell Bates, *The Mango and the Palm* (London, 1962), 51–53.

55. K. D. Leaver, "The 'Transformation of Men to Meat' Story," NADform Information Sheet no. 20, Native Affairs Department, Salisbury, November 1960, p. 2, National Archives, Zimbabwe; Brelsford, "The 'Banyama' Myth," 54–55. Similar stories about pigs were commonplace in the southern Belgian Congo in the 1940s; see Ceyssens, "Mutumbula," 586–87.

56. Author's field notes, 18 August 1986.

57. N. W. Cavendish, Commissioner, Kenya Police, to Chief Secretary, Nairobi, 11 March 1939, KNA/CS/1/19/4, Fire Fighting in East Africa, 1933–46; see also the Luganda newspaper *Matalisi*, 25 March 1925, 6–7, Makarere University Library; *Uganda Herald*, 24 April 1931, 1; *Uganda Police Annual Report, 1950* (Kampala, 1951), 29–30; *Uganda Police Annual Report, 1951* (Kampala, 1952), 34; *Uganda Police Annual Report,*

1952 (Kampala, 1953), 33–34; Works and Public Health Committee, 10 May 1938, KNA/PC/NBl/2/53, Municipal Nairobi Council Minutes, 1938.

58. Nichodamus Okumu Ogutu, Uhuyi Village, West Alego, Siaya District, Kenya, 28 August 1986.

59. Nairobi Fire Commission, 1926, KNA/AG4/3068; J. B. Powell, Superintendent, Nairobi Fire Brigade, Annual Report, 1935, KNA/PC/NB1/2/50, Nairobi Municipal Council Minutes, January–June 1936.

60. "'Human Vampire' Story Incites Mombasa Mob's Fire Station Attack," *East African Standard*, 21 June 1947, 3; Kenya Colony and Protectorate, *Report on Native Affairs, 1939–47* (London, 1948), 83; George to Elspeth Huxley, 20 January n.d., Elspeth Huxley Papers, Rhodes House, Oxford, RH MSS. Afr. s. 782, box 2/2, Kenya (1).

61. William H. Friedland, "Some Urban Myths of East Africa," in Allie Dubb, ed., *Myth in Modern Africa* (Lusaka, 1960), 94.

62. In 1959 in Kampala a man was sentenced to three years in prison for attempting to sell another man to the fire station, but the fear of the fire station and the fire brigade in and of itself never entered the oral record in Uganda. See "Three Years for Attempt to Sell Man," *Uganda Argus*, 16 February 1959, 5; "Firemen Do Not Buy People," *Tanganyika Standard*, 16 February 1959, 3.

63. Eric Mottram, *Blood on the Nash Ambassador: Investigations in American Culture* (London, 1983), 62ff. Such concerns are articulated in popular idioms in diverse contexts; see Barbara Allen, "'The Image on Glass': Technology, Tradition, and the Emergence of Folklore," *Western Folklore* 41 (1982), 85–103; and Caroline Walker Bynum, "Material Continuity, Personal Survival, and the Resurrection of the Body: A Scholastic Discussion in its Medieval and Modern Contexts," *History of Religions* 30, no. 1 (1990): 51–85.

64. See for example Jan Harold Brunvand, *The Vanishing Hitchhiker: American Urban Legends and Their Meanings* (New York, 1981), 19–46; and *The Choking Doberman* (New York, 1984), 50–68.

65. Stewart Sanderson, "The Folklore of the Motor-Car," *Folklore* 80 (1969): 241–42.

66. See Sanderson's collection of rumors about the Rolls-Royce, ibid., 246–47; and F. H. Moorhouse, "The 'Work' Ethic and 'Leisure' Activity: The Hot Rod in Post-War America," in Patrick Joyce, ed., *The Historical Meanings of Work* (Cambridge, 1987), 244.

67. Warren James Belasco, *Americans on the Road: From Autocamp to Motel, 1910–1945* (Cambridge, Mass., 1981), 8.

68. See Mary Douglas, *Purity and Danger: An Analysis of the Concepts of Pollution and Taboo* (London, 1984), 35, 85.

69. In 1935 nine and a half hours of a Nairobi fireman's day were devoted to "station duties" and maintaining equipment, and the nightly lookout had to report "every fifteen minutes. . . . This is salutary from a disciplinary point of view, as well as keeping the guard awake"; J. B. Powell, Superintendent, Nairobi Municipal Fire Brigade AE, 1935, Nairobi Municipal Council Minutes, January–June 1936, KNA/PC/NB12/50.

70. Daniel Sekirrata, Katwe, Uganda, 22 August 1990.

71. Dead bodies transported in vehicles were another matter, however. Corpses were purchased from hospitals and driven to Zaire. Several men "transported dead bodies in the back seat of his car. These bodies were always smartly dressed." A few others sold corpses "to Senegalese who used them to safely transport their gold in. These dead bodies were cut through the skin, opened inside, and then gold could be

dumped there. If the authorities tried to arrest them, these people could claim they were taking sick relatives for treatment." Ahmed Kiziri, Katwe, Uganda, 20 August 1990; Musoke Kopliumu, Katwe, Uganda, 22 August 1990; Daniel Sekirrata, Katwe, Uganda, 22 August 1990; Gregory Sseruwagi, Lubya, Uganda, 28 August 1990.

72. Sepirya Kasule, Kisenyi, Uganda, 28 August 1990.

73. George Ggingo, Kasubi, Uganda, 15 August 1990.

74. Noah Asingo Olungu, Goma Village, Yimbo, Siaya District, Kenya, 22 August 1986.

75. Simbwa Jjuko, Lwaze, Uganda, 20 August 1990.

76. Peter Hayombe.

77. Domitila Achola, Uchonga Ukudi Village, Alego, Siaya District, Kenya, 11 August 1986; Alozius Kironde, Kasubi, Uganda, 17 August 1990.

78. Alozius Kironde, Kasubi, Uganda, 17 August 1990.

79. Margaret Mwajuma, Ndegro Uranga Village, Alego, Siaya, Kenya, 11 August 1986.

80. Brelsford, "The 'Banyama' Myth," 54–56.

81. Gregory Sseruwagi, Lubya, Uganda, 28 August 1990.

82. Anyango Mahondo.

83. See White, "Bodily Fluids," 425–31.

84. Ludmilla Jordanova, *Sexual Visions: Images of Gender in Science and Medicine Between the Eighteenth and Twentieth Centuries* (London, 1989), 92–93.

85. Washington, D.C., fire fighters routinely complained that the public's ignorance of fire fighting increased the likelihood of fires while maintaining that the techniques and challenges of their work made it too esoteric to make public; see Robert McCarl, *The District of Columbia Fire Fighters' Project: A Case Study in Occupational Folklife* (Washington, 1985), 131–36.

86. Bates, *Mango and Palm*; 53–54.

87. George Ggingo; see also Mangarita Kalule, Masanafu, Uganda, 20 August 1990; Juliana Nakibuka Naloongo, Lubaga, Uganda, 21 August 1990; Joseph Nsubuge, Kisati, Uganda, 22 August 1990; Musoke Kopliumu, Katwe, Kampala, Uganda, 22 August 1990; Gregory Sseruwagi, Lubya, Uganda, 28 August 1990.

88. Karl Marx, *Capital, A Critique of Political Economy*, vol. 1 (Harmondsworth, Eng., 1976), 279–80.

89. Alec Okaro, Mahero Village, Alego, Siaya District, Kenya, 12 August 1986.

90. McCarl, *District of Columbia Fire Fighters' Project*, 39, 136–40. Apprenticeship, however, was often parodied by religious movements in colonial Zaire; see Edouard Bustin, "Government Policy Toward African Cult Movements: The Cases of Katanga," in Mark Karp, ed., *African Dimensions: Essays in Honor of William O. Brown* (Boston, 1975), 117.

91. J. B. Powell, Superintendent, *Nairobi Municipal Fire Brigade Annual Report, 1935*, Nairobi Municipal Council Minutes, January–June 1936, KNA/PC/NB1/2/50.

92. Anyango Mahondo.

93. Brelsford, "The 'Banyama' Myth," 55.

94. Jack Santino, "'Flew the Ocean in a Plane': An Investigation of Airline Occupation Narrative," *Journal of the Folklore Institute* 15, no. 3 (1978): 202–7.

95. A miner quoted in June Nash, "The Devil in Bolivia's Nationalized Tin Mines," *Science and Society* 36, no. 2 (1972): 227; for another interpretation, see Taussig, *Devil and Commodity Fetishism*, 207–13.

96. Jeff Guy, "Technology, Ethnicity, and Ideology: Basotho Miners and Shaft Sinking on the South African Gold Mines," *Journal of Southern African Studies* 14, no. 2 (1988): 260–69.

97. Alec Okaro.

98. Sepirya Kasule. In Buhaya, just across the border in Tanzania, in the 1980s it was said that anyone who opened a door that warned "hatari umeme!" (danger electricity!) would die at once, and his body tossed in a pit in back. See Brad Weiss, "Electric Vampires: Haya Rumors of Wealth" (Paper presented at American Ethnological Society, Memphis, March 1992).

99. Guy, "Technology, Ethnicity, and Ideology," 269, gives a particularly graphic example of a point that has been made both by Antonio Gramsci ("The history of industrialism has always been a continuing struggle . . . against the element of 'animality' in man") and in studies of anti-vivisection movements; see Antonio Gramsci, *Selections from the Prison Notebooks*, ed. and trans. Quintin Hoare and Geoffrey Nowell Smith (New York, 1971), 297–98; Coral Lansbury, *The Old Brown Dog: Women, Workers, and Vivisection in Edwardian England* (Madison, Wisc., 1985), 83–119; and Susan Sperling, *Animal Liberators: Research and Morality* (Berkeley, 1990), 141–43.

100. Quoted in Lloyd William Swantz, "The Role of Medicine Men Among the Zaramo of Dar es Salaam" (Ph.D. diss., University of Dar es Salaam, 1972), 336.

101. John Higginson, "Steam Without a Piston Box: Strikes and Popular Unrest in Katanga, 1943–1945," *International Journal of African Historical Studies* 21, no. 1 (1988): 101–2.

102. Timotheo Omondo, Goma Village, Yimbo, Siaya District, Kenya, 22 August 1986.

103. Anyango Mahondo.

104. This point comes from two articles by Jack Santino: "Miles of Smiles, Years of Struggle: The Negotiation of Black Occupational Identity Through the Personal Experience Narrative," *Journal of American Folklore* 96, no. 382 (1983): 394–412; and "Occupational Ghostlore: Social Context and the Expression of Belief," *Journal of American Folklore* 101, no. 400 (1988): 207–18.

105. In the classic sense, misfortune is something that requires an explanation, such as why a granary in Azande country collapsed on specific people; see E. E. Evans-Pritchard, *Witchcraft, Oracles, and Magic Among the Azande* (Oxford, 1976), 22–23. Vampire accusations do not explain disappearances or deaths; indeed, the fact that someone had disappeared was offered as "proof" that the firemen did kidnap people; see page 31 of this essay.

106. Nyakida Omolo, Kabura, West Alego, Siaya District, Kenya, 19 August 1986.

107. F. H. Moorhouse, "The Marxist Theory of the Labour Aristocracy," *Social History* 3, no. 1 (1978): 64–66.

108. Daniel R. Headrick, *The Tools of Empire: Technology and European Imperialism in the Nineteenth Century* (Oxford, 1981); and Michael Adas, *Machines as the Measures of Men: Science, Technology, and Ideologies of Western Dominance* (Ithaca, N.Y., 1989).

109. See Ivan Karp, "Other Cultures in Museum Perspective," in Karp and Steven D. Levine, *Exhibiting Cultures: The Poetics and Politics of Museum Displays* (Washington, 1991), 373–85.

110. *Mutende* (Lusaka) no. 38 (1936), NAZ/SEC2/429, Native Affairs: Banyama; Eustace Njbovu, Kapani, Luangwa, Zambia, 22 July 1990.

111. Ceyssens, "Mutumbula," 491.

112. Quoted in Swantz, "Medicine Men," 336.

113. Gary Allen Fine, "The Kentucky Fried Rat: Legends and Modern Society," *Journal of the Folklore Institute* 17, nos. 2–3 (1980): 237; Allen, "'Image on Glass,'" 103; Bynum, "Material Continuity," 64.

114. Lansbury, *Old Brown Dog*, 99–111.

115. Moretti, *Signs Taken for Wonders*, makes a similar point about horror literature, particularly *Frankenstein* and *Dracula*: both represent the extremes of a society, he argues; "The literature of terror is born *precisely out of the terror of a split society*, and out of the desire to heal it" (83).

116. See Jordanova, *Sexual Visions*, 111.

117. Samuel Mubiru.

118. *Embalasassa*, the mythical "poisonous reptiles that politicians never wanted to talk about publicly," were said to be sent by Milton Obote during his first regime to kill the Baganda people; they could also breed in machines. "Somewhere . . . near Kaziba market [on the Tanzanian border] there was something made out of an old army tank that the villagers broke into only to discover *embalasassa* eggs inside"; Jonah Waswa Kigozi, Katwe, Uganda, 16 August 1990; Alozius Matovu, Kasubi, Uganda, 17 August 1990; see also W. B. Banage, W. N. Byarugaba, and J. D. Goodman, "The *Embalasassa* (*Riopa fernandi*): A Story of Real and Mythical Zoology," *Uganda Journal* 36 (1972): 67–72.

119. Timotheo Omondo; E. E. Hutchins, District Officer, Morogoro, vol. 1, part A, sheets 25–26, August 1931, film MF 15, TNA. D. Willis, Provincial Commissioner, Kasama, "Report on Banyama," 24 March 1931, NAZ/ZA1/9/62/6/1; Geoffrey Howe, Provincial Commissioner, Northern Province, Kasama, "Confidential Memo to All DCs, Northern Province," 24 April 1944, NAZ/SEC2/429, Native Affairs: Banyama.

120. See Moretti, *Signs Taken for Wonders*, 90–104; and Gabor Klaniczay, *The Uses of the Supernatural: The Transformation of Popular Religion in Medieval and Early Modern Europe*, trans. Susan Singerman (Princeton, N.J., 1990), 168–238.

Part VI
The Circulation of Knowledge

[18]

Global Knowledge on the Move

Itineraries, Amerindian Narratives, and Deep Histories of Science

By Neil Safier*

ABSTRACT

Since Bruno Latour's discussion of a Sakhalin island map used by La Pérouse as part of a global network of "immutable mobiles," the commensurability of European and non-European knowledge has become an important issue for historians of science. But recent studies have challenged these dichotomous categories as reductive and inadequate for understanding the fluid nature of identities, their relational origins, and their historically constituted character. Itineraries of knowledge transfer, traced in the wake of objects and individuals, offer a powerful heuristic alternative, bypassing artificial epistemological divides and avoiding the limited scale of national or monolingual frames. Approaches that place undue emphasis either on the omnipotence of the imperial center or the centrality of the colonial periphery see only half the picture. Instead, practices of knowledge collection, codification, elaboration, and dissemination—in European, indigenous, and mixed or hybrid contexts—can be better understood by following their moveable parts, with a keen sensitivity toward non-normative epistemologies and more profound temporal frameworks.

D URING A CONTEMPLATIVE MOMENT in the late eighteenth century, along the shores of a sizable tributary of the Amazon River, a Brazilian-born naturalist named Alexandre Rodrigues Ferreira (1756–1815) paused to consider how native peoples of that region conceptualized geographical matters. Along with a gardener and two sketch artists, Ferreira had amassed an encyclopedic collection of botanical, faunal, and ethnological specimens during his decade-long journey (1783–1792) through the South American

* Department of History, University of British Columbia, 1873 East Mall, Room 1297, Vancouver, British Columbia V6T 1Z1, Canada.

I would like to thank Michael Dettelbach, Florence Hsia, and Neil Whitehead for early conversations on this topic; the Department of History's Science and Technology Studies Cluster at the University of British Columbia for comments on an early draft of this essay; Simon Schaffer, Jim Secord, and the participants at the May 2009 CRASSH seminar in Cambridge for their queries and suggestions; Bernie Lightman for his editorial observations; and Sujit Sivasundaram for organizing both the Cambridge meeting and this Focus section and for having graciously invited me to participate.

134   FOCUS—ISIS, 101 : 1 (2010)

tropics. Like most travelers in the tropical forest, he depended largely on indigenous local guides and native informant-intermediaries to help him navigate the ever-changing conditions of Amazonia's fluvial labyrinth. So it is especially striking that in order to understand native geographic practices he couched his reflections in decidedly European terms: "What," he asked, "might a European raised like one of these *tapuia* do if asked [to describe] a river, its direction, its tributaries, [and] the number of villages that sit upon it, being ignorant of the existence of geometry, geography, hydrography, etc.?" The question he posed that day about native skills seems to have been more about epistemological commensurability than about indigenous prowess. It appeared to compare abilities acquired through the social and cultural conditions that reigned in the tropical lowlands of South America with those skills for comprehending science that would have been innately available to a European. For Ferreira, the geographical sciences he cited were European domains of understanding, intellectual guideposts that those who lived in these parts— such as the *tapuia* (a generic European term for certain indigenous populations of Brazil)—would necessarily have lived without. Ferreira never answered his own rhetorical question. Instead, he described an object created by an Amerindian who marked out a river—along with its tributaries and population centers—using a series of cords and knots. This set of twists and turns made with pieces of rope or string did not constitute what Ferreira considered to be a map. Whatever practical or experiential knowledge it reflected, and however useful or accurate it may have been, the material representation of the river did not rise to the level of science in Ferreira's eyes, at least not a science that he could easily recognize or describe.[1] (See Figure 1.)

Despite its extensive duration and the extraordinary harvest of plants, insects, birds, reptiles, native masks, and human skeletons it acquired, the Ferreira expedition to the Brazilian Amazon was but one in a number of officially sponsored Portuguese exploratory missions undertaken in the second half of the eighteenth century. As such, it should be considered in the global context of an aggressive Portuguese scientific expansion to other fluvial sites—including the Cunene River in Angola and the Sena and Sofala Rivers in Mozambique—as well as Atlantic island environments like Cape Verde and coastal settings in Asia, namely Goa. Ferreira's expedition to Amazonia was also inextricably linked to South American boundary disputes, a direct legacy of the 1494 Treaty of Tordesillas divvying up the world between the two Iberian powers. For these reasons, Ferreira felt that acquiring geographical information was just as important as collecting the leaves, barks, and fruits that made up the native pharmacopeia. But local populations were never far from view.[2]

Since the sixteenth century, imperial powers that were engaged in the conquest and

---

[1] Alexandre Rodrigues Ferreira, "Observações gerais e particulares sobre a classe dos mamíferos observados nos territórios dos três rios, das Amazonas, Negro, e da Madeira," in *Viagem filosófica pelas capitanias do Grão Pará, Rio Negro, Mato Grosso e Cuiabá: Memórias: Zoologia e botânica* (Rio de Janeiro: Conselho Federal de Cultura, 1972), pp. 67–204, on pp. 93–94 (here and throughout this essay, all translations are my own unless otherwise indicated). On Alexandre Rodrigues Ferreira, Portuguese colonial science, and Amazonian colonization see Ronald Raminelli, *Viagens ultramarinas: Monarcas, vassalos, e governo a distância* (São Paulo: Alameda, 2008); and Ângela Domingues, *Quando os índios eram vassalos* (Lisbon: CNCDP, 2000). On the subject of Ferreira's interaction with indigenous geographical concepts see Neil Safier, "The Confines of the Colony," in *The Imperial Map: Cartography and the Mastery of Empire*, ed. James Akerman (Chicago: Univ. Chicago Press, 2009), pp. 133–183.

[2] On these Portuguese expeditions see Raminelli, *Viagens ultramarinas*; and William J. Simon, *Scientific Expeditions in the Portuguese Overseas Territories (1783–1808) and the Role of Lisbon in the Intellectual-Scientific Community of the Late Eighteenth Century* (Lisbon: IICT, 1983).

FOCUS—ISIS, 101 : 1 (2010) 135

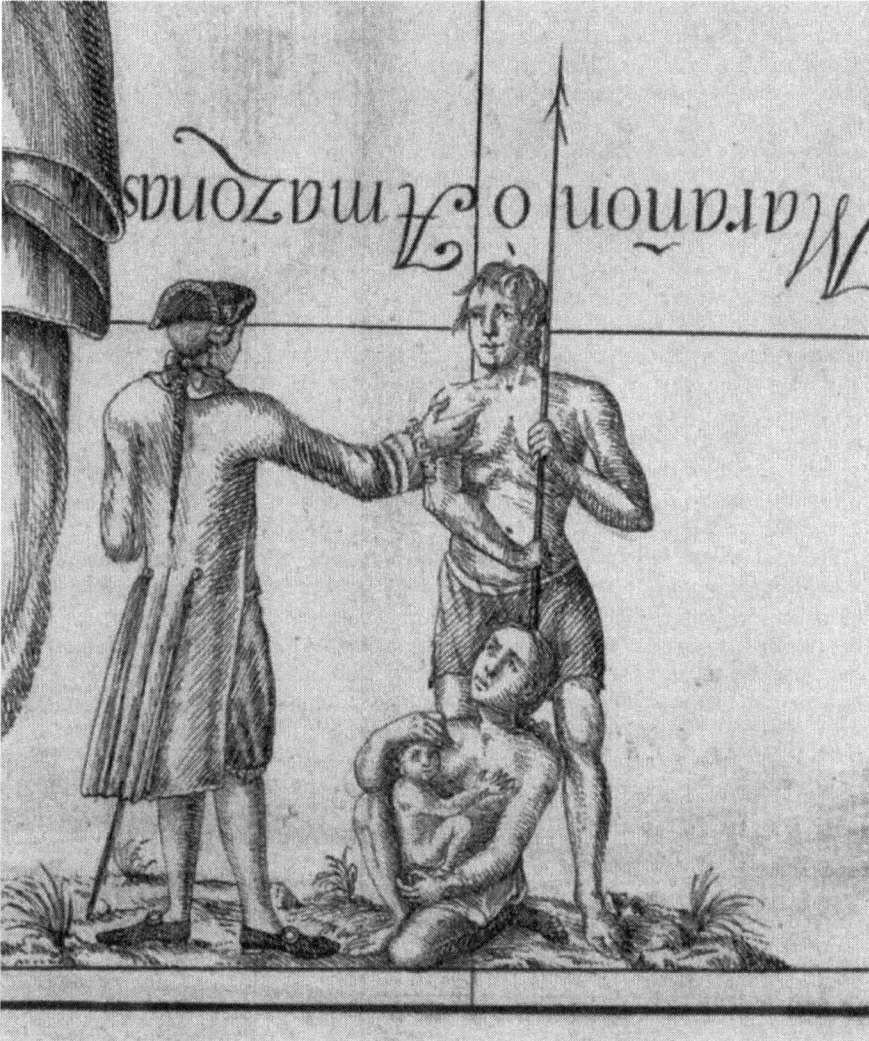

Figure 1. With his back to the viewer, a fully clothed European man engages in conversation with an Amerindian family. The exchange of geographical knowledge about the Amazon River and its tributaries often took place in ephemeral moments like the one depicted here even though Europeans frequently denied that Amerindian knowledge was commensurable with European scientific norms. Francisco Requena, "Mapa de una parte del Rio Yapura: Comprehendida desde su entrada en el Rio Marañon por su boca mas occidental hasta el pueblo de San Antonio de Maripi," detail. Courtesy of the Geography and Map Division, Library of Congress, Washington, D.C.

colonization of the Americas recognized that coming to terms with the customs, beliefs, and techniques of local populations—including their own self-referential systems of knowledge—was an important component of the overall project. As one Spanish cosmographer explained in instructions he gave to New World travelers, "You should seek

136   FOCUS—ISIS, 101 : 1 (2010)

out information regarding [indigenous] practices with regards to science, or what they understand [*sienten*] about the creation of the world and the movement and composition of the heavens." And yet, the broader question of the epistemological commensurability between European and indigenous systems of knowledge has become a fundamental issue for historians of science only in the last few decades. It was Bruno Latour's classic discussion of a local Sakhalin island map used by the French naval officer La Pérouse as part of a global network of "immutable mobiles" that encouraged scholars to correlate knowledge produced in the metropole with similar processes that were taking place within or beyond the colonial fold. Increasingly, historians of science have come to recognize that knowledge acquired by European expeditions overseas included at least some portion of knowledge derived from indigenous sources and that in many cases imperial reconnaissance depended entirely on these contacts with local cultures. Historians and anthropologists have redefined scientific knowledge collected at the so-called "periphery" and processed at the imperial "center" in myriad ways, ranging from knowledge that is hybrid or "mestizo" in character to a kind of "middle ground" knowledge.[3] The manner by which indigenous peoples of the Americas and elsewhere actually contributed to processes of collection, codification, and dissemination of inquiries into the natural world has in turn become a core issue for those attempting to write more integrated and global histories of science.

Such integrated histories—which view both European and non-European forms of knowledge as legitimate systems of understanding—must by necessity take into account the paucity of sources that shed reliable light on indigenous methods for interrogating and responding to the natural world.[4] But how? Expanding the archive and sites through which traditional narratives of encounter and exchange can be recounted is one option.[5] Another is expanding the scale within which these historical processes are examined, moving away from an overly constrained emphasis on laboratories and academies—the *sine qua non* of the constructivist approach—to consider knowledge that is by definition mobile or itinerant.[6] The call for historians of science to "concentrate on the multidimensional . . . *local*

---

[3] Alonso de Santa Cruz, *Obra cosmográfica*, Vol. 1, pp. 70–71, cited in María P. Portuondo, *Secret Science: Spanish Cosmography and the New World* (Chicago: Univ. Chicago Press, 2009), p. 112; and Bruno Latour, *Science in Action* (1987; Cambridge, Mass.: Harvard Univ. Press, 2003), pp. 215–219. For redefinitions of the scientific knowledge collected at the "periphery" and processed at the "center" see Serge Gruzinski, *La pensée métisse* (Paris: Fayard, 1999); and Richard White, *The Middle Ground: Indians, Empires, and Republics in the Great Lakes Region, 1650–1815* (Cambridge: Cambridge Univ. Press, 1991).

[4] See Sujit Sivasundaram's contribution on this topic to this Focus section: "Sciences and the Global: On Methods, Questions, and Theory."

[5] In her study on glaciers, Julie Cruikshank fluidly merged textual narratives of exploration with oral accounts and songs from the Tlingit and Athapaskan tradition; see Cruikshank, *Do Glaciers Listen? Local Knowledge, Colonial Encounters, and Social Imagination* (Vancouver: UBC Press, 2005), p. 258. Other scholars have rejected such practices as "upstreaming," using contemporary oral accounts to read present practice into past behaviors. See White, *Middle Ground* (cit. n. 3), p. xiv. See also Daniel Richter, *Facing East from Indian Country* (Cambridge, Mass.: Harvard Univ. Press, 2001).

[6] On the portability and circulation of knowledge in the Atlantic context see James Delbourgo and Nicholas Dew, eds., *Science and Empire in the Atlantic World* (New York: Routledge, 2008); Antonio Barrera-Osorio, *Experiencing Nature: The Spanish American Empire and the Early Scientific Revolution* (Austin: Univ. Texas Press, 2006); Delbourgo, *A Most Amazing Scene of Wonders: Electricity and Enlightenment in Early America* (Cambridge, Mass.; Harvard Univ. Press, 2006); Neil Safier, *Measuring the New World: Enlightenment Science and South America* (Chicago: Univ. Chicago Press, 2008); and Londa Schiebinger, *Plants and Empire: Colonial Bioprospecting in the Atlantic World* (Cambridge, Mass.: Harvard Univ. Press, 2004). For Asia and the Indian Ocean region see Fa-Ti Fan, *British Naturalists in Qing China: Science, Empire, and Cultural Encounter* (Cambridge, Mass.: Harvard Univ. Press, 2004); Carla Nappi, *The Monkey and the Inkpot: Natural History and Its Transformations in Early Modern China* (Cambridge, Mass.: Harvard Univ. Press, 2009); and Kapil Raj,

contexts of scientific endeavor" has to some degree been answered, removing the so-called peripheries from the strict purview of colonial historians and displacing the imperial centers from their privileged position at the forefront of the history of science's grand narrative.[7]

But many challenges remain. Narratives of exploration and encounter—like those that Ferreira and La Pérouse provided their contemporaries—often yielded mixed results when used as legitimate records of indigenous behaviors. Narrative conventions, special interests, and cultural prejudices regularly clouded the eyes of proto-ethnographers. What is more, the populations early modern Europeans described and the terms they used were often fabrications based on preexisting European categories, the very term "Indian" being the most obvious example. These terms then became fixed and were appropriated by the very people to whom they were initially applied. As two Brazilian anthropologists have noted, "artificial and generic as they were at the time of their creation, these labels have progressively come to be 'inhabited' by flesh-and-blood people."[8]

Native populations were flesh-and-blood people in the past as well, and they had their own notions of history that, like their cultures, developed and changed over time. Therefore, they should in no way be relegated to a timeless past, their histories springing to life only when European actors happened to provide descriptions of them in images and texts.[9] In this essay, I suggest three possible frames that may help to create more seamless histories of science that include indigenous actors and categories: an emphasis on itineraries and connected histories; attempts to redefine traditional indigenous knowledge on its own terms; and, with specific reference to Amazonia, the use of deep history to rethink more remote strands of science and its histories in a global frame. These approaches and their respective disciplinary perspectives are offered here as a preliminary route map toward reconstructing the histories of non-European knowledge systems: a scientific history of South American subalterns whose stories have for too long been hidden from our view.

BROKERS, ITINERARIES, AND CONNECTED HISTORIES

Among attempts to integrate non-Western perspectives into the broader Western narrative of the history of science, a comparative approach has been the most common. Seeking to examine the similarities and parallels between scientific developments along national lines, specialists have often reached across the aisle to vastly different cultural traditions.

Relocating Modern Science: Circulation and the Construction of Knowledge in South Asia and Europe, 1650–1900 (New York: Palgrave Macmillan, 2007). In the African context see Mary S. Morgan, "'On a Mission' with Mutable Mobiles" (Working Papers on the Nature of Evidence: How Well Do 'Facts' Travel? No. 34/08), London School of Economics, Aug. 2008.

[7] David Wade Chambers and Richard Gillespie, "Locality in the History of Science: Colonial Science, Technoscience, and Indigenous Knowledge," in *Nature and Empire: Science and the Colonial Enterprise*, ed. Roy MacLeod, *Osiris*, 2nd Ser., 2000, *15*:221–240, on p. 240.

[8] Manuela Carneiro da Cunha and Mauro W. B. de Almeida, "Indigenous People, Traditional People, and Conservation in the Amazon," *Daedalus*, 2000, *129*:315–338, on p. 316.

[9] Marshall Sahlins, *Islands of History* (Chicago: Univ. Chicago Press, 1987); Stuart Schwartz and Frank Salomon, "New Peoples and New Kinds of People: Adaptations, Adjustments, and Ethnogenesis in South American Indigenous Societies (Colonial Era)," in *Cambridge History of the Native Peoples of the Americas*, 2 vols., ed. Schwartz and Salomon (Cambridge: Cambridge Univ. Press, 2000), Vol. 2, pp. 443–501; Peter Nabokov, *A Forest of Time: American Indian Ways of Knowing* (Cambridge: Cambridge Univ. Press, 2002); and Carlos Fausto and Michael Heckenberger, "Indigenous History and the History of the 'Indians,'" in *Time and Memory in Indigenous Amazonia: Anthropological Perspectives*, ed. Fausto and Heckenberger (Gainesville: Univ. Press Florida, 2007), pp. 1–43.

138   FOCUS—ISIS, 101 : 1 (2010)

The world's preeminent scientific civilizations—including India, China, and the Islamic world—are frequently included in broad, global surveys of science and its history. But rather than placing these civilizations at the center of their own respective local (or indeed global) histories, such surveys often deal with them strictly in relation to contemporaneous developments in Western cultures. One scholar discussed the "fructifying effect" that Arabic-Islamic civilization had on the course of Western intellectual development, arguing that the "success of modern science in the West" was due to "neutral spaces" that were "free from the incursions of political and religious censors."[10] This emphasis on "successful" civilizations (read: the West) tends to displace those groups or individuals that have made heterogeneous contributions to science or that conceptualize the natural world in less traditional ways.

New approaches emphasizing the mobile and interconnected nature of knowledge have questioned the definition of science as an institutionally driven and socially bound activity. Against the "intercivilizational" approach, this new orientation emphasizes the connections between individuals and groups with varying degrees of political autonomy, rather than between large and vague "civilizations." Looking through the prism of shape changers, beguilers, and shifty personalities has highlighted the contingent processes inherent in scientific practices on both the European and the non-European ends of the table, providing a stimulating window through which to understand histories of science in a globalized and interconnected world.[11]

Other recent volumes offer encouraging points of departure for theorizing the relationship of go-betweens to the broader history of scientific practices.[12] So does Sanjay Subrahmanyam's paradigm of "connected histories"—in contradistinction to comparative histories—which argues for connecting stories *between* empires and geographical regions and for "reconfiguring" early modern history by transforming the way we think about temporal categories.[13] A perspective emphasizing extraimperial connections expands the range of actors who participated in the production of scientific knowledge, not only as "pathfinders" and porters in the literal sense but also as individuals who shaped and organized data according to their own developed standards of expertise.

In my own work, itineraries reveal pathways linking individuals, objects, and impulses between sites that are often taken for granted in the Atlantic system of knowledge production and that frequently lie outside the purview of metropolitan institutions and imperial capitals. Removing the strict limitations of a single national or imperial frame reveals other processes beyond the traditional loci of scientific production. I refer to these processes as "scientific commemoration"—the myriad activities by which empirical observations are transformed into tangible, memorable products. In order to garner authority, early modern scientific experiments needed to be replicable and persuasive, and those who recorded data and shaped experimental material into a communicable form needed to know how such activities would become memorable for a distant audience. The

---

[10] Chambers and Gillespie, "Locality in the History of Science" (cit. n. 7), p. 233; and Toby E. Huff, *The Rise of Early Modern Science: Islam, China, and the West* (Cambridge: Cambridge Univ. Press, 1993), pp. 13, 11.

[11] See Simon Schaffer *et al.*, eds., *The Brokered World: Go-Betweens and Global Intelligence, 1770–1820* (Uppsala: Science History Publications, 2009).

[12] In addition to *The Brokered World*, see Delbourgo and Dew, eds., *Science and Empire in the Atlantic World* (cit. n. 6); and *Itinerario*, 2009, *33*(1), which includes an excellent essay on this theme by Lissa Roberts entitled "Situating Science in Global History: Local Exchanges and Networks of Circulation" (pp. 9–30).

[13] Sanjay Subrahmanyam, "Connected Histories: Notes towards a Reconfiguration of Early Modern Eurasia," *Modern Asian Studies*, 1997, *31*:735–762.

FOCUS—ISIS, 101 : 1 (2010) 139

inscriptive, narrative, and material techniques used to "commemorate" experiments can be used to tease out different stages in the elaboration of scientific texts and treatises. Mobile, interconnected, and brokered forms of knowledge can thus allow nontraditional actors to emerge from within unexpected, often ephemeral sources: from sloppy notes taken in a muddy field to the proof-sheets of an edited compendium fabricated within European printing houses and learned societies.[14]

DEFINING INDIGENOUS KNOWLEDGE

But connected histories between individuals or regions can have limitations. While specific stories reveal the mobile nature of scientific knowledge in the early modern period and the myriad actors involved in its production, they usually emerge as the result of European accounts. In order to bring other sources to bear on received narratives in the history of science, strategies from the anthropologist's ken are fruitful as well. One obvious point of interest is the anthropologist's attention to the material object, something historians of science have been keen on recognizing as a locus of both literal and phenomenological meaning. One anthropologist has written that "material things index the human productive activity that went into them, [and] they materialize social and cosmological structures that would otherwise elude direct experience." This focus on the material object has recast many encounters that took place between non-European populations and European travelers. For instance, whale bones served as a pretext for the sustained contact between William Parry and the Inuit in northern Canada from 1821 to 1823, a crucial period in Parry's expedition in search of a northwest passage. Fueled by the social and economic needs of the Inuit to trade with passersby, this interaction produced extensive geographical and ethnological knowledge for the British, while at the same time fostering oral accounts of the British passage in the social memory of the Inuit. As such, whale bones served as a point of intersection for both groups, enabling us in retrospect to perceive the encounter as one that was propelled as much by indigenous agency as by supposedly intrepid European curiosity.[15]

In the South American context, indigenous medicinal practices offer a similarly striking example of the contrast between "traditional" and "Western" scientific narratives. The Brazilian anthropologist Manuela Carneiro da Cunha has described a school for shamans established by a group of Krahó Indians in the central Brazilian state of Tocantins. These ritual leaders and expert dealers in traditional medicine came together to oppose an accord that had been reached between a prestigious medical school in São Paulo—which was interested in the neurological effects of some of the native plants of the region—and another group of shamans that considered themselves authorized to speak on behalf of all shamans who had such knowledge. This conflict

---

[14] On the notion of "scientific commemoration" more broadly see Safier, *Measuring the New World* (cit. n. 6).

[15] Webb Keane, "Subjects and Objects," in *Handbook of Material Culture*, ed. Chris Tilley *et al.* (Thousand Oaks, Calif.: Sage, 2006), pp. 197–202, on pp. 201–202; and Michael T. Bravo, "Ethnological Encounters," in *Cultures of Natural History*, ed. N. Jardine, J. A. Secord, and E. C. Spary (Cambridge: Cambridge Univ. Press, 1996), pp. 338–357 (on the interactions of Parry and the Inuit). On anthropologists' attention to the material object see the Focus section on "Thick Things," edited by Ken Alder: *Isis*, 2007, *98*:80–142. See also Lorraine Daston, ed., *Biographies of Scientific Objects* (Chicago: Univ. Chicago Press, 2000); Daston, ed., *Things That Talk: Object Lessons from Art and Science* (New York: Zone, 2004); Amiria Henare, Martin Holbraad, and Sari Wastell, eds., *Thinking through Things: Theorising Artefacts Ethnographically* (London/New York: Routledge, 2007); and Nicholas Thomas, *Entangled Objects: Exchange, Material Culture, and Colonialism in the Pacific* (Cambridge, Mass.: Harvard Univ. Press, 1991).

140   FOCUS—ISIS, 101 : 1 (2010)

reflected differing notions about how traditional indigenous knowledge should be shared with modern institutions, as well as about who had the right to speak on behalf of those who are party to such knowledge. Carneiro da Cunha has also argued that because many traditional societies have a private understanding of their own cultural heritage, they find themselves necessarily at odds with Western society, where knowledge is both protected and exchanged in the public domain. For her, Western scientific knowledge and traditional knowledge are not necessarily commensurable, but "this incommensurability does not reside in their respective results." Rather, it resides in the aspiration to universality that characterizes Western knowledge: the need to discover laws that are applicable at all times and in all places. Traditional knowledge systems work according to different criteria, and, once again, physical objects are revelatory of these differences. Carneiro da Cunha uses the example of a community in Acre (Brazil), some of whose residents believe that stones are living organisms: "It may be that where you live, stones are not alive," said one resident to another, "but here they grow and for that reason are living."[16] The underlying idea is that entirely valid systems of knowledge—be they Western or traditional—do not necessarily function according to the same criteria for internal truth or consistency; nor is it always clear who controls access to the information these systems protect.

Although certain features of indigenous practice may indeed diverge from the universalizing tendency of Western science, empirical and experimental behaviors abound within native traditions, whether as millenarian or modern practices. How these native knowledge practices are treated and valued by travelers or encroaching cultures can be seen as a chapter in the politics of indigenous rights, especially through the form most closely associated with the history of science and techniques— namely, intellectual property. There has been a vigorous debate among those seeking to protect indigenous rights as to whether intellectual property protection—a set of laws enshrined in a Euro-American framework and normally related to new rather than old knowledge—is the appropriate way to secure profits accruing from indige- nous cultural or intellectual patrimony. This debate has often been couched in global terms using territorial metaphors. According to one scholar, the search for such protection has been "stimulated by the desire to secure possession, in terms that will have *international* legal purchase, of natural resources and ways of life in the face of *encroachment*."[17] The patrimony of indigenous populations, despite being locally acquired and organized, is perceived as being "encroached" upon by other groups and other legal systems with transnational interests. Therefore, the protection against such threats needs to be conceived outside of a local or national framework as well.

An eighteenth-century anecdote suggests that such questions have historical roots. In discussing a curious proposal to erect a set of pyramids at the ends of a geodetic baseline outside Quito (present-day Ecuador), Antoine-François Prévost argued that Latin should not be the sole language in which the pyramids' inscriptions were written: "It seems that our traveling savants will have commerce with men who are capable of reasoning and feeling, and that . . . they should at the very least translate

---

[16] Manuela Carneiro da Cunha, "De Charybde en Scylla: Savoirs traditionnels, droits intellectuels et dialec- tique de la culture," XXVIème Conférence Marc Bloch, Paris, 10 June 2004, accessed at http://cmb.ehess.fr/ document110.html (27 Apr. 2009); and Carneiro da Cunha, "Relações e dissensões entre saberes tradicionais e saber científico," *Revista USP* (São Paulo, Brazil), 2007, *75*:76–84, on p. 78.

[17] Marilyn Strathern, "Potential Property: Intellectual Rights and Property in Persons," *Social Anthropology*, 1996, *4*:17–32, on p. 21 (emphasis added).

FOCUS—ISIS, 101 : 1 (2010) 141

their inscription into the language of Peru."[18] This nod to the enfranchisement of the native populations as part of a project in which, directly or not, they had a stake is only one example we can look toward in determining how native rights were articulated in an era before modern commercial and legal protection for scientific knowledge was established. Using indigenous narratives to determine the ways in which their knowledge should be protected conforms both to the conditions in which such knowledge was produced and to the contexts and geographic range in which that knowledge would eventually be deployed.

AMAZONIA AT THE CROSSROADS OF TIME

During its long history of contact with the wider world, Amazonia has often served as a laboratory for the production of European knowledge about indigenous cultures and societies. In the eighteenth and nineteenth centuries, myriad travelers made observations regarding the "character" of the Amazon's native populations. In the twentieth century, the southern portion of the Amazon River basin served as a field site for Claude Lévi-Strauss during his first ethnographic forays in the 1930s and 1940s. Along the Andean cordillera, recent disciples of Lévi-Strauss (notably the anthropologists Philippe Descola and Anne-Christine Taylor) have carried out fieldwork on the Achuar peoples of the Ecuadorian Amazon, concluding that transspecies interaction and a fluid boundary between the human and the "natural" speak to an epistemology—purportedly universal but appearing with particular force in certain South American indigenous groups—that operates beyond a paradigm opposing Nature to Culture.[19] In and around the island of Marajó, near the headwaters of the Amazon, archaeologists have also discovered ceramic artifacts (so-called Marajoara pottery) that radically reformulated previous assumptions about the carrying capacity of the Amazonian ecosystem and the cultural development of the region's inhabitants, with important implications for lowland urbanization patterns and the history of indigenous technologies.[20]

Other archaeological and anthropological work has challenged established regimes of historical temporality by using indigenous frames and deeper historical cross-sections to understand aspects of native culture that earlier ethnohistorians had been unable to access. Indigenous notions of temporality have thus come to challenge certain linear Western paradigms of history. Because Western historiography has been so dependent on a sacred historical time frame, and its own seemingly inexorable progression of socioeconomic and cultural advances, it has not been able to integrate long-term historical models from anthropology or alternative non-Western ideas for conceptualizing temporal processes.[21]

[18] Prévost's argument appeared in *Le Pour et Contre*, 1735, 77:35. For a detailed discussion of the pyramid controversy, and its implications for the enfranchisement of native laborers who participated in the project, see Safier, *Measuring the New World* (cit. n. 6), Ch. 1.

[19] Philippe Descola, *Par-delà nature et culture* (Paris: Gallimard, 2006); and Anne-Christine Taylor, "The Soul's Body and Its States: An Amazonian Perspective on the Nature of Being Human," *Journal of the Royal Anthropological Institute*, 1996, 2:201–215. See also Eduardo Kohn, "How Dogs Dream: Amazonian Natures and the Politics of Transspecies Engagement," *American Ethnologist*, 2007, 34:3–24.

[20] See, e.g., Anna Roosevelt, *Moundbuilders of the Amazon: Geophysical Archaeology on Marajo Island, Brazil* (San Diego, Calif.: Academic, 1991); and, more recently, Michael J. Heckenberger et al., "Amazonia 1492: Pristine Forest or Cultural Parkland," *Science*, 2003, 301:1710–1714.

[21] On the challenges and barriers to writing outside of a sacred historical frame see Daniel Smail, "In the Grip of Sacred History," *American Historical Review*, 2005, 110:1337–1361.

This assertion raises the question: What time line should be adopted for a global history of science? And according to whose criteria—indigenous or European—should such a paradigm be established?

In the case of the Amazon, archaeologists in Brazil, the United States, and elsewhere have advocated for a history of the region that reveals long-term changes in the natural ecosystem and in the deeper structures of human cultures and societies. Rejecting the myth that Amazonia prior to 1492 was a balanced, harmonious, and untouched ecological paradise, scholars now recognize that it was a place of cultural and ethnic flux, a crossroads for groups that, migrating between the Andean highlands and the Colombian plateaus, brought with them their arts, culture, and technical skills. The study of landscapes bearing deep records of human passages has been crucial for this history. As Carole Crumley has written, landscapes maintain the mark of the activities that affected them: "[Human] practices are maintained or modified, decisions are made, and ideas are given shape; a landscape retains the physical evidence of these mental activities."[22] These kinds of traces in the material landscape complement other evidence recorded by archaeologists, including large road systems, attractive spears, and elaborate funerary urns. These discoveries have served to dispel the previous idea of small, technically primitive groups of itinerant peoples in Amazonia who were incapable of producing sophisticated material cultures.

Anthropologists have also been effective in recovering indigenous conceptions of space and time, shedding light on long-term changes wrought by human and nonhuman denizens of Amazonia.[23] Amazonian societies changed dramatically in the last two millennia—well before the arrival of Europeans—and those changes can be understood by looking more deeply at native populations' own concepts of time and historical change. Jean-Pierre Chaumeil has proposed a "cumulative conception of time" that escapes from the more traditional cyclical model through the use of sacred flutes, mortuary remains, and "layers" of history between living and dead generations. Chaumeil discusses "mythic journeys" that inscribe notions of time onto spatial landscapes, a form of "topographic writing" and historical memory that traditional sources have ignored. The Yanesha of eastern Peru also used topographic writing to inscribe their memories and rituals. For the Yanesha, the historical present is a period between a timeless past and a timeless future, and they use sacred music in addition to topography to counteract the "suffering, pain, death, and oblivion" associated with this epoch.[24]

Nothing should prevent historians from using similar analyses to understand natural knowledge through the prism of a deeper historical past. By focusing on the ritual aspects of food preparation, healing practices, astronomical observations, botanical remedies, or tools to alter the landscape, historians of science can reconstruct past

---

[22] Carole Crumley, "Historical Ecology: A Multidimensional Ecological Orientation," in *Historical Ecology: Cultural Knowledge and Changing Landscapes*, ed. Crumley (Santa Fe, N.M.: School of American Research Press, 1994), pp. 1–13, cited in William Balée and Clark L. Erickson, "Time, Complexity, and Historical Ecology," in *Time and Complexity in Historical Ecology: Studies in the Neotropical Lowlands*, ed. Balée and Erickson (New York: Columbia Univ. Press, 2006), pp. 1–17, on p. 2.

[23] Fausto and Heckenberger, eds., *Time and Memory in Indigenous Amazonia* (cit. n. 9); Balée and Erickson, eds., *Time and Complexity in Historical Ecology*; and Neil L. Whitehead, ed., *Histories and Historicities in Amazonia* (Lincoln: Univ. Nebraska Press, 2003).

[24] Jean-Pierre Chaumeil, "Bones, Flutes, and the Dead: Memory and Funerary Treatments in Amazonia," in *Time and Memory in Indigenous Amazonia*, ed. Fausto and Heckenberger, pp. 243–283; and Fernando Santos-Granero, "Time Is Disease, Suffering, and Oblivion: Yanesha Historicity and the Struggle against Temporality," *ibid.*, pp. 47–73, on p. 47.

FOCUS—ISIS, 101 : 1 (2010) 143

practices as well. As Carlos Fausto and Michael Heckenberger have remarked, the topics studied by anthropologists have changed from "kinship, politics, economy, or religion" to "subjectification, embodiment, empowerment, agency, and identity."[25] These latter categories are in no way incompatible with recent work in the history of science. An attention to the technical aptitudes of indigenous peoples and the broad range of knowledge they bring to interactions with the natural environment can enhance our understanding of the codependence of ritual, power, and natural knowledge, in Amazonia and beyond.

THE SCIENTIFIC IMPERIALISM MODEL REVISITED

So how might these different approaches assist historians of science in teasing new global histories out of an arguably limited documentary corpus? What I hope to have shown are some ways of fusing recent methodologies in history, anthropology, and archaeology with the history of science in order to achieve this goal. These methods allow us to escape from a narrow temporal and territorial view of history and incorporate other peoples and places within the received narrative of scientific "expansion." The "imperial" model of global scientific production—with European empires at the forefront of natural knowledge acquisition, codification, calculation, and dissemination—should make way for a more expansive definition of scientific enterprise on a global scale. Clearly, we do not need to discard the studies that have usefully examined imperial institutions for their role in connecting colonized worlds with the European metropole. But we may wish to look toward alternative models that do not reinforce the omnipotence of the imperial center at the expense of local or moving platforms of knowledge creation.

Questions of commensurability (or the co-production of knowledge) have their relevance for this expanded frame, just as they did during the colonial period. Europeans often sought to efface indigenous knowledge in order to buttress their own claims, aided by the supposition that native informants were not reliable eyewitnesses. Innate cultural prejudice that developed during Europe's interactions with other parts of the non-European world, including Asia and Africa, led the bulk of European travelers in the Americas to speak in tremendously pejorative terms of indigenous knowledge systems. From Charles-Marie de La Condamine to Cornelius de Pauw, native residents of the Americas were perceived as retrograde human specimens whose inferiority was marked on their characters from birth. Alexandre Rodrigues Ferreira was no exception. Referring to Amerindians' knowledge of mathematics, he explained that "for those who do not have moveable goods for their descendants to inherit, nor money to count, nor extended calculations to carry out either about time or space, clearly arithmetic is of no use."[26] For these Europeans, the idea of indigenous science was akin to the indigenous use of mathematics: something so rudimentary that it was only worth mentioning in order to ridicule.

The explicit comparison between European and Amerindian systems of knowledge was not limited to the realm of science. The traits and cultural mores of Amerindians were prominent features of many European narratives describing their cultural encounter with

---

[25] Fausto and Heckenberger, "Introduction," in *Time and Memory*, ed. Fausto and Heckenberger, pp. 1–43, on p. 4.

[26] Ferreira, "Observações gerais e particulares sobre a classe dos mamíferos observados nos territórios dos três rios, das Amazonas, Negro, e da Madeira" (cit. n. 1), p. 92.

Figure 2. *"Yuripuxuna Indian." Alexandre Rodrigues Ferreira attempted to classify the indigenous populations he encountered in Amazonia according to their technical skills and the tools they used. Courtesy of the Fundação Biblioteca Nacional, Rio de Janeiro, Brazil.*

native peoples of the Americas. (See Figure 2.) In the case of the Guaicuru Indians, for example, Ferreira came away particularly impressed with their treatment of slaves, in contradistinction to the contemporaneous European participation in the slave trade: "We call [the Indians] barbarous [*bárbaros*]; and yet, in this region, they do not dishonor humanity as do the most refined nations of Europe, who despite having rationality that is

FOCUS—ISIS, 101 : 1 (2010) 145

fed by philosophy and illuminated by revelation, seem nonetheless to have chosen the heaviest means to control the yoke of African slavery in the Americas."[27] Such texts by Europeans certainly served the role of integrating non-European populations into a more inclusive history of natural knowledge production on a global scale. But ethnographic data drawn from necessarily biased sources needs to be supplemented by other strategies, including following itineraries across linguistic and imperial boundaries, borrowing from conceptual categories in other disciplines, and looking for ways that "prehistorical" categories can inform historical development in the past and in the present. What is required are modes of inquiry that highlight particular local contexts in a system of exchanges that was perpetually in motion. A grand, linear narrative seems harder to maintain when our own scholarly itineraries through these knowledge networks reveal connections that were not immediately apparent to those whose worlds we later imagine and reconstruct.

[27] Alexandre Rodrigues Ferreira, "Guaicurus," in *Viagem ao Brasil de Alexandre Rodrigues Ferreira: Coleção etnográfica*, 3 vols. (Lisbon: Kapa, 2005), Vol. 3, pp. 22–27, on p. 26.

[19]

A commonwealth of science: the British Association in South Africa, 1905 and 1929[1]

Saul Dubow

Setting

On 15 August 1905 a party of some 200 official members of the British Association for the Advancement of Science arrived in Cape Town on board the Union Castle Liner, *Saxon*. The voyage had been pleasantly uneventful and the visitors occupied their time with an extensive programme of lectures and discussions, games and entertainments, and scientific experiments besides.[2] The boundaries between amusement and scientific investigation were not rigidly maintained. It was in the jovial spirit of scientific adventure, we must therefore assume, that the head of the president of the Association, the mathematician and astronomer George Darwin (son of Charles) consented to having his head measured with a pair of calipers as he reclined on deck in a comfortable cane armchair.[3]

The ostensible purpose of the visit of the British Association was to hold its annual meeting together with the newly formed South African Association for the Advancement of Science, members of which had been enrolled as associates of the British Association by special arrangement. But there were important ideological issues involved too and these constitute the focus of this chapter. In looking closely at the visits of the British Association to South Africa, first in 1905, and again in 1929, I wish to address some of the complex relationships between science, imperialism and colonial nationalism, and to touch as well on the place of science in constructions of racial and ethnic identity. These issues, I argue, were of central concern to the organisers of the British and South African Associations. They raise questions about science, conceived of as a universalistic, transcendent and objective set of practices, and its use as a means of promoting particularist and partial political purposes in the period of transition from empire to commonwealth.

A precedent for overseas meetings of the British Association had been set with its visits to Montreal in 1884 and Toronto in 1897. However, whereas previous gatherings took place in a single city, the 1905 visit involved travelling through the country and was therefore thought of – in a phrase redolent with meaning – as a 'South African meeting'.[4] A total subvention of £6,000 was provided by the colonies of the Cape, Transvaal, Orange Free State and Natal towards the sea passages of most of the overseas visitors, whose numbers totalled some 380. The head of the Union Castle Mail Steamship Company, Sir Donald Currie, offered reduced fares for the Atlantic crossing, and pledged his personal support for the enterprise on the grounds that it was 'thoroughly in accord with the spirit of Imperialism'. A private South Africa Fund was subscribed in Britain to cover additional expenses, and free railway passes were granted to cover the extensive internal travel arrangements.[5]

The expedition was a major undertaking, with the official proceedings held over the course of two weeks in both Cape Town and Johannesburg. Visits were also arranged to centres such as Durban, Pietermaritzburg, Bloemfontein and Kimberley, at which lectures were delivered and civic receptions laid on. Optional side tours were arranged to Victoria Falls, Bulawayo and Beira. Elaborate arrangements for the visit were made by the specially constituted South African committee of the British Association in London which had the responsibility of directing overall planning. The burden of much of the preparatory work was borne by the Cape Town-based committee, consisting of the Royal Astronomer and founding president of the South African Association, Sir David Gill, and the marine biologist John D. F. Gilchrist. To ensure high-powered political support, several vice-presidents of the British Association were appointed, including the High Commissioner for South Africa, Lord Selborne, and his predecessor, Lord Milner; the Governors and Lieutenant-Governors of the four colonies of South Africa; the Administrator of Southern Rhodesia; and the mayors of cities included in the Association's itinerary.[6]

The visit of the British Association was marked by lavish hospitality on the part of private individuals and the royal progress of the scientists was punctuated by a succession of enthusiastic civic welcomes. Towns competed with each other in fussing over their illustrious guests and bid to be included in the offical programme. At every stop reception committees were busily active, local excursions were arranged, and a profusion of toasts, votes of thanks and enthusiastic tributes were traded between local and visiting dignitaries. Great pride was taken in the precision of the organisation and its planning. Every

68   SCIENCE AND SOCIETY IN SOUTHERN AFRICA

visitor was allotted a particular seat on one of the four special trains; on arrival at any of the towns at which they were staying, hosts were able to assemble on the platform in the order in which their guests would alight.[7]

In Johannesburg, the visit was marked by one of the greatest social events ever held in the city: a mayoral party given at the Wanderers' Hall attended by a 'brilliant crowd' of some 1,800 notables.[8] One of the most remarked upon outings was a visit to the Mount Edgecombe sugar mill outside Durban where the scientists delighted in photographing a dance performed by hundreds of 'Zulus' in the presence of the Governor of Natal. The railways as well as local publicity organisations printed lavish programmes with illustrated essays highlighting the special features of particular regions and cities.[9] Sightseeing was evidently as much a priority as serious scientific discussion, a fact attested to by the rather low attendance rates at sectional meetings.[10] Indeed, one visitor extended his warmest gratitude to his South African 'kinsmen', drily thanking those 'who helped to make our trip to their continent such a delightful and enjoyable picnic'.[11]

If elements within the British Association were concerned by the apparent lack of serious scientific purpose in the visit, their fears were outweighed by the enthusiasm and publicity that was generated. The objects of the British Assocation were always wider than purely academic and, since its foundation in 1831, the organisation had proved adept in reinventing itself to suit new realities and constituencies. Originally conceived in the age of parliamentary reform as a bridge between specialists, practitioners and the general public, the British Association proved responsive to shifts in the political climate. In the early 1880s it had been beset by a sense of malaise and decline, reflected in falling attendances at yearly meetings. One way in which the Association reinvigorated itself was by reaffirming links with provincial and amateur scientific societies. A parallel initiative, graphically symbolised by the decision to meet in Canada in 1884, was the decision to cultivate links with the empire. This reorientation was given particular impetus by the Association's growing realisation that it was losing its way as scientific endeavour in Britain became increasingly specialised and professionalised. Involvement in the empire therefore offered new possibilities for the British Association to reassert its prestige and to fulfil its historic role as a populariser of scientific method and culture.[12]

Michael Worboys places particular emphasis on the British Association's growing concern with empire in terms of the economic and political imperatives of late nineteenth-century social imperialism, a doctrine which sought to contain domestic tensions and crises both

A COMMONWEALTH OF SCIENCE   69

by projecting these outwards into the empire and by drawing the colonies into closer economic contact with Britain. The Association's self-proclaimed 'imperial mission' was an ideological and cultural expression of these processes. Thus, Worboys indicates how the Association, in identifying itself with the 'universality of science' and ideas of progress, served as a metaphorical embodiment of the idea of empire.[13] In the case of Canada, as Gale has shown, the 1884 meeting of the British Association marked 'a dramatic demonstration of the important role which science could play in peacefully federating the interests of the nation states of the empire', while at the same time 'boosting and reaffirming the Association's role as an organizing centre of research within the provinces and the Empire at large'.[14]

A similar point can be made in the case of South Africa. The 1905 visit was intended to confer status on the newly constituted South African Association for the Advancement of Science (S2A3) whose immediate history went back to a meeting held in Cape Town in July 1901 at which a proposal was made by Theodore Reunert to establish an annual congress of engineers. The term 'Engineer' was defined in the broadest of terms so as to encompass 'not only those engaged in the utilization of Science, but those also whose lives and interests are occupied in the pursuit of Science for its own sake'.[15] The idea of forming an association similar to the British Association was canvassed at the gathering and, at a further meeting, it was resolved to constitute the S2A3 on this model.

In 1900 Sir David Gill attended a meeting of the Council of the British Association which had expressed interest in holding one of its annual meetings in South Africa. As a fellow of the Royal Society, as joint president of the S2A3 and the South African Philosophical Society, and with his recent knighthood, his prestigious position as royal astronomer and his extensive connections, Gill was well placed to bring this about. From 1902 he became actively engaged in gathering support for the visit from the mayors and corporations of Cape Town and Johannesburg, the Chambers of Commerce of these cities, the stock exchange and the Chamber of Mines. The end of the Anglo-South African War now made such a visit possible. The prime minister of the Cape, Gordon Sprigg, was therefore approached with a view to bringing out the British Association in 1905. He agreed and promised to provide material assistance. Gill was also successful in securing the support of Joseph Chamberlain who visited South Africa at the beginning of 1903. He informed the colonial secretary that the British Association would be going 6,000 miles to help the 'work of conciliation in South Africa'.[16] In his address to the S2A3 that year, Gill underlined the role that science could play in healing the bitterness of war and in cementing the imperial connection. 'Science', he argued, 'knows no nationality, and forms a meeting-ground on which men of every race are brethren, working together for a common end – and that end is truth.'[17]

The 1905 meeting

The British Association arrived in 1905 to a traumatised country poised uneasily between the experience of high-handed imperial domination and the beginnings of self-government and political renewal. The recent departure from South Africa of Milner as High Commissioner, the formation of the Het Volk Party and the publication of the Lyttelton Constitution providing for self-government in the Transvaal, pointed to a measure of rejuvenation in the political process. There were also welcome signs of economic recovery after the harsh commercial depression that followed the end of war. On the other hand, Campbell-Bannerman's victory in the British general election – and the decisive effect that this would have on the domestic political situation in South Africa – lay some months in the future. The British Association's visit therefore occurred during a delicate political hiatus. As the assistant secretary of the British Association delicately put it in an interview with the *Morning Post*: 'The South African colonies are passing through rather a trying period in their history. It is a matter of common knowledge that times are none of the best.'[18]

This sense of unease was reflected in the cautious approach taken by the British Association. A recurring theme in the many speeches delivered at public functions celebrating its visit was the healing role that science could play, but this sentiment was principally directed to 'British' South Africans with gestures of reconciliation directed only obliquely to 'Boers'. The tone was set by the Governor of the Cape, Sir Walter Hely-Hutchinson, when he welcomed the British Association to Cape Town at the start of its visit. Noting that the occasion was 'of no ordinary importance, whether in the history of scientific inquiry or in the history of the relations of the United Kingdom with the British dominions beyond the seas', he expressed hope that an 'important step had been taken in drawing closer together the bonds of the brotherhood of science' and, in so doing, 'promoting and developing brotherly feeling between his Majesty's subjects in South Africa and the motherland'.[19]

The idea that science had no political boundaries undoubtedly sent out a message of inclusiveness. But, for the most part, this sense of unity was cast in the context of a shared sense of imperial belonging. In Johannesburg, the Lieutenant-Governor of the Transvaal, Sir Arthur

Lawley, expressed regret that South Africa was a land encircled by walls constructed from 'prejudices of caste, colour, and race' born of past feuds and divergent interests. And he suggested that, like Jericho, such walls 'were only to be levelled by trumpet blasts of knowledge and of the wisdom which knowledge bore in its train'.[20] Likewise, Sir Richard Jebb hoped that, in promoting mutual understanding, the visit of the British Association would not only strengthen imperial ties, but would also facilitate more cordial relations between the 'two white races in the continent'.[21] Others were more inclined to jingoistic triumphalism. Thus, Col. Sir Colin Scott Moncrieff spoke 'as a Briton to Britons' even as he noted that 'science was of no nation'. By this he meant that the Association's visitors included scientists from America, Europe and even far-off Japan. His expression of 'kindly sympathy with the brave people who were but lately their enemies, but now the subjects of the King', can only be interpreted as a form of smug condescension.[22]

In the many tributes to the Association's role in reaffirming 'our English-speaking brotherhood', the 'strengthening of ties between the South African colonies and the Mother Country', and the formation of more links in the 'chain of civilization',[23] there is a distinct sense that the Association was determined to cement imperial unity and to reiterate the fact of British supremacy. The extensive programme of travel satisfied the needs of tourism, but it was also designed to encompass the imperial domain. Care was therefore taken not to marginalise areas of the country which, though visited, remained beyond the official scientific programme, and the existence of inter-colonial rivalry was recognised in placatory fashion.[24] Inevitably, choices had to be made and some towns were left out of the itinerary. Despite its historic English character and its strong claims to be an educational centre, the invitation from Grahamstown was declined. So, too, was an opportunity to visit the Lovedale Institution where Gill promised 'they would see more than 1,000 natives of the different races and obtain from Dr. Stewart (who is probably the most interesting living authority on the subject) all his views with regard to their capacity, the possibilities of their future, etc.'[25]

Some of the most poignant and affecting excursions were those arranged to the battlefields of the recent war. At Colenso, the visitors arrived in luxury trains and were able to spend time finding cartridges, unspent bullets and shell fragments. James Stark Browne noted approvingly that the war graves were being maintained in beautiful condition by the Guild of Loyal Women.[26] At Paardeberg, the scene of General Cronjé's surrender, skeletons of horses, meat and biscuit tins and other raw war debris were abundantly evident. Both the *Star* and

72   SCIENCE AND SOCIETY IN SOUTHERN AFRICA

The Times reported that the visitors 'were generally delighted with their experience'. As if to underline the sense of victory and the restoration of political order, a party of intrepid scientists trekked across the veld to Kimberley; they were guided by a farmer named 'Joe' who was said to have fought with Cronjé but now gamely entertained them by singing Boer songs around the fire.[27] The *Diamond Fields Advertiser* echoed this theme: whereas 'the Fates' had previously decreed that 'the only missions to achieve any large measure of success in our direction should partake of a somewhat warlike nature', the new mission came 'in the peaceful and cosmopolitan garb of science'; it was to be hoped that their 'patriotic aspirations' would ultimately be realised.[28]

A distinct note of imperial triumphalism was sounded when the Association visited the Victoria Falls in Southern Rhodesia. The president of the Association, Professor George Darwin, was given the honour of opening the new railway bridge over the Zambezi for passenger travel. Referring to the occasion as the 'crowning glory of the tour', Darwin took the opportunity to reflect on the achievements of Cecil Rhodes and the technological marvels of modern railway travel. He found himself unable to resist quoting from his great-grandfather, Erasmus Darwin, who had anticipated the potential wonders of steam, and he proceeded to muse about how his illustrious ancestor would react if he could see his great-grandson 'declaring a railway bridge open in the heart of Equatorial Africa'. A telegram from the British South Africa Company underlined the unmistakeable symbolism with the words: 'Very fitting that foremost representative of science should be associated with inauguration of modern engineering. Regret founder of country is not alive to witness realization of part of his great ideal.'[29]

The 1905 meeting was widely considered to have been a great success in all respects; thus there were many tributes to the contribution made by the British Association in helping to advance the development of scientific work in South Africa, as well as to the generosity of the South African hosts. The papers delivered by the Association's visitors covered a typically wide range of subjects and the characteristic balance between pure and applied science was consciously maintained. Papers with a particularly South African focus were prepared for publication in four special volumes (with the co-operation of the South African Association) though their quality gave rise to concern.[30] A few even made it into the general *Report of the British Association*.

Reflecting the pre-eminence and leading organisational role of the South African Association's foremost scientist, Sir David Gill, there was a large concentration of papers on astronomy and geodesy. The tradition of astronomy in South Africa was, indeed, one of the foremost and earliest examples of science in South Africa (if not always science of South Africa). One of the concrete results of the Association's visit was a renewed commitment to complete the geodetic survey of Africa from south to north which had been inaugurated by Lacaille during his time at the Cape in the 1750s. This programme was one of a number of ambitious survey projects initiated by Gill from the 1880s onwards. It had bearings on theoretical questions relating to the size and shape of the earth and its distance from the heavens, as well as having vital practical implications for the processes of triangulation and mapping of colonial boundaries.[31] South African related material was also prominent in Sections C (Geology) and E (Geography) owing in part to the country's rich array of mineral deposits and the development of the diamond and gold mining industries from the 1860s. Nineteenth-century pioneers of South African geology such as Andrew Geddes Bain, Andrew Wyley, P. C. Sutherland, G. W. Stow and E. J. Dunn were well known to the British Association visitors. The timely publication in 1905 of the first comprehensive textbook on the geology of South Africa was indicative of the relative maturity of scientific work in this field.[32]

A considerable boost to anthropological and ethnological work was provided by the presence of A. C. Haddon who attempted to survey the existing field and to map out directions of further research.[33] Yet the disparate nature of the contributions to Section H (Anthropology) indicates how undeveloped South African anthropology was at this time – notwithstanding contributions by scholars such as L. Péringuey on the 'Stone Age in South Africa', Henry Balfour on 'The musical instruments of South Africa' and H. A. Junod on 'The Thonga tribe'. Perhaps the most significant – and certainly the most controversial – paper in this section was David Randall-MacIver's report on Great Zimbabwe which concluded that 'the Rhodesian ruins were the work of a native race closely akin to those at present inhabiting the country'. Great Zimbabwe, MacIver maintained, was all the more interesting as a product of the southern African region rather than as a 'parasitic growth from Arabia' – even if this conclusion destroyed the romance of its supposed links with biblical antiquity.[34]

From a political point of view the most notable contribution was in Section F (Economic Science and Statistics) where Howard Pim delivered an address entitled 'Some Aspects of the Native Question'. The importance of this paper in defining and outlining the concept of racial segregation in South Africa is now well established and it attracted considerable attention in the press at the time.[35] So, too, did Sir

Richard Jebb's presidential address to Section L (Educational Science) on 'University Education and National Life'. In the course of his discussion of the writings of Newman, Huxley, Arnold and Sidgwick, Jebb insisted on the interdependence of scientific and literary culture. Jebb's remarks on the need for a teaching university in South Africa and his positive comments on the achievements of the new civic universities (especially Birmingham) in satisfying the demand for professional, technical and scientific as well as general education, were widely noticed – particularly in Johannesburg.[36]

Despite the importance of the British Association's 1905 visit in drawing attention to, and providing a focus for, intellectual endeavour in South Africa, systemic weaknesses were all too evident. As Jebb's remarks made clear, there was as yet no fully fledged teaching university in the country, there were few professional bodies and organisations in existence, resources were scarce and there was little if any overall coordination of research. The indebtedness of South Africa to the British Association was therefore all too evident and the latter did little to downplay its elevated status. Although kindly remarks were made about the progress of South African science these were mostly delivered in the form of gestural encouragement.[37] In short, the British Association was on display and the gratitude of the locals sometimes came close to obsequiousness.[38]

Institutions and nationhood

In the absence of large-scale institutions dedicated to the production and dissemination of basic intellectual and scientific knowledge, the S2A3 and the Philosophical Society were important bodies. They were in turn supported by a number of professional organisations which helped to foster the development of intellectual communities and scientific awareness. Many of these were established during the final decades of the nineteenth century, including the Institute of Mechanical Engineers and the Association of Engineers and Architects (1892), the Chemical and Metallurgical Society of South Africa (1894), the Geological Society of South Africa (1895), the South African Society of Electrical Engineers and the Transvaal Medical Society (1897).[39] The medical profession was an especially important focus of scientific activity. Doctors were often amateur scientific investigators of note and, importantly, they were based in the country towns and hamlets as well as the cities. Publications like the *South African Medical Journal* and the *South African Medical Record* existed principally to promote the collective interests of doctors but they also functioned as a vital outlet for the discussion and dissemination of medical and associated scientific research. A similar mix was evident in the *Cape Law Journal* which played a vital role in regulating the legal profession, circulating law reports and contributing to a national tradition of jurisprudence.

Another significant focus of scientific activity was the cluster of museums which grew up in the second half of the nineteenth century. The oldest and most prestigious was the South African Museum in Cape Town which traced its origins back to 1825 but which was re-established almost from new in 1855. The Albany Museum in Grahamstown was founded in the same year. In Natal, museums were established at Durban in 1877 and Pietermaritzburg in 1904. The Boer republics boasted similar institutions: a National Museum of the Orange Free State had been created in 1877, while the South African Republic created its Staats Museum in 1892. These museums were principally civic institutions but they could also serve as a focus for broader national aspirations. The initiative for the Staats Museum, for example, had come from W. J. Leyds, a Dutch-born cultural entrepreneur and close associate of Kruger. Although developed as a general museum with a strong emphasis on natural history, it was specifically intended to promote the republican cause by stressing Afrikaner cultural history and it attracted considerable popular interest as a result.[40] Competition between the South African and the regional museums was often keen. One index of such rivalry, together with an increasing concern with professional standards of museology and research, can be seen in the development of house-journals, beginning with the *Annals of the South African Museum* in 1898. By 1907 similar publications were being produced by the Albany, Natal government and Transvaal museums.

In the context of regional rivalries the newly formed S2A3 played a significant role helping to sew the sinews of a wider national scientific identity. Amongst its declared constitutional aims was 'to promote the intercourse of Societies and individuals interested in Science in different parts of South Africa' and 'to obtain a more general attention to the objects of pure and applied Science'.[41] From the outset, therefore, the S2A3 sought to include not only those with a professional or academic interest in science, but also amateurs and enthusiasts.[42] Its catholic approach was reflected in its impressive growth in membership figures: 268 'foundation members' in 1902; well over 700 members and associates at the end of the first meeting in 1903; and 1,322 in 1906[43] – a figure never surpassed in the twentieth century. Theodore Reunert recalled that it was founded as an 'act of faith' 'at a time of great and universal despondency'.[44] Its leaders saw their mission, at least in part, in terms of drawing South Africa together and

76   SCIENCE AND SOCIETY IN SOUTHERN AFRICA

in assuaging the bitterness of war. This emerged as a major theme in David Gill's 1903 presidential address wherein he argued that periods of political turmoil were almost invariably followed by 'intellectual progress and development' and that the Association could help to facilitate this process.[45] This politically inclusive but avowedly imperial-centric view of science was reiterated in 1907 by the Grahamstown-based journal, *African Monthly*, when the four South African colonies were beginning to explore actively the possibilities of unification. At a time when symbols of national unity were being keenly sought after, it noted the importance of a unitary parliament if the 'ideal of a South African nation, British in character, and therefore Imperial in tendency' were to prevail. Equally important in breaking down 'petty localism' and establishing 'true' nationality was the common desire on the part of individuals to cooperate with one another; the creation of S2A3, it noted, was welcome evidence of this process.[46]

Although it is not clear whether the *African Monthly* envisioned the S2A3 as a metaphorical South African parliament, had it done so it would only have been echoing a recurrent image of the British Association as the 'parliament of science'. That view reflected the British Association's desire to serve a range of scientific constituencies and interests and underlined the fact that, in acting as an advocate for science, it inevitably participated in the realm of politics; indeed, parallels were drawn between the foundation of the British Association in 1831 and the passage of Russell's first Reform Bill a year later.[47] The S2A3 may not have seen itself in quite the same terms. But it did play a significant role in the politics of symbolic unity, particularly as far as anglophone South Africans were concerned. This was implicit in the very structure of the S2A3 which was made up of local committees and governed by a Council composed of members drawn from the major centres of the country. By the time of Union the S2A3 had met in all four colonies. It was thus one of only a few nationwide organisations (including, perhaps, the churches and the medical profession) enjoying local as well as international links.

The focus on scientific advancement was a conspicuous feature of the reconstruction period following the Anglo-South African war. It has often been noted that, whatever the specific failures of Milner's cultural and political efforts to anglicise South Africa (with respect to educational and immigration policies, for example), his campaign to reorder the social, economic and administrative structure of the country was both extensive and marked by a high degree of success. The impetus given to modernisation placed a premium on the role that science and technology should play in the creation of a new society and this had both ideological and practical dimensions. For Milner and his followers technical competence was not only proof of the transformative and progressive capacity of a reawakened British imperialism, it also had the advantage of being capable of being represented as the politically acceptable face of state intervention.

An important index of the post-war technocratic tendency of government was the encouragement of scientific methods in agriculture which, as Donald Denoon points out, was the one aspect of Milner's work for which Louis Botha was willing to praise the post-war administration.[48] The creation in the Transvaal of a department of agriculture in 1902 under the direction of F. B. Smith provided an important stimulus to the adoption of modern scientific methods which attracted the particular interest of ambitious young Afrikaner modernisers.[49] Immediately following the grant of self-government to the Transvaal in 1908 and on the invitation of Botha, now prime minister, Dr Arnold Theiler, a Swiss-born zoologist and bacteriologist, created a new and well-funded veterinary institute at Onderstepoort near Pretoria. After Union, Onderstepoort came to coordinate veterinary research work in South Africa, absorbing the existing laboratories in Grahamstown and Natal as satellites.[50] Its achievements in applied agricultural and veterinary research, together with the creation of a centralised Department of Agriculture in 1911, came to be celebrated in the modernising nationalist idiom of man's progressive technical mastery over nature and, by implication, of white South Africans' special scientific knowledge of, and control over, a hostile African environment.[51]

Aside from new departments of state such as the Agriculture department, a number of nationally significant scientific institutions and projects were inaugurated in the immediate post-Union era. Amongst the most important were the South African Institute for Medical Research (1912), jointly funded by Union government and the mining industry; the Geological Survey of South Africa (1910);[52] the first national statistical survey (1911), the Meteorological Office (1912); and the National Botanic Gardens in Kirstenbosch (1913). The creation of national scientific institutions required delicate political balancing acts because provincial rivalries were often aroused in the process of forging a wider sense of national identity. Regional institutions often competed for favour and funding and, inevitably, some lost out as a result of national consolidation. In the case of museums, for example, unification secured the premier position of the South African Museum in Cape Town which, together with the Transvaal Museum, now benefited from a Union government grant and were awarded premier status. Conversely, the new national dispensation worked to the detriment of institutions like the Albany Museum which now came under the aegis of the provinces and were treated as being of secondary importance.[53]

The establishment of Kirstenbosch is especially revealing of the complex interaction between local, national and imperial connections. Its immediate origins go back to the 1880s and 1890s when a renewed phase of locally oriented botanical activity was inaugurated by researchers such as Harry Bolus, Peter MacOwan and Rudolph Marloth at the Cape, John Medley Wood in Natal, and Selmar Schonland in the eastern Cape.[54] Writing in *The State* in 1909, a literary and political venture created by members of Milner's kindergarten to advance the political cause of closer union, Bolus couched his appeal to preserve the Cape's distinctive flora in terms of the awakening of 'a higher patriotism in South Africa'. He feared that Table Mountain was rapidly being denuded of heaths, orchids and anemones by flower sellers and casual pickers and, in calling for the creation of a special reserve in order to protect the country's native flora, he cited the example of the Yellowstone Park in the United States and the National Trust in England.[55]

This plea was reinforced by Harold Pearson who came from Kew Gardens in 1903 to take up the newly established Bolus chair of botany at the South African College. Along with Neville Pillans, Pearson was the leading figure in the move to establish the Kirstenbosch botanic gardens and was personally responsible for selecting its site. He couched his appeal for a state botanical garden partly in the familiar language of utilitarian objectives (commercial and economic possibilities, medical and agricultural research) but principally on the grounds that the pursuit of 'science for its own sake' was a mark of civilised society. Tying this ideal to the quest for national identity, he portrayed the natural world as uniquely expressive of the nation, arguing that there was 'nothing more truly "South African" than its indigenous flora'.[56] Thus:

> The South African Botanic Garden cannot be merely an economic undertaking; it must also be an expression of the intellectual and artistic aspirations of the New Nation whose duty it is to foster the study of the country which it occupies, to encourage a proper appreciation of the rare and beautiful with which Nature has so lavishly endowed it.[57]

The creation of Kirstenbosch as a National Botanic Garden (encouraged by the S2A3 and aided by a small grant from the Botha government) gave expression to this national sentiment and reflected the brief blaze of optimism which characterised the immediate post-Union period. From the beginning, the cultivation, display and study of the indigenous flora of South Africa was the raison d'être of the

Kirstenbosch. In this sense it was distinctive because, unlike botanic gardens elsewhere in the empire which were devoted to the collection and study of foreign flora and which were closely tied into the colonial network of which Kew formed the hub, Kirstenbosch was additionally intended 'to be a Garden for the study of the flora of South Africa itself – the country in which it was situated'.[58] The establishment of Kirstenbosch at the side of Table Mountain can therefore be seen as the culmination of a process whereby the flora of South Africa, which had previously attracted the enthusiastic attentions of botanists and collectors as 'marvels' or 'curiosities', now became truly indigenised and were seen as valuable in their own right.[59] As a garden featuring unique and local rather than exotic botanical specimens, Kirstenbosch proclaimed South African nationhood. At the same time it could also be seen to express a more restricted and specific sense of Cape-ness.[60]

Also bound up with the struggle for national and regional identity was the movement to create a system of tertiary education. At the time of the British Association's 1905 visit there was only one 'university', the University of the Cape of Good Hope, whose foundation in 1873 was one of the first tangible rewards for the grant of responsible government to the Cape. In reality it was little more than an examining body (modelled on the old University of London) designed to serve the disparate teaching colleges spread about the country. There were thus, in 1905, around 50 teaching staff and fewer than 600 students. By contrast, when the British Association next visited South Africa, in 1929, the university system consisted of around 500 lecturers (of whom nearly half were professors) and the residential student body had grown to more than 7,000.[61]

This rapid growth (albeit from a small base) was both conditional upon and indicative of the process of political unification. Propagandists of closer union in the first decade of the century made much of the need for a national policy on university education. For some, like Chief Justice J. H. De Villiers, the creation of a national teaching university was 'a necessary first step under Union'.[62] From 1908, when an inter-colonial conference was called in Cape Town in order to discuss the future of tertiary education, various government commissions considered what had become known as the 'University Question' – though with a conspicuous lack of success. In 1916 several key university acts were passed as a result of which the modern distribution of anglophone and Afrikaner white tertiary educational institutions was established. But the initiative to create a single national university proved a failure, partly because of the individual aspirations of the existing educational institutions, but also because of ongoing regional competition for cultural and political primacy between the Cape and the Transvaal and, in particular, because of growing sectarian conflict between English- and Afrikaans-speakers.[63] The 1928 Van der Horst Commission considered that the ideal of a single national university in South Africa had proved impractical and that the historical trend was in the opposite direction.[64] Eric Walker shrewdly commented at this time: 'Politically and economically, South Africa had just moved centripetally; academically, in the very act of political union, it had rushed confusedly in the opposite direction.'[65]

One of the most articulate and persuasive interwar champions of South African science and, especially, of its role in the creation of nationhood, was Jan Smuts. His understanding of this link was bound up in his personal holistic vision whereby the local and the particular was also part of the transcendent and the universal. Whereas many extreme forms of nationalism seek to root themselves in mystic notions of the soil, forest or landscape, Smuts's 'patriotism of place' and sense of national belonging was defined through the more detached perspective of the philosopher and naturalist.[66] As a noted botanist and philosopher Smuts considered himself qualified to pronounce on science as a whole – just as he used his position as a leading South African politician to project himself as a statesman of the world. Thus, on losing political office to Hertzog in 1924, Smuts devoted much energy to scientific affairs and to the S2A3 in particular. In his 1925 presidential address to the Association he sought to reorient science away from the 'habits of thought and the viewpoints characteristic of its birthplace in the northern hemisphere', pointing instead to the country's distinctive position in the southern African subcontinent and the southern hemisphere more generally. Employing a geological metaphor, Smuts posited Africa as the 'great "scientific divide" among the continents': a high exposed watershed (like the Witwatersrand) separating great drainage areas, where 'future prospectors of science may yet find the richest veins of knowledge'.[67]

Smuts began his 1925 address by describing the implications of the 'Wegener hypothesis', named after the German geophysicist whose *Origin of Continents and Oceans* (1915) pioneered the theory of continental drift. His use of Wegener's ideas – which were far from commonly accepted at the time – allowed Smuts to posit Africa as the 'mother-continent' of the southern hemisphere from which South America, Madagascar, India and Australasia originally split away or 'calved off'. In placing southern Africa at the centre of the southern hemisphere, it now became possible to correlate scientific developments across a range of disciplines in new and creative ways which might have far-reaching implications for 'universal science'.[68] In geology, for example, several Cape formations appeared to be mirrored by similar formations in India and South America; the pattern of mineral deposits, such as diamonds and coal, illustrated a similar symmetry.[69] Botany posed particularly interesting problems. For, whereas most South African flora was evidently of tropical origin, the southwestern Cape was characterised by a distinct temperate flora which could not – as was then widely believed – have derived from northern Europe. Instead, Smuts suggested, Cape flora might have come from ancient Gondwanaland, the continent which was now covered largely by the South Atlantic Ocean and which used to encompass much of Africa, Australia, India, South America and Madagascar. This theory could explain botanical affinities between South African flora and flora belonging to other countries in the southern hemisphere.[70] Continuing with the implications of the Wegener hypothesis for the understanding of climatic changes and meteorology, Smuts came to astronomy. Here he mentioned the outstanding pioneering work of Lacaille, Henderson and Gill, concluding that South African astronomy 'has the distinction of being responsible for the determination of both great astronomical standards of measurement – the distance of the sun and the distance of the fixed stars'.[71]

Finally, Smuts paid tribute to the developing field of human palaeontology, paying special attention to Raymond Dart's recent work on the Boskop and Taung skulls and their profourd implications for the understanding of human evolution. Significantly, he lent support to Dart's novel and highly controversial claim that the Taung specimen (*Australopithecus*) represented a critical evolutionary 'missing link' in hominid development and he speculated that 'South Africa may yet figure as the cradle of mankind, or shall I rather, say, one of the cradles'. The idea that Africa might harbour some of mankind's earliest progenitors was a clear reference to Darwin but in speculating about 'cradles' in the plural form, Smuts might also have been gesturing towards polygenetic or multilinear theories of evolution. Whatever the case, Smuts certainly lent credence to the racialised form of anthropology that Dart did so much to promote. Thus, in arguing for South Africa's distinctive interest as a field of anthropological research, he ventured the opinion that 'Our Bushmen are nothing but living fossils' – analogous to the status of the country's cycads in the field of botany.

The notion that the aboriginal races of the country represented the end of an evolutionary line, that Bushmen could be likened to the indigenous flora and fauna of the country, and that they should be preserved primarily as evolutionary curiosities, had important implications for the development of racial science in South Africa and they were also reflective of racial attitudes during the segregationist era.[72] In this light, it is a matter of considerable irony – though by no means a contradiction – that Smuts prefaced his 1925 presidential address by affirming the ethnically inclusive spirit of the S2A3:

> In the Association both official languages of the Union enjoy equal privileges, and papers and addresses in either language are treated absolutely alike for purposes of publication or otherwise. It is the aim and object of this Association to bring together and unite all South Africans, irrespective of race and language, who are interested in the general scientific culture of South Africa.[73]

By 'irrespective of race and language' Smuts was obviously referring to English- and Afrikaans-speakers – not necessarily through a conscious act of excluding blacks, but simply because they would not have figured in this definition of 'South African'. Put more sharply, and considered in the light of the political prominence of segregationist legislation at this time, Smuts's appeal for unity amongst white South Africans reflected his unquestioning assumption of the need to maintain white supremacy and to deny African claims to common citizenship.

The 1929 visit

In 1929, at the invitation of the South African Association, the British Association returned to South Africa. This time there were more than 500 overseas visitors, funding having been secured from the South African government, individuals and commercial organisations based in Britain, as well as a contribution from the Rhodes Trust. The delegation was high-powered in scientific terms with some forty-four Fellows of the Royal Society attending, including its president, the atomic physicist Sir Ernest Rutherford.[74] Ten 'representative' scientists were invited to accept the hospitality of the Union. Thus, '[w]ith punctilious regard to the Union's racial traditions' three guests each were asked from England and Holland, the remainder coming from France, Austria, Italy and the United States.[75]

There were superficial resemblances with the 1905 meeting: as before, the official programme was split between Cape Town and Johannesburg (with optional excursions further afield), there were enthusiastic civic welcomes, extensive press coverage and evidence of considerable public interest in the proceedings. But the tone, context and intent of the 1929 meeting was markedly different from 1905. In the intervening quarter of a century, South Africa had been politically transformed. Instead of four separate British colonies under the overall

A COMMONWEALTH OF SCIENCE   83

control of a British High Commissioner, the ex-Boer war general J. B. M. Hertzog was now leader of a unitary state which had recently achieved the status of full sovereignty within the British Commonwealth. In the months before the Wall Street crash, the economy seemed buoyant. And the focus of white politics appeared to be turning away from tensions between English- and Afrikaans-speakers and towards the 'solution' of the 'native question'; indeed, only a few months before, Hertzog had fought – and decisively won – a general election on the issue of the 'black peril'.

By comparison with 1905, a new sense of national pride and self-confidence was widely evident. The composition of the nation was still a matter of dispute, but substantial consensus existed over two fundamental principles: that South Africa would continue to remain as an independent state within the Commonwealth, and that racial segregation between white and black was to be upheld and entrenched. Within these parameters the symbolic power of science and technology could easily be accommodated for it could be seen to exemplify the dynamism of a new society with independent standing in a wider community of nations. The British Association was keenly sensitive to the delicateness of the situation. If, in 1905, the British Association felt that it could afford to be imperious in keeping with its imperial role in the world, in 1929 it was now much more conscious of functioning within the emerging consensus politics of the Commonwealth and of its leading, but less elevated, position within the commonwealth of knowledge.

This spirit was evident from the outset. In his first address, the president of the British Association, Sir Thomas Holland, chose to quote from W. J. Viljoen's Afrikaans translation of Percy Fitzpatrick's *Jock of the Bushveld*, adding that 'the translation is in a language capable of expressing virile sentences'.[76] This gesture did not only play to the literary icon of South African Englishness; Holland's willingness to speak in Afrikaans struck an obvious chord with his audience, as did his tribute to Viljoen (who had died suddenly a few days before). A noted scholar of the Afrikaans language and leading educational administrator in the Cape as well as the Orange Free State, Viljoen was an exemplar of pragmatic moderation in the fraught arena of language and educational policy.[77] Thus, to reinforce the message of conciliation, Sir Ernest Rutherford made the point that the British Association gathering was a 'representative' one, noting that Sir Thomas was a Canadian while he himself was a New Zealander.[78] This formula was evidently successful for, on the Johannesburg leg of the journey, Holland again quoted in Afrikaans from *Jock*, adding that the book accurately 'reproduced the spirit of the veld'. And, at a mayoral reception attended by some 4,000 guests a couple of days later, the back of the city hall stage was hung with both the Union Jack and the new South African flag, below which the words 'Welcome/Welkom' were outlined in coloured lights.[79]

The 1929 meeting provided an ideal opportunity to reflect on South Africa's achievements since the beginning of the century. The fact that sectional meetings of the British Association could be held on the imposing new Groote Schuur campus of the University of Cape Town was a source of considerable civic pride; thus, the excellence of the university's facilities and architectural design (it was conceived by J. M. Solomon, a local Cape artist and follower of Herbert Baker, and built with the help of Edwin Lutyens) were widely remarked upon.[80] More broadly, science was explicitly called into the service of an inclusive white South African nationhood based on shared values of intellectual, cultural and material progress. This was frequently coupled with a firm commitment to international cooperation, especially in the context of the Commonwealth. Implicitly excluded were the extreme fundamentalism of Christian nationalism and, by a process of neglect and peripheralisation, the claims of African nationalism. The defining sentiments of this sense of moderate white nationhood were fittingly articulated by General Smuts's rising protégé, Jan Hofmeyr, the politician-scholar who would, in the 1930s and 1940s, come to personify the political hopes of the increasingly marginalised white liberal intelligentsia.

In welcoming the British Association to Cape Town on behalf of the South African Association (of which he was then president), Hofmeyr delivered a widely reported address entitled 'Africa and science' which the *Rand Daily Mail* referred to as brilliant, inspirational and visionary.[81] Hofmeyr began by recalling the remarkable intellectual progress which had taken place in South Africa since the previous visit of the British Association in 1905. He recorded the development of the university system, the growth of specialist and professional scientific societies, as well as the expansion in state-sponsored and applied scientific work.[82]

Hofmeyr's central theme was what he referred to as the 'South Africanisation' of science. Whereas in 1905 science in South Africa could be called 'exotic' in the sense that it depended on imported expatriates, its personnel was now, whether by adoption or birth, 'essentially South African'. But, although South Africans evinced great pride in their science because it was 'distinctively ours', Hofmeyr noted that there was 'nothing narrow about its South Africanism. Were it otherwise, it would have been false to the spirit of Science.'[83] South African science had succeeded in drawing the attention of the world to the country; it also had much to offer. Thus, Hofmeyr went on to express the view that the next task was even bolder, namely, to 'Africanise' science. This ambition was expressed in terms of a curious brand of intellectual sub-imperialism whereby whites, as the natural representatives of European civilisation in Africa, were bound to discharge their obligations to that great continent from their base in the south. In tones heavily reminscent of the evangelical nineteenth-century imperial mission Hofmeyr declared:

> It is by way of this Southern gateway that Science itself can most effectively be made to permeate Africa. And to you, having so come, to you, the ambassadors of Science, I present – Africa. It is Africa and Science, which, I would like to think, are to-day met together. Happy indeed should be the fruits of the mating.[84]

In closing, Hofmeyr described the 'development of Science in Africa, of Africa by Science' as a 'Promised Land'.[85] The optimism of this expansive African vision may have been misplaced, but it was not entirely without foundation as the concurrent opening in Pretoria of the Pan-African Agricultural Veterinary Congress as well as the International Geological Congress vividly illustrated.[86]

The sense of national pride and mission within which Hofmeyr conceived of South African science was enthusiastically taken up in the English-language press. It was reiterated by Smuts at the inaugural meeting of the Association in Johannesburg. On this occasion Smuts reminded his audience of the social and intellectual transformation which had taken place in South Africa since the previous visit of the British Association in 1905 to a country 'devastated and laid bare in a great war'. The reconstruction of the country, the achievement of political unity and the yet-to-be-achieved ideal of united nationhood, were matters of considerable pride. Smuts went on to say – with perhaps a permissible measure of exaggeration – that it was science that was largely responsible for recreating a 'new South Africa'. In areas such as mining, agriculture and manufacturing, science had provided the technology for overcoming animal and plant diseases and for exploiting natural resources in new and original ways. Whereas general members of the public had previously been sceptical about science, they were now appreciative and enthusiastic converts to its cause. Indeed, Smuts went so far as to suggest with double-edged irony – reflecting his suspicion of the mass technological age – that science had become 'the new magic . . . the great intangible power, the imponderable which in the long run carries everything before it'.[87]

With these remarks Smuts touched various bases: his words lent added weight to Hofmeyr's Cape Town address, they endorsed the

86 SCIENCE AND SOCIETY IN SOUTHERN AFRICA

intrinsic association of white nationality with rational progress and material achievement, and (clever politician that he was) reminded his audience that he himself was both a broad-minded man of science and a central figure in the process of national conciliation and renewal.

Smuts also took the opportunity to underline the message of Sir Thomas Holland's presidential address in Johannesburg, appropriately on the mineral resources of the world and their importance as a factor in the maintenance of civilisation and world peace. Holland had stressed the role of applied science in the advance of material and cultural progress, linking the control of natural resources to international politics and arguing that if the British empire and the United States would jointly exercise a 'mineral sanction' on countries infringing the Kellog Pact, no war could last very long. His clear message, therefore, was that South Africa was a valued member of the Commonwealth and that the gold mining industry was of pre-eminent significance from both a domestic and an international perspective.[88] This idea was calculated to appeal to Johannesburg's industrial and business community, flattering their sense of importance and reminding them of their debt to science at one and the same time. It also served more generally to remind South Africans of their international obligations and responsibilities.

Holland's address can be seen as the culmination of a wider effort on his part to secure a broad base of support for scientific research. In a public debate on 'science and industry' held in Cape Town a week before, attention had been focused on the relationship between scientific research and economic prosperity. Stressing the beneficial effects of science to the community at large, Holland emphasised science as a democratic and popular, rather than an arcane and elitist, activity. Thus he sought to undercut both the condescending attitudes of pure scientists towards applied work, as well as the suspicion on the part of 'captains of industry' that scientific research was a useless if harmless activity undeserving of their backing.[89] In this regard Holland was not only addressing a South African constituency: like previous leaders of the British Association, he was alert to the need to reposition the organisation with regard to public and professional opinion back in Britain. In the 1920s, as Collins and Macleod have shown, the British Association found itself under renewed pressure. It had to respond to post-war public scepticism towards the idea that scientific research was an unqualified good; it needed to be seen to be serving the public interest; and, within the profession, it had to maintain the delicate balance between a commitment to pure and applied research – or, in other words, to justify the concerns and interests of the few, while satisfying the needs and understanding of the many.[90]

Just as South Africa's geopolitical significance within the Commonwealth was highlighted in speeches and comments at the 1929 meeting, so South African scientists were seen to be part of an international community and the production and dissemination of knowledge was understood as a reciprocal and cooperative process. Fittingly, therefore, the South African content of the 1929 conference was much more extensive and its profile significantly higher than in 1905. In fields ranging from zoology, botany and geography, to economics, anthropology, psychology and education, South African material was widely evident and discussed in some depth. As if to prove that South African scholarship could hold its own in international terms, mirroring its status as a nation amongst nations, General Smuts was invited to expound on his theory of 'Holism' at one of the prestigious set-piece events. His paper, grandly titled 'The nature of life', was given prominent coverage in the press and Smuts must have been gratified that scientists of the stature of J. S. Haldane, Wildon Carr, A. S. Eddington and Lancelot Hogben presented formal responses.[91]

In the wake of Dart's claims for the significance of *Australopithecus* as well as Robert Broom's lifetime of internationally recognised work on human and reptile fossils, anthropology and prehistory was accorded considerable attention. Several international luminaries in the field of prehistory were present in 1929, including Leo Frobenius, Henri Breuil, Gertrude Caton Thompson, John Myres and Henry Balfour. The latter, who was curator of the Pitt Rivers museum in Oxford and president of the anthropology section, paid tribute to the advances which had been made in South African prehistory since his first visit in 1899. And he stressed the national and international significance of South Africa's archaeological heritage.[92]

There were two especially keenly watched papers in the anthropological section, both with the potential to excite controversy. The talk by the German ethnologist and exponent of *kulturkreis* theory, Leo Frobenius, was well trailed in the press since he was expected to offer startling evidence for the existence of a great and civilised race which had apparently lived for over 7,000 years in the area between Great Zimbabwe and Lake Malawi, worshipping the stars and the moon. But Frobenius may have received advanced warning of Gertrude Caton Thompson's rather more prosaic findings about the origins of Great Zimbabwe; in the event his talk on the different styles and types of Bushman rock art – though suggesting Carthaginian influence in characteristic diffusionist mode – was presented in careful academic style and caused no sensation.[93]

The presentation of Caton Thompson's findings, by contrast, was no damp squib. As a respected archaeologist and Egyptologist, she had

88   SCIENCE AND SOCIETY IN SOUTHERN AFRICA

been commissioned by the British Association (with funding from the Rhodes Trustees) to settle the long-running popular and scholarly debate about the origins of the Zimbabwe ruins. Unlike Randall-MacIver's report to the 1905 meeting, Caton Thompson was firmly of the opinion that all aspects of the Zimbabwe civilisation were the results of indigenous African endeavour.[94] This finding, which unambiguously rejected theories ascribing the authorship of Zimbabwe to mysterious ancient visitors from the Near East, helped to puncture a key aspect of white settler mythology: that Africans were incapable of creating a significant material culture on their own. Needless to say, her views were not accepted by all. A determinedly dissenting note was sounded by the acclaimed anthropologist Raymond Dart whose fundamental commitment to cultural diffusionism caused him to launch an intemperate attack on Caton Thompson.[95]

Another controversial paper with a strong bearing on contemporary racial thought was E. G. Malherbe's discussion of 'Education and the poor white' which raised fears about the long-term capacity of the ruling white race to maintain its dominance. Drawing on the preliminary results of the landmark Carnegie Commission into poor whiteism (of which he was a leading member) the ambitious young Columbia-trained educationist shocked public opinion by referring to the poor white problem as a 'skeleton in our cupboard'. As a result of an unconscious feeling of vulnerability, Malherbe suggested, whites experienced a psychological 'inferiority complex' which led them to lay the blame for their own predicament on blacks. Mechanisms to protect the lowest ten per cent of whites from the upper fifty per cent of blacks would only serve to jeopardise the country's future.[96] Malherbe's address drew highly favourable comment by some and was widely seen as a courageous and authoritative intervention into an area of increasing social and economic concern. Dr C. W. Kimmins, president of the Educational Section, resorted to eulogy, and the *Cape Times* called it 'brilliant'.[97] Malherbe's mentor and colleague Fred Clarke, then professor of education at the University of Cape Town, wrote him a congratulatory letter in which he praised the young man for displaying 'Clear-headedness, courage & a genuine patriotism that was ready to face martyrdom'.[98]

By genuine patriotism, Clarke meant Malherbe's willingness to speak as a 'good South African' rather than an Afrikaner sectarian. Clarke's assessment of the attendant dangers proved correct when the Afrikaans press tore into Malherbe for betraying his Afrikaner loyalties. *Ons Vaderland*, mouthpiece of the Transvaal nationalists, accused Malherbe of 'professorial superficiality' and 'thoughtless stupidity'. The attack was ostensibly focused on Malherbe's methodology and the quality of his research, but the newspaper was clearly stung by the suggestion that whites were somehow psychologically fearful of blacks and highly sensitive about his calumnious airing in public of a problem which might reflect negatively on the standing of the Afrikaner *volk*.[99] *Die Burger* joined in with an editorial titled 'Pure nonsense', and *Die Volksblad* was likewise hostile.[100] Underlying the negative reaction lay an even deeper fear: that Afrikaner poor whites were becoming biologically and mentally enfeebled through eugenic deterioration.

Greatly concerned that the Carnegie enquiry was becoming dangerously politicised, a statement was communicated to the press by its leading investigators, J. F. W. Grosskopf, E. G. Malherbe and R. W. Wilcocks – all of whom were respected Afrikaner academics – stressing that their primary task was objective 'fact finding' and carefully affirming the commission's political neutrality. Malherbe was forced into a convoluted attempt to defuse the tension by distancing himself from the interpretation that had been placed on his words. This 'clarificatory' explanation was accepted by *Die Burger* which duly responded with an editorial acknowledging the importance of the commission's work and expressing confidence in its commitment to 'bring the facts to light'.[101] But *Ons Vaderland* remained uncompromisingly hostile and was especially concerned at the negative impression that would be created by Malherbe's presentation of so-called 'facts' to the British Association as well as to his American backers.[102]

Political controversy thus intruded into the 1929 meeting, but it did not overwhelm the event. In the many reflections and tributes to the success of the 1929 meeting, both the British and the South African Associations expressed themselves well pleased with the way in which things had gone. A special meeting to reflect on the proceedings was convened by the Royal Empire Society in December. Here, the editor of *Nature*, Sir Richard Gregory, reiterated the modern utilitarian role of science in promoting imperial cooperation, economic development and human well-being. In an age 'when nearly all the problems of development of natural resources and guidance of life are scientific, yet the control of the factors of progress is in the hands of administrators who have no first-hand knowledge of science', it followed that science should rank in importance with the 'administrative and fighting services' and be regarded 'as an indispensable part of the machinery of government and not as a luxury to be dispensed with in times of financial stringency.'[103] In South Africa, a genuine mood of buoyant

90   SCIENCE AND SOCIETY IN SOUTHERN AFRICA

confidence in the country's achievements was evident. The *Cape Times* captured the spirit when it proclaimed in an editorial on 'Savants and servants':

> When last the British Association met in Cape Town its delegates were the guests of the Government of the Cape Colony, then a separate State in the South African group of colonies. But science knew no political boundaries, and in 1905, as in 1929, it held its meetings in the chief centres of what now constitutes the Union, and in doing so it contributed its share to that strong sense of South African unity which was then beginning to take shape and form.[104]

The idea that science knows no politics was of course a convenient fiction. Aside from Malherbe's intervention into the causes of poor whiteism, one of the striking features of the 1929 programme was the number of papers dealing directly or indirectly with racial science and eugenics. Amongst these, one might mention the contributions of visitors like R. Ruggles Gates on 'racial crossing' and H. J. Fleure on 'racial drifts'. Even more directly pertinent to South African conditions were the raft of papers on physical anthropology and human origins, the heated public debate on the origins of Great Zimbabwe, as well as papers dealing with comparative racial intelligence quotients and the purpose of native education.

I have argued elsewhere[105] that the dispassionate qualities of science were frequently invoked at this time in regard to the desire to find a 'solution' to the 'native question'. In Hofmeyr's 1929 address, for example, he maintained that science had an important role in 'determining the lines along which white and coloured races can best live together in harmony and to their common advantage'.[106] The appeal to – and appeal of – scientific objectivity can also be seen as a counterpart to the (disingenuous) wish of leading politicians to prevent the 'native question' becoming an issue in party politics. If blacks were in the process of being excluded from common citizenship via the landmark segregation bills then under parliamentary consideration, justification for their exclusion was in part founded on the idea that African culture was incompatible with the values of Western rationality and natural progress. Science could therefore be used both to evaluate Africans' rights as citizens, and also to constitute white citizenship and nationality.

As the Malherbe incident illustrated, the terms upon which white nationhood would be constituted was becoming increasingly bitterly contested. A resurgent Afrikaner nationalism operating both within and beyond the realm of parliamentary politics sought to define South African nationality in ways that went much further than the 'two

A COMMONWEALTH OF SCIENCE   91

streams' policy of Prime Minister Hertzog. The objective of radical nationalists who sought ultimately to establish a Boer republic without any trace of the imperial connection was not yet fully articulated. But the tendency was registered in the only significantly discordant note sounded in reaction to the British Association's 1929 visit – that of the Afrikaans press.

The reception granted to the British Association by *Die Burger*, the mouthpiece of Cape Afrikaner nationalism, in 1929, was cool rather than overtly hostile. Notably, the newspaper chose to emphasise the European rather than British profile of the visitors, paying particular attention to the presence of individuals like Professor Freudenberg of the University of Heidelberg. In subdued tones of selfless patriotism, the paper expressed willingness to learn from their overseas guests, noting that the visit was in South Africa's best interests and that it would improve the international status of the country.[107] It was on this basis, too, that *Die Kerkbode*, the influential organ of the Dutch Reformed Church, came to terms with the Association's visit. *Die Kerkbode* was uncomfortable, however, with the fact that there was no explicit theological dimension to the meeting, but comforted itself with the observation that religion was an intrinsic part of everyday intellectual life and existence. Exception was taken, however, to Hofmeyr's opening address in which he referred to the exciting possibility that Africa might, as Darwin predicted, turn out to be 'the scene of Nature's greatest creative effort', namely, the evolution of mankind. Quoting Hofmeyr's account of recent palaeontological and anthropological discoveries, *Die Kerkbode* therefore expressed disappointment at his acceptance, in defiance of scriptural orthodoxy, of evolutionist theory. Notwithstanding this complaint, the Dutch Reformed Church organ was pleased to welcome the scientists: it warmed to the promise that science could help to advance South Africa's agriculture and industry, and noted with satisfaction Thomas Holland's efforts to speak in Afrikaans.[108]

If Afrikaner opinion-formers were inclined to accept the British Association, they would only do so on their own terms. They were thus extremely sensitive to any appropriation of the visit by supporters of Smuts's South African Party, or to anything which could be interpreted as a slight on the Afrikaner volk. It is therefore unsurprising that the British Association provided a convenient subject for party political sniping. In anticipation of the British Association's arrival the *Cape Times* (a staunch supporter of Smuts's South African Party) published a crude cartoon by Whyndam Robinson. This depicted two of Hertzog's ministers, F. W. Beyers and D. F. Malan, dressed as cavedwellers, with Beyers chewing on a bone (or meat) inscribed 'hatred'.

The caption read: 'Those members of the British Association especially interested in relics of the Stone Age will not have far to look.'[109] This provocation did not go unnoticed. *Die Burger* responded in an editorial by the nationalist ideologue A. L. Geyer entitled 'scandalous'. Addressing itself to the learned visitors, the paper generously sought to assuage any embarrassment they might suffer; the *Cape Times*, it assured them, was a jingoistic newspaper which could not best claim to represent British values and culture. Nor should the *Cape Times* be seen as a yardstick of South African culture. Afrikaners – whether English- or Afrikaans-speaking – were ashamed that the visitors should encounter a tasteless newspaper which venomously attacked the nationalist government that had been responsible for inviting them. For those guests accustomed to reading accounts of 'Dutch' racial hatred in British newspapers, the *Cape Times'* cartoon revealed where the source of such sentiment was truly to be found.[110] In sum, Geyer's editorial skilfully sought to invert accusations of race hatred, to distance the British Association from Smuts's South African Party and to align Afrikaner nationalism with South Africanism. This tactic was endorsed in an article by C. J. Langenhoven, the noted Afrikaner poet and critic, who claimed the high-ground of cultural and intellectual achievement for the National Party, and attacked those who viewed Smuts as a great world statesman who suffered domestically from an unappreciative nation of 'backvelders' and blinkered race-haters.[111]

Notably, the hostility of the Afrikaner press was directed to specific issues and did not extend to a direct attack on the British Association itself or, indeed, on western scientific traditions. Pride in South African scientific achievement was widely shared and actively courted. Anger was instead directed inwards and targeted towards moderate South African Party-supporting Afrikaners like Malherbe, Smuts and Hofmeyr, whose ease with the international community of scholars was in itself perceived as a threat.

Conclusion

The visits of the British Association to South Africa in 1905 and 1929 highlight marked shifts in the relationship between South Africa and the imperial metropole. In 1905 the British Association was greeted by a newly constituted country whose experience of war had left it economically shattered and politically fragmented. Discussions about future political cooperation between the four British colonies were only beginning but, aside from the centralised authority of the colonial administration, there existed few national institutions out of

A COMMONWEALTH OF SCIENCE 93

which South Africa could be fashioned as a meaningful entity. At least as far as the anglophone establishment was concerned, the joint scientific meeting of the British and South African Associations offered an excellent opportunity to proclaim the virtues of peaceful cooperation and reconstruction. Such an event could demonstrate the connection between Britain and its southern African colonies, as well as the internal links between those colonies. And it would do so in a manner that was neither official nor politically provocative: under the guise of the universality of science and the search for objective truth, the universality of the British empire and the transcendent virtues of British values could be implicitly affirmed. By expressing Englishness (or, more properly, Britishness) in the neutral language of universal progress, prosperity and security, the risk of giving political offence was minimised.

In the Victorian era the notion of civilisation had served as a key discursive justification of British imperialism, building variously on evangelical Christianity, racial supremacy and social evolutionism. But the civilising ideal carried unwanted historical baggage in the shape of John Philip, Exeter Hall and the humanitarian tradition. These aspects of the civilising project were acceptable neither to Afrikaners, nor to those forward-looking English-speaking South Africans who sought an answer to the country's problems in political reconciliation between Boer and Briton and racial segregation between black and white. One promising way out of this ideological impasse was to secularise and neutralise the idea of civilisation, stripping it of its moralistic and culturally specific overtones and recasting it (and imperialism more generally) in the guise of scientific progress and technological prowess. Portraying government policies in this light was precisely what Milner and his followers sought to do in the postwar reconstruction period. Equally, because science was an apparently neutral and objective activity committed to the realisation of the common good, it was also readily adopted by politicians like Botha and Smuts to aid the creation of an independent and unitary state under Afrikaner leadership.

Science and technology can therefore be said to have played a notable role in the process of political reconciliation between Boer and Brit. Indeed, in the years after Union the creation of a range of scientific and educational institutions came to symbolise the growing confidence of a new South African nation which, though independent, was nevertheless still firmly tied into the wider imperial network. However, the rise of Afrikaner nationalism in the immediate post-Union era under the leadership of General Hertzog, increasingly challenged the ideology of South Africanism championed by the governing

South African Party. With the electoral victory of Hertzog's National party in 1924 this challenge became more overt. Hertzog's 'two-stream' ethnic policy, coupled with his quest to assert South Africa's parity within the empire, was initially accommodated within the newly developing white commonwealth. Nevertheless, when the British Association revisited South Africa in 1929 the changed political milieu could be measured in terms of discernible shifts in the relationship between imperial and colonial science. South African patriotic pride and confidence were registered by a demonstrably enhanced scientific and technical ability to master the African environment (and, in the case of anthropology, Africans themselves). For politicians like Smuts and Hofmeyr science was therefore both a source of national pride in South Africa's achievements as well as visible proof of its claims to international status: it was, in this sense, both a tangible expression of, and a metaphor for, commonwealth.

In the sphere of domestic politics, political moderates hoped that scientific rationality would triumph over ethnocentric prejudice and emotion (and for many of the same figures a belief in scientific rationality extended to efforts to 'solve' the 'native question'). As the proceedings of the 1929 meeting revealed, however, this optimistic vision of the dispassionate benefits of scientific research was tainted by the nationalist sensitivities which surfaced in discussions about poor-whiteism and evolutionist theory, and in stereotypes of Boer backwardness. But although such disputes questioned the extent to which political reconciliation was an accomplished fact, they did not overly detract from the broader success of the British Association in developing a supra-white sense of national identity. Rather, they pointed to intensifying debates about the position of the Afrikaner volk within the body politic of South Africa as well as its broader relationship to the outside world. These debates were, however, not only about the terms of inclusion within white South African identity; increasingly, they referred to the basis upon which blacks would be excluded from common citizenship. And here, too, science played a conspicuous role.

Notes

1   My thanks to Jocelyn Alexander, William Beinart and Libby Robin for their comments on earlier versions of this chapter.
2   *The Times*, 2 September 1905.
3   See photograph album, A17 fol., British Association for the Advancement of Science, Historical Papers, University of the Witwatersrand.
4   Archive of the British Association for the Advancement of Science (BAAS) Bodleian Library, Oxford. Box 205, *Engineering*, 28 July 1905, p. 119.

A COMMONWEALTH OF SCIENCE   95

5   O. J. R. Howarth, *The British Association for the Advancement of Science: A retrospect 1831–1931* (London, 1931), pp. 128–30; *The Times*, 16 August 1905; BAAS box 203, Donald Currie to Professor Dewar, 11 June 1903.

6   *The Times*, 16 August 1905; 2 February 1905.

7   BAAS box 420; *Morning Post*, 30 October 1905.

8   *Star*, 29 August 1905.

9   See e.g. BAAS box 198, *Glimpses in Natal*.

10 *Star*, 28 August 1905; *The Times*, 17 August 1905.

11 James Starke Browne, *Through South Africa with the British Association* (London, 1906), p. 275. It was precisely because of a perception that the 1884 meeting in Montreal would amount to 'a glorified picnic of important men of science, who could have no serious purpose in visiting Canada', that objections to overseas meetings were registered in England. See Howarth, *The British Association*, p. 121. See also *Star*, 28 August 1905 (editorial).

12 This paragraph is drawn from R. Macleod, 'Introduction', in R. Macleod and P. Collins (eds), *The Parliament of Science: The British Association for the Advancement of Science 1831–1981* (Northwood, 1981), pp. 17–19, 32–4. See also A. Gale, 'Science at the margins: the British Association and the foundations of Canadian anthropology, 1884–1910', Ph.D. thesis, University of Pennsylvania, 1986, pp. 67, 187–9.

13 M. Worboys, 'The British Association and empire: Science and social imperialism, 1880–1940', in Macleod and Collins (eds), *Parliament of Science*. The classic analysis of social imperialism remains B. Semmel's *Imperialism and Social Reform* (London, 1960).

14 Gale, 'Science at the margins', pp. 22–3.

15 Address by Sir David Gill to the S2A3, in *Report of the South African Association for the Advancement of Science: First Meeting Cape Town 1903* (Cape Town, 1903), p. 17.

16 *Ibid.*, pp. 18–19. BAAS box 201, Gill to secretary British Association, 5 August 1902; Gill to Garson, 9 March 1903; Gill to Silva White, 25 January 1904.

17 Address by Sir David Gill to the S2A3, p. 36. cf. the words of Gill's fellow astronomer John Herschel who did pioneering work at the Cape between 1834 and 1838 and who was also a leading light in the early years of the British Association (serving as president in 1845): 'Let selfish interests divide the worldy; let jealousies foment the envious; we breathe a purer Empyrean air. The common pursuit of truth is of itself a brotherhood.' Cited in R. Macleod, 'Retrospect: The British Association and its historians', in Macleod and Collins (eds), *Parliament of Science*, p. 4.

18 *Morning Post*, 30 October 1905, in BAAS box 420.

19 *The Times*, 16 August 1905.

20 *The Times*, 31 August 1905.

21 *Star*, 2 September 1905.

22 *Ibid.*

23 *Star*, 28 August 1905 (editorial); *The Times*, 23 August 1905; *The Times*, 14 September 1905.

24 *The Times*, 23 August 1905 (speech by Professor Darwin); *The Times*, 6 September 1905; *Star*, 2 September 1905 (speech by Professor Darwin). *The Friend*, 4 September 1905.

25 BAAS box 201, Gill to Silva White, 14 March 1905; Gill to Silva White, 28 March 1905; James Stewart to Gill, 24 March 1905.

26 *The Times*, 28 August 1905; Browne, *Through South Africa*, p. 69.

27 *Star*, 5 September 1905; *The Times*, 6 September 1905; Browne, *Through South Africa*, pp. 127–8; *Bloemfontein Post*, 6 September 1905.

28 *Diamond Fields Advertiser*, 5 September 1905.

29 *The Times*, 13 September 1905.

30 H. T. Montague Bell (ed.), *Addresses and Papers Read at the Joint Meeting of the British and South African Associations for the Advancement of Science Held in*

96   SCIENCE AND SOCIETY IN SOUTHERN AFRICA

South Africa 1905, 4 vols (Johannesburg, 1906). See e.g. BAAS box 202, William Cullen to David Gill, 24 May 1905. Cullen took exception to Gill's suggestion that the editors were having to 'cadge' for papers, but admitted that abstracts were not coming in quickly and that some sub-standard papers 'have managed to slip in'.

31   A. C. Brown (ed.), *A History of Scientific Endeavour in South Africa* (Cape Town, 1977), pp. 417, 442–3; B. Warner, *Astronomers at the Royal Observatory Cape of Good Hope* (Cape Town, 1979), pp. 104–5. These surveys were massive enterprises. Gill's project to measure, by triangulation, the 30th east meridian (the longest measurable arc of meridian) stretching from South Africa to Norway, was only completed in 1955. See also Howarth, *The British Association*, p. 130; D. Gill, 'On the origin and progress of geodetic survey in South Africa, and of the African arc of meridian', in *Report of the Seventy-Fifth Meeting of the British Association for the Advancement of Science: South Africa 1905* (Cape Town, 1906), pp. 228–48.

32   Presidential address by T. Reunert, *Report of the South African Association for the Advancement of Science: 3rd and 4th meeting 1905–6* (Cape Town, 1906), p. iv; Review of F. H. Hatch and G. S. Corstorphine, *The Geology of South Africa* (London, 1905), in *Star*, 29 August 1905.

33   A. C. Haddon, 'Anthropology', in *Report of the Seventy-Fifth Meeting of the British Association*, pp. 511–27.

34   *Ibid.*, p. 304. Notably, MacIver's paper was the only anthropological contribution with reference to South Africa printed in the main section ('Reports on the state of science') of this volume.

35   *The Times*, 2 September 1905; Pim's address was reported at length in *Star*, 1 September 1905. For the significance of Pim's writings, see S. Dubow, *Racial Segregation and the Origins of Apartheid in South Africa, 1919–36* (London, 1989).

36   Richard C. Jebb, 'Educational Science', in *Report of the Seventy-Fifth Meeting of the British Association*, pp. 597–605; for comments on the significance of this address, see M. Boucher, *The University of the Cape of Good Hope and the University of South Africa 1873–1946* (Pretoria, 1974), p. 67.

37   *The Times*, 2 September 1905: Professor Darwin, in his closing address, referred to the 'number of important papers bearing on South African matters'.

38   See e.g. *Star*, 28 August 1905 (editorial): 'We flatter ourselves, moreover, that this visit has been looked forward to no less eagerly by them than by the Colony'; also *Star*, 2 September 1905 (editorial): 'It is also something gained if the visit has enabled them to gather – though few of them were likely ever to have entertained doubts on the point – that the British element in South Africa is neither worse nor better than the members of the stock from which it has sprung'; *Bloemfontein Post*, 2 September 1905 (editorial): 'We are indeed very sensible of the honour and privilege of entertaining, though it be for a moment, the representatives of old-world learning though we regret that our own advancement makes us worthy of being little else than a pied a terre between greater centres.'

39   S. M. Naudé and A. C. Brown, 'The growth of scientific institutions', in Brown (ed.), *A History of Scientific Endeavour*, p. 70.

40   N. J. Dippenaar (ed.), *Staatsmuseum 100* (Pretoria, 1992). When the British ousted the Kruger government from Pretoria in 1900 it was rapidly renamed the Pretoria (and later, again, the Transvaal) Museum.

41   *Report of the South African Association for the Advancement of Science: First Meeting ... 1903*, p. 9.

42   The S2A3 was cautious not to be seen as in any way interfering with the premier scientific status of the South African Philosophical Society which dated back to 1877 and of which Gill was also president in 1903. The relationship between the two organisations is comparable to that existing between the Royal Society of London and the British Association. The superior position of the Philosophical Society, though never really in doubt, was confirmed when it received the Royal Charter in 1908 and changed its title to the Royal Society of South Africa.

43 'Report of the Council for the period ended May 2nd 1903', in *Report of the South African Association for the Advancement of Science . . . 1903*, p. 517; B. J. F. Schonland, 'The South African Association for the Advancement of Science, its past and future', *South African Journal of Science* (hereafter *SAJS*), 49:3–4 (1952), 61. Membership was drawn from the whole of South and southern Africa.

44 Presidential address by T. Reunert, in *Report of the South African Association for the Advancement of Science . . . 1905–6*, p. i.

45 Address by Sir David Gill to the South African Association for the Advancement of Science, in *Report of the South African Association for the Advancement of Science . . . 1903*, p. 36.

46 *African Monthly*, 2:8 (1907), 227.

47 Macleod and Collins (eds), *Parliament of Science*, pp. v, 17.

48 D. Denoon, *A Grand Illusion* (London, 1973), pp. 68–9. See also J. Krikler, *Revolution from Above, Rebellion from Below: The agrarian Transvaal at the turn of the century* (Oxford, 1993), pp. 66, 76 and ff.

49 See W. Beinart, 'Agricultural science, conservation and nationalism: H. S. D. du Toit in South Africa', paper presented to conference on 'Science and Society in Southern Africa', University of Sussex, 1998.

50 B. C. Jansen, 'The growth of veterinary research in South Africa', in Brown (ed.), *A History of Scientific Endeavour*, pp. 166–70; F. Stark (ed.), *Pretoria: 100 Years* (Pretoria, 1955), pp. 161–5. In 1980, Theiler was the first recipient of the S2A3's South African Medal.

51 D. M. Joubert, 'Agricultural research in South Africa: An historical overview', in Brown (ed.), *A History of Scientific Endeavour*, pp. 266–8.

52 The national survey arose out of a merger between the Geological Commission of the Cape Colony and the Geological Survey of the Transvaal. The Geological Survey of Natal and Zululand ceased to exist some years before Union. See Dippenaar, *Staatsmuseum 100*, p. 62.

53 R. F. H. Summers, *A History of the South African Museum, 1825–1975* (Cape Town, 1975), p. 92; N. Fowler, 'A history of the Albany Museum, 1855–1958', unpublished MS, 1968, Albany Museum, pp. 183–4.

54 E. Percy Phillips, 'A brief historical sketch of the development of botanical science in South Africa and the contribution of South Africa to botany', *SAJS*, 27 (1930).

55 H. Bolus, 'The native flora of South Africa and its preservation', *The State*, 2:7 (1909), 105–6. See also, 'The proposed national botanic garden', *Report of the Eighth Annual Report of the South African Association for the Advancement of Science: Cape Town 1910* (Cape Town, 1911), pp. 421–3.

56 H. H. W. Pearson, 'A state botanical garden', *The State*, 5:5 (1911).

57 H. H. W. Pearson, 'A national botanic garden', *Report of the Eighth Annual Report . . . of the South African Association*, p. 54.

58 R. H. Compton, *Kirstenbosch: Garden for a nation* (Cape Town, 1965), pp. 33, 50.

59 *Ibid.*, p. 31.

60 Although Kirstenbosch was founded as a National Botanic Garden, this status was only uneasily maintained. Cape dignitaries provided a great deal of impetus for its creation and it was more closely linked for research purposes to the University of Cape Town than to a government department (like that of agriculture). At a meeting on 8 March 1912 attended by many Cape notables it was resolved to establish 'a National Botanic Garden within the Cape Peninsula'. In 1923 a new herbarium was established under the aegis of the department of agriculture at Pretoria as an embryo 'Kew'. This initiative was regarded as a snub to Kirstenbosch. Local Cape opinion was indignant at what it saw as regional competition and an unwelcome instance of state centralisation. See Compton, *Kirstenbosch*, pp. 43, 80–1; also D. P. and E. McCracken, *The Way to Kirstenbosch* (Cape Town, 1988), chs 11 and 12.

61 These figures should be treated as indicative rather than entirely accurate; there are inconsistencies in the sources from which they have been drawn: J. H. Hofmeyr, 'Africa and science', *SAJS*, 26 (1929), 4; E. G. Malherbe, Memo on

98   SCIENCE AND SOCIETY IN SOUTHERN AFRICA

'Educational development in the Union 1905–1930', Killie Campbell Library, Durban, KCM 56973 (305) file 427/7, p. 5; E. G. Malherbe, *Education in South Africa vol. II: 1923–75* (Cape Town, 1977), p. 727.

62   Boucher, *The University of the Cape of Good Hope*, p. 124; R. P. B. Davis, 'University reconstruction in the Cape Colony', *African Monthly*, 3:18 (1908); J. Edgar, 'Union and the university question', *The State*, 3:4 (1910); 'The case for a national university', *The State*, 4:1 (1910).

63   M. Boucher, *Spes in Ardus: A history of the University of South Africa* (Pretoria, 1973); E. G. Malherbe, *Education in South Africa vol. 1: 1652–1922* (Cape Town, 1925); H. Phillips, *The University of Cape Town 1918–1948: The formative years* (Cape Town, 1993).

64   UG [Union Government publication] 33-'28, *Report of the University Commission* (Pretoria, 1928), paras 48, 105–6 and 'summary of conclusions'.

65   E. A. Walker, *The South African College and the University of Cape Town 1829–1929* (Cape Town, 1929), p. 78.

66   See S. Dubow and S. Marks, 'Patriotism of place and race: Keith Hancock on South Africa', paper delivered Keith Hancock symposium, Australian National University, Canberra, 1998.

67   J. C. Smuts, 'South Africa in science', *SAJS*, 22 (1925), 3–4.

68   *Ibid.*, pp. 4–5.

69   *Ibid.*, pp. 5–6.

70   *Ibid.*, pp. 6–7.

71   *Ibid.*, pp. 14–15.

72   See e.g. R. J. Gordon, *The Bushman Myth* (Boulder, 1992); S. Dubow, 'Human origins, race typology and the other Raymond Dart', *African Studies*, 55:1 (1996).

73   Smuts, 'South Africa in science', p. 1.

74   Howarth, *The British Association*, p. 143; *The Times*, 22 July 1929.

75   *Cape Times*, 11 March 1929.

76   *The Times*, 23 July 1929.

77   *Cape Times*, 20 July 1929 (editorial).

78   *The Times*, 23 July 1929.

79   *Rand Daily Mail* (hereafter *RDM*), 23 July 1929; *RDM*, 25 July 1929.

80   See e.g. *Cape Times*, 27 July 1929 (editorial); Phillips, *The University of Cape Town*, p. 8.

81   *RDM*, 23 July 1929 (editorial). See also *Cape Times*, 23 July 1929 (editorial); *The Times*, 5 August 1929 (editorial).

82   Hofmeyr, 'Africa and science', pp. 2–5. Cf. press reports of Hofmeyr's talk in, e.g., *The Times*, 27 March 1929.

83   Hofmeyr, 'Africa and science', pp. 6–7.

84   *Ibid.*, p. 9.

85   *Ibid.*, p. 18.

86   *RDM*, 3 August 1929 (editorial); *Cape Times*, 29 July 1929. Some of the meetings of the Geological and Agricultural sections of the British Association were held in Pretoria in conjunction with these other international conferences.

87   *RDM*, 1 August 1929. See also *RDM*, 2 August 1929 (editorial).

88   *RDM*, 1 August 1929.

89   *RDM*, 24 July 1929; 25 July 1929 (editorial); 2 August 1929 (editorial); 5 August 1929 (interview with Holland). Among the participants in this discussion were Richard Gregory, D'Arcy Thompson and Daniel Hall. They covered subjects such as science's contribution to industry, fisheries and soil fertility. See *Cape Times*, 24 July 1929.

90   Macleod, 'Retrospect' and P. Collins, 'The British Association as public apologist for science, 1919–1946', in Macleod and Collins (eds), *Parliament of Science*, pp. 5–6, 211–15.

91   *The Times*, 26 July 1929; W. K. Hancock, *Smuts, vol. 2: The fields of force* (Cambridge, 1968), pp. 190–1. Hogben, in typically pugnacious fashion, was less respectful than most. He dismissed Smuts's metaphysical approach, maintaining

that Holism could only be treated seriously if it could be presented in a form capable of being tested.

92 *The Times*, 2 August 1929. Balfour also visited South Africa in 1905 as part of the British Association.
93 *RDM*, 20 July 1929; 31 July 1929; *Cape Times*, 1 August 1929.
94 *Star*, 2 August 1929; *RDM*, 3 August 1929.
95 For more on Dart and the racial paradigm he promoted, see S. Dubow, *Scientific Racism in Modern South Africa* (Cambridge, 1995); also Dubow, 'Human origins, race typology and the other Raymond Dart'.
96 *Cape Times*, 24 July 1929. See also E. G. Malherbe, 'Education and the poor white', *SAJS*, 26 (1929).
97 *Cape Times*, 24 July 1929; 24 July 1929 (editorial); 25 July 1929.
98 E. G. Malherbe papers, KCM 56973 (47), Fred Clarke to E. G. Malherbe, 24 July 1929. Clarke later became professor of education at the University of London.
99 *Ons Vaderland*, 26 July 1929 (editorial).
100 *Die Burger*, 26 July 1929 (editorial); *Die Volksblad*, 30 July 1929 (editorial).
101 *Die Burger*, 30 July 1929.
102 *Ons Vaderland*, 7 August 1929 (editorial).
103 BAAS box 261, 'Science and the empire' address given by Sir Richard Gregory on 3 December 1929.
104 *Cape Times*, 22 July 1929 (editorial).
105 Dubow, *Racial Segregation*; Dubow, *Scientific Racism*.
106 Hofmeyr, 'Africa and science', p. 16.
107 *Die Burger*, 19 July 1929; 20 July 1929 ('Suid-Afrika en die wetenskap').
108 *Die Kerkbode*, 31 July 1929 ('Die "British Association" ').
109 *Cape Times*, 17 July 1929.
110 *Die Burger*, 18 July 1929 ('Skandelik', editorial by A. L. Geyer).
111 C. J. Langenhoven, 'Aan stille waters', *Die Burger* (I am unable to find the precise date).

[20]

Visible empire: scientific expeditions and visual culture in the Hispanic enlightenment

DANIELA BLEICHMAR

An unsigned portrait painted at the turn of the nineteenth century in the city of Bogota, now the capital of Colombia, depicts José Celestino Mutis, one of the foremost botanists working in the Spanish Americas at the time (Figure 1).[1] Born and trained as a physician and surgeon in Spain, in 1760 Mutis crossed the Atlantic as the personal physician to the newly appointed viceroy to the New Kingdom of Granada—a territory which occupied the north-west corner of South America, roughly corresponding to present-day

Figure 1.
Salvador Rizo? (Royal Botanical Expedition to the New Kingdom of Granada), *José Celestino Mutis (1732–1808)*, *c.* 1800, oil on canvas, 48.8 × 36.2 in. (124 × 92 cm). Real Academia Nacional de Medicina, Madrid.

Venezuela, Colombia, Panama, Ecuador, and part of Peru. Mutis arrived in New Granada at the age of 29 and never returned to Europe, remaining in the Americas until his death in 1808.

For about twenty years after arriving in New Granada, Mutis worked as a physician and as a professor of mathematics, astronomy, and natural philosophy at the *Colegio Mayor de Nuestra Señora del Rosario*, the kingdom's institution of higher learning, where he was reputedly the first person to teach Copernicus and Newton in the Spanish Americas. After the expulsion of the Jesuits from all Spanish territories in 1767, he actively participated in the kingdom's educational reform. Mutis also served as a mine administrator for almost ten years, from 1766 to 1770 and from 1777 to 1782. Despite these varied occupations, his principal interest was the study of the kingdom's natural history. Mutis conducted botanical and entomological investigations and collected specimens, becoming an expert on multiple aspects of New Granadan nature. He composed long lists of the Latin names of the plants of the region, and kept meticulous observation journals with notes on everything from local customs to the mating behavior of ants to the disappearance of a favorite household cat and the resulting invasion of mice in his living quarters.[2] Mutis relied not only on his own observations but also on conversations with a wide range of people from various social and ethnic groups, whom he questioned about their knowledge of local flora and fauna and their medicinal uses. Mutis recorded their responses in his journals, though he seems to have valued them mostly as an opportunity to scornfully rail against the stupidity of popular knowledge. A hot-tempered, somewhat cantankerous man who complained of 'the bitterness produced by dealing with people,' Mutis far preferred the solitary study of nature and the type of disembodied conversations he maintained with a vast network of correspondents throughout the Americas and Europe—among them the most famous naturalist of his time, Carl Linnaeus—as well as with the books in his impressive library.[3]

Today, Mutis is celebrated in Colombia as the founding father of national science and a source of patriotic pride. He is the type of figure to have public institutions named after him, as is the case with the botanical garden in Bogota, and to be featured in currency, as he was in both Colombia and Spain. The bicentennial of his death in 2008 was commemorated with multiple exhibitions and press coverage in both countries. This renown is due to his leadership for twenty-five years of the Royal Botanical Expedition to the New Kingdom of Granada. Mutis launched the expedition in 1783 and led it until his death in 1808; the project continued haltingly for almost ten more years and was terminated in 1817 when, in reaction to the wars of independence, the Spanish government commissioned an officer to send all of the expedition's materials to Madrid.[4] The materials are held today in the archive of Madrid's Royal Botanical Garden.

The Royal Botanical Expedition to the New Kingdom of Granada formed part of an ambitious project to renew the Spanish empire through the application of natural history to political economy. This initiative included many other expeditions, as I will discuss. Mutis and his patrons envisioned that the expedition would promptly yield useful and valuable information in the form of natural commodities. To this end, he assembled a team composed of *herbolarios*, or plant collectors, as well as artists and botanical contributors. Working together, members of this team diligently attempted to locate American varieties of cinnamon, tea, pepper, and nutmeg—Asian natural commodities traded with great profit by the British and the Dutch—as well as new types of the valuable antimalarial cinchona (*Cinchona officinalis*), the source of quinine and a prized Spanish monopoly. In this, Mutis shared the global and imperial economic aspirations of other eighteenth-century botanists, most notably Carl Linnaeus, Joseph Banks at Kew Gardens, and the staff at the Paris Jardin du Roi—an approach that has been richly analyzed by Richard Drayton, Lisbet Koerner, Staffan Müller-Wille, and Kapil Raj, among others.[5]

There is no question of Mutis's genuine interest in economic botany. He spent years studying different types of cinchona, and became embroiled in a heated priority dispute regarding a new variety of the plant.[6] He monitored European periodicals to keep track of British trade in tea, and located a South American plant that he tirelessly and unsuccessfully promoted as a potential substitute, the so-called 'Bogota tea.'[7] He also investigated American varieties of cinnamon and pepper. But Mutis also devoted enormous efforts to another end, one with less obvious economic or utilitarian applications: the production of visual representations of American plants (Figure 2). Over the years, the expedition employed over forty artists, thirty of them working simultaneously at one point. While Mutis and a handful of botanical collaborators penned only about 500 plant descriptions, the much larger artistic team created a staggering total of almost 6,700 finished folio illustrations of plants and over 700 detailed floral anatomies.[8]

In today's world of online image databases and laser printers, it can be hard to grasp the dedicated labor it took to craft a single one of these paintings, let alone thousands. A single image involved a close collaboration among plant collectors, botanists, and entire teams of artists who specialized in the various steps it took to achieve a finished illustration. This process took several days. Each image embodies not only a plant but also multiple decisions, negotiations, and types of expertise. Mutis did not work alone, as his portrait suggests, but rather supervised a large operation. He hired artists from Bogota, from Madrid, from Quito; he obsessed about how to train them and control their work, imposing a strict work schedule based on a nine-hour day, six days a week, for forty-eight weeks out of the year. Mutis had strong ideas about both botanical and artistic aspects of the images, and got into monumental fights with those painters whose work ethic or results did not satisfy him. He recruited Spanish artists from Madrid's prestigious San Fernando Academy of Fine Arts, only to realize later on that they actually had strong opinions about art and were not as malleable as he had hoped. After dismissing a particularly bothersome Spanish artist from the expedition, Mutis attempted to have him kicked out of the kingdom, writing to the viceroy that this man posed a threat to the social order. His solution to the problem of finding a large number of docile painters was to establish a

444   DANIELA BLEICHMAR

Figure 2.
Nicolás Cortés (Royal Botanical Expedition to the New Kingdom of Granada),
Gustavia augusta, tempera painting. Archivo del Real Jardín Botánico, Madrid, III,
2673.

free drawing school where young boys could be trained as botanical
draftsmen.[9] Some of these artists worked in the expedition for the greater
part of their lives.

Given the existence of this extensive visual archive, the enormous efforts
to which Mutis went to employ, train, and supervise his painters, and the
frequent discussion of the production and uses of natural history illustrations in his journals and correspondence, it is clear that for Mutis images
were of central importance to the exploration of American nature. And he
was not alone in his visual voraciousness. While his patriotic fame might
suggest that this expedition was unique, it was not an isolated phenomenon
but rather part of a large-scale scientific program throughout the empire that
resulted in a flurry of related expeditions and investigations. Historians
Antonio Lafuente and Nuria Valverde have calculated that between 1760
and 1808 there were at least fifty-seven scientific expeditions to and through
the viceroyalties.[10] Seven of them focused on botany (Table 1), and every
single one of them, without exception, employed artists who produced a
large number of illustrations. Indeed, the bulk of their work consisted in the

Table 1. Natural history expeditions in the Spanish empire, 1777–1816

Expedition	Dates	Region	Naturalists	Artists
Royal Botanical Expedition to Chile and Peru	1777–1788	Chile and Peru	Hipólito Ruiz, José Pavón, Joseph Dombey	José Brunete, Isidro Gálvez
Royal Botanical Expedition to the New Kingdom of Granada	1783–1816	New Kingdom of Granada (Colombia, Venezuela, Ecuador, Peru, Panama)	José Celestino Mutis + associates (inc. Diego García, Eloy Valenzuela, Francisco Antonio Zea, Sinforoso Mutis, Francisco José de Caldas, + others)	Salvador Rizo, Francisco Matis, >40 others
Botanical explorations in the Philippines	1786–1801	The Philippines	Juan de Cuéllar	Anonymous Philippine and Chinese artists
Royal Natural History Expedition to New Spain	1787–1803	Mexico and Guatemala	Martín de Sessé, José Mariano Mociño, Vicente Cervantes, José Longinos	Atanasio Echeverría, Vicente de la Cerda
Malaspina expedition	1789–1794	South, Central, and North America; Australia; the Philippines	Thaddeus Haenke, Luis Née, Antonio Pineda	José del Pozo, José Guio, Juan Ravenet, Fernando Brambila, José Cardero, Tomás de Suria, José Gutiérrez, Francisco Lindo, Francisco Pulgar
Expedition to Cuba	1796–1802	Cuba	Baltasar Manuel Boldó, José Estévez	José Guio (prev. Malaspina expedition)
Expedition to Ecuador	1799–1808	Ecuador	Juan Tafalla	Francisco Pulgar, Francisco Xavier Cortés (prev. Mutis expedition)

production of visual materials: the expeditions created many more pictures than collections or textual descriptions, manuscript or published. As a group, these expeditions alone created over 10,000 finished drawings.[11]

This essay takes that enormous visual archive as a starting point for rethinking expeditions that remain almost completely understudied in the Anglophone literature. What do we make of these images? What is this strange beast, the scientific expedition as artistic workshop, painting as exploration? Why did naturalists care so much about images? What work did images do for them? Methodologically, how can we use these visual materials as historical sources? These questions have not really been asked; for the most part, scholars have not thought hard about these images, looked at them closely, or connected them to either scientific or imperial practices.[12] In this essay, I argue that these expeditions operated on multiple connected levels: they were concerned with economic botany, with political economy, with Linnaean taxonomy, and with visualizing the empire. Images formed part of a globalizing project that was common to European science at the time, which consisted in creating and circulating abstracted natural facts in multiple media. And it is precisely visual culture that allows us to understand how the expeditions achieved these multiple goals: it is what brings the various aspects together.

Focusing on this visual archive allows us not only to rethink the natural history expeditions that created it, but also to ask broader questions about the role of images in constituting and communicating facts in the Spanish empire, and about the production and circulation of knowledge in long-distance systems in general. The story I outline in this essay, and develop more fully elsewhere, is partly about the Hispanic world, and partly about the operation of eighteenth-century colonial and imperial science.[13] Just as Spanish naturalists and administrators shared an interest in economic botany with many European counterparts, they were also not alone in their visual emphasis— other European imperial naturalists likewise traveled with artists and valued observation and representation as instruments of reconnaissance and possession. That said, the degree to which visual evidence was pursued in the Hispanic world, and the long tradition of using images for combined scientific and administrative purposes from the turn of the sixteenth century uninterruptedly to the turn of the nineteenth, are particular to the Spanish case.[14]

The colonial machine: natural history and political economy in the Hispanic enlightenment

The Spanish enlightenment expeditions make clear the enormous scientific, political, and economic importance of natural history, and of botany in particular, in the Spanish empire in the second half of the eighteenth-century—a vast topic that I will address only briefly given that my main goal in this essay is to analyze the role of visual culture, but one that has been examined in great detail.[15] These expeditions are related to a series of reform policies instituted in the Spanish empire by the new Bourbon dynasty that came into power at the beginning of the eighteenth century, particularly during the reign of Charles III (r. 1759–1788). The Bourbon reforms attempted to revitalize the empire economically and politically by strengthening Spanish industry and reshaping the relationship with the viceroyalties.[16] Scientific expeditions and investigations of the empire played an important role in these efforts. The Bourbon administration sought to revisit sixteenth- and seventeenth-century successes with mineral riches by now exploiting profitable natural commodities. Ministers and naturalists alike hoped that a better known and efficiently administered empire could furnish rich revenues by allowing Spain to compete with trade monopolies maintained by other nations. This climate of international economic and political competition created opportunities for naturalists to sell their services to interested patrons. Botanical expertise became a highly valuable form of practical knowledge. As Londa Schiebinger has argued, in the eighteenth century botany was big business and big science.[17]

In the Spanish empire, this big science operated on a large international scale that connected administrative and scientific networks throughout the empire. Most of these expeditions were massive undertakings that stretched over many years, and involved not only the deployment of numerous personnel but also the active participation of the whole imperial administrative apparatus, so that from town to town in the Americas, governors, treasury officials, physicians, pharmacists, clergymen, and many other local populations were all involved in these projects.[18]

The historians James McClellan and François Regourd have introduced the concept of a 'colonial machine' to describe the apparatus of state-sponsored science in France and its colonies in the eighteenth century.[19] The expression vividly captures the complexity of a type of system that was very much in operation in the Spanish empire, dating back to the early sixteenth century and re-strengthened in the second half of the eighteenth century.[20] This apparatus involved the participation of government ministers and advisers, political thinkers, imperial administrators in the peninsula and throughout the viceroyalties; new institutions such as the San Fernando Royal Academy of Fine Arts (f. 1752), the Royal Botanical Garden (f. 1755), the Royal Natural History Cabinet (f. 1776), and the Royal Cabinet of Machines (f. 1788); and long-standing but recently reinvigorated institutions like the Royal Pharmacy and a network of army and naval hospitals, observatories, pharmacies, and personnel. Parallel institutions contributed to the effort in the colonies, among them the San Carlos Royal Academy of Fine Arts (f. 1781) and the Royal Botanical Garden (f. 1788) in Mexico City, a botanical garden and natural history cabinet in Guatemala City (both f. 1796), and a botanical garden in Havana (f. 1816, with activity and proposals going back to the early 1790s).[21] Thus, the Spanish empire participated quite actively in the world of colonial science involving widespread networks of gardens and other institutions, which has been so well studied for the French and British cases but remains little known among Anglophone scholars of science and empire who are not specialists in the region.[22]

This is not to suggest that the Spanish empire functioned in exactly the same ways as the British or French. One important difference is that in the Hispanic world these expeditions were not understood as radically new types of endeavors but rather as part of a long-standing tradition that had a deep historical dimension. As Antonio Barrera-Osorio has shown, over the course of the sixteenth century the exploration, exploitation, and governance of Spain's New World territories led to the creation of new institutions that compiled and deployed useful information, and that fostered research and innovation in technology, natural history, medicine, and industry.[23] While the expeditions are connected to Enlightenment ideas about the public utility of science, the arts, and trades, also—and in ways that were symbolically much more powerful—they constituted ways of revisiting sixteenth-century glories. The New Spain expedition, for instance, was envisioned as a continuation of the trip undertaken to the same region between 1570 and 1577 by Francisco Hernández, Philip II's physician.[24] The eighteenth-century expeditions represented a new wave of an old phenomenon: the rediscovery and reconquest of the Americas. The author of an article published in 1793 in the *Mercurio Peruano*, a journal published in Lima between 1790 and 1795, voiced this belief in a statement whose eager hopefulness matches the exalted name of the society that published the periodical, the *Sociedad Académica de Amantes del País* (Academic Society of Lovers of the Country). 'Scientific expeditions,' the writer declared, 'should erase the sad memories of bloody expeditions. They lead far-away towns to culture, order, the arts, and countless goods.'[25] If Madrid considered the expeditions a way of reaching back to glorious times of conquest and political might, Spanish Americans found in them the promise of reconfiguring and moving away from that past.[26]

This rediscovery was often enacted by Americans themselves.[27] The expeditions were as likely to originate in Mexico City, Lima, or Bogota, as in Madrid, if not even more so. Throughout this vast global empire, administrators and learned men agreed that the exploration and exploitation of natural resources was central to the fortunes of the empire, at both local and systemic levels. Enlightened *criollos* (American-born descendants of Spaniards) shared European ideals of science as useful to both economic and moral improvement. For them, however, this improvement was connected to a sense of ownership over the territory—a patriotic identity with multiple political, religious, epistemological, and cultural aspects that has been discussed by scholars including Solange Alberro, David Brading, Jorge Cañizares-Esguerra, and Bernard Lavallé.[28] We find frequent visual and textual statements from the time about *criollos'* privileged capacity for investigating and understanding the Americas. Expeditions often combined imperial, metropolitan, and local colonial agendas, operating on multiple levels at once. While the Spanish empire competed against the British, French, and Dutch, different regions of the empire vied with each other for privileged status.[29]

Learning to see and seeing to know: visual epistemology in eighteenth-century natural history

The second aspect of the expeditions that I want to explore in this essay concerns the practices of eighteenth-century natural history, and it is here that visual culture becomes truly central to the story. In thinking about visual culture rather than only about illustrations, I want to suggest that the expeditions' high regard for representation was closely connected to attitudes towards the role of observation. Representation and observation were intrinsically connected in the persona and the practices of the naturalist.

Mutis's portrait (Figure 1) depicts a naturalist deeply engaged in the pursuit of his craft. He sits before a work table, his focused gaze fixed on the viewer with weary patience, as if we had just burst into his study of muted grays and browns and interrupted his silent labor. He has lifted his head but his body remains hunched over in concentration, eager to resume the examination of the flower he holds up towards him. A branch of the same plant lies ready to be pressed between the pages of a notebook and thus become a herbarium specimen; books scattered around the table serve as sources of corroboration in describing and classifying this plant. The magnifying lens that Mutis holds in his right hand connects the naturalist's instrument—his eyes—to his subject of study, a symbol of the acute observational capacities that characterize him as a botanist. This is not simple looking but rather expert, disciplined, methodical observing. The flower Mutis so carefully considers is no other than *Mutisia clematis*, a New Granadan species that Carl Linnaeus the younger named in Mutis's honor.[30] Thus, the portrait celebrates Mutis's talents as botanical discoverer and connects them to his capacities as an observer.[31] The painting elucidates that for Mutis—as for other naturalists at the time—representation and observation were intimately connected, part of a comprehensive understanding of visuality as a mode of knowing appropriate for studying natural history, as well as a useful tool for the various tasks and demands of scientific work, including training, patronage, discovery, transportation, and persuasive communication.

Being a botanist implied seeing in specific ways. A botanist's worth was appraised according to the finesse of his visual skills, what Mutis variously described as the 'botanical eyes,' 'lynx eyes,' or 'very delicate eyes' that characterized great botanists and made their observations trustworthy.[32] Collecting and classifying, the twin obsessions of eighteenth-century natural history, were predicated on the ability of the trained eye to assess, possess and order. The process of becoming a naturalist revolved around visual training, and relied heavily on images—particularly printed images (Figure 3), as I have described elsewhere.[33] Illustrated books provided a visual and verbal vocabulary that was shared by naturalists throughout and beyond Europe. They presented standards against which naturalists could gauge the value of their own work, as well as models for them to emulate or react against. Thus, books helped to define and arbitrate a community of competent and relevant practitioners.[34]

Printed images also defined the traveling naturalists' job by demarcating what they should accomplish in their voyages, namely, to describe any local productions not included within the European printed inventory of global nature, to rectify any discrepancies, and to resolve incomplete or erroneous descriptions. Books provided naturalists with the illustrations they needed to

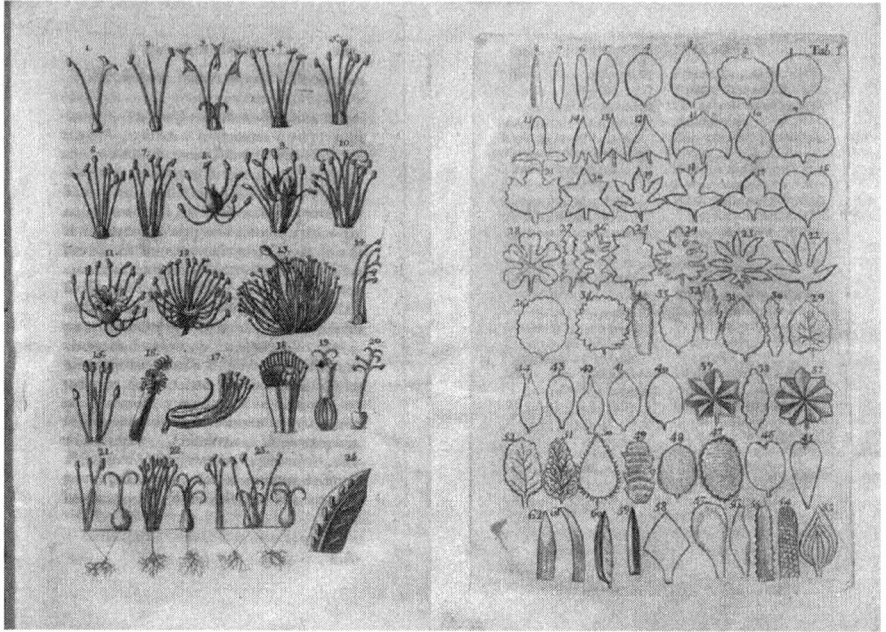

Figure 3.
Unsigned engravings depicting (left) the twenty-four classes in the Linnaean system of botanical classification and (right) sixty-two types of simple leaves, adapted from Linnaeus's publications to appear in in Casimiro Gómez Ortega, *Curso elemental de Botánica, dispuesto para la enseñanza del Real Jardín Botánico de Madrid* (Madrid, 2nd edn, 1795), *Parte práctica* (left) and *Parte teórica* (right). These engravings are copies of the illustrations in Linnaeus's publications. Copies such as these helped to publicize and gain recruits to Linnaean taxonomy, and also to create a visual culture shared by botanists in different places. The plate on the right reveals itself as a copy by inverting the order of the images, which in the original engraving are numbered from left to right and not from right to left, as in this version.

approach nature, with parameters for producing new images, and with a medium for presenting their own contributions to natural history. The traveling naturalists' way of seeing involved a constant triangulation among image, text, and specimen, using books to interpret what they saw in the field and producing their own texts and images to respond to what they read as well as to contribute new information. In the eighteenth century, images provided an entry point into the exploration of nature, functioned as a key instrument for producing knowledge, and constituted one of the foremost results of natural investigations.

Naturalists also found images useful in more practical ways: they were central to the culture of gift exchange and reciprocity that regulated almost any type of transaction at the time.[35] When soliciting additional funds, reassuring an anxious patron or courting a new one, requesting that an acquaintance based in Europe send them recently published books (illustrated, of course), or attempting to enter into correspondence with a world-renowned naturalist, travelers knew to send pictures along with their letters. Mutis, for instance, shipped several sets of drawings and herbarium specimens to Carl Linnaeus, the ultimate arbiter of botanical worth at the time (Figure 4).[36] Mutis also repeatedly needed to present samples of his artists' work in order to reassure increasingly impatient officials in New Granada and Madrid of the expedition's progress.

Images functioned not only as the result of observations but also as part of the process. Naturalists drew often; and often, they drew well. Their writings are peppered with sketches. Their eyes and hands worked in tandem, aiding each other: drawing allowed them to see, to think, and also to communicate.[37] When working out a taxonomical point for themselves, naturalists produced notes that tend to include diagrams to clarify the problem at hand as well as its solution. When writing letters, especially to correspondents who had never been in the region they were describing, naturalists appended drawings to get their point across. For example, when characterizing four varieties of cinchona by differentiating among leaf shapes, using words to describe their forms—spear-shaped, oblong, heart-shaped, oval—was not enough. A drawing (Figure 5) proved necessary to make the point clear beyond error. And so here we have the meeting point of the three areas of enquiry I identified as the primary concerns for the Spanish naturalists: economic botany, taxonomy, and visuality. Naturalists used observations and illustrations in their attempts to determine whether these four different plants, growing in four different regions of South America, could all be legitimately traded as cinchona, or, to give another example, whether a plant commonly deemed 'pepper' in South America could really be considered the same species as the 'true' pepper that the Dutch imported from East Asia. Since Linnaean classification was based on visually-determined criteria (the number and position of pistils and stamens), images served an important role in identity disputes.

The fact that naturalists were happy with casual sketches in their own notes but preferred to send colleagues images produced by more skilled artists provides yet another reason for their great care in selecting and overseeing draftsmen. It is telling that although the naturalists from the various Spanish expeditions only rarely corresponded with one another, the very few letters that they did exchange invariably mentioned their painters. In late 1788, Vicente Cervantes, a naturalist in the New Spain expedition, replied to a letter in which Mutis had asked about the talents of two Mexican artists who had recently joined the team. Cervantes answered the query not only with words but also by sending images that would demonstrate the draftsmen's skills.[38] Similarly, the lone letter that naturalist Luis Née, member of the Malaspina circumnavigation expedition, sent to Mutis addressed the incorporation of a botanical draftsman into the team. Writing from Ecuador in 1790, Née expressed satisfaction with the artist's work:

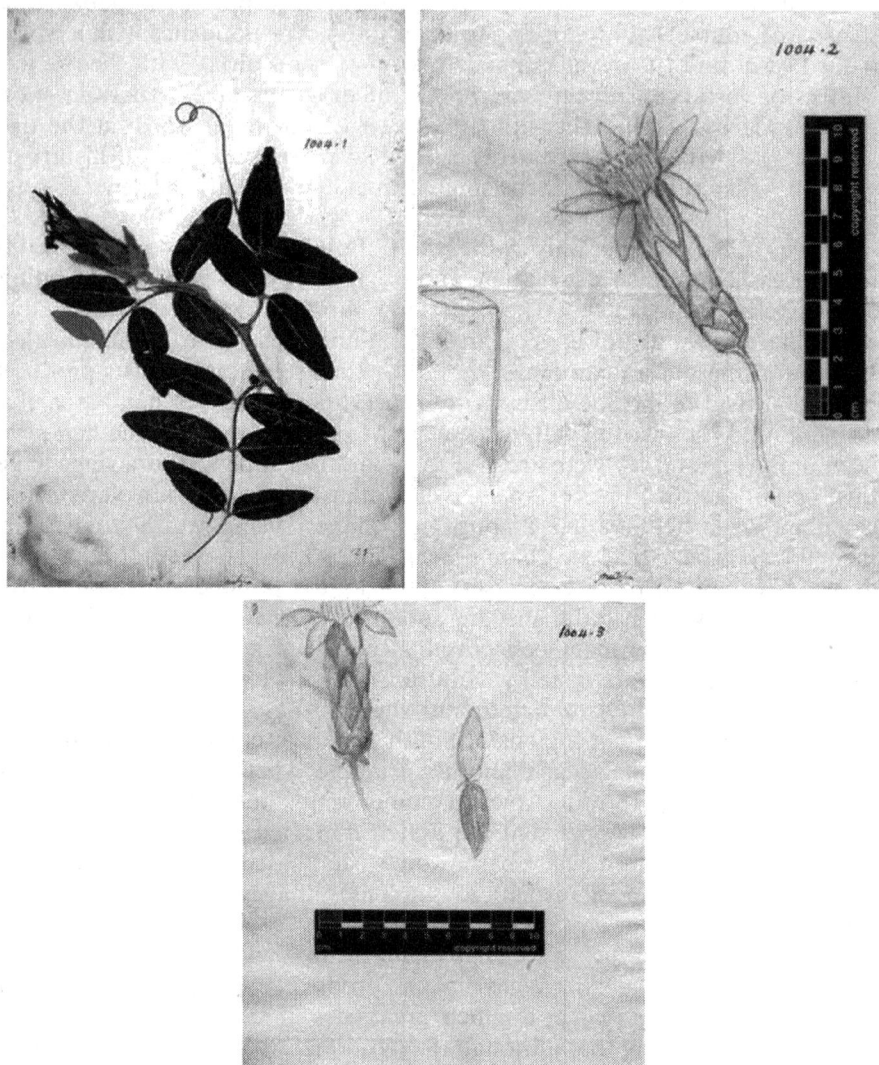

Figure 4.
Herbarium specimen and two pencil drawings of the *Mutisia* that José Celestino Mutis sent to Carl Linnaeus. Linnaean Society, London LINN 1004.1, 1004.2, and 1004.3 (Herb Linn).

> The botanical draftsman who has arrived is good and patient. He knows the principles of botany and can very well define the parts of a plant, especially the fructification parts. The drawings I have taken care to direct to this day include nothing beyond what is necessary for any systematist to know the [plant's] class and order. Adding a methodical description [to the drawing] seems sufficient to know the plant that is being presented.[39]

Figure 5.
Unsigned pen and ink drawing on paper showing José Celestino Mutis's four cinchona types, distinguished by color (orange, red, yellow, and white) and leaf shape. Royal Botanical Expedition to the New Kingdom of Granada. Archivo del Real Jardín Botánico, Madrid, III, 2, 3, 110.

It is worth noting that Née writes of 'directing' the painter's work, indicating that while artists were crucial members of an expedition they were ultimately subservient to the authority of naturalists. The artist was the expedition's hand, hired to produce the images that the naturalist indicated, while the naturalist acted as the expedition's eyes, selecting the objects to depict, indicating which elements the artist should include and which he should ignore, and imposing the specific vision with which to approach and represent nature. The botanist controlled the artist's work schedule, the contents of his work, the materials he needed, and even his body, deciding where and when the artist should travel. The desired image was a botanical object, not an artistic creation, and thus botanists oversaw that the illustrations including only 'what is necessary' (as Née put it) to determine the plant taxonomically, preventing their artists from using a decorative pictorial style in their work. Botanical considerations dictated the content, style, and even the size of an image. Naturalists supervised and directed the artist's work, evaluating whether a drawing was satisfactory or needed emendation. For instance, Née reviewed a watercolor painted by José Guío (Figure 6) and wrote a correction directly across the image, in this way canceling it out. Née determined, 'The fruit should be green, the painter is mistaken.'[40] According to naturalists, artists could simply not work without their direction. As Hipólito Ruiz, from the Chile and Peru expedition, explained,

> I do not doubt that the draftsman ... can draw in a satisfactory manner [*algo regular*] whatever aspect of plants the botanist ordered. But since the botanist carries the weight of the project, if he were not appropriately appointed, it would be useless for the other [the artist] to trace a plant without somebody to indicate to him the requirements necessary for composing a good drawing. Because making a perfect drawing is not a matter of representing the visible parts of a plant but of knowing which situation, direction, scale, and shape to give it, without adorning the drawing with suppositions, and without omitting anything in the plant, no matter how negligible it may seem, because the perfection [of the

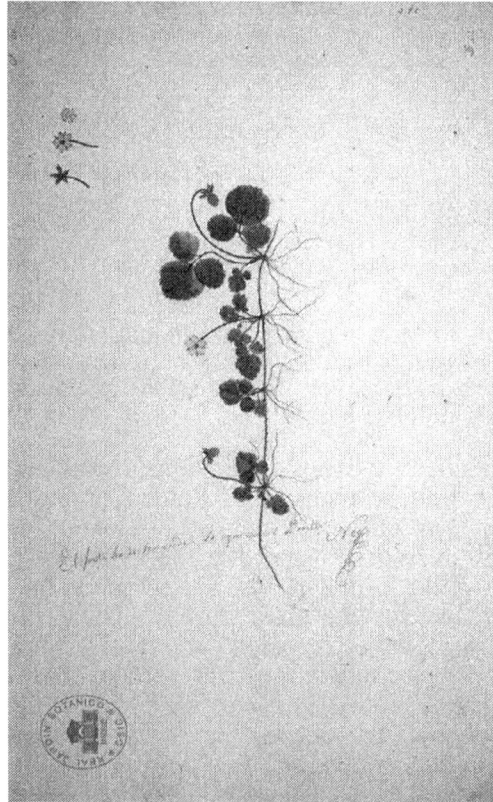

Figure 6.
José Guio (Malaspina expedition), *Rubus radicans Cav.*, watercolor, 1790, 11.8 × 19.3 in. (30 × 49 cm). A manuscript annotation from botanist Luis Née indicates, 'The fruit should be green the Painter is mistaken' (*El fruto ha de ser verde, se equivoca el pintor*). Archivo del Real Jardín Botánico, Madrid, VI, 40.

drawing] and the genuine knowledge of the plant depend precisely on these [details], which are the hardest to notice and draw.[41]

The botanists considered themselves to be the true authors of the illustrations, treating the artists as necessary but subordinate manufacturers.[42]

Long-distance looking

The third aspect of the expeditions that I will discuss in this essay is their capacity to abstract, visually incarnate, and mobilize plants that remained in key ways unseen and unknown, even three centuries after Spaniards first encountered New World nature. The most important work that images did for eighteenth-century natural history was to transport nature across distances. The explicit purpose of natural history expeditions consisted in producing field notes, herbarium specimens, and drawings made on the ground, often in the form of quick and abbreviated sketches, and then transforming these materials into published textual and visual representations. It is worth emphasizing the importance of all three aspects— images, words, and objects—since naturalists triangulated among all three media in their work. However, although all three media were important, it was widely acknowledged that images presented considerable advantages over pressed specimens when attempting to transport nature—the difference between a 'live' and 'dead' specimen. Compare, for instance, painter Nicolás Cortés's lively and colorful depiction of a *Gustavia augusta* (Figure 2) with the herbarium specimen in Linnaeus's collection (Figure 7). Although the herbarium specimen constituted the reference type for Linnaean nomenclature, there were aspects of plant life that images could transport in ways that pressed specimens could not.

With this in mind I want to return one last time to Mutis's portrait (Figure 1). Because thinking about these trajectories from the field to the cabinet, from South America to Europe, highlights the choice to depict Mutis inside a completely enclosed study, without even a window through which we might see the landscape out of which the plants were plucked in order to be brought into the room. The production of scientific facts is thus rendered as a process privileging the intellectual and physical tasks of observing and classifying over the manual labor of procuring the specimens themselves or of painting their portraits, and the indoor cabinet displaces the outdoor field. American nature is literally out of the picture.

Juxtaposing Mutis's portrait to another painting produced by an artist from his workshop elucidates that this indoor representational choice is linked to the issue of the transatlantic circulation of people, specimens, and images (Figure 8). The portrait depicts Antonio José Cavanilles, a renowned Spanish botanist and author, the director of the Madrid Royal Botanical Garden between 1801 and 1804, and a long-time correspondent and supporter of Mutis.[43] The two portraits share much in common: both were painted in Bogota at the turn of the nineteenth century, both highlight the role of observation in natural history, and both relate visual acuity to the

Figure 7.

Herbarium specimen of *Gustavia augusta,* sent by Carl Gustaf Dahlberg to Carl Linnaeus from Surinam. Linnean Society, LINN 863.1 (Herb Linn).

honor of a discovery. Both portraits also allow us to reflect on the relationship among place, visibility, and invisibility. Cavanilles is shown in profile, dressed in his black priestly habit and sitting before a work table. His left hand points to the botanical illustration that Cavanilles examines with imperturbable attention, which is clearly recognizable as one of the expedition's own. Cavanilles studies the drawing with great concentration, observing the various parts of the plant and transforming this visual analysis into a written taxonomic description, which he writes with a pen in a notebook that lies open and ready on the table. Eye and hand work in coordination; image yields text. The white page of the illustration contrasts with the dark background and the rich black of Cavanilles's dress, a luminous flash that attracts the viewer's eye. The botanical drawing is as much a protagonist of this painting as the naturalist, and it serves the important function of connecting the botanist in Spain with the painter in America by reducing the distance that separated them. Although, like Mutis's portrait,

Figure 8.
Salvador Rizo? (Royal Botanical Expedition to the New Kingdom of Granada), *Antonio José Cavanilles, c.* 1800, oil on canvas, 33.9 × 26 in. (86 × 66 cm). Museo Nacional, Bogota, Colombia.

this painting is not signed, the artist incorporated himself through a clever mechanism: the name 'Rizoa,' visible at the top of the image, identifies both an American plant and a painter from the same region, Salvador Rizo (1762–1816), the expedition's head artist and Mutis's second-in-command. By including the plant's drawing and name, the portrait celebrates the naturalist as well as the artist, who through this work thanks Cavanilles for having baptized this American genus with his name.[44]

Rizo's portrait of Cavanilles uses a botanical identity to pay tribute to both a naturalist and an artist, in the same way that Mutis's portrait honors him through the *Mutisia.* An important difference between the two paintings is that in Rizo's portrait the botanical drawing has displaced the specimen, in order to demonstrate the way in which Mutis and Rizo expected the expedition's images to be used in Europe. Mutis, based in South America, could observe numerous fresh specimens year after year and collaborate with the artist to create an image that would function as a composite mosaic of those multiple observations. That would have been impossible for someone who only had access to a single dried specimen, which would inevitably include the accidental particularities of that particular plant—a leaf that was torn or eaten away by an insect, a wilting flower, a specimen collected when

458   DANIELA BLEICHMAR

the flower had not fully bloomed. Herbarium specimens were fragile, they could rot, be infested with insects, get damaged and have portions fall off. In contrast, the drawing incarnates not only a plant genus but also the multiple specimens and observations that had allowed the naturalist and the artist to produce an idealized type version.[45] Ideally, Mutis's paper composite specimen would make it unnecessary for any other naturalist after him to travel to America. Thanks to the drawing, Cavanilles is able to sit at his desk in Europe and conduct 'first-hand' observations of foreign nature, using the image to classify and name American flora.

A letter that Mutis wrote in 1783 demonstrates that he had precisely this use in mind for his images. The letter articulates the potential of images to allow long-distance knowing by seeing, explaining:

> no plant, from the loftiest tree to the humblest weed, will remain hidden to the investigation of true botanists if represented after nature for the instruction of those who are unable to travel throughout the world, so that even without seeing plants in their native soil they will be able to know them through their detailed explanation and living image.[46]

Three years later, Mutis wrote to Casimiro Gómez Ortega, then director of Madrid's Royal Botanical Garden:

> If I am not deceived by my own passion [...] I can promise myself that any image coming from my hands will not need any retouching by those who come after me, and that any botanist in Europe will find represented in it the finest characters of fructification, which are the a-b-c of science—of botany in the Linnaean sense—without the need to come see them [American plants] in their native ground.[47]

Images preserved the impermanent and transported the distant. More than illustrations or representations, they came to stand in for the objects they depicted, providing European naturalists with visual repertoires that allowed them to gather and compare natural specimens from around the world within the enclosed spaces of their studies. The botanical illustration supplants the very act of travel, erasing geography and distance in the same manner as the two portraits, in placing the naturalists within similar indoor settings, make it impossible to know that Mutis conducted his observations in Bogota, New Granada, while Cavanilles carried out his own observations long-distance from his desk in Madrid.

In addition to erasing place and distance, the portraits of Mutis and Cavanilles also eliminate time and labor. Time, in collapsing sequential acts of travel, collection, representation, transport, observation, and description, presenting them as simultaneous events. Labor, in their focus on the individual naturalist, rendering invisible the collective nature of long-distance observation. The paintings erase the enormous team of botanists and artists who worked with Mutis, as well as Cavanilles's ample network of correspondents, excising them out of the image in the same way as Stalinist photography could make a suddenly undesirable comrade disappear. While botanical observation was the work of many, this numerous cast disappeared and the credit went to a single man.[48] In the process that Lorraine Daston and Peter Galison have described as 'collective empiricism' there is an inherent tension between the necessity to establish extensive networks and the tradition of crediting a single individual as the author of an observation—a tension that traveling naturalists often felt keenly, as they saw their European correspondents become the 'authors' who published descriptions of new genera based on the field work that had cost the travelers such great efforts.

Natural history was fundamentally a visual discipline, based on the observation and representation of specimens that sometimes were 'out there' in the field, other times 'in here' in collections, and yet other times in the hybrid domesticated space of the illustration, where exterior and interior, the field and the collection, were collapsed into a single paper nature that was always and perfectly available for virtual exploration. But, like the portrait, the natural history illustration both communicates and erases (Figure 2). When one examines large numbers of natural history illustrations from the sixteenth, seventeenth, and eighteenth centuries, what becomes truly striking is the amount of white space there is in these images. For the most part, they consist of a few traces on a largely blank page. Given the impressive powers of the naturalist's eyes to identify and classify, it is remarkable just how much these trained eyes chose not to see and not to show. The naturalist's gaze was extraordinarily selective not only about what it noticed but also about what it disregarded. For that reason, the visual culture of natural history presents a great paradox: the very point of the publications in which these images appeared was to place before European eyes little-known natural productions from distant lands. These plants were collected, described, drawn, and published precisely because they grew in South America. However, this information was not included in their depictions.

More than mere representations, images acted as visual avatars replacing perishable or immobile objects that would otherwise remain unseen and unknown outside of their local setting.[49] Images defined nature as a series of transportable objects whose identity and importance was divorced from the environment where they grew or the culture of its inhabitants. Pictures were used to reject the local as contingent, subjective, and translatable, favoring instead the dislocated global as objective, truthful, and permanent. The Linnaean system proposed a totalizing, universal way of seeing as well as of classifying. Faced with a multitude of overlapping taxonomies and nomenclatures, naturalists were relieved to have a single system, a single naming method, and a single visual approach that remained operative regardless of where it was employed or by whom. Images showed decontextualized specimens, uprooted from their native soils, expunged from any use or cultural context. The appropriation of nature was predicated upon a selective vision that produced scientific facts through the erasure of local information. What this process made visible was not only or not primarily the specimen itself but rather the naturalists' observations. What it made invisible was distance and place. The ordered list of Latin names and descriptions and the illustration of isolated specimens on blank pages served to cleanse the soil out of nature, transforming local productions into delocalized natural specimens that could circulate on a global stage.

A watercolor painted in Mexico in 1791 by Juan Ravenet, an artist with the Malaspina expedition, articulates these questions of seeing and not seeing, discovering and hiding, observation and representation—that is, of distance and closeness (Figure 9). Mexico City lies in the distance, a spread of minuscule clay-colored buildings at the feet of the volcanoes that surround the central valley of Mexico. The empty flatness of the landscape leading to the city matches the muddy sky, making the blue mountains stand out majestically. While the backdrop of mountains pulls our eye towards the far background, a tree emerging onto the picture from the left jolts us back to the immediate foreground. The watercolor is an exercise in closeness and distance, focusing not on the city but on what lies far beyond it and far before it. The foreground, much closer to the viewer than to the city, stretches all across the image creating a parallel plane to both the city and the mountains. This frontal strip of space is punctuated by groups of people who populate it. In the bottom right of the image, two women in a small hut go about their daily chores. Moving from right to left, we see two men struggling with the mules that draw a carriage, a couple with a small child tending animals, and a horse-rider seen from the back. In the bottom left corner, in a privileged space that is vertically anchored by the tree and physically elevated by a small hill, four figures surround a man holding a spyglass (Figure 10). He holds the long instrument to his face with both hands, using it to bring the distant city close before his eyes—another play on closeness and distance, and on the role of vision in filling that space. A light-skinned figure, he is identified as a member of the Malaspina naval expedition by his attire and instrument. Concentrated in his observation, he remains oblivious to the figures surrounding him, a barely-clad indigenous couple with their three children. To the left of the observer (our right), a small boy looks up at him with great interest, arms crossed, while to his right (our left), his sister extends

Figure 9.
Juan Ravenet (Malaspina Expedition), 'View of Mexico City from Guadalupe,' 1791, watercolor, 16.3 × 42.9 in. (41.5 × 109 cm). Museo de América, Madrid.

Figure 10.
Detail, Juan Ravenet (Malaspina Expedition), 'View of Mexico City from Guadalupe,' 1791, watercolor, 16.3 × 42.9 in. (41.5 × 109 cm). Museo de América, Madrid.

her arm, reaching out towards the white man and thus mirroring with her arm the horizontal line created by the man's spyglass. Physically close, she reaches out to him; at a distance, he visually reaches out to the city. As a member of the Malaspina expedition, this man has traveled a great distance to see and record the city, and in turn to be recorded doing so. His meticulous, trained observation is extremely selective: giving his full attention to the restricted view framed by his instrument, the man in the corner fails to see the ground on which he stands or the people around him. His concentrated, expert vision represents an achievement both in observation and in willful blindness, and suggests that efforts to make the empire visible always involved making parts of it invisible.

Acknowledgements

I am grateful to Suman Seth for the invitation to present an earlier version of this material at the Science and Technology Studies Colloquium at Cornell University, to graduate students and faculty in that department for their helpful questions and feedback, and to two anonymous reviewers for their thoughtful readings of an initial version of this essay and their insightful suggestions for revising it. The material discussed in this essay is treated in much greater detail in my forthcoming monograph, *Visible Empire. Colonial Botany and Visual Culture in the Eighteenth-Century Hispanic World* (University of Chicago Press, 2010).

This project received research funding from the Princeton University History Department, the Mellon Foundation, the USC-Huntington Early Modern Studies Institute, the Del Amo Foundation, the University of Southern California (ASHSS grant), and the Getty Foundation.

462   DANIELA BLEICHMAR

Notes

[1] The standard biography is A Federico Gredilla, *Biografía de José Celestino Mutis* [1911], intro. Guillermo Hernández de Alba, Bogotá: Plaza & Janés, 1982.

[2] José Celestino Mutis, *Diario de observaciones de José Celestino Mutis (1760–1790)*, transcr. and intro. Guillermo Hernández de Alba, 2 vols, Bogotá: Instituto Colombiano de Cultura Hispánica, 2nd edn, 1983, I: 369.

[3] Gredilla, *Biografía*, p 272. On Mutis's library, see Julio Humberto Ovalle Mora, 'El fondo José Celestino Mutis de la Biblioteca Nacional de Colombia,' *Boletín de Historia y Antigüedades*, XCIII(833), June 2006, pp 359–374.

[4] Among the vast literature on Mutis and the expedition, see Daniela Bleichmar, 'Painting as Exploration: Visualizing Nature in Eighteenth-Century Colonial Science,' *Colonial Latin American Review*, 15(1), June 2006, pp 81–104; Marcelo Frías Núñez, *Tras El Dorado vegetal: Jose Celestino Mutis y la Real Expedición Botanica del Nuevo Reino de Granada (1783–1808)*, Seville: Diputación Provincial de Sevilla, 1994; Gonzalo Hernández de Alba, *Quinas amargas, el sabio Mutis y la discusión naturalista del siglo XVIII*, Bogota: Academia de Historia de Bogotá, 1991; Enrique Pérez Arbeláez, *José Celestino Mutis y la Real Expedición Botánica del Nuevo Reino de Granada*, Bogota: Instituto Colombiano de Cultura Hispánica, 2nd edn, 1983; María Pilar de San Pío Aladrén (ed), *Mutis y la Real Expedición Botánica del Nuevo Reino de Granada*, 2 vols, Barcelona: Lunwerg Editores, 1992.

[5] Lucile H Brockway, *Science and Colonial Expansion: The Role of the British Royal Botanical Gardens*, London: Academic Press, 1979; Richard Drayton, *Nature's Government: Science, Imperial Britain, and the 'Improvement' of the World*, New Haven: Yale University Press, 2000; Lisbet Koerner, *Linnaeus. Nature and Nation*, Cambridge, MA: Harvard University Press, 1999; Staffan Müller-Wille, 'Nature as a Marketplace: The Political Economy of Linnaean Botany,' in Neil De Marchi and M Schabas (eds), *Oeconomies in the Age of Newton*, Durham, NC: Duke University Press, 2003, pp 154–172, and 'Walnut-Trees at Hudson Bay, Coral Reefs in Gotland: Linnaean Botany and its Relation to Colonialism,' in Londa Schiebinger and Claudia Swan (eds), *Colonial Botany: Science, Commerce, and Politics in the Early Modern World*, Philadelphia: University of Pennsylvania Press, 2005, pp 34–48; Chandra Mukerji, *Territorial Ambitions and the Gardens of Versailles*, Cambridge: Cambridge University Press, 1997; Kapil Raj, *Relocating Modern Science: Circulation and the Construction of Knowledge in South Asia and Europe, 1650–1900*, New York: Palgrave Macmillan, 2007; Schiebinger and Swan, *Colonial Botany*; Emma C Spary, *Utopia's Garden. French Natural History from Old Regime to Revolution*, Chicago: University of Chicago Press, 2000.

[6] Gonzalo Hernández de Alba, *Quinas amargas, el sabio Mutis y la discusión naturalista del siglo XVIII*, Bogotá: Academia de Historia de Bogotá, 1991.

[7] Marcelo Frías Núñez, 'El té de Bogotá: un intento de alternativa al té de China,' in Marie Cécile Bénassy, Jean-Pierre Clément, Francisco Pelayo and Miguel Ángel Puig-Samper (eds), *Nouveau monde et renouveau de l'histoire naturelle*, 3 vols, Paris: Presses de la Sorbonne Nouvelle, 1993, 3, pp 201–219.

[8] For a detailed discussion of the expedition's image-making practices and the illustrations' stylistic characteristics, including an analysis of their stylistic departures from European conventions of botanical illustration, see Bleichmar, 'Painting as Exploration.'

[9] Carmen Sotos Serrano, 'Aspectos artísticos de la Expedición Botánica de Nueva Granada,' in San Pío Aladrén, *Mutis y la Real Expedición Botánica*, vol 1, pp 121–157.

[10] Antonio Lafuente and Nuria Valverde, 'Linnaean Botany and Spanish Imperial Biopolitics,' in Schiebinger and Swan, *Colonial Botany*, p 136.

[11] Among the enormous bibliography on these expeditions, see *La expedición Malaspina, 1789–1794*, 9 vols, Madrid: Lunwerg Editores, 1987–1996; María Belén Bañas Llanos, *Una historia natural de Filipinas: Juan de Cuéllar, 1739–1801*, Barcelona: Ediciones del Serbal, 2000; Andrew David (ed), *The Voyage of Alejandro Malaspina to the Pacific 1789–1794*, London: The Hakluyt Society, 2001; Alejandro Díez Torre *et al* (eds), *La ciencia española en ultramar*, Madrid: Doce Calles, 1991; Iris H W Engstrand, *Spanish Scientists in the New World. The Eighteenth-Century Expeditions*, Seattle: University of Washington Press, 1981; Andrés Galera Gómez, *La ilustración española y el conocimiento del nuevo mundo. Las ciencias naturales en la expedición Malaspina (1789–1794): La labor científica de Antonio Pineda*, Madrid: CSIC, 1988; Antonio González Bueno (ed), *La Expedición botánica al Virreinato del Perú (1777–1788)*, Madrid: Lunwerg, 1988; Virginia González Claverán, *La expedición científica de Malaspina en Nueva España (1789–1794)*, Mexico City: Colegio de México, 1988; María Dolores Higueras Rodríguez (ed), *La Botánica en la Expedición Malaspina, 1789–1794*, Madrid: Turner Libros, 1989; Antonio Lafuente and José Sala Catalá (eds), *Ciencia colonial en América*, Madrid: Alianza Editorial, 1992; Xavier Lozoya, *Plantas y luces en México. La Real Expedición Científica a Nueva*

España (1787–1803), Barcelona: Ediciones del Serbal, 1984; Félix Muñoz Garmendia (ed), *La botánica al servicio de la corona: la expedición de Ruiz, Pavón y Dombey al virreinato del Perú*, Madrid: Lunwerg Editores, 2003; Mauricio Nieto Olarte, *Remedios para el imperio: historia natural y la apropiación del Nuevo Mundo*, Bogota: Instituto Colombiano de Antropología e Historia, 2000; Juan Pimentel, *La física de la monarquía. Ciencia y política en el pensamiento colonial de Alejandro Malaspina (1754–1810)*, Madrid: Doce Calles, 1998; Belén Sánchez, Miguel Ángel Puig-Samper and J de la Sota (eds), *La Real Expedición Botánica a Nueva España 1787–1803*, Madrid: V Centenario, 1987; María Pilar de San Pío Aladrén (ed), *La expedición de Juan de Cuéllar a Filipinas*, Madrid: Lunwerg and Real Jardín Botánico, 1997; María Pilar de San Pío Aladrén (ed), *El águila y el nopal. La expedición de Sessé y Moziño a Nueva España (1787–1803)*, Madrid: Lunwerg Editores, 2000; María Pilar de San Pío Aladrén and María Dolores Higueras Rodríguez (eds), *La armonía natural. La naturaleza en la expedición marítima de Malaspina y Bustamante (1789–1794)*, Madrid: Lunwerg Editores, 2001; and Arthur Robert Steele, *Flowers for the King. The Expedition of Ruiz and Pavon and the Flora of Peru*, Durham, NC: Duke University Press, 1964; as well as the works cited in note 4.

[12] The few existing publications tend to be catalogues or short pieces, and not detailed analysis of the role of images in the expeditions. Carmen Sotos Serrano, *Los pintores de la expedicion de Alejandro Malaspina*, 2 vols, Madrid: Real Academia de la Historia, 1982 and 'Aspectos artísticos de la Expedición Botánica de Nueva Granada,' in San Pío Aladrén, *Mutis y la Real Expedición Botánica*, 1, pp 121–157; José Torre Revello, *Los artistas pintores de la expedicion Malaspina, Estudios y Documentos para la Historia del Arte Colonial*, vol. II, Buenos Aires, Universidad de Buenos Aires, 1944; Lorenzo Uribe Uribe, 'La Expedición Botánica del Nuevo Reino de Granada: su obra y sus pintores,' *Revista de la Academia Colombiana de Ciencias Exactas, Físicas y Naturales* 19, 1953, pp 1–13, and 'Los maestros pintores,' *Flora de la Real Expedición Botánica del Nuevo Reino de Granada (1783–1816)*, 50 vols, Madrid: Ediciones de Cultura Hispánica, 1954–, I, pp 102–106.

[13] Bleichmar, *Visible Empire*.

[14] Bleichmar, *Visible Empire*, esp. chapter 1.

[15] Carmen Añón Feliú, *Real Jardín Botánico de Madrid, sus orígenes 1755–1781*, Madrid: Real Jardín Botánico, 1987; María de los Ángeles Calatayud Arinero, *Pedro Franco Dávila. Primer director del Real Gabinete de Historia Natural fundado por Carlos III*, Madrid: CSIC/Museo Nacional de Ciencias Naturales, 1988; Jorge Cañizares-Esguerra, 'Eighteenth-Century Spanish Political Economy: Epistemology and Decline,' *Eighteenth-Century Thought*, 1, 2003, pp 295–314; Paula S De Vos, 'Research, Development, and Empire: State Support of Science in the Later Spanish Empire,' *Colonial Latin American Review*, 15(1), June 2006, pp 55–79, 'Natural History and the Pursuit of Empire in Eighteenth-Century Spain,' *Eighteenth-Century Studies*, 40(2), 2007, pp 209–239, and 'The Rare, the Singular, and the Extraordinary: Natural History and the Collection of Curiosities in the Spanish Empire,' in Daniela Bleichmar *et al* (eds), *Science in the Spanish and Portuguese Empires, 1500–1800*, Palo Alto: Stanford University Press, 2008, pp 271–289; Antonio Lafuente and Nuria Valverde, *Los mundos de la ciencia en la ilustración española*, Madrid: Fundación Española para la Ciencia y la Tecnología, 2003; Francisco Javier Puerto Sarmiento, *La ilusión quebrada. Botánica, sanidad y política científica en la España Ilustrada* (Madrid: CSIC, 1988), and *Ciencia de cámara. Casimiro Gómez Ortega (1741–1818), el científico cortesano*, Madrid: CSIC, 1992.

[16] David Brading, 'Bourbon Spain and its American Empire,' in Leslie Bethell (ed), *The Cambridge History of Latin America*, New York: Cambridge University Press, 1984, pp 389–440; Jean Sarrailh, *L'Espagne éclairée de la seconde moitié du XVIII siècle*, Paris: Imprimerie Nationale, 1954; Stanley J Stein and Barbara H Stein, *Apogee of Empire: Spain and New Spain in the Age of Charles III, 1759–1789*, Baltimore: Johns Hopkins University Press, 2003.

[17] Londa Schiebinger, *Plants and Empire. Colonial Bioprospecting in the Atlantic World*, Cambridge, MA: Harvard University Press, 2004.

[18] Lafuente and Nuria Valverde, 'Linnaean Botany and Spanish Imperial Biopolitics,' p 136.

[19] James E McClellan and François Regourd, 'The Colonial Machine: French Science and Colonization in the Ancien Régime,' in Roy Macleod (ed), *Nature and Empire: Science and the Colonial Enterprise*, *Osiris*, 2nd series, vol 15, 2000, pp 31–50.

[20] Antonio Barrera, *Experiencing Nature: The Spanish American Empire and the Early Scientific Revolution*, Austin: University of Texas Press, 2006; Juan Pimentel, 'The Iberian Vision: Science and Empire in the Framework of a Universal Monarchy, 1500–1800,' in Roy Macleod (ed), *Nature and Empire: Science and the Colonial Enterprise*, *Osiris*, 2nd series, vol 15, 2000, pp 17–30.

[21] Engstrand, *Spanish Scientists*; Miguel Ángel Puig-Samper and Mercedes Valero, *Historia del Jardín Botánico de la Habana*, Madrid: Doce Calles, 2000; John Tate Lanning, *The Eighteenth-Century*

464   DANIELA BLEICHMAR

Enlightenment in the University of San Carlos de Guatemala, Ithaca, NY: Cornell University Press, 1956, pp 162–164.

[22] Lucile H Brockway, *Science and Colonial Expansion: The Role of the British Royal Botanical Gardens*, London: Academic Press, 1979; Drayton, *Nature's Government*; Donald P McCracken, *Gardens of Empire: Botanical Institutions of the Victorian British Empire*, London: Leicester University Press, 1997; Chandra Mukerji, *Territorial Ambitions and the Gardens of Versailles*, Cambridge: Cambridge University Press, 1997; Spary, *Utopia's Garden*.

[23] Antonio Barrera-Osorio, *Experiencing Nature: The Spanish American Empire and the Early Scientific Revolution*, Austin: University of Texas Press, 2006.

[24] On Hernández, see Raquel Álvarez Peláez, 'Estudio introductorio,' in Francisco Hernández, *De materia medica novae hispaniae, libri quatuor. Cuatro libros sobre la materia médica de Nueva España. El manuscrito de Recchi*, intro. Raquel Álvarez Peláez, trans. and transcr. Florentino Fernández González, 2 vols, Madrid: Ediciones Doce Calles, 1998, 1, pp 15–138; José María López Piñero, *El Códice Pomar (ca. 1590): el interés de Felipe II por la historia natural y la expedición Hernández a América*, Valencia: Universitat de València/CSIC, 1991; José María López Piñero and José Pardo Tomás, *Nuevos materiales y noticias sobre la Historia de las plantas de Nueva España de Francisco Hernández*, Valencia: Universitat de València/CSIC, 1994, and *La influencia de Francisco Hernández (1515–1587) en la constitución de la botánica y la materia médica modernas*, Valencia: Universitat de València/CSIC, 1996; Simon Varey (ed), *The Mexican Treasury. The Writings of Dr. Francisco Hernández*, Stanford, CA: Stanford University Press, 2000; and Simon Varey, Rafael Chabrán and Dora V Weiner (eds), *Searching for the Secrets of Nature. The Life and Works of Dr. Francisco Hernández*, Stanford, CA: Stanford University Press, 2000. The standard biography is Germán Somolinos d'Ardois, *Vida y obra de Francisco Hernández*, vol 1 in Francisco Hernández, *Obras completas*, 3 vols, Mexico: UNAM, 1959.

[25] *Mercurio Peruano* IX: 25, reproduced in Jean-Pierre Clément, *El Mercurio Peruano, 1790–1795*, 2 vols, Madrid: Iberoamericana and Frankfurt am Main: Vervuert, 1997, p 118.

[26] The connections among natural history, nationalism, and the Latin American wars of independence are explored in Thomas Glick, 'Science and Independence in Latin America (with Special Reference to New Granada),' *Hispanic American Historical Review*, 71, 1991, pp 307–334.

[27] Jorge Cañizares-Esguerra, *How to Write the History of the New World: Histories, Epistemologies, and Identities in the Eighteenth-Century Atlantic World*, Palo Alto, CA: Stanford University Press, 2001; Susan Scott Parrish, *American Curiosity: Cultures of Natural History in the Colonial British Atlantic World*, Chapel Hill: University of North Carolina Press for the Omohundro Institute of Early American History and Culture, 2006; Neil Franklin Safier, *Measuring the New World. Enlightenment Science and South America*, Chicago: University of Chicago Press, 2008.

[28] David Brading, *The First America. The Spanish Monarchy, Creole Patriots, and the Liberal State, 1492–1867*, New York: Cambridge University Press, 1991; Bernard Lavallé, *Las promesas ambiguas: criollismo colonial en los Andres*, Lima: Instituto Riva Agüero, 1993; Solange Alberro, *El águila y la cruz. Orígenes religiosos de la conciencia criolla: México, siglos XVI–XVII*, Mexico City: Colegio de México/Fondo de Cultura Económica, 1999; Cañizares-Esguerra, *How to Write the History*; John R Fisher, Allan J Kuethe and Anthony McFarlane (eds), *Reform and Insurrection in Bourbon New Granada and Peru*, Baton Rouge: Lousiana State University Press, 1990.

[29] The 'colonial machine' is of course an abstraction, and as such a simplified model that does not reflect the multiple frictions that existed within projects as well as between institutions, individuals, the metropole and the colonies, various colonies, or regions within a colony. Colonial science was intensely competitive, as I analyze in detail in Bleichmar, *Visible Empire*, esp. chapters 1, 5, 6 and 7.

[30] On the importance of naming plants honorifically at the time, see Schiebinger, *Plants and Empire*, pp 194–225, and Nieto Olarte, *Remedios para el imperio*, chapter 2.

[31] My interpretation of this painting is supported by another surviving portrait of Mutis, which also depicts him in an enclosed study, sitting with a sprig of *Mutisia* in his hand and in front of a table on which rests a microscope. On scientific portraiture, see Ludmilla Jordanova, *Defining Features: Scientific and Medical Portraits*, London: Reaktion, 2000.

[32] Mutis, *Diario de observaciones*, II: 65 and 537–538; José Celestino Mutis, *Archivo Epistolar del Sabio naturalista Don José C. Mutis*, ed. Guillermo Hernández de Alba, 4 vols, Bogotá: Instituto Colombiano de Cultura Hispánica, 2nd edn, 1983, 1, pp 154–156.

[33] I discuss the acquisition of visual expertise in 'Training the Naturalist's Eye in the Eighteenth Century: Perfect Global Visions and Local Blind Spots,' in Cristina Grasseni (ed), *Skilled Visions. Between Apprenticeship and Standards*, New York: Berghan Books, 2006, pp 166–190.

[34] Paula Findlen describes a similar role for books in sixteenth-century natural history in 'The Formation of a Scientific Community: Natural History in Sixteenth-Century Italy,' in Anthony Grafton and Nancy Siraisi (eds), *Natural Particulars. Nature and the Disciplines in Renaissance Europe*, Cambridge, MA: MIT Press, 1999, pp 369–400.

[35] For detailed analyses of gift-exchange among sixteenth- and seventeenth-century naturalists, see Paula Findlen, *Possessing Nature: Museums, Collecting, and Scientific Culture in Early Modern Italy*, Berkeley: University of California Press, 1994; and Brian Ogilvie, *The Science of Describing: Natural History in Renaissance Europe*, Chicago: University of Chicago Press, 2006. While eighteenth-century practices had changed by the late eighteenth century, nevertheless principles of gift-giving, obligation, and reciprocity continued to prevail, as discussed for instance in Drayton, *Nature's Government*; Parrish, *American Curiosity*; and Spary, *Utopia's Garden*.

[36] The drawings, specimens, and correspondence are held today in the archive of the Linnaean Society of London, and include a set of thirty-two very fine drawings (Mss. BL 1178). Botanical exchange networks are described in Spary, *Utopia's Garden*; see also John Gascoigne, *Science in the Service of Empire: Joseph Banks, the British State and the Uses of Science in the Age of Revolution*, Cambridge: Cambridge University Press, 1998.

[37] On the acquisition and uses of drawing skills at the time, see Ann Bermingham, *Learning to Draw: Studies in the Cultural History of a Polite and Useful Art*, New Haven: Yale University Press, 2000.

[38] 'Satisfago a la discreta curiosidad de Vm. sobre dibujantes con dos plantas trabajadas por los dos que hemos conseguido en esta Academia de Sn. Carlos [...] Son jóvenes muy tiernos, dóciles, y vivísimos en el trabajo, con cuyas circumstancias, y los principios que manifiestan confiamos no desmerezcan a los que pudieran haber venido del Perú, que no los juzgo más adelantados.' Vicente Cervantes to José Celestino Mutis, Mexico, 27 December 1788, Archivo del Real Jardín Botánico de Madrid (hereafter ARJBM), III, 1, 1, 83, ff. 6r–6v. Reproduced in Mutis, *Archivo Epistolar*, 3: pp 219–223. Sessé praised Echeverría's talents and sent especially fine samples of his work to Spain; Martín de Sessé to Casimiro Gómez Ortega, Mexico City, 27 June 1788, ARJBM, 5, 1, 1, 23, ff. 2v–3r.

[39] 'El dibujante de plantas que ha venido, es bueno y de paciencia; tiene sus principios de botánica y sabe muy bien definir las partes de una planta, en especial las de la fructificación. Los dibujos que hasta hoy he tenido cuidado de dirigir, no están cargados sino de lo preciso, para que cualesquiera sistemático pueda conocer la Clase y Orden. Unido a éste [a el dibujo] la descripción metódica, parece que es suficiente para conocer la planta que se presenta.' Luis Née to José Celestino Mutis, Guayaquil *c.* 22 October 1790. ARJBM, III, 1, 1, 230, f. 2r. *Archivo Epistolar*, 4: pp 74–76.

[40] At times, artists talked back: Lorraine Daston and Peter Galison, *Objectivity*, New York: Zone Books, 2007, pp 93–94.

[41] Hipólito Ruiz to Jorge Escobedo, *Superintendente General de Real Hacienda*, Huánuco, 9 July 1786. Archivo del Museo Nacional de Ciencias Naturales, item 125 in María de los Ángeles Calatayud Arinero, *Catálogo de las expediciones y viajes científicos españoles a América y Filipinas (siglos XVIII y XIX)*, Madrid: CSIC, 1984; reproduced in Hipólito Ruiz, *Relación histórica del viage, que hizo a los reinos del Perú y Chile el botánico D. Hipólito Ruiz en el año 1777 hasta el de 1788, en cuya época regresó a Madrid*, ed. Jaime Jaramillo Arango, 2 vols, Madrid: Real Academia de Ciencias Exactas Físicas y Naturales, 2nd edn, 1952, pp 466–472.

[42] While most naturalists aspired to having complete control over their artists, work relationships seldom proved that one-sided in practice. For a more detailed discussion of the complex relationships between naturalists and artists, including specific case studies, see Bleichmar, *Visible Empire*, chapters 2 and 3; Daston and Galison, *Objectivity*, chapter 2, esp. pp 84–98; and Kärin Nickelsen, *Draughtsmen, Botanists, and Nature: The Construction of Eighteenth-Century Botanical Illustrations*, Archimedes Series, vol. 15, Dordrecht: Springer, 2006.

[43] Antonio González Bueno, *Antonio José Cavanilles (1745–1804): la pasión por la ciencia*, Madrid: Fundación Jorge Juan, 2002; José María López Piñero *et al*, *Antonio José Cavanilles (1745–1804). Segundo aniversario de la muerte de un gran botánico*, Valencia: Real Sociedad Económica de Amigos del País, 2004.

[44] Cavanilles described the new plant and dedicated it to Rizo in his 'Descripción de los géneros Aeginetia, Rizoa y Castelia,' *Anales de Ciencias Naturales*, 3, 1801, pp 132–133.

[45] On the choice of representing types or specimens, see Lorraine Daston and Peter Galison, 'The Image of Objectivity,' *Representations*, 40, 1992, pp 81–128, and *Objectivity*, esp. introduction and chapters 1 and 2.

466   DANIELA BLEICHMAR

[46] José Celestino Mutis to Juan José de Villaluenga, President of Quito, *Audiencia*, 10 July 1786, ARJBM, III, 2, 2, 196 and 197; reproduced in *Archivo Epistolar*, I: p 316.

[47] José Celestino Mutis to Casimiro Gómez Ortega, 3 January 1789, *Archivo Epistolar*, I, pp 439–440.

[48] On participation and credit in Atlantic science at the time, see Parrish, *American Curiosity*, esp. chapters 3, 5, 6, 7; and Safier, *Measuring the New World*, esp. chapters 2–5.

[49] My understanding of the mobilizing role of images owes much to the work of Bruno Latour, in particular *Science in Action: How to Follow Scientists and Engineers through Society*, Cambridge, MA: Harvard University Press, 1987, esp. pp 215–257. However, Latour's model has problems, criticized in Michael Bravo, 'Ethnological Encounters,' in Nicholas Jardine, James A Secord and Emma C Spary (eds), *Cultures of Natural History*, Cambridge: Cambridge University Press, 1996, pp 338–357; and Daniela Bleichmar, 'Atlantic Competitions: Botanical Trajectories in the Eighteenth-Century Spanish Empire,' in Nicholas Dew and James Delbourgo (eds), *Science and Empire in the Atlantic World*, New York: Routledge, 2008, pp 225–252.

Name Index

For Product Safety Concerns and Information please contact our EU
representative GPSR@taylorandfrancis.com
Taylor & Francis Verlag GmbH, Kaufingerstraße 24, 80331 München, Germany